FIRST VOICES
an aboriginal women's reader

FIRST VOICES
an aboriginal women's reader

EDITED BY

PATRICIA A. MONTURE AND PATRICIA D. MCGUIRE

INANNA Publications and Education Inc.
Toronto, Canada

Published in Canada by Inanna Publications and Education Inc.
210 Founders College, York University
4700 Keele Street, Toronto, Ontario M3J 1P3
Telephone: (416) 736-5356 Fax (416) 736-5765
Email: inanna@yorku.ca Website: www.yorku.ca/inanna

 Canada Council   Conseil des Arts    ONTARIO ARTS COUNCIL
for the Arts   du Canada   CONSEIL DES ARTS DE L'ONTARIO

The publisher gratefully acknowledges the support of the Canada Council for the Arts and the Ontario Arts Council for its publishing program.

The publisher is also grateful for the kind support received from an Anonymous Fund at The Calgary Foundation.

Front Cover Design: Val Fullard
Front Cover Artwork: Christi Belcourt, "Tree Spirits Leaving Before the Fire,"
  acrylic on canvas, 61 x 91.5 cm, 2007 <www.christibelcourt.com>
Interior Design: Luciana Ricciutelli

Printed and Bound in Canada.

Library and Archives Canada Cataloguing in Publication

        First voices : an Aboriginal women's reader / edited by
Patricia A. Monture and Patricia D. McGuire.

Includes bibliographical references and index.
ISBN 978-0-9808822-9-2

        1. Native women--Canada--History. 2. Native women--
Canada--Social conditions. 3. Native women--Canada--
Biography. 4. Native women--Legal status, laws, etc.--Canada.
I. Monture, Patricia A. (Patricia Anne) II. McGuire, Patricia D.
(Patricia Danielle), 1960-

E78.C2F58 2009   305.48'897071   C2009-904941-4

For our past and the women who helped us be who we are today.
For our present and the sisters we stand strong with.
For our future, our children.

For Kate Monture, 1993-2009.

I am only what I make myself
I can only think for myself
I am me.

Mohawk is what makes me
Strong, independent,
Woman.
It flows through my blood
To my heart.

—*Kate Monture, 2009*

CONTENTS

IDENTITY

INDIGENOUS KNOWLEDGES

ACKNOWLEDGEMENTS

THIS IS A PROJECT WE TOOK ON because we believe in the need to share the stories that Aboriginal women hold with a wider audience. We believe in teaching, learning, and sharing. Our families, traditional teachers, and Elders have taken the time to ensure that we understand the importance of traditional values such as sharing our experiences and the value of stories. Of courses, the mistakes made are ours and we are committed to continuing to learn and grow. We also want to acknowledge and thank each of the authors who permitted us to republish their work in this volume. Their gifts and creativity make this reader an accomplishment. We are happy to have played a small part in sharing their wisdom and knowledge.

Between the two of us, there would be a very long list of names to thank that could well go on for pages. We have been surrounded by kindness, support, and encouragement over the course of bringing this project to completion but also over the years. The list is too long but we know that you know who you are. So a big *miigweetch* and a big *nia:wen* to you all.

This reader came to be because of the vision, dedication, and hard work of Luciana Ricciutelli. Her skills as editor (and task master!) continue to amaze us. We want to acknowledge the comfort we take knowing that this Canadian sister truly understands and fights alongside us laying our words on these pages. Creating an index is not easy task (and it's not a lot of fun). We thank Sheila Molloy for her hard work to make this addition to our text and her willingness to volunteer for the job. We are also grateful to the Board of Inanna Publications for making our contribution to the knowledge people have about Aboriginal women possible. Their dedication to women's publishing allows these kinds of contributions to knowledge to occur. *Miigweetch* and *nia:wen* to you all.

Lastly, we each want to thank our children. The Monture clan are Justin, Michael Blake, Kate, and Jack. The Mcguire's are Cora Lee, Tony, and grandchildren, Andrew, Tyra, Victoria, Jordan, Audi, and Winner. They have made many sacrifices when our work took us away from them or we burned the midnight oil working on this project or that. More importantly, we have learned so much from them as they have shared their wisdom with us. It is for you and your children and their children that we have time and again found the energy to keep going.

—*Patricia A. Monture and Patricia D. McGuire*

PATRICIA A. MONTURE AND PATRICIA D. MCGUIRE

INTRODUCTION

THE STORIES OF ABORIGINAL WOMEN have been told since long before this land became a country known as Canada. For many of those decades since the land became known as Canada, the stories of Aboriginal women were ignored. Historians wrote about men as though women idly waited for the men to return with the "meat and the treaty" (Fog 76). But Aboriginal women have not forgotten the stories. In writing about stories LeAnne Howe (Choctaw) notes: "Native stories are power. They create people. They author tribes. America is a tribal creation story, a tribalography" (29). Our stories are woven into the land and shape the way we raise our daughters. In recent decades, the number of Aboriginal women who have chosen to share our stories in writing has grown considerably. As we reviewed the published papers in *Canadian Woman Studies/les cahiers de la femme (CWS/cf)* written by or about Aboriginal women, we were impressed by the talent of our many sisters. Their creativity carries us as women and carries our nations.

The papers in this book have all been peer-reviewed and previously published in an issue of *CWS/cf.* They date back to the 1980s; long before it was vogue to publish the writings of Aboriginal women. Almost none of the articles have been updated. Readers can trace over a period of nearly 30 years the developments in our work and the way the issues have changed (or sometimes, not changed very much). Not all of the authors are Aboriginal. The non-Aboriginal authors show us that both "cross-cultural" understanding and solidarity is possibility. The nation of each Aboriginal author is noted in most of the biographies. This information can be used to keep the teachings that are shared in this book "straight." By comparing the stories of the Haudenosaunee women or the Anishnaabe women, you can learn more about each of those nations' beliefs, teachings, traditions, and knowledge systems. Even though you will find similarities among the diverse Indigenous nations, it is important to acknowledge that we do come from specific nations and each of our complex national structures have unique traditions, ways of being, and ways of knowing. To really know us is to keep the knowledge of the Anishnaabe together, separate from the knowledge of the Cree or the Inuit.

It is always important to remember that the words Aboriginal, Native, In-

1

digenous, or Indian are colonial words imposed upon many diverse nations. They are not our own words for who we are and from this position it does not matter which colonial word you choose to use now. You will find in this text that they are all used, which is often a reflection of the time the article was written. Generally, Aboriginal draws its meaning from Canada's constitution where we are defined as the "Indian, Inuit, and Métis." "Indian" is the correct legal term when used to describe any person registered under the rules found in Canada's *Indian Act*. Often these "registered" Indians are called "status" Indians. So those who are not registered under the Act do not have status, and frankly we find that reference to others disturbing. All persons have "status" as a human being and should have equality.

Indigenous stories should not be seen as mere entertainment but rather they are the first literatures of this land. These stories document our knowledge about our peoples. There are many different forms of story that ground Indigenous knowledge systems. There are sacred stories that are only shared by specific people—the people who own those stories (really the stories own them)—at certain times of the year after appropriate (and nation specific) protocols have been met. Readers will not find these stories in this book although some authors make reference to these sacred knowledges and stories. Access to sacred stories is provided in the oral tradition through relationships with Indigenous communities. Indigenous peoples also have stories about their histories including family stories. These are the tribalographies mentioned earlier. There are stories that share life lessons and provide "counselling" opportunities. Sometimes we just make up stories about the things that have happened to us and tell them just because we need to laugh! Sometimes, at gatherings, there will be an informal storytelling contest. Who can tell the funniest stories? There are the stories we tell as academics and publish in scholarly books and journals because we can adapt our ways of knowing and being to different forms. This is really what Indigenous scholarship is. And we are sure that a number of Indigenous women who are reading this are naming different kinds of stories that we have forgotten to mention. Our goal here is not to name every form of storytelling our peoples have, but to make the point that our lives and worlds as Indigenous people are full of all kinds of stories. Although there has been much destruction, our storytelling ways have not been destroyed nor have we been de-storyed.

This book begins with a section of papers that reflect the great diversity of Aboriginal women. Not only do we come from different nations, each of whom have their own traditions, ceremonies, laws, and languages but, Aboriginal women also interact with the world in multiple ways. Some are interested in politics while others write. Some dance and paint and create. We all share experiences with the colonial history of Canada and with present-day experiences of discrimination. This shared colonial history often makes us look the same when really it is the imposed colonial oppression that we have survived that is the same—the same strategies laid over the people and the land from coast-to-coast. The profiles of the women presented in the first section allow the reader to meet a few us, know us a little, and recognize our diversity. From meeting a few of us us, the book proceeds to share how we look at the world. Each of the sections is built around a concept that is key in our worldviews, epistemologies, and the structure of our knowledge systems.

Many times we have heard the Elders say: "You must know where you have come from to know where you are going." This simple statement teaches that we must know our histories to know who we are. Identity is one of the core components required for the stable structuring of social, political, legal, and knowledge systems in Aboriginal nations. The second section, therefore, presents papers where authors share and examine their own identities. Through studying these stories you can begin to know the complexities of our identities. There is no single "authentic" Aboriginal identity or Aboriginal woman's identity. That is a viscous stereotype that has done much harm to our peoples.

The land is who we are as peoples. To know who you are you must also know where you come from. This means understanding the relationship you have with the territory of your people. Indigenous women understand the land that has become known as Canada in a different way from the common geographical one learned about in the public education system in this country. We know whose territory we are in. It might be the land of the Blackfoot, the Salish, or the Maliseet. You must know where you are as your behaviour in another's territory reflects on your people. There are different ways to behave when you are a visitor in another nation's territory. For many Aboriginal nations, it was women's duty to protect the land. Thus, the papers in this section titled, "Territory," are essential to building an understanding of who we are as Aboriginal women. Many Aboriginal women are deeply troubled by the devastation wrought on the land as the papers in this section demonstrate. As you will also read, Aboriginal women not only have particular relationships and responsibilities to the land, but in many of our traditions we have a special relationship and responsibility to the waters.

The largest section in this reader is the section on activism. It is a very narrow construction, which views Aboriginal women as the victims of oppression. Woven throughout our history are the stories of many, many women who have stood up against oppression and discriminations. As the papers in this section demonstrate, activism has come in many forms and involves multiple forms of discrimination. Challenges have been brought in the health care field, education, employment, politics, and the legal system. The fact that we have survived colonial oppression and continue to fight is a key message in this section of the book. We are not passive people who have had colonialism done to us. Rather, we are active agents. Aboriginal women are subjects not objects of oppression. We hope this text allows you to consider these important differences in how we have been treated in academic literatures and research. Although we are often not heard, we do have voices. And this is the idea that is reflected in the title of this book we are sharing with you.

The stories in the section titled, "Confronting Colonialism," are all about the ways Aboriginal women have struggled to take back their power. This section documents the many different forms of racialized and sexualized violence that we have survived. It comes after the section on activism, because we needed to emphasize that we are subjects not objects before we discussed the impacts of colonialism. The impacts of colonialism, which often lead to the need for activism, are far too often about having both the strength and courage to resist. But resisting is not a condition of life that we are satisfied with. Simply put Aboriginal women deserve more. We deserve lives where we do not fear for our safety, survive violence ourselves, or fear for our daughters. Similarly, we do not believe that to decolonize our minds, bodies, lives, and communities is sufficient.

One of the most significant ways in which our lives and communities have been devastated is through the application of Canadian laws on our people. Although, the problems that are created by the *Indian Act* are often acknowledged, the conflict between Canadian laws and Aboriginal peoples are far more complicated and widespread. The papers in this section offer an examination of the struggles with the criminalization of Aboriginal women and our efforts to reform the Canadian correctional system. They also examine the struggle for rights that has coalesced around the Constitution of Canada. In our efforts to advance our claims and resist oppression, many Aboriginal women's groups now turn to international human rights standards to press our claims. This section is intended to encourage the reader to challenge what is taken for granted and pursue an advanced understanding of the ways Canadian laws operate to oppress Aboriginal women.

Finally, the book sets out eight powerful papers about the structure of our Indigenous ways of knowing. In this last section of the book, we return to papers that pick up some of the ideas and traditional values set out in the first section. We choose to present papers that are based on our ways of knowing last because it is in our own knowledge systems where we find the hope for the future. The gap left in our lives from constantly resisting is filled by the hope that our traditional ways bring. As the two papers from the earlier volumes show, we have valued these ways of knowing and let them shape our lives for a very long time. The last three papers show how Aboriginal women have developed our understandings of our own ways of knowing and combined them with our other pursuits be those creative or academic.

With this book, we offer our prayers for the future for our children and our children's children.

Patricia A. Monture, Aye-wah-han-day, is a citizen of the Mohawk Nation, Grand River Territory (near Brantford, Ontario). She is mother, sister and auntie. Since 1994, she has been employed at the University of Saskatchewan. Patricia is presently a full professor in the Department of Sociology where she is also the academic director of the Aboriginal Justice and Criminology Program. Her research interests include crime, law and justice studies; the rights of Aboriginal peoples and a deep commitment to equality rights for women. She has published numerous papers and several books. In 2008, in acknowledgement of her commitment of women's activism in the university, she received the Sarah Shorten Award from the Canadian Association of University Teachers and an honourary doctorate of laws from Athabasca University. In 2009, she received an honourary LL.D. *from Queen's University. Her award-winning publications include* Thunder in My Soul *and* Journeying Forward: Dreaming First Nations Independence.

Patricia D. McGuire, Kishebakabaykwe Bizhiw indoodem, is a mother and grand-mother. She is citizen of Bingwi Neyaashi Anishinaabek but shared summers as a child with her relatives at Kiashke Zaaging Anishinaabek in Ontario. She has worked with Anishinaabek communities developing and teaching in post-secondary education programs for more than twenty years. Patricia is on leave from Negahneewin which is located at Confederation College in Thunder Bay Ontario. She teaches in the area of Indigenous Studies, law, sociology and development. She is currently working on a Canadian Institute of Health Research grant dealing with Aboriginal resilience in Canada with CIET. *She is a Ph.D. student at the University of Saskatchewan. Her thesis work is on developing social theory and Indigenous knowledge from her home territory.*

REFERENCES

Fog, Gunlog. "Some Women are Wiser than Some Men: Gender and Native American History." *Clearing a Path: Theorizing the Past in Native American Studies.* Ed. Nancy Shoemaker. New York: Routledge, 2002. 75-103.

Howe, LeAnne. "The Story of America: A Tribalography." *Clearing a Path: Theorizing the Past in Native American Studies.* Ed. Nancy Shoemaker. New York: Routledge, 2002. 29-48.

PROFILES OF ABORIGINAL WOMEN

PATRICIA A. MONTURE

KOHKUM WOULD BE MAD AT ME

kohkum would be mad at me
if she were still here.
for dying my hair
hiding the gray
(hey, I'm not 50 yet)
wearing make-up
and fancy clothes.
supposed to love who you are
and how the Creator made you.
not supposed to try and change that.

Kohkum would be mad at me
if she were still here.

kohkum never had to live with
white people
least not how I have live with white people.
i have them every day, all day,
at work.
(maybe I have it wrong, maybe they got me)
kohkum just had the indian agent
telling her what to do
every now and again
reserve used to be refuge
(maybe it still is)

but, see
I listened to what the white folk told
get an education
got me a job
in a fancy university

I hide my hair and the evidence
of gray injun wisdom.
I hide my face, behind a mask
of revlon "easy, breezy, beautiful"

I hide.
(Or maybe, I just like "war paint")

Originally published in Canadian Woman Studies/les cahiers de la femme, *"Indigenous Women in Canada: The Voices of First Nations, Inuit and Métis Women," 26 (3 & 4) (Winter/Spring 2008): 199. Reprinted with permission of the author.*

Patricia A. Monture is a citizen of the Mohawk Nation, Grand River Territory. She is currently teaching in the Sociology Department at the University of Saskatchewan where she coordinates the Aboriginal Justice and Criminology Program. She is a committed activist/scholar who continues to seek justice for Aboriginal peoples and especially Aboriginal women and girls.

RESPONSE TO CANADA'S APOLOGY TO
RESIDENTIAL SCHOOL SURVIVORS

ON JUNE 11, 2008, PRIME MINISTER Stephen Harper, on behalf of the Canadian government, made a Statement of Apology to former students of residential schools. All Opposition leaders, Stephane Dion, Jack Layton and Gilles Duceppe, also made statements of apology. All Aboriginal leaders of the National Aboriginal Organizations responded to the Statement of Apology. All of the National Aboriginal leaders met with the Prime Minister fifteen minutes prior to the Statement made in the House of Commons, was provided with a copy of the Statement to review and was advised at that time that we would be providing responses on the floor of the House of Commons.

As the National President of the Native Women's Association of Canada, I was given a responsibility that day to make a statement that the rest of the world would hear. I was honoured to represent Aboriginal women in Canada and speak from the heart regarding the impacts of the residential school system, specifically on Aboriginal women in Canada. It was one of the most powerful experiences that I have ever had not only personally but professionally as well. The following is the statement that I made in response to the Prime Minister's Statement of Apology. After I reviewed the written statement, the affect was not the same, so I have made a few minor additions to provide further context to my statement.

***

I began with an introduction of myself by speaking in my language. What I said in my Mohawk language is, "Greetings of peace to you." My nation is Mohawk of the Haudenosaunee Confederacy, Bear Clan. And my real name is Gowehgyuseh, which means "She is Visiting."

I am here to represent the Native Women's Association of Canada and the women that we represent have a statement. It is about the respect of Aboriginal women in this country.

Prior to the residential schools system, prior to colonization, the women in our communities were very well respected and honoured for the role that they have in our communities. Women are the life givers, being the caretakers of the spirit that we bring into this world, Our Mother earth. We were given those responsibilities by the Creator to bring that spirit into this physical world and to love, take care of and nurture our children.

The government and churches' genocidal policies of the residential schools caused so much harm to that respect for women and to the way women were honoured in our communities. There were ceremonies for young men and for young women that taught them how to respect themselves and each other. These ceremonies were stolen from them for generations.

Despite the hardships, we have our language still. We have our ceremonies. We have our elders. And now we have to revitalize those ceremonies and the respect for our people not only within Canadian society but even within our own peoples.

I want to say that I come here speaking from my heart, because two generations ago, my grandmother, being a Mohawk woman, was beaten in residential school, sexually beaten and physically beaten, for being a Mohawk woman. She did not pass on her traditions. She did not pass it on to my mother and her siblings. That matriarchal system that we have was directly affected. Luckily, I was raised in a community where our knowledge and our ceremonies have been kept by all of our mothers.

I want to say that as mothers, we teach our boys and our girls, equally. That is what I am here to say, that although I represent the Native Women's Association, we also represent men and women because that is our traditional responsibility. It is not just about women's issues. It is about making sure that we have strong nations again. That is what I am here to say.

We have given thanks to you for your apology. I have to also give you credit for standing up and starting to tell the truth. I did not see any other governments before today come forward and apologize, so I do thank you for that. But in return, the Native Women's Association wants respect.

I have just one last thing to say. To all of the leaders of the Liberals, the Bloc and NDP, thank you as well. I thank you for your words. But it is now about our responsibilities today. Words must turn into action. The decisions that we make today will affect seven generations from now. My ancestors did the same seven generations ago. While they tried hard to fight against you, they knew what was happening. They knew what was coming.

We have had so much impact from colonization and that is what we are dealing with today. Women have taken the brunt of it all. In the end it must be about more than what happened in the residential schools. For women, the truth telling must continue.

Thank you for the opportunity to be here, at this moment in time, to talk about those realities that we are dealing with today. But at the end of it, I am left with questions. What is it that this government is going to do in the future to help our people? Because we are dealing with major human rights violations that have occurred to many generations. These violations have impacted on my language, my culture and my spirituality. I know that I want to transfer those to my children and my grandchildren, and their children, and so on. What is going to be provided? That is my question. I know that is the question from all of us. That is what we would like to continue to work on, in partnership. *Nia:wen.* Thank you."

***

I had to prepare emotionally, mentally, physically and spiritually to make this statement. I first began to realize the impacts of the residential school system fourteen years ago when I made a decision in law school to write a major research paper about the residential school system. It was one of those papers where I read story after story of the most horrific abuses against Aboriginal children. It was a time when residential school survivors were just beginning to open up and to disclose the various forms of abuses.

I then had to reflect on my own personal upbringing and heard about the horrendous abuses that my own grandmother and her siblings had to endure while they attended the "Mush Hole," the Mohawk Institute in Brantford, Ontario. I also reflected and reviewed my matrilineal family and the affects that these abuses had on my mother, her siblings and their families. My grandmother and mother had already passed away when I began to realize the intergenerational impacts, so I wasn't able to have direct conversations with them about this issue. I am not sure my grandmother would have wanted to talk about it anyway. I was, however, able to sit with my uncle, my grandmother's brother, and he told me many horrible stories. I began to understand how much was stolen from my matriarchal family as a result of my grandmother attending the Mush Hole. It became a reality that our traditional form of educating our children through language and traditional teachings that were supposed to be taught to us by our grandmother was stolen from her; her language was sexually beaten from her and her spirit was beaten by a system designed to destroy her. She was a Mohawk girl whose life was taken from us by genocidal policies of the Canadian government and religious denominations of churches.

The most detrimental effect is that this systemic form of assimilation occurred to thousands and thousands of families throughout at least six generations, a hundred years, a century. As you can imagine, the transference of traditional knowledge and languages was directly impacted and replaced with a violent cycle of abuse. Every Aboriginal person has been affected whether a family member attended residential school or not. When a systemic process is created to destroy a people by erasing a language, a culture and a spirit, every single person is affected. When this system attacked children, the heart of our Nations, the heart of our Mothers and Grandmothers, it attacked every single person.

Despite the blatant attacks on our people to try to erase our existence, the process didn't work. As noted in my Response to the Apology, I believe that we have to celebrate the fact that we still have our grandmothers, grandfathers, mothers and fathers, aunties and uncles, that have been able to keep the traditional values, beliefs and language. Although most Indigenous languages in Canada are becoming extinct, the processes to revitalize has begun. Our people have survived cultural genocide through their resilience and strength of those people who have ensured that the language and culture continue. We have done this because of our belief in our spirituality and it has been through the strength of spirit that our culture and tradition is alive.

Damage has been done, though. Many generations of families have been affected. Languages are becoming extinct. It is now up to the federal government to provide the resources needed to Aboriginal peoples today and in the future. It is ironic that the Conservative minority government apologized for its wrongdoing in the creation of the residential school system; but yet, it eliminated language revitalization programs. It would seem to me that what is needed now, as noted in my response, that action is needed. This government must provide direct resources to Aboriginal communities to continue programs and services that will enable the continued transference of Indigenous traditional knowledges and languages.

Most Canadians became a little educated on June 11, 2008 about the assimilationist policy of the Canadian government. Being that this is one of the most troubling "black marks" against Canada, every Canadian person should be knowledgeable that the human rights violations that occurred against Aboriginal children is as a result of Canada's genocidal policies. Every Canadian person should know its impacts on Aboriginal peoples, and more specifically on Aboriginal women. Everyone should know that the negative issues of the poverty, alcoholism, drug addiction and the cycle of violence can be traced back to Canada's policies. We can even trace the issue of missing and murdered Aboriginal women to the residential school system. All of this must be mandatorily taught in all Canadian schools. It shouldn't have taken until the year 2008 for most Canadians to be educated about the residential school system.

When such action is taken by the Canadian government to not only apologize, but to create a process in which it actually acknowledges the harms its done, then we can accept the Apology. A process needs to ensure that the financial resources are in place to deal with all of the impacts we are dealing with today. When our languages are fully revitalized, then we will know that change has occurred. When Aboriginal women are no longer targets of violence, then we know that change has occurred. When our Nations our flourishing and no longer living in poverty, then we know that change has occurred. I look forward to the day when we are no longer fighting for equality because we have reclaimed our way of being.

Originally published in Canadian Woman Studies/les cahiers de la femme, *"Indigenous Women in Canada: The Voices of First Nations, Inuit and Métis Women," 26 (3 & 4) (Winter/Spring 2008): 223-225. Reprinted with permission of the author.*

Beverley Jacobs is past President of the Native Women's Association of Canada (2004-2009).

ALICE OLSEN WILLIAMS

A PORTRAIT OF GLADYS TAYLOR

S HE IS UNTAINTED, UNSPOILED by the education system of the dominant society. She's a person of raw strength and earthiness. Gladys Taylor is a seventy-five-year-old Elder who has spent all her life in Curve Lake Reserve, twenty miles north of Peterborough, Ontario. She has ten children. "I lost three, but I've still got seven," she proudly claims. I asked her how many grandchildren she has. As soon as I said that. her eyes twinkled and we both started laughing as we both realized she didn't know off-hand. Laughingly she explained, "Oh-oh-oh-oh-oh-I should really count them up."

As we watched our TV soap, she took a writing-pad and counted up her grandchildren. Seventeen she has. She also has seven great-grandchildren.

Gladys is a deeply religious woman, who has loved God all her life. Several years ago, the Native Ministry of the United Church of Canada made her the Leading Elder for all of Canada.

The following are excerpts from her record of thoughts, ideas, prayers, sermons, diaries and poems:

Bizindan weweni (Listen carefully). It's not right to ask an Elder to repeat a story again. You get knowledge by listening.

In a treasured picture-frame, Gladys Taylor has this poem and a photograph of all her children.

What Are Our Children Worth?

All people place a value,
On things they call their own,
Their clothes and cars and jewelry,
Their friends, their health and home.

The possession of greatest value,
We will ever have on earth
Makes me ponder this question,
What are our children worth?

So gather your children around you,
Guard and guide them with hand and heart,
For all too soon will come the day,
When you and they must part.

Then all your days will be lonely,
You will miss their youthful mirth,
All our love and all our life,
That's what our children are worth.

August 31, 1988

Today I seen on TV a "Advert." It showed numerous items but the one that caught My fancy was a large bowl. Around the edge was Nice Smooth lumps of glass and sort of frilly lace which reminded me of when I had a play-house as a small girl, and I had a Very Special Friend who was Very dear to me. We shared everything. When He was Sad I was Sad too. He could put his head on my shoulder and we would sit this way till the hurt was gone, and one day he brought me a large piece of this Kind of bowl for Our play-house. I really treasured this; it was frosted green. And when you turned it, it would have golden and blue tinges. I always kept this polished. Now I only have the Memories because my Special Friend went away and I can only go back to childhood days. Now I'm grateful, even when friends part they can't take away Memories. They leave them behind; they're Consolations on blue days.

My First Thoughts This Evening

As I look back over the years, even as far back as my childhood, I see so many changes. Some good. Some bad. Others that will never change, such as being Indian. But I love being Indian because I love challenges. Naming some, I'm the first Native woman to get a license to Serve Communion to my people without going through college and I didn't study theology. I'm sure I wouldn't have ever been any use if it had to be on account of knowing English ways. Because I didn't go to school long, I was working by the time I was eleven years old.

March 15, 1986

Last night before I went to sleep, I was thinking back, many years ago when I was a Young Mother. How good it was to rock my baby to sleep; to Sing those Ojibwa hymns and hear the even breathing of My Little One, Who felt so safe in My arms. Now alone in this big house there's Nothing. Only Memories. But some time during the night, Something woke me. I could feel baby breath on My Withered Cheek and hear that even breathing. Once more: life is so good tome. It's great to be alive.

This was when I was Very sick and was here all alone. My time rolled backwards that night.

Smoke Signals Across the Lake

I see the Smoke of three Camp fires
On this Sunny March Morning.
They come from the fires, built on the Shore
By the Weedigo's of the four Corners
They meet here Once a year to decide
The ways of livelihood of their Nations
To Smoke the pipe of peace.
They must have Come to a good understanding
Because I see the Sign of one Single Smoke
Where they have each put bits of tobacco.
That says there will be peace and under standing
With Our Indian Nations.
So let us lift up Our arms to embrace
The warm Sunshine of our Mother Earth's love
Let us : feel the pulse of Nature's heart beat
We will have the good feeling of Belonging to our land, and live to
Keep it that way.

Sunday, December 4

Today has been a good day. Cold, Clear and Windy. Some snow fell, and big patches of ice formed on the lake, smooth paths among the waves. It's dark now; the wind is still strong. My Children were all home, also my Grandchildren, even little Anna.

Wednesday, December 21, 1988

We had lots of Snow earlier in last week but it has rained and now it looks like a green Christmas. I remember when I was a small girl and the Nish Nobs would go hunting for food. Some times when it was a mild spell and the porcupine would be out they would kill it for the quills. And also the meat is real good, but they had to fetch it from a long ways. And it being so sharp. And nearby they would drag it, they would cut a branch from the tree that had sort of a hook. They would pull it through its mouth and drag it home. Then the Old Ones would get mad and scold them. They believed when you done it that way you were bringing on a big snow storm. I'm afraid if I tell this to the White people they will make me drag a porcupine up and down the ski slopes to prove Our beliefs (hee hee).

Memories of Yester Years...

I'm glad of this opportunity to share this Sunday Service with the people of the United Church. I work in Our church when there's no Minister to take Our Service. Although My Services are different because I usually Speak in My Native language. But I have to use English too because we have people in Our Church who aren't Native or Some who don't Speak or Understand it, but when I give Communion it's done in Ojibwa. I feel so good about it all, its just like balm to Our Souls. I 'm also a leading Elder for all of Canada's Natives. When they get Ordained I attend the Ordination.

Wednesday, February 15, 1989

I visited a big Church this week, took part in its Service. I was One of the three who were asked to take part and was also the last one to speak. As I sat there listening, they talked about Money and the cost of everything, the drought, the Ozone layer, the Earthquake Victims, Acid rain. But no one spoke about the One who is the head of that building.

Saturday, October 24

Mom's birthday; nothing can measure my loneliness today.

I was sitting beside the bleachers feeling Very lost and friendless when a big black car came toward me blaring its horn. I moved out of the way and as I looked at the people in it, I seen Chief get out and walk toward me. He folded me to his breast with tears streaming down his face. He said, Mom it's nice to see you. He was sick looking and his clothes didn't fit but he was clean. He had a blue wind breaker. In the pocket was a hair ornament: a baby's face, it held a nice white feather. He said, Mom it's for your hair, and there was also a small bottle of something that looked like sand-coloured seeds. As we talked he said, Mom I come for you, You'll come to live with me. Granma came with me. Let's go and see her. We went. She was busy cleaning her little house. She had made a birchbark flower pot and it wasn't finished yet I felt so happy, Then Chief said, Mom lets go. I said, don't leave yet. Well I came after you Mom. I'll have to go now. I turned to speak to Mom. She wasn't there. The only thing I seen was two figures flying toward the east. I can feel my hopes and heart crumble. I called out, Wait Chief. I'll go. But they just kept on going. I woke up Crying.

The International Year of the Child

What does it mean? Who is it for? It must be for the whole World, the neglected, the abandoned, parentless, beaten and bruised, the molested, the murdered, the homeless, the retarded, the crippled. Why is it such a big celebration? It must be for the healthy child that's lucky to enjoy the good things of life: good clothes, lots of toys, three good meals a day, a vacation, later on a car, Credit Cards, Booze, dope, lots of Friends, Money, Beach parties, drag racing. But where does it all end? It ends in the earth. Where all humanity came from in the beginning of time. There was a time when such a day was unheard of for every day was a day of the child in the eyes of and life of an

Gladys Taylor. Photo courtesy of Patti Shaughnessy.

Indian grandmother. My heart beats slow: like the beating of the drum: when they sang the death Chant even my steps are slow. I walk with my head down: there are times I lift up my eyes to observe the beauty of Our earth and wish I could see into the future.

Equal Rights?

Do you know what that means? Do you understand what it stands for? My foot steps follow the path of the evening sun : I'm getting on in Years now, but all my life ever since I've understood a bit of the English language, I hear my people say, we want equal rights. I don't think they know either. Here's what I think, why is it so right when a Indian man sells his Indian blood for a white woman. She gains also in the bargain, every Indian right, when she gets settled snugly into the band her demands are big if she has Children, maybe by her previous marriage or out of wed-lock. Why are they always given a better opportunity than the honest-to-goodness Indian Kid? But when a Indian woman marries a White man she is looked upon as a non-Indian. How

19

can anyone change who you are? I was born Indian, if I was a white woman, how can I become an Indian because I married one? If these are equal rights, I think when an Indian man takes a white woman for his wife he should lose his rights as well as an Indian women. The scale that weighs out human rights should balance equal, because when the Indian woman and her white man have kids they are called Metis. Again the white man gets all kinds of help; because he calls himself Metis too, he builds a nice home, nice furniture, turns himself inside out to be a good Indian. I don't know. I guess they are just used to pushing. The reason they get ahead.

October 7, 1987

This day is overcast and my outlook is just as grey and dreary. My heart ache from last evening still hangs on, those days come often now. It makes me wonder if it's any use trying to fit into the white world of my children. My roots are very obvious, my ways, my thinking, even my looks. I'm just as unique as an arrowhead.

As I look upon this ordination I feel honoured, to be a part of it. I have been looking back at the time when we first started the Native Ministry in 1981. We were a weak people, but we put all Our faith and our expectations at the Feet of God. We knew we couldn't do it on our own. So we figured if we put Him in first place with everything we do He would see us through. That's why we have come this far. We are looking at the rewards of our Faith. I remember, when I witnessed my Calling we had gone to White Bear Resserve. I couldn't understand why I was asked to go but there was my letter and it said my plane ticket would be at the terminal. Then a few days later we went on a sight seeing tour. The bus stopped between two high Mountains. I got off and as I looked up past the timber line, up past the boulders to the snow caps on top, I felt so small and useless just like the small bugs crawling on the ground. I felt so humble looking at his vast creation, and thinking I'm apart of this. What Can I do? Then like the gentle breeze that blows over the Mountain's grasses, I heard God's Call. As small and useless as you feel, I have work for you to do. Feed my Sheep. The closeness of Him was so real. I felt His hand on my head again as I did one other time, and I know it will again, when my life's work is ended as He whispers in Soft Ojibwa,

You're Home my child, you're Home. Come rest in the shadow of My love and all the tired will be gone.

Originally published in Canadian Woman Studies/les ahiers de la femme, *"Native Women," 10 (2 & 3) (Summer/Fall 1989): 21-23. Reprinted with permission of the author.*

Alice Olsen Williams was born in Trout Lake, 150 miles north of Kenora, in the

traditional territory of her mother's people from time before memory. She received her teaching certificate from Lakehead Teacher's College, which is now the Faculty of Education at Lakehead University in Thunder Bay, Ontario. Having taught in Thunder Bay and at Pic Mobert First Nation, Alice and her husband, Doug, moved to Curve Lake First Nation just north of Peterborough, Ontario, where Doug was born and raised. While looking after their four children and their home, Alice completed her B.A. from Trent University as well as developing her skills in beadwork and sewing. In 1980 she discovered quilting, mastering the techniques which allow her to create the meticulous hand-quilting in her bed coverings and wall hangings. Gradually Alice formed the concepts which would be the basis for her distinctive style and work. Blending her cultural heritage into a unified whole, she envisions the central motif to depict the symbols and themes of Anishinaabe culture, surrounded by the conventional North American quilting blocks and patterns which were developed and continue to be evolved by those women and their descendants who came to this Land from Europe, the legacy of her father's people. Through her understanding of the teachings of the Elders, Alice has created her own Life symbol. She continues to grow as an artist, searching for new ways to express the Spirit of Creation in the images of her designs.

THE LIFE OF A CHIEF

An Interview

NORA BOTHWELL IS CHIEF OF THE Alderville First Nation, a community of 250 Mississauga Indians located on the shores of Rice Lake in southeastern Ontario.

Nora lost membership in her band on her marriage to a non-Indian and was reinstated following passage of Bill C-31 amending the *Indian Act* in 1985. She was elected Chief in 1987. Nora holds a certificate in Native Economic Development and Small Business Management and a Bachelor of Arts degree in Native Studies. She talked to *Canadian Woman Studies* about her life experience and her work as Chief.

Have you always been interested in politics?

No. Believe me, no, but it grows on you. I always worked in the community, even when I was growing up. I was brought up around older people, at the west end of the reserve, and I carried in wood and water for neighbours. My mom was a single parent. Helping and sharing was part of everyday life. Then when I married and became non-status I became an underdog. At the time I married I didn't understand the implications of no longer being "Indian." I continued to work in the community, but it angered me when I saw job postings which said "must be a band member." I can see making Native ancestry a preferred requirement for a job but lots of our people out there are resourceful and qualified and if they came home they could make a real contribution. I know what it is to be on the reserve and have resources available to me and I also know what it is to be on the other side. I got my education while I was non-status and grants weren't available to me. That all helps me now to understand and make decisions as a result of looking at all sides of an issue.

You went back to school as a mature student. What motivated you to do that?

I first went to Sir Sandford Fleming College to take a refresher course in bookkeeping. My goal was to become a book-keeper. I worked for a couple of summers, one summer at the college, and I enjoyed meeting people, but sitting behind a desk, typing, was not for me. It wasn't lively enough. The turning point for me came when I enrolled in the Native Economic Development and Small

Business Management Program in 1982. It was a one-year program sponsored by the Métis and non-status Indian organization in this zone and students were supported by the Local Employment Assistance Program of C.E.I.C. I was really interested in the community development part of the course and I found it easy to understand. I could identify with what was being taught because I could see how the instructor's experience out west corresponded to what I had seen at Alderville. My community development instructor encouraged me to on to further education. I said "Oh, no. I'm too dumb." But he told me "Determination is what counts."

I enrolled at Trent University in Native Studies, but only after thinking about it for several months and talking it over with my kids. My daughter was eleven and my son was four when I went back to school in 1982.

How did you manage as a single parent?

I had a great mother. If it wasn't for her I would never have been able to make it with babysitting costs. There have been tough times. It wasn't easy to go to school and then come home and do all the things that you have to do, keep the house. do the laundry, feed your kids and read them a bedtime story, and make sure they got a little part of you, and then start doing your homework.

Night courses were the worst. I used to be perturbed when I would drive 50 miles through a storm to get to class and students living right in Peterborough couldn't make it. Then I would think: "But I'm the one who is going to gain for this." I am lucky that I have determination. When I make a decision I stick by it, and having a goal in mind is like seeing the light at the end of the tunnel. And when you get to the end of that tunnel there is another tunnel, so there are never-ending tunnels. But that's okay because you just go one tunnel at a time.

Tell us about a day in the life of a chief.

My day often starts with the phone ringing; someone needs something or wants to meet me at the office. Then there are the kids to get off to school. I am usually at the administration office by 9:00 a.m. three or four days a week. I get the mail at 10:00 and there is always a lot of correspondence that has to be done. I keep an open door and make myself available if people want to drop in. I am especially pleased when older members of the community come in and talk about what they would like to see happen here.

Letters and other communications with government could be a daily activity. For example, this past week I was tracking down the person in the Department of Indian Affairs who was responsible for a survey on the success of post-secondary students. When D.I.A. asked our opinion on the terms of reference for the survey, I wrote saying the information available was not satisfactory, but they went ahead and called our students directly. They had no right to question our students without permission of Chief and Council, but by the time I reached the woman in charge of evaluation, the telephone survey had already been carried out and the woman in charge had never seen my letter objecting to the process. Your people don't know about the day-to-day work you do and it is difficult to put out information in a positive manner. It is important for people to know how they are affected by the political process, so they will take an interest in what goes on. For example, a lot of our people don't understand treaties. In our last newsletter I went over very briefly how each treaty refers to us at Alderville, leaving it open that anyone interested in learning more could find information at the administration office. One person did follow up on it.

I'm trying to digest the *Indian Act* and in my spare time I am going through documents on land issues. We have had land taken from the reserve over the years and we don't know whether or not it was taken honestly. We are working on developing a resource centre and library for our young people and one of our women is taking training to manage that. Someday, in our plans, there will be a museum, and we are in the feasibility stage of a community centre.

Those are day-to-day things that come up. We are meeting tomorrow with a consultant who is doing a land use study for the reserve.

Is there reserve land not being used at present?

Yes. As a council we are trying to see I what would be the best use of land owned by the Band. There is some agricultural land which you can rent out, but the income is small. We obtained a grant to hire a forestry technician who did soil samples. He will work with the land use consultant to plot the land and give Council advice on the best site for new housing, instead of everyone building just anywhere. We have lakefront property and a park. Over the years there has been no planning done, whether to have holding tanks for water, or setting boundaries for building sites. With the passage of Bill C-31 we have had a lot of people come back to the reserve. They want lots, and they should rightfully have them, but where will we put them? Council has passed a by-law establishing lot sizes and we are having a surveyor come in this spring.

It sounds like Council is working towards having a development plan.

We eventually want to have the plan up on the wall. Here is the reserve. Here is what we would like to see. We have been drawing up by-laws and policies. The reality is that even though you are on a reserve, there are certain rules that have to be observed. We have had community meetings to discuss proposed changes, and of course there were people who didn't come. So we are hearing rebuttals from some. It takes a lot of work to put new policies in place.

The media report on chief's meetings discussing self-government. How does that connect with the local concerns you've been talking about?

Self-government means that we are supposed to have control over our own services and resources. Right now we don't even have a real consultation. What happens nine times out of ten is that government presents a policy, a draft policy they call it, and they don't listen to what we say, just as the evaluator I spoke about earlier didn't listen when I said "No! this survey is unacceptable." How can a researcher decide whether one of our students is successful? She may not have graduated from a college or university, but she could still take something from the course and do something valuable in our eyes. Whose standard of success is going to be applied?

Communities are supposed to be able to establish their own membership codes under Bill C-31 but we have already been notified that the federal government will pay for local services only for those members who qualify under the Indian Act. If we at Alderville have all our people back without restrictions, we will always have a community. If we abide by Indian Act regulations, some families, including my own, perhaps, will disappear from the community in two generations. We need economic development so that we can make the choice for ourselves.

Do you think you could have been a Chief six or eight years ago?

No, because I really didn't have any goals, formal education or most importantly, the self-confidence. I know that basically I always wanted to help my people. I just didn't know how to go about it.

What helped prepare you for your present responsibilities?

That first community development course was where I started to take hold. I learned a lot from interacting with students in the small business course, but even when I went to Trent I wasn't sure where I was going. Interacting at university with Native students from all over the country made me realize that the problems on my reserve weren't any different than anyone else's problems. I began to think: "Wow! Maybe I could change that. Maybe I could be the one."

So fine, you can sit there and talk 'til you're blue in the face, but what are you going to do about it? You come home and get involved in the community, because you care. Caring is a grassroots value that I learned from my mom and that she learned from her mom. During the summers while I was a student and after I graduated, I worked with status, non-status and non-Native women to set up and incorporate a crafts co operative at home. Through my formal education I learned how to plan, how to research, and most important, how to delegate responsibility. I used to be on committees and do everything, but I learned in community development that if people are going to grow, they have to make their own mistakes. This is important, to let them go, but there must be a guide.

The co-op still operates in the summer season. We have talked about enlarging the business, but like in any organization, people move on. One of the lessons we learned was that when you start something and teach people things, they leave to do other things. You are left with a new core, so you always have to be teaching.

That's a useful insight. Instead of bemoaning the fact that people you train move on, you gear up for the change and keep teaching new generations of organization members.

Native women traditionally were the teachers. I believe that they have to be initiators and motivators as well. Women have the quality that they can do a hundred things at once. You have to when you have kids and have to run a household on a limited budget. Women can push. If it weren't for women taking the initiative, we wouldn't have our status back.

Are there sacrifices involved in doing the things you have done?

You bet! You're never really free because if you are really committed you will give up your time. If someone calls on a week-end and says "Nora, I need help with this," I am there because I feel it's my duty. You don't realize until you get into the position what a responsibility it is. You have to be respected and you also have to take a lot of criticism, not always to your face! But that's O.K. If people talk, you know you are doing something.

I've put a lot of stress on my kids. My daughter has taken a lot on herself. She can control the whole household. She is talking about going into a law and security program at college, or she may go into social work. My son is more sports-minded.

What would you say are the qualities necessary for a young person who wants to make a contribution to the community, perhaps in a position of leadership?

I didn't set out to be a chief, but I knew I could do something because I was determined. So I think you have to be determined. You have to have goals. You have to be able to share. And you have to be patient. I keep a turtle with me wherever I go as a reminder. People don't always accept change. However, I feel that through communication with your community members, through giving insights into problems, etc. and how we intend to deal with them, one can make things happen in Indian country. Most importantly, you must always stress that "this is your community and the future depends on you, so get out there and get involved."

Originally published in Canadian Woman Studies/les ahiers de la femme, *"Native Women," 10 (2 & 3) (Summer/Fall 1989): 33–35. Reprinted with permission of the author.*

Prior to joining Rama Mnjikaning Nation, Nora Sawyer was Chief of the Alderville First Nation for seven of the nine years between 1987 and 1995. In her position as Director of Health and Social Services, Chippewas of Rama First Nation, Nora Sawyer has overseen the implementation and growth of a number of successful health initiatives. She has held a number of senior administrative and political posts throughout her working life and continues to be a champion for the Aboriginal community in health and community matters.

LANA WHISKEYJACK

A NICE STORY OF NOHKOM

Dedicated to Nohkom Caroline Whiskeyjack

So many memories of *Nohkom* and me
summers of stretched hide in the dancing trees
rez dog licking my wounded knee
galloping horses in storms they flee
long walks behind that ol'canvas tent
passed a tall birch was crooked and bent
Rusted t-ford to potbelly stove
places we played, moments I love
Tea and bannock by the kitchen window
sitting by her side as she played bingo
and ohhhh those handgames late into the night
drumming, laughing till the early morn light
rolling hills, silver sage, painted sky
picked purple berries in bacon grease they fry
together as a child *Nohkom* and me
traveling, visiting, being so free
I'd be of support feed her horse named buckskin
burnt down her smokehouse '*Whawaa*' what a sin
tried to help with a big load of laundry
no more after that ol'ringer caught me
but there's no other place I'd rather be
than by her side
Nohkom and me.

Summer ended I started school
with a smile she said "Education is your tool"
then off we'd walk half a mile or so
chewing gum, spitballs flying down the bus aisle
speeding down narrow gravel roads
all us rez kids sent to town-school by the loads

*Lana Whiskeyjack, "Nohkom", mixed media
(plaster, acrylic, colour photocopy, hide, gem and pastels), 2002.*

wore hand-me-downs all stained and torn
at lunch eat frybread and Indian popcorn
and oohhh during those long lunch hours
kids all aggressive full of imitated power
a slap, a whack, all chanting "whiskeybottle"
come home scratched, bruised, get a cuddle
in her strong arms she'd whisper to me
"Go back my girl, be strong, don't flee
don't turn the other cheek, it's respect you seek."
swelled with confidence, tough as teak
came home next day bit battered but smiling
after that there was no more bullying
like there's any other place I'd want to be
than by her side
Nohkom and me.

I grew up the way she planned
strong, loving and independent
then one day as if it were meant
a phone call from a woman who was pregnant
she—a non-native—pleaded to me

"It's his, your ex, won't you let him be
he still calls your name deep in his sleep
his heart's not yours but mine to keep
so take back your love medicine
that is what he said you'd do to win"
I gasped then laughed in disbelief
being blamed for something I'd never weave
I called *Nohkom* with tears in my eyes
cried and muttered "That man's full of lies!"
then she told me like I already knew
lovingly consoling me like she experienced a few
"The only medicine we have is between our legs."
an instinctive wisdom a life-giving force begs
enlightened by knowledge forever there
mistahi respect, love, wisdom to share
worked hard like she did clearing fields
studying, writing, creating, those are my shields
and like there's any other place I'd rather be
than by her side
Nohkom and me.

Finished school, worked, fell in love
our nations capital is where we moved
walked and talked in unrecognized territory
humour like hers provokes social foray
so far from home an emptiness reappears
then moments of gathered memories soothe my fears
visions of healthy relations, animate landscapes
veiled ancient teachings my wondrous gaze
swiftly I return to my many colourful places
of mountains, pow wows, medicines, and old faces
still haunted, challenged as restlessness consumes
the wisdom and spirit of *Nohkom* blooms
"*Kiyam*, don't worry, do your best and share"
powerful words of hers remind me to care
gift-giving of paintings, buffalo stew and laughter
ways I offer love—my desired character
an earthy role strengthens my intrinsic ember
sweetgrass smolder carries thanksgiving of her
her rhythmic visits of songs, stories and humour
teaches us women to grow strong and together
sometimes we listen many times we don't
eventually we learn to balance as others won't
but we're here for each other together as one

collective roles our children's continuum
and there's no other place I'd rather be
than by my family's side
Hiy-hiy to *Nohkom* and me.

The artwork on the previous page is a casting of my seven-month pregnant belly. The image within the casting is of my nohkom Caroline. I transferred my favourite picture of her so that her heart is centred on my belly button.

Originally published in Canadian Woman Studies/les cahiers de la femme, *"Indigenous Women in Canada: The Voices of First Nations, Inuit and Métis Women," 26 (3 & 4) (Winter/Spring 2008): 215-216. Reprinted with permission of the author.*

Lana Whiskeyjack is a nehiyaw (Cree) from Saddle Lake Cree Nations. She is an artist/art actionist who resides in Alberta.

CARRYING THE PIPE

Maliseet Elder, Healer and Teacher, Imelda Perley

PRESENT-DAY NEW BRUNSWICK and Maine are home to the Maliseet,[1] Algonkian speakers who call themselves *Welustuk*, "people of the beautiful river," a reference to the Saint John River. In the post-invasion period as they lost their hunting lands and river access, the Maliseet were concentrated on five reserves: Oromocto, Fredericton, Kingsclear, Woodstock, and Tobique. There were 4659 registered Maliseet in 1996.[2] The Maliseet face many of the problems other Indigenous peoples try to cope with (Hamilton and Owston), including high suicide and accident rates, and widespread unemployment and poverty. However, as in most Indigenous communities, there are many people working and innovating on these and other issues. Many of these leaders are women (Laronde; Anderson and Lawrence) and one of them is Imelda Perley, *Opo-lahsomuwehs* (Moon of the Whirling Wind), of Tobique, New Brunswick.

Like many Indigenous women leaders, Imelda is not paid for most of her "work" (quotation marks hers). She is the volunteer co-founder of the *Wolas-toqey* Language and Culture Centre, located in Tobique and at St. Mary's First Nation. The Centre runs a long list of programs, including Family Harmony Weekends, an anti-violence initiative incorporating the ceremonial and cultural practices. Imelda's nineteen-year-old son committed suicide last year and she and her husband, David Perley (who is running for a band council position this year), hope to establish an anti-suicide program. Her paid work includes teaching language and culture at the University of New Brunswick and the University of Maine at Houlton.

Imelda advises Indigenous nations to give priority to language revival, maintenance, and preservation, promoting language in every aspect of community life. She says that each nation should have a language policy to protect language rights.

Besides reflecting her own resilience and strength, Imelda Perley's work and her approach say a great deal about Indigenous women's ways of analyzing health and healing. For Imelda, violence, addiction, and sickness are community, not individual, problems, rooted in losses that are multiple, multi-generational, and collective. In Imelda's work, there is much adaptation and compromise, some of it quite creative. Such an approach is necessary, for Imelda is a Fourth World woman living and working in a colonized setting. This, of course, frames and limits her agency, despite her deeply held beliefs, remarkable personal strength, and optimism. In this, her experience reflects that of Indigenous women leaders all over Canada and beyond.[3] I spoke to Imelda, a Maliseet Elder, just after she had finished a four-day fast with her neighbours, the Mi'kmaq of Big Cove. Imelda and the others fasted and danced from dawn until dusk to free their communities from violence and addictions, reflecting the beliefs that energy is shared and that making sacrifices can lead to community healing.

I met Imelda at a gathering of Indigenous women in Winnipeg sponsored by the Native Women's Association of Canada. We came from all across Canada to identify and define concepts of Indigenous health and the factors that contribute to Indigenous health. I am an urban Newfoundland woman of English, Irish, French and Mi'kmaq ancestry in her early forties. I have spent much of my life and career learning about and from my Indigenous roots—and those of others as I work on land claims/rights, policy analysis, and policy development for Mi'kmaq, Innu, Inuit, and other Indigenous communities and organizations. More than ritual, more than songs and books, I find that listening to female Elders like Imelda connects me to that which is Indigenous, in me and in all of us. Being with female Elders brings me back into relationship with my own deceased aunts who unassumedly practiced Mi'kmaq medicine and healthways. It also also brings me into relationship with the very land I come from. Because I am introverted and formally educated, I learn by listening and writing. Imelda, too, is formally educated but her focus is the spoken word and she likes the more the traditional format of speaking to an attentive listener; hence, this transcribed discussion between the two of us about Imelda's work.

There are so many challenges facing Indigenous people—land claims, the effects of residential schools, language loss, health issues—multiple, collective losses. It seems everything is uphill at times with little progress. How do you identify what to tackle, or which issue or problem to focus on?

My family warns me I'm doing too much, always travelling, always working. They're always telling me this. But if you are a pipe carrier for the community, you have already given yourself to the community.

My focus is language. As a language carrier, it is my duty to transmit the gift of language to others. We've lost so many (*Wolastoqey*/Maliseet) speakers. There are so many people who don't know who they are and where they came from because of this. Let me give you an example of what language loss means. The Maliseet word for the "moon" is "Grandmother." When we call Grandmother "the moon" in English, we are objectifying her and this separates us from her—we lose that connection to her.

There has never been a time I didn't use language. One woman came to me in a crisis. Her husband was drinking and holding a gun; he wanted to kill himself. The woman wanted me to go to him and I said to her, "He doesn't know me, so how can I help?" She said, "No, he doesn't know you, but he's heard of you." There was some power in this. So I went to him, bringing my eagle feather, and I saw the gun. I knew he was a (Maliseet) speaker so I told him we didn't want to lose another speaker, it's too important, and we have lost so many. I asked him how the language would be passed on to his children without him because his wife didn't speak Maliseet. He said he hadn't thought of it that way. Then he put the gun down and we smudged. My work is about going where I know I can make a difference.

I know that you see language as healing in itself, as medicine—in fact, you see it as very central to the healing of Indigenous women, men, children, Elders, and communities. How have you used language in promoting healing?

Our language is our ancestral breath. We can't lose that. Language is who we are and who we will be; it is the centre of my learning and teaching and a gift from creation.

I do a lot of plays as a way of teaching, involving the whole community. Our plays have messages. We had animal characters who observed a treaty being signed and they talked about what the treaties meant, what rights and responsibilities the treaties recognized. Now, the treaties were written in the English language, not ours. So that's a problem and it might have been different if they were in our language. So that's in the play, too. I want the kids to know their language because they will one day be responsible for the treaties. The treaties were signed with the Maliseet nation but without our language; we won't be a nation anymore.

In 1994, I asked if I could teach a Maliseet first-language course in New Brunswick high schools. At first, the parents said, "What's the use? It's better to learn French to get a good job." Then I did home visits and I told the parents the kids have to know who they are so they can learn better. We have to teach each student as a whole person. Even if their mom is non-native, they're still Maliseet and they have to know what that means. That's how they become whole. I remember one kid got kicked out of school but he still did a project for my class; the language meant something to him.

"Culture," including language, of course, is often put forward as a solution or a method of healing. But there is also the argument from Australia and elsewhere (Brady) that cultural practices alone cannot heal because Indigenous people remain in oppressive political and economic contexts, for example, in Fourth World situations. What are your thoughts on this?

Right now our politics are separate from our culture. Everything changed after contact (with Europeans); for instance, we began to hunt with guns and then our whole hunting concepts and methodology changed. I grew up in a completely Maliseet-speaking milieu and now I am teaching Maliseet as a second language once a week for three hours. Men are now responsible for politics and women are now responsible for culture. We have been so badly affected by assimilation policies. Sharing is missing now.

We are trying to find a way to integrate culture and politics. When people speak at band council meetings, they should hold an eagle feather. They should avoid profanity and speak with respect to Elders, with no yelling. We should open our meetings with prayers. All these things are traditional; they are part of who we are as Maliseet.

The hierarchy of current politics is foreign to us. There is power at the top and things are enforced, not the result of consensus. There is a lot of big spending and borrowing but, you know, there is a way of living without money. Some are being rewarded by this system, by the way our communities are administered, and they don't want to change it. On our band council of 12, there are four who think like me.

Culture can heal our community and our governments; it builds self-esteem. I think of the kindergarten kids I have given spirit names. I had to find a way to make our culture appealing to them; I didn't want it to be like just another class. One boy was misbehaving and I gave him the spirit name of wolf and I told him how the wolf behaves. I gave each kid whatever spirit name worked for them. Now these kids are in middle school, they're about 13, and I'm taking five of them on a fast in August. I'm asking them not to take drugs or drink. I don't want them confused about who they are or about how to handle the struggles in their lives. I am very hopeful about this.

There were some kids getting into drinking and I had an Elder give a sweat lodge on a Tuesday night. They had to be sober for four days prior to that. Some of them thought they couldn't do it; they thought four days was too long and it included the weekend, which was deliberate on my part. They had to learn to be clean; they had to learn that discipline for their adult lives. Sixteen out of the 23 kids I invited made it to the sweat. That was in 1995 and six of them have never touched a drop of alcohol to this day. I think our leadership can be healed, too.

I'm struck by how you have been so successful in bringing outside resources to bear on your goals. You've built or supported various projects successfully by inviting well-resourced institutions into your community and you've worked hard at making alliances that can assist the Maliseet and other Indigenous people.

Some of it is small. I got a small grant from the New Brunswick Arts Council a few years ago to collect stories of the little people and shamans. My goal is to develop these stories into curriculum.

In 1997, I visited the Maori in New Zealand and learned a lot about language nests, sites in which there is complete immersion in the Indigenous language. Now we have seven language nests in New Brunswick with language education from the womb to beyond the grave. Mothers learn how to talk to their baby in Maliseet before the baby is born.

I invited the Massachusetts Institute of Technology to our community because they have a program that enables Aboriginal students to become linguists and they're trying to save languages through texts. We need to leave written texts for the generations that will come after us. Three MIT staff came here to Tobique and spent a week with our Elders and had daily talking circles in Maliseet. MIT wanted me to do my Masters degree there but I didn't want to leave my Elders. Meanwhile, they are trying to recruit Aboriginal people to do their undergraduate degrees with MIT paying for their studies. They're also giving us ideas on how to expedite the preservation of our stories.

I have good connections (internationally). For example, the Indigenous Language Institute out of Santa Fe, New Mexico has been very generous to us, donating clocks and watches and other items in our language. They have given us DVDs aimed at helping with language retention.

I also joined the NDP provincially and federally. I realized that non-Aboriginal MPPs and MPs are making decisions on behalf of Maliseet and other Indigenous people. I asked the NDP candidates to put up campaign signs in Maliseet and they did. The candidates met with our youth and Elders in talking circles. (Federal NDP leader) Jack Layton came to our territory and he was respectful of where he was. I was impressed by this.

I campaigned for Allison Brewer (New Brunswick NDP leader), who has worked with the Inuit. I invited her to our community for a circle and she listened. She said she had no idea how difficult things are in our community; I felt her truth, honesty, and sincerity.

Not all politicians are like Allison. When (Liberal) Andy Scott was Minister of Indian Affairs, he came to a debate at the University of New Brunswick and said, "I know a lot about Aboriginal people." I waited, I was just an observer, but then I spoke and I said to him, "You know a lot about Aboriginal *policies* because you write them." I told him, "Our logs are going to build your summer homes while we live in prefab houses, which is not our traditional way." I invited him to spend one night in a single mother's home in Tobique and to drink our water and eat our fish because we can't do it, but I never heard from him afterwards.

I've never been politically inclined and I normally wouldn't vote in a provincial or federal election. But I see how I have to become involved to protect the rights of my grandchildren. Maybe I'll run for office one day but first I want to concentrate on healing my community.

I've found that Indigenous women's work often gets to the heart of the matter. Women may not occupy as many official leadership positions as men, as you say, but I see so many Indigenous women leaders doing their work in other capacities. Do you see women's leadership roles changing? What do Indigenous women bring to leadership roles?

Clan mothers were always important to us, and that is a tradition we have to bring back. Clan mothers were responsible for the well-being of the whole community. The purpose of ceremonies was to support the clan mothers in their duties. We've revived the ceremonies to promote the spiritual, emotional, and physical well-being of our women. And we do this for the sake of our families, our communities, and our nations.

Indigenous women are the first teachers and there is something gentle about their teachings. Indigenous women maintain that connection to the earth, our land, our ancestors. Traditionally, we buried the placenta of every baby to keep connected. Today I encourage women to do this. We have revived puberty ceremonies for girls—"Honouring Grandmother Moon." Women need our language to stay connected to what keeps us alive and to be supported in our work.

The sacred pipe teaches us about balance. One of the teachings is that I carry a male spirit within me, too. Everyone has both spirits and each spirit has to be respected and nurtured. This gets forgotten.

If women and Elders played more of a role in official politics, there would be more healing and then better decisions. We would be returning to our roots and honouring them. We would be sharing and becoming whole Maliseet people. That's not happening yet.

I wonder what motivates you, and what inspires you to do this work? Have your motivations or inspirations changed over the years?

My grandmother was my biggest influence. She raised me. For her, being a grandmother was a profession. She took care of the sick and the Elders; she made blankets for new babies; she worked at the church and she gardened, always giving food away to whoever needed it. For Grade Seven, I went to an off-reserve school and the teacher asked all the students what we wanted to be when we grew up. I said I wanted to be a grandmother. Well, they all laughed. When I told my grandmother, she said, "They just don't understand." I understood her quite well and I wanted to be of service myself.

Another influence on me is Rita Joe (the Nova Scotia Mi'kmaw poet). Reading her poems was a turning point for me. Rita acknowledges the influences on her and she is now giving back, sharing the things that have shaped her.

Of course, I continue to be inspired by the people who want to learn the Maliseet language. I tell them that our language is endangered, yes, but it is very much alive on the *ktahqomiq* (land) where we survive, it is our *npisunol* (medicine) that heals us. You know, it is the songs yet to be sung and in the generations yet to be born. As I tell you these things, I feel that generations of women in my past, present, and future are guiding my responses.

Originally published in Canadian Woman Studies/les cahiers de la femme, "Indigenous Women in Canada: The Voices of First Nations, Inuit and Métis Women," 26 (3 & 4) (Winter/Spring 2008): 200-203. Reprinted with permission of the author.

Maura Hanrahan, Ph.D., is an independent anthropologist who works with Indigenous people's organizations in several provinces and at the national level. A Newfoundlander of English, Irish, French, and Mi'kmaq ancestry, Maura is a member of the Sip'kop Mi'kmaq Band, St. Alban's, Newfoundland. She is the author or editor of ten books in several genres. Her latest book is Spirit and Dust: Meditations for Women with Depression *(2009). Maura is also an award-winning painter. Her website is <www.maurahanrahan.com>.*

[1]Formerly spelled "Malecite."

[2]1996 Census, Statistics Canada, Government of Canada. Note also that the Maliseet are not part of the Mi'kmaq nation, as is sometimes wrongly assumed in the popular press and elsewhere.

[3]For a better understanding of these issues, see Anderson and Lawrence as well as Laronde.

REFERENCES

Anderson, K., and B. Lawrence, eds. *Strong Women Studies: Native Vision and Community Survival.* Toronto: Sumach Press, 2003.

Bailey, A. G. *The Conflict of European and Eastern Algonkian Cultures, 1504–1700.* Toronto: University of Toronto Press, 1969.

Blair, S. *The Wolastoqiyik Ajemseg: The People of the Beautiful River at Jamseg.* Fredericton: New Brunswick Culture and Sport Secretariat, Heritage Branch, 2003.

Brady, M. and K. Palmer. *Alcohol in the Outbreak: Two Studies of Drinking.* Canberra: Australian National University, North Australia Research Unit, 1984.

Hamilton, W. D. and R. D Owston. *School in Crisis: the Tobique Education Evaluation Report.* Fredericton, NB: np.1982.

Herrison, M. R. P. *An Evaluative Ethno-history Bibliography of the Malecite Indians.* Ottawa: National Museums of Canada, 1974.

Kelm, M-E. and L. Townsend, eds. *In the Days of Our Grandmothers: A Reader in Aboriginal Women's History.* Toronto: University of Toronto Press, 2006.

Laronde, S., ed. *Sky Woman: Indigenous Women Who Have Shaped, Moved or Inspired Us.* Penticton: Theytus Books, 2005.

McGee, H. F., ed. *The Native Peoples of Atlantic Canada: A History of Ethnic Interaction.* Toronto: McClelland and Stewart, 1974.

Wallis, W. D. and R. S. Wallis. *Anthropological Series* 40, 148. Canada Department of Northern Affairs and National Resources. National Museum of Canada, Ottawa, 1957.

GARRY KLUGIE

THE POVERTY AND THE POETRY

A Native Woman's Life History

MY MOTHER, MARGUERITE ROSE KLUGIE, a Loucheux woman of the T'licho tribe in the Northwest Territories, could have remained a misunderstood heartache to me if it hadn't been for a life-history project that gave me the opportunity and tools to understand her experiences and life in the context of gender-role prejudices and social inequalities. For years I had refused to identify with my mother, even though she was my only real parent. So many of Marguerite's problems and qualities that were confusing and unacceptable to me I dismissed as both isolated and insignificant. As a result of analysing Marguerite's life in a feminist context, I realized how common her experiences are and that there is nothing insignificant about inequality, prejudice, and oppression. In sharing this rewritten version of Marguerite's life history, I hope that others will expand their sense of involvement in the status of minority women in Canada.

The struggle for a feeling of belonging and self-identity began early for Marguerite as a result of a series of losses. As Marguerite recounts, in 1936, after she was born, Marguerite and her mother were involved in an airplane accident which her mother did not survive and in which Marguerite suffered severe head and body injuries. Shortly afterward her father sent Marguerite's younger brother and older sister to the Fr. Resolution Grey Nun Mission to join Marguerite, who was there recovering. Recuperating in a private room for the next few years, Marguerite's whole life was guided by older women and men: the nuns, nurses, and doctors who cared for her. Everyone in her isolated adult environment provided models that combined responsibility, piousness, independence, chastity, nurturing, and altruism. These replaced what would have been her family values. The Grey Nuns had done a good job of teaching her exaggerated female behaviour. Years later Marguerite commented that she always pushed me to be free because she felt that her own childhood rambunctiousness had been stifled.

Practices of sexual segregation and cultural repression had a strong effect on Marguerite's life. The Canadian film *Somewhere Between* portrays the effect of early missionary educational practices on Indian women of British Columbia: alienation from their own people, loneliness, and a sense of helplessness are reported by many other native Indian women. In the residential schools they could neither play with nor speak their own language with their own brothers. It seems very likely that this segregation has not only isolated generations of native Indian women—and men—from their culture but also from understanding each other, both inside and outside a family situation.

Adolescence pitched Marguerite into another stage of questioning and painful growth. Formal education, which had begun for Marguerite when she was seven, continued until she was sixteen, when she finished grade nine. Her peers often felt that because Marguerite needed special medical attention, she was spoiled. Her teachers also seemed to be insensitive to her background. These attitudes of her peers and teachers often made schooling a humiliating and awkward time that taught Marguerite to keep her inner feeling to herself. However, with one friend Magdalena, she shared her feelings and dreams. What might have been a great comfort turned into another loss when young Magdalena died of tuberculosis. Marguerite recalls comforting Magdalena during her last days: "We would hold each other and cry… I prayed to her then, saying that all my life would be a sacrifice… I replaced her suffering and death with my life."

Marguerite's sense of being a woman was marked by changes in her sexuality. Marguerite's first period was not a time of celebration but rather an experience that brought on isolation and shame. Like all of the other young women, Marguerite had not been prepared for the change. When it occurred each girl was taken from the larger dormitory for a few days and given a rag for cleaning herself—nothing was explained. Marguerite's treatment of her own daughter's menstruation was different. She made a conscious effort to make the change a time of celebration instead of punishment.

During Marguerite's youth explosive conflicts with the nuns were common for many of the children. One such encounter left Marguerite with many shattered teeth that were not repaired for years. Because of her appearance, she says she didn't "bother with men" for a long time.

Marguerite left the convent when she was twenty-one years old. She recalls that that occasion was the first time she consciously considered herself a woman; consequently, she needed to begin a new way of life. Marguerite and Magdalena's older sister, Geraldine, moved to Fort Smith for work. Being self-supportive was difficult but it was much more fulfilling than living in the convent. After only one year of the new independence and growth Marguerite contracted tuberculosis. Not only did she have to wear a body cast for over two years but also she was also once again dependent on others for her physical and emotional needs. Yet Marguerite's attitude remained powerfully understanding, almost healing "it just happened so I accepted it did what I liked."

Geraldine remained a friend to Marguerite through her illness, and when Marguerite was finally released she and Geraldine trained as nurses together until they decided to take jobs as cooks in a Yellowknife mine. Here both women "tried to nurture a good life. We were very independent economically.

I was in control and this allowed me to express my freedom." Soon, though, Marguerite realized that being a woman almost certainly meant becoming a mother, regardless of her hopes and dreams.

Marguerite knows, from painful experience, the truth of Buffy Saint Marie's song "Better to Find Out for Yourself":

Ev'ry baby that's been born, been spanked, and made to cry,
Ev'ry young woman that's been loved, been shaken, and made to sigh,
Ev'ry woman that' sever been loved, has told me, told me true,
Take his heart and run away, as he would do to you....

Marguerite's first sexual relationship with a man ended in pregnancy and abandonment. From the outset Marguerite learned that childbearing and childrearing were left to be woman's work; fatherhood was relatively meaning-less. Paul, Marguerite's first child, was born in 1956 in an Edmonton winter, 2,000 miles from Yellowknife, without a prospective father. Her decision to give birth in Edmonton and then to put Paul up for adoption was a reaction to the unavoidable social attitude which, in the north at least, labelled single pregnant women as promiscuous misfits. Both of these judgments, that chil-dren are the responsibility of women and that unmarried pregnant women are promiscuous, protected the men in Marguerite's life from criticism when and from taking responsibility for I their own sexuality.

The cycle of abandonment did not stop until after the birth of three more children: me, my brother James (whom I have never met), and my sister Barbara; even then, in the long run, there seemed to be little comfort. Like Paul and Marie, Rose, James, and Barbara were eventually put up for adoption, more because of poverty than social pressure this time.. When Eugene was born, the father, Stanley Johnson, decided to stay with Marguerite to "start" a family. Now Marguerite, the childbearer and child caregiver, had one more to look after: Stanley. In this respect she seems to fit a common pattern.

In an analysis of twenty-two life histories of women, Marjorie Mitchell found that after marrying, many women found themselves "burdened not only with the responsibilities of child care … but also with longer standing responsibilities of husband care" (mimeo, Camosun College, Victoria, B.C., 1978). Accepting the extra physical, sexual, and emotional demands was, for Marguerite, a means of fulfilling her own needs. Her comments on why she remained in the relationship after they both began drinking and Stanley began beating her makes this very clear: "I would be very angry and sad, but I had no alternatives. I needed him so I could keep the children … no one else would have me."

Repeated incidents of loss and physical violation are indications of Marguerite's status as a Canadian native Indian woman. Between the ages of twenty and forty, when Marguerite had her last child, Monica, she had given birth to eleven children. Five were put up for adoption and two others, Benjamin and Douglas, died before they were two years old. Only four children have remained with her. After eleven natural births, in which Marguerite always had an episiotomy, her doctor requested that she undergo a hysterectomy.

Yet the circumstances were less than professional. Instead of acknowledging Marguerite's right to control her body, her doctor asked Stanley for permission to perform the operation. Marguerite cried for weeks afterward, feeling empty, defeated, and outraged. "It wasn't fair … the power they had. Stan secretly arranged the whole thing. I guess he thought that after that I couldn't get pregnant so he could have as much sex as he wanted, but I said no."

In 1974, Marguerite took my brother, two sisters, and me from Edmonton to the Yukon, where Stanley had been working for over a year. Again Marguerite reminded me of the hardship of being a single parent. While Stanley was away she had to explain to the younger children where their father was and undertake all of the household and social demands we created. But in the Yukon there was a stronger sense of family and the children grew up in a clean, quiet, natural setting. Today Marguerite is waiting and working to support a family of three. She is going through the last motions of childrearing, after which she can use her own time, energy, and love for herself: "I'm not worried about growing old … I'm looking forward to having a house on a lake, living by myself, doing some sewing, and starting to paint again."

Though fashionable liberal ideologies maintain that individuals have freedom of access to all the social institutions that bring personal progress or growth, it seems truer to say that access to these institutions varies according to sex and race.

Originally published in Canadian Woman Studies/les cahiers de la femme, "Multi-cutlure," 4 (2) (Winter 1982): 39-41. Reprinted with permission of the author.

Marguerite Klugie has retired to two homes: one in Fort Resolution, North West Territories, and the other in Pelly, Yukon. She and her partner of over 50 years, Stanley Johnson, were to celebrate their 50th anniversary in 2008, when he passed away suddenly. Most of Marguerite's children, many of whom she lost to foster care, have been close to her over these many years, including Paul (Patrick, raised in Chicago), Rose, Garry, Barbara, Nyla, Styd, and Monica. Marguerite is happy to work in her communities, to cook and bake for everyone, to take photographs of the country and animals of her home lands, and to walk along the Pelly River, sometimes accompanied by two foxes. She is cared for by all of her family.

Garry Klugie is the happy father of three girls and step-father of two girls. He has taught in B.C. public schools for over 16 years and in B.C. First Nations schools over the last eight years. He has just completed a five-year term as founding Principal and Senior Secondary teacher for the Skeetchestn Community School in B.C. He is planning on relocating back to his Burns Lake home with his wife Teanne and hopes to return to regular classroom teaching, to writing, and to playing with family.

KIM ANDERSON

AN INTERVIEW WITH KATSI'TSAKWAS ELLEN GABRIEL, OF THE KANIEN'KEHÁ:KA NATION, TURTLE CLAN

PRESIDENT OF QUEBEC NATIVE WOMEN'S Association since October 2004, Ellen Gabriel advocates on behalf of Aboriginal women so they may gain their rights back in the wake of sexist policies coming from the Indian Act. This work includes assisting women to carry their messages to provincial, national, and international levels. Ms. Gabriel was chosen by the People of the Longhouse and then her community to be a spokesperson during the 1990 "Oka" Crisis, which involved protecting the Pines from the expansion of a nine-hole golf course in Oka. She has traveled across Canada, to the Hague in Holland, to Strasbourg in France to address the European parliament, and to Japan. In her travels she has worked to educate people about the 1990 events in her community and to sensitize the public on the history, culture, and identity of Aboriginal people.

Ellen has a Bachelor of Fine Arts degree from Concordia University. She worked as an illustrator/curriculum developer for Tsi Ronteriwanónha ne Kanien'kéka/ Kanehsatà:ke Resource Center in Kanehsatà:Ke and also worked as an art teacher for the Mohawk Immersion School for grades 1-6. Ellen has also worked on videos illustrating some of the legends of the Iroquois people and the local stories of the community of Kanehsatà:ke. She believes that education is one of the ways Aboriginal people can overcome oppression while still maintaining Indigenous languages, cultures, traditions and traditional forms of political structure.

Kim: *Can you talk a little bit about your work as the President of Quebec Native Women's Association, and how you got involved?*

Ellen: I observed that the work being done by the Association was effective and well respected; as well, I admired the past presidents who strengthened the work of the organization so I decided to join. Plus I'm motivated to be an agent of social change and I was interested in continuing to do advocacy work outside of my community and nation. I started attending Quebec Native Women's Association meetings and now I've become the President. In between all that, of course, I've tried to maintain my artistic side and keep that creative ideas flowing because that has been a good outlet for me.

Kim: *Quebec Native Women has always struck me as one of the most dynamic Native women's organizations in the country. What are some of the initiatives you've been working on?*

Ellen: Well, first of all, the organization was really well established before I came on. It has been nourished by the dedicated women who have been part of the organization, accompanied by some dynamic individuals who have dedication, passion, and care for the women in the communities and at the urban level. That is why I think the Quebec Native Women has always been one of the more active associations, like you said. We are well organized and we have people who are very dedicated and don't mind a low-paying job. I'm not too sure if it's also because the French-English situation has caused us to struggle more than other provinces to maintain our identity. There have also been some interesting allies along the way that have helped the Aboriginal women's movement in Quebec become so well-established. Like the late Rene Levesque, as well as some of the major women leaders of the women's movement in Quebec.

In 1988, QNWA was the first [Native] group in Canada to publicly denounce the violence happening in our communities, and that work has continued to this day. When I came on, there were new projects, such as the sexual abuse file, matrimonial real property, Native Women Shelters network, amongst others. We're going into our third year with that. There's a youth program, justice and public security, employment and training, a health file, and an international file. QNWA creates research to make tools that frontline workers can use in their work. The board is comprised of nine out of eleven nations in the region as well as an urban women's representative and a youth representative.

Kim: *Can you describe some of the international work of QNWA?*

Ellen: The international file was one of the things that was just starting when I got on. Now we have partners in Latin America. It has been eye-opening to see the impact colonization has had, and to see how similar our experiences are with other Indigenous peoples. One striking effect is the impact of machismo on our languages, cultures, and identities amongst all our people, and in particular how it is affecting the lives of Indigenous women in Latin America.

We now have a partner in Panama who's developed a course on leadership for Indigenous women, as well as on the United Nations Declaration on the Rights of Indigenous Peoples. We would like to see an on-line course on writing a business proposal and how we in the North can help Indigenous women entrepreneurs partner with women [from other countries] to help create a market for our goods. Presently, we are working with a consultant that works with the Asia-Pacific Economic Council to create different kinds of market models so that Indigenous women can become more self-sufficient, because anywhere in the world Indigenous women are marginalized, and are the poorest of the poor. We also want to submit an economic development proposal to CIDA this year, to partner with some businesswomen in Panama and maybe some other parts of Latin America. We'd like to do an exchange; bring some

Ellen Gabriel, 2005. Photo: Kenneth Deer.

of their products up here, help them write business proposals, have a partner in Canada, and so on.

Kim: *I've always been interested in leadership and Indigenous women. What's involved in the course you offer?*

Ellen: Well, it's all in Spanish right now, and it's a computer-based course. There are over three hundred participants so far. There are little sections and each one is a scene. Participants talk about social issues of violence as well as how to use international instruments to lobby our governments, how to give a speech, how to do research on issues—so there's some really interesting things that are being developed. I find that the women in Latin America are very well organized. They don't have funding, but they march in the thousands, and they're very vocal. They do work with men's groups too. It's interesting to see the differences between us and the passion we share for social justice issues.

Kim: *Is there anything distinct about they way they teach leadership?*

Ellen: I remember attending a three-week workshop in Peru in 1985, and it really covered the gamut of identity. They'd say, "Okay what is so special about you region?" Women would bring in plants. If they didn't have the plants they would bring in vegetables like corn; they would bring in whatever they had. They would talk about their language; they would talk about their home, their family, their ceremonies, their spirituality. These are the things they talked about as necessary for defining the characteristics of a leader. A leader should know where they come from, who they are, and have a link to their ancestry. I found it really refreshing, as opposed to what we learn up here: how to be a good administrator, how to write proposals to government, how to do your budget and stuff like that. They teach them that too, but we don't see the other stuff.

Kim: *That's a very different type of grounding.*

Ellen: Yes, very much. They did a lot of bonding exercises to get to know one another. The solidarity is really evident there. There's a unity. Like before Apartheid was broken in Africa, people would march in demonstrations in the hundreds of thousands. They had this collective experience. For Aboriginal people in Canada at least, the collective experience is gone. The collectivity remains in the past and we're not using it now, unless we organize blockades.

Kim: *Let's talk a little bit about Oka and what's changed, because that was a defining moment for a lot of people across the country. And of course, you had people coming from all over to unite. It really flared up with that and it's never happened in that way again. As you think back over the last twenty years, what has changed in terms of activism?*

Ellen: Well, I think what was interesting was that people behind the barricades had no clue what was going on in the rest of Canada until a few weeks after it started. I mean, television was not our priority. I think we could catch the eleven o'clock news if we had time. And so when we heard about the support, it was really empowering for us because it was a time in everybody's lives—I'll just speak for myself—where there was so much unknown. *There could be a gun battle any second. Am I going to make it through this experience? What's going to happen to me afterwards? Am I going to jail and am I going to jail for a long time?* There were a lot of uncertainties, so when we heard about protests and when we had people from all over Canada sneaking in behind the barricades to come and tell us: "Our community supports you, our community donated food," it brought back our faith in people and humanized us again. Because the media certainly took that away from us, and the government certainly took that away from us. And so morally, spiritually, we needed that.

Then afterwards, it took a few months for me to realize that the youth were really affected by this and nobody was there for them. Their impression was that being a Mohawk meant being a warrior and being a warrior meant being a badass. And this is the problem that we have today; I find that my community has gone backwards in growth, rather than forwards, whereas a lot of the other communities have grown.

Kim: *You mean communities that weren't actively engaged had more opportunity to grow from this experience? Maybe people that were witness to it, but necessarily not right in the middle of it?*

Ellen: Well, it surprises me, because even now I get people telling me what was happening to them during that time, and it's eighteen years later! People seem to have the need to tell me what was going on for them; that Oka was such a good thing that happened for everybody. Meanwhile I'm thinking, "Well no, not for my community." But it did that; it inspired pride, empowerment—and people became more aware on the state of our languages, for example, which is really important to me. I think it also empowered other communities to say, "Okay, well we're not taking this anymore. We're going to put up blockades." And they know how to use the media now, which was not there before. So there were a lot of positive things that happened for Aboriginal people.

I think it was a good thing and it was worth the sacrifice. Just to know at least we did something that might help one little community that no one has ever been aware of before. I guess it's difficult to say how deep it goes, not just for me personally, but for others.

Kim: *Well, and for non-Aboriginal people too right? Because I know both Native and non-Native people who told me that it was a life-changing experience. I have non-Native friends who left Quebec as a result of what happened. They were so appalled at the reaction that they lost their faith in the province. Of course, the federal government was involved too, but I guess they thought that Quebec was better than that. So it had such a profound effect on all different types of people. But it's interesting to hear you talk about what happens to a community after all the press and the people go away.*

Ellen: Yes … there were programs for healing. We had a lot of people that came to us. Some said, "We'll do sweats for you," but what they were thinking about was power. Kanehsatake was like a magnet, bringing together a diversity of people. There were those who wanted our stories; who wanted to take something from us that they thought was power. There were a lot of charlatans, people who saw money opportunities, maybe thought that we were like hicks or hillbillies that would fall for their storyline. But we were very careful and cautious because we made decisions as a group.

It was also a little scary at the time, because the whole idea was to stop development of a golf course. The issue was our rights to that land. And people came in with their own agendas that we didn't know about.

Kim: *Was Oka your first foray into activism? How did you get involved?*

Ellen: Well, there was a certain faction of the Longhouse that decided to maintain the barricades after all the injunctions came in against us, and I was close to that family. I had taken an oath when I joined the Longhouse to uphold those laws and those values. So when this came along, I thought: *it's not like I have a decision or a choice; I have to do this.* And I learned as I went along. I learned from my Elders who were there. I learned from people who had some experience in negotiation and so I'm really thankful for them.

Kim: *So you hadn't been a leader in that sense before? You hadn't had experience negotiating?*

Ellen: People might be surprised when I say this, but I'm very much an introvert. I think most artists are; they like time alone right? I always had problems doing presentations and I hated talking in front of a class, so some time afterwards, I met some of my university professors who were really surprised at what I was doing. So I was very fortunate to receive caring support and feedback from my Elders. I had just graduated from Concordia, and so it was a kind of tough summer school. Survival 101, kind of thing. It was pretty much a war zone: you were denied food; you were denied medicine; people were being beaten and tortured; and you really didn't have time to think about yourself. You just need to do what you have to do. The whole process was: *I'm on automatic mode, here.* So I had maybe one time during the whole summer when I broke down and then I got back up and did my work.

But it wasn't until years later that I really started taking care of myself and getting rid of some of the stuff I felt was poisonous to keep. The philosophy behind our traditions is one of the things that has kept me strong. Having good support systems, my family, my Elder and his family. Another thing that kept me going was my respect for nature. I've always loved nature and the environment and I have always been into preserving the environment, even as a young child. So I feel it's important to be part of the efforts regarding the issue of defending Indigenous peoples' rights, especially now that we're looking at climate change and global warming. I look at our traditions, our Indigenous knowledge sources from around the world. I'm trying to see how we can get the international community to accept, respect, and value Indigenous knowledge. For me I go back again to that obligation, when I took that oath. What do we want to preserve for future generations? What I may contribute may be a very small pebble in the whole ocean of water, but whether I do it through my art or my activism doesn't matter, as I think this is probably something I'll do for the rest of my life. I think that's what I took with me from Oka.

Kim: *Can you talk about how your art and activism come together?*

Ellen: I was fortunate that as a child, my parents supported and encouraged my artistic endeavours. It gave me a solid base from which to express myself and to hone my craft. I have always been attracted to imagery that reflects my identity as an Indigenous person and so historical images and traditional forms of art are obvious icons that help me convey my message. Art is a non-threatening from of expression that can spark discussion, curiosity, it can be aesthetically pleasing or not, and can convey a message which can introduce an issue without necessarily overwhelming the audience. Consequently, as I became more politically active, it was a natural progression for me to incorporate my activism into my art work. I like the affect that my socio-political work has upon viewers and their interpretation of my work. And because I am visual, I like to utilize images as either symbols or icons of both contemporary and historical references to get my point across. Coming from a people who have always fought against colonization and oppression, it seems natural in a way, that I would incorporate my activism with my art. But I am an artist and so as my work evolves, so does my choice of medium, iconography and motivation. It is important for me to continue using my art as a form of cultural sensitiza-tion but as well, to continue creating art such as landscapes, portraits, etc, for the sheer pleasure of expressing myself without the use of words.

Kim: *Before we go, I wanted to know if you had any reflections on some of the activism that has been going on in recent years. What are your observations based on your own experience?*

Ellen: I can see problems sometimes when that machismo element comes in, because it clouds the mind. I think, again, it goes back to people wanting their fifteen minutes of fame, which means they are not there for the right reasons. I think it's so important now to be aware of the issues; to be able to argue without fault. To justify your actions of why you are doing something. It's not enough to block a road or to block a railroad; you have to justify and have a complete understanding of what you are doing and why. Because that's the nature of our relationship with Canadians and their government—we as Indigenous peoples have to continuously teach them about us, our perspectives, our history, our identity, and why they are important to us; why we want to perpetuate our languages, and why we want to continue being stewards of the land. And most times people don't have enough of that knowledge or opportunities to share information. I believe that change will come with the people of this country, not the politicians or governments who have, in the past, been motivated to protect the bottom-line or interests of the corporations exploiting our lands and resources.

Kim: *Well, it's interesting to think about it in the context of youth, too.*

Ellen: The youth need guidance, and they need role models. They need reassurances that it's okay to be "Indian," "Native," or "First Nations" and that they don't need drugs, alcohol, or the latest fashions to be proud of who they are. There is not enough in our school systems to reinforce that pride in their identities. Science, math, and all those things that are taught in school are important, but there must also be something that teaches them about who they are as Indigenous peoples. Otherwise, in the future, the only way they will see or live their identity will be through museums, in documentaries, or in books. We have a duty to the future generations to perpetuate traditional knowledge and teach this in the schools because lots of youth don't have that opportunity at home. In conjunction with school curriculums, we should start encouraging our youth to learn their culture and languages, start creating those books and filming those documentaries, otherwise, future generations will be people with Indigenous ancestry but without living the experience of being Indigenous.

Kim: *Well you certainly have been a role model for many of us. Thanks for sharing with us here.*

Originally published in Canadian Woman Studies/les cahiers de la femme, *"Indigenous Women in Canada: The Voices of First Nations, Inuit and Métis Women," 26 (3 & 4) (Winter/Spring 2008): 52-58. Reprinted with permission.*

Kim Anderson is the author of A Recognition of Being: Reconstructing Native Womanhood *(2000) and the co-editor, with Bonita Lawrence, of* Strong Women Stories: Native Vision and Community Survival *(2003).*

ROLE MODELS

An Anishinaabe-kwe Perspective

AANII. RENÉE ELIZABETH Mzinegiizhigo-kwe Bédard *ndizhinikaaz. Waabzheshii ndodem. Dokis First Nation ndoonjibaa.* I was always told to introduce myself by my Elders and my family. My name is Renée Bédard. I am Ojibwe (Anishinaabe-kwe) and Marten Clan, from Dokis First Nation, along the French River. I am an Indigenous Studies Ph.D. candidate at Trent University, studying the creative processes of Anishinaabe women artists. I write and paint about the Anishinaabe women I know, grew up with, and see in Anishinaabe communities. My passion as an Anishinaabe woman scholar and artist is to highlight the voices and experiences of Indigenous women in a positive manner.

I send out a *miigwech* (thank you) to all the Indigenous women who have crossed my path, offering knowledge and experience on how to be a "good" Indigenous woman. I have had many Indigenous women role models. My mother, my aunties, my granny or grannies, my cousins, my sisters, and my friends were my best role models on how to be a strong Anishinaabe-kwe (woman). Anishinaabe women Elders have also been influential role models for learning what is the best path to being a "good" woman. The Elders speak of the concept of *mino-bimaadiziwin*, which speaks of a "good mind," a "good way," or a "good path" that an individual takes in order to live a healthy and well-rounded life as an Anishinaabe. I look to the women in my family and the Anishinaabe women Elders who have walked before me for examples of how to live *mino-bimaadiziwin*, as well as grow into a responsible Anishinaabe-kwe who can help her family, community, and Nation.

In the Anishinaabe seven stages of life, I am still in somewhat of the "wandering and wondering" stage , full of questions, looking for teachers and answers to what are the secrets of life. In my late twenties, I am young enough to appreciate the freedom of my youth and yet I feel the doors opening up to a new stage of life that includes knowing my future goals, and starting my own family . I find myself looking back and around me at the Indigenous women who have informed my sense of womanhood. It is those Indigenous women who have come before me that inspire and encourage me to be a "good" role model for the young girls who follow in my footsteps.

49

Over the years, I have spent time with Anishinaabe women Elders, listening, watching, and internalizing any guidance or knowledge they might share. It is the importance of Elders as role models that I wish to talk about first in order to highlight the important work they do for us young women. Through Elders, Anishinaabe women and girls learn a sense of community, love, family, and esteem (for self and others). After the passing of many of the older Anishinaabe women in my own family, I realized that the knowledge of those generations who came before me would only continue on into the future if I took action and made the effort to learn and remember as much as I could from my Elders. For myself, I feel it is a treasure to spend time with Elders; it is a gift. Anishinaabe women Elders do more than just educate our young women and girls. They shape our feminine identities as Anishinaabe-kwewag (women) in ways that lay the foundations for a sense of self-worth and self-respect.

The *Gathering Strength* volume of the *Report of the Royal Commission on Aboriginal Peoples* (RCAP) states that Elders are important because they are the: "Keepers of tradition, guardians of culture, the wise people, the teachers. While most of those who are wise in traditional ways are old, not all old people are elders, and not all elders are old" (3: 527).

The knowledge and experience of women Elders teaches us how to be a strong, responsible, Indigenous woman. Their wisdom is not only personally learned, but also comes from the shared knowledge and experiences of their ancestors and their Elders, which is described by Pam Colorado (Oneida) as a "collective effort to know throughout time" (58). As Joseph Couture (Cree/Métis) points out, the ways of knowing expressed by Elders guides people to learn to live in balanced relationships with all other living things:

> There is an observable Elder "psychology" implicit in what they do and say, Elders, as highly aware persons, and as carriers of oral tradition, are the exemplars, the standing reference points. When guided by Elders, the apprentice learns to perceive and understand something of such dimensions as the nature itself of the knowledge, of the centrality of primal experiences, of the "laws of Nature," as this in Elder sayings.... Evolved Elders arrive at and preserve a sense-rooted thinking which knows the world as a spiritual reality. He who "knows," experiences a spiritual nature in the perceived world. Reality is experienced by entering deeply into the inner being of the mind, and not by attempting to break through the outer world to a beyond. This positions the Native person in "communion," within the living reality of all things. His "communion" is his experience of the ideas within, concentric with reality without. Thus, to "to know," to "cognize," is experiential, direct knowing. (57)

As an Anishinaabe-kwe, I have been taught that Anishinaabe women Elders are significant for the development of Anishinaabe knowledge, worldview, and ways of being or interacting with the world. Colorado explains that: "Elders guide us through our experiences, usually by identifying appropriate rituals or processes so that we gain insight and understanding of ourselves, the universe and our place in it" (56). Elders are our historians, philosophers, helpers, leaders, teachers, and healers (Cajete; Colorado; Castellano; Simpson 1999, 2000). Elders are our experts, specialized in traditional cultural knowledge and experiences (Colorado). The Elders' role at the community level is to act as "cultural" guides and models for how to live life in a healthy, well-rounded manner.

As well as our valued Anishinaabe women Elders, many of us Anishinaabe-kwewag (women) look to our mothers, gannies, aunties, cousins, sisters, and friends as our most influential role models. The adult Indigenous women around us who we meet and spend time with can be significant role models for us . Many of these Indigenous women might not even be related to us, might not be from our Nation, but still they inspire, teach, and guide us when we need someone to steer us towards the future. The Anishinaabe women in my family taught me about my identity as an Ojibwe or Anishinaabe-kwe, my history as a member of Dokis First Nation, and my sense of connection to the lands of my people along the French River.

Odawa Elder Liza Mosher says:

> I have no heroes. I have lots of role models. My mother was my best role model. My grandparents were my best role models, so was my father. Because your Spirit chooses those as your parents as your Spirit leaves the greater side. You learn from those parents, that's what you came for. It's good even though you go through a lot of pain. (148)

Sometimes we need not look farther than the women directly around us in our families to find role models. Sometimes all we have to do is look beside us to our sisters and friends to find someone to inspire and look up to. For myself, my older sisters and my now deceased Ojibwe mother and grandmother have remained the constant reminders of what my responsibilities are as a young woman and as a young Anishinaabe-kwe.

I find myself building a web of relationships with other Indigenous women in order to learn what are my responsibilities as an Indigenous woman. The adult Indigenous women in my life are role models of how to respond to, act, and live out my responsibilities as an Indigenous woman. Many Indigenous women define themselves through responsibilities of family, community, and nation. We rely on each other as Indigenous women to show each other how to survive, raise our families, and attend to our community obligations. Indigenous women's identities are tied to the inter-relationships we have with the women in our families, communities, and connections we make with Indigenous women outside our communities; oftentimes our friends, Elders, teachers, and acquaintances. Together, as Indigenous women, we work to determine our identities and responsibilities as women by talking and spending time with each other.

Together we share both our happy times and hard times. Each connection, each relationship helps shape our knowledge of our feminine responsibilities in the world and makes us stronger. Indigenous women look to other Indigenous women in their lives as the most immediate and profound role models.

Besides Elders and other adult women we share our lives with, it is important to note the influence of the young girls, children, and babies in our lives. It is often through the eyes of the young that we learn to value our lives as women. Have you ever noticed how women often rush to hold a newborn? Babies are close to the Spirit world and the Creator. Liza Mosher notes: "At the first stage, the child is half Spirit and half human. It's more in the Spirit world than in this reality…" (156). The young are special and cherished—a reminder for women that they are the creators of life.

Women feel the pull of that closeness to the Spirit world, which is pure and open to new experiences. Being able to bring a new life into the world and raise-up the young is something we need to thank the young for. The young give many gifts to women. It is through the very young that we learn how to be mothers, aunties, and grannies. Without the young, Indigenous women would not experience these roles and responsibilities so key to our feminine identities. The young teach us compassion, humility, generosity, and kindness. As women we need to look up to the very young as the grandmothers and grandfathers of the next generation (244). In this way, babies, children, and youth are also our role models.

With all the negative images of our women bombarding us in the media, and with the rise of other forms of violence against women in our families, communities, and western institutions (e.g., prison system), it is important to highlight the "good work" women do in our communities. I am inspired by the women I see raising awareness about the *Lost Sister's*, our women missing or lost due to violence and murder. The *Lost Sister's* campaign has made me want to write and paint images of the women I know, love, and look up to, to change how others see Indigenous women. We need not look further than our family and friends or the faces of our young children to find healthy and strong images of Indigenous women around us.

If we want to change how our Indigenous mothers, sisters, friends, aunties, and grannies are seen and treated by the world, we, as Indigenous women need to speak out. Indigenous women need to show the world our faces, share our voices, opinions, and acknowledge each other, so that there are role models for the young women to look to in the future. We have to say to the world, "I am an Indigenous woman," and "I am Anishinaabe-kwe." I am not the Pocahontas as portrayed in the Disney movie, dressed in skimpy clothing to be rescued by a man or objectified as a sex object. I am a smart, passionate, and fearless woman. I and other Indigenous women will not be abused or violated or mistreated. I will be honoured, respected, and treated with value by the world. As an Indigenous woman, an Anishinaabe-kwe from Dokis First Nation, I am proud to acknowledge the many Indigenous women role models who have had an impact on my life and send out a *Gchi-miigwech* (Big thanks!) to all of them. I, in turn, will be a role model for the young girls and women who follow behind me.

Originally published in Canadian Woman Studies/les cahiers de la femme, *"Indigenous Women in Canada: The Voices of First Nations, Inuit and Métis Women," 26 (3 & 4) (Winter/Spring 2008): 190-192. Reprinted with permission of the author.*

Renee E. Mzinegiizhigo-kwe Bedard is Anishinaabe, marten clan and a member of Dokis First Nation in northern Ontario. As an Anishinaabe woman academic, she pursues issues and topics that are important to Anishinaabeg women and the Anishinaabeg community. She holds a B.A. from Nipissing University, an M.A. from Trent University and is currently completing her Ph.D. in Indigenous Studies at Trent University.

REFERENCES

Anderson, Kim. *A Recognition of Being: Reconstructing Native Womanhood.* Toronto: Second Story, 2000.

Canada. *Gathering Strength.* Vol. 3 of *Royal Commission on Aboriginal Peoples: Report of the Royal Commission on Aboriginal Peoples.* Ottawa: The Commission, 1996.

Cajete, Gregory. *Native Science: Natural Laws of Interdependence.* Santa Fe, New Mexico: Clear Light Publishers, 2000.

Castellano, Marlene Brant. "Updating Aboriginal Traditions of Knowledge." *Indigenous Knowledges in Global Contexts: Multiple Readings of Our World.* Eds. George J. Sefa Dei, Budd L. Hall, and Dorothy Goldin Rosenberg. Toronto: University of Toronto Press, 2000. 1-13.

Colorado, Pam. "Bridging Native and Western Science." *Convergence* 21(2/3) (1988): 49-68.

Couture, Joseph. "Explorations in Native Knowing." *The Cultural Maze: Complex Questions on Native Destiny in Western Canada.* Ed. John W. Friesen. Calgary: Detselig, 1991. 53-57.

Mosher, Liza. "We have to go back to the Original Teachings." *In the Words of the Elders: Aboriginal Cultures in Transition.* Eds. Peter Kulchyski, Don McCaskill, and David Newhouse. Toronto: University of Toronto Press, 1999. 141-167.

Simpson, Leanne. "Anishinaabe Ways of Knowing." *Aboriginal Health, Identity and Resources.* Ed. Jill Oakes, et al. Winnipeg: Department of Native Studies, Native studies Press, 2000.

Simpson, Leanne. *The Construction of Traditional Ecological Knowledge: Issues, Implications and Insights.* Diss. University of Manitoba, 1999.

LINA SUNSERI

SKY WOMAN LIVES ON

Contemporary Examples of Mothering the Nation

MY GRANDMA, DOROTHY DAY, passed over two years ago. I remember her as a gentle, smiling woman who seemed happiest when surrounded by all her children and grandchildren. She often said that family was the most important thing and that we should try our best to see each other as often as we could, even if our lives demanded that we be physically far apart from each other. She kept reminding us that we must always be respectful of one another and to help family and friends in need. She lived her life according to those wise words. In doing so, she was well connected to the Native community in London, Ontario, to the Oneida Nation, and other friends within the broader London area. Her house was open to all of us in the family; I don't recall her door ever being locked. That is what Grandma Day wanted: for her home to be open to her family and friends who needed a comforting place. She had many friends; in fact whenever I say to others that I am her granddaughter, people have stories to tell and remind me of what a loving, caring woman she was. Grandma Day had a hard life, but that never hardened her or made her speak badly of those who caused her pain. She did not want bad energy to fill her heart and soul. She raised all her children on her own, helped to raise many grandchildren, and helped out with her great-grandchildren when needed. She worked hard and helped out in her community throughout her life, especially in the Native community, and with those who had challenges, as she herself had a vision disability.

Months after her passing, the N'Amerind Friendship Centre in London opened a new library and learning resource centre and named it the Dorothy Day Learning Centre. At the opening day ceremony, the executive members of N'Amerind explained that they decided to name it after my grandmother in order to remember and honour a lifelong member of the centre and community. She was remembered as someone who gave so much to the community, who loved all unconditionally, and who who wanted all Natives to feel proud of their identity and to cherish their culture. She was one of the original founders and a long-time volunteer at the centre. Like many other Native women, my grandma loved and nurtured the community and expected little in return. To be recognized through the naming of a new learning centre is suitable.

Grandma Day believed the youth were our future and that they need to be nurtured. She believed we need proud youth, educated in Native worldviews, in order to build strong communities That is what the new learning centre has become: a place where all forms of knowledge are enriched and respected, and whose principle aim is to revitalize Native cultures and knowledge. My grandma is happy, I am sure of that. Her spirit lives in the centre with those who are learning everyday, guiding them into a good way. As a gentle, yet strong Oneida woman, she helped me to understand and appreciate the meaning of Native womanhood. Thank you, grandma. We love you and are carrying on as best as we can.

***

Another remarkable Oneida woman is my aunt, Donna Phillips. About two years ago, her birthday party was held at the N'Amerind Friendship Centre so that all her beloved family and friends could be present. After all the food was eaten and the presents opened, a number of people said a few words about what aunt Donna meant to them. Her daughters spoke about her kindness, her unconditional love, her unwavering support throughout their lives, and of how their mother had been an inspiring role model for them. Other family members shared how they learned from her how to be strong, caring, and proud of their Oneida ancestry. One community member spoke of how aunt Donna helped her throughout her life. This person learned to live as the Creator meant for us to live: by following the principles of respect, reciprocity, honesty, and caring. My aunt Donna has lived by these principles all her life and many people at the party shared examples of how she represents these principles. My aunt Donna is a well-recognized member of not only the Oneida community, but also of the larger Native community on Turtle Island. She has served her nation well. She has taught many people about the richness of our culture, the history of Oneida, and of women's role(s) in our communities. She has taken the responsibility of being an Oneida woman of the Turtle clan seriously, by being an activist for social justice for our people and for others who have suffered injustices. She has been an active member of the Native Women Association of Canada and other Native organizations in Canada. She has travelled across the globe to share and learn about Indigenous histories and cultures so that she could pass on that knowledge to the future generation. She has never been afraid of hard work, even if there has been, in turn, little financial reward or recognition. She does all of this because it needs to be done and because she loves her people. At her birthday party those present recognized her dedication to her community publicly and affirmed how she has been a positive role model for many, especially Native women. She is a good example of an Oneida woman or mother of our nation—someone who nurtures its members and inspires them to cherish the individual gifts they have been given by the Creator. Through her lived examples, we can learn to give back to our nation in our own unique way. I know that a large reason for my academic success is from having witnessed my Aunt Donna's strength, shared her vision, and watched her care for her people. This has instilled in me a sense of pride about my Oneida background, and a belief that the women in our communities are truly the heart of our nation. As the Sky Woman who fell from the Sky, both Aunt Donna and Grandma Day are typical mothers of our nation: they have shaped us into who we are and they guide us into reclaiming our independence and freedom as original peoples of beautiful Turtle Island.

***

I wanted to share these two stories in order to provide concrete examples of the strength that has existed within Oneida women despite the many forms of oppression they have had to endure. Many Indigenous scholars have analyzed the current conditions of Indigenous women and traced these back to a destructive colonial history (Anderson; Ladner; Laroque; Lawrence; Mihesuah; Monture-Angus; Stevenson; Voyageur). Although I will touch upon some of the negative legacies of colonialism that still invade our communities, the main purpose of this paper is to present positive empowering images of Indigenous women, specifically of the Oneida nation. Oneida Nation is one of the six Nations of the Haudenosaunee League, also known as the Six Nations or Iroquois Confederacy. I intend to show that Indigenous women's lives are rich with strength and determined spirit, gifts that the Creator has given them so that as warriors they can face the battles they encounter as they work toward pulling down barriers that impede them as women, as First Nations, as well as those that impede our communities.

EMPOWERING MOTHERHOOD

Both my grandma and my aunt cared, nurtured, and fought for their loved ones and for their community as strong mothers of the nation. The way motherhood is understood here stands against the mainstream dominant ideology of patriarchal motherhood. Patriarchal motherhood is an ideology that has controlled, constrained, and degraded women (O'Reilly). This is because such an ideology constructs "good" mothers as ones who are "naturally" willing to put their family's needs first, at the expense of their own interests (O'Reilly). "Good" mothers sacrifice and conform to an institution of motherhood that is male-defined and a site of oppression (O'Reilly). Although my grandma and my aunt did love and care for their families, they also cared for their own lives and pursued their own interests. My aunt Donna's years of activism while a mother is an example of her not conforming to a patriarchal ideology of motherhood that expected her to push aside her own interests and needs. Motherhood did not imply a subservient and submissive role, rather it gave her strength to be a type of woman that her children, grandchildren, and all other Oneida people could look up to. An alternative to patriarchal mother-hood has always existed in Indigenous communities, as Indigenous women "have historically, and continually, mothered in a way that is 'different' from the dominant culture, [and this] is not only empowering for our women, but is potentially empowering for all women" (Lavell-Harvard and Corbiere Lavell 3). This empowered mothering recognizes that when mothers practice mother-ing from a position of agency rather than of passivity, of authority rather than of submission, and of autonomy rather than of dependency, all, mothers and children alike, become empowered (O'Reilly Collins).

Consequently, motherhood becomes a political site, wherein mothers can effect social change and reduce the patriarchal nature of institutions (Collins). Acts taken by my grandma, for example, can be seen as political sites: offering her home to those in need was a political act, as her home came to be a refuge from the pain experienced by those surviving in an environment which was—and still is—hostile to Indigenous peoples. Her home was also a place where her loved ones knew that they were accepted as gifts from the Creator, even when acts by others made one question that reality. Being a "good" mother did not mean women had to push aside their own needs in order to give exclusive at-tention to their children. Thus, the relationships formed by mothers and their children, and especially by mothers and daughters in Indigenous communities, are not characterized by oppressive patriarchy (O'Reilly). By being surrounded by strong and independent, yet still gentle and caring women, as children we learned to value the feminine spirit and to respect and treat women, our moth-ers, as equal to men (O'Reilly). From an Indigenous standpoint, this kind of mothering contains a commitment to "prepare and equip the next generation to bring about an Indigenous resurgence based on Indigenous interpretations of our traditions" (Simpson 26). Grandma and aunt's daughters witnessed the independence, autonomy, and strength of their mothers, and this provided them with the knowledge of the sacredness of Indigenous womanhood.

MOTHERING THE NATION IN THE CASE OF ONEIDA WOMEN

Often Indigenous women are negatively portrayed as the stereotypical "sav-age," who has been historically constructed from the early period of contact between Indigenous and non-Indigenous people (Acoose; Stevenson). Hence, encountering real women that are in opposition to the stereotypical images presented in a racist society is crucial for the development of a positive Indig-enous identity for the daughters of Indigenous women. Meeting strong and independent Indigenous women provides younger women with the strength needed to live as Indigenous peoples in an environment that still does not ac-cept them as equal. At my aunt's birthday party, those of us who expressed to her what a good role model she has been recognize that she has educated us about the value of Indigenous cultures that historically have been characterized by powerful Indigenous women. Indigenous women like my aunt and grandma have offered us the opportunity to grow and develop in a positive way by giving us a space—our family—of resistance against racism and colonialism.

As Patricia Hill Collins argues, in this type of mothering, home and family are not oppressive spaces for women, but spaces where our identity is affirmed and valued, and where healthy lives are constructed. Indeed, for Indigenous women, families are our "foundations of resistance" because they give us the strength needed to survive and defy oppressive experiences (Anderson). It is within our families that we come to learn and appreciate our Indigenous histories and cultures, and where we acquire the tools needed to fight against the negative images of Indigenous peoples that bombard mainstream Canadian society. As Kim Anderson maintains, "strong, independent female role models provide Native girls with the sense that they can overcome whatever obstacles they will inevitably encounter ... the bond between Aboriginal girls and their grandmother is notably strong, and this relationship has taught many lessons about resistance" (118). This strong bond is one that is evident within my family: most girls are attached to their grandmothers, and in many cases, the grandmother is the primary caregiver, as both my grandmother and aunt have been. In families like this, "native girls witness both the social and the economic decision-making power of older women in their communities" (Anderson 118). What these girls have witnessed is women performing necessary and important work in the community so that it can survive and grow. As the example of my grandmother shows, Indigenous women have often been the ones who have helped to create urban organizations that serve the specific cultural needs of our nations' members. As Lee Maracle points out, "the majority of these women grew up poor, under educated, and struggled with their schooling, [but nevertheless successfully] mothered children, built organizations and served the community while reclaiming culture, doing healing work on themselves and others" (56). This concept of mothering is one that is both empowering and culturally specific. Within an Oneida and other Haudenosaunee, and likely among other Indigenous worldviews, mothering refers to much more than simply bearing one's own biological children.

Similar to the way that Collins describes community mothering, Oneida women see mothering as a political act, as a way to participate in the sustainability of the self and the community. They do so by bearing and nurturing their own children, taking care of others' children, and providing for the whole community, in order to resist forms of racial discrimination and cultural genocide. In this way, they ensure our nations are healthy and strong. These various forms of mothering are political acts and can be traced back to the creation stories of our peoples. In our Oneida creation story, the origin of earth is attributed to Sky Woman, who fell from the sky carrying the seeds of creation (the three sisters of corn, squash, and bean, and the medicines of tobacco and strawberry) and after lying on top of the turtle, created earth. Later she gave birth to the Lynx woman who eventually gave birth to the first humans created and born on Mother Earth. The story of Sky Woman is a testimony of the rich powerful roles held in our nation by women as Mothers of the Nation. This important responsibility was later reaffirmed in the way men and women share responsibilities in the leadership of our councils as spelled out in the Great Law of Peace that governs our nations.

Due to our creation story, in the Haudenosaunee socio-political structure, the hereditary line of the clans is passed through the females. Each Clan Mother assumes many responsibilities, such as holding title to the land, appointing/removing hereditary chiefs, adopting members to the nation, and overseeing the overall practice and transmission of culture. This gave Haudenosaunee women responsibility in all spheres of life as mothers of the nation, and set up matrilineal structures as governing principles. For Oneida women and other Haudenosaunee women, responsibility towards one's own clan members and one's own nation is central to their identity as woman/mother of the nation, as the examples of my grandmother and aunt also illustrate. As mothers of their nation they carried their responsibility to serve their community and to help maintain a strong Oneida culture despite attempts at cultural assimilation by mainstream society.

SOME DANGERS IN THE IDEOLOGY OF MOTHERING THE NATION

The identification of women as mothers of the nation extends beyond an Oneida context and, in many cases, the imagining of women as mothers of the nation is full of complexities and contradictions. Women as mothers and are often "called upon to literally and figuratively reproduce the nation" (Loomba 214). The complexity of this identification is seen in the ways in which as mothers of the nation, women can become either empowered or controlled and constrained (Banerjee; De Mel; Loomba; McClintock; Thapar-Bjorkert and Ryan; Yuval-Davis). As biological reproducers of the nation, as reproducers of national boundaries, as transmitters of culture, as symbolic signifiers of national differences, and as participants in nationalist struggles, women have held contradictory positions in nationalist movements. In some cases they have exerted agency and become empowered while transforming a previous male-dominated nationalist movement, but at other times, their "mothering the nation" role has become a justification for their oppression and control over their bodies, either because they have to ensure that the future children of their nation have "pure" blood, or they must abide by strict, fixed, and essentialist notions of culture and identity.

Consequently women have responded in various ways to the construction of motherhood and their roles as mothers. As Ania Loomba points out, women have either appropriated the iconography of motherhood to pursue their own vision of the future nation, or fought together with their male nationalists, or attempted to open new conceptual spaces for women by moving into public space as mothers of the nation and negotiated and/or challenged existing notions of mothers and female roles.

CONCLUSION

Mothering of the nation can be either an empowering or an oppressive act. Within an Oneida/Haudenosaunee perspective, it can, in fact, be both. As my examples and the narrative of the Sky Woman show, there are instances of an empowering feminine spirit that exists and nurtures the concept of mothering. Our creation story is a positive source of strength for women and for the whole community. Yet, after years of colonialism and sexist patriarchy, we have seen changes in the image of Indigenous womanhood and traditional gender relations (see Anderson; Ladner; Lawrence; Monture-Angus; Stevenson; Sunseri). A persistent negative legacy of colonialism is the sexism that now lives in many of our Native organizations and communities.

Through European influence, power was legally removed from Oneida and other Haudenosaunee clan mothers; as a result, the clan line was no longer passed through the female line in the *Indian Act*. This led to a devaluation of Indigenous womanhood and is at the heart of the unequal gender relations that currently exist in our communities. With regards to the concept of mothering and other "traditional" aspects of our cultures, we now see a "colonial" version of traditionalism that justifies the subordination of Indigenous women (Martin-Hill). This distorted traditionalism has stripped women of their historical roles and authority and devalued them. Tradition, rather than a source of strength, is now used to subordinate and silence women and to mainly serve the interests of men. Sky Woman has been transformed into a "traditional" Indigenous woman who is silent and submissive (Martin-Hill).

However, as the lives of my grandmother and aunt illustrate, there still many empowered women who follow the teachings of the Sky Woman. These women are fulfilling their responsibility of mothering the nation by participating in the ongoing struggle of decolonization, by working for the revitalization of our cultures and political systems, and by nurturing our communities. In the process, when they deliver the message of Peace, as provided by the Creator, they recall the spirit of Sky Woman. Further, they assure that the symbols associated with the "mother of the nation" are not just rhetoric, but are expressed in the material reality of everyday life. Women have always done the work of mothering as asked of them through the creation stories, but often have not been recognized or valued accordingly. Yet, as the example of the new learning centre named after my grandmother and the testimony of those who attended my aunt's birthday show, people in our community are listening again to the drumbeat of our nation as it is sung by women. We still have much work to do to repair the damage that colonialism has done to our communities, but all of us together walking in balance can restore equal relations as the teachings of the Sky Woman story and the Great Law of Peace demand of us.

Originally published in Canadian Woman Studies/les cahiers de la femme,

"Indigenous Women in Canada: The Voices of First Nations, Inuit and Métis Women," 26 (3 & 4) (Winter/Spring 2008): 21-25. Reprinted with permission of the author.

Lina Sunseri is of the Oneida Nation of the Thames, Turtle Clan. Her Longhouse name is Yeliwi:saks, which means Gathering Stories, Knowledge. She also has Italian ancestry from her father's side. She is Assistant Professor, Dept. of Sociology, Brescia University College, at the University of Western Ontario.

REFERENCES

Acoose, Janice. *Iskwewak: Kah'ki Yaw Ni Wahkomakanak. Neither Indian Princesses nor Easy Squaws.* Toronto: Women's Press, 1995.

Anderson, Kim. *A Recognition of Being: Reconstructing Native Womanhood.* Toronto: Second Press, 2000.

Banerjee, Sikata. "Gender and Nationalism: the Masculinization of Hinduism and Female Political Participation in India." *Women's Studies International Forum* 26 (2) (2003): 167-179.

Collins, Patricia Hill. *Black Feminist Thought: Knowledge, Consciousness, and the Politics of Empowerment.* New York and London: Routledge, 1990.

de Mel, Neloufer. "Agent or Victim? The Sri Lankan Woman Militant in the Interregnum." *Feminists Under Fire: Exchanges Across War Zones.* Eds. W. Giles, M. de Alwis, E. Klein and N. Silva. Toronto: Between the Lines, 2003. 55-74.

Ladner, Kiera L. "Women and Blackfoot Nationalism." *Journal of Canadian Studies* 35 (2) (2000): 35-60.

LaRoque, Emma. "The Colonization of a Native Woman Scholar." *Women of the First Nations.* Eds. C. Miller and P. Chuchryk. Winnipeg: University of Manitoba Press, 1996. 11-18.

Lavell-Harvard, D. Memee, and Jeannette Corbiere Lavell, eds. *"Until Our Hearts Are On the Ground": Aboriginal Mothering, Oppression, Resistance and Rebirth.* Toronto: Demeter Press, 2006.

Lawrence, Bonita. *"Real" Indians and Others: Mixed-Blood Urban Native Peoples and Indigenous Nationhood.* Lincoln and London: University of Nebraska Press, 2004.

Loomba, Ania. *Colonialism/Postcolonialism.* London and New York: Routledge, 1998.

Maracle, Lee. "Untitled." *Sky Woman: Indigenous Women Who Have Shaped, Moved or Inspired Us.* Ed. Sandra Laronde. Penticton: Theytus Books, 2005. 55-60.

Martin-Hill, Dawn. "She No Speaks and other Colonial Constructs of the 'Traditional Woman.'" *Strong Women Stories: Native Vision and Community Survival.* Eds. K. Anderson and B. Lawrence. Toronto: Sumach Press, 2003. 106-120.

McClintock, Anne. *Imperial Leather: Race, Gender and Sexuality in the Colonial Contest*. New York and London: Routledge, 1995.

Mihesuah, Devon Abbott. *Indigenous American Women: Decolonization, Empowerment, Activism*. Lincoln and London: University of Nebraska Press, 2003.

Monture-Angus, Patricia. *Journey Forward: Dreaming First Nations' Independence*. Halifax: Fernwood, 1999.

O'Reilly, Andrea. "Introduction." *Mother Outlaws: Theories and Practices of Empowered Mothering*. Ed. A. O'Reilly. Toronto: Women's Press, 2004. 1-28.

Simpson, Leanne. "Birthing an Indigenous Resurgence: Decolonizing Our Pregnancy and Birthing Ceremonies." *"Until Our Hearts Are On The Ground": Aboriginal Mothering, Oppression, Resistance and Rebirth*. Eds. D. Memee Lavell-Harvard and Jeannette Corbiere Lavell. Toronto: Demeter Press., 2006. 25-33.

Stevenson, Winona. "Colonialism and First Nations Women in Canada." *Scratching the Surface: Canadian Anti-Racist Feminist Thought*. Eds. E. Dua and A. Robertson. Toronto: Women's Press, 1999. 49-80.

Sunseri, Lina. "Moving Beyond the Feminism versus Nationalism Dichotomy: An Anti-Colonial Feminist Perspective on Aboriginal Liberation Struggles." *Canadian Woman Studies/les cahiers de la femme* 20 (2) (2000): 143-148.

Thapar-Bjorkert, Suruchi, and Louise Ryan. "Mother India/Mother Ireland: Comparative Gendered Dialogues of Colonialism and Nationalism in the Early Twentieth Century." *Women's Studies International Forum* 25 (3) (2002): 301-313.

Voyageur, Cora J. "Contemporary Indian Women." *Visions of the Heart*. Eds. D. A. Long and O. P. Dickason. Toronto: Harcourt Brace and Co., 1996. 81-106.

Yuval-Davis, Nira. *National Spaces and Collective Identities: Borders, Boundaries, Citizenship and Gender Relations*. London: Greenwich University Press, 1998.

IDENTITY

HEALING IS

a purple flower that unfolds
on my face leaving a bruise
whereupon entering the therapist's
office there was none before
but she had to ask
where did my father
      hit   me
before I even speak   on the exact
spot where he hurt me   it appears
an old memory forcing itself to the surface
to speak a language I didn't know I had in me
sounds of emotions resurface to reclaim
their rightful place to sing their songs
and rejoice in freedom   up I go
a swaying of mitosak in the wind
blowing so hard it
grabs   twists   yanks
my breathe away
leaving only a prayer in my heart
the creator can hear

Therapists Psychiatrist state there is nothing
more western medicine can do so I turn to the east
follow the red road
start my journey in the sweat lodge
people murmuring their prayers
red   spotted   skin
     drenched   drained
the Elder says he saw the spirits return home
with the tobacco offerings in their hands
kicking up their heels
new colourful blankets wrapped around their shoulders

our prayers following behind them
                                        my anguish taken
now carried by the Creator
then I remember the old ones believed
the grass is humble no matter what happens
iskote'wo   stampede   pouring
of concrete into squares the grass comes again
I am strong no matter how
tired   sore   burdened
my ribcage aches from each breath
after days of sobbing over the terrors of childhood
my spirit knows I return like the grass on the prairie
        wild   free
as the drum in my heart beats
this woman's heart and yours is not on the ground
this nation has not fallen from the prairie a distant
song calls out
miywasin
                miywasin
                                miyawasin

Originally published in Cnadian Woman Studies/les cahiers de la femme, "Indigenous Women in Canada: The Voices of First Nations, Inuit and Métis Women, 26 (3 & 4) (Winter/Spring 2008): 13. Reprinted with permission of the author.

Isabel Louise O'Kanese is a Cree non-status Indian living in Edmonton. She began journal and poetry writing at the age of ten. She is a radio announcer at CJSR since 1999. She is currently working as a Community Disability Support Worker and works with disabled adults.

PATRICIA D. MCGUIRE

WIISAAKODEWIKWE ANISHINAABEKWE
DIABAAJIMOTAW NIPIGON ZAAGA'IGAN

Lake Nipigon Ojibway Métis Stories About Women

I WAS RAISED ON MY MOTHER'S and father's stories of Lake Nipigon. Although, other old people shared stories in Macdiarmid, Ontario were I lived, my parent's stories were my baseline. In the community of Kiashke Zaaging Anishinaabek, I was presented with the rich tradition of oratory in my summers spend there. I was blessed with listening to the stories told. *Anishinaabe Diabaajimtow Nandagikenim*—stories are the mainstay of Anishinaabe knowledges. They speak to us of our life. Stories told me how to deal with the world, how to learn, and how to behave. Stories told me who I was, where my territory was, and who my people were. Other worlds were described to me in stories, worlds that could only be reached by sacrifice and vision. Stories talked to me about community, featuring our relationships to one another as paramount for our survival. Stories told me about emotions such as love, loss, and grief, but also the importance of laughter. Stories detailed how our society changed but described what our foundations were. Stories challenged us to look and think other ways and to remember who we are. Stories give us memory. These ideas about stories are the subject of this discussion.

Wassaygijig was my mother's grandfather. Just before he died, my mother watched him building a sweat-lodge. It was built to fit one person. He worked on making the frame, collecting the rocks, and preparing the fire. He did this all day, she said. She watched him go in, heard him singing, and waited for him to come out. When he came out, she saw him smoking a pipe. He then called her to him and said that when he was praying he saw what she would see in her life. She would have many different experiences. In the future, she would witness significant changes in the Anishinaabe society. The last substantial change was that the women would be the leaders. The women are known as the Anishinaabekwe in my language.[1] Stories about women in Indigenous communities offer awareness for our current historical and contemporary context as Anishinaabe.[2] *Anishinaabekwe Ogimakaanag*—women are the leaders and we need to remember this.

There is paucity of information available that discusses the experience of the Anishinaabe populations in Northwestern Ontario. The dearth of information about the Wiisaakode Anishinaabe, Métis, is even more pronounced and there is none about Anishinaabekwe. What is available is generally from western academic traditions. These perspectives studied what were perceived to be either dying or static populations. These stories do not capture the spirit and beauty of the stories from this area of Ontario and missed the tenacity and strength of women's stories.

Western traditions misread the social standing of women in the societies they studied. Women in Anishinaabe societies were thus misinterpreted in the historical record (Morriseau and Dewdney; Vanderburgh; McGuire; Geystick and Doyle; Johnston). In texts written by European missionaries, traders, folklorists, and academics, women were viewed as either absent or invisible or portrayed in a stereotypical manner reflecting western ideas of women (Hungry Wolf; Cruikshank et al; Accoose). Instead, Anishinaabekwe had authority and power within our societies that was equal to that of men. A more egalitarian relationship existed between men and women in Anishinaabe society. This authority, power, and egalitarianism in Anishinaabe societies were not apparent to representatives of European patriarchal societies. When this social reality became evident, Anishinaabekwe were targeted in other ways.[3] Anishinaabekwe occupied a central position in society. They had many responsibilities ranging from sacred duties to leadership to distribution of resources. Anishinaabekwe had a sphere of influence that included the feminine but did not make that the central force. A discussion of women and land begins my retrospective of stories that I have heard from various members of my community. My context informs my stories much like my parents' and others' stories were influenced by the social and political environment in which they lived in.

My mother and father told me stories about Lake Nipigon. The community of MacDiarmid, Ontario is on the shores of this water. The lake is spring fed and it is beautiful, cold water. It is said that when the Creator gave Nanabush his job of naming all of creation, he stopped in this area. He was tired and so he sat down while placing his axe at his side. It is from the hole created by his axe that this spring water erupted and became Lake Nipigon. This lake is the feeder lake for all the waters that flow into Lake Superior.

My sisters and I often go back home for community events, mostly funerals. Once, when I was home, my sisters and I went to the water by the big dock. It was a clear day with the sun shining down on the remnants of ice that were still on the lake. As we were talking, I unwrapped a cigarette. I placed this tobacco in my hand as I silently prayed. My sisters asked me what I was doing. I said offering tobacco to the water because it was springtime. One of my sisters told my mom what I had done and my mother asked me why. I told her that same thing that I told my sisters. She started telling me a story about my maternal grandmother, who the French called Queen Anne. The French called her this because my grandfather, a leader in the community, would not allow any meetings to take place without my grandmother being present. My grandfather deferred to her. She was bossy. *Nii Nokomis*, my grandmother, was asked to go to Fort William Indian reserve on Lake Superior to conduct spring ceremonies. These ceremonies involved her making the water dance[4] and giving offerings to the water for safe journey for the Anishinaabe. She was the keeper of this ceremony and was called upon frequently to conduct it. It was Anishinaabekwe responsibility to do this ceremony before the ice left. I did not know this story before I placed an offering in the water. When you are where you are supposed to be, the land that countless generations of your ancestors have occupied, you are told what you are supposed to do. This offering was needed for the water spirits.

Chi niibii, water is women's responsibility. In one of the Anishinaabe creation stories, water was given to the women to care for because only women have the ability to create water and sustain life within our bodies. Women have this ability as well as the ability to nurture spirit and interact with the spirit world. Spirits choose to live and be cared for within women. The respect that was accorded to women due to these abilities has been forgotten in some communities. Our biology is who we are and we have the ability to give life. Women have been honoured by the Creator to do this. Women are at the center of creation. These and similar teachings have been attacked by government and religion deliberately for a long time. The consequence of these continued assaults is that even the Anishinaabekwe are forgetting what their responsibilities are and who they are. These stories I present here concern social issues that we must talk about openly so that they can be stopped.

Anishinaabe in many communities in Northwestern Ontario are oppressed and in turn behave in oppressive manners ways toward one another. A couple of years ago, one of my students came to interview me about Indigenous women's issues. We talked about how the collective spirit of women needed to be nourished and nurtured like precious seeds. The week before I had heard about another rape of a young girl in one of our communities. Sexual assaults are a common feature of life for many women in communities in Canada, not just Aboriginal women. Hearing that Anishinaabe men and boys are doing this is like an open wound on my spirit and I grieve for our past respect as Anishinaabekwe. My student talked about a recent rape of a young girl in her community and it appeared that she and others in her community were not only blaming the victim, but blaming the mother of the victim! Talk about evading community responsibility. She mentioned that a woman who lived next to the house where this girl was being raped noted that this young girl was the only girl at a party with lots of men, and what do you expect? I asked what this woman did to prevent the rape. There was no answer. I told my student that gossiping is not a response to rape and is not an Anishinaabe response to rape.

If we did not accept responsibility for girls and women in our communities, no one will do it for us. For too many years gossip has been used as a social control mechanism, especially when the gossip is directed at the wrong parties. Gossip is not directed at the men who commit the sexual assaults. There is a lack of community responsibility that is disturbing. The violence that is directed at our girls and women has its roots somewhere else. The disrespect that is shown to women and that we show to one another is a form of self-loathing and hatred. It is a part of intergenerational trauma that we all have to deal with. Colonialism is still in force in our communities. This is apparent when you explore the treatment of Anishinaabekwe.

At numerous cultural gatherings, I always find girls and women outside of circles. I always lightheartedly tease them and ask why, although I know the reason; they are 'on their time.'[5] Their biology is used to exclude them. I am told that it is a sign of respect for womanhood. It is funny how exclusionary practices are deemed to be respectful. When I was a young girl, I was told that there are certain times of the month when women cannot step over certain objects such as guns, axes, bundles.... I was never told that I could not participate in meetings, spiritual gatherings, and ceremonies because of my biology as a Anishinaabekwe. Sometimes, at gatherings women are not allowed to touch the traditional foods and be near the Sacred drums. They are centered out.

Many gatherings talk about women's "time of the month." Oftentimes, it is men who are talking about "women's time." Men and women have separate teachings that belong to their Sacred bundles. When this is going on, Anishinaabekwe practice our so-called cultural value of non-interference. This means silence on this practice by women. Apparently, this non-interference is a cultural value that cannot be interfered with as there will be dire consequences ... like maybe change? This is why I believe the interpretation of the value of non-interference came from outside of our communities. Anishinaabe were very comfortable with change.

The idea of non-interference may be related to forced education practices of the various colonial governments. My parents told me stories about the strictness of the nuns. They described how the sisters in boarding school obeyed the priests without question. Boarding schools were a form of residential schools. I wonder how much of the negative attitude toward and disrespect for women that I see at gatherings is a result of the residential school system. If women were at the center of creation in the Judeo-Christian worldview, maybe women would have been respected, instead of being blamed for the downfall of mankind with the mark of the "fall from grace" apparent every month. This was not our way to treat one another as Anishinaabekwe. A woman's time of month was considered sacred. The notion that women are responsible for "original sin" is the underlying factor for much turmoil in our societies but its worst impacts are seen on our spiritual beliefs.

I was traditionally adopted by a couple from Cree territory when I was in my twenties. They have taught me much over the years and I must admit that I am not an easy person to teach. The one lesson that I always remember is to use your commonsense. One that I remember but always intentionally forget is always wear a dress or skirt to cultural gatherings. Skirts are assumed to be respectful apparel for women and girls. There are no such restrictions on either men or boys apparel. This practice is frequently announced at cultural gatherings and sometimes enforced by shaming. You must be strong to ignore what is being said to you. I have seen women asked to leave gatherings. I have seen women get up and leave. I get up and leave sometimes. I use my commonsense and ask myself what am I really being taught here? There are fundamentalist ideas at work here that are disturbing to me.

A number of years ago, I was invited to go to a women's circle. This was early in my learning and it was one of the first women's circles that I attended. Only Indigenous women would be talking and giving teachings that were specific to women. I was so excited! I knew that if it were all women attending, we would be respected. Was I ever wrong. Women were being told what to do and how to do it. We were given a verbal rule book that told us how we were supposed to act as women. We were talked down to and deliberately made to feel inferior. Many women were crying in this circle. I was filled with disgust that women would be doing this to other women. My anger served me to see clearly. Being in that circle felt like being at a revival meeting for a fundamentalist sect where the first thing to do is break down is the psychological defenses and then you re-build from there. This was not how I was told to do things and like no stories about Anishinaabe practices that I had ever heard of.

There are degrees of fundamentalism in every spiritual practice. A conversation with my son about Muslims illustrated to me how people manipulate spiritual understandings. Women are centered out for control when orthodox mentalities interpret spiritual understandings. Women become the symbols of how respect and honour are interpreted, even when they are not treated in either a respectful or honourable manner. When I am asked, "Where is your skirt?" I reply, "Oh, I forgot that the spirits can only recognize me with a skirt on … I wonder if spirits wear skirts." A spiritual practice that relies on rules of behaviour is motionless like stagnant water. It does not have to be this way. Our stories can create social transformation(s) in our societies. *Mindimooyeg,* older women in our society have abilities that we need today. These stories have to do with tenacity and strength amidst the challenges of life and living. There is grief and loss but it not so overwhelming that laughter isn't heard.

My mother and aunties were talking. I was upstairs listening to them. They are all widows. They were talking about family violence. One of my aunts was invited to speak at a gathering where this would be the topic. One of them asked what this was about. My aunt who was speaking at this gathering replied, in Anishinaabemowin, that it was about fighting within and between family members. My other aunt replied, "Then we wrote the book on family violence." I could hear their laughter upstairs. My mom is the eldest sister; she is 86. They have seen a lot in their lifetimes. My mother raised sixteen children, my youngest aunt eleven, and my other aunt five children. My mother used Anishinaabe midwifes for eleven children; only five were born in the hospital.

My father's sister, my aunt Agnes, died a couple of years ago. In the last five years of her life, my aunt buried three sons, all unexpectedly. I do not know how she was able to cope. My mom told me a story about my aunt, who was married to a farmer outside Nipigon, Ontario. She was pregnant and alone on

Agnes McGuire, Patricia McGuire's paternal grandmother, and her great great grand-mother, Picakoushekwe. Photo courtesy McGuire Jackfish Island collection.

the farm with just her kids. When the baby came, something was wrong and the baby died. This happened to my aunt twice. Both times she was alone. This meant that she had to prepare her babies for burial and bury them herself. My mom and dad went to visit her after one of the deaths. She told my mother what happened and showed her the little graves that were on either side of the garden. My aunt worked hard her whole life even when she was finally able to leave that farm. These women had tremendous strength and tenacity. They did what they had to do in spite of all of the loss and grief they experienced. They met their responsibilities.

In Aboriginal communities across Canada, loss, grief and trauma are prevalent. The impact of government policies on education and child welfare that resulted in the taking away of children will be with us for a long time. I was about seven when my friend was taken away by the Children's Aid Society in MacDiarmid, Ontario in 1967. This is a small Wiisaakode Anishinaabe and Anishinaabe community on Lake Nipigon. Lots of children began to disappear. When my friend was taken, I cried. My father found her by accident as her foster home was close to Fort William, now called Thunder Bay, Ontario. We were reunited. Nothing, but death, would do this again to us. She had been my friend since childhood. Life is not the same without the knowledge that she is there. She remembered when we were small kids. She said that she held these memories close to her when she was apprehended. When she was in care, she said that she remembered me more than her family. We were together than much when we were children. My friend, Ramona Nobis died of an accidental overdose in 2005. This death is still difficult to talk about. She and her family were still looking for their baby sister at the time of her death. This child was the last one who disappeared. The federal and provincial policies that enabled this to happen across the country have much to answer for.

Stories can help us heal from tragic losses. Stories can help us with our grief. My stories of loss and healing are from another source that the ones that I grew up hearing. The social and political context is different. The province started stealing children from their families and communities in the late 1950s. Communities were coming back to life and healing from residential school policies when these child welfare policies took effect. The Children's Aid Society, under the guise of protecting children, aided in creating overwhelming loss in community. Yet, the children who survived were able to effect social change in their communities once they re-discovered who they were. An example of someone who was able to do this was Sandra Kakeeway.

I first met Sandra Kakeeway in 1974. Her sister, Sam[6] invited me over to meet her. Sandra looked at me and asked Sam, "What are you doing bringing Indians around here?" I looked behind me but realized that she was talking about me. We laughed about this for years. It became a way for Sandra to introduce dialogue on cultural identity and the consequences of cultural displacement in her workshops across Canada and the United States. When I met her, she said that she saw an Italian woman when she looked in the mirror as she was raised with Italians. She was Anishinaabekwe. Her expertise was in child welfare, sexual abuse, substance abuse, and Aboriginal healing practices. This story about identity became her way to talk about Aboriginal children in child welfare. Sandra and her siblings were apprehended when she was five years old. Sandra was a survivor of child sexual abuse that occurred when she was in foster care. The government paid for this foster care for her, and her brothers and sisters. She attempted to file charges and initiated a lawsuit after she had dealt with and began to cope with this abuse.[7] This attempt at charges and a lawsuit went nowhere. Unfortunately, her case is not unique in Canada.

Some Aboriginal communities lost all the children in communities in the 1960s and 1970s. Many of these children are still trying to find their way home. Sandra helped foster children not only find their way home but find their way back to themselves. She was responsible for finding and reuniting almost all her brothers and sisters, except for one, Grace. She was still searching for her sister at the time of her unexpected death. This was the motivating force behind her many activities aimed at educating Canadians about child welfare policies and the effect they had on Aboriginal communities across Canada.

On Rat Portage Indian reserve, there is a place by the poplar trees where the eagles dance in the sky. It is wood tick season and I was on the lookout for their little ugliness. This is the place where Sandra wanted to be buried and this is the place where her wishes were followed. She wanted to be by her father, Sandy Kakeeway, who was from this territory. Sandra always talked about her dad. She had missed meeting him because he had committed suicide. Substance abuse affected her family. This hopelessness was a consequence of child welfare policies in the 1950s and 1960s. The despair and despondency many parents felt as their children were stolen and they, their parents, could do nothing to stop it caused the intergenerational trauma that we have to overcome today. Many communities are still struggling because of these colonial policies and genocidal practices. Sandra helped her people overcome oppression and internal colonization. She refused to be a victim. Her life was a testament to the tenacity of the human spirit and the power of forgiveness. I was awed that she was able to forgive people who behaved horrendously towards her. Her mission in life was to help our people, especially the youth of our communities, to be supported to live in a strong and responsible manner.

My friend's gift and medicine was her laughter and her smile. This was her bundle. It is hard to put on paper the power of laughter; the healing that results in honest laughter. We talked many times of Indigenous communities that had forgotten how to truly laugh and celebrate life no matter how challenging. These were communities we worked with that experienced record high suicides and lateral violence. Sandra and I used to talk about how do you help people and communities to heal from generations of pain and suffering? How do you get secrets out in the open so that they lose the power to hurt? How do you heal the hidden? How do you get people to speak the unspeakable?

When you heal, you help others too. You show that some things are just not worth carrying anymore. These things lose their power when they are confronted and spoken about. As Anishinaabekwe, we have a responsibility to make our stories heard. Our stories are about how we are viewed in our societies. It is up to us to ensure that these stories are told the way that we want them told.

In Indigenous worldviews, knowledge is collectively based and is active. Knowledge is a dynamic process. It is not based on experts and does not proceed in a linear fashion. The western tradition of linear and expert based knowledge is as foreign as the idea of owning knowledge. The Anishinaabe who are keepers and custodians of traditions of storytelling do not admit to knowing everything or owning the knowledge that they safeguard and transmit. There is an openness and willingness for knowledge creation. It is this openness that enables collective generation of new knowledge.

Land is the defining and stabilizing feature of the Anishinaabe knowledge systems. Stories about our land compel us to have a personal relationship to it. Land and relationships are central to Indigenous knowledge(s). Relationships and connections to others and to the land inform how we behave. It is this first relationship then that becomes the mirror for our social world. Story telling provides the nuance to our collective selves. Hearing stories is the beginning of establishing our relationships within our societies.

The process of telling a story is very different than the process of arguing that one paradigm about the world is privileged and, therefore, more believable because it is based on so-called scientific fact. Scientific facts themselves are generated in a social context; they are not neutral (Denzin and Lincoln). In light of this, in contemporary academia, there has been a proliferation of writing by colonial and post-colonial writers that discuss scholarly works written about them rather than by them. New stories emerge that speak to different and varied truths. Colonial stories are being challenged by this more distinctive and balanced telling (Smith). As Ted Chamberlin and Hugh Brody state,

> Stories ... give us a sense of who we are, and where we belong. They sometimes go by the name of history, sometimes by the name of myth and legend, sometimes by the name of law and philosophy and politics and economics, sometimes by the name of story and song and dance, sometimes by the name of science. Each story belongs to a tradition, and each tradition has its own criteria of authenticity and authority. (1)

Theories are stories that are told within social contexts for social purposes and from the teller's social standpoint (Denzin and Lincoln; Smith). People who have benefited from the social theory as science viewpoint stand to lose their privileged status (Smith). The view that someone from another cultural perspective can represent Indigenous realities more accurately than we can is disappearing as a scholarly activity.

We maintain that Indigenous ways of life are distinct. Our ontological realities and epistemologies are distinctive (Bastien; Alteo; McLeod).[8] Our knowledge(s) are not frozen in time. They are robust and active. We have to explore our ways of being and our ways of learning about the world, if we want our stories to continue into our future. The manner in which these stories are told may change but these stories must be told. In our process of theory generation, our ways of making sense of the world will be paramount. Anishinaabe theories will be describing, making sense of our experience, and evaluating those experiences, as they will be embedded in our specific social realities (Mannheim). As Mary Rogers notes, " 'I' announces a biographical creature whose experiences grow out of and beyond an array of social roles and subject positions. Its presence presses against the traditional boundaries of social theory and raises awareness of the multiple sites of consciousness where theory originates and takes shape (13).

The Self must be part of this theory creation as this is the site in which Indigenous social theory can imagine a different way of being, one that is rooted in our past but meets our collective future with intellectual rigour. The "I" may be interpreted differently in Indigenous contexts as the collective self may be of more importance, than an individualist view (Smylie). If we are to meet our responsibilities as Anishinaabekwe, we have to use available contemporary tools to ensure that our stories live on. They can offer a counterbalance to the historical record and add to the development of Indigenous-based written theories and methods. Indigenous theories about the world exist and they are transforming. The idea is not new. Yet, we must exercise care in how and what we do with our stories as we are telling them. Mary Ritchie said,

> When we speak the language of the oppressor, we must be aware of how we are being swallowed up by concepts we did not create, and that as members of a non-dominant community, we must exercise caution and restraint in our attempts to develop our communities and enter the multi-cultural arena. (309)

In the social construction of theory, we must be cognizant that our efforts will ensure understanding occurs for both us and our neighbours in Canada. In the varied understandings about the world, our stories offer our understanding. It is time to share them with one another and with people willing to listen. Anishinaabekwe can exercise our leadership this way.

Originally published in Canadian Woman Studies/les cahiers de la femme, *"Indigenous Women in Canada: The Voices of First Nations, Inuit and Métis Women," 26 (3 & 4) (Winter/Spring 2008): 217-222. Reprinted with permission of the author.*

Patricia D. McGuire is a mother and grandmother. She is completing a Ph.D. in Sociology at the University of Saskatchewan as well as being a professor with Negahneewin at Confederation College.

[1]*Niin gaagwe nitaa anishinaabemowin*—I am learning how to speak Ojibway. My mother said that I spoke Ojibway as a child but like all of my brothers and sisters, I stopped one day. She said that something happened at school. Even though, my parents could speak different dialects, I struggle to remember. My parents did not force the language on us because they thought we would have an easier time if we just spoke English.
[2]My daughter and I often talk about the importance of stories. I see her as an example of Anishinaabekwe Ogimaa. She is a leader and is bossy like her grandmothers.
[3]This was mainly through legislation such as the Indian Act, especially membership provisions. The Native Women's Association of Canada has addressed these issues in many publications over the years. (see http://www.nwac-hq.org/).
[4]My grandmother actually made the water by Lake Superior dance. I just was told the story. I have no idea how she accomplished this.
[5]"On their time" means female menses.
[6]Jessie Goodchild named this group of children, Sandra, Sandria, and Sandford.

Their father's name was Sandy.

[7]The foster mother who abused her was president of the foster parents association for many years. The lawsuit did not go anywhere. Sandra was told that the foster mother was too old when she pushed for charges to be laid.

[8]Bastien, Alteo and McLeod discuss the distinctiveness of their communities' worldview and how this influences how the world is perceived and acted upon.

REFERENCES

Accoose, J. *Iskwewak Kah'KiYaw NiWahkomakanak: Neither Indian Princesses Nor Easy Squaws.* Toronto: Women's Press, 1995.

Alteo, E. R. *Tsawalk: A Nuu-chad-nulth Worldview.* British Colombia: University of British Columbia Press, 2004.

Bastien B. *Blackfoot Ways of Knowing: The Worldview of the Siksitaitsitapi.* Alberta: University of Calgary Press, 2004.

Chamberlin T., Brody H. *Aboriginal History.* Background workshop. Royal Commission on Aboriginal Peoples; Ottawa, 1993.

Cruikshank, J., Sidney, A., Smith, K., Ned, A. *Life Lived Like a Story.* Lincoln: University of Nebraska, 1990.

Denzin N. K. and Y. S. Lincoln, eds. *The Landscape of Qualitative Research: Theories and Issues.* New Delhi: Sage Publications, Inc., 1998.

Geystick, R., and Doyle, J. *Te Bwe Win −Truth.* Toronto: Impulse Editions, Summerhill Press, 1995.

Hungry Wolf, B. *The Ways of My Grandmothers.* New York: Quill, 1980.

Johnston, B. *The Manitous- The Spirit World of the Ojibway.* Toronto: Key Porter Books, 1995.

Mannheim, K. *Ideology and Utopia.* Trans. L. Wirth and E. Shils. New York: Harcourt Brace Jovanovich, 1936.

McGuire Sr., P. *My Life in the North.* Unpublished Manuscript, 1988.

McLeod, N. *Cree Narrative Memory: From Treaties to Contemporary Times.* Saskatoon: Purich Publishing, 2007.

Morriseau, N. and S. Dewdney. *Legends of My People: The Great Ojibway.* Toronto: Ryerson Press, 1965.

Ritchie, M. "Whose Voice Is it Anyway? Vocalizing Multicultural Analysis." *Multicultural Education, Critical Pedagogy and the Politics of Difference.* New York: Suny Press, 1995.

Rogers, M. F. *Multicultural Experiences, Multicultural Theories.* New York: McGraw-Hill, 1996.

Smith, L. T. *Decolonizing Methodologies- Research and Aboriginal Peoples.* New York: St. Martin's Press, 1999.

Smylie J. Aboriginal Health Research Methods Class Discussion, University of Saskatchewan, 2006.

Vanderburgh R. M. *I Am Nokomis Too: The Biography of Verna Patronella Johnston.* Don Mills: General Publishing Co. Limited, 1977.

SURVIVING AS A NATIVE WOMAN ARTIST

IT IS ONLY A HUNDRED years since our ancestors lived in teepees, hunted the buffalo, and invented beef jerky. It is only a hundred years and some since your ancestors herded us onto reserves, washed us with scrub brushes and lye soap, and chopped our hair off, uniforming the children in religious residential schools in an attempt to knock out the savagery. Our ancestors were beaten for speaking their language, their mother tongue: now we have major political battles in this country over whose mother tongue is the most important. It is only a hundred years and now we stand before you in this institution with our art work on the walls. Now we are civilized, aren't we?

We have come from a culture that has developed in one hundred years to the space age, something that has taken your collective cultures thousands of years. Yet still our people are criticized. We have to try harder than anyone else because we are diplomats for each other. We cannot afford one drunk in the street, one panhandler; we are stereotyping each other every day with our actions. People ask me questions about other Native people in this country, they ask me what they think; they think we are connected by some form of microchip. This country is as full of as many diverse nations and languages as the continent of Europe. If Native people across the country appear to agree on issues it is because the issues are all the same: land, education, money, culture, language rights, and the environment.

I am here as an artist, as a communicator, as a maker of visual imagery; one of the most powerful forms of communicative expression that we have. I have included words for those of you who have a hard time with pictures; there is no excuse for you not understanding what my work is about if you take the time to really look and see, as I have been doing. I feel a responsibility to communicate.

In 1983 I travelled to Stonehenge fulfilling a childhood dream. I travelled through landscape that could have been in British Columbia. Arriving, I saw huge stones in a circle erected by a then primitive people. It was while standing near these huge landmarks that I thought of the very ancient consideration of the future that was a part of this Indigenous culture and I realized how very harmonious this beginning was with the Indigenous peoples of North America.

We too have erected stone landmarks of astronomical size, some many thousands of years old. These are, however, not revered, as is Stonehenge—many saw their demise with the beginning of agriculture, others more recently at the hands of the developers, many only exist in the memory of the people or as a part of archaeological record, some are displayed in part as curiosities.

For thousands of years our culture respected nature and only took from the environment what it needed. It did not need mandates to understand the balance of nature but took its direction from the dictates of nature. It was a culture that took note when the leaves fell, when the snow fell, how much rain there was in a year, how the coats of the animals looked. It was a culture that did not make divisions between life, art, and religion.

My part in the preservation of a seemingly invisible culture—on the plains we don't have totem poles—is as a receptor or translator, one who would point out what there once was, what there still is, and the importance of all this to us. If it only serves to interest the viewer on the level of "nice pictures," that's fine with me, but it is made with the intent of serving many viewers on many levels and as a form of expression that I must take.

I am here out of respect for my people—the people that were unknown to me for most of my life. Other people knew more about me than I knew about myself. "You're an Indian!" the kids screamed at me at school. "You're a half-breed!" they said as they got older and had listened to their parents' dinner conversations. "You're a Métis!" they started to whisper in the 1970s, gentrifying the term "half-breed" or "mixed blood."

With all these people knowing more about me than I did, I thought it required a closer look. I was coming from a position of weakness, which is what lack of knowledge is. I found out that my father and his brother had had Indian names. I found out that my great grandmother had lived in Rocky Mountain House in the 1950s. We used to go blueberry and Saskatoonberry picking there and my father would disappear for hours—gone to visit his grandmother. I found out that I had relatives at Morley and a whole other family in southern Alberta.

I found out other things too. I found out that Indian people couldn't vote until after 1960. I found out that if they wished to leave the reserve they had to pay for a pass. I found out that most of the government-issued meat that came to the reserves disappeared and either no meat or rotten meat was distributed. I found out that smallpox blankets were distributed to the Indians from the United States. I found out that whole villages filled with death lodges were left on the prairie, filled with thousands of people who had died from smallpox. I found letters in the Canada sessional papers that talked about funding for residential schools and the disparaging influences camped around the schools—parents trying to see their children who were taken away to become statistics.

In a museum in Rocky Mountain House, I found the Tree of Life chart drawn by pious Father Lacombe, who started Dunbow school near Calgary. I found the pathway to heaven known only to one Indian. The rest came along the path where one of the seven deadly sins—that of slothfulness—had been depicted. You can see this chart on the third floor of the museum. It has every Indian going to hell.

I found out that being an Indian was determined by treaty right and I found out that a lot of the people in the cities, the urban Indians, were non-status and that I was one of them.

I started asking questions in my artwork, drawing pictures of all those chiefs, those Canadian heroes with their Victoria medals burning a hole in their chests for the generations to come. I did these paintings from 1969 to 1973. I drew and painted very personal statements then.

As the years went by and I continued to work I began to see a pattern among other peoples of the world. People united to form lobby groups to save Africa, and to help the people in India, and people began to emigrate here from war-torn countries. I kept hearing about the Third World. Finally in 1984 on a trip to Ottawa I asked the question of International Development for Education in the Arts (CIDEA): what are you doing for our Third World country that exists in Canada?

My work began to take a more political—as some people called it—bent. It seems anything involved with Native people is categorized as being political or an artefact. I began to make contemporary artefacts in protest against the National Gallery's treatment of artists of Native heritage.

I started to like myself. I began to take a stand. I was proud of my heritage. I had always been taught by my parents to be proud of who I am and I extended it to be proud of my people. I liked the person I saw in the mirror, but I noticed that the sight of me brought a kind of shifty-foot-changing attitude. I was watched in stores. I stood for a long time at counters waiting to be waited on. I heard people talk about my people in the streets, the panhandlers, the drunks, the stories about needing a bus ticket to visit the wife in hospital. I remembered the boys joking in high school through clenched teeth about picking up a squaw at Smokey Lake. I remembered my biology teacher talking about oriental eye-folds and telling us he could see a few in the class.

But things are different now, aren't they?

Not much. Look at the exhibition, "The Spirit Sings," at the Glenbow in Calgary. During a time when the world's eyes are on us, a major exhibition is created that travels across the country freezing the Native people into a romantic notion of the seventeenth-century. Look at the exhibition in the Vancouver Art Gallery: "Beyond History: 10 Little Indians." Here we're three.

Don't misunderstand me. I have absolutely no problem exhibiting my work with my own kind. But I am different. You have all made me different. You taught me about the discipline of art and being a professional and to me that means it is art that is shown in this category of "New Alberta Art." I have been around a long time. It's a good thing I left the country and the province with my work or I may never have been shown at the Glenbow. It's a good thing that the assistant curator is from the east. It's pretty hard to deny excellence when other people celebrate it and recognize it.

That is not really the part I have the problem with because it is pretty standard for artists not to be appreciated in their hometown; in fact it is fairly standard among all creators. What I have a problem with is the categorization of Native Artist in a museum that does not separate other Canadian artists in exhibitions according to their race.

It seems Native people cannot do anything without that adjective in front of their name.

The other artists in the exhibition, George Little Child and Jane Ash Poitras, may not share my views. That is understandable; they are just beginning their careers. For me it has been a constant battle since entering art college in Calgary in 1962. Nothing has been handed to me on a silver platter, but I have drawn the energy from all this negativity and turned it into a positive force. The racism I have suffered has only focused me more on the battle against racism. It is one of the warshirts that I wear now. I know there is a purpose for me on this earth and I will make a difference.

To my fellow exhibitors: I am proud to exhibit my work with you and to know that even though your road will be rough that I will have helped to create some smooth patches for you as those artists I have listed on the blackboards have done for me and for us all.

To those people whose life is affected by racism, I say—as my father taught me—"Just take a stand, just fight and never give in, never give in to those bastards."

This article is an excerpt from a speech given by the author at the opening of "Diversities," an exhibition of the work of George Little Child, Jane Ash Poitras and Joane Cardinal-Schubert at the Glenbow Museum in Calgary in October 1989.

Originally published in Canadian Woman Studies/les cahiers de la femme, "Feminism and Visual Art," 11 (1) (Spring 1990): 50-51. Reprinted with permission of the author.

Joane Cardinal-Schubert passed away on September 17, 2009, after a long and courageous battle with cancer. Although best known for her paintings and installations, Cardinal-Schubert, throughout her long and successful career, engaged in an range of other activities such as curator, writer, lecturer, poet, and activist for First Nations artists and individuals engaged in the struggle for Native sovereignty. Her painting and installation practice is prominent for its incisive evocation of contemporary First Nations experiences and examination of the imposition of EuroAmerican religious, educational, and governmental systems upon Aboriginal people. She was a lobbyist for the Society of Canadian Artists of Native Ancestry (SCANA) and an outspoken advocate of Native causes.

ALEX WILSON

N'TACIMOWIN INNAN NAH'

Our Coming In Stories

MY FAMILY IS FROM THE Opaskwayak Cree Nation, a community several hours north of Winnipeg. The Swampy Cree dialect of our community has no word for homosexual and no gender specific pronouns.[1] Rather than dividing the world into female and male, or making linguistic distinctions based on sexual characteristics or anatomy, we distinguish between what is animate and what is inanimate. Living creatures, animate objects, and actions are understood to have a spiritual purpose (Ahenakew). Our language and culture are rooted in this fundamental truth: that every living creature and everything that acts in and on this world is spiritually meaningful.

This understanding is reiterated in the term "two-spirit," a self-descriptor used by many Cree and other Aboriginal lesbian, gay, bi, and trans people. When we say that we are two-spirit, we are acknowledging that we are spiritually meaningful people. Two-spirit identity may encompass all aspects of who we are, including our culture, sexuality, gender, spirituality, community, and relationship to the land.

As a two-spirit woman, I know that an understanding and expression of my own identity is very different from those that prevail in most other Canadian cultures and I am very grateful for this. For me, two-spirit identity is empowering. As an educator and psychologist, I wanted to learn more about what our identity means to other two-spirit people and how this empowered identity appears within the context of the sustained racism, homophobia, and sexism that most of us have experienced. This article presents findings from a qualitative research project that explored those questions.

"MAKE SURE YOU GET YOUR WORDS RIGHT"

The Shoshone two-spirit writer Clyde Hall entitled his contribution to an anthropological collection about two-spirit people: "You anthropologists make sure you get your words right" (Jacobs, Thomas, and Lang 272). This admonishment is long overdue. Anthropologists and gay historians have produced a substantial body of work on sexuality and gender in Indigenous North American communities (Angelino and Shedd; Callender and Kochems;

Driver; Gutierrez; Jacobs; Jacobs, Thomas, and Lang; Lang 1996, 1998; Lewis; Parsons; Roscoe 1987, 1991; Simms; Steffenson; Thompson; Balboa, Chanca, Castillo, and Las Casas in Trexler; Williams). While this work has formed the basis of a critique of Western cultural assumptions about sexuality and gender, it has only rarely focused on or been informed by the lives of contemporary two-spirit people (Wilson 1996). Similarly, while this work may have helped to create a more comfortable and safe living space for non-Aboriginal lesbian, gay, bi, and trans people,[2] only a few of these authors appear to have thought about how their work might contribute to the well-being of contemporary two-spirit and other Aboriginal people.[3]

Two-spirit people have also been underserved by other social science disciplines, which historically viewed gender, sexual, and racial identity as discrete developmental strands (Wilson 1996). Feminist researchers have examined ways in which cultural constructions of the self are produced (Gever), the multilayered texture of identity for women of colour (Etter-Lewis), and conscious community identity as a liberation strategy (Robinson and Ward; Salazar). This proxy literature may help us work through some of the theoretic density of two-spirit identity. However, if we want to understand the ways in which two-spirit identity effects self-discovery, political resistance, and social change for Aboriginal people and communities, we need to talk to two-spirit people (Keating 1993).

INDIGENOUS RESEARCH METHODOLOGY

The research described here began as an exploration of the question, "How does the empowered identity of a two-spirit person appear within the context of sustained homophobia, sexism, and racism?" This question could only be answered by two-spirit people and that, if I wanted them to share their knowledge and experiences, I needed to work in ways that were congruous with their values, ethics, and practices.

The design and methodology of this research were guided by teachings from Cree and Ojibway cultures, the communities to which most of the research participants belong. These principles, which include the communality of knowledge (knowledge does not belong to any one individual), relational accountability (we are accountable to each other for everything that we do), reciprocity (we give back to our communities and each other), and holism (we must care for all of being, including the physical, emotional, mental, and spiritual elements), have informed and guided other Aboriginal scholars' research design[4] (Cardinal; Hermes; Martin; Meyer; Native Women's Research Project; Steinhauer 1997; Steinhauer, E. 2003; Weber-Pillwax 2001, 2003; Wilson 1996, 2000, 2001; Wilson, S. 2004).

Research activities also incorporated community research protocols developed by Aboriginal community members in Manitoba (Graveline, Wilson, and Wastasecoot). These protocols include accountability, respect for and adherence to an Aboriginal worldview, relationship building, and giving back to the community. Respect for an Aboriginal worldview requires a researcher to respect the integrity and authenticity of Aboriginal peoples' knowledge, experience, understandings, and voice. I sought to preserve the authority of Aboriginal voices by inviting two-spirit community members to participate in personal interviews and group discussions and collaborate in all stages of the research process, from data collection through analysis to the presentation of findings.

Research activities were based in Northern Manitoba and in Winnipeg. Eight people who identify as two-spirit and who were willing to reflect on and share their experiences joined me for individual open-ended and unstructured interviews and group discussions. The participants, who ranged from eighteen to fifty plus years of age and represented a continuum of gender identities, were encouraged to explore and share in detail their lived experiences as two-spirit people. The information they shared was recorded and then analyzed using a voice-centred relational method. As the data was reread and discussed, I recognized a shared narrative arc in the participants' stories. Early in their lives, they had been relatively comfortable with who they were. Around or soon after they reached school age, their sense of self began to fragment and they responded by cutting themselves loose in some sense. Eventually, a more integrated sense of self began to return and, finally, they came into their identities as two-spirit people.

BEGINNING TOGETHER

At the start of our first meetings, participants were asked to introduce themselves in whatever way they were comfortable. In addition to their name, almost every participant also mentioned their home community and/or the First Nation to which they belonged. Others offered more detail. For example, after stating her name, one participant then identified the First Nation community in which she was born and the communities from which each of her parents came. She offered her family clan name and identified the home community of her partner. Introductions such as these made it clear that participants' identities extended well beyond any individuated sense of self. They revealed identities in which their sexualities, families, histories, communities, place, and spiritualities are inseparable from each other and understood in the context of their whole lives.

Many of the participants grew up in northern bush communities. As children in these and other small and isolated communities, they relied heavily on creativity and imagination in play, with activities that reflected a close connection to family and place. They played with siblings and cousins and neighbours, at family and friends' homes, in the bush, acting out their own plays or playing doctor, chef, house, and Sasquatch. As children, many participants were able to slip unchallenged across, between, and along gender boundaries. These same participants, however, were later reined in for gender trangressions:

I just liked playing [games] with girls. I had what could be called a "girl-friend" at 13 but somehow I didn't see myself as a lesbian or even attracted to girls. I just saw it as affection.... I didn't even know there was a word for it until high school. But what the hell was a "les-be-friends" anyway?

FRAGMENTATION

While early in their lives, participants had found comfort and safety grounded in family and place, there also came a time when those things began to fracture. Although only two participants had attended residential schools, each referred to the devastating impacts that residential schools have had on their lives, families, and communities. Many of us have heard stories about residential schools, but it is easy to forget how totalizing that experience was:

... The first thing they did was divide us by boy/girl. Girl go this way, boy go this way. Girl wear pinafores. Boy wear pants. All hair cut.... I didn't really know which side to go to. I just knew that I wanted to be with my sisters and my brother. I had never worn a dress before so I went with my brother.... It was like a little factory—one priest shaved my head while the other tore off my clothes. I was so scared. I covered my area. It didn't take long for them to notice.... That was my first beating.

The schools were designed to strip Aboriginal children of their language, spirituality, and any other connections to their culture, community, or family. Children at the schools did not get to learn the simple daily "how-to" of affection, caring, communication, and love—lessons that our families and communities ordinarily provide.

As one woman who had not attended the schools noted, "All the residential school shit was repeated on [us]!" Some participants talked about being sexually, emotionally, and/or culturally abused by family members and others and their own struggles with depression, anger, and self-destructive behaviours. As they moved towards their teens and their racial, sexual, and gendered identity became more apparent, participants had typically encountered racism, homophobia, and sexism. For some, this began in their family homes. One light-haired, blue-eyed participant was teased by older siblings who suggested she was not her father's child. Another participant described how their family life changed when their mother remarried:

A white man raised us. He did not know or care about Aboriginal people, nor did he encourage us to retain our culture. We had a very abusive and rigid upbringing. We weren't allowed to speak Cree and soon forgot it. As my siblings got older they were systematically driven from the house. So eventually I alone had to deal with the violence and [my parents'] alcoholism on a daily basis.... I remember often feeling awkward and uncomfortable around most people. I never knew what to say or how to act.... I didn't know why I felt so different. I never wanted to do what other girls were doing. It just didn't interest me.... Boys were incredibly boring and might as well have been from another planet.... And the rules of my life at school or home or church were baffling. I just didn't feel like I fit anywhere.

For many participants, the sustained experience of racism, homophobia, and sexism separated them from their family and community and diminished their belief and confidence in who they were and their place in their worlds:

I remember thinking that [gay] was a dirty word because everyone around me said it was. I took a long time to even say and admit that I was gay. And when I did, I still had lingering thoughts on the subject.... Nno matter what I did to try and prevent being gay, I was very recognized from others that I was.

I knew I was gay but ... I wanted to fit in with my family and friends. It was not until I was thirty-five that I started to live my gay life for myself. This was after both my parents passed away.... I denied them knowing who the real me was and is.

In my community, you are the butt of all jokes. And they would tease me about setting me up with the rubbies in the community. That is what really turned me away from myself because I didn't want to be made fun of. I didn't want people to look at me differently or treat me differently.

Some inscribed their fractured sense of self on their skin: "I have a little row of scars on my arm from cuts because of all this," said one participant. Another lamented, "I reached the point where I was stifled. I could not move. I cut myself. Nothing I did made sense anymore. I knew I was on the wrong track." Others numbed themselves with alcohol and drugs. One related that, "The first time I got drunk I was eight and starting drinking with my mother regularly by fourteen. By seventeen, I was drinking and taking drugs on a weekly basis with my friends or at home." Turning thirteen proved traumatic for another participant who drank, took drugs, and smoked for the first time: "I remember crying and crying. I was all fucked up—not a pretty sight."

CUTTING LOOSE

As a first step towards reclaiming an integrated identity, the participants had looked for ways to escape and get safe. Some found this within their home communities. Some had immersed themselves in creative activities like writing or music. Some had found support networks. Most, however, did not feel safe enough to actively and openly explore their sexuality until they had left their communities. One participant described the aftermath of her move to the city: "I started to really think and feel things about my sexual identity. I thought about all the ramifications and had all the same doubts, denial, fears, anger, acceptance, and finally joy." While it does not seem unusual for Aboriginal people who are gay to be overwhelmed by their struggle to find a place to comfortably be themselves in the unfamiliar culture of a new city, it may also be a place where they find important supports and opportunities to explore their identity.

COMING TOGETHER: FINDING OUR SELVES AGAIN

Several participants described points in their lives when they recognized their own ability to interpret their experiences and choose their identity. In one group discussion, a participant offered this response to another person's description of their confusion about identity:

I think we all went through that. It sucks! And it still does, but we have to try to remove those chains—kind of like Black people had to—and admit it, say it: We are the only ones that enslave us now.

Many participants came to this recognition with guidance and support from other people. Participants described how their own understandings of sexuality, gender, spirituality, and "traditional" culture emerged and merged:

When I first came out, I came out as a lesbian, I thought I had to "pick a side."... That was okay for a while. I was comfortable with having relationships with women. But the more emotionally/mentally/spiritually/physically healthy and confident I became, the more I recognized that I was also attracted to men—which is not to insinuate healthy equals straight but that I became more aware of myself and who I am.

When I started learning about Aboriginal spirituality it all seemed so "mystical." There was a sacredness that seemed so much more pure.... I had a high school teacher who also became my traditional teacher. He explained that it is not just that things are done, but also how and why. He always encouraged me to question and debate.... He said if ever you ask someone why and they have no answer or say, "because that is the way it has always been done," run away from them.

My spirituality is a cross between the Bible and Native spirituality.... You can believe in some aspects [of the Bible] but not let it run you. On a spiritual side, I have come to acknowledge that we are a very powerful people. History states that we had our ways of living in harmony with the land. It makes sense to me and yet, that Bible influence will always be there to remind me of where I grew up.

Assuming control of their experiences and identity (particularly with respect to their sexuality and spirituality) empowered participants and brought them closer to an integrated sense of self. So too has their naming. The self-descriptor "two-spirit' clearly resonates for participants, drawing together the cultural, sexual, spiritual, and historic aspects of their identities:

I first heard the term during a two-spirit gathering.... At the time I was about two years into my coming out process, very comfortable with it. But I was really searching for how my culture fit into the queer culture. I didn't see myself anywhere in the pride marches, demonstrations, gay scene, or support groups. So when I heard our own histories around being gay I was thrilled. It just made sense to me that we would have a place, a purpose in our nations.... I identify with it more than any other label, like bi-sexual, which is too centred on sex.... I am more than that.... Two-spiritness [is] someone who has both masculine and feminine energies rather than man and woman spirits. It may be semantics but to me the words "man" and "woman" are separate and opposite from one another therefore it suggests gender roles and rules ... a very white, middle-class, Christian construct— man is aggressively in charge and women is a passive follower. Not very cultural as our nations tended to be balanced. But when you say masculine and feminine energies that could mean anyone or anything.

Being two-spirited is an identity that I have to acknowledge on a personal level. I know I am and I can say to myself that I am.... To my knowledge, there was no Cree word for gay.... Not understanding gays and lesbians is something we are struggling with. But we are getting better at it.... I love telling others about the history of our people. I would say that I am gay.... To be specific though, I would also mention that I am two-spirited. I think that it's important to let others know that there is the term.... I first heard of the term in 1997 when I started coming to the Pride parades.... I am proud to be a First Nations person; it was kind of like icing on a cake to know that we had our own identity within an identity.

COMING-IN

... On the wall of the main cabin a sign was posted: it said, "Pow-wow, Saturday night." When I read it, I felt dizzy, overwhelmed by my imagining what the dance might be. Two-spirit people dancing. I have lived with dreams of dancing, dreams where I spin around, picking up my feet. I have many feathers on my arms and on my body and I know all the steps. I turn into an eagle. Arms extended, I lift off the ground and begin to fly around in big circles. Would this be my chance? I waited patiently for Saturday night to come, listening....When the drumming started, I was sitting still, listening and watching...And then a blur flew by me and landed inside the circle of dancers that had formed.... It was a two-spirit dancing as it should be. After that, more two-spirits drifted into the circle. I sat and watched, my eyes edged with tears. I knew my ancestors were with me; I had invited them. We sat and watched all night, proud of our sisters and brothers, yet jealous of their bravery. The time for the last song came. Everybody had to dance. I entered the circle, feeling the drumbeat in my heart. The songs came back to me. I circled the dance area, and in my most humble moment, with the permission of my ancestors, my eleven-year-old two-spirit steps returned to me.... (Wilson 1996: 316)

As my friend Wayne Badwound said, "Coming in"—"that's what two-spirit people do." As a final step toward the development of their identities as two-spirit people, participants began to take responsibility for and control of the meaning of their own experiences and identities. Their reflections on sexual identity, traditional culture and spirituality revealed that rather than trying to fit themselves into an established identity, they were embracing and developing identities that fit who they are, including two-spirit identity. Participants described the fit between two-spirit identity and their own understandings of the distinct cultures, histories and traditional knowledges of Aboriginal peoples. Two-spirit identity is one that reflects Aboriginal peoples' process of "coming in" to an empowered identity that integrates their sexuality, culture, gender and all other aspects of who they understand and know themselves to be.

As the two-spirit people who participated in this research make clear, their understanding of sexuality is inseparable from their culture and socio-historical position. For two-spirit people, who typically live with sustained racism, homophobia and sexism, the process of "coming in" to their identity is likely to be very different from the conventional "coming out" story circulated in mainstream Canadian (GLBT) culture. In these narratives, "coming out" is typically a declaration of an independent identity: an GLBT person musters their courage and, anticipating conflict, announces their sexuality to a friend or family member—at the risk of being met with anger, resistance, violence or flat-out rejection or abandonment. In the narratives of two-spirit people, however, "coming in" is not a declaration or an announcement. Rather, it is an affirmation of interdependent identity: an Aboriginal person who is GLBT comes to understand their relationship to and place and value in their own family, community, culture, history and present-day world. "Coming in" is not a declaration or an announcement; it is simply presenting oneself and being fully present as an Aboriginal person who is GLBT.

The two-spirit people who collaborated in this project described times when they felt grounded and whole and stated what their identity means to them:

> *I feel like I am really a part of the circle, like I belong to something bigger … to the Great Mystery.*
>
> *It is a Mystery or Creator or whatever, but things seem to make sense once I found the two-spirit community. It was and is healing. Two-spirit is healing.*
>
> *Things started to clear.… I realized that it wasn't about colonization and oppression.… It wasn't about measuring up and comparing and not being good enough or smart enough.… It wasn't about wasn'ts.… It is about our strength, our land…our hearts.*

The final word goes to a participant who more often than not preferred to listen and observe during our discussions, but closed our last group meeting with this statement:

> *It has taken me a long time to see that I am valuable. Now that I see it and feel it, everything seems possible. I looked to so many places by travelling and even dating "exotic" people. But here the answer was right within me, and the answer is in our communities. We are our communities and they are us. Being two-spirited means I am always at home.*

CONCLUSION

The narrative arc of these stories of two-spirit people is really about journeying along a circular path. It is our nature to be whole and to be together. We are born into a circle of family, community, living creatures, and the land. Our encounters with racism, homophobia, and sexism may disturb our balance and we sometimes lose our place in the circle. For those of us who lose our place, our traditions, history, memories, and collective experience of this world will still guide us. Two-spirit identity is about circling back to where we belong, reclaiming, reinventing, and redefining our beginnings, our roots, our communities, our support systems, and our collective and individual selves. We "come-in."

Originally published in Canadian Woman Studies/les cahiers de la femme, *"Indigenous Women in Canada: The Voices of First Nations, Inuit and Métis Women," 26 (3 & 4) (Winter/Spring 2008): 193-199. Reprinted with permission of the author.*

Alex Wilson, Opaskwayak Cree Nation, is an Assistant Professor in the College of Education at the University of Saskatchewan. She is passionate about social justice and research and is particularly focused on Indigenous methodologies. She enjoys kayaking, fishing, and spending time at home on her Nations traditional territory.

[1]The Cree name *Aayahkwew* was used by anthropologist D. Mandelbaum to describe a Plains Cree person who seemed to defy western gender roles.

[2]For example, Williams (1996) argues that one anthropologist's sexual experiences in the field privileged him with information about "Indigenous" sexual practices that can now be incorporated into mainstream safe-sex literature for gay men.

[3]For example, in articles included in *Out in the Field* (Lewin and Leap) none of the anthropologists who had conducted research with two-spirit people described ways they had contributed positively to the communities in which they had conducted research—none, that is, other than Williams, who described himself as a "status symbol" for the Mayan man who was both his lover and his informant.

[4]Specific Indigenous scholars have identified respect, reciprocity, and responsibility as three basic principles of Indigenous research methodology.

REFERENCES

Ahenakew, Freda. *Cree Language Structures: A Cree Approach.* Winnipeg: Pemmican Publications, 1987.

Angelino, H., and C. L. Shedd. "A Note on Berdache." *American Anthropologist* 57 (1995): 121-26.

Blackwood, E. "Sexuality and Gender in Certain Native American Tribes: The Case of Cross-Gender Females." *Signs: Journal of Women in Culture and Society* 10 (1984): 27-42.

Callender, C. and L. M. Kochems. "The North American Berdache." *Current Anthropology* 24 (4) (1983): 443-470.

Cardinal, L. "What is an Indigenous Perspective?" *Canadian Journal of Native Education* 25 (2) (2001): 180-183.

Driver, H. *Indians of North America.* Chicago: University of Chicago Press, 1961

Etter-Lewis, G. "Black Women's Life Stories: Reclaiming Self in Narrative Texts." *Women's Words: The Feminist Practice of Oral History.* Eds. S. Gluck and D. Patai. New York: Routledge, 1991. 42-58.

Gever, M. 1990. "The Names We Give Ourselves." *Out There: Marginalizations and Contemporary Cultures.* Eds. R. Ferguson, M. Gever, Trinh T. Minh-Ha, and C. West. Cambridge: MIT Press. 191-202.

Graveline, J., S. Wilson, and B. Wastasecoot. 2002. *Indigenous Community Research Protocol Conference: Final Report.* Brandon University.

Gutierrez, R. *When Jesus Came, The Corn Mothers Went Away: Marriage, Sexuality, and Power in New Mexico, 1500-1846.* Stanford: Stanford University Press, 1991.

Hermes, M. "Research Methods as a Situated Response: Towards a First Nations' Methodology." *Qualitative Studies in Education* 11(1) (1998): 155-168.

Jacobs, S. E. "Berdache: A Brief Review of the Literature." *Colorado Anthropologist* 2 (4) (1968): 25-40.

Jacobs, S., W. Thomas, and S. Lang. *Two-Spirit People.* Chicago: University of Illinois, 1997.

Keating, A. "Myth Smashers, Myth Makers: (Re)Visionary Techniques in the Works of Paula Gunn Allen, Gloria Anzaldúa, and Audre Lorde." *Critical Essays: Gay and Lesbian Writers of Color.* Ed. E. S. Nelson. New York: Harrington Park Press. 1993. 73-95.

Lang, S. *Men As Women, Women As Men: Changing Gender in Native American Cultures.* Austin: University of Texas Press, 1998.

Lang, S. 1996. "Traveling Woman: Conducting a Fieldwork Project on Gender Variance and Homosexuality Among North American Indians." Eds. E. Lewin and W. Leap. *Out in the Field.* Urbana: University of Chicago Press. 86-107.

Lewin, Ellen and William Leap 1996. *Out in the Field.* Urbana, Ill: University of Illinois Press.

Lewis, O. 1941. "Manly-Hearted Women Among the North Piegan." *American Anthropologist* 43: 173-87.

Mandelbaum, D. *The Plains Cree.* New Haven: Yale University Press, 1936.

Martin, K. "Ways of Knowing, Being and Doing: A Theoretical Framework and Methods for Indigenous and Indigenist Re-search." *Voicing Dissent: Journal of Australian Studies* 76 (2007): 203-214.

Meyer, M. *Native Hawaiian Epistemology: Contemporary Narratives.* Unpublished doctoral dissertation. Harvard Graduate School of Education: Cambridge, MA, 1998.

Native Women's Research Project. *Community-Based Analysis of the U.S. Legal System's Intervention in Domestic Abuse Cases Involving Indigenous Women.* Washington: National Institute of Justice, 2003.

Parsons, E. C. "The Zuni la'mana." *American Anthropologist* 18 (1916): 521-528.

Robinson, T. and J. V. Ward. "'A Belief in Self Far Greater Than Anyone's Disbelief': Cultivating Resistance Among African American Female Adolescents." *Women, Girls and Psychotherapy: Reframing Resistance.* Eds. C. Gilligan, A. Rogers, and D. Tolman. New York: Harrington Park Press, 1991. 87-103.

Roscoe, W. "Bibliography of Berdache and Alternative Gender Roles Among North American Indians." *Journal of Homosexuality* 14 (3/4) (1987): 81-171.

Roscoe, W., ed. *Living the Spirit: A Gay American Indian Anthology.* New York: St. Martin's Press, 1988.

Roscoe, W. *The Zuni Man-Woman.* Albuquerque: University of New Mexico Press, 1991.

Salazar, C. "A Third World Woman's Text: Between the Politics of Criticism and Cultural Politics." *Women's Words: The Feminist Practice of Oral History.* Eds. S. Gluck and D. Patai. New York: Routledge, 1991. 93-106.

Simms, S. C. "Crow Indian Hermaphrodites." *American Anthropologist* 5 (1903): 580-81.

Steffenson, K. *Manitoba Native Peoples and Homosexuality: Historical and Contemporary Aspects.* Winnipeg: The Council on Homosexuality and Religion, 1987.

Steinhauer, D. "Native Education: A Learning Journey." Unpublished master's thesis. University of Alberta: Edmonton, Canada, 1997.

Steinhauer, E. "Thoughts on an Indigenous Research Methodology." *Canadian Journal of Native Education* 26 (2) (2003): 69-81.

Thompson, M. 1994. *Gay Soul: Finding the Heart of Gay Spirit and Nature.* San Francisco: Harper.

Trexler, R. *Sex and Conquest: Gendered Violence, Political Order, and the European Conquest of the Americas.* Ithaca: Cornell University Press, 1995.

Weber-Pillwax, C. *Identity Formation and Consciousness with Reference to Northern Alberta Cree and Métis Indigenous Peoples.* Unpublished doctoral dissertation. University of Alberta: Edmonton, Canada, 2003.

Weber-Pillwax, C. "Indigenous Research Methodology: Exploratory Discussion of an Elusive Subject." *Journal of Educational Thought* 33 (1) (1999): 31-45.

Weber-Pillwax, C. "What is Indigenous Research?" *Canadian Journal of Native Education* 25 (2) (2001): 166-174.

Williams, W. L. "Being Gay and Doing Fieldwork." *Out in the Field.* Eds. E. Lewin and W. Leap. Urbana: University of Chicago Press, 1996. 71-85.

Williams, W. L. *The Spirit and the Flesh: Sexual Diversity in American Indian Culture.* Boston: Beacon Press, 1986.

Wilson, Alex. *Dashing Berdache—The Two-Spirit Race: A Review of the Literature.* Unpublished qualifying paper. Harvard Graduate School of Education: Cambridge, MA: 2001.

Wilson, Alex. "How We Find Ourselves: Identity Development and Two-Spirit People." *Harvard Educational Review* 66 (2) (1996): 303-317.

Wilson, Alex. *Living Well: Aboriginal Women, Cultural Identity and Wellness.* Winnipeg: Prairie Women's Health Centre for Excellence, 2003.

Wilson, Alex. "Two-spirit People." *Encyclopedia of Feminist Theories.* Ed. L. Code. New York: Routledge, 2000: 477-478

Wilson, S. *Research is a Ceremony.* Toronto: Fernwood, 2008.

TRIPLE JEOPARDY

Aboriginal Women with Disabilities

PEOPLE WITH DISABILITIES ARE disadvantaged in the areas of education, access, transportation, housing, employment opportunities, recreation, cultural opportunities, etc. Women with disabilities speak of double jeopardy. I believe that Aboriginal women who have a disability are in a situation of triple jeopardy. You may be familiar with many of the concerns that Aboriginal people in Canada have—poor housing conditions, lack of adequate medical care, and substance abuse. When you add to this disability and being female, you have a situation of extreme disadvantage.

For example, when it was time for me to start school, I had to leave my home in Manitoba to attend a special school for visually-impaired children in Ontario. Not only did I have to leave my family, but I was in a different culture with its own language and norms. Like all the children there, I experienced the negative effects of being educated in a segregated institution, but for me there was the additional burden of being in a different culture. This is still happening today. There are many Aboriginal children from remote communities in the North who must come to the South for educational or rehabilitative services.

WHO WE ARE

Aboriginal peoples are not a homogeneous group. Just as you cannot talk about "the disabled" with any clarity, you must remember that Canada's Aboriginal population can be divided into the following groupings—Status, Non-status, Treaty, Métis, and Inuit. Aboriginal people are urban and rural dwellers; some live on a reserve while others live off the reserve; and many still live in the North. This means that there are many varying circumstances and realities for Canada's Aboriginal population.

SELF-GOVERNMENT

Self-government is the number one priority for Aboriginal people. It is seen as the best way to improve their status in Canadian society. While Aboriginal persons with disabilities are in agreement with self-government, there is the concern that their needs as persons with disabilities may not be included in the process of self-government. I saw evidence of this when doing the interviews which comprise the Coalition of Provincial Organizations of the Handicapped (COPOH) report "Disabled Natives Speak Out."

JURISDICTIONAL PROBLEMS

It is often said that for disadvantaged groups, education is the key to escaping poverty, dependency on welfare, unemployment, etc. Aboriginal people with disabilities are being denied access to the services that would enable them to get the education that assists in obtaining employment. Employment is crucial if an individual is to have an independent and financially secure lifestyle. What is denying us that access?

That access is being denied by jurisdictional quagmires. For those of us who have status or treaty rights, we have always been viewed by service agencies as being the responsibility of the federal government. This means that provincial rehabilitation resources that are available to other Canadians with disabilities are not always available to us. For example, in Manitoba, the Society for Manitobans with Disabilities, formerly the Society for Crippled Children and Adults, does not include people with Status in their mandate. This makes it very difficult for Aboriginal people to get needed services.

I have my own personal example in this area. I was told by one worker at the Canadian Institute for the Blind (CNIB) in response to my request for a closed circuit TV reader, which I needed for my education, that as an Aboriginal person with status that I was not eligible for VRDP allocated equipment, and that VRDP students had first priority to these devices. The worker told me that as an Aboriginal person I was not eligible for VRDP and as a status Indian I was the responsibility of Indian Affairs and it was to them that I should make the request. However, not more than two days prior to that I had been told by someone from the education department of Indian Affairs that there was no money in their budget for these devices and that I was registered with the CNIB and that I should make my request to CNIB. This is just one example of a situation where the lack of clarity and the bureaucratic-run-around prevents Aboriginal people with disabilities from getting adequate services.

Now that Aboriginal people have started to set up their own education services, the whole situation has become just that much more complex. Despite the fact that Indian Affairs has a policy on Aboriginal people with special needs, this policy is not clear or well understood by many of these organizations. As a consequence, they do not know how to access the funds that are theoretically available to meet the rehabilitation needs of Aboriginal persons with disabilities. So who is the loser in all this? It is ultimately the person with the disability, of course.

Just as there is a lack of clarity in the education area, there is a lack of clarity in the area of Medical Services. I have come across many situations where a person with a disability whose health is stabilized and who is eligible for assistance from other programs, is rejected by those programs because those programs assume that Medical Services should be taking care of all their needs. We are running up against the domination of the medical model. This is something that non-Aboriginal people with disabilities were fighting in the early '70s when the consumer movement was born. Aboriginal people with disabilities are still fighting that battle. Often, these people end up going home to their reserve with nothing, because none of the programs would accept responsibility for them.

These are just a few examples of the bureaucratic problems which Aboriginal people with disabilities encounter when they attempt to access necessary services. Add to that coming from a different culture, speaking a different language, having to deal with non-Aboriginal bureaucrats, and you will get an idea of some of the obstacles encountered by Aboriginal people with disabilities and why I am talking to you about a situation of triple jeopardy.

ISOLATION

Recently, I attended a conference which focused on the concerns of parents of children with disabilities from the North. There were a number of women at the conference who were single parents. These women felt that their needs, and the needs of their disabled children were not being met. For the most part, these women were living in poverty and it was difficult for them to meet the dietary needs of a child with a disability.

I heard many accounts from parents whose children were living in Southern institutions. These children have come from Northern isolated communities to Southern settings to get needed services which are unavailable in the North. I heard about how these children lose contact with their families and their communities. The length of time spent away from family and community can be months and even years. The only way for parents to see their children is to fly down. Flying from North to South is very expensive. It is impossible to make frequent trips. This is particularly true if you have a low income or are on social assistance. The end result is that you lose contact with your child. You have really no choice in that matter, because there are no services in your community. If the child is to get those services, she/he must come South.

TRANSITIONS

People can become disabled as children or it can happen later in life. If you have a disability as a child and you have to leave your community to get access to services or for education, the more time spent away from your community and family the more assimilated into white culture you become. Earlier I made a reference to going away to school. I spent six and a half years of my childhood away from my family and community, and during that time I lost most of my language, a lot of my cultural roots, and perhaps the most devastating to me was the loss of family contacts and bonds. While language and culture are important, these are something I think one can re-learn. But not growing up in a family atmosphere is not something that you can make up for in later years. Being assimilated into another culture makes you a stranger in your own culture, but it does not make you belong in the other, so in a sense you belong in neither culture. Ultimately, if you have different norms and values than that of your family, it makes it harder for you to be part of your own family, so you tend to be isolated.

When you are disabled as an adult, you have to learn to adjust to your disability while simultaneously adjusting to white culture in order to receive services. If you need services to assist you with these adjustments, they are very difficult to find. There are very few service providers who have the necessary understanding of both the cultural factors and the disability factors to assist a person in coping with the transitions they are experiencing in their life. Non-Aboriginal disability organizations do not always have culturally appropriate programs to help people who are Aboriginal. Aboriginal organizations do have these programs, but they often do not have the understanding of disability issues.

We need to aim some of our attention at Aboriginal women's organizations, so that they become sensitive to the issues and concerns of their Aboriginal sisters who have disabilities.

CONDITIONS ON RESERVES

I have met a number of Aboriginal women and men with spinal cord injuries at 1010, a housing project in Winnipeg for disabled people. These women and men were preparing for a life in Winnipeg, because there are no options at home on their reserves. There are no accommodations on their reserves to assist them to live in that setting with their disability—ramps into buildings, modified living units that are accessible, accessible transportation, etc. The condition of existing facilities on reserves can make independent living difficult. For example, gravel roads that are poorly maintained are difficult to travel on when using a wheelchair. These individuals had no choice but to live in the city.

People who live in isolated communities in the North get into the community either by winter road or by air. During spring when the ice is breaking up there is total isolation, because the winter roads are not usable and you can't fly in. So you are stuck either in or out. That makes it difficult for a person with a disability. It doesn't make it easy for you to live in your community. Situations such as this also force people into urban settings.

SUBSTANCE ABUSE

It is well known that the high rate of substance abuse leads to disabilities. For example, children born with fetal alcohol syndrome can have learning disabilities. People become disabled in accidents that are brought on by substance abuse. Furthermore, drug dependency does not end with disablement. Many treatment facilities are inaccessible. This is particularly true when it comes to women's treatment facilities. We need to work to see that these facilities become accessible and have programs which are culturally appropriate for Aboriginal women with disabilities.

Substance abuse is a contributor to domestic violence. There are many Aboriginal women who are survivors of violence. As the Disabled Women's Network (DAWN) report indicates, violence can lead to disability. Shelters for abused women need to be made aware of the needs of Aboriginal women with disabilities. Non-Aboriginal shelters for abused women need to be encouraged to have culturally appropriate programs for Aboriginal women with disabilities.

MEDICAL CONDITIONS

Aboriginal people are susceptible to certain kinds of diseases and medical conditions such as diabetes, which can cause loss of limbs, blindness, etc. These medical conditions are exacerbated and triggered by poor living conditions on reserves—i.e., malnutrition, poor housing, etc. Many reserves still have poorly constructed houses which lack plumbing, water systems, and adequate heating systems. These living conditions make it difficult for a person with a disability to live independently, and it is particularly difficult for women who are raising children. You can imagine how difficult it is for an Aboriginal woman who is a wheelchair user to raise her children in a house which does not have indoor plumbing.

Inadequate health services on reserves compound the problem. There are examples of people who are more disabled than they need to be because they were treated by people who were poorly trained, under-qualified, etc. in limited facilities with poor diagnostic equipment.

It would seem to me that clarity of jurisdiction, clear lines of responsibility, and a better internal understanding of the lines of responsibility would improve the situation immensely. Some recommendations are as follows:

•Clarify methods for accessing services and make this information well known at the individual level. If people understand better how to access services, it is easier for consumers to get the services that they are looking for.

•Decentralize services. Services should be available on reserves so the

people living there would not have to leave their community.
Improve access on reserves. For example, schools could be made accessible. Make access to people with disabilities a priority everywhere—including on reserves.

•Develop information programs, so that the people who need this information can get access to it. Aboriginal organizations need to have an understanding of their funding process so they can get the funds to provide the services they require.

•We must do public education with Aboriginal women's organizations, so they become aware of the issues and concerns of Aboriginal women with disabilities. We must also encourage non-Aboriginal women's organizations to provide culturally appropriate programs which meet the needs of Aboriginal women with disabilities.

A version of this article was presented at a conference held by COPOH *in Toronto in 1989. Originally published in* Canadian Woman Studies/les cahiers de la femme, *"Women and Disability," 13 (4) (Summer 1993): 53-55. Reprinted with permission of the author.*

Doreen Demas was born and spent her early years living in her home community of Canupawakpa Dakota nation, but has made Winnipeg her home for many years. She attained a degree in Social Work from the University of Manitoba, and is the current Director of the First Nations DisAbility Association of Manitoba. She has been actively involved in the disability community for more than two decades. She has worked with First Nations organizations, provincial and federal governments, and persons with disabilities as a consultant, policy analyst, and writer on issues related to disability, in areas such as health and poverty. She participated in the Canada Aboriginal Peoples' Round Table sessions where she contributed in the areas of healthcare, education, employment ,and housing from a disability perspective. Of late, she freelances and is working with the Assembly of Manitoba Chiefs and the First Nations Education Resource Centre on their disability services' model for on-reserve First Nations children and adults with disabilities and their families. An award winner, she has published and spoken nationally and internationally on disability issues. When not working, she enjoys spending time with her two dogs and two cats, and is involved in rescue programs and shelters for animals.

VALERIE ALIA

INUIT WOMEN AND THE POLITICS OF
NAMING IN NUNAVUT

IN THE PAST TWENTY-FIVE YEARS, Inuit—women and men aged nineteen to ninety—have told me that despite centuries of interference by visitors to the North, traditional ways of naming are very much alive.

It has been a time of great change in the eastern Arctic, since the official launch of Nunavut (Inuktitut for "Our Land") in 1999. Inuit women played a major role in the process of creating this Inuit-majority public government. Among the key players were Rosemarie Kuptana, then president of the national organization Inuit Tapirisat of Canada (now Inuit Tapiriit Kanatami); Nellie Cournoyea, then Northwest Territories government leader; Martha Flaherty, then president of Pauktuutit Inuit Women's Association; Mary Simon, then head of the Inuit Circumpolar Conference (now the Inuit Circumpolar Council); and her successor, Sheila Watt-Cloutier. In February 1984, Pauktuutit held its tenth annual general meeting in Iqaluit.

> *Between changing diapers and calming rambunctious children, they talked about rape and the failings of the northern justice system. They wept for the loss of Inuit culture and traditional skills. And they demanded that [the issues] be addressed....* (Gregoire 7)

When I spoke with Martha Flaherty in Iqaluit in June, she spoke of the deep meaning of names in her life, and the traditions that have survived generations of interference and change. Her extended family was celebrating the birth and naming of its newest member.

> *The name never dies.... The name which I have is the same one that was carried by my ancestors for a very long time....* (Robbe 46)

> *Before I was born, my mother had to decide who would be involved at my birth... The first person who has to be there is a mid-wife, man or woman.*[1] *In my case it was my grandmother.... Also present at my birth was the person I was named after, my other grandmother ... we called each other* sauniq, *name-sake, bone-to-bone relation.* (Freeman 72)

In Inuit culture, names insure the continuity of the lives of individuals, families, and communities. Names are passed from one generation to the next without regard for gender. The same namesake can live through several new people, male or female. The ties are so strong that until puberty, kinship terms, dress, and behaviour often follow the namesake relationship, rather than biological sex or conventional gender identification.

> *No child is only a child. If I give my grandfather's atiq [soul-name] to my baby daughter, she is my grandfather. I will call her ataatassiaq, grandfather. She is entitled to call me grandson.* (Brody 33)

"Discovered" by seventeenth-century explorers, the Canadian Arctic has known traders, governments, and European religions since the early 1900s. These visitors persisted in interfering with the ways Inuit define and experience genders and families, and name themselves and their land.

> Although the missionaries were sure that they were doing the right thing, their actions sometimes brought confusion and sorrow. Those who stopped the drum dancing, forbade the Coppermine Inuit to wear lip ornaments, and christened children with foreign names were little by little helping to destroy independence and pride....
> (Crowe 148-9)

Like the missionary activities, the history of government intervention also reveals discrepancies between intention and effect. Efforts by government to save Inuit lives and administer important services were grounded in paternalism and framed in inappropriate terms. The various missionaries and public officials gave religious or bureaucratic explanations for changing Inuit names. They sought to baptize and bring Inuit into the faith (whichever faith it happened to be). Or they found the absence of surnames "confusing" and the Inuktitut names difficult to pronounce and accurately record (Alia).

After Anglican and Catholic clergy had carried baptismal naming throughout the North, government got into the act. Numerous complaints (many of them from government representatives) short-circuited a fingerprinting program which was begun in the 1930s. Next, Inuit were issued identification, or "disk" numbers. In 1944, census fieldworkers were told that each Inuk (Inuit person) was to receive a disk whose number would appear on all birth, marriage, and death certificates. The Arctic was divided into twelve districts, separated into West and East. Each number started with "E" for East or "W" for West; Inuit in the eastern Arctic still refer to their "E-numbers."

Many *Qallunaat* (non-Inuit) and Inuit expressed resentment of the disk number system. However, negative reactions were far from universal, as some *Qallunaat* suggest. For example, Derek G. Smith's fascinating discussion, although grounded in genuine social concern, is out of touch with reality.

Following the trend of embracing ethnohistory and avoiding live interviews (in part, a response to challenges levelled at past anthropological practice), he assumes that that all Inuit are affronted by the disk system, framed as "structural violence" (citing Johan Galtung) or "cultural genocide." If he had left the archives behind, and talked to people living in Nunavut, he would have heard another story. Inuit from different age groups, communities, and experiences have told me they much preferred the disk system, which was minimally disruptive to identity traditions, to other bureaucratic interventions. The interviews reveal a range of Inuit perspectives, from acceptance (even attachment) to the disk system to resentment. At a 1986 meeting of Pauktuutit, several women expressed different attitudes about the disk numbers, including one remark that "I wish they'd give us back our disk numbers."

Smith's assumption raises a significant methodological problem: it is easier to apply theory to dead publications than to live people. Of course, the fitting of data to theory occurs in interview-based research as well. The challenge is to listen to, or read accounts of, a variety of people and then try to discover whether any theory covers the range of their experiences and views. Thousands of people vividly remember the introduction of disk numbers and were entirely ignored in the research and theory-making process.

CENSUS AND CERTIFICATION: RESHAPING THE INUIT FAMILY

Census-taking was filled with inconsistencies and absurdities. Lists followed official standards for "the Canadian family," with no attempt to understand Inuit family structures of traditions, which would have made it clear that much of the census structure was irrelevant. Some of the "standard" categories have no parallels in Inuit culture. There are no titles such as "Dr.," "Mr.," or "Ms." and no gender-specific pronouns. An *Inuk* is a male or female person.

Children who were full family members according to Inuit practice were designated "boarder," "step," or "adopted," by census-takers. *Qallunaat* policy-makers have yet to acknowledge that today's "new" policies allowing adopted children access to their biological families were followed by Inuit for centuries. In 1969, The Northwest Territories Council tried (unsuccessfully) to move the other way and make adoptions "confidential" (i.e., secret). Today, Inuit "custom adoption" remains common and is gaining legitimacy in the *Qallunaat* legal system.

The concept of "head of family" or "head of house-hold," essential to government documentation, is alien. In an Inuit extended family, the "father/husband" is not necessarily the central or most powerful person. In 1994 in Iqaluit, a woman told me the idea seemed silly to her. "My mother was the head of the household—my father was always out hunting; she ran things at home. So why wouldn't they list *her* as the 'head' of the family?"

Bob Hodge says birth certificates express state control, and portray the official image of a "normal" family. They carve identities into the record, and

From left to right, Annie Okalik—midwife and mother of Paul Okalik, first Premier of Nunavut—and Rosie Veevee, Pangnirtung, 1984. Photo: Valerie Alia.

convey privilege or subjugation that can last more than a lifetime (Hodge). Birth certificates issued to Inuit contained wrong names, nonexistent family relationships, irrelevant dates. They listed precise times and locations of births that had never been recorded, for people who travelled widely and identified time and place in non-southern ways.

I have heard many stories of the sometimes comical, sometimes harmful inaccuracies. Some people have failed to receive retirement and other benefits. In the 1980s in a Baffin Island community, twins were listed as having been born several years apart.

Elise Attagutaluk told me she was stunned when, as a young adult, she suddenly received a birth certificate with her *husband's* surname on it. "I sent it back and asked for correction and they just sent it back to me unchanged." Frustrated by the still unresolved situation, she told me the story one afternoon when we were in Ottawa for a meeting. Not long after, Elise died with that name.[2]

Inuit families feature close ties, grounded in the intricate, intimate naming system. The distinction between a "real" and a "common-law" spouse is meaningful only in *Qallunaat* terms, for southern law. Many families follow neither religious nor legal marriage rites. "There are hardly any marriages here," one woman told me. People mostly live together in what southerners would call "common-law marriages." Women tell me the missionaries in the early days insisted on marriage.

PROJECT SURNAME

Surnaming has always been tied to class and power. A surname can be a sign of power or powerlessness. It can mark inheritance of family, status or property, or subjugation of one class or gender by another, signifying person-as-property. In western tradition, a woman's renaming at marriage represents the transfer of "property" (the woman) from father to husband. Inuit tradition does not include this kind of marriage tie or re-identification of the woman through her husband's identity. Following criticisms of the disk number system (many of them by *Qallunaat*), Inuit in the Northwest Territories were given surnames out of a misguided idea this would give them more power by making them like other Canadians. Commissioner Stuart Hodgson made it an official project of the 1970 Territorial Centennial and hired Abraham (Abe) Okpik to carry out the military-sounding "Project Surname." In 13 months, Okpik travelled more than 45,000 miles and interviewed some 15,000 people.

In a culture without gender-specific naming, titles, or other status designations, surnaming was absurd. Despite assurances that all was "voluntary," many people had no say. In fact, many of them were not even present for the program in which they presumably participated. "Kids came home and were told 'You're somebody else,'" Elise recalled.

Women were renamed in their absence, by men. One Elder remembered her confusion when her husband came home and announced their new name. It made no sense. Women didn't take their husbands' names, yet suddenly, both she and her husband had his father's last name. The new name was not just a confusion or an inconvenience, it undercut the relationship between name, name-avoidance, and respect in the family. In many communities, a woman may not speak the name of her husband's father. In order to follow traditional practice, a woman surnamed for her husband's family would now have to avoid speaking her own last name.

Canada was not the first country to develop a surnaming program for Indigenous people. The Soviet government gave surnames to the Yuit in the 1930s. Today, amidst an emerging movement of Siberian peoples, Yuit are finding ways to counter the assimilationist results of such programs. In the 1960s, Polar Inuit were given surnames by the Danish Ministry of Ecclesiastical Affairs. In the 1980s, after 15 years of home rule, Greenland took over responsibility for the names of its people.

Despite culture and language loss and change, agony, and anomie (especially in younger generations), Inuit culture remains remarkably strong. Cultural continuity is particularly evident with regard to naming. "Underground" practices (such as using the Inuktitut name in private and putting a *Qallunaat* name on the birth certificate) have moved back aboveground.

As I predicted in 1989, Nunavut ushered in an era of cultural renewal, and increasing acknowledgment that contact among cultures is never one-way. Despite the outward appearance of acculturation, traditions are strong, in constant flux, and never pure except in the minds of scholars. We must respect the rights of different Canadians to experience and express their cultures, families, and identities in different ways.

Originally published in Canadian Woman Studies/les cahiers de la femme, *"Women of the North," 14 (4) (Summer/Fall 1989): 11-14. Updated and reprinted with permission of the author.*

Valerie Alia is the author of Names and Nunavut: Culture and Identity in Arctic Canada *(2007) and* The New Media Nation: Indigenous Peoples and Global Communication *(2009). She is Adjunct Professor in the Doctor of Social Sciences Programme at Royal Roads University (BC), former Running Stream Professor of Ethics and Identity at Leeds Metropolitan University (UK) and inaugural Distinguished Professor of Canadian Culture at Western Washington University.*

[1]Thanks to recent developments, midwives are again able to practice. Martha Greig, formerly head of Pauktuutit, is a midwife who was instrumental in developing programs to bring traditional and western medical practice together. It was she who first told me Inuit had male midwives; her grandfather was one.

[2]Elise died in 1986 (ironically and tragically, at the hand of her husband, whose name she had been given), shortly after we made plans to worth together. Her life continues through names, through the important work of her sister, Alexina Kublu, and through the policies and projects she initiated or inspired, in Igloolik and nationally.

REFERENCES

Alia, Valerie. *Names and Nunavut: Culture and Identity in Arctic Canada.* New York: Berghahn Books, 2007.

Brody, Hugh. *The People's Land.* Harmondsworth, England: Pelican, 1975.

Crowe, Keith. *A History of the Original Peoples of Northern Canada.* Kingston: McGill-Queen's University Press, 1991.

Freeman, Minnie Aodla. *Life Among the Qallunaat.* Edmonton: Hurtig, 1978.

Gregoire, Lisa. "A Show of Strength for Women." *Arctic Circle* Spring 1994.

Hodge, Bob. "Birth and the Community." *Language and Control.* Roger Fowler et al. London: Routledge and Kegan Paul, 1979.

Robbe, Pierre. "Les Noms de personne chez les Amassalimiut." *Etudes Inuit Studies* 5 (1) (1981) (author's translation).

Smith, Derek. "The Emergence of 'Eskimo Status': An Examination of the Eskimo Disk List System and Its Social Consequences, 1925-1970." *Anthropology, Public Policy and Native Peoples in Canada.* Eds. Noel Dyck and James B. Waldram. Montreal: McGill-Queen's University Press, 1993.

AGNES GRANT

FEMINISM AND ABORIGINAL CULTURE

One Woman's View

A S A CAUCASIAN FEMINIST working almost exclusively in First Nations communities, with First Nations people who are predominantly women, I have been plagued for many years by the contradictions in some feminist agendas. From firsthand experience and through dialogue with Aboriginal colleagues I know that there is little equity for women in First Nations communities.

However, it is not always possible to subscribe to the feminist agenda as presented by some women's groups, especially the National Action Committee on the Status of Women (NAC), as the agenda must be acceptable in First Nations communities. For example, I was forced to take sides during the Charlottetown Accord referendum debate over the issue of First Nation's right to self-government.

Like many Canadian women, I was not absolutely convinced that NAC was right to come out against the Accord. Nor was I absolutely sure that the First Nation's position (supporting the Accord) would help them achieve the right to self-determination.

With NAC's cavalier statements about First Nations being able to achieve self-government through other channels, the die was cast for me. NAC had obviously learned little from the Oka crisis. Through Oka we saw just how far the Mohawks were prepared to go to protect their rights and how far Canadians were prepared to go to suppress those rights.

First Nations people will eventually achieve self-government but it will not be without cost to Canadian society. For a group like NAC, which is so used to struggling for equality, to make light of another group's efforts serves only to alienate people.

I have come to reject single-issue positions since they tend to over-simplify the issue at the expense of others. Such an approach is not within my vision of feminism, and though I understand the urgency of women's issues, I cannot work only for women's issues.

The feminist movement has been justifiably criticized in the past for being white and middle-class, but it must be recognized that many feminists have earnestly sought ways to involve women from other races and cultures. What has not been understood or acknowledged is the profoundly racist nature of

Canadian society. Caucasian women need never concern themselves with racism unless they consciously choose to do so. Many privileged (white) members of society are completely unaware of the complex relationships that exist between white and minority people. This is not to say that white feminists are unfair or racist, but many of us do operate in cooperation with a racist system.

Having worked for over twenty years in northern communities training Aboriginal teachers, I have noticed the hostility many Aboriginal women feel when pressured to join Caucasian feminists. I have seen the pain of Aboriginal women as they have attempted to seek equality within women's groups. A few have succeeded but many more have experienced their involvement in the feminist movement as another demonstration of marginalization. A few examples will demonstrate my point.

At the 1985 World Conference in Nairobi, Aboriginal women did not participate in activities with "Canadian" women. At a workshop conducted by Aboriginal women, I listened with acute embarrassment as Caucasian women discussed their difficulty in communicating with minority women. This was puzzling, as the Aboriginal women had just presented to them a multitude of commonalities. At another conference I watched as an Aboriginal guest speaker was shouted down by a Caucasian woman who had not agreed with the speaker's comments. The guest speaker left the building in tears and stood on the curb waiting for a taxi as local women in groups of two and three brushed by her.

It is not my intention to be critical or negative toward my sisters. I cite the above examples not as proof that feminists are racist and unfeeling but as specific examples of what it can be like to be a First Nations woman in our midst.

Various women's initiatives have made real attempts and progress at grappling with First Nations issues. Bill C-31, the bill that gave status First Nations women equality with First Nations men, would likely never have been passed if it had not been for the support of other women. Undoubtedly, Aboriginal women have benefited from the actions of feminists and in our hearts I know that we all rejoice that this is so.

A cursory examination of key feminist issues, however, reveals worlds that are separated by such chasms they appear irreconcilable. It is only a minority of Aboriginal women who can take for granted adequate food, housing, and sanitation for their children; adequate police protection; justice from the courts; non-coercive health care; and, an education system that respects their cultures and spirituality. Reproductive choice and abortion? Abortion is not an issue when the highest infant mortality rate in Canada is found among Aboriginal children under a year old. Equality in the workplace is not an issue when some First Nations communities have a 75 percent or higher unemployment rate. Sexual orientation? Long before Europeans invaded this continent there was acceptance of a person's sexual orientation as a matter of course and respect.

The bottom line is that in a racist society women are as much the enemy as men. When the Canadian government/army fired tear gas at innocent Mohawk women and bayoneted a 14-year-old girl in the breast as she was attempting to go home, we needed to make that an issue. At stake was not a "Native issue," nor a "women's issue." At stake was a justice issue for a minority group.

First Nations women see the destruction of their culture as the major barrier to equality and a productive life. They see the destruction of their men by colonial powers as the most devastating of all factors. First Nations women will tell you that the concepts they have of themselves as mothers, as the bearers of children, the keepers of the family unit, and the transmitters of culture, has remained comparatively intact. There is no such equivalent cultural identity for their men. While Aboriginal women may feel that they have suffered greatly at the hands of their men as well as men from outside their culture, they believe that Aboriginal men have suffered more. The woman who is battered suffers great mental and physical anguish. The man who batters is a man who has lost his soul. He has lashed out at what is the core and root of his culture, the respect for Mother Earth, and by extension, woman.

Through my association with First Nations people I have come to value myself as a woman in a way I had never imagined possible. First Nations spiritual belief places Mother Earth, and by extension all women (through their ability to give birth), at the centre of all life. No amount of Christian dogma has shaken this reverence for womanhood.

Rarely have I heard "put down" comments about women by First Nations men the way we are so used to hearing in our culture. Never have I heard sexually explicit, exploitative jokes about women. That is not to say that sexually explicit jokes don't exist. The difference is that they acknowledge sexuality as a healthy, mutually enjoyable activity and the jokes are told with great candour instead of leering and innuendo. And there is meticulous adherence to when and where such joking is permitted.

The prestige and value of First Nations women increases with age. The devaluing of age by white society is a contradiction manifested in many feminist activities and actions that can be particularly painful to First Nations women. White women who make derogatory comments about their mothers, or even aunts, are viewed with shock and pity, for surely these are women who are lost on their spiritual journey.

When I walk into a crowded room and a young First Nations woman rises to give me her chair I have learned not to say, "I'm not that old!" I take the chair humbly and gratefully, acknowledging that I am respected because of my years. I am being shown that I am an important person who is valued for the experience I have acquired in my journey through life. I am also being told that I am loved because of my age. And because I am older, it is incumbent upon me to remember my position as an older woman in the family of humanity and interact with the people around me in an appropriate and respectful fashion.

That brings me full circle to my opening comments.

When we become strident, single-issue women, we are not serving anyone, least of all ourselves. "Female power" is not about gender; it is fundamental to the real humanity in us. If we allow ourselves to be seduced by the patriarchal methods by which our country functions today—the confrontation, the adversarial way of resolving issues, the power struggles—we may win some battles, yes, but we will have already lost the war.

Originally published in Canadian Woman Studies/les cahiers de la femme, *"Racism and Gender," 14 (2) (Spring 1994): 56-57. Reprinted with permission of the author's family.*

Agnes Grant worked for Brandon University for 28 years as a professor and administrator for off-campus programs on reserves and Hutterite colonies. She edited and authored several professional books, including Our Bit of Truth, No End of Grief *and* Finding My Talk. *She also wrote a novel,* May There Be No Sadness of Farewell, *which will be published posthumously in fall of 2009.*

SHIRLEY O'CONNOR-ANDERSON, PATRICIA A. MONTURE,
AND NERISSA O'CONNOR

GRANDMOTHERS, MOTHERS, AND DAUGHTERS

A S THE LEADERS AND FUTURE LEADERS of the Ontario Native Women's
Association (ONWA), we often question and discuss what the role of the
association is and what the future for First Nation's women in Ontario is. As
traditional women, we understand the role of the association to be the same
as our roles as women, mothers and grandmothers. This is what we strive to
have the association reflect. Women are warm, loving, and caring. We are the
first teachers.

I have had the unique opportunity to speak to two women, Shirley, who is
a mother and a grandmother, and one of her daughters, Nerissa. As I spoke
to them both, I realized they both repeated many times "as I have come to
understand this." I also realized that many of the Elders and traditional people
I have heard speak, speak in this way. There is no force or persuasion involved.
I think this is very important to understand if you want to understand what
traditional people are all about.

It is also important for you to know that I have put the spoken words of both
Shirley and Nerissa into my own in the process of writing this down. Any inac-
curacy or vagueness must become my responsibility as the one who has woven
this article together. The other explanatory note I wish to add is that the use
of the term "First Nations" is my own personal choice. It is a political choice
which reminds the people who came to this country and their descendants
of a truth in history that is often forgotten. This is our home and we are the
original people of this land. Many times when Nerissa and Shirley spoke they
used the word "Indian." I have changed their language into a consistent form.
For me, when I was growing up "Indian" is the word I learned to describe who
I was. Since then I have come to understand that it is a word that has a strict
legal meaning. I have, therefore, decided to try to use "Indian" only in that legal
way. This is much easier to accomplish in my writing than it is in my speaking.
My use of First Nations includes all of the original people of this land. This
includes the Métis people. As I have come to understand it, the Métis are the
descendants of the people who made a stand in the Riel Rebellion in Manitoba.
I do not believe a useful definition of Métis is anyone who is a "half-breed." All
First Nation's people of mixed blood come from specific nations, even though

sometimes through adoption and assimilation they have lost this knowledge. I believe that all individuals who have become lost to their First Nations, still maintain a rightful place in that nation.

Shirley: In order to ensure the survival of First Nation's women, and all people for that matter, we must ensure that we are helping Mother Earth heal. There are two ways we can accomplish this. We can work to ensure that First Nation's voices will be included in the decision-making processes in this province and this country. We also believe that we can only ensure our futures by understanding our own history.

Life today is so confusing. Many of us feel overwhelming helplessness. This is reflected in high suicide rates, alcohol and drug abuse, and over-incarceration. When an individual is able to understand from where we came, from proud and strong people, it is not so bad anymore. When we look at our present through our history, then we can see a future that is good.

There are many points to be made. It is like looking at a puzzle and we as First Nations must begin to understand how the puzzle goes together. There are issues of justice, health, land, and pollution. All the things in the air that are affecting all living things. Slowly our bodies, our minds and our spirits are being poisoned. We cannot sit back and wait for the government to wake up. Everywhere we look there is depletion and crisis. A good example is all the fish that used to live in the waters around Kenora. The sturgeon are now gone. White people panic in the face of crisis. They worry. But Indian people are strong. We have faced so much oppression and so many efforts to assimilate us. As "Indians" we must learn to respect ourselves and each other. We have a very important job to do and that is to teach. We can teach how all nations must begin to work together. This is where the future of the Ontario Native Women's Association rests.

Nerissa: We must go back to the grassroots. This is where you get strength and knowledge. There is such an emptiness inside when you are without your traditions. How can you help someone else when you are not yourself whole? Traditions and wholeness just have to be done.

Women are the strong ones. We are strong because we are the givers of life. You learn from your Elders your aunties and uncles, grandmothers and grandfathers. That is where to go looking for your answers. That is where our youth will again find their answers and their strength.

Shirley: Being a grandmother now means that I have a second chance to teach. As a child I was brought up in a good way. If we think about our children, we know that they test us. They do not always listen to us. And that is the way they are meant to be. We tell a toddler whose job is to explore, "don't touch!" But, they touch anyway. We tell our teen-age women, "don 't go out with that boy!" But they go anyway. We always challenge life no matter how old we get. It is only when you have your own children that it begins to make sense. We then do what our mothers and grandmothers taught us to do. Life repeats itself.

The hardest thing to do in life is to let go of your own children. When you become a grandmother, you then understand you have a second chance. This is why grandmothers are always accused of spoiling. Grandmothers have learned a kind way because they have learned to let go. They are no longer responsible for the disciplining of those children in the same way as a mother is.

Even as grandmothers, we never stop learning. We go to our Elders and to our daughters and to our grandchildren. We see that there is continuous teaching all around us. We know that you can learn important lessons from the smallest living thing to the most vicious human being or animal.

The means to survival is to find the positive pieces of the puzzle and improve. Without that insight you become bitter. We must always be reminded to look for the beauty in yourself. If you cannot see that, then you will not be able to see the beauty around you.

It is necessary to share your experience to be able to find the beauty in yourself and in others. This is where we come back to the Ontario Native Women's Association. The association is one way we are able to share with each other. ONWA is like family to me. Each child in a family is different. We each have different gifts. Every woman who is involved with ONWA, I can learn from. ONWA is kept together by sharing a common vision. As President, the women around me are my children. When they do not behave it is my responsibility to pull us all back together again. And my strength to do this comes from knowing my traditions and going to the Elders for help.

Sometimes we are told we are a political organization. I have wondered what politics are. As I have come to understand it, politics come naturally from within. In the traditional way of life, politics, education, spirituality, family, do not come apart. We cannot separate them. Politics is like a beautiful flower. When we cut it off from the rest of the plant by picking it, it will eventually die. That is what "government politics" reminds me of sometimes, the control and the removal of beauty. That kind of politics is just like a picked flower. It will lose its beauty and die. If you do not pick that flower, but water it and nurture it instead, it will grow. That is the beauty that the First Nation's way teaches. What should be is a strong woman who sees the beauty within. And politics should be the woman who sees true justice.

Originally published in Canadian Woman Studies/les cahiers de la femme, *"Native Women," 10 (2 & 3) (Summer/Fall 1989): 38-39. Reprinted with permission of the authors.*

At the time this article was written, Patricia A. Monture was a law student at York University. She was First Vice President of Ontario Native Women's Association representing the southern region. Shirley and Nerissa O'Connor are mother and daughter. They are from the Lac Seul First Nation in northern Ontario and reside in Sioux Lookout. They have both been active at the community level. Shirley was President of the Ontario Native Women's Association in the late 1980s.

BROWN GIRL DANCING

WHEN I WAS A LITTLE GIRL, I loved pink. I even wanted all my clothes to be pink. Imagine, growing up in the bush near Turtle Lake on the Thunderchild First Nation and I wanted pink jeans—not dark pink, pastel pink! My love of pink would always make my mother's face twist and contort. My mom has always said that I knew my own mind from the minute I was born.

On a trip to the library at Thunderchild School when I was in kindergarten, I found a book with a little girl in the cover in a pink leotard and tutu. I loved pink! I grabbed the book and went running to the teacher to ask her what the little girl was doing. She told me she was a ballerina. I asked my teacher to read me the book and she did. It was about the little ballerina going off to ballet school. When she was done, I told my teacher: "That's what I want to be when I grow up! A ballerina!" My teacher laughed and that made me mad. I went home and told my mom and dad, "I want to be a ballerina!"

Until I was eight years old, I kept up with the idea that I wanted to be a ballerina. From the time I was two I was powwow dancing and I learned all three women's styles. I especially like jingle-dress dancing. My mom said she would often see people pointing at me and saying things like "that girl just floats when she dances. It hardly looks like her feet are on the ground." So my family knew I was a good dancer.

On the reserve, just about any reserve on the prairies and not just the Thunderchild First Nation where I grew up, you cannot take ballet classes. There are no dance schools. So the opportunities that many children have who grow up in cities are not available for First Nations children. Sometimes I think about the other children who have dreams to be something, like my dream to be a ballerina, who can't live their dreams because there aren't opportunities on the reserve or their families are poor.

My mom listened to my constant "I want to be a ballerina" demands and turned our lives around so I could take dance lessons. In the summer of 2001, when I was eight, she found a town house in the city and moved us to town. My brothers and dad stayed on the reserve. It was funny living in the city and I was scared of everything. The cars drove so fast and there were so many of them that whenever we walked downtown I walked with my shoulder almost against

Watch her, listen,
She speaks to us.
The swaying grass under her feet
The sun shining,
Hitting her dress
As she dances with the wind.
For her people, she teaches us,
Her beautiful ways of life.
But the clouds come, they tell us he
And she stops,
The rhythm she had, her teaching
Are gone.
The rain comes

And
She
Dances.
—*Kate Monture, 2009*

Kate Monture in her jingle dress. Photo courtesy Monture family collection.

the buildings. All my family made sacrifices so I could dance my dream.

That fall I started dance classes in both jazz and ballet. I loved it! My mom laughs all the time because as soon as I started classes I never walked anywhere again. We'd go to the grocery story and those big long aisles looked like a place to do a series of chassés in jazz or gallops. I danced through parking lots and in the halls at school. I am grateful that I have a mom who listens and went to school for a long time. I know she would rather be watching lacrosse or hockey than ballet. But she has always supported me and my dream to dance. We aren't poor like a lot of people I know on the reserve. So I have had the chance to be a brown girl dancing ballet.

One of the stories that gets told about me happened at one of the very first dance competitions I went to. I was sitting beside my mom in the audience in between my own dance numbers watching the other dances. I was nine years old. After a while of watching, I leaned over and asked my mom: "Where are all the other brown girls dancing? I have only seen one other brown girl." My mom explained to me that dance was expensive and often First Nations families often don't have the money to enroll their children in dance. And she also explained about having to move away from the reserve for me to have the opportunity. It made me very sad that all the brown girls couldn't dance and another dream was born. As I get older, I want to find ways to help make opportunities for other brown girls to dance.

Sometimes it is not easy being a brown girl dancing. I am often the only girl in my classes who is First Nations. It is sometimes isolating and I feel very alone. I have had opportunities to dance with the Royal Winnipeg Ballet, the National Ballet School of Canada, and Quinte Ballet School. When I was eleven, I went to Winnipeg to dance. When we walked into the school, I felt like I had been slammed into a wall of white. There were at least a hundred dancers there and I saw only one other dancer who was not white. I have had to learn how to deal with this isolation and I sometimes have to remind myself that there is nothing the matter with me. The reason I don't fit is because I have crossed cultures and boundaries. I am a brown girl dancing ballet.

Sometimes, the white people I dance with make it clear that I don't fit—sometimes through their words and actions. But most often, just by how they look at me. Other times, other First Nations people treat me like I am odd. But what I know in my heart, Creator gave me the gift to dance—jazz, jingle, ballet, and sometimes even hip hop! And I will always be a brown girl dancing.

Originally published in Canadian Woman Studies/les cahiers de la femme, *"Indigenous Women in Canada: The Voices of First Nations, Inuit and Métis Women," 26 (3 & 4) (Winter/Spring 2008): 177-178. Reprinted with permission of the author.*

Kate Monture was 15 years old and in Grade 11 when she wrote this article. She is Mohawk from Grand River Territory and also has ties through her father to the Thunderchild First Nation (Cree) in Saskatchewan.

PATRICIA A. MONTURE

WOMEN'S WORDS

Power, Identity and Indigenous Sovereignty

IN THE WAY OF MY PEOPLE, the Haudenosaunee, I tell stories. My people, as are other Indigenous nations, are people with a storytelling tradition. Our histories, our laws, the ways Creator gave us, are all contained within our stories and our languages. And, for us, the storytelling tradition is a complex idea. There are the sacred stories. Stories that are only told after certain protocols (such as the passing of gifts or traditional medicines) are followed. We do not tell these stories when there is work to be done. Winter is the time for telling stories. Our stories tell our family, tribal, and national histories. LeAnne Howe (Choctaw) writes: "Native stories are power. They create people. They author tribes. America is a tribal creation story, a tribalography" (29). Through our stories we learn who we are. These stories teach about identity and responsibility. These are stories about how to live life, how to be a good "Indian." And sometimes we just tell stories for fun, to laugh, because laughter is healing. Coming from this storytelling tradition, it is odd to know that our stories are sometimes excluded from the material scholars call "literature."

For me the issue is much simpler, I write so I am a writer. I have published books and articles in legal journals, Native Studies reviews, and more recently I have published as a sociologist. I have chapters in books about literary criticism, criminology, and in feminist and Native Studies readers. I have spoken in forums organized by political scientists, sociologists, criminologists, and historians as well as scholars who study law, religion, and English literature. This may be seen as interdisciplinary work but I prefer to see it as trans-disciplinary. My work crosses traditional disciplinary boundaries because the discipline I follow is the laws and ways of my people, the Haudenosaunee. My writing is not anchored in my profession. I don't write like an academic. Not because I can't, but because I don't. Because that does not fill the silence that has existed between "Indian"[1] nations, our citizens, the women, and power. When I struggle and I cannot for the life of me write a sentence or have a complete thought, I write jagged lines and call it a poem. On these days, I am writing to survive. Some days, I resist with my words. I speak to power to take back our power, the power of Indigenous women.

116

Other days I write dreams and hopes and prayers. They are the words of life and of living. My words are my strength. They are my women's power. That question, what is Native literature,[2] is simple. For me, so is the answer. I am a writer. I tell stories.

In the last three decades, the words of Indigenous women who live on the land that has become the country known as Canada, have found their way to bookstore shelves in quite a dramatic way. Maria Campbell's 1973 work, *Halfbreed*, is often seen as the work that marks the start of this trend. Since then there have been novels and books of both short stories and poems by Lee Maracle (Coast Salish); Lenore Keeshig-Tobias (Anishnabe); Eden Robinson (Haisla); Louise Halfe (Cree); Jeanette Armstrong (Okanogan); Rita Bouvier (Métis); Beth Brant (Mohawk); and Ruby Slipperjack (Anishnabe). There are also numerous works by academic authors and Indigenous scholars such as Darlene Johnston (Anishnabe); Patti Doyle-Bedwell (Mi'kmaq); Kim Anderson (Cree/Métis); Marie Battiste (Mi'kmaq); Andrea Bear Nicholas (Maliseet); Bev Jacobs (Mohawk); Emma LaRocque (Métis); Dawn Martin-Hill (Mohawk); Kiera Ladner (Cree); Bonita Lawrence (Mi'kmaq/Métis); Lina Sunseri (Oneida); and so many others. Thinking this list and speaking it out loud to myself, calling up the names even in English, empowers me and it is equally an act of power. It is my circle of women with the gift of words. Those of us gifted with words in Indigenous traditions know stories are not really a new phenomenon among "Indian" people (Grant x). Further, the ability to write stories down is one that should neither be accredited to this century, or the last.

E. Pauline Johnson (Tekahionwake, 1861-1913) (Mohawk) had her work published, first in Ontario newspapers, in the late 1800s and early 1900s (Gerson and Strong-Boag xiii). In her short story, "A Red Girl Reasoning," written in 1906, Johnson wrote of an Indian woman's thoughts on her marriage to a white man:

> …I tell you we are not married. Why should I recognize the rites of your nation when you do not acknowledge the rites of mine? According to your own words, my parents should have gone through your church ceremony as well as through an Indian contract; according to my words, we should go through an Indian contract as well as through a church marriage. If their union is illegal, so is ours. If you think my father is living in dishonour with my mother, my people will think I am living in dishonour with you. How do I know when another nation will come and conquer you as you white men conquered us? And they will have another marriage rite to perform, and they will tell us another truth, that you are not my husband, that you are but disgracing and dishonouring me, that you are keeping me here, not as your wife, but as your—your—squaw." That terrible word had never passed her lips before, and the blood stained her face to her very temples. (cited in Gunn Allen 33)

Johnson's written words are now more than one hundred years old. Woven through her words are not just anger but racialized analysis. Indigenous women have been naming and standing against the irony of colonialism and its impact on our lives as women for a very long time. I find great strength in the words of the women who walked before me. I find encouragement because unlike what is written in the historical record, I know my people understood white ways and were always able to offer a critique of it.

Some might choose to see Johnson's work as feminist but as Paula Gunn Allen concludes, her work is best seen as part of the "Native narrative tradition" (9). Carole Gerson and Veronica Strong-Boag wrote that while Johnson was never known as a public supporter of women's suffrage "as far as we know" (xvii), they nonetheless characterize her in the following way: "Pauline Johnson can now be seen as one of Canada's turn-of the-century bright New Women, part of the generation of her sex who pursued independent lives as they contested the boundaries of respectable femininity" (xvii).

This is misleading in several ways. Haudenosaunee women have always led independent lives, at least prior to the coming of Europeans who brought laws and ways that subordinated women. It is ironic that Johnson is taken by "white" women as an icon of their own. Johnson situated herself with her people, and, thus, in many of her poems used Haudenosaunee imagery. White wampum, moccasin-making, the Grand River, Joseph Brant, corn planting, and lacrosse are only a few of the varied Haudenosaunee images borrowed from her people and found in her work. She described one of her goals as: "to upset the Indian Extermination and noneducation theory—in fact to stand by my blood and my race" (cited in Gerson and Strong-Boag xvi). Clearly Johnson saw herself as Mohawk when she wrote below the title "The Iroquois Women of Canada," "By one of them" (Gerson and Strong-Boag 203).

Today, there are voices of many Indigenous women now recorded in print and lining the shelves in Canadian bookstores. It is important for the academy to see this development as a small and recent piece of a much longer history. And within this recognition, it is essential to see voice as a complicated phenomenon. There is no unified subject that can be identified as "Indian" (Ladson-Billings 261). Indigenous voice(s) is a complex matter of gender and multiple consciousness(es) (such as being an "Indian" academic). Each of the distinct First Nations, such as the Mohawk, Cree, Dene, Métis, Saulteaux, Mi'kmaq, Gitksan and so on, have their own languages and traditions. These distinct peoples each have their own knowledge systems. There are similarities but care must be taken not to make unitary that which is rich and diverse. Today, First Nations in "Canada" share many problems and experiences largely as a result of the common treatment that comprised the federal policy of "civilizing" us (Ladson-Billings 261). The sharing of the common experiences of colonialism cause connections among First Peoples, but it is the shared experiences that make us appear monolithic.

Voice is also complicated by the international boundaries we know today. The line, which makes the country of my birth Canada and not the United

States, is a line that bisects the territory of my people the Haudenosaunee. It bisects other nations such as the Cree, Blackfoot, Maliseet, Mi'kmaq, and Anishnabe. To speak just to the "Canadian" experience draws an artificial boundary as pointed out by Rene Hulan in her work appropriately titled, *Native North America*.[3] In the introduction she notes that the borders of nation-states have not eradicated the circles of Indigenous people and we write not only as resisters and survivors but as people who continue to attest "to the strength and confidence of" the Native American literary traditions (9).

To understand Native literature one must understand something of the person's tribal tradition as this grounds who they are, as well as the symbols and styles they will use. To understand my sharing, you must know that I am Mohawk from Grand River, a direct descendant of Joseph Brant. I am a Monture but am related to the Smith's, Hill's, and Brant's. My Indian name is Aye-wah-han-day.[4] It means "speaking first." My name grounds me in the gift of words Creator gave me. It is both identity and direction. It is strength and responsibility. It is this location, as Mohawk citizen and woman, which guides the way I see the patterns that in turn ground my understanding of who I am and what I know.

As scholars, we want to make patterns and personal understandings into larger structures such as theories or knowledges. Literature has such a structure and often that structure is not welcoming to the written words shared by Indigenous authors and storytellers. If, for example, you choose not to write but only speak your stories, remaining "pure" in your commitment to the oral tradition, you will not ever be counted as a literary great. Craig Womack considers this an illiteracy campaign similar in nature to the burning of the Mayan codices in the 1540s (13). In educational institutions, in Canada and elsewhere, this exclusion of oratory as a tradition of value, has a particular consequence compounded by the way in which scholars of literature cling to their own cultural traditions. Those traditions that exclude oral literature are equally grounded in culture, despite the fact that the academy fails to acknowledge this fact. Agnes Grant explains:

> A fundamental reason that traditional Native literature is not included in many programs is that looking at Native literature, and literature of all minority cultures, requires a change in perspective by the reader. The absence of the familiar European form, style and content, too often leads to the criticism that such literature is inferior. The possibility of different but equal merit is seldom, if at all, entertained (vii).[5]

It is the required shift in perspective that poses the problem for some readers. Writing, then, for many Indigenous authors is often the act of naming both power and exclusion, as one rarely exists without the other. Often, this act of naming is seen as an act of resistance when most often it is an act of (re)claiming.

The discussion of Native literature as literature is also confounded by certain other assumptions that are tangled into the web surrounding the authenticity debate. Assimilationist ideas and ideals are part of this tangle. Creek scholar Craig Womack, a self-identified two-spirited person, discloses another assumption:

> ...it is just as likely that things European are Indianized rather than the anthropological assumption that things Indian are always swallowed up by European culture. I reject, in other words, the supremacist notion that assimilation can only go in one direction, that white culture always overpowers Indian culture, that white is inherently more powerful than red, that Indian resistance has never occurred in such a fashion that things European have been radically subverted by Indians. (12)

Extending this realization to a structural premise, imaginative literature such as fiction and poetry is, as Lakota scholar Kelly Morgan argues "a more accurate gauge of cultural realities than the ethnographic, anthropological, and historical record" (cited in Womack 15).

Resistance and authenticity are common themes in the body of work known as literary criticism discussing the written words of First Nations. Questions of authenticity ("Are you a real Indian?") are questions that are most frequently raised externally, by those at a distance from our communities. As Marilyn Dumont (Métis) argues, the authenticity debate simplifies and is disrespectful to the great diversity of Aboriginal experiences. She writes:

> ...there is a continuum of exposure to traditional experience in Native culture, some of us have been more exposed to it than others, but this does not mean that those who have been more exposed to it are somehow more Indian, as if we are searching for the last surviving Indian (47).

The debate about authenticity requires a gaze that looks at individuals. We, as Indigenous people, do not see ourselves as separate from our people or our land. This gaze, which has authenticity as its central focus is contrary to Indigenous epistemologies where identity is not an isolated phenomenon.

First Nations identity is a function of community and belonging to that community. It is a fundamental component of both Indigenous knowledge(s) and the voices that breathe life into those knowledge(s). In discussing racialized discourses, Gloria Ladson-Billings writes:

> When René Descartes[6] proclaimed that he thought himself into being, he articulated a central premise upon which European (and Euro-American) worldviews and epistemology rest—that the indi-

vidual mind is the source of knowledge and existence. In contrast, the African saying "Ubuntu," translated "I am because we are," asserts that the individual's existence (and knowledge) is contingent upon relationships with others. (257)

This contrast in the location of knowledge of Europeans and African Peoples is one that will resonate with First Peoples as well. I am because I know my name, my family, my clan, and my nation.

Non-Indigenous scholars studying the writing of First People are often confused by and then impose their understanding of identity upon us. Pauline Johnson is described as a "Mohawk-Canadian," a description few Mohawks will claim. She is called "mixed-race" (Gerson and Strong-Boag xiii) or a half-breed. She is indeed the daughter of Mohawk father (a condoled chief) and a white woman, but this in the eyes of Mohawks does not necessarily distance her from the identity she claims as Mohawk, or Iroquoian woman, as discussed earlier. She was born into the community and on the territory. In an ironic twist, she was also known to the public as a "Mohawk Princess" (xvii). The location she is attributed even though she identifies herself as standing by "her blood and her race" provides insight not into the life of Ms. Johnson, but into the lives and belief patterns (including the demand for authenticity) of the white people who have written about her.

Osage scholar, Robert Warrior, notes that the focus of much of the scholarship called literary criticism operates to "reduce, constrain and contain American Indian literature" (xix). This is precisely what the authenticity debate accomplishes. In this way the criticism promulgates essentialist categories. Craig Womack (Creek), relying on Warrior's earlier work on intellectual sovereignties, disputes these are the most important categories and notes that:

> ...I will concentrate on the idea that Native literary aesthetics must be politicized and that autonomy, self-determination, and sovereignty serve as useful literary concepts. Further, I wish to suggest that literature has something to add to the arena of Native political struggle. (11)

Womack asserts that, "without Native American literature, there is no American canon" (7). Agnes Grant noted: "No Canadian literature course can be truly representative of Canada without literature written by [A]boriginal Canadians themselves" (vi). I am in full agreement because to declare otherwise is to de-story the land.

The authenticity debate is one form of containment. A second is the propensity to declare that Indigenous writings are acts of resistance. The characterization of Indigenous writing as resistance is too simplistic. There is no doubt that some writing by First Nations is about resistance. But it is rarely limited to resistance as our lives are never just resistance. To focus solely on our resistance is to place colonialism at the centre of the discussion. We can never be or dream more than resistance and survival. It also operates to freeze our cultures and peoples in the time immediately before contact. It reinforces the campaign to see culture and tradition in a hierarchy of superiority.

The truth of the matter is, Indigenous peoples around the world have made significant contributions to the development of the states that now enclave them. The influence of my people on the United States' constitution would be but one example (Johansen). Our understanding of the place Indigenous oral and literary traditions hold in the history of the world can be recovered through understanding the ways in which Indigenous writers locate themselves. And this location is always more specific than a claim to "Indian" identity.

Understanding this, Womack argues that the understanding of Native literature, whether contemporary or ancient, must be nation specific. In *Red on Red,* his gaze is therefore turned to his own people, the Creek (1). And, my gaze equally is grounded in the words of Haudenosaunee authors and thus the focus on E. Pauline Johnson. As Kelly Morgan argues, gender must also be a central element of the analysis. As Lakota women are absent from the historical record—except as "docile drudges"—the imaginative writings of Lakota women are vital (Morgan cited in Womack 15). This is a form of nation (re)building.

Womack asserted that autonomy, self-determination, and sovereignty are the fundamental units of analysis in Indigenous literary criticism. Sovereignty is a word that has gotten Indigenous nations into a lot of trouble. It threatens states. This occurs simply because there is an assumption in western thought that there is a single form and system of knowing and therefore sovereignty must have a single meaning. And that meaning is now enshrined in international standards. This is not what I understand Haudenosaunee people to be saying when we talk about sovereignty. It is the power to not only determine your being but also the power to be responsible to that identity. In Indigenous epistemologies, sovereignty means access to well-being for all our citizens. It means being assured of safety (and we cannot ever be sure we are safe).[7]

It may appear that the promise of my title, "Women's Words," has been lost in this discussion. In part this is (or perhaps was, as colonialism has left a large ugly footprint over my own people's gender knowledge) because gender is not constructed among my people in a way that is oppressive. Gender is not a hierarchical distribution of power, where men have more and women less. Gender is not a binary and perhaps we should consider that there are more than two genders (Cannon). Gender is a state that balances Haudenosaunee social systems. My understanding always comes from a woman's place, a mother's place, an auntie's place, a sister's place, and a *kohkum's* place. And each of these are sets of responsibilities, not roles. One of the most devastating impacts of colonialism has been directed at the women.

It is important for me to share with you some of what it means to be a Mohawk woman. In the creation story of the Haudenosaunee, this is how people came to the world:

In the beginning, there was nothing but water, nothing but a wide, wide sea. The only people in the world were the animals that lived in and on water.

Then down from the sky world a woman fell, a divine person. Two loons flying over the water happened to look up and see her falling. Quickly they placed themselves beneath her and joined their bodies to make a cushion for her to rest upon. Thus they saved her from drowning.

While they held her, they cried with a loud voice to the other animals, asking their help. Now the cry of the loon can be heard at a great distance over water, and so the other creatures gathered quickly.

As soon as Great Turtle learned the reason for the call, he stepped forth from the council.

"Giver her to me," he said to the loons. "Put her on my back. My back is broad." (Ella Elizabeth Clark[8] cited in Grant 15).[9]

And this is how this land mass came to be known as Turtle Island to my people. It is on the back of that great turtle. The story of creation continues but for my purposes here, this little piece of the story tells of the central position that woman held in creation and how woman were, and are, situated in our worldview. Human life on this earth sprang from this woman's fall. And when she died, from her body grew the plants of the earth. From her head grew the squash, her breasts the corn, and her limbs the bean. These plants are known to my people as "the three sisters." And the creation story locates women's relationship with agriculture and the land for it is the women who "own" those fields. Without these understandings of how the world came to be in the minds of the Haudenosaunee, one cannot understand the words that we choose to write.

I want to close by borrowing the words of another Mohawk author, Beth Brant (Degonwandonti). She wrote these words in the introduction to *A Gathering of Spirit*, and this collection of writing by North American Indian women was the first collection of its kind I came across in the university bookstore when I was an undergraduate student. Over the years it has brought me much solace and it is a cherished collection. She wrote: "We started something, sisters. Our testament is out there now, part of the wind, part of the people's minds and hearts. *We have always been here. We will always be here*" (15).

This paper was given in 2004 at the National University of Mexico as the Margaret Atwood/Gabrielle Roy Chair in Canadian Studies.

Originally published in Canadian Woman Studies/les cahiers de la femme, *"Indigenous Women in Canada: The Voices of First Nations, Inuit and Métis Women,"* 26 (3 & 4) (Winter/Spring 2008): 177-178. Reprinted with permission of the author.

Patricia A. Monture is a citizen of the Mohawk Nation, Grand River Territory. She is currently teaching in the Sociology Department at the University of Saskatchewan where she coordinates the Aboriginal Justice and Criminology Program. She is a committed activist/scholar who continues to seek justice for Aboriginal peoples and especially Aboriginal women and girls.

[1]One of the first discussions I have with my students is on naming. Aboriginal, Indian, Indigenous, First Nations, and so on, are all terms of colonial imposition. Depending on whom you talk to, any of those names can get you into trouble. There is no "right" choice.

[2]See my discussion in "Native America and the Literary Tradition."

[3]See also Thomas King's "Borders" in *One Good Story That One* (131-145). I mention this story because Dr. King, a man, has created such a wonderful and strong female character. There he tells a story of a Blackfoot woman crossing the border from Canada to the States. As she refuses to identify herself as anything other than Blackfoot, she spends days being bounced back and forth between border crossing buildings. On more than one occasion I have had a border crossing guard impatiently say to me some version of: "So just tell me what side of the line you can't see you live on!" Post 9/11, I wonder if such "tolerance" still exists.

[4]Paula Gunn Allen (Laguna, Sioux, Lebanese) wrote: "The problem of names, common in Indian Country, is an extension of the general problem of identity for people who are overwhelmed by alien invaders who not only rename human beings but the land and all its features" (14).

[5]See also Rita Joe's "The Gentle War," in *Canadian Woman Studies/les cahiers de la femme* 10 (2,3) (1989): 27-29.

[6]"I think, therefore I am" in *Discours de la Méthode*, 1637.

[7]The most recent example where I live would be the Stonechild Inquiry.

[8]Note Ella Elizabeth Clark is a non-Indigenous woman who collected the "myths" of peoples she thought were vanishing.

[9]The Seneca version of this creation story as told by J. J. Cornplanter (1889-1957) is recorded in *Legends of the Longhouse*. I am choosing to work from creation stories that others have written down as this article may be read at any time of the year and is not told following the completion of the appropriate protocols.

REFERENCES

Allen, Paula Gunn. *The Sacred Hoop: Recovering the Feminine in American Indian Traditions.* Boston: Beacon Press, 1994.

Bell, Betty Louise. *Faces in the Moon.* Norman: University of Oklahoma Press, 1994.

Brant, Beth (Degonwadonti). *Writing as Witness: Essay and Talk.* Toronto: Women's Press, 1994.

Brant, Beth (Degonwadonti). *A Gathering of Spirit: A Collection by Native American Indian Women.* Toronto: Women's Press, 1988.

Clark, Ella Elizabeth. *Indian Legends of Canada.* Toronto: McClelland and Stewart, 1960.

Cornplanter, Jesse.J. *Legends of the Longhouse.* Ohsweken: Irocrafts Limited, 1938.

Descartes, René. *Discourse on Method.* Cambridge: MIT Press, 2004. First published in 1637.

Dumont, Marilyn. "Popular Images of Nativeness." *Looking at the Words of Our People: First Nations Analysis of Literature.* Ed. Jeannette Armstrong. Penticton: Theytus Books. 1993. 49-50.

Gerson, Carole and Veronica Strong-Boag. E. Pauline Johnson T*ekahionwake: Selected Poems and Selected Prose.* Toronto: University of Toronto Press, 2002.

Grant, Agnes. *Our Bit of Truth: An Anthology of Canadian Native Literature.* Winnipeg: Pemmican Publishing, 1990.

Howe, LeAnne. "The Story of America: A Tribalography." *Clearing a Path: Theorizing the Past in Native American Studies.* Ed. Nancy Shoemaker. New York: Routledge, 2002. 29-48.

Hulan, Rene, ed. *Native North America: Critical and Cultural Perspectives.* Toronto: ECW Press, 1999.

Joe, Rita. "The Gentle War." *Canadian Woman Studies/les cahiers de la femme* 10 (2,3) (1989): 27-29.

Johansen, Bruce E. *Forgotten Founders: How the American Indian Helped Shape Democracy.* Boston: Harvard Common Press, 1982.

King, Thomas. *One Good Story, That One.* Toronto: Harper-Collins, 1993.

Ladson-Billings, Gloria. "Racialized Discourses and Ethnic Epis-temologies." *Handbook of Qualitative Research.* Eds. Norman K. Denzin and Yvonna S. Lincoln. Thousand Oaks: Sage Publications, 2000.

Monture-Angus, Patricia. "Native America and the Literary Tradition." *Native North America: Critical and Cultural Perspectives.* Ed. Rene Hulan. Toronto: ECW Press, 1999. 20-46.

Shoemaker, Nancy, ed. *Clearing a Path: Theorizing the Past in Native American Studies.* New York: Routledge, 2002.

Warrior, Robert A. *Tribal Secrets: Recovering American Indian Intellectual Traditions.* Minneapolis: University of Minnesota Press, 1995.

Womack, Craig S. *Red on Red: Native American Literary Separatism.* Minneapolis: University of Minnesota Press, 1999.

TERRITORY

RITA JOE

I LOST MY TALK

I lost my talk
The talk you took away.
When I was a litle girl
At Shubenacadie school.

You snatched it away:
I speak like you
I think like you
I create like you
The scrambled ballad, about my world.

Two ways I talk
Both ways I say,
Your way is more powerful.

So gently I offer my hand and ask,
Let me find my talk
So I can teach you about me.

Originally published in Canadian Woman Studies/les cahiers de la femme, *"Native Women," 10 (2 & 3) (Summer/Fall 1989): 28. Reprinted with permission of the author's family.*

KAAREN OLSEN DANNENMANN

REFLECTIONS FROM A NAMEKOSIPIIWANISHINAAPEKWE

My Trout Lake, Your Trout Lake

IT IS 2006 NOW AND I AM remembering how I came to think about my Trout Lake being your Trout Lake. Since the death of my brother in 1998, I had been going through a particularly difficult time. We had been partners in the reclamation of Trout Lake and we had dedicated our lives to this work. We saw our role in Trout Lake, in part, as bringing our relatives back home, or making our homeland once again accessible to them—those that had been displaced and dispossessed by the residential schools, the Great Scoop of the 1960s and '70s, by commercial fishing, by tourism on the lake.

I came back to Trout Lake in 1981, after having been away for fifteen years. I had two daughters and was expecting a third child. Trout Lake was my life's dream, to learn the life ways of my mother's people and to find and rebuild our place on the lake. The rocky shores and sand beaches, the islands and channels, swamps and bays, poplars, birches, and pines, the wind and waters—all were calling me home. I ached for the taste of *kaaskiiwak, moonsochaash, atikame-konakishiin*, the food of my home place. I ached for the smells of its hot dusty trails, warm sticky buds, forest beds of balsam fir. With every bird song and loon call transporting my soul back home, I quit my job and packed up my little family and left the city forever. I soon found my childhood memories fused with those of my grandmothers, grandfathers, great-grandparents, aunts, uncles, and cousins. The memories of their experiences flowed through my consciousness while the hills echoed their ancient voices.

My brother's small trap line was at the west end of the lake and he and I spent the first summer building a log cabin. Over the years, we built other cabins and worked with our cousins, hunting, trapping, fishing, learning the lake and learning how to live on the lake. We held Trout Lake's first sweat lodge ceremony in over seventy years, and brought the drum back. We reclaimed the daily practices and ceremonies that we had been taught and that characterized our relationships with the animals, plants, and trees, giving back as we were being given, a reciprocity that ensured a sustained life on Trout Lake. My brother and I brought young children, youth, and young adults to the trap line, showed them the way we lived, taught them what we knew about traditional life on the Land, had a lot of fun, a lot of laughter. When we told our mother about these excursions, she was so happy, she said that once again, maybe, the ice on Trout Lake would be full of the tracks of children. We kept those words in mind, keeping our resolve that our people would one day come back to Trout Lake to stay.

One of the ways to bring people back was to develop courses that would be delivered in Trout Lake. My brother and I were both trapper instructors, survival course teachers, and wilderness excursion leaders. We were working on a program called Indigenous Knowledge Instructors Program (IKIP) that was the vision of Treaty #3 trappers. I continued with this project after my brother died. One day, I was at a meeting to talk about the implications of the program to the community and one of the questions I was asked was if the program could be called "your program" and I was immediately put off by the question, remembering all the trappers and Elders I had met and interviewed and so, I said, no, it could not. Then I was asked if it could be said that I was the proprietor of the program. Again, I said, no, it could not. I was intrigued by the questions and, just as intrigued by my answers, at the internal voice that would not let me acquiesce. At the end of the meeting, I returned to the questions and said that, for the present time, it could be said that I was responsible for the program.

For a long time afterward, I thought about that, especially when I was in Trout Lake. I knew that there was a huge lesson I was about to be taught and that I had to be still and be receptive. That was often difficult. Being an Anishi-naapekwe in Trout Lake was often challenging, my right to be there disputed. I did not have the credibility that had come automatically to my brother and to my male cousins. But gradually, Trout Lake started sharing with me its knowledge. Answers came to me, into my heart and soul, into my life's blood, quietly into my veins. My hands knew these answers as I reached out to pick berries, reached for moss, rocks, and medicines. In order to articulate these lessons, I tried to weave around the English words I had to use, around the nuances of the phrases of this foreign language, and I was especially challenged to find a way around the seemingly impenetrable ideas of private ownership, individual rights, and the separation of rights from responsibilities.

For the Anishinaape People, in our ancient languages, the words "my" and "our" do not mean possession or ownership as they do in English. In English, these words are even identified as being *possessive* adjectives. For Anishinaapek, these words mean something very different. Traditional teachers tell us, for example, our homes, our canoes, our tools and equipment are not ours but are on loan to us. Even the articles of our clothing are on loan to us. Our very bodies are on loan to us. Our children are not ours but are on loan to us. Our partners are on loan to us. We are very carefully taught that everything on loan to us must be cared for and then returned in the condition, or even better condition, than it was when we acquired it.

For Anishinaape People, then, the words "my," "our," "your," "his," or "hers" are not about ownership or possession but about a relationship. When I say, or when any NamekosipiiwAnishinaape says, "Trout Lake is my home," or "my Trout Lake," we do not mean that we own Trout Lake, that we possess it (and therefore you do not and neither does anyone else) but rather, it means Trout Lake is that part of our great Mother the Earth with which we have a very special relationship. This relationship includes those with whom we share that home—our aunts, cousins, etc., the moose, bear, gulls, ravens, mice, moles, flies, mosquitoes, fish, the trees, the grass, rocks, etc. This relationship is characterized by a spirituality and sacredness, an intimate knowledge and huge reciprocal respect and reverence where we all know our rights and responsibilities. This very amazing relationship involves a give and take that requires consciousness and constant nurturing. My Trout Lake takes care of me, is very gentle with me, and teaches me everything I need to know. In turn, I take care of my Trout Lake to the best of my ability, and I remain open to its teaching and growing.

When I think about my Trout Lake, the words of Salish Chief Sealth come back to me. My Trout Lake is about the web of life, about the interdependence and interconnectedness of time and space and love. In my mind, I hear the words of the great orators and paraphrase them to describe my Trout Lake. Every rock and every tree and every blade of grass on my Trout Lake tell me the stories of those who long ago walked these trails. It is said that the clear cold waters of my Trout Lake carry the memories of my grandmothers and grandfathers. It is said that the whispers of the wind in the trees, the murmurs of the waves against the sand beaches, the songs and sounds of the forested islands are the voices of the future, the voices of our children's children and their children. This is my Trout Lake, and I lay my claim to say that, but it can also be your Trout Lake.

So, when I say "your Trout Lake," I mean that you also can cultivate a deeply personal and sacred relationship to Trout Lake, and treat it like you would treat your brother or your child, your mother or your grandmother. There is a huge responsibility attached to that relationship. Your obligations are just beginning. Furthermore, Trout Lake being your Trout Lake does not give you the right to interfere with, or damage in any way, my sacred relationship with Trout Lake. You do not have personal rights that supercede the collective rights of all our relations on Trout Lake, its islands, forests, hills, swamps, bays, inlets, etc. You will have to learn your place in Trout Lake and learn to love that place.

Our story, and their story, of the past 514 years, the smallpox blankets, open warfare, theft of our lands, the residential school system, assimilation—all have made their marks on us. It is no wonder that we are confused about our rights, and how we must take care to know that rights are inseparable from responsibilities. This is one of the first lessons we learn from the Land. This is the circle we have to pass on to our children, our children who are thirsting for this knowledge, who are demanding to be taught and given their birthright.

We women, especially, have to take this up as our sacred responsibility.

Originally published in Canadian Woman Studies/les cahiers de la femme, *"Indigenous Women in Canada: The Voices of First Nations, Inuit and Métis Women," 26 (3 & 4) (Winter/Spring 2008): 213-214. Reprinted with permission of the author.*

Kaaren Olsen Dannemann (Ma'iinkan) is an Anishinaapekwe from Namekosipiink (Trout Lake) in Northern Ontario. She is a mother of three and a grandmother of five precious little ones. Her life is instrinsically connected to her homeland, her family and her community. She is a trapper and a trapper instructor and manages a camp for Aboriginal youth and children as well as offering other land-based trainings and activities. She works tirelessly to keep traditional culture and knowledge alive for the next generations, with language classes, trips to the trap line, games, ceremonies and special events and gatherings. Kaaren is a strong anti-racism worker and has developed partnerships with non-Aboriginal people and organizations to conduct de-colonizing / undoing racism workshops. She is committed to peace and justice and is part of several international efforts that support Indigenous peoples' struggles for recognition of rights to land, language, culture, and economies.

DEBORAH MCGREGOR

ANISHNAABEKWE,
TRADITIONAL KNOWLEDGE AND WATER

Water is a sacred thing. This is reflected in many traditional beliefs, values, and practices.
—Ann Wilson, Anishnaabe Elder, Rainy River First Nation

FOR THOUSANDS OF YEARS, Aboriginal people have created and passed on knowledge resulting in sustainable relationships with all of Creation. Ann Wilson's words serve to remind us that we still have this knowledge and a responsibility to pass it on in order to maintain such relationships.

In the course of Aboriginal history in Canada, significant compromising of Aboriginal peoples' ability to make decisions based on traditional knowledge has only occurred within the last 150 years. Since that time, deliberate, systematic attempts to eradicate Aboriginal worldviews, philosophies, traditional knowledge and values have seriously undermined traditional forms of governance and related processes (Mercredi and Turpel; RCAP). Many First Nations, having suffered the oppressive forces of colonization, are now revitalizing their customs, values, and knowledge so as to re-establish a relationship with Creation based on their own traditions. This process forms an important part of the day-to-day as well as the political lives of First Nations peoples.

A key component of this revitalization is the recognition that the role of women in traditional Aboriginal societies has been one of the most impacted as a result of colonization processes. Aboriginal women have been ignored, and their knowledge and contributions to sustaining Creation have been devalued by colonial society (Clarkson, Morrissette and Régallet; Lawrence and Anderson). Aboriginal women now have to interact with a society which functions in a reductionist, compartmentalized ways and that also struggles to see how everything is related to the whole.

If Aboriginal women's contributions to sustainability do not currently have a place of honour in dominant western society, they are increasingly given this honour in Indigenous society as Aboriginal peoples and communities continue the process of decolonization and re-creation. I have seen the recognition, acknowledgment, and respect of women's knowledge in Indigenous communities through my work. At the June 2006, Canadian Water Resources Association 59th Annual Conference in Toronto, Ontario, for example, where discussion centred on the dominant western worldview that the "water crisis" can be solved by science and technology, the session chair, Haudenosaunee scholar Dan Longboat, invited Elder Edna Manitowabi, Grandmother and Professor Emeritus at Trent University, to speak on Anishnaabe women's views of water. It was most welcome to hear a woman of Edna's distinction remind us that Aboriginal women have traditionally played important roles with respect to water and that their voices must be included in present-day discussions. Without the invitation extended by Mr. Longboat, however, the participants would never have been exposed to these views.

In another recent meeting with a prominent community leader in which I was exploring the role of Aboriginal knowledge in urban contexts, I was told that Aboriginal knowledge is alive and well, even in urban centres like Toronto. I was provided with the specific example that there are many Aboriginal women living in Toronto who take their roles seriously, honouring the water by conducting moon ceremonies within the city itself. I myself was part of a water ceremony conducted by Elder and Grandmother Pauline Shirt in a workshop convened specifically to discuss the role of traditional knowledge and water in March 2006.

I hope that by sharing my experiences working on environmental issues, especially those concerning water, I am fulfilling an important responsibility as an Anishnaabe woman. As a mother, a clan member, a member of a First Nation, and as a teacher, I have a responsibility to share knowledge. This reflection paper is based on my work with Elders and traditional knowledge holders in Ontario in relation to the role of traditional knowledge in protecting water. The information presented here is largely derived from three major projects on this topic with which I have been involved in recent years.

ROLE OF TRADITIONAL KNOWLEDGE IN PROTECTING WATER

In May of 2000, seven people died in Walkerton, Ontario, due to contamination of the local water supply. The Walkerton Inquiry was subsequently established to examine both the immediate and systemic causes of this incident (O'Connor 2002a). The Walkerton situation, while it was ongoing and when the Inquiry's findings were released, shocked the country, and rightly so. Sadly, however, tragedies associated with environmental contamination are far from being new to Aboriginal people in Ontario. A significant number of First Nation communities have been living under boil water advisories such as that issued for Walkerton for years (Gelinas; O'Connor 2002b). The recent evacuation of Kashechewan First Nation in north-eastern Ontario due to water contamination further reminds us that such issues are relatively commonplace in Aboriginal communities.

To help shed light on Ontario's "water crisis" from a First Nations perspective, the Chiefs of Ontario in 2000 prepared its own report to the Walkerton Commission Part 2 Inquiry. I was asked to undertake a research project on traditional knowledge as part of the preparation of this report. From the Elders who were interviewed, a clear message emerged: women play an important role in First Nations cultures as spokepersons for water and carrying the primary responsibility for protecting that water. This message was confirmed and expanded upon during various research collaborations between Environment Canada and the Chiefs of Ontario between 2005-2008, aimed at better understanding the role of traditional knowledge and water protection from an Elders' perspective. During workshops held across the province involving over forty Elders and traditional knowledge holders, the prominent role of women was repeatedly raised and recommendations emerged to support women's involvement in all water-related decision-making.

These initiatives focused on gaining an understanding of First Nations' traditional views on caring for water, and how this knowledge can contribute to community and government-level source water protection planning in Ontario. Further key findings of this work are summarized below.

THE MEANING OF WATER

In attempting to express the meaning of water as a discrete concept, we risk obscuring the meaning that is associated with water in traditional Aboriginal philosophies. For many Aboriginal people and their ways of life, water offers "life-giving" forces, accompanied by certain duties and responsibilities. This knowledge must be lived to have meaning.

Key points frequently raised by Elders and traditional knowledge holders were summarized in D. McGregor and S. Whitaker's 2001 study "Water Quality in the Province of Ontario: An Aboriginal Knowledge Perspective," and are paraphrased below:

•Water finds significance in the lives of First Nations people on personal, community, clan, national, and spiritual levels. Whatever the level at which it is considered, water is understood as a living force which must be protected and nurtured; it is not a commodity to be bought and sold.
•Water is, and always has been, viewed by Indigenous people as something precious: a fundamental life-giving force. Concern for water is not new in Aboriginal communities.
•Water in Aboriginal traditions has cleansing and purifying powers. It is the giver of life with which babies are born. Water has tremendous significance before birth, during the birthing process, and after birth.
•It is imperative to keep the water clean so it can continue to fulfill

its purpose. Respect must be shown to water. This is frequently done by offering tobacco to the water.

•Recognizing the vital importance of water to survival is the beginning of a healthy perspective. Water is the blood of Mother Earth. Similar to blood, which circulates throughout our bodies, nutrients flow into the land via water. Without our blood serving its proper functions, we would die. It is the same with water. If it cannot perform its functions, we, as part of the Earth, will perish.

•In addition to people, water supports the lives of other beings or aspects of Creation that are important in the whole web of life. Again, Indigenous people benefit from this life-giving support. For example, there are medicines under and around the water. Water is the basis of life; we cannot live without it.

•Water was also used as a medicine, or as a part of medicines. It has medicinal properties and should be collected in certain ways.

•Although there are shared perspectives and teachings between men and women in Aboriginal societies as to the importance of water, and although overall responsibilities to care for water are collective, women have a special relationship to water.

•Aboriginal Elders who are men recognize the special role women have in relation to water. In workshops held with Elders in 2006, participants repeatedly stated that women, as life-givers, have a special connection with water.

•Many of the Elders who participated in the projects talked about the medicinal and spiritual properties of water and most of them identified these teachings as coming from their Grandmothers.

WOMEN'S ROLES AND TRADITIONAL KNOWLEDGE

Everyone has a responsibility to care for the water. Women, however, carry the responsibility to talk for the water.

—Ann Wilson

In the Aboriginal worldview, water has been closely associated with the female. Kim Anderson writes:

Symbols of female and male balance can be found everywhere in the Aboriginal world. We have brother sun and Grandmother moon; father sky and mother earth. We talk frequently about the significance, the properties and the energies of water (equated with the female) and fire (equated with the male). We know that both water and fire are critical to our survival and the balance between these properties must be respected, as each has the ability to consume the other. (174)

137

According to the Haudenosaunee and the Anishnabe peoples, the moon is viewed as Grandmother, and represents continuous rebirth and renewal. The Grandmother is a leader and she is respected in this way. Kasti Cook states:

> We are grateful to her and continue to extend to her our greatest esteem, attention and appreciation for all that she does. She has a special relationship to the waters of the Earth, big and small. From the waters at the doors of life, such as the follicular fluid that bathes the primordial ovum, the dew on the grass in the dawn and at dusk, to the waters of the great oceans, she causes them all to rise and fall. Her constant ebb and flow teaches us that all Creation is related, made of one breath, one water, one earth. The waters of the earth and the waters of our bodies are one. Breastmilk is formed from the blood of the woman. Our milk, our blood and the waters of the earth are one water, all flowing in rhythm to the moon. (139-140)

Women thus have a special relationship with water, since, like Mother Earth, they have life-giving powers. Women have a special place in the order of existence. They provide us, as unborn children, with our very first environment—in water. When we are born water precedes us. With this special place in the order of things come responsibilities. No one is exempt from caring and paying respect to the water, but for women there is a special responsibility. In some ceremonies, women speak for the water.

The voice of Aboriginal people remains largely absent in the discourse around water protection in Ontario. Of major concern is the lack of recognition of the role of women and their knowledge regarding water. However, Aboriginal women are not waiting for permission to act, nor are they waiting for public policy and legislation to recognize them; they are going ahead and fulfilling their responsibilities to water according to their own traditions and worldviews. The two examples below are wonderful and inspiring illustrations of this, and help to create awareness of the important role that women play in regards to water.

AKII KWE: ABORIGINAL WOMEN WHO SPEAK FOR THE WATER

We are the voice for the water.
—Akii Kwe, Bkejwanong Territory (Walpole Island)

I had the privilege of meeting with this amazing group of women as part of research I was conducting a few years ago. Akii Kwe is an informal grassroots group of women speaking out on what they know about how to protect water in their territory. They began by protesting what was happening to the water, in particular by responding to Imperial Chemical Industries' indication that they wanted to dump more pollution into the waters flowing around Bkejwanong Territory. The women decided to speak for the water and try to stop such actions. Below are insights shared by Akii Kwe as expressed during the meeting I had with them and in a position paper they provided to me.

For many years, Indigenous women in the Bkejwanong territory have noticed changes in water quality, particularly because they have a close and special relationship to the water. It is part of the Anishnaabe-Kwe tradition that women speak for the water. In the process of rediscovery, revitalization, and healing, the Anishnaabe-Kwe of Bkejwanong Territory organized themselves to speak for the water. Akii Kwe members stated that in Bkejwanong, nature provides the foundation of the Anishnaabe culture and the ways in which the people conduct themselves (systems of governance). It is because of this that people have a responsibility to act on behalf of the water. Akii Kwe members have, over the years, observed birth defects and other changes in animals. One particular example was that the meat of the snapping turtle began to turn yellow. Such changes in the environment (food chain) were attributed by the women to problems with the water, and yet they were told that the level of contamination was "acceptable." The women know this not to be true. The water was not okay, and what was happening to the water was not okay. What was and is happening to the whole environment was and is not okay.

Water is continuously being poisoned. Akii Kwe members conduct their work from a spiritual plane and rely on traditional teachings to guide then through their work; such guidance comes from ceremonies and Elders. The women state that it is their responsibility to protect the water and thus fulfill their roles as women and as members of their respective clans. They say, "We view our fight for water as a spiritual journey. It is part of our collective and individual growth as people" (McGregor and Whitaker 24).

Akii Kwe members see their strength as lying in their spirituality. Western science does not have this in its methods. When the women focus on the spiritual plane, they are not bogged down with bureaucracy. They do not need "permission" to do what they know is right. Their approach is holistic, and considers emotional, physical, intellectual, and spiritual aspects. While scientists, environmentalists, and politicians frequently ignore or only permit marginal representation of Aboriginal women in their discussions of water, Akii Kwe are working to affirm that their unique and powerful ties to water and should be integral to any such processes.

THE GREAT LAKES MOTHER EARTH SPIRIT WALK

Anishnaabe Grandmothers, Josephine Mandamin and Irene Peters are inspiring role models. These women are taking matters into their own hands in order to help preserve the water in and around the Great Lakes. They are doing so by leading awareness-raising walks around the Great Lakes. The first walk—a 1,300 kilometre trek around Lake Superior—took place in 2003. Each walk is lead by a Grandmother ("Mother Earth Water Walk") and begins annually in the spring with a water ceremony, feast, and celebration and. Routinely covering distances of over 1,000 kilometres, the goal of each walk is to raise awareness about water and try to change the perception of water as a resource to that of a sacred entity whichmust be treated as such. The 2006 walk involved two groups of Anishnaabe men and women travelling around Lake Ontario and Lake Erie simultaneously. By the summer of the 2009, Josephine Mandamin walked over 17,000 kms, around each of Great Lake and the St. Lawrence River. Grandmother Mandamin's epic journey is also featured in a National Film Board film, *Waterlife.*

On these journeys the Grandmothers carry with them a vessel of water and an eagle staff. Supporters of the Mother Earth Water Walk maintain a web site and are always happy to receive assistance from supporters. The beauty of this project is that it is led by women who are fulfilling their role and trying to engage as many people as they can in raising awareness of the spiritual and cultural significance of water. The walks have inspired Anishnaabe women in other communities to organize their own water walks.

FUTURE DIRECTIONS

The guidance received from Elders and traditional knowledge holders in the work I have been involved in clearly states that women should have a special place in decision-making about water: as it stands, women's important link to water is largely ignored. For example, most recently, the Government of Canada's Minister for Indian Affairs and Northern Development, Environment Canada, Health Canada, and the National Chief of the Assembly of First Nations announced the creation of a panel of experts that will examine options for a regulatory framework to ensure safe drinking water in First Nations communities. There are no Aboriginal women on this panel (INAC). Such exclusion is even occurring in many Aboriginal communities, where Aboriginal women have essentially been denied their inherent connection to water in western-imposed systems of "water management." Moreover, with respect to efforts to share and understand traditional knowledge, it was found that, "Without the equal input of women, the Elders were able to only give half of the knowledge available" (Lavalley 34). It was therefore recommended that "…women receive special mention in the invitation to discuss important matters, such as water" (Lavalley 34) Any discussion about water protection must ensure that women are equitably represented.

Gains are slowly being made, in part due to the efforts of the Mother Earth Walk, in March 2007, the Anishinabek Nation announced the creation of a Women's Water Commission aimed in part at providing input to the Ontario government on Great Lakes water issues (UOI). The foundation of the Anishinabek Women's Water Commission, "…is the traditional role of the Women in caring for water" (UOI 1). It was established in recognition of this traditional role along with the need to include women as part of the decision-making processes in formal environmental and resource management. This commission, led by none other than Josephine Mandamin, gained momentum with the appointment of political representative Chief Isadora Bedamash in March 2008. Chief Bedamash's appointment is seen vital in the effort to, "...strengthen our leadership role in the area of water policy in Ontario, and enhance the leadership of the Women's Water Commission itself" (UOI 1).

Through its work not only with member First Nations but also with Ontario government agencies, it is hoped that this Commission will provide valuable insights into the approaches required for the ongoing protection of the Great Lakes. While only time will tell as to the efficacy of women's voice in such an arrangement, it is nevertheless a positive step forward.

In summary, Aboriginal women have a special connection to water that mainstream society has not considered in formal decision-making processes. This lack of recognition has not stopped Aboriginal women from fulfilling their obligations. They continue to do as they have always done, guided by spiritual teachings, traditions, values, and ceremonies. My hope is that by sharing with you my experiences working with Elders and Grandmothers, I too have in part fulfilled my responsibilities as an Anishnaabe woman.

Originally published in Canadian Woman Studies/les cahiers de la femme, *"Indigenous Women in Canada: The Voices of First Nations, Inuit and Métis Women,"* 26 (3 & 4) (Winter/Spring 2008): 26-30. Reprinted with permission of the author. Updated by the author in 2009.

Deborah McGregor is Anishinaabe from Whitefish River First Nation. She is currently Associate Professor in Aboriginal Studies and Geography at the University of Toronto. She is the mother of two boys and currently lives in Toronto. She holds a B.Sc. in Psychology from the University of Toronto, a Master of Environmental Studies from York University and a Ph.D. from the University of Toronto's Faculty of Forestry. She has been an educator and trainer at both the university and community levels and have been involved in curriculum development, research and teaching. For two decades, her focus is on Indigenous knowledge in relation to the environment.

REFERENCES

Akii Kwe. "Minobimaatisiiwin: We Are to Care for Her." Position Paper from Women of Bkejwanong First Nation. Walpole Island, ON, 1998.

Anderson, K. *A Recognition of Being: Reconstructing Native Womanhood.* Toronto: Second Story Press, 2000.

Clarkson, L., V. Morrissette and G. Régallet. *Our Responsibility to the Seventh Generation: Indigenous Peoples and Sustainable Development.* Winnipeg: International Institute for Sustainable Development, 1992.

Cook, K. "Grand Mother Moon." Haudenosaunee Environmental Task Force. *Words That Come Before All Else: Environmental Philosophies of the Haudenosaunee.* Haudenosaunee Environmental Task Force. Cornwall Island: Native North American Travelling College, 1999. 139-142.

Gélinas, J. *Chapter Five: Drinking Water in First Nation Communities. Report of the Commissioner of the Environment and Sustainable Development.* Ottawa: Office of the Auditor General of Canada, 2005. Online: <www.oag-bvg. gc.ca/dominao/reports.nssf/html/c20050905ce.html>.

Kamanga, D., J. Kahn, D. McGregor, M. Sherry, and A. Thornton 2001. *Drinking Water in Ontario First Nation Communities: Present Challenges and Future Directions for On-Reserve Water Treatment in the Province of Ontario.* Submission to Part II of the Walkerton Inquiry Commission. Chiefs of Ontario, Brantford.

Indian and Northern Affairs Canada (INAC). *Backgrounder: Creation of a Panel of Experts for the Development of Options for a Regulatory Framework to Ensure Safe Drinking Water in First Nations Communities.* May 31 2006. Online: <http://www.ainc-inac.gc.ca/nr/prs/m-a2006/02764bk_e.html>.

Lavalley, G. "Aboriginal Traditional Knowledge and Source Water Protection: First Nations' Views on Taking Care of Water." Toronto: A Report prepared for the Chiefs of Ontario and Environment Canada, 2006. Online: <http://www.chiefs-of-ontario.org/environment/index.html>.

Lawrence, B. and K. Anderson. "Introduction to Indigenous Women: The State of Our Nations." *Atlantis* 29 (2) (2005): 1-7.

McGregor, D. and S. Whitaker. "Water Quality in the Province of Ontario: An Aboriginal Knowledge Perspective." Prepared for the Chiefs of Ontario. Toronto, 2001.

Mercredi, O. and M. E. Turpel. *In the Rapids: Navigating the Future of First Nations.* Toronto: Penguin Books, 1993.

"Mother Earth Water Walk." 2008. Online: <www.motherearthwaterwalk. com>.

O'Connor, D. *Report of the Walkerton Inquiry Part One: A Summary—The Events of May 2000 and Related Issues.* Ontario Ministry of the Attorney General. Toronto: Queens Printer for Ontario, 2002a.

O'Connor, D. "Chapter 15: First Nations." *Report of the Walkerton Inquiry Part Two: A Strategy for Safe Drinking Water.* Ontario Ministry of the Attorney General. Toronto: Queens Printer for Ontario, 2002b. 485-497.

Royal Commission on Aboriginal Peoples (RCAP). "People to People, Nation to Nation: Highlights from the Report of the Royal Commission on Aboriginal Peoples." Ottawa: Minister of Supply and Services, 1996.

Union of Ontario Indians (UOI). "First Nations Appoint New Women's Water Commissioner." News Release, February 26, 2008. Online: <www.ansihinabek.ca>. Accessed April 8, 2008.

ISABEL ALTAMIRANO-JIMÉNEZ

NUNAVUT

Whose Homeland? Whose Voices

MANY POLITICAL CHANGES OF the twentieth century have involved the rhetoric of nationalism, which continues to play a crucial role in present-day political discourses. In recent decades, Indigenous peoples' demand to be recognized as nations has stressed territory and power as fundamental collective rights. Despite the rich separate literature on nationalism and Indigenous peoples, little effort has been done to study the possible relation between the two. Even lesser attention has been paid to the relationship between Indigenous nationalism, gender, and tradition. This article explores how these connections have unfolded in Nunavut, Canada. An analysis from a nationalist perspective is useful to examine how tradition and gender are crucial boundary makers in the construction of Indigenous national identities and to consider what roles women play in the rhetoric of nationalism.

This article advances three related arguments. First, it argues that the construction of Indigenous nationalism is a political process in which traditional and historical models are evoked; gender roles are constructed; and symbols, customs, and political and social practices are selected in the assertion of the right to a homeland and self-determination. Second, the deliberative reconstruction of tradition mimics the rigid identity criteria demanded from Indigenous peoples by the nation state. In the case of Nunavut this is expressed in the contested visions of tradition, gender roles, and the ongoing struggle to maintain Inuit identity and symbolic control within non-Inuit forms of governance. Third, both Indigenous nationalist discourses and colonizing polices include boundaries of exclusion and silence that entrap men and women differently.

I suggest that an analysis of the connections between nationalism, gender, and tradition is essential for a textured understanding of Indigenous women's realities and political actions. There is an ambivalent position between nationalism and women. On the one hand, nationalism has promoted women's activism and visibility; on the other hand, it has limited women's political actions and horizons, especially when women's aspirations are considered to divide the nationalist movement (Hall 100). The nation requires a sense of sameness, unity, and strong commonality based upon tradition when representing itself through the language of nationalism.

INDIGENOUS NATIONALISM, TRADITION, AND WOMEN

In their efforts to turn their cultural difference into a political resource, Indigenous peoples have integrated tradition into politics transforming such tradition into a significant symbolic capital with different functions and values according to different contexts. In Indigenous nationalist discourses, forms of everyday tradition and historicity tend to be superseded by political and economic readings of tradition (Schroeder 13). In contrast to lived tradition that is place-specific, the abstract conception of tradition celebrated in the nationalist narrative is generalized and distant from its diverse local footing so that it can conform to rigid definitions of Aboriginal peoples and historical continuity.

From this perspective, the national narrative reconstructs traditional history as a meta-narrative of timeless cultural continuity that, nonetheless, clashes with dynamic cultural practices and social relations. According to Schröder (12) by being imbued with political, hegemonic meaning, tradition loses its very embeddedness in everyday life and is objectified as reflexively constructed and deployed. Thus, the codification of tradition is among the more effective sources of social and political control and approval as it is aimed at persuading the members of a community that their commonalities are more relevant than their differences (Schochet 309). The question is not whether there is such a thing as a homogeneous tradition or past, rather, the question is who is mobilizing what in the articulation of the past, deploying what identities and representations, and in the name of what political purposes (Shohat 110).

The codification of tradition and its enforcement can therefore be understood as attempts from the dominant group to institute homogeneity and conform to the identity demanded by the Western settlers. In this context, difference is often expressed in simple terms of black and white, and internal difference is rendered equally problematic. However, while this process is imagined in relationship with local subjects, the logic upon which this process is founded inhibits efforts to understand or empower those individuals who live "out of the way" (Tsing) or those who have a different understanding of tradition. Dominant discourses of tradition are aimed at concealing the conflicting power relationship between gender and tradition and at legitimizing the status quo, which generally excludes Aboriginal women and their concerns.

Indigenous nationalist movements construct women's rights and aspirations as "unauthentic," "untraditional," or threatening to the political and cultural liberation of Aboriginal peoples. Often, gendered struggles against colonialism have been reduced to "women's issues" by the formal male leadership and then presented as a wholesale threat to Aboriginal sovereignty (Lawrence and Anderson 3). Women's demands for inclusion and equality have been dismissed and conceived of as "individual concerns." Several scholars (LaRocque; Dion Stout; Green; Ramirez) have demonstrated that formal male leadership has refused to address colonialism when women, rather than men, are its target. Consequently, the mobilization for Indigenous self-determination in these circumstances does not necessarily include the emancipation of Indigenous women.

From this perspective, dominant groups also control the rhetoric on tradition as well as subordinate groups whose discourse differs from that of the dominant. As the contestable issue of gender remains submerged in political struggles emphasizing self-determination, cul- tural difference, and experiences of material and social inequalities, Indigenous women's voices remain "muted." Nevertheless, as Shirley Ardener has explained in her introduction to *Defining Females*, muted groups are not deficient in their capacity for language, nor are they necessarily quieter than the dominant group. Rather, the "mutedness" of one group may be regarded as the "deafness" of the dominant group. Moreover, the latter group's deafness forces subordinated groups such as Indigenous women to create alternative spaces of action and strategies aimed at challenging the legitimacy and hegemony of such discourses and power.

Therefore, gendering Indigenous struggles helps to explain how Indigenous women relate to nationalism, tradition, and feminism. Andrea Smith notes that the discussion on Indigenous women's struggles and Indigenous nationalist movements have usually been framed in quite simplistic terms, emphasizing a gap between feminism and Indigenous women. Despite appearances, Indigenous women are complex figures to feminists, not only because of these women's double racial and gender identities but also because Indigenous women's actions and political positions seem to point in contradictory directions.

INDIGENOUS WOMEN AND FEMINISM

Postcolonial feminists (Spivak; Mohanty; Stasiulis) have contributed greatly to the discussion of the "double marginal" and have challenged other feminists to consider the intersections with other axes of difference. Nonetheless, Indigenous women differ in important ways from those of the so-called Third World analyzed by postcolonial feminism.

Chandra Mohanty's influential essay "Cartographies of Struggles" for example, redefines Third World not within any geographical boundaries but within particular socio-historical conjectures. Mohanty perceives important commonalities between Third World women and women of colour in the First World. However, as Radhika Mohanram argues, such redefinition reproduces a homogenous conception of the Third World by emphasizing global economy as an organizing principle. At the same time, it also underlines alliances that are relevant in multicultural contexts. This emphasis, however, tends to bypass Indigenous rights and to position Indigenous peoples just as any other minority. Although in the literature the term Third World has been superseded by the term postcolonial, which encompasses different national-racial formations, this term continues to neglect Indigenous colonization experiences.

The different issues that postcolonial feminists and Indigenous women raise are important when considering their perceptions of nationalist projects. Critical differences between the perspectives of Indigenous women and postcolonial feminists result not only from their different racial experiences but also from their different worldviews. Indigenous women underline the continuation of colonialism—even within the context of independent national states—and gender equality by drawing on both cultural constructions honouring and valuing womanhood and non-Indigenous perspectives as well (McIvor 173). Indigenous traditions portrayed by women generally place women at the centre of communities, families, and political and cultural practices including the participation of the collective in achieving balance and consensus. Therefore, from Indigenous women's perspectives, issues surrounding the social reproduction of their collective identities and communities are crucial and connected to their struggles for self-determination.

However, an important body of literature reveals contradictions and ambiguities in Indigenous women's lives that defy easy generalization. Indigenous women within a community may experience a wide range of differences in their status, cultural settings, and voices, while individual women encounter considerable changes in their political position consequent to changing kinship status (Conte). These discrepancies between the actual functions Indigenous women perform and the roles imposed on them create further paradoxes in women's status relative to men. Despite the contradictions women have experienced and their unequal access to essential resources, women have often used their domestic functions and status as a means to facilitate rather than hinder their opportunities for political participation. Furthermore, while some Indigenous women have centred on building and reproducing communities as an extension of Indigenous women's responsibilities towards their communities, others have adopted other forms of political action in the political sphere.

As Indigenous nationalism may force communities to preserve a past and conform to the image and representation of resistance, emergent internal movements mobilize "discrepant" traditions in struggles around identity, place, and power. Indigenous women's resistance illustrates the conflicting relation between the representation of binary formulations and the mobilization of alternative visions of tradition. As a subordinate group, Indigenous women act to transform the interface between the discourses of place, tradition, and politics in Aboriginal decolonization struggles. In this process, Indigenous women are not merely subject to unified racial and gendered identities, but are agents claiming to construct and mediate meaningful complex subjectivities. Their discourses both reproduce Indigenous tradition and resist the hegemony of dominant representations of tradition.

Nunavut and Inuit nationalism is a relevant case in which the institutionalization of a new relationship between Indigenous peoples and the government was accompanied by important efforts and debates to redefine Indigenous traditions, self-government, and women's relationship to their communities. In this context, Indigenous women have emphasized the gendered experiences of colonialism. While formal male Indigenous leadership has associated resistance and self-determination with land claims, constitutional protection, and western forms of governance, female activists have identified self-determination to a variety of issues connected to the community including cultural and economic development and gender-balanced relationships.

NUNAVUT: WHOSE HOMELAND?

Thanks to an active Inuit nationalist movement that started in the 1970s, on April 1, 1999, the eastern Arctic, equivalent to one-fifth of Canada's landmass, became a new territory: Nunavut ("Our Land" in Inuktitut), in which 85 percent of the population is Inuit. Under the language of nationalism, Inuit tradition and culture were closely associated with the homeland and the hunter. The economic, political, and identity focus given to the land and its resources positioned Inuit men's concerns at the centre of the nation-building process. Hunting is a social and cultural institution, so it is not surprising that the image of the hunter is a central expression of Inuit tradition and identity (Searles 124-25). Through this image, hunting skills and the ability to survive in the Arctic's harsh climate are condensed to portray a male-centered Inuit identity while women's dynamic social, cultural, and economic roles are left out.

The centrality of the image of the hunter and the economic and cultural emphasis on the continuation of traditional practices and subsistence used under the nationalist language contributed to place women and women's activities in a less valued position than that of men or, at least, in a position no longer considered "traditional."

Furthermore, the apparent neutrality of social and political institutions helps to conceal internal power structures and to make the contestable issue of gender taken for granted. For example, the political movement that gave birth to Nunavut emphasized the collective right to exercise authority over the land, which has been a traditional male domain (Schweitzer et al. 18). However, as Mark Nuttall argues, women in Arctic hunting societies fish, gather plants, hunt small animals, collect birds' eggs, and process meat, hence making vital contributions to the social and economic vitality of their communities. Thus, the construction of land use and occupancy as male-centred when the Nunavut land claims were negotiated has had important negative consequences for women.

When dealing with "traditional" land use and occupancy, the Canadian government asks Aboriginal peoples to demonstrate that they were at a certain level of social organization and that they had some notions of "property" in order to claim territorial rights (Pinkoski and Ash). At the same time, land claims processes are embedded in colonial representations of women as landless and domestically placed. As a result, negotiations have focused on validating statements of male traditional, and continuing, land use and occupancy of the specific areas claimed, rather than on both men's and women's contributions to hunter-gatherer economy. From this perspective, a male-centred nationalist

147

discourse is related and reinforced by the rigid definition of Indigeneity and historical continuity adopted by the Canadian state. This approach is also consistent with conventional southern Canadian notions of development, which emphasize the exploitation of non-renewable resources.

The indirect consequences of the gendered land claims negotiation process extend beyond the actual contents of a land claim. Inuit women had expressed concerns about an emphasis on the economic, social, and political roles and issues for men at the expense of those of women in Nunavut (Pauktuutit Inuit Women's Association). For instance, as part of the Nunavut land claims the Tungavik Federation of Nunavut (TFN) negotiated wildlife income support with the Northwest Territories (NWT) government. The TFN agreed to narrow the scope of the program from the "household" to the "hunter" as this focus fit within an existing government initiative providing hunters (primarily men) with small amounts of funds to subsidize gas and repairs to machines used for harvesting (Archibald and Crnkovich 8). Although there may be income support programs for men whose livelihood of hunting is interrupted, the Inuit Women Association stated that no such programs for the interruption of women's labour in the harvest exist.

Thus, the shift from the "household" to the "hunter" not only values the continuation of men's traditional activities as opposed to women's but also contributes to conceal important economic and social transformations experienced by Inuit society. For example, Inuit women have increasingly become the main economic supporters of the household by stepping into the wage economy and continuing with their traditional activities such as harvesting. This suggests a clash between the reconstruction of traditional history as a metanarrative and the dynamism of live tradition, cultural practices, and social relations.

Besides the conceptualization of gendered territorial struggles, other events involving the creation of national institutions also reveal the gendered vision of the nation and the constant struggle of the Inuit to maintain their identity and symbolic control within non-Inuit forms of governance.

The fundamental idea behind the Nunavut land claims was that territorial institutions, state structures, and political process should reflect the nature, values, and tradition of Inuit society. However, such nationalist aspirations had to be accommodated into a public model of self-government. In the context of institution-building, the Inuit leaders also introduced the gender-parity vote proposal. While the public model of government was successfully adopted, the gender-parity proposal failed in the middle of a heated debate around the meaning of tradition and its role in contemporary Inuit society. Although the discussion focused mainly on these intersections, I argue that the outcome of the referendum was also closely related to the competition between unelected and elected leaders for political legitimacy and the institutionalization of contemporary Inuit politics and government.

In 1994, the Nunavut Implementation Commission (NIC), the entity in charge of overseeing the creation of a government for the new territory, released a document proposing that the new government should be gender-balanced by creating two-person constituencies, with one male and one female representative (Nunavut Implementation Commission). The proposal recognized the systemic barriers to women's participation in the political process and governance structure within Inuit society and outlined the need to eliminate such barriers in order to create balance and mutual respect between men and women in the decision-making process (Nunavut Implementation Commission Report).

The centrality of gender and tradition in the national institution-building process in Nunavut was articulated clearly during the gender-parity referendum. On May 26, 1997, the inhabitants of Nunavut voted on a proposal that would have guaranteed gender parity within the Nunavut Legislative Assembly. However, the proposal was rejected by 57 percent of the voters (Bourgeois; Hicks and White; Laghi). The proposal, a radical and unique idea in the world, and the public debate that developed previous to the vote, contested not only the relationship between men and women, but also their place in modern Inuit society.

Three arguments were put forth during the debate regarding the gender-parity proposal: (1) gender parity would help restore traditional equal value between women and men; (2) gender equality is foreign to Inuit society; (3) the proposal is against the "Inuit spirit," which is based on commonality not individualism; and (4) equality is best ensured by ignoring gender and racial differences.

Inuit male and female leaders who negotiated the land claims endorsed the first argument. During the weeks leading up to referendum representatives for Nunavut Tungavik Incorporated (NTI), NIC, and Pauktuutit (the Inuit women's organization) ran a campaign and visited a number of communities in the territory. These **organizations** argued that Inuit tradition used to be gender-balanced. According to this argument, gender roles were different yet complementary. Therefore, gender equality in the legislature would best reflect the division of labour and equal sharing of responsibility between women and men in Inuit society before westernization ended this society's nomadic lifestyle. However, the plebiscite results do not indicate that the campaign had any positive effect. In fact, many people felt intimidated by what they perceived was a one-sided campaign. Some people questioned who had paid for the campaign and why the opponents were not part of it. Furthermore, while Inuit tradition invokes complementary gender roles, increased unemployment among men and participation of women in wage labour is such that men saw gender parity as a further limitation to the traditional role of men as providers (Steele and Tremblay 36).

The second argument was used by conservative groups to oppose the proposal. They claimed that the notion of equality between the sexes was foreign to Inuit society and instead invoked Christian gender roles as part of their argument. Accordingly, men belonged to the outside world and, as hunters, they were the providers. Women, in contrast, belonged to the household and were in charge of childbearing, skin cleaning, midwifery, and sewing. According to this argument, the role of women within the nation was limited to their roles within the home. To elect women to the legislative assembly would have meant taking women out of the home and preventing them from fulfilling their duties. Many Inuit women lined up with this argument for fear that female participation in politics would increase violence and social problems. Jens Dahl (46) points out that Inuit women's opposition to the proposal reflected their commitment to maintain strong families and also their fear of increasing social problems.

The third argument was also used by the opponents of the proposal to argue that women could not be seen as a separate collectivity, because such a perception jeopardized the viability of the whole. According to this point of view, community decisions are geared towards unanimous consensus even if that means exercising strong forms of discipline among the members of a community. Since individuals cannot be abstracted from the community, the whole goal of statecraft is to transcend individual interests and to work for the community's public good.

The fourth argument was also advanced by the opponents of the gender-parity proposal, who took a liberal view of democracy. Among the most vocal opponents were the elected politicians, including the Director of Community Affairs and the Women's Directorate, MLA Manitok Thompson. The assumption behind this argument was that equality was best ensured by ignoring sexual or other differences and by emphasizing individual merit and commitment to advance general interests. From this perspective, good laws and public policy were viewed as a means to secure the equal opportunity of all individuals to compete for the role of representing the society at large. As Jackie Steele and Manon Tremblay argue, equal representation was, in this position, measured in terms of the procedural equality of competition. The fact that a prominent Inuit female advanced this view and the idea that the proposal was discriminatory both against men (by reserving seats for women) and against women (by assuming women could not win without representational guarantees) increased concerns as to who constitute a legitimate voice of women's equality concerns.

Although the debate preceding the gender-parity referendum focused on issues regarding gender roles, collective versus individual rights, and descriptive versus substantive representation, the proposal was part of the nationalist process of creating government institutions and legitimizing political leadership. The proposal was advanced by the old leadership, who negotiated the land-claims agreement and who sought to retain some symbolic control within non-Inuit forms of governance. In contrast, many of the vocal opponents were elected politicians who had been socialized in the NWT liberal mindset. From this perspective, the debate prior to the referendum was also a battleground about the power accorded to elected leaders as opposed to unelected leaders operating within Inuit forms of governance and, about the legitimization of elected leaders, who would better fit Nunavut's "Canadianized" government institutions and principles. Ultimately, the debate around the gender-parity proposal was a battle over who has the right to speak on behalf of whom. In the end, the gender-parity initiative failed, showing that Inuit nationalism is not only a political process in which tradition and gender are highly implicated, but also an ongoing struggle to maintain cultural identity and symbolic control within non-Inuit forms of governance. Furthermore, it is a struggle about different visions of the nation. While elected leaders may move more comfortably within a public government, for many Inuit, Nunavut the idea of "homeland," continues to be unfulfilled promise."

CONCLUSIONS

This article argues that the construction of nationalism is a political process in which historical models are evoked, gender roles are constructed, and symbols, customs, and political and social practices are selected in the assertion of the right to a homeland. In nationalist discourses, gender does not constitute a legitimate component because Indigenous nationalism's emphasis is on the distinction between "them" and "us" and on conforming the terms demanded from Indigenous peoples by the national states. From this perspective, both Indigenous nationalist discourses and colonizing polices include boundaries of exclusion and silence that entrap men and women differently and contributes to the unequal representation of men and women.

While the adoption of a public model of government did not represent a challenge to Inuit "tradition," the gender-parity proposal and its debate centred on the theoretical foundations of gender equality, the contested visions of Inuit tradition, and on who has the right to speak on behalf of whom. From this perspective, the political choices facing Inuit society are not between self-determination and fragmentation or between collective rights versus democratic individual rights. Rather, they are about different ways of understanding self-determination, nationhood, Inuit identity, and the place of men and women within the nation.

Originally published in Canadian Woman Studies/les cahiers de la femme, *"Indigenous Women in Canada: The Voices of First Nations, Inuit and Métis Women," 26 (3 & 4) (Winter/Spring 2008): 128-134 Reprinted with permission of the author.*

Isabel Altamirano-Jiménez is an Indigenous Zapotect from Oaxaca, Mexico and Assistant Professor in the Department of Political Science and the Faculty of Native Studies at the University of Alberta.

REFERENCES

Archibald, Linda, and Mary Crnkovich. "If Gender Mattered: A Case Study of

Inuit Women, Land Claims and the Voisey's Bay Nickel Project." 1999. Online: <http://www.swc-cfc.gc.ca.pubspr/0662280024/199911_06622800_e.pdf>. Accessed 04 Nov. 2005.

Ardener, Shirley. "Introduction." Ed. S. Ardener. *Defining Females.* New York: Wiley, 1978.

Bourgeois, Annette. "Nunavut Rejects Equity Plan: Eastern Arctic Residents Vote Down Proposal to Elect a Man and a Woman from each Riding." *Canadian Press* 27 May 1997.

Conte, Christine. "Ladies, Livestock, Land and Lucre: Women's Networks and Social Status on the Western Navajo Reservation." *American Indian Quarterly* 6 (1-2) (1982): 104-124.

Dahl, Jens. "Gender Parity in Nunavut." *Indigenous Affairs* 3-4 (1997): 46-47.

Dion, Stout. "Fundamental Changes are Needed to End Violence." *Windspeaker* November 20 (1994).

Green, Joyce. "Taking into Account Aboriginal Feminism." *Making Space for Indigenous Feminism.* Ed. Joyce Green. Winnipeg: Fernwood Publishing, 2007. 20-32.

Hall, Catherine. 1993. "Gender, Nationalisms and National Identities: Bellagio Symposium, July 1992." *Feminist Review* 44 (1993): 97-103.

Hicks, Jack, and Graham White. "Nunavut: Inuit Self-Determination Through a Land Claim and Public Government?" Eds. Jens Dahl et al. *Nunavut: Inuit Regain Control of Their Lands and Lives.* Copenhagen: International Work Group for Indigenous Affairs, 2000. 30-117.

Laghi, Brian. "Eastern Arctic Residents Reject Gender-Equal Plan: Supporters Said it Would Reflect Balance of Work in Traditional Inuit Society." *The Globe and Mail* 27 May 1997.

LaRocque, Emma. "Re-Examining Culturally Appropriate Models in Criminal Justice Applications." Ed. Michael Ash. *Aboriginal and Treaty Rights in Canada: Essays on Law, Equity, and Respect for Difference.* Vancouver: University of British Columbia Press, 1997: 75-96.

Lawrence, Bonita, and Kim Anderson. "Introduction to 'Indigenous Women: The State of Our Nations.'" *Atlantis* 29 (2) (2005): 1-8.

McIvor, Sharon Donna. "Self-Government and Aboriginal Women." *Scratching the Surface: Canadian Anti-Racists Thoughts.* Eds. Enakshi Dua and Angela Robertson. Toronto: Women's Press. 167-186.

Mohanram, Radhika. "The Construction of Place: Maori Feminism and Nationalism in Aotearoa/New Zealand." *NWSA Journal* 8 (1) (1996): 50-69.

Mohanty, Chandra. "Cartographies of Struggle." *Third World Women and the Politics of Feminism.* Eds. Lourdes Torres, Ann Russo, Chandra Mohanty. Bloomington: Indiana University Press, 1991: 1-48.

Nunavut Implementation Commission. "Two Member Constituencies and Gender Equality: A Made in Nunavut Solution for an Effective and Representative Legislature." *Footprints in the Snow.* Iqaluit, 1994.

Nunavut Implementation Commission Report. *Nunavut Legislature and First Election*. Iqaluit, 1996.

Nutall, Mark. *Arctic Homeland: Kinship, Community and Development in Northwest Greenland*. Toronto: University of Toronto Press, 1992.

Pauktuutit Inuit Women Association of Canada. *Arniat: The Views of Inuit Women on Contemporary Issues*. Ottawa: Pauktuutit, 1991.

Pinkoski, Marc and Michael Ash. "Anthropology and Indigenous Rights in Canada and the United States: Implications in Steward's Theoretical Project." *Hunter-Gatherers in History, Archeology and Anthropology*. Ed. Alan Barnard. New York: Palgrave Macmillan, 2004.187-200.

Ramirez, Renya. "Race, Tribal Nation and Gender: A Native Feminist Approach to Belonging." *Meridians: Feminism, Race and Transnationalism* 7 (2) (2007): 22-40.

Schochet, Gordon. "Tradition as Politics and the Politics of Tradition." *Question of Tradition*. Eds. Mark Salber Phillips and Gordon Schochet. Toronto: University of Toronto Press. 2004. 296-320.

Schröder, Ingo W. "The Political Economy of Tribalism in North America: Neo-Tribal Capitalism?" *Anthropological Theory* 3 (4) (2003): 435-456.

Schweitzer, Peter P., Megan Biesele and Robert K. Hitchcock. *Hunters and Gatherers in the Modern World: Conflict, Resistance and Self-Determination*. New York: Berghahn Books, 2000.

Searles, Edmund. "Fashioning Selves and Tradition: Case Study on Personhood and Experience in Nunavut." *The American Review of Canadian Studies* 31 (1-2) (2001): 121-136.

Shohat, Ella. "Notes on the 'Post-Colonial.'" *Social Text* 31/32 (1992): 99-113.

Smith, Andrea. "Native American Feminism, Sovereignty and Social Change." *Feminist Studies* 31(1) (2005): 116-132.

Spivak, Gayatari Chakravorty. *The Post-Colonial Critic: Interview, Strategies, Dialogues*. New York: Routledge, 1990.

Stasiulis, Daiva K. "Relational Positionalities of Nationalisms, Racisms and Feminisms." *Between Woman and Nation*. Eds. Caren Kaplan, et al. Duke: Duke University Press, 1999. 182-218.

Steele, Jackie, and Manon Tremblay. "Paradise Lost? The Gender Parity Plebiscite in Nunavut." *Canadian Parliamentary Review* 28 (1) (2005): 34-39.

Tsing, Anna Lowenhaupt. *In the Realm of the Diamond Queen*. Princeton: Princeton University Press, 1993.

BRENDA MCLEOD

FIRST NATIONS WOMEN AND SUSTAINABILITY
ON THE CANADIAN PRAIRIES

IN PRE-COLONIAL TIMES, First Nations[1] across Canada engaged in agriculture, hunting, trapping, fishing, and gathering to survive and trade for goods with other Aboriginal nations in the Americas (Dickason). First Nations engaged in these activities primarily as hunting and gathering societies but also within larger complex social settings along the West Coast and Eastern Woodlands areas of Canada where it was possible to grow or access a localized food supply. Activities were primarily carried out at a subsistence level that promoted sufficiency over accumulation, based on their spiritual and material attachment to their homeland (Chamberlin). The colonization of Canada changed the way that land and resources were used and interfered with First Nations' ways of life.

First Nations across Canada share a common experience of colonial encounter that has left them economically marginalized, politically weakened, and culturally stigmatized. The effects of the colonial experience include a loss of land base and access to resources that allowed First Nations to engage in a sustainable livelihood in pre-colonial times. Furthermore, the loss of sustainable livelihood has been accompanied by environmental degradation of the remaining homelands where significant numbers of First Nations people still reside. The overall effect for First Nation communities has been the endemic presence of social, mental and physical illness in communities that were once self-sustaining and environmentally sustaining. The key to changing the present conditions in First Nation communities lies in sustainable development that meets the needs of the communities as defined by them and respects their value systems while providing sustainability.

Women in First Nation communities share concerns with other women for social change that will return sustainability to their communities. Although still important, the concerns of most First Nations women, unlike many Canadian feminists, are not embedded primarily in gender issues; due to the subjugation of First Nations peoples in Canada, the issues of First Nations women are most often grounded in national and community issues. Inherent in these issues is the legacy of colonialism that has displaced First Nations from traditional lands and resources, accompanied by the subjugation of

154

traditional economies and customs that have culminated in an overall loss of a way of life for men and women alike. The social, political, and economic disadvantage that First Nations women experience in their communities can be attributed to gender bias that originated with missionaries who introduced male domination and hierarchy into an egalitarian social system. First Nations women experience racism and discrimination within the larger society as Aboriginal persons and as women but also discrimination within their own communities, because they are women. These conditions translate into less access to jobs, support, training programs, and a reduced ability to affect and change their circumstances, as well as lower life expectancy than non-Aboriginal women.

The physical loss of lands and resources for First Nations, accompanied by repressive government policies, have separated First Nations from their lands and resources, either through harvesting resources with little or no return to First Nation communities or by restricting access and economic development for the benefit of those same communities. Economic development for individuals and communities outside of First Nation communities have provided few employment opportunities for Aboriginal people and resulted in environmental degradation—reducing sustainability in terms of livelihood and health. Such negative impacts lead to despair and a sense of degradation and dehumanization as people are forced to depend on state programs to survive.

This paper explores historical events experienced by First Nation communities in Saskatchewan focusing on the objectives of treaty-making between First Nations and the Crown with reference to sustainability. Treaty promises of access to lands and resources to sustain First Nations' livelihood will be measured against the actual conditions for sustainable development that resulted from these treaties—particularly considering the promise and the pitfalls of contemporary treaty land entitlement agreements. The paper will conclude by pointing to the need for exploring sustainability from the perspectives of First Nations, particularly women, in order to provide a basis for social, mental and physical well-being.

THE TREATY RELATIONSHIP BETWEEN SASKATCHEWAN FIRST NATIONS AND THE CROWN

During the first 200 years after Europeans first came to North America, First Nations built relationships with newcomers through the fur trade. Later, the Crown required access to lands held by First Nations, to facilitate its colonization agenda of settlement and agriculture through immigration. Elders in the five treaty areas of Saskatchewan recall the settlement of Europeans in their lands being foretold through the prophecies of their ancestors (Cardinal and Hildebrandt). This knowledge assisted First Nations in preparing to accommodate newcomers in their traditional lands. As a result,

[i]t was decided long before the White man arrived that the First Nations would treat the newcomers as relatives, as brothers and sisters ... that they should live in peace and that they would share the land. The sacred earth could never be sold or given away, according to the principles of First Nations, but it could be shared ... to the depth of a plough blade ... so everyone could peacefully co-exist. (Elder Peter Waskahat qtd. in Cardinal and Hildebrandt 31)

The treaty process was chosen to facilitate this sharing as it was familiar to both First Nations and Europeans. Beginning in 1870, a number of treaties were made that covered the area of what would later become the three Prairie provinces. Essentially, for First Nations, the various treaties were agreements to ensure peaceful relations between the Crown and First Nations and arrange a sharing of territory (Cardinal and Hildebrandt).

First Nations sought to secure a Crown guarantee that their relationship with the Creator would be treated with respect and integrity (Cardinal and Hildebrandt). A number of principles were affirmed in the treaties signed between the Crown and First Nations. These principles include a joint acknowledgement of the supremacy of the Creator; a joint commitment to the maintenance of peace; a mutual agreement to create a perpetual familial relationship; a guarantee of each other's survival and stability based on mutual sharing; and finally, that the sharing arrangement guarantee a continuing right of livelihood to First Nations (Cardinal and Hildebrandt). Thus, First Nations looked to treaties as an economic future but also a wider base of sustainability where their values towards the use of land and resources would ensure long-term survival as well as a livelihood.

Conversely, for the Crown, the main objective in making treaties with First Nations was to secure clear title to particular geographic areas and resources for settlement (Tough). Settlers required lands for agriculture but timber and hay resources were valuable to settlers and government alike. Settlers counted on timber, hay and grazing to subsidize and enhance ranching and agriculture operations while government coffers expanded through revenues generated from leases and permits for the use of these resources (Lambrecht). The Crown's objective depended upon the alienation of vast tracts of land and resources from First Nations in Saskatchewan and Manitoba. In exchange for the taking of lands and resources, the Crown provided "gifts" of cash, hunting and trapping supplies, agricultural supplies, cloth, and Reserve[2] lands for the exclusive use of Indian peoples. In the treaties covering Saskatchewan and Manitoba, the Crown promised to pay annuities and provide for the needs of First Nations in the context of a fiduciary relationship.

The nature of this relationship between sovereign nations was based on the Crown's duty of care to act in the best interests of First Nations, which I argue requires a commitment to the sustainability of First Nations. The Crown and First Nations sealed treaties in spiritual and state ceremonies with each party committing to enduring obligations and responsibilities. Treaty commissioners carried out the negotiations on behalf of the Crown but treaty implementation was the responsibility of government officials. The "official representatives" in the treaty negotiations were male Band members who where 21 years and older. First Nations women were certainly present at the time of treaty negotiations but were not permitted a vote or voice in the negotiations with Commissioners. Under the *Indian Act*, First Nations women were not recognized legally as persons; a woman's status as an Indian and her Band membership was determined by her father or her husband, who were assigned her political and social powers (Voyageur).

TREATY IMPLEMENTATION

Treaties continued to be negotiated until the early 1900s but were never ratified by parliamentary process in Canada. By 1876, the Dominion government consolidated all previous legislation about Indian peoples into *The Indian Act*. Within four years, the Department of Indian Affairs (DIA) was created to administer the new Act and implement the terms of the treaty negotiated with the registered Indian population in Canada. Interpretation of the terms of the treaties was left to government officials who tended to provide a very literal interpretation to the terms; missing from the literal text of the treaties was the spirit and intent under which those treaties were negotiated. However, that context is retained through the oral histories of First Nations and still exists today with Elders. Considerable differences exist between literal interpretation of the promises made in treaties and what First Nations believed they had agreed to. DIA officials were influenced in their interpretations by the bureaucratic machinery of not only their own department, but also the larger Department of the Interior, of which the DIA was a part.

The Department of the Interior was structured so that one Deputy Minster was responsible for all of the settlement/homestead lands and all of the resources under the *Dominion Lands Act*. The DIA had its own Deputy Superintendent General whose responsibilities included all of the lands reserved for Indians and their accompanying resources. Both of these Deputy Ministers reported directly to the Minister of the Interior, while ideally managing two distinct land classifications independently. This ideal quickly broke down when Treaty First Nations began to make Reserve selections in areas that were coveted by settlers and colonization companies or were desired for commercial purposes. Competing government policies of the DIA, *Dominion Lands Act* and private interests led to land surrenders of entire Reserves or major portions of Reserve lands and sometimes relocation to land that was insufficient in quantity and quality to engage in a sustainable livelihood of agriculture or subsistence activities (Carter). These events served to create unsustainable conditions for First Nations, thus failing to meet the duty of care promised at treaty negotiations.

Elders from Treaty Four and Six areas refer to the Cree concept of "*pimâcihowin* (the ability to make a living)" (Cardinal and Hildebrandt) that describes the spiritual, physical, and economic connection of First Nations as key to being able to make a living with the land. This integral concept informs traditional doctrines, laws, principles, values, and teachings about the sources of life and the accompanying responsibilities including "those elements seen as necessary for enhancing the spiritual components of life and those associated with making a living" (Cardinal and Hildebrandt 43). Elders indicated that the capacity of land to provide a livelihood is not only due to its material capabilities but also the spiritual powers inherent in it. Thus, physical separation from land and resources entails spiritual and economic separation of First Nations from lands and resources that were once available to sustain them.

Treaty Elders in Saskatchewan view the treaties as

> guaranteeing the continuing right of First Nations livelihood, and the continuing right to maintain a continuing relationship to the land, and its resources [which] constitutes one of the irrevocable and unchanging elements of the treaty relationship. (Cardinal and Hildebrandt 46)

The length of time it has taken for government to recognize and begin to rectify First Nations land and resource loss is evidenced by the signing of Treaty Land Entitlement (TLE) Framework Agreements in Saskatchewan and Manitoba in 1992 and 1997, respectively. TLE agreements were finalized to end over 100 years of outstanding land debts owed to signatory First Nations. These agreements were made to ensure that the lands owed to entitled First Nations at the time of signing or adhering to a treaty were finally awarded. The agreements attempted to address the issues of loss of use of lands and resources over that long time period.

Agreements in Saskatchewan and Manitoba allow entitled First Nations to add to their land base but differ in the extent to which they provide resources to entitled First Nations to be able to build up their communities to a level of sustainability. For instance, Saskatchewan's TLE agreement provided for shortfall acres to be acquired to constitute land that should have been included in the original Reserve as well as equity acres. Equity acres were derived from a formula that sought to account for the increase in a community's population as well as the loss of use over time. These acres were then converted into a cash payment to be used for Band development, agriculture, recreation and culture, and education (Canada 23). In contrast, the majority of TLE Bands in Manitoba received small cash settlements that are not adequate for further development of lands and resources acquired under TLE agreement (Henley).

The loss of lands and resources that accompanied treaty implementation compromised sustainability for First Nations. Numerous scholars have studied First Nation populations and generated statistics about social and economic conditions in terms of health status, living conditions and overall well-being by age, gender, geographic location and government status.[3] James Frideres portrays First Nations communities as having high unemployment and dependency on state funding; high infant mortality rates; high rates of suicide and substance abuse; lower levels of education and income; substandard housing accompanied by overcrowding and poor sanitation; a general lack of potable and safe water; poor transportation routes and accessibility as well as low levels of long-term economic development (Frideres and Gadacz). These conditions are directly related to a loss of land and access to resources as well as their health of the land (Adelson).

OPPRESSION OF FIRST NATIONS WOMEN

Vandana Shiva, in discussing similar conditions in India, refers to imperialists who viewed land and resources as commodities for exploitation for profits by separating nature from humans. The effect of this separation is that nature is viewed as an external surrounding and not the sustainer of human existence. Shiva attributes this concept to Cartesian philosophy, a paradigm leading to development based on exploitation and domination of nature and the subjugation of ecological knowledge of colonized peoples. She further maintains that women, as the givers and producers of life, are in a privileged position to appreciate the principles of sustainability from not only a biological basis, but also historical and cultural bases because of "their role as providers of sustenance, food and water" (42). Shiva points to the work of Alice Schlegel who demonstrated that this role is present in subsistence societies where the roles of males and females are interdependent and complementary; conditions that create diversity but not necessarily inequality. It is the diversity of these roles that are destroyed by colonization.

The roles of First Nations women suffered the greatest subjugation when land and resources became a commodity. The effects of this subjugation are evident at a personal, community, and national level. Beginning in 1869, legislation began to discriminate against First Nations women in terms of their "status"[4] as registered Indians who were extended Aboriginal and, where applicable, treaty rights (Ouellette). Essentially, the identity of any First Nation woman was determined by her father's status and upon marriage, her husband's status (Brizinski). If a First Nation woman married a man who did not have status or was not an Indian, she became disenfranchised of her rights and benefits; First Nations men were not affected by this legislation. After a number of attempts, Indian women successfully lobbied for change to the *Indian Act* to remove this discrimination in 1985 with the passing of Bill C-31.

While this legislation gives disenfranchised individuals the right to have their status reinstated, the federal government controls the degree to which benefits and rights may be passed on to their descendants by separating persons with reinstated status into "Full" and "Half" status (Brizinski 182). The responsibility for passing on status lies now with First Nations men and women who have status but causes subjugation at a community level as increased membership in communities have not been accompanied by increased funding, housing and land. Women who seek to return to Reserve communities are faced with a severe lack of housing and in some instances, membership codes that deny them the right live on the Reserve and access services (Voyageur). Within their communities, Aboriginal women hold administrative but not decision-making positions. Most community decisions are determined at the level of chief and council where "[t]here are only a handful of women chiefs" (Voyageur 98) perhaps because women are unable to gain sufficient community support to become chiefs or they are waiting until three are more women in council before holding the position of chief (Voyageur). Past experiences of First Nations women who have spoken out about inequality or injustice in their communities have reinforced their subjugation as they "are labeled as troublemakers and can face barriers in the subsequent encounters with the band" (Voyageur 99).

At a national level, First Nations women have organized themselves politically to speak on behalf of their concerns, out of necessity. During constitutional talks, The Native Women's Association[5] demanded a seat at the negotiation table and a portion of the funding allocated to male-dominated political organizations to ensure their issues would be addressed (Voyageur). For their troubles, male leadership, ironically elected and operating within the *Indian Act*, accused them of going against tradition by pursuing individual rights over the rights of the collective. As Grace Ouellette notes, the *Indian Act* "as an act of colonization in the subjugation of Indian people has often been overlooked" (31) making the struggles of Aboriginal women "[not] soley against male domination but rather one of liberation from the colonial policies and national oppression" (51). This complex agenda figures heavily in the pursuit of self-government by First Nations as women want to ensure that they have active participation in determining how their communities will be governed.

SUSTAINABLE DEVELOPMENT AS A BASIC RIGHT—RESTORING HUMANITY

Given the legacy of colonization in all aspects of the lives of First Nations, communities in Saskatchewan might well ask how they are to achieve sustainability on their newly acquired lands under TLE. Perhaps an effective way to approach this dilemma is to look at sustainable development as a basic right of individuals and communities rather than primarily as an economic strategy. Traditional models of sustainable development tend to be based on concepts of individualism, rational choice, and market-based competition, thereby keeping the focus on commercial economic development rather than holistic measures of sustainability (Hessing). Furthermore, Melody Hessing concludes that such models have not lead to more sustainable societies but have damaged the social and ecological foundations of those they were trying to help.

While Hessing and other feminist researchers seek to emphasize ecological and social dimensions to sustainability, it is important to note that First Nations in Canada face some unique constraints in trying to achieve their goals of sustainability. Ouellette, in her study of Aboriginal women's feminist perspectives in Canada states that some of these restraints include the *Indian Act*, provincial and federal legislation about lands and resources, and a colonial experience resulting in economic marginalization, political weakness, and cultural stigmatization within their own homelands. The conditions First Nations women find themselves in within their ancestral homelands raises unique issues of racism, national oppression, and colonialism that many Aboriginal women feel are best acted on by their own organizations. As Ouellette points out, principles of liberal feminism are neither appropriate nor applicable to most Aboriginal women due to their circumstances, politics, and conceptions of human nature. One contentious point is the place of motherhood and its responsibilities, viewed by most feminist theory as the source of women's subjugation. In contrast, for Aboriginal women, the ability to give life and nurture and care for others is a powerful key to the survival of Aboriginal peoples (Ouellette).

The *Indian Act*, as a colonial instrument of oppression, continues to affect the process of achieving sustainability in First Nation communities by providing legislative authority for policy decisions about First Nations' lands, resources, and livelihood. As Ouellette points out, "Despite many revisions, the *Indian Act* continues to define and regulate the lives of Indian people [in Canada] in every respect. It is legislation designed exclusively for them" (31). In addition, provincial and federal legislation govern the use of lands for subsistence activities and place limits on quantities of resource harvests in the interests of balancing conservation concerns, Aboriginal rights to resources and the promotion of sport/pleasure/tourism access to resources.

In Saskatchewan, treaty rights were consolidated in 1930 with the passage of the *Natural Resources Transfer Act* that gave the provinces the right to make legislation regarding lands and resources outside of federal lands (including Indian Reserves) and to control resource harvest within their respective provincial boundaries. Under this legislation, Indian peoples in Saskatchewan and Manitoba are now restricted to hunting and fishing for food only, and not for commercial purposes, on a year-round basis. While treaty rights to hunt and fish have been restricted, some scholars have pointed to the expansion of harvest rights to cover the entire area of a province rather than being confined to a treaty area (Issac).

However, this "generous" move on the part of the Crown did not take place with the consultation of First Nations, thereby ignoring the conditions under which First Nations governed resource harvest amongst their traditional territories. If a First Nation wanted to harvest resources outside of their treaty or traditional area, protocol dictated that an agreement to enter another First Nation's territory and harvest resources required a negotiated agreement to share that territory (Cardinal and Hildebrandt). Provincial legislation provides authority to government bureaucracy to redefine relationships without the consent or input of First Nations communities. In turn, conflict has resulted when these arrangements have been altered, leading to overharvesting of resources in some areas and subsequent restrictions applied by provincial legislation in the name of conservation.[6] In the end, those who suffer the greatest hardship are those who can least afford it—First Nations communities whose members depend on harvested resources for economic, social, and cultural survival.

An example of the effects of redefining relationships has occurred in north central Saskatchewan in the community of Witchekan Lake First Nation. In 1947, the community was assigned a trapping block, for their exclusive use, prior to their adhesion to Treaty Six in 1950. The six-mile square area was a portion of the community's traditional lands used for trapping, hunting, fishing, and foraging as well as social gathering and healing. In the 1960s, the community was approached and gave permission for grazing leases in the trapping block. Problems arose when a grazing lease was issued during the 1970s to a rancher under a revised *Wildlife Act* that gave the rancher the authority to deny access to anyone to his leased area. A lawyer from Saskatchewan Justice stated that "The radical changes to the rights of the trappers made in 1979 was apparently done without notice to them and, perhaps, without any real consciousness of what was being done to their interests" (Crane as qtd. in McLeod 109).

The rancher erected fences, and harassed trappers from Witchekan Lake First Nation. Trappers complained to authorities about being shot at, having traps stolen and finding traps flung into trees. At the same time as he was denying access to trappers from Witchekan Lake First Nation, the rancher was himself trapping, without a license. He admitted to trapping 200 beaver in at least two trapping seasons. No one came to the aid of the trappers between 1972 and 1992. The results of these activities was that trapping by the First Nation community ceased in the northern half of their trapping block while the southern half remained inaccessible because of swampy terrain and lacked a road. Thus, community members had a sharp decline in subsistence activity vital to their survival. They were forced to trap around the immediate are of Witchekan and Sylvander Lakes, which provided primarily muskrats and a few beaver for furs and food. The resource rich area of the larger trapping block was made unavailable for subsistence activities, social gathering and healing.

In an attempt to settle over 20 years of conflict, an agricultural lease was created in 1992 for the northern half of the trapping block that provided the rancher and trappers with separate access periods to the area. The agreement is for a 33-year period but does not guarantee access for trappers at this point in time. Provincial conservation officers have tended to respond enthusiastically to concerns of the rancher's family about hunting carried out by First Nations people, even outside of the rancher's access period. This atmosphere has left community members from Witchekan Lake apprehensive about exercising their rights to the trapping block but also angry at what they perceive to be the destruction of their way of life.

To further demonstrate the lack of consultation and redefining of relationships, the southern half of the trapping block is now under a grazing lease with a number of different ranchers. The rancher with the largest grazing lease owns land adjoining the trapping block and has been permitted to fence the road allowance with a locked gate that allows him to grant and deny access to the trapping block. The provincial government departments of Saskatchewan Environment and Resource Management (SERM) and Saskatchewan Agriculture and Food permitted this condition in response to the landowner's concerns about illegal hunting when his cattle are in the leased area.[7] The community of Witchekan Lake First Nation was not consulted about this lease or the denial of access to the trapping block. In fact, the community is not aware of when the southern half of their trapping block came under a grazing lease.

Interviews with the women of Witchekan Lake First Nation demonstrated hidden effects of the bureaucratic conflict over the trapping block. Some women in this community expressed concern for the safety of the hunters and trappers.[8] Although none of the women spoke of being directly harassed by SERM officers, they viewed the diligence of SERM officers as a threat to providing additional food and proper nutrition for their families. As well, they were concerned about the safety and comfort of their husbands on overnight trips as SERM has consistently prohibited the construction of a cabin or shelter on the trapping block for the use of community members. The lack of proper road access to the trapping block and lack of cabin or shelter for their husbands, placed a burden on some women, especially those with young children. These women drove their husbands to the edge of the trapping block so they could hunt during the day, returning later in the day to pick their husbands up, which usually coincided with the arrival of the school bus. When women were not able to drive their husbands, hunting ceased and families became dependent on store bought groceries.

Witchekan Lake First Nation sees the trapping block as vital to their survival and well-being, even though they have been unable to make a viable living from trapping. Not one person interviewed in the years between 1997 and 2001 stated that the trapping area should be let go from the community. In contrast, each individual wanted to see the area retained by the community for a variety of reasons. Some people saw the area as a refuge if the welfare system ever collapsed while others saw it as a vital area for retaining teachings about the land and relationships. Others still regarded the Bland Lake area as a place to heal physically, emotionally and mentally and to regain an overall sense of well-being and cultural pride. These reasons clearly demonstrate the nature of sustainability to Witchekan Lake First Nation and the importance of the land in achieving and maintaining sustainability. However, their experiences with government officials and ranchers have all too clearly reminded them of their economic marginalization, political weakness and cultural stigmatization in voicing their rights to the trapping block as a source of subsistence.

As clearly demonstrated by the situation at Witchekan Lake, First Nations, as Reserve communities, have continuous and intimate knowledge of their traditional lands. First Nations' definitions and perspectives on sustainability in terms of, among others, the socioeconomic, ecological, epistemological, psychological and political conditions that are necessary for sustainability should be heard.[9] Employing a purely economic model of sustainable development is akin to modernization strategies of "fixing" the socioeconomic situation in First Nations communities by generating revenue through economic growth. To be sure, economics are important to the sustainability of First Nation communities, but so are other aspects of community survival and sustainability that require a more holistic approach that must come from inside and not outside of communities.

Perhaps the greatest source of information for achieving this goal lies with First Nations women in their communities who employ a pragmatic and respectful approach towards the environment. John G. Bretting and Diane-Michele Prindeville note that unlike Indigenous women of Spanish descent, Native American women do not see themselves as only environmental stewards but also as spiritually connected to nature which provides them with direction for living (155). Interestingly enough, Manitoba's *Principles and Guidelines of Sustainable Development* lists stewardship as its second principle, describing Manitobans as "caretakers of the economy, the environment, human health and social well-being for the benefit of present and future generations" (Manitoba). This document does not consider the possibility of the environment being the caretaker and maintains the separateness of humans from the environment with the latter requiring the management skills of humans.

The National Round Table on the Environment and the Economy (NRTEE) focused heavily on management aspects in developing resource policy around the sustainability of Aboriginal communities in Canada. Its report entitled *Aboriginal Communities and Non-Renewable Resource Development* points to the 1998 document *Gathering Strength: Canada's Aboriginal Action Plan* objectives of renewing the partnerships between Aboriginal peoples and the government, strengthening Aboriginal governance, developing a new fiscal relationship and supporting strong communities, people and economies (116). While NRTEE claims to have relied on Aboriginal experience in developing its policy, the document reflects little of the spiritual relationship between Aboriginal peoples and the resources. Policy remains focused on economic benefits while promoting capacity-building of Aboriginal peoples in land, environment and resource management through co-management.

Capacity building in First Nations communities cannot stop at providing leadership and work skills for economic participation. First Nations are entitled to meaningful and long-term participation that allows for sustainability, as defined by their communities. This definition will vary from community to community based on needs, lands, resources and each community's vision of sustainability for its members, lands and resources. First Nations communities are not a homogeneous group nor does each community have the same type of land and resources. Therefore, blanket solutions for sustainability cannot be applied to First Nations communities, particularly when there is a lack of knowledge about the visions and constraints First Nations hold for a good life in their communities.

CONCLUSION

First Nations communities made arrangements to receive newcomers and shared the land with them, negotiating treaties to ensure that the traditional ways of life for First Nations would be upheld and respected. Economics was a valid concern as treaties and settlement of the lands followed on the decline of the fur trade, signaling a change in land and resource use for First Nations and newcomers alike. Although relatively few attempts have been made to capture the essence of First Nations' perspectives on treaty-making, Elders in Saskatchewan have been clear about the continuous rights of First Nations to maintain a connection to land and resources in a way that guarantees the survival and well-being of the present and future generations. In essence, this concept broadly defines sustainability.

However, what is lacking is the knowledge of how First Nations envision sustainability today. Like feminist research that points to the importance of broadening sustainable development beyond the economic to include social and ecological dimensions, First Nations communities consider these dimensions important to sustainability. However, First Nations are faced with creating a good life in the face of economic marginalization, political weakness, and cultural stigmatization, as nations, in their own homelands. Exploring the visions and strategies of these communities in their struggle can contribute to a wider understanding of sustainability.

In the face of the colonial experience, First Nations women retained their traditional roles to maintain culture, care for future generations, and steady their communities (Voyageur). In addition, First Nations women have spoken out about the conditions they face, advocating and working for political and social change, balanced with cultural values of harmony, mutual respect, and equality.

Originally published in Canadian Woman Studies/les cahiers de la femme, *"Women and Sustainability," 23 (1) (Fall /Winter 2003): 47-54. Reprinted with permission of the author.*

Brenda McLeod is currently a Ph.D. student at the Natural Resources Institute, University of Manitoba. Her past research includes a land use and occupancy study of one

First Nation and the Settler population in the Witchekan Lake area of Saskatchewan as well as land claims research. Her current research project explores sustainability from First Nations perspectives in Saskatchewan through community-based research with treaty land entitlement communities.

[1] The term First Nations is used in this paper to refer to Indian peoples who are descendants of the original treaty signatories in Saskatchewan and Manitoba. The term Aboriginal is used to include Indian, Metis, Non-Status Indian and Inuit peoples in Canada. The term Indigenous refers globally to Aboriginal peoples.

[2] The term "Reserve" is capitalized throughout this paper in an attempt to decolonize the term while dispelling ethnocentric perceptions about its diminished social significance. A Reserve is the remaining homeland of a First Nation in Canada and is a distinct outcome of a defined process and as such, is a proper noun.

[3] See the works of Frideres and Gadacz. Previous editions of this work document the conditions and lack of change in the social and economic status of Aboriginal communities in Canada.

[4] The term status refers to a government designation that an Indian person is registered under the *Indian Act* as an Indian and who is entitled to rights and benefits as well as restrictions. Signatories to treaties and their descendants are considered to be registered Indians with these entitlements as well as the rights and benefits of the treaty they are attached to.

[5] The mandate of the Native Women's Association of Canada (NWAC) is "a collective goal to enhance, promote, and foster the social, economic, cultural and political well-being of First Nations and Metis women within Aboriginal and Canadian societies" (qtd. in Ouellette 53). In discussing organizational structure, Ouellette notes that in 1989, 14 years after its inception, NWAC moved from a hierarchical structure to one modeled after the Four Directions.

[6] Elders interviewed in the Witchekan Lake area in north central Saskatchewan in 1997 questioned the quotas set for the community on the number of moose they can hunt on an annual basis. Moose, a staple of traditional diet, is currently highly prized for food. For a number of years, SERM has been concerned with a declining moose population in the province, implementing conservation measures by restricting hunting quotas and areas.

[7] Personal communication with a SERM official December 10, 2001.

[8] I conducted these interviews in 2001 for a research report for the community.

[9] I am borrowing this list of conditions from Wackernagel. However, First Nations may have differing or additional conditions regarding sustainability.

REFERENCES

Adelson, Naomi. *"Being Alive Well": Health and the Politics of Cree Well-Being.* Toronto: University of Toronto Press, 2002.

Bretting, John G. and Diane-Michele Prindeville. "Environmental Justice and the Role of Indigenous Women Organizing Their Communities. In *Environmental Injustices, Political Struggles: Race, Class and the Environment*. Ed. David E. Comancho. London: Duke University Press, 1998. 141-164.

Brizinski, Peggy M. *Knots In A String: An Introduction to Native Studies in Canada*, 2nd ed. Saskatoon: University Extension Press, 1993.

Canada. *The 1992 Saskatchewan Treaty Land Entitlement Framework Agreement*.

Cardinal, Harold and Walter Hildebrandt. *Treaty Elders of Saskatchewan: Our Dream Is That Our Peoples Will One Day Be Clearly Recognized As Nations*. Calgary: University of Calgary Press, 2000.

Carter, Sarah. *Lost Harvests: Prairies Indian Reserve Farmers and Government Policy*. Montreal: McGill-Queen's Press, 1990.

Chamberlin, J. Edward. "Culture and Anarchy in Indian Country." *Aboriginal and Treaty Rights In Canada: Essays on Law, Equity, and Respect for Difference*. Ed. Michael Asch. Vancouver: University of British Columbia Press, 1997. 3-37.

Dickason, Olive P. *Canada's First Nations: A History of Founding Peoples From Earliest Times*, 3rd ed. Toronto: Oxford University Press, 2002.

Frideres, James S. and Rene R. Gadacz. *Aboriginal Peoples In Canada: Contemporary Conflicts*, 6th ed. Toronto: Prentice Hall, 2001.

Henley, Thomas. Natural Resources Institute, University of Manitoba. Personal Communication, February, 2003.

Hessing, Melody. "Sustainable Livelihoods, Part I: Introduction." Online: Gender and Sustainable Development. Online: <http://www.royalroads. ca/ste/research/gender/AB_Live1.html>. Retrieved 25 May 2003.

Issac, Thomas. *Aboriginal Law: Cases, Materials and Commentary*, 2nd ed. Saskatoon: Purich Publishing, 1999.

Lambrecht, Kirk N. *The Administration of Dominion Lands, 1870-1930*. Regina: Canadian Plains Research Center, 1991.

Manitoba. Manitoba Conservation. Environmnetal Stewardship Division. Sustainable Resource Management Branch. Online: <http:// www.gov. mb.ca/conservation/susresmb/principle-susdev/index.html>. Retrieved 2 February 2003.

McLeod, Brenda V. "Treaty Land Entitlement in Saskatchewan: Conflicts in Land Use and Occupancy in the Witchekan Lake Area." Unpublished Thesis, University of Saskatchewan, 2001.

National Round Table on the Environment and the Economy. *Aboriginal Communities and Non-Renewable Resource Development*. Ottawa: National Round Table on the Environment and the Economy, 2001.

Ouellette, Grace. *The Fourth World: An Indigenous Perspective on Feminism and Aboriginal Women's Activism*. Halifax: Fernwood Publishing, 2002.

Shiva, Vandana. *Staying Alive: Women, Ecology and Development*. New Jersey: Zed Books, 1987.

Tough, Frank. *"As Their Natural Resources Fail": Native Peoples and the Economic History of Northern Manitoba, 1870-1930.* Vancouver: University of British Columbia Press, Press, 1996.

Voyageur, Cora J. "Contemporary Aboriginal Women in Canada." *Visions of the Heart: Canadian Aboriginal Issues,* 2nd ed. Eds. David Long and Olive P. Dickason. Toronto: Harcourt Canada, 2000. 81-106.

Wackernagel, Mathias. "Framing the Sustainability Crisis: Getting From Concern to Action." October, 1997. Online: Sustainable Development Research Institute. Online: <http://www.sdri.ubc.ca/publications/discussion_papers.cfm>.

WINONA LADUKE

THIRD WORLD HOUSING DEVELOPMENT
AND INDIGENOUS PEOPLE IN NORTH AMERICA

HOMELESSNESS IS AN INDICE of under development and of lack of access
to capital and other resources with which to shelter one's family. Housing
is also a basic cornerstone for development work in any community, as the need
for food, clothing and shelter are prerequisites to the health and well-being
of a community. It is within this context that I have undertaken this profile
of housing initiatives in third world development, and their implications for
Native communities in North America.

Housing is a critical problem in Native communities in North America.
Many Indian people live in overcrowded conditions or in homes without
proper sewer and sanitation systems. In addition, the lack of infrastructure whether roads, electricity or sewers in many reservation communities
continues to mark a level of underdevelopment not present in adjacent
non-Indian communities. There are a great number of similarities between
Native communities in North America and third world communities
internationally. However, in terms of housing, one significant distinction
between North American Native communities and many poor communities
in the third world is the existence and prevalence of the so-called informal
housing sector. In many third world communities, the lack of access to land
and capital has meant that people have constructed shanty-towns, usually on
the outskirts of large cities. Many development organizations are working to
upgrade the housing of people in these areas. There is, of course, a so-called
informal housing sector in Native communities in Canada, but more prevalent
(largely in the past two decades) has been the emergence of federal housing
programs, so-called cluster and band or reserve housing. This type of housing
for Native people is a result of a colonial policy different from that in the third
world. These housing projects, similar to urban public housing projects, pose
a new set of problems and challenges to Native people.

While Native communities have distinct interests and needs in terms
of homes, and may not have an interest in replicating the amenities of the
dominant Euro-American society, most communities would like to have
modest homes, enough space for all family members, and adequate plumbing,
electricity or other services to fit their needs. The fact is, this is a dream, not

a reality in most Indian communities. However, the present conditions, and the basis from which we have to work to meet the need for shelter is a result of a long historic process of colonialism, and an underdevelopment process in which the Native communities and their ability to meet community housing needs have been adversely affected.

In the past 100 years, many Native communities have faced forced removals and relocations from their traditional territories and homes. This has had significant social, mental and economic consequences on these communities. The impact of forced relocation on Indigenous communities has come under discussion by the World Bank, an institution that has played a significant role in many relocations internationally. In outlining some resettlement guidelines for projects, The Bank has noted that

> The very nature of involuntary resettlement gives rise to special social and technical problems.... A feeling of powerlessness and alienation is often engendered in those who are relocated, especially when entire communities are uprooted from familiar surroundings. To the extent that pre-existing community structures and social networks disintegrate and tightly knit kin groups are dispersed to new relocations, social cohesion is weakened and the potential for productive group action is diminished. (Cernea 7)

Most Native communities are living with problems that began with the initial involuntary resettlement, whether it was 100 years ago or ten. Many Native communities are facing feelings of disempowerment and disorganization and are struggling to reorient and reorganize themselves to meet the challenges posed by the lack of a cohesive socio-political infrastructure.

The problems resulting from involuntary relocation have been further exacerbated by a number of governmental and sometimes donor/church initiatives. There have been two major facets of the new problem. First, the structure and resources of the community have been altered so that they no longer are able to meet local community needs in housing, food or other basic requirements. Second, communities and individuals have become dependent upon paternalistic institutions for many of their basic needs.

Pliny Fisk, of the Centre for Maximum Potential Building Systems, discusses the impact of colonialism on the ability of communities to house themselves. He notes, in a discussion of Miskito Indian communities in Puerto Cabezas, Nicaragua, that colonialism

> has resulted in a skills and equipment shift that no longer fully relates to the capabilities of the region. This gap between what is presently used, and what could be used is reflected in housing deficiencies, skills deficiencies and equipment mismatches which in the end culminates in an identifiable economic deficit in the region. (n.p.)

In other words, many communities are "outward facing." Skills are directed towards exterior job/economic interests and reservation resources are directed towards off-reservation markets. In the effort to regain control of housing on the reservation, Fisk and other practitioners have sought to rebuild internal infrastructures and alter the outward-facing economic and resource system.

A second significant problem is the emergence of dependency in many third world communities. This is also apparent in the Indian reservations and reserves. Michael Cemea, in The World Bank report, comments on the impact of the "dependency syndrome" on relocated villages. He notes:

> People subjected to relocation are prone to develop the syndrome of settler dependency if paternalistic help policies are applied.... Such policies discourage self-mobilization, and undermine the settlers commitment to self support and development. (7)

A key issue is mobilizing the participation of people who are affected by dependency for the purposes of self-determination and self-directed development. It is clear that the underlying social impacts of relocation and the resulting structural disorientation pose a long-term challenge for new development initiatives in the Native community.

These underlying problems have not been addressed by Canadian and U.S. federal initiatives undertaken in the past 20 years to mitigate the problem of homelessness. Housing initiatives undertaken by such organizations as the Canadian Mortgage and Housing Corporation (CMHC), Housing and Urban Development (HUD) and other federal agencies are essentially "top-down" programs, and as a result, have in many cases been mismatched with local values, land use patterns and needs, and reinforce problems of dependency and feelings of powerlessness.

These problems are illustrated in a case study done on the Grassy Narrows Reserve in Ontario by a group of CMHC consultants. The study, entitled "A Culturally Sensitive Approach to Planning and Design with Native Canadians," offers insight into a recent relocation and a new housing program in a Native community.

The Ojibway sense of community derives from the cultural and kinship bonds of a group of people, not necessarily from physical proximity. Historically, many Ojibway or Anishinabeg people have lived most of the year at hunting, trapping or harvesting camps in the bush, returning to a major village for the purposes of trading and ceremonial activities. The European concept of community is quite different from this, and is derived primarily from the proximity of a number of houses to a central village and commercial or cultural centre. Anthropologists have termed the Ojibway community "dispersed settlement pattern," compared to the "urban" or "concentrated" settlement patterns of European communities.

With the contamination of their water and food supplies by mercury leaching from the Reid paper plant at Dryden, the Grassy Narrows community was forced to relocate. Centralized water and sewage systems were developed by the Canadian government, and new houses were built for the community. As A. G. Leslie, chief of the Agencies Division of the Department of Indian Affairs and Northern Development (DIAND) remarks,

> It is desirable that housing on Indian reserves be on a community planned basis so that all services such as stores, schools, etc. will form part of the housing community. Many times in the past, houses have been constructed for the convenience of the individual, and when we try to provide roads, water and sewage systems, it is a most difficult problem. (qtd. in Simon 65)

The new project, based on the economies of scale, is contrary to the Anishinabeg sense of community and space. This has caused social problems and a disruption of order. The people feared "losing the traditional way of life and were disturbed by the design of the new village, with its prefabricated buildings laid out in symmetrical patterns of congestion. They debated the advantages and disadvantages. The people were proud of the old village. It had been built by them."

Today, people speak with regret of leaving the old community, and with a helplessness toward what has been imposed on them from the outside.

> On the old reserve, your closest neighbour was maybe a quarter of a mile away. What we don't have now is space. When you are all bunched up like we are now, problems start. We're too crowded, too close. We don't live like the White man, that's not our way. The white man lives close together, but we don't. We like to live far apart in families. (qtd. in Simon 69-70)

While the case study is of one Ojibway reserve in Ontario, the implications are accurate for many Indian communities. The governmental housing initiatives of the 1960s to the present have had the effect of moving many people into identical HUD houses in close proximity. The programs have met the technical requirements of providing housing for the Indian community, but have caused a social and physical disruption of the economic, cultural, political and social aspects of the community at the same time.

The year 1988 was declared by the United Nations as the International Year for Shelter for the Homeless (IYSH), and as such generated a great deal of discussion and work internationally on the problem of homelessness. A home is one of the last vestiges of self-determination. To have the ability to determine the plan and location of a home are a basic exercise of a personal right to self-determination. The United Nations, in its General Assembly Resolution on the IYSH, also looked at homelessness as a part of an overall series of social and economic problems. The IYSH recognized that "the housing shortage and the situation of the shelterless is not really a disease, but rather a symptom of the larger dimension of poverty." It is within that context that most work in this discussion appears to fall.

In the study on housing, from which this paper is derived, the researcher reviewed development literature, consultants' work, United Nation documents, and the work of a number of international organizations concerned with housing and construction. A number of themes underlie the overall discussion. These include:

1. *The relationship between landlessness and homelessness.* Millions of people, including millions of Indigenous people, continue to be dispossessed of their land on a yearly basis. Others cannot gain access to land because of laws, economic interests or other institutions that restrict or have expropriated access. This problem is international, and is within the borders of the U.S. as well. In the Native community, the present dispossession of groups like the Dine of Big Mountain (and their pending forced relocation to urban areas like Flaggstaff) has been documented as a cause of homelessness. In the non-Indian community, the plight of rural farm families and the subsequent relocation of these families to urban areas is also an indication of the relationship between landlessness and homelessness. We cannot address one issue without the other.

2. *Homelessness is intimately related to other issues such as poverty.* Housing initiatives that have the most success (in this survey) were combined with integrated community development initiatives. Critical issues such as access to credit, infrastructure, community education, organizational and individual empowerment and employment all need to be addressed in consonance with housing for the effort to have a long-term successful impact on the community.

3. *The most successful housing initiatives are those which are highly participatory.* Top-down, "donor controlled" housing initiatives exacerbate the problem of powerlessness and disenfranchisement of the already disenfranchised. The more participation by homeowners, community groups and other community members in the project, the more linkages in the project and the stronger the potential for its success.

4. A *critical and often overlooked issue in housing development is the role of women.* The IYSH noted that 15 million people die annually from malnutrition and disease, and that the highest incidence of this is in slums. These deaths are directly related to inadequate shelter, water supply and inadequate waste disposal. Women and children are the

majority in these areas. And women in particular, because of their double and triple workloads (and lack of access to political power, money, skills and other resources), are least likely to be able to make improvements in their shelter conditions. In many cases, women and children are those who stay the most significant portion of time in these "shelters." Integrated and comprehensive shelter strategies are needed, with special emphasis on women and their meaningful participation.

5. Sustainable housing development strategies are intimately linked with use of ecologically sound technologies and local resources, whether physical or human, and as a part of an overall integrated development program.

Originally published in Canadian Woman Studies/les cahiers de la femme's *issue on "Women and Housing" 11 (2) (1990): 12-14. Reprinted with permission of the author.*

Winona LaDuke, an Ojibway from White Earth Reservation in Minnesota, is an activist, environmentalist, economist, and writer. She is currently the Executive Director of both Honor the Earth and White Earth Land Recovery Project.

REFERENCES

Cernea, Michael, "Involuntary Resettlement in Development Projects Policy Guidelines in World Bank Financed Projects" World Bank Technical Paper Number 80 (1988).

Fisk, Pliny, "Indigenous Building Systems for the Miskito Community of the Atlantic Coast of Nicaragua." Centre for Maximum Potential Building Systems. Austin, TX [Mimeo], 1985.

Simon, J. C. et al. "A Culturally Sensitive Approach to Planning and Design with Native Canadians." Ottawa: Canadian Mortgage and Housing Corporation, External Research Program, August 1984.

ELIZABETH BASTIEN

MATRIMONIAL REAL PROPERTY SOLUTIONS

MATRIMONIAL REAL PROPERTY (MRP) refers to the house or land that a couple occupies or benefits from while they are married or living in a common-law relationship. Provincial and territorial family law sets out standards and processes for the disposition of matrimonial real property following the breakdown of a marriage or common-law relationship. The Supreme Court of Canada ruled in *Derrickson v. Derrickson*, [1986] that these provincial and territorial family laws do not apply to land located on First Nations reserves. The federal *Indian Act* also does not contain any direction that applies to MRP on these lands. This gap in the law has had serious consequences, especially for Indigenous women who experience the breakdown of their marriage or common-law relationship.

The Native Women's Association of Canada (NWAC) has advocated for a resolution to the matrimonial real property situation for over twenty years. During this time extensive research on MRP has been published, including reports by the Standing Senate Committee on Human Rights (Government of Canada 2003), the Standing Committee on the Status of Women (Government of Canada 2006), and the Royal Commission on Aboriginal Peoples. Unfortunately, the extent of the federal government's activity on this issue was limited to the publication of research. Other interested parties took action: NWAC filed a lawsuit against Canada alleging that the legislative gap on MRP violates the human rights of Aboriginal women that are guaranteed by the *Canadian Charter of Rights and Freedoms*. As well, some First Nations addressed the issue of matrimonial real property through various mechanisms including Band Administration Housing Policies or Band Council By-Laws,[1] Land Codes and/or Matrimonial Real Property Codes under the *First Nations Land Management Act* (INAC 2004) or under Self-Government Agreements.[2] The number of communities that enacted such policies, codes, or by-laws has been limited, and the federal government has not recognized the authority of actions that do not fall within the purview of the *Indian Act* or other legislation (INAC 2006b).

In 2006, the federal government worked with stakeholders to design and implement a process to develop consensus on solutions to the MRP issue in

First Nations communities. On September 29, 2006, the Department of Indian and Northern Affairs Canada (INAC), NWAC, and the Assembly of First Nations (AFN) jointly announced an initiative to develop MRP solutions. This announcement marked the beginning of a series of consultation and dialogue sessions on MRP conducted by each of the three parties across Canada. The Minister of Indian and Northern Affairs appointed a Ministerial Representative to be responsible for facilitating the process of developing solutions based on the findings of the consultation and dialogue sessions, and for preparing and submitting a report with recommendations to the Minister. These recommendations were to indicate the consensus reached by NWAC, the AFN, and INAC if possible: if consensus could not be reached, then the Ministerial Representative was responsible for making recommendations to the Minister on the best way forward. Although INAC stated that the goal of the process was "identifying and implementing a mutually acceptable solution" (INAC 2006a) the federal government also noted in a media backgrounder document prepared for the launch that their objective was "to introduce a legislative solution in the House of Commons in the spring of 2007" (INAC 2006a). This focus on one particular approach by the federal government at the start of the consultation and dialogue process provided an early forewarning of an already determined outcome, and perhaps makes it less surprising that the consensus process eventually failed.

NWAC, the AFN, and INAC received submissions and conducted meetings, interviews, and sessions with their respective constituents from October 2006 to January 2007. A Working Group consisting of representatives from each organization met on a regular basis throughout this period to investigate in greater depth specific issues associated with MRP. The Ministerial Representative also convened expert panels on topics including land management systems and family law, which the Working Group representatives were invited to attend. It should be noted that the sessions, focus groups, and workshops organized by NWAC and the AFN were attended by a representative from INAC: however, the organizations funded by INAC to hold independent sessions or workshops were not required to invite NWAC or the AFN representatives to those meetings, although a record of their findings was provided to NWAC in the first quarter of 2007.[3]

NWAC used its funding to meet with Aboriginal women across Canada to hear first-hand their voices and experiences. NWAC was careful to ensure that the ideas for solutions came from women who had personal experience with MRP, and reflected their experiences, knowledge, and culture. While many women were interested in contributing their views, various factors prevented their full participation. The limited timeframe for the sessions to be conducted—only four months between October 2006 and January 2007—combined with winter weather conditions made travel and attendance difficult. Women living in remote or isolated communities found it costly to make travel arrangements on short notice, and women who needed to arrange childcare or an absence from work also experienced difficulties due to the short timeframes. Many women expressed frustration with the limited window available to them to become familiar with the options under consideration: they advised NWAC that they needed more time to reflect, discuss, and consider the implications before providing an opinion. Some women feared that engaging in the discussion process would jeopardize their personal safety or security, or their job tenure. NWAC made every effort to help women to participate safely and ensure that their privacy was respected. Even so, attending a session may have placed some women at risk, and the decision to participate could not be guaranteed to be a private matter. The women who did manage to participate told NWAC that they saw value in the process, but were concerned that the voices of many other women were not being heard (NWAC 2007).

The issues and concerns that women reported to NWAC around MRP were grouped into six key themes: the intergenerational impacts of colonization; violence; justice and access to legal services; accessibility of supports for women and children, especially those who move away from the reserve; communication and education; and legislation, but not as a stand-alone tool (NWAC 2007). NWAC clearly and consistently heard from the women that solutions must address both the lack of legislation that directly affected women's ability to remain in the family home and the lack of non-legislative supports for women facing MRP issues. Women expressed concern about losing their opportunities and rights that residence on-reserve made possible for the individual, and identified specific circumstances that negatively affected their ability to access legal or other remedies. Women who could only find housing off-reserve after the end of their marriage or relationship spoke of their loss of access to Band administered programs and services, as well as their loss of access to family, culture, language, and community. These difficulties were especially acute for women who lived in remote, northern, or isolated communities, where the cost of transportation, seasonal limitations on travel, and the limited availability of programs and services provided additional barriers. NWAC found that women generally expressed only muted support for the use of federal legislation to address MRP in the short term, until the First Nations were able to put their own legislation into place.

NWAC developed a series of short, medium, and long-term solutions to address each of these six key areas of concern identified by Aboriginal women. The intergenerational impacts of colonization require solutions that address membership and citizenship issues, the use of a culturally relevant gender-based analysis, and repatriation programs and redress for the lack of protections women and their families experienced under the *Indian Act*. Solutions for issues associated with violence against women include measures such as increased transitional, affordable, and emergency housing, and the use of collective, culturally relevant approaches to resolving conflict. Improvements in access to justice include an assessment of the impact of MRP measures implemented under the *First Nations Land Management Act*, training for legal professionals, and the implementation of alternative dispute resolution practices where appropriate. Increasing communication and education for Aboriginal women and their communities about MRP was also identified as a key area for improvement, as was ensuring that Aboriginal women could access programs and supports, both on and off-reserve, including those women who live in remote, rural, or isolated communities. It was entirely clear to NWAC after talking to Aboriginal women across Canada that MRP, and by extension the opportunities and rights that living in the family home made possible, encompassed a wider set of issues than simple possession or compensation for investments.

NWAC brought these messages from Aboriginal women forward to the Working Group meetings that continued throughout the spring of 2007. Following these meetings the Ministerial Representative submitted her report to the Minister of Indian and Northern Affairs in March 2007: it contained comprehensive recommendations for action but also reflected the lack of consensus on key points between the three stakeholder organizations. Despite this initial lack of consensus, the three organizations indicated that they were willing to continue working on MRP issues, so a series of meetings continued for the balance of 2007. It later became evident that the rationale for continued participation was not based on the same premise for all three organizations. NWAC and the AFN reviewed draft legislation put forward by INAC and continued to advocate for non-legislative solutions and changes to the approach that would reflect the concerns of their constituents and respect traditional First Nations practices, laws, and governance. INAC, however, was solely interested in moving forward draft federal legislation on MRP. Considerable effort was expended on reviewing draft materials put forward by INAC in an attempt to ensure the content met standards that included the duty to consult, respecting Aboriginal rights, the equality of women and men, international law, the *Canadian Human Rights Act*, First Nations sovereignty, and First Nations laws. NWAC raised concerns about the provision of resources and capacity for First Nations to enact their own legislation, and further suggested that federal legislation should include an opt-out clause for First Nations who developed their own MRP laws.

At the same time, NWAC continued to press for non-legislative solutions. Legal rights do not exist in a vacuum, and a solely legislative solution would not be sufficient to assist Aboriginal women who could not access justice because of poverty, the effects of systemic oppression, or geographic isolation. Despite the ongoing insistence of NWAC and the AFN that the proposed draft legislation was not adequate as a stand-alone solution, the federal government continued to focus on this to the exclusion of other options. INAC representatives were unable to discuss in any concrete terms implementation options or other solutions that would assist Aboriginal women, although they acknowledged that implementation measures were being designed by the federal government, in isolation from the Working Group process.

This failure of the policy development process to achieve agreement could perhaps have been foreseen, given the short timeframe and other limitations placed on the initiative as well as the stated objective of the federal government at the time the initiative was announced. At a meeting in January 2008, the INAC representatives advised the other parties at the table that the federal government would soon introduce a federal bill on MRP. The INAC representatives stated that any further input provided by NWAC and the AFN would not influence the federal bill: given this check on their effectiveness NWAC representatives declined to be involved any further in a process that they no longer saw as viable or effective. On March 4, 2008, the federal government tabled Bill C-47: *An Act respecting family homes situated on First Nation reserves and matrimonial interests or rights in or to structures and lands situated on those reserves* (Government of Canada 2007).

What began as a joint policy initiative ended as a unilateral announcement by the federal government of new legislation. In stark contrast to the tripartite announcement at the beginning of the MRP initiative in September 2006, the Minister of Indian and Northern Affairs announced the introduction of MRP legislation in March 2008 without the presence or support of any of the other stakeholders. This clearly demonstrated how INAC's decision to move ahead with one specific action despite recommendations to the contrary by the two other parties in the process caused the loss of support for the initiative by NWAC and the AFN. An analysis of the overall process and the impacts and outcomes of engaging in it for each organization will have to wait until it is known whether Bill C-47 will be passed, what the full extent of the government implementation plans associated with the legislation will be, and how the participating organizations and First Nations react to the end results. At this point in time, it appears that NWAC and the AFN may have overestimated how much influence and input into the process they could achieve, as well as the extent to which the federal government intended to use their input to develop and shape the policy outcomes. In turn, the federal government may have underestimated the extent to which NWAC and the AFN would engage in the process, as well as the extent to which they were able to identify shared goals and principles. The INAC representatives may also not have expected to face such a unified opposition, nor one that was so well-informed.

NWAC continues to recommend that the implementation of MRP legislation must be accompanied by non-legislative solutions that address the intergenerational effects of colonization, access to justice, reduction of violence, communication and education about MRP, and the accessibility of supports for Aboriginal women both on and off-reserve. Despite the lessons learned while participating in this process over the past year, NWAC believes that the potential benefits that could be achieved for Aboriginal women require the organization to continue to work at improving the federal government's approach to MRP. NWAC suggests that the federal government re-engage all those involved in the initial process to complete further consultations with First Nations communities that includes women, elders, youth, and leaders in those communities. In addition, an appropriate implementation plan that includes non-legislative options, adequate resources, and a capacity building process that will support and enhance the proposed MRP legislation must also be created, in order to fulfill the promise of the initial announcement of a tripartite process to devise solutions to Matrimonial Real Property.

Originally published in Canadian Woman Studies/les cahiers de la femme, *"Indigenous Women in Canada: The Voices of First Nations, Inuit and Métis Women," 26 (3 & 4) (Winter/Spring 2008): 90-93 Reprinted with permission of the author.*

Elizabeth Bastien is a member of Wikwemikong Unceded First Nation. She joined the Native Women's Association of Canada in 2006 to work on the MRP initiative following the completion of her Master's in public policy from Simon Fraser University. Elizabeth is currently working on NWAC's Sisters in Spirit initiative.

[1]For example, the Squamish Nation *Housing Policy* (2001, revised 2003).
[2]For example, the Westbank First Nation Self-Government Agreement between Her Majesty the Queen in Right of Canada and Westbank First Nation.
[3]The organizations that conducted sessions included the Advisory Council of Treaty 6 Women, the Assembly of Manitoba Chiefs, the National Association of Friendship Centres, the Nishnawbe Aski Nation Women's Council and the Congress of Aboriginal Peoples.

REFERENCES

Derrickson v. Derrickson, [1986] 1 S.C.R. 285. Online: <http://scc.lexum. umontreal.ca/en/1986/1986rcs1-285/1986rcs1-285.html>. Accessed: 10 March 2008.
Government of Canada. *A Hard Bed to Lie In: Matrimonial Real Property on Reserve.* 2003. Standing Senate Committee on Human Rights. Ottawa. Online: <http://www.parl.gc.ca/37/2/parlbus/commbus/senate/Com-e/ huma-e/10app2-e.pdf>. Accessed: 10 March 2008.
Government of Canada. House of Commons. Seventh Report, Standing Committee on the Status of Women. 39th Parliament, 1st Session. 2006. Online: <http://cmte.parl.gc.ca/Content/HOC/committee/391/fewo/re-ports/rp2311018/FEWO_Rpt07-e.html#TopOfPage>. Accessed: 10 March 2008.
Government of Canada. Bill C-47: *An Act respecting family homes situated on First Nation reserves and matrimonial interests or rights in or to structures and lands situated on those reserves.* 39th Parliament, 2nd Session. 16 October 2007. Online: <http://www.parl.gc.ca/legisinfo/index.asp?Language=E&L

ist=list&Type=0&Chamber=C&StartList=2&EndList=200&Session=15>. Accessed: 10 March 2008.

Indian and Northern Affairs Canada. (INAC). *First Nations Land Management Act*. 2004. Online: <http://www.ainc-inac.gc.ca/pr/pub/matr/fnl_e.html>. Accessed: 10 March 2008.

Indian and Northern Affairs Canada. (INAC). "Backgrounder: On-Reserve Matrimonial Real Property." 2006a. Online: <http://www.ainc-inac.gc.ca/wige/mrp/cnp_e.html>. Accessed: 10 March 2008.

Indian and Northern Affairs Canada. (INAC). "First Nation Law-making Activity." 2006b. Online: <http://www.ainc-inac.gc.ca/wige/mrp/fni_e.html>. Accessed: 10 March 2008.

Native Women's Association of Canada. (NWAC). *Reclaiming Our Way of Being: Matrimonial Real Property Solutions. People's Report: "What We Heard."* Ottawa: NWAC, 2007.

Royal Commission on Aboriginal Peoples. *Report of the Royal Commission on Aboriginal Peoples*. 1986. Online: <http://www.ainc-inac.gc.ca/ch/rcap/sg/sgmm_e.html>. Accessed: 10 March 2008.

Westbank First Nation Self-Government Agreement between Her Majesty the Queen in Right of Canada and Westbank First Nation. 2003. Online: <http://www.ainc-inac.gc.ca/nr/prs/s-d2003/wst_e.pdf>. Accessed: 10 March 2008.

ACTIVISM

MONIQUE MOJICA

AN INVOCATION/INCANTATION TO THE
WOMEN WORD-WARRIORS FOR CUSTOM-MADE SHOES

International Women's Day 1989
No, I didn't go to the march
feelings of ambivalence,
rage
time to free up some fury
unstick some spit and piss and vinegar
place them in a sacred manner
around me
unearthed unshrouded
Because even our rage must be given its due respect.

It's International Women's Day.
A Black voice echoes:
Ain't I a woman?

… unanswered.

time to roll up the chunks of hurt
resentment/rejection
like so much mucus
congested accumulated
Over the decades of trying to fit into feminist shoes.

O.K., I'm trying on the shoes; but they're not the same
as the shoes in the display case. The shoes I'm trying
on must be crafted to fit these wide, square brown
feet. I must be able to feel the earth through their soles.

So, it's International Women's Day, and here I am among
the women of the theatre community — my community.
Now, I'd like you to take a good look — I don't want to

185

be mistaken for a crowd of Native women. I am one. And
I do not represent all Native women. I am one.

And since it can get kinda lonely up here, I've brought
some friends, sisters, guerrilleras — the women word-warriors,[1]
to help fill up the space.

I've brought *Chrystos* to tell you that:
"I am not your princess...
I am only willing to tell you how to make frybread
1 cup flour, spoon of salt, spoon of baking powder
Stir Add milk or water or beer until it holds together
Slap piece into rounds Let rest
Fry in hot grease until golden." [2]

I've brought *Cherrie* to let you know that:
"...the concept of betraying one's race through
sex and sexual politics is as common as corn." [3]

I've asked *Gloria* to come to say:
What I want is an accounting with all three
cultures — white, Mexican, Indian. I want the freedom
to carve and chisel my own face, to
staunch the bleeding with ashes, to fashion my own
gods out of my entrails. And if going home is
denied me, then I will have to stand and claim my
space, making a new culture — una cultura mestiza —
with my own lumber, my own bricks and mortar and
my own feminist architecture.

I've brought *Diane* to describe that to hold a brown- skinned lover means:
"We embrace and rub
the wounds together."

She also says:
"This ain't no stoic look.
This is my face." [4]

There is a Cheyenne saying that:
A Nation is not conquered
Until the hearts
of its women
are on the ground.

I dedicate my presence here tonight to my two sons; to
Bear who is here on the earth with me and to
Yocallwarawara who has passed over to the other side.
I thank them for the gifts and the teachings they have brought me.
It is for them, and for the unborn generations that I am here
wearing shoes that have not yet molded to my feet and
asking *Lillian*[5] to set a place for me at her tea party.

A Nation is not conquered
Until the hearts
of its women
are on the ground.

Nya weh —
Nuedi

This monologue was written for hosting Fern-Cab, the Five-Minute Feminist Cabaret, March 1989.

Originally published in Canadian Woman Studies/les cahiers de la femme, *"Native Women," 10 (2 & 3) (Summer/Fall 1989): 40. Reprinted with permission of the author.*

Monique Mojica is an actor and published playwright from the Kuna and Rappahannock nations. Her play "Princess Pocahontas and the Blue Spots" was produced by Nightwood Theatre and Theatre Passe Muraille in 1990, on radio by CBC and published by Women's Press in 1991. She is the co-editor, with Ric Knowles, of Staging Coyote's Dream: An Anthology of First Nations Drama in English, *Vols. I & II (Playwrights Canada Press). Monique is a long-time collaborator with Floyd Favel on various research and performance projects investigating Native Performance Culture. She was also he Artist in Residence for American Indian Studies at the University of Illinois in Spring 2008. She continues to explore art as healing, as an act of reclaiming historical/cultural memory and as an act of resistance.*

[1]From Paula Gunn Allen, *The Sacred Hoop*, Beacon Press, 1986.
[2]Chrystos, from *Not Vanishing*, Press Gang, 1988.
[3]Cherríe Moraga, from *Loving in the War Years*, South End Press, 1983.
[4]Diane Burns, from *Riding the one-eyed Ford*, Contact II Publications, 1981.
[5]See Lillian Allen's album, *Revolutionary Tea Party*.

LYNN M. MEADOWS, WILFREDA E. THURSTON AND LAURA E. LAGENDYK

ABORIGINAL WOMEN AT MIDLIFE

Grandmothers as Agents of Change

ABORIGINAL WOMEN PLAY A vital role in the health of their communities and families as mothers, workers, and community leaders (Health Canada). Yet, in spite of that growing body of knowledge at a population health level, the local contexts and causality of health disparities that affect the day-to-day well-being of Aboriginal women in this population are under-researched and poorly understood. While there is no lack of documentation on the multiple oppressions experienced by Aboriginal people and the effect of those oppressions on health and well-being (Romanow; Stout and Kipling; Tjepkema; Young; Cardinal, Schopflocher, Svenson, Morrison, and Laing), as well as on the particular vulnerabilities of Aboriginal women who have high rates of multiple risk factors including poverty, violence and substance abuse (Colman; Romanow; Stout, Kipling, and Stout), strategies for advocacy and action to improve Aboriginal women's health continue to lack the relevancy and community grounding needed to remedy the current situation (Thurston and Potvin). Including Aboriginal perspectives about the underlying factors that affect their health, such as social context (e.g., racism and socio-economic differences), are critical (Ellerby, McKenzie, McKay, Gariépy, and Kaufert; O'Neil, Reading, and Leader) but often overlooked (Young) as plans for health interventions or community programs are developed. Furthermore, women's perspectives may also be overlooked if a gendered analysis and inclusion of women is not deliberate (Deiter and Otway; Dickson; Gittelsohn *et al.*; Sayers and MacDonald; Anderson).

Our study of midlife Aboriginal women thus focused on the question, "What are the mechanisms through which health determinants affect women's day-to-day experiences of well-being?" We sought women's narratives that described their health and the life circumstances that affected it, and wanted to provide an opportunity for descriptions of a holistic view of health focused on physical, spiritual, and emotional well-being (Svenson and Lafontaine). In our study of over 40 women in several Aboriginal communities, there is evidence to suggest that women who focus on the future for either themselves or their grandchildren may be change agents that help improve health not only for themselves but for their families and communities as well.

DESIGN AND METHODS

This qualitative study used elements from ethnography (Creswell) to explore Aboriginal women's experiences and perceptions of health and well-being at midlife, defined in our program of research as ages 40 through 65 years. The Conjoint Health Research Ethics Board at the University of Calgary granted approval for the research. Techniques to enhance the rigor of the study included methodological congruence and methodological purposiveness (Meadows, Verdi, and Crabtree; Morse and Richard). Strategies of ensuring validity included situating the study in the literature, bracketing, sampling strategies, and methodological cohesion (Meadows and Morse; Meadows, Verdi, and Crabtree; Patton).

In each location in which we spoke with women, permission for data collection was obtained through a process of community engagement and review by the appropriate authorities (Meadows, Lagendyk, Thurston, and Eisener). Purposive sampling was used to include women both on and off reserves, in rural and urban areas (Kuzel) with potential participants identified using multiple strategies (Meadows, Lagendyk, Thurston, and Eisener) such as attending health fairs, snowball sampling (Kuzel) and opportunistic encounters. Aboriginal and non-Aboriginal interviewers were employed to conduct the group and individual interviews using an interview guide that was revised as new issues arose or contexts differed. Where possible, interviews were audio recorded with permission of the participants, and transcribed verbatim. Textual data were read into a qualitative analytic software program (QSRN6®) to aid in data summary, management and analysis (Meadows and Dodendorf). The multidisciplinary research team met frequently to discuss the analysis, contributing to within-project validation (Denzin; Kuzel and Like; Lincoln and Guba; Meadows and Morse). Data analysis and interpretation progressed through a number of stages: immersion/crystallization to identify general issues and topics (Borkan; Crabtree and Miller 1999a); identification of relationships and the contingencies that affected them among identified areas; and further examination for alternative interpretations, to reconcile discrepancies, and situate interpretation in the literature (Borkan; Crabtree and Miller 1999b; Meadows, Verdi, and Crabtree).

RESULTS

The data used in this analysis were collected in group, focus group, and individual interviews conducted in English with over 40 women who lived in a variety of locations including on reserves and in urban or rural areas throughout Alberta. We found that women's discussion of health and wellness, consistent with existing data, was not always merely individual but connected to their community and their family (Meadows, Thurston, and Melton; Adelson; Svenson and LaFontaine).

One of the most strikingly different aspects of this study compared to our previous research in midlife women's health (Meadows, Thurston, and Berenson; Meadows, Thurston, and Melton; Meadows and Mrkonjic) was that many of the participants were grandmothers[1] and great-grandmothers at what seemed to us a relatively young age. For many of the women interviewed, assuming the role of grandmother was marked by reflection that included consideration of their own well-being as well as that of their families. Women also reported committing to decisions that enhanced their well-being such as seeking formal training or education to give them tools for change and expand the choices in their lives. Some explored traditional knowledge and ways, and began to teach others in their communities about them as a way of healing. Women illustrated a strong positive role in promoting well-being within themselves, within their families and within their communities.

RACISM AND CULTURAL HARM

The Aboriginal women in our study talked about health in the context of residential schools[2] and their ongoing sequelae. The great harm and multigenerational effect on physical, spiritual, and emotional well-being of children being torn from their families of origin was evident throughout the data. Some of the experiences were personal and direct such as feelings of constant hunger and sparse meals of "burnt porridge and sour milk," being forced to scrub floors with toothbrushes, having their knuckles scrubbed until they bled, and being humiliated over natural processes such as the onset of menstruation. Several women also reported experiences of sexual abuse. Others spoke of the cultural harm perpetrated at the residential schools by being forbidden to speak their own languages and instead forced to learn and speak English. Many of the women who attended residential schools reported the schools' minimal emphasis on formal academic education, often stopped at grade eight or earlier. Although some women credited the schools with teaching them the basics of housekeeping, personal hygiene and self-discipline, many felt the schools limited women's education through emphasis on non-academic skills.

It took women years to recognize and overcome these experiences, and many felt their understanding of what had happened to them came too late for them to be able to make a difference in the lives of their own children.

> *I wasn't told anything about parenting, being a parent. I didn't know how to be a parent. And then, when I was on my journey, I did find out that what I missed at the school was "love." How to love another person.... I was in that school for eight years, and I was very lonely growing up. I was sexually abused in the residential school.* (Mary)

Women talked about the consequences of their experiences that resulted in adult addictions and a perceived inability to parent well, and how they saw their actions as having consequences for the lives and well-being of their children and grandchildren.

> *I put my daughter and my older kids into all this alcohol scene. I was drinking at that time and, and I used to come home drunk, you know, and I used to yell at them and everything. They were terrified of, you know, of me. But, now, I don't drink. I don't do anything. I'm trying to be a good mother. Whereas I should have done that when I was young. Right from the start. But that's where the residential school has a ripple effect on our children. Like, my grandchildren still feel that effect. 'Cause I didn't teach my kids parenting. I started to learn [parenting] as an adult....* (Mary)

Even women who did not attend residential schools were able to critically reflect on the more subtle, indirect effects for subsequent generations.

> *When I asked [Mom] about her experience, she said that she never experienced anything really negative in school. But as a child, as her child now, I think, yes, she did experience some things. But she doesn't recognize, you know, what it was. And some of the things that I've picked out of that, is like, for instance, not teaching us the language. I think that has a lot to do with her experiences with the school system. As well as, um, hugging! Like hugging's something that, I'm sure as Native people we had before ... it's just something that she doesn't realize what was taken away from her.* (Barb)

Many women spoke of the lack of respect for Aboriginal ways of life and perceived or visible differences between Aboriginal and non-Aboriginal people, sometimes exacerbated by socioeconomic circumstances, and the ways in which this impacts their sense of well-being.

> *We were one of two Indian families that lived in the town and that was really, really not a great experience cause we suffered a lot of discrimination and whatnot. So that wasn't great but also being kinda from a poorer family it was tough... not having what everybody else had and, you know, not even having the proper equipment and supplies and whatnot that we needed for school and all of that kind of thing.* (Doreen)

Some women recalled struggles to deal with a hostile and racist environment and the challenges of mastering school work or obtaining higher education in their youth.

> *...[B]ecause we were stupid Indians, my cousin and I wanted to take matric [university entrance courses] and we were told "Natives just do general programs." And my cousin and I said, "We're taking matric. And,*

*we showed them.... So (small chuckle) I was very defiant. And I know I
carried this rage, and this anger for years.* (Marge)

Racism was common and also had direct implications for the women's physical health and well-being, as one participant indicated.

*When I lived in the city, this one doctor, would give you, he'd just always
give prescription for pills ... basically like, "Just get out of my office," you
know? Who cares? "Who cares that you're got a hole in your lip, and your
eye's black," you know? He didn't even check to see if I had eye damage or
anything, just wrote me up these prescriptions for drugs....And, I told him
[how I got the injuries] ... he just right away wrote me a prescription ...
which I threw in the garbage as I walked out of his office.* (Cilli)

As women reflected on how these experiences affected their lives and their well-
being they revealed how these attitudes and behaviours persist even today.

*If you are exposed to racist comments enough times, I think it affects your
self-esteem. Even my own daughter experienced it already. And, I, you
know, as her mother, I have to explain to her that there are people out
there that see different, [that see us] as different, and they can't accept that
it is anything similar. So ... she even said to these girls one day, they were
calling her, [and] they said, "We don't like you because you're Native." And
she said, "But, you don't even know me." And they said, "So, you're just
Native, we don't need to know you."* (Barb)

Women described for us the life-long impact of cultural harm and racism
experiences, including in their encounters with people in both educational and
medical roles. Thus, those who could potentially be health resources were at
times instead detriments to their health. Yet, at midlife many women recon-
ciled the experiences, moved past them, and were also determined to mediate
them for others.

(GRAND)MOTHERING

In our sample one 49-year-old woman already had 22 grandchildren and a
few women were great-grandmothers before their sixtieth birthday. Women's
narratives described their involvement with their grandchildren as a "new start,"
improving on their past parenting practices.

*It's my fault that you guys [referring to her children] don't know how to do
parenting, 'cause I didn't show you how.... And, it's not too late.... Sure
I didn't do that for you guys but I do accept it and I accepted the blame
but, it's never too late for me to start telling you how to take care of your
children.* (Mary)

Women also described how their relationship with their grandchildren was different from the relationship they had with their children:

> *The elderly say, "Once you become a grandparent, you love your kids but there's a greater love with your grandchildren." And I see that now.* (Millie)

> *My kids always get jealous of my grandson, hey?* (Clara)

> *The only difference between a grandmother and a mother, is the grandmother didn't have the labour having the baby, and they get the labour* after *the baby (laughs).* (Dorothy)

Some women took on a parenting role for their grandchildren because their own children did not have the means (whether for health reasons, addictions, or low-income) to care for the children themselves. As they cared for their grandchildren, some women struggled with memories of separation from their parents while at residential school.

> *I don't know what to do. I don't want to let him go, yet I feel that he should be with his mother. Because, he'll be going through what I went through. Not being, you know, being at the school [and] not being with my mom. We had no bond. That's what I feel like, you know. Maybe I should let him go back. But, then she [boy's mother] will leave him all over the place [because she won't be able to take care of him].* (Mary)

As women entered midlife, however, they took inventory and consciously made decisions that would enhance their well-being and help encourage the physical, spiritual, and emotional well-being of their families as well.

> *And that's what I want to be healthy for, cause I want to be around for my grandkids.... And, that's what I teach my grandchildren. I want to make sure that my grandchildren are very healthy. Are in good health. I don't want them to go through what I went through.* (Lila)

> *Oh, I just hope to be, to be healthy enough to enjoy my grandchildren. Because some of my little, my little granddaughters are shocked that I can even run. And, they find out I can run if I have to chase them. (Laughing) Oh, I have fun with them.* (Ila)

Some reflected on past practices and circumstances that were detrimental to their health that they changed after becoming a grandmother.

> *I used to drink, too. That is different when you start having grandchildren ... and especially when I'm a great grandma now.* (Dorothy)

When describing her past and her thoughts of suicide after the death of five of her seven children, one woman said:

> *I still look forward, look ahead, to old age. Because I'm not only thinking of myself, I'm thinking of my two sons, my grandchildren and now my great grandchildren. 'Cause they have nobody to call* Kokum *[grand-mother], if I decide to lay back and give up. Who's going to be there for them?* (Evonne)

Women's narratives demonstrated their desire to break old patterns themselves and work with their families and communities for change.

> *I'm helping other women understand their past. Where they came from. Their hurt, their pain. The abuse they witnessed. And that they can still be happy and content with their life and go on. And not the exact same cycle.* (Linda)

> *Oh we would learn lots of things, like how to ah, look after yourself ah, like how to be, and how to ah, oh, and then we were expected to come back home and teach our families. Other people listened to me, but my kids didn't.* (Elaine)

> *I take part in traditional ceremonies, so, that part of my upbringing, I still keep it and I'm passing it onto my two sons. And my grandchildren and now I have great grandchildren so, I'm more or less role modeling it because I don't want to lose it, I don't want my family to lose it.* (Evonne)

Ultimately women wanted to encourage a supportive environment that could promote and enhance the health and well-being of their families, their communities and themselves.

DISCUSSION

The findings of this study illustrate the complexity of the determinants of health across the lifespan as they have affected the health and well-being of our sample of Aboriginal women at midlife. For many of the women in our sample, positive influences on their healthy child development, educa-tion, physical environment, and culture were systematically eroded through experiences and institutional realities of their youth. Yet in midlife, women were using their gendered roles and their life knowledge to create positive experiences and environments that mediated these effects on their own well-being and that of their families and communities, allowing them to work toward healthier futures.

Previous research has shown that women can use adult insight to reconcile past experiences including abuse (Meadows, Thurston, and Lackner), evidenced again in the current study and stories the women shared with us. There was also evidence that women were tired of repetitive cycles of poverty, lack of education, and lost traditions, and that they were determined to redress the past through educating themselves and their families for the present and future.

In our study, women acknowledged the harmful effects of past experiences but they have also embraced attitudes and actions that celebrate future potential. These women saw that they had a second chance to be parents of a healthy Aboriginal community. They turned their primary attention to their grandchildren, but they continued to love and teach their own children, as well as pursue opportunities that enhanced their own health and well-being. Somehow the effects of discrimination and loss of traditional roots and values, and personal or family experiences with residential schools, substance abuse, violence or death have become an impetus to focus on a healthier approach to life and/or a decision to move beyond the past and into the future.

Kirmayer, Brass and Tait discuss at length the need for identity development and community empowerment in Aboriginal youth, as well as strategies to engage youth in community development. This study suggests that grandmothers may play an important role in creating the personal skills that youth will need in order to participate. The challenge is to recognize the potential these resourceful, strong, and determined women have and work with them in their communities. The increasing self-confidence apparent in some of the women with whom we talked has already increased their community capacity, but this needs to be systematically harnessed and joined with other assets in the community (whether people, resources or knowledge) (Thurston, Scott, and Vollman) to strengthen the existing social capital.[3]

There is an ongoing need for increased capacity building in Aboriginal communities, to add to the skills and competencies that women in our study have individually pursued at community levels (Thurston, Scott, and Vollman; Deiter and Otway; Dickson; Gittelsohn *et al.*; Sayers and MacDonald; van Uchelen, Davidson, Quressette, Brasfield, and Demerais; Voyageur; Walters and Simoni).

Among these communities, with their ongoing disparities in health and well-being, the grandmothers are pockets of resilience and improvement. These positive aspects of their lives and potential for health improvements should be complemented by formal resources for further education and partnering with health care professionals (Browne and Fiske; Browne and Smye; Colomeda and Wenzel; Stout and Kipling). In the process of health promotion and community mobilization, the history and consequences of colonialism must be acknowledged and taken into account, along with the other complex and interacting determinants of health such as gender (Moane; Deiter and Otway; Dickson). As community perspectives on health issues are identified, we can work with Aboriginal grandmothers as agents of change to move toward improved health and make positive change within communities sustainable.

This study was supported by a grant from the Alberta Heritage Foundation for Medical Research Health Research Fund. We thank the Aboriginal women and communities who worked with us on this study, our Aboriginal community interviewers, Donna Vukelic for her transcription, Amanda Eisener who provided important research assistance on the project, and Kathy Dirk, our project's co-ordinator.

Originally published in Canadian Woman Studies/les cahiers de la femme, *"Women's Health and Well-Being" 24 (1) (Fall 2004): 159-165. Reprinted with permission of the authors.*

Lynn M. Meadows is Associate Professor in the Department of Community Health Sciences at the University of Calgary and is currently Acting Graduate Education Co-ordinator. Wilfreda E. Thurston is Professor in the Department of Community Health Sciences, Faculty of Medicine; Adjunct Professor in the Faculty of Nursing; and Director of the Institute for Gender Research. Laura E. Lagendyk is employed in the Knowledge Management Department of Alberta Health Services.

[1]We are using "grandmother" here in the formal sense of familial relationship. Often in Aboriginal culture, children unrelated to a woman will be called grandchildren.
[2]Residential schools existed in Canada from about 1920 to 1998. For a description of the residential school system, see Law Commission of Canada; Schissel and Wotherspoon; and Milloy.
[3]Social capital is defined variously as the quality and quantity of social relations embedded within community norms of interaction (Coleman) and "the norms and networks that enable people to act collectively" (Woolcock and Narayan 226).

REFERENCES

Adelson, N. "Health Beliefs and the Politics of Cree Well-Being." *Health: An Interdisciplinary Journal for the Social Study of Health, Illness and Medicine 2* (1998): 5-22.
Anderson, K. *A Recognition of Being: Reconstructing Native Womanhood.* Toronto: Second Story Press, 2000.
Borkan, J. M. "Immersion/Crystallization." *Doing Qualitative Research.* Eds. B. F. Crabtree and W. L. Miller. Thousand Oaks, CA: Sage Publications, 1999. 179-194.
Browne, A. J. and J. Fiske. "First Nations Women's Encounters With Mainstream Health Care Services." *Western Journal of Nursing Research* 23 (2001): 126-147.

Browne, A. J. and V. Smye. "A Post-Colonial Analysis of Healthcare Discourses Addressing Aboriginal Women." *Nurse Researcher* 9 (2002): 28-41.

Cardinal, J. C., D. P. Schopflocher, L. W. Svenson, K. B. Morrison, and L. Laing. *First Nations in Alberta: A Focus on Health Service Use.* Edmonton, AB: Alberta Health and Wellness, 2004.

Coleman, J. S. *Foundations for Social Theory.* Cambridge, MA: The Belknap Press of Harvard University Press, 1990.

Colman, R. *A Profile of Women's Health Indicators in Canada.* Prepared for the Women's Health Bureau, Health Canada, 2003.

Colomeda, L. A. and E. R. Wenzel, "Medicine Keepers: Issues in Indigenous Health." *Critical Public Health* 10 (2000): 243-256.

Crabtree, B. F. and W. L. Miller. "The Dance of Interpretation." *Doing Qualitative Research.* Eds. B. F. Crabtree and W. L. Miller. Thousand Oaks, CA: Sage Publications, 1999a. 127-144.

Crabtree, B. F. and W. L. Miller. *Doing Qualitative Research.* 2nd Edition. Thousand Oaks, CA: Sage Publications, 1999b.

Creswell, J. W. *Qualitative Inquiry and Research Design: Choosing Among Five Traditions.* Thousand Oaks, CA: Sage Publications, 1998.

Deiter, C. and L. Otway. *Sharing Our Stories on Promoting Health and Community Healing: An Aboriginal Women's Health Project.* Winnipeg: Prairie Women's Health Centre of Excellence, 2001.

Denzin, N. K. *Interpretive Interactionism.* Newbury Park, CA: Sage Publications, 1989.

Dickson, G. "Aboriginal Grandmothers' Experience With Health Promotion and Participatory Action Research." *Qualitative Health Research* 10 (2002): 188-213.

Ellerby, J. H., J. McKenzie, S. McKay, G. J. Gariépy, and J. M. Kaufert. "Bioethics for Clinicians: 18. Aboriginal Cultures." *Canadian Medical Association Journal* 163 (2000): 845-850.

Gittelsohn, J., S. B. Harris, A. L. Thorne-Lyman, A. J. G. Hanley, A. Barnie, and B. Zinman. "Body Image Concepts Differ by Age and Sex in an Ojibway-Cree Community in Canada." *Journal of Nutrition* 126 (1996): 2990-3000.

Health Canada. *Closing the Gaps in Aboriginal Health.* Health Policy Research Bulletin 5, 2003.

Kirmayer, L. J., G. M. Brass, and C. L. Tait. "The Mental Health of Aboriginal Peoples: Transformations of Identity and Community." *Canadian Journal of Psychiatry* 45 (2000): 607-616.

Kowalsky, L. O., M. J. Verhoef, W. E. Thurston, and G. E. Rutherford. "Guidelines for Entry into an Aboriginal Community." *The Canadian Journal of Native Studies* 16 (1996): 267-282.

Kuzel, A. "Sampling in Qualitative Inquiry." *Doing Qualitative Research.* Eds. B. F. Crabtree and W. L. Miller. Thousand Oaks, CA: Sage Publications, 1999. 33-46.

Kuzel, A. and R. Like. "Standards of Trustworthiness for Qualitative Studies in Primary Care." *Primary Care Research: Traditional and Innovative Approaches.* Eds. P. G. Norton, M. Stewart, F. Tudiver, M. J. Bass, and E. V. Dunn. Newbury Park, CA: Sage Publications, 1991. 138-158.

Law Commission of Canada. *Restoring Dignity: Responding to Child Abuse in Canadian Institutions: Executive Summary.* Ottawa: The Commission, 2000.

Lincoln, Y. S. and E. G. Guba. *Naturalistic Inquiry.* Newbury Park, CA: Sage Publications, 1985.

Meadows, L. M. and D. M. Dodendorf. "Data Management and Interpretation Using Computers to Assist." *Doing Qualitative Research.* Eds. B. F. Crabtree and W. L. Miller. Thousand Oaks, CA: Sage Publications, 1999. 195-218.

Meadows, L. M., L. Lagendyk, W. E. Thurston, and A. C. Eisener. "Balancing Culture, Ethics and Methods in Qualitative Health Research With Aboriginal Peoples." *International Journal of Qualitative Methods* 2 (2003): 1-14.

Meadows, L. M. and J. M. Morse. "Constructing Evidence Within the Qualitative Project." *The Nature of Qualitative Evidence.* Eds. J. M. Morse, J. M. Swanson, and A. Kuzel. Thousand Oaks, CA: Sage Publications, 2001. 187-200.

Meadows, L. M. and L. Mrkonjic. "Breaking – Bad News: Women's Experiences of Fractures at Midlife." *Canadian Journal of Public Health* 94 (2003): 427-430.

Meadows, L. M., W. E. Thurston, and C. A. Berenson. "Health Promotion and Preventive Measures: Interpreting Messages At Midlife." *Qualitative Health Research* 11 (2001): 450-463.

Meadows, L. M., W. E. Thurston, and S. Lackner. "Women's Health Study: Women's Reports of Childhood Abuse." *Health Care for Women International* 22 (2001): 439-454.

Meadows, L. M., W. E. Thurston, and C. Melton. "Immigrant Women's Health." *Social Science and Medicine* 52 (2001): 1451-1458.

Meadows, L. M., A. J. Verdi, and B. F. Crabtree. "Keeping Up Appearances: Using Qualitative Methods in Dental Research." *Journal of Dental Education* 67 (2003): 981-990.

Milloy, J. S. *A National Crime: The Canadian Government and the Residential School System, 1879-1986.* Winnipeg: University of Manitoba Press, 1999.

Moane, G. *Gender and Colonialism: A Psychological Analysis of Oppression and Liberation.* London: Macmillan Press Ltd., 1999.

Morse, J. M. and L. Richards. *Readme First for a User's Guide to Qualitative Methods.* Thousand Oaks, CA: Sage Publications, 2002.

O'Neil, J. D., J. R. Reading, and A. Leader. "Changing the Relations of Surveillance: The Development of a Discourse of Resistance in Aboriginal Epidemiology." *Human Organization* 57 (1998): 230-237.

Patton, M. Q. *How to Use Qualitative Methods in Evaluation.* Newbury Park, CA: Sage Publications, 1987.

Romanow, R. J. *Building on Values: The Future of Health Care in Canada. Final Report* Commission on the Future of Health Care in Canada, 2003.

Sayers, J. F. and K. A. MacDonald. "A Strong and Meaningful Role for First Nations Women in Governance." *First Nations Women, Governance and the Indian Act: A Collection of Policy Research Papers.* Eds. J. F. Sayers, K. A. MacDonald, J. A. Fiske, M. Newell, E. George, and W. Cornet. Ottawa: Status of Women Canada, 2001. 1-54.

Schissel, B. and T. Wotherspoon. *The Legacy of School for Aboriginal People: Education, Oppression, and Emancipation.* Don Mills, ON: Oxford University Press, 2003.

Stout, M. D. and G. Kipling. *The Health Transition Fund Synthesis Series: Aboriginal Health.* Ottawa: Health Canada, 2002.

Stout, M. D., G. D. Kipling, and R. Stout. "Aborginal Women's Health Research." *Canadian Women's Health Network* 4/5 (2002): 11-12.

Svenson, K. A. and C. Lafontaine. "The Search for Wellness." *First Nations and Inuit Regional Health Survey.* First Nations and Inuit Regional Health Survey National Steering Committee, 2003.

Thurston, W. E. and L. Potvin. "Evaluability Assessment: A Tool for Incorporating Evaluation in Social Change Program." *Evaluation* 9 (2003): 453-470.

Thurston, W. E., C. M. Scott, and A. R. Vollman. "Developing Healthy Public Policy: The Role of the Public." *Canadian Community as Partner.* Philadelphia: Lippincott Williams and Wilkins, 2003. 124-156.

Tjepkema, M. "The Health of the Off-Reserve Aboriginal Population." *Health Reports* 13 (2002): 1-17.

van Uchelen, C. P., S. F. Davidson, S. V. Quressette, C. R. Brasfield, and L. H. Demerais. "What Makes Us Strong: Urban Aboriginal Perspectives on Wellness and Strength." *Canadian Journal of Community Mental Health* 16 (1997): 37-50.

Voyageur, C. J. "Contemporary Aboriginal Women in Canada." *Visions of the Heart: Canadian Aboriginal Issues.* 2nd ed. Eds. D. Long and O. P. Dickason. Toronto: Harcourt Canada, 2001. 81-106.

Walters, K. L. and J. M. Simoni. "Reconceptualizing Native Women's Health: An 'Indigenist' Stress-Coping Model." *American Journal of Public Health* 92 (2002): 520-524.

Woolcock, M. and D. Narayan. "Social Capital: Implications for Development Theory, Research, and Policy." *The World Bank Research Observer* 15 (2000): 225-249.

Young, T. K. "Review of Research on Aboriginal Populations in Canada: Relevance to Their Health Needs." *BMJ* 327 (2003): 419-422.

MICHELLE CAMERON

TWO-SPIRITED ABORIGINAL PEOPLE

Continuing Cultural Appropriation by Non-Aboriginal Society

"I UNDERSTAND WHAT YOU'RE SAYING," she said. "But saying non-Ab-originals shouldn't use the term two-spirited, it reminds me of a lawsuit I heard where Xerox sued someone to make them quit using the word Xerox as a verb." I looked at her, and saw hundreds of years of colonization at work. This woman was queer, educated, and feminist, yet still was not questioning her own privilege. How could she compare cultural appropriation to corporate copyright infringement? She was completely missing the point.

I have noticed an increasing trend of non-Aboriginals beginning to self-label using the term two-spirited. "So what's the problem?" you may wonder. A non-Aboriginal self-labelling as two-spirited is an example of continuing cultural appropriation by mainstream society. The term two-spirited has a *specific* cultural context, and removing it from that context simply because one likes the meaning of it is an act of colonization and must be resisted. Eduardo Duran and Bonnie Duran discuss the need for Aboriginals to "create counterhege-monic discourses" (27). The term two-spirited is part of our counterhegemonic discourse and reclamation of our unique histories.

Aboriginal people coined the term two-spirit and are using it to reflect our past, and the direction of our future. We are using the term. It is ours. Paula Gunn Allen discusses the Native American concept of ownership, when she states, "possession was seen as a matter of *use*, not a matter of eternal right" (19 [my emphasis]). She continues, "People couldn't steal something that belonged to someone else because only one person can use something at a time" (19). My assertion is that Aboriginal people are using the term two-spirited, and out of respect, other groups should refrain from self-labelling with it while we are using it.

Two-spirited Aboriginal people experience intersecting oppressions that im-pinge upon their unique identity in the queer community. Two-spirited people have typically been seen only as an add-on or subset of other queer categories like bisexual or transsexual, rather than as their culturally specific and unique selves. For example, in the LGBQT component of one of my third year social work classes, two-spiritedness was not adequately discussed, and the term was left dangling unexplained under the term bisexual up on the blackboard. Then in our Aboriginal-specific social work class, there was *no* two-spirit content at all. Two-spiritedness tends to fall between the cracks in academic curriculum. University courses do not adequately cover the concept of two-spiritedness in their LGBQT content, which only adds to the general lack of knowledge within the queer community and society at large.

This also has created a rift in the queer community between non-Aboriginals who feel entitled to use the term two-spirited freely, and Aboriginals who believe it is yet another egregious example of cultural appropriation by the dominant society. In this paper, I will analyse the history of two-spiritedness, the identity politics operating behind the use of the term, and articulate why it is inappropriate for non-Aboriginal queers to self-apply the terminology.

HISTORICAL CONTEXT

Prior to European contact, many (but not all) Aboriginal groups had two-spirit members who were integral parts of the community, occupying positions of honour and communal value. Sabine Lang states that two-spirit people were "seen as being neither men nor women, but as belonging to genders of their own within cultural systems of multiple genders" (114). Aboriginal sexuality was based on multiple genders, at least three, but up to six. For example, there were male, female, and not-male/not female (two-spirited). Some groups conceived of six genders. For example, a two-spirited woman who had a female partner was a different gender than a two-spirited woman who had a male partner.

Terry Tafoya states, "gender orientation and sexual orientation are two separate categories" (194). The difference between the modern constructs of gay/lesbian/bi is that they are based on *sexual orientation*, whereas two-spiritedness is based on *gender orientation*. This is a difficult concept for people indoctrinated with western binary (male/female) concepts of sexuality. Sexual orientation is based on physical sex characteristics. Gender orientation is not based on physical sex characteristics, but rather on the roles the person chooses to align with. I will use myself as an example to clarify the distinction here. I completed an Aircraft Engine Mechanic program. Now, whether I chose to be with a man or a woman, if you go by the two-spirited concept, I would *still* be considered two-spirited either way despite my "male" choice of gender role. Yet, because my partner is a woman, I am considered homosexual in the western sexual dichotomy. Sabine Lang states, "a same-sex relationship in many Native American cultures, at least traditionally, is not necessarily at the same time a same-gender relationship" (104). This is because a female with a male gender role was considered to be a completely different gender than a female with a "normal" female gender role. As such, traditionally my partner and I would not be considered homosexual, because we have two different gender roles.

Paula Gunn Allen, a First Nations scholar, states that "we do not fit easily into pre-existing officially recognized categories is the correlative of our culture of origin" (6). She continues, "neither does our thought fit the categories that have been devised to organize Western intellectual enterprise" (6). Two-Spirited Aboriginals do not subscribe to or neatly fit into the western dichotomies of human sexuality. We are not either/or; we are neither/nor. Traditional western discourse is not an adequate framework for the complexities involved in two-spiritedness.

ANALYSIS OF EFFECTS OF THE RESIDENTIAL SCHOOL SYSTEM

Gil Lerat has pointed out that "the religious dogma of the Residential Schools have erased a proud and rich history of Two-spirit people in most Aboriginal communities" (5). This is one of the unacknowledged side effects of the horrific sexual, emotional, and physical abuse that many Aboriginal children encountered in the residential school system. Many Aboriginals who experienced same-sex sexual abuse as a child equate this abuse with being gay, or gay sex. It is well established that pedophilia is not the same thing as being gay, lesbian, bi, or two-spirited and that, in fact, most child molesters identify as heterosexual men (Groth and Gary 147). However, in the mindset of three generations of residential school survivors, this distinction has not been drawn. As Fiona Meyer-Cook and Diane Labelle state, "Two-Spirited people are seen in the same light as sin and sexual abusers" (39).

Our Elders—the gatekeepers of knowledge in Aboriginal communities—have not passed down their teachings regarding two-spirited people's place in our communities. Either there is complete silence on the issue, or there is blatant denial and homophobia incorporated in their teachings. This has had the unfortunate effect of generations growing up with no concept of what it historically meant to be two-spirited and this has led to the erasure of this history from the collective mindset of the residential school generations, and subsequent generations thereafter. Heterosexist and homophobic thought has permeated the teachings of some of our Elders due to the imposition of Christian values imposed on them in the residential schools. These sentiments often remain unchallenged when spoken by an Elder, due to the respect they have in the community.

Colonization and the residential school system wreaked havoc on traditional Aboriginal beliefs and customs. The dehumanization suffered by our elders and our communities in the residential schools has had an intergenerational effect on Aboriginal communities, and especially on two-spirited members of the community. The association of two-spiritedness with sin, and the erasure/denial of their very existence is the dominant culture/colonizer speaking with the voices of our Elders.

RECLAIMING AS RESISTANCE

Kathy Absolon, a First Nations academic, urges us to "decolonize our minds and hearts" (16). Linda Tuhiwai Smith's text *Decolonizing Methodologies* describes various approaches to achieving this decolonization of mind, heart, and work. Smith is a Maori academic, and as such her writings and discourse can be relevant and transferable to the Canadian Aboriginal context.

Smith discusses the concept of *claiming*. She states that claiming and reclaiming "teach both the non-Indigenous audience and the new generations of Indigenous peoples an official account of their collective story" (144). Aboriginal two-spirited people are in the midst of reclaiming their stolen history and identity within their communities. More Aboriginals are identifying as two-spirited and embracing the history behind the term. They are digging out their history from obscurity, and creating an official account of their collective history through academic discourse and writings (see especially Jacobs, Thomas and Lang), and gatherings such as the Second Annual Saskatchewan 2-Spirit Conference in June 2005 to share ideas and knowledge that was withheld/unknown by the gatekeepers.

Another concept discussed by Smith is *remembering*. She states: "This form of remembering is painful because it involves remembering not just what colonization was about but what being dehumanized meant for our own cultural practices" (146).

Our Elders, our communities, need to remember the way things were *before* the imposition of the dominant culture and religion. Decolonizing our collective minds includes an honest acknowledgement of the way things were, and of the valued place two-spirited people should have in our communities.

Smith also states: "To resist is to retrench in the margins, retrieve what we were and remake ourselves" (4). The concept of two-spirited encapsulates this perfectly. As stated in the introduction to *Two-Spirit People*, Aboriginals attending the ThirdNative American/First Nations gay and lesbian conference in Winnipeg coined the term "two-spirit" in 1990 (Jacobs, Thomas and Lang 2). Sue-Ellen Jacobs, Wesley Thomas and Sabine Lang state the decision "to use the term two-spirit was deliberate, with a clear intention to distance themselves from non-Native gays and lesbians" (3). The term two-spirit is thus an Aboriginal-specific term of resistance to colonization, non-transferable to other cultures. There are several underlying reasons for two-spirited Aboriginals' desire to distance themselves from the mainstream queer community.

Sabine Lang states that for Aboriginal people, their sexual orientation or gender identity is secondary to their ethnic identity. Lang states, "at the core of contemporary two-spirit identities is ethnicity, an awareness of being Native American as opposed to being white or being a member of any other ethnic group" (115). I agree with Lang's statement. My core identity is First Nations; being two-spirited is wrapped and surrounded by this core identity and cannot be separated from it.

I identify as a Carrier First Nation two-spirited woman when I am talking to other Aboriginals. When talking to non-Aboriginals, I identify as a lesbian. This is a very conscious decision on my part because it gets tiring to explain the concept to everyone who is unfamiliar with the term two-spirited. However, I do not feel the term lesbian adequately represents the whole reality of my experience.

Lang states, "whereas white gay and lesbian activists often feel alienated from white society and its homophobia, two-spirit activists will usually not reject Native American cultures, even though such cultures may manifest homophobia" (115). At queer conferences that I have attended, none of the discussions with other two-spirited people involved rejection of their communities, no matter how homophobic or hostile these communities were.

In her book *Outlaw Culture*, bell hooks discusses the "demand that difference be appropriated in a manner that diffuses its power" (16). The point of using the term two-spirited was to emphasize our difference in our experiences of multiple, interlocking oppressions as queer Aboriginal people. When non-Aboriginal people decide to "take up" the term two-spirit, it detracts from its original meaning, and diffuses its power as a label of resistance for Aboriginal people. already there is so much of First Nations culture that has been exploited and appropriated in this country, and now even our terms of resistance are targeted for mainstream appropriation and consumption.

There is a long history of debate around the issue of cultural appropriation. Vine Deloria states, "Before the white man can relate to others he must forego the pleasure of defining them" (174). Two-spirited is a reclaimed term designed by Aboriginals to define our unique cultural context, histories, and legacy. When people do not see the harm in "sharing" the term, they are missing the point. And refusing to recognize that appopriating the term will inevitably alter its cultural context.

There are many reasons why cultural appropriation occurs. Vine Deloria's text, *God is Red,* examines the issues of cultural appropriation of Indigenous culture and religion. Deloria criticizes "the intense interest in tribal religions by non-Indians and the seemingly wholesale adoption of some of their beliefs and practices by significant segments of white society" 38). This ties in with the "culture-vulture" phenomenon, with whites constantly seeking the new and exotic to be pilfered from non-white cultures. Loretta Todd alludes to this when she comments, "Nothing is authentic or autonomous, therefore everything is fair game. Couple this with a still-vague yearning for meaning and for the past and what do you get? Most often, appropriation of "tribal" cultures throughout the world" (74).

There is an inherent beauty in the term two-spirited that others identify with. If you Google the term two-spirited, it is unfortunately extremely easy to find some New Age non-Aboriginal who strongly feels they are entitled to take the term two-spirited, and use it however they want. Usually they trot out some alliance with an actual First Nations person who condones their appropriation of the term.

Nevertheless, this can be seen as a form of "cultural invasion" as discussed by Paulo Freire. He states,

> the invaders penetrate the cultural context of another group, in disrespect of the latter's potentialities; they impose their own view of the world upon those they invade and inhibit the creativity of the invaded by curbing their expression. (152)

When the colonizer or dominant society culturally invades Aboriginal society, it must be resisted; otherwise meanings are lost or distorted. This is how the original words for the two-spirited concept were lost in so many Nations to begin with. Beatrice Medicine states that we "must be aware of the ways language is changed and the meaning of Native terms altered and then used to meet the needs of disenfranchised groups and individuals as a possible response of self-interest" (147).

In her book *Outlaw Culture*, hooks mentions "the ways differences created by race and class hierarchies disrupt an unrealistic vision of commonality" (75). Some would argue that focusing on differences contributes to the fracturing of an already vulnerable and marginalized queer community. The myth of a hegemonic queer community needs to be dispelled. We are *not* all the same. Our diversity should be celebrated, honoured, and respected. For two-spirited First Nations, this means respecting our jurisdiction over the term two-spirited, a *culturally specific* term we created to reclaim our unique heritage.

CONCLUSION

Aboriginal two-spirits have identities that operate outside of the western dichotomy of sex orientation and gender. Many of the words for two-spirited were lost from various First Nation groups due to the imposition of Christianity, and dominant society. Eduardo Duran and Bonnie Duran state: "The process of self-determination starts with the ever-evolving processes of self-identification and self-construction" (156). When Aboriginal queers decided to begin using the term two-spirited, it was a sign of reclamation of the historical legacy that is unique to our First Nations. Two-spirited identity then can be viewed as a counterhegemonic identity, and as a term of resistance to colonization.

Originally published in Canadian Woman Studies/les cahiers de la femme, *"Lesbian, Bisexual, Queer, Transsexual/Transgender Sexualities," 24 (2 & 3) (Winter/Spring 2005): 123-127. Reprinted with permission of the author.*

Michelle Cameron is a Dakelh-ne (Carrier) First Nations two-spirited woman. She completed her Master of Social Work in 2007, and is currently working as an analyst for the federal government. Her research interests include two-spirit/LGBQTTI issues, Indigenous feminist discourse, counter-hegemonic thought, and Indigenous forms of resistance and protest. This paper was originally presented at Cornell University's "Quotidian Queerness" conference in Ithaca, New York on April 29-30, 2005.

REFERENCES

Absolon, K. *Healing as Practice: Teachings from the Medicine Wheel.* A commissioned paper for the WUNSKA network, Canadian Schools of Social Work. Unpublished manuscript, 1993.

Deloria, V. (Jr.) *Custer Died For Your Sins.* New York: University of Oklahoma Press, 1988 [1969].

Deloria, V. (Jr.) *God Is Red* (30th Anniversary Ed. Golden, Colorado: Fulcrum Publishing, 2003 [1973].

Duran, E. and B. Duran. *Native American Postcolonial Psychology.* Albany: State University of New York Press, 1995.

Freire, P. *Pedagogy of the Oppressed.* New York: Continuum International, 1970.

Groth, A. N. and T. S. Gary. "Heterosexuality, Homosexuality and Pedophilia: Sexual Offenses Against Children and Adult Orientation." *Male Rape: A Casebook of Sexual Aggressions.* New York: AMS Press, 1982. 143-152.

Gunn Allen, P. *Off the Reservation.* Boston: Beacon Press, 1998.

hooks, b. *Outlaw Culture: Resisting Representations.* New York: Routledge, 1994.

Jacobs, S. E., W. Thomas and S. Lang. *Two Spirit People: Native American Gender Identity, Sexuality, and Spirituality.* Chicago: University of Illinois Press, 1997.

Lang, S. "Various Kinds of Two-Spirit People: Gender Variance and Homosexuality in Native American Communities." *Two Spirit People: Native American Gender Identity, Sexuality, and Spirituality.* Eds. S. E. Jacobs, W. Thomas and S. Lang. Chicago: University of Illinois Press, 1997. 100-118.

Lerat, G. *Two-Spirit Youth Speak Out! Analysis of the Needs Assessment Tool.* Vancouver, Urban Native Youth Association, 2004.

Medicine, B. "Changing Native American Roles in an Urban Context and Changing Native American Sex Roles in an Urban Context." *Two Spirit People: Native American Gender Identity, Sexuality, and Spirituality.* Eds. S. E. Jacobs, W. Thomas and S. Lang. Chicago: University of Illinois Press, 1997. 145-155.

Meyer-Cook, F. and D. Labelle. "Namaji: Two-Spirited Organizing in Montréal, Canada." *Journal of Gay and Lesbian Social Services* 16 (1) (2004): 29-51.

Smith, L. T. *Decolonizing Methodologies: Research and Indigenous Peoples.* Dunedin: University of Otago Press, 2002.

Tafoya, T. "M. Dragonfly: Two-Spirit and the Tafoya Principle of Uncertainty." *Two Spirit People: Native American Gender Identity, Sexuality, and Spirituality.* Eds. S. E. Jacobs, W. Thomas and S. Lang. Chicago: University of Illinois Press, 1997. 192-200.

Todd, Loretta. "What More Do They Want?" *Indigena: Contemporary Native Perspectives.* Eds. G. McMaster and L.A. Martin. Vancouver: Douglas and McIntyre, 1992. 71-79.

MARY SILLETT

ENSURING INDIGENOUS WOMEN'S VOICES ARE HEARD

The Beijing Declaration of Indigenous Women

WOMEN FROM 189 NATIONS MET in Beijing from August 30 September 8, 1995, for the non-governmental organization (NGO) Forum on Women. They gathered to lobby the United Nations Fourth World Conference on Women, which was held simultaneously, to define agendas for the twenty-first century that would chart a course for the future of women around the world.

The NGO Forum on Women builds on the three previous Women's Forums and United Nations Conferences that marked the Decade for Women: the first in Mexico (1975); the second in Copenhagen (1980); and the third in Nairobi (1985). This Forum, unlike the others, also builds on the major issue-based world conferences that took place since that time: the United Nations Conference on Environment and Development (1992); the World Conference on Human Rights (1993); the International Conference on Population and Development (1994); and, the World Summit for Social Development (1995). Recognizing these issues and forging critical links between the conferences, women became central players on the international stage. Their activities at the conferences now affect the lives of women globally.

The NGO Forum at Huairou had a number of different processes occurring simultaneously, and in the middle of the Forum the UN Conference officially began, which further complicated the processes. At the Forum, I concentrated on the daily Indigenous Caucus sessions and when time permitted, I attended workshops. The UN Conference also had an Indigenous Working Group, and in the final days of the Forum there was discussion between the two groups. This discussion was absolutely essential so that the Indigenous persons at the Conference could represent the positions developed by the NGO Indigenous Caucus.

PAUKTUUTIT'S POSITIONS FOR THE NGO FORUM

Before going to Beijing as a representative of Pauktuutit, a national organization representing the interests of Inuit women, I was asked to focus on the following issues:

1. The Inuit Circumpolar Conference (ICC) has worked extensively within international forums to have Inuit and other Indigenous peoples' collective and individual rights recognized as essential components of international human rights work.

2. Of particular importance is the establishment of a permanent forum for Indigenous Peoples in the United Nations system and the need to continue to change and strengthen the institutional framework of the United Nations to recognize the increasing importance of the issues affecting Indigenous Peoples.

3. On November 4, 1991, the Council of European Communities adopted EEC Regulation No. 325491. The Regulation not only prohibits the use of leghold traps in the EEC, it bans the import of the fur products of thirteen species from countries that ither employ leghold traps or utilize trapping methods that do not meet international humane trapping standards.

The Regulation took effect on January 1, 1995. The Regulation provided a "year of grace" if the EEC determined that by July 1, 1994, sufficient progress was being made in developing humane methods of trapping. This "year of grace" expired on December 31, 1995. Twelve of the species listed in the Regulation are trapped in Canada.

Hunting and trapping is a way of life for tens of thousands of Aboriginal peoples across Canada. A ban on the import of wild fur into the EEC is not just a matter of economics or the maintenance of a standard of living. It is a question of human rights. Aboriginal peoples harvest twelve of the species on the EEC list and many of them have already suffered from the downturn in the hunting and trapping economy.

In Canada, an Aboriginal Task Force was created to look into the issue. Amongst their recommendations, they felt that at the international level, the following issues must be addressed: work towards gaining a "year of grace" from the Regulation; ensure that Aboriginal interests are adequately represented in the entire decision-making processes; develop a long-term strategy to deal with the EEC Regulation and related initiatives, including communications programs; ensure that there is permanent and accountable representation in Europe to communicate and provide current information on issues related to the fur trade; ensure a united front at the political level; develop alternative markets; and, ensure EEC compliance with the Regulation.

4. Since the creation of the United Nations, there has been an ongoing debate about which term should be used to refer to Indigenous Peoples. We insist on the usage of Indigenous Peoples (with an "s") because under international law, "peoples," not people, have the right

to self-determination. Peoples have collective rights. People have individual rights. Some nations, including Canada, have refused to recognize this language.

THE BEIJING DECLARATION OF INDIGENOUS WOMEN

The Indigenous Women's Caucus held daily sessions at the Huairou site where groups of Indigenous women from over thirty countries worked on a draft declaration to influence the United Nations Platform for Action—a strategic plan that guides the long-term activities of the UN. The collective effort of our group resulted in the Beijing Declaration of Indigenous Women, which covers issues of concern to Indigenous peoples around the world: self-determination, land and territories, health, education, human rights violations, violence against women, intellectual property rights, biodiversity, the Human Genome Diversity Project (HGDP), and political participation.

We agreed the two most important issues were the right to self-determination, and the need to voice strong objection to the patenting of Indigenous genetic materials through the HGDP. On the first issue, we stated that the UN must recognize Indigenous Peoples with an "s" as peoples with the right to self-determination granted them under international law and as peoples with collective rights, not as people with individual rights.

On the second issue, the Human Genome Diversity Project is an international consortium of scientists, universities, governments, and other interest groups in North America and Europe organized to take blood, tissue samples (cheek scrapings or saliva), and hair roots from hundreds of so-called "endangered" Indigenous communities around the world. On the assumption that Indigenous peoples are facing extinction, this consortium is gathering DNA samples from living peoples. Genetic manipulation raises serious ethical and moral concerns with regard to the sanctity of life. The Caucus opposed the patenting of all genetic materials and urged the international community to protect all forms of life from genetic manipulation and destruction.

The Beijing Declaration of Indigineous Peoples was given to Madeleine Dion Stout, an Indigenous representative at the United Nations governmental conference so that she could use it in attempts to influence the drafting sessions of the Platform for Action. As well, the Indigenous Caucus drafted a message to the G-7 that concentrated on the themes that we are peoples with the right of self-determination, that we have rights and responsibilities to protect the earth, and that we need economic justice based on Indigenous values—not on western values.

WORKSHOPS

In addition to the Indigenous Caucus sessions, I was able to attend, among others, a workshop on the struggle for recognition of Aboriginal rights. The facilitators from the Frog Lake Indian Band in Alberta were unable to attend so two other women from Canada actually led the workshop. There were two issues that clearly dominated this session. One was the Indigenous Peoples with the "s" issue, and the other was whether or not there should be separation of women's issues from Indigenous Women's issues.

There was general agreement that the United Nations must recognize the self-determining and collective rights of Indigenous peoples. It was acknowledged that Canada was not a supporter of that position and that efforts have to be made domestically and internationally to change that position.

Two participants (out of about forty) felt that we must struggle to achieve fundamental human rights for women worldwide because women's issues are the same everywhere. Women worldwide want to be free from inequality, underdevelopment, war, and oppression, and we should not underestimate this effort by dividing women into different categories such as women, Indigenous women, displaced women, immigrant women, etc. Debra Harry, an Indigenous woman from the United States led the other side of the argument (which was widely supported by the rest of the participants) stating that there was a need in all forums to recognize the special circumstances of Indigenous peoples. Indigenous peoples, unlike others, have been objects of legislation; have been colonized; have been treated as minorities, displaced peoples, insular objects, and never as peoples with human rights, with self-determining rights, or any rights at all. It is for these reasons Ms. Harry believes that Indigenous women need extraordinary recognition.

Another workshop was on sustainable development and biodiversity by Indigenous women from South America. The speaker talked about the traditional Indigenous knowledge of her people and how this knowledge has been exploited by outsiders for profit. She was detailed in her presentation about the knowledge and medicines of her peoples and she expressed anger at outsiders who, instead of respect, showed disrespect for the contributions they have made to the world. This issue was frequently raised by many Indigenous women throughout our gatherings and its obvious importance is highlighted in the intellectual property sections of the Indigenous Declaration.

CONCLUSION

The "peoples" issue was one identified by all the participants in the Indigenous Caucus and it is well represented in all of the documents resulting from the Forum. The fur issue is reflected in the subsistence issue of the Declaration. In the fall of this year, the European Parliament will be voting to see if they will accept the report done by experts from different countries regarding a process to determine "humane trapping standards." The outcome of this vote will determine international humane trapping standards and the regulations with respect to the import of wild fur products.

Excerpted from a report prepared for Pauktuutit Inuit Women's Association.

Originally published in Canadian Woman Studies/les cahiers de la femme, *"Post-Beijing" 16 (3) (Summer 1996): 62-64. Reprinted with permission of the author.*

Mary Sillett was born in Hopedale, Labrador, and graduated in 1976 with a Bachelor of Social Work from Memorial University of Newfoundland. She has worked on Inuit and Aboriginal issues in community, regional, provincial, national, and international settings. She is a past President of the Inuit Women's Association of Canada and was a Commissioner on the Royal Commission on Aboriginal Peoples. She is the mother of two sons.

PATTI DOYLE-BEDWELL

"WITH THE APPROPRIATE QUALIFICATIONS"

Aboriginal People and Employment Equity

The truth about stories is that that's all we are.
—Thomas King (2)

IN THE TRADITION OF MY Mi'kmaq ancestors, I believe in equity and fair-ness. In traditional times, the circle symbolized the need for all diversity to create the circle. No part could exist without the other. Moreover, in Mi'kmaq culture, my lived experience must also be included in any story about employ-ment equity. I do not think my experiences differ from other Aboriginal faculty. We all sit in the circle. I am a Mi'kmaq woman, lawyer, teacher, and Director of the Transition Year Program (TYP) at Dalhousie University College of Continuing Education. I also taught at Dalhousie's law school for two years and directed its Indigenous Blacks and Mi'kmaq Program.[1] I no longer teach at the law school and therein lies part of my story.

The first group of Mi'kmaq women graduated from Dalhousie Law School in 1993. I am the only Mi'kmaq woman with an LL.M. from Dalhousie Law School. I say this, not to brag, but to illustrate how recently we achieved law degrees and how far we have to go to achieve equity in the legal profession. Being part of the first group, my experience has been a mixed bag of outright racism to tremendous support.

I chose the title, "With the Appropriate Qualifications," because it was the title of the job ad for the Director of the Program for Indigenous Blacks and Mi'kmaq. The job ad indicated that the successful candidate would be allowed to teach law if s/he had the "appropriate qualifications." To me, this spoke volumes about the judgment calls made by those in power about our abilities. Inherent in assessing applicants for a job is subjectivity. The morals and values that we place on people and their knowledge create the judgment placed on any applicant. What is "appropriate?" The most important part of employment equity involves the deconstruction of those value judgments that tend to impede employment equity principles.

Despite the many statutes and even constitutional documents that propose to implement a society free of racism and discrimination, immense barriers still exist that prevent us from reaching our full potential. The Canadian government has implemented measures to ensure that employment equity becomes a reality. The four designated groups—women, Aboriginal Peoples,[2] visible minorities, and people with disabilities—have statutory and constitutional measures designed to increase their employment. The focus of this paper, Aboriginal Peoples, reflects my experience as a Mi'kmaq woman facing barriers to employment due to my race/gender. I will critically analyze the barriers and propose suggestions for change.

This paper also explores the construct of employment equity in Canada. First, I examine the vision of employment equity through legislation and constitutional instruments and explore the law in Canada that supports employment equity. Second, I explore the reality that Aboriginal faculty encounter in the workplace. I will delineate the barriers that block our progress. Dominant institutions tend to create poisoned work environments when they do not understand our cultures or our experiences of oppression, poverty and racism. I will also explore barriers that Mi'kmaq people confront as we face racism on a daily basis. I most likely will not approach this in a strictly legal way. According to Patricia Monture-Angus (1995), "What I am concerned about is that the First Nations ways of understanding and learning are not the same as those that are accepted within the dominant institutions of learning in this land, especially within legal institutions, including law schools. The understanding and respect of these different ways must be recognized and respected if we are truly going to make any headway in race relations" (26).

I believe strongly that my experience and that of others in marginalized positions must be shared and listened to in order to effect change. I conclude with my vision of healing from racism, and the need to confront issues of racism head on in the workplace without defensiveness and without shame. Dalhousie University, as an institution, has made significant progress on issues facing Aboriginal faculty. I have also found my place where I can flourish. I have moved towards healing.

MOVING TOWARDS EQUITY: THE VISION IN LAW

In Canada, treating people equally has always meant accommodating difference, not treating people the same. According to Judge Rosalie Abella,[3] in her report *Equality in Employment: A Royal Commission Report*:

> Equality in employment is not a concept that produces the same results for everyone. It is a concept that seeks to identify and remove, barrier by barrier, discriminatory disadvantages. Equality in employment is access to the fullest opportunity to exercise individual potential. Sometimes equality means treating people the same, despite their differences, and sometimes it means treating them as equals by accommodating their differences. Formerly we thought that equality only meant sameness and that treating persons as equals meant

treating everyone the same. We now know that to treat everyone the same may be to offend the notion of equality. Ignoring differences may mean ignoring legitimate needs. It is not fair to use the difference between people as an excuse to exclude them arbitrarily from equitable participation. Equality means nothing if it does not mean that we are of equal worth regardless of differences in gender, race, ethnicity, or disability. The projected, mythical and attributed meaning of these differences cannot be permitted to exclude full participation. Ignoring differences and refusing to accommodate them is a denial of equal access and opportunity. It is discrimination. To reduce discrimination, we must create and maintain barrier-free environments so that individual can have genuine access free from arbitrary obstructions to demonstrate and exercise fully their potential. This may mean treating some people differently by removing the obstacles to equality of opportunity they alone face for no demonstrably justifiable reason. (3)

Canada has embraced Judge Abella's vision through court decisions, notably *Andrews v. the Law Society of British Columbia*,[4] and through various pieces of legislation, notably the *Employment Equity Act*, proclaimed shortly after the Abella Report. Accommodation of differences means that we must also identify the barriers that prevent members of the designated groups from reaching their full potential. But still, the unspoken, underlying premise of employment equity assumes that the barriers that prevent us from reaching our full potential are not culturally bound but are individual flaws in the groups themselves.

In Canada, the four designated groups receive legal protection through both provincial and federal legislation as well as the *Constitution Act of 1982*. Section 15 of the *Constitution Act of 1982* (the equality provision) states: (1) "Every individual is equal before and under the law and has the right to the equal protection and benefit of the law without discrimination and, in particular, without discrimination based on race, national or ethnic origin, colour, religion, sex, age or mental or physical disability." The Courts have not closed these categories. Unlike the U.S. experience, the Charter allows for the development of equity programs in s. 15(2) which states: (2) Subsection (1) "does not preclude any law, program or activity that has as its object the amelioration of conditions of disadvantaged individuals or groups including those that are disadvantaged because of race, national or ethnic origin, colour, religion, sex, age, mental or physical disability."

Morley Gunderson, Douglas Hyatt, and Sara Slinn illustrate the differences between the United States and Canada:

Employment equity means different things to different people—ranging from the general concept of equity or fairness at the workplace

214

to more specific concepts pertaining to requirement to achieve particular representations of target groups in the internal workforce of the organization. The term *affirmative action* is more commonly used in the United States, while employment equity is the term used in Canada, coined by the Abella Commission (1984) in part to differentiate from the earlier U.S. affirmative action initiatives that were often associated with rigid quotas. (6-7)

In *Andrews,* the Supreme Court defined discrimination as:

Discrimination may be described as a distinction, whether intentional or not but based on grounds relating to personal characteristics of the individual or group, which has the effect of imposing burdens, obligations, or disadvantages on such individual or group not imposed upon others, or which withholds or limits access to opportunities, benefits, and advantages available to other members of society. Distinctions based on personal characteristics attributed to an individual solely on the basis of association with a group will rarely escape the charge of discrimination, while those based on an individual's merits and capacities will rarely be so classed. (Abella 174-75)

S. 15(2) also, unlike the United States, allows for programs that are aimed at the amelioration of conditions facing disadvantaged groups (Hassmann 255). There is no question that for Aboriginal Peoples, language, culture, poverty, isolation, illness, disease, racism, lower education, and segregation from mainstream, all serve to act as disadvantages in the mainstream labour market.[5]

I had hoped that the adoption of Abella's vision would ensure that our community ties would be respected, where we would have the opportunity to overcome the barriers, by the active participation of those people who created those barriers. But the means to overcome those barriers meets resistance from those in the mainstream.

Canada has implemented many legal mechanisms that focus upon employment equity. Responsibility for remedying discrimination flows from the division of powers in s. 91 and s. 92 of the *Constitution Act of 1867*, which divided human rights responsibility by federal responsibilities set out in s. 91 and provincial responsibilities set out in s. 92. As a result, we have federal legislation, the *Canadian Human Rights Act,* which deals with issues under federal jurisdiction. The *Canada Labour Code* applies to areas of federal responsibility as well. Provinces have enacted their own human rights legislation governing discrimination within their own spheres.

Canada has also implemented the *Employment Equity Act* that identifies four groups that require support: women, Aboriginal Peoples, visible minorities, and people with disabilities. But the *Employment Equity Act* does not reach all members of the labour market. Gunderson, Hyatt, and Slinn find that legislated employment equity exists mainly in the federal jurisdiction, which covers about five to ten percent of the Canadian workforce (146).

The *Employment Equity Act* requires employers with more than one hundred employees, under the Federal Contractors Program, to create an employment equity plan for the four target groups if the federal government has business with that particular employer. For example, under the Federal Contractors Program, the business must report its numbers to the Human Resources Development Corporation (a federal government department) in order to be in compliance with the Act. Yet enforcement under the federal legislation is generally regarded as weak. Penalties under the legislated program exist only for failing to file a report with the Federal Human Rights Commission and these are minimal (maximum of $10,000 for a single violation and $50,000 for repeat violations).

The Canadian Human Rights Commission approved a new policy in February 1990 called the Aboriginal Employment Preference Policy, which states: "Within its area of jurisdiction, (federal) the Canadian Human Rights Commissions will not, as a general rule, consider as discriminatory preferential hiring, promotion or other treatment of Aboriginal employees by organizations or enterprises owned and /or operated by Aboriginal people" (CHRC policy guideline). This applies to band councils and other Aboriginal organizations to allow them to hire Aboriginal Peoples without being subject to discrimination accusations by non-Native people.

Aboriginal Peoples, despite massive efforts of the Government to disconnect us from our cultures and assimilate us into the mainstream, have maintained a strong presence in Canada. We have secured constitutional protection of our treaty and Aboriginal rights.[6] Over one million people identify as Aboriginal. As for Status Indians, there are over 660 reserves in Canada with approximately 719,496 in population (*Registered Indian Population* xiii). Disagreements continue to rage over the definition of "Aboriginal," which contributes to the difficulties in counting Aboriginal Peoples.[7] So right off the bat, it is difficult to ascertain the exact numbers of Aboriginal Peoples in Canada. The difficulty arises in counting Aboriginal people in a particular workforce. People have the right to self-identify or not. In the Mi'kmaq country, our leaders have yet to determine clear parameters as to who is a beneficiary/member. From the employment side, this leads to people with little or no connection to the community self-identifying as Aboriginal, and taking advantage of employment equity programs for Aboriginal Peoples. The burden is left to the employee to self-identify or not and people do not have to provide proof of ancestry. Many times that proof is lost in the eons of time.

Focusing on the Status Indians, those who have legal recognition under the *Indian Act*, we know that only two percent of status Indians have ever earned a degree. Most of those with degrees are women. In Nova Scotia, the provincial government workforce has only one percent of its workforce identifying as Aboriginal. Often, for us to gain employment, we must be better qualified than someone in the mainstream. In the next section, I explore the reality of employment equity, beyond the numbers.

MOVING TOWARDS EQUITY: THE REALITY

Facing our social conditions, created and sustained from colonialism, ensures that multiple employment barriers exist that prevent us from realizing our full potential. Linda Smith eloquently paints a picture of the social conditions faced by Aboriginal Peoples:

> Whilst Indigenous communities have quite valid fears about the further loss of intellectual and cultural knowledges, and have worked to gain international attention and protection through covenants on such matters, many Indigenous communities continue to live within political and social conditions that perpetuate extreme levels of poverty, chronic ill health and poor educational opportunities. Their children may be removed forcibly from their care, adopted or institutionalized. The adults may be as addicted to alcohol as their children are to glue, they may live in destructive relationships which are formed and shaped by their impoverished material conditions and structured by politically regressive regimes. While they live like this they are constantly fed messages about their worthlessness, laziness, dependence and lack of "higher" human qualities. This applies as much to Indigenous communities in the First World nations as it does to Indigenous communities in developing countries. Within these sorts of social realities, questions of imperialism and the effects of colonization may seem to be merely academic; sheer physical survival is far more pressing. The problem is that constant efforts by governments, states, societies and institutions to deny the historical formations of such conditions have simultaneously denied our claims to humanity, to having a history, and to all sense of hope. To acquiesce is to lose ourselves entirely and implicitly agree with all that has been said about us. To resist is to retrench in the margins, retrieve who we were and remake ourselves. The past, our stories, local and global, the present, our communities, cultures, languages and social practices—all may be spaces of marginalization but they also have become spaces of resistance and hope. (3-4)

Employment equity focuses on the removal of barriers that prevent access to employment. Imagine living with such stereotypes and realities. I am convinced that employment equity measures in Canada that focus simply on monitoring the numbers of the four designated groups in businesses that fall under the *Employment Equity Act* does not go far enough to ensure equality. I base this on my own experience of barriers and the difficulties I have encountered at

Dalhousie's law school, both as a student and an academic.

Smith argues that research for/about Indigenous Peoples requires academics to recognize our social conditions. I would take that one step further and argue that employers must also recognize the social conditions that affect our employment. Truly, the very fact that we must survive often takes precedence over "achieving career goals." If we add the fight to remain employed and to overcome multiple barriers that years of colonialism placed in our path, the journey may very well appear hopeless.

Given that I come from this background, this is a story. It is my story. It is a story about law, about me, about racism. This narrative illustrates my attempt to weave law into my story, the need to share my "legal" career, my experience. As Thomas King states, "Stories are wondrous things. And they are dangerous" (9). Telling my story is dangerous but at the same time, necessary. Telling our stories that bring into question the values held dear to all Canadians is dangerous. Exposing racism through personal experience is dangerous. While my story sounds hopeless, and the social conditions that shape and govern my reality look bleak, I have not given up on my dream of writing and teaching.

The danger lies in exposing my inner truth to those in power who do not often understand my truth and the social reality that surrounds me. As Patricia Monture-Angus (1992) states:

> Truth, in non-Aboriginal terms, is located outside the self. It is absolute and may be discovered only through years of study in institutions that are formally sanctioned as sources of learning. In the Aboriginal way, truth is internal to the self. The Creator put each and everyone here in a complete state of being with our set of instructions to follow. Truth is discovered through personal examination, not through systemic study in formally sanctioned institutions. (106)

As a Mi'kmaq woman, I must honour my traditions that demand that I begin with the truth located in myself. At the same time, my truth or my story may not matter to anyone. After all it is my story. My story may not resonate with anyone. I am not telling the story to garner sympathy about the plight of "poor oppressed people."[8] Speaking from my cultural traditions in a modern context tells me that we have survived the dominant society's outward attempts at colonialism and genocide but there is no question that we still live in a colonial world that does not respect our presence. However, in a country such as Canada, which holds the vision of equality and fairness to all, I think it is important to place that law under the magnifying glass, to see if the implementation of the law fits the vision.

Aboriginal experiences do not fit within the dominant legal framework. My experience has not fit into the dominant legal framework. Trying to fit our experience into a legal system mired in colonialism and racism is where the danger comes in. I have based my research and teaching on my cultural understandings. As a result, I often face scepticism from those of the dominant culture. James Henderson states that "Aboriginal perspectives are just now being heard in Canada in a climate that is not mired in racial discrimination and hostility to our very presence" (245). Mi'kmaq values demand that I find the truth in myself, but within a climate; at least at Dalhousie's law school, which has hostility and discriminates against my presence.

I am told by Dalhousie's law school that I am not a lawyer. I am not a legal academic. I cannot teach at the law school. I write barely enough papers for the academy to consider me a researcher. I occupy some type of middle ground. I am too political, too controversial, too focused on the plight of the "poor oppressed people." Coping with racism that cuts to one's very soul takes its toll on one's mental health. I became tired of the complaints, the racism, and issues in my own life that meant I could no longer fight the good fight. While I am not at the law school now, the fact that I lack academic talent from the perspective of the law school has shamed me to no end.

Stereotypes and racial profiling continue to have negative impacts upon our working and learning environment. I direct educational equity programs at Dalhousie. Particularly at the law school, accepting minority and Aboriginal applicants means "watering down" the qualification, meaning that we constantly need to prove our abilities. If you are accepted to law school, not only do you have to jump through all the same hoops as mainstream students, (LSAT, degree, and grades), you must also attend a pre-law program. Stereotypes such as drunk, disorderly, welfare bums, dumb, illiterate, and others too painful to mention, rule the mainstream mindset. Sadly, these stereotypes often shape my reality.

Negotiating the university climate, weighed down by these negative images reminds me of Mount Everest and its crevices. Climbing Mount Everest through the Khumbu Icefall is an apt analogy for tracking one's way through the maze of academia. Jennifer Banker, a professor at the Dalhousie law school, constructs and describes employment barriers as a "steel ceiling." However, as one who has experienced racism, I believe the Mount Everest analogy reflects more of my experience. Some Aboriginal people make progress, and some even make it to the summit, but on the way, some of us have felt defeated and alone; not unlike being the first Mi'kmaq to achieve anything in the mainstream world.

Climbing Mount Everest demands rigour, preparedness, a sound heart and body, as well as a deep desire to succeed. In spite of the best-laid plans, the icefall can kill in an instant. Despite the best knowledge, one can never predict the movement of the icefall. I liken this to navigating the constantly changing paths of academia. Rules change and barriers appear, often without warning. As a result, I looked for advice from more experienced teachers. But mixed messages meant that the school accused me of doing too much work by reading the students' papers and being too available for them.

I have often discovered new crevices as I have struggled to reach my potential. Often, these crevices appear quickly and without warning. As Patricia Monture-Okanee (1995) states:

As a professor, I wield a certain amount of power. I do not deny this. It is true. I decide whether a student passes or fails; if an "A" or a "C" is earned. However, when I stand in front of a class, many of the individuals have more privilege and power than I can ever imagine having. This power is carried as a result of their skin-privilege, or their gender or their social status or family income. The Law School, however, functions solely on the view that I am the powerful one. Students are protected against any "alleged" bias by any professor by the grade appeal process. However, I am not any professor. I am not male, white, and my family is not economically advantaged. I am heterosexual, able bodied, and a mother of five. I am Mohawk and follow my ways. There is not protection available for me in any policy of either the law school or the university if the situation arises where I experience a student who discriminates against me based on my gender, culture, or race. (21).

As a professor at the law school, I encountered many students who complained about my lack of "appropriate qualifications." Students brutally assassinated my character, my abilities, and my soul. When I had Aboriginal students in the class, the law school ignored their positive evaluations because, of course, Aboriginal students would automatically rate me highly as a teacher. When I had negative evaluations from white students, the school put them out for all to see as the school thought the white students had rated me objectively as a poor teacher. Everyday, I faced that hostility and racism. I felt alone and without support as no one at the school could understand my experience of racism.

Workloads often differ for Aboriginal faculty. During my time at the law school, I sat on the studies committee, Indigenous Blacks and Mi'kmaq Program committee and Advisory Board, Employment Equity Council, and the TYP Advisory Board. I also had to finish my LL.M. I am also expected to know everything "Aboriginal." But of course, I did not know enough to teach law to mainstream students.

I had to teach constitutional law and public law—required courses that most students did not see as advantageous to their career path. Having a brown face teaching these courses set some students off on a path of racial harassment. I went to the Dean with my issues and she did nothing to support me. In my second year of teaching, another professor attended my lectures with her class. Again, the school told me that students had complained about my teaching style. But at that time, I had another professor observing my class. The school did not pursue the complaints when the Dean learned that another professor in the class with me provided feedback and could disprove the allegations of poor teaching. I had support from other colleagues who affirmed my role as a teacher. The administration anticipated that I would not have support from others and had counted on my isolation.

In my first year of graduate studies, I had two part-time jobs, took a full course load, and taught one course. I also had my family and extended family responsibilities to deal with. I am also diabetic which can derail me. At the same time, many of my colleagues did not face the same challenges of poverty, illness, and racism. I had no release time for my thesis until 2001. When I became the Director of the Indigenous Blacks and Mi'kmaq Program in 2000, the Dean promised to allow me to teach a course in the law school once I achieved my Master's degree. I did complete my LL.M. but then was told that I could not teach. This was a result of the law school's judgment that I failed as a first and second-year law teacher in 1995-96.

Unfortunately, despite achieving my Master's degree in law, I did not have the opportunity to teach a course in the law school after those painful two years of teaching. I found out that due to my grades (or perhaps my thesis, I am not sure), I would never be allowed to teach at the law school. Despite my experience in many areas, the Dean in no uncertain terms, told me that I would never be allowed to teach at the law school again, as apparently I did not have the "appropriate qualifications." I felt so confused because the rules changed midstream as to my job, my duties, and my responsibilities with respect to my former law school position. So another crevice appeared, without warning.

Mainstream judgmental barriers face all Aboriginal people in the Dalhousie law school. I have wondered what is wrong with me. I cannot overcome these hurdles. Other times, I become filled with rage over the unfairness of it all. I cannot put into words the despair I experienced or the lack of confidence I suffered during those two years. I could fill a book with my negative experiences. I am so grateful to have tremendous support in my current position, as director of the Transition Year Program. I had little or no support in the law school.

Due to the lack of support, I left the law school to work in my community. I couldn't handle the racism anymore—the veiled judgments about minority students in the Indigenous Blacks and Mi'kmaq Program as being "less than" other students. Having grown up in my community, I live my life in a Mi'kmaq way, which means, in the school's mind, as "less than." My Mi'kmaq way did not fit into the law school. Mainstream culture focuses upon the individual. The Mi'kmaq culture focuses upon family and community responsibility. To juggle conflicting values while trying to adapt to mainstream culture becomes difficult when the institution does not take seriously our cultural connection to our communities. Institutions tend to devalue Aboriginal scholars whose work focuses upon community unless non-native people pursue such research. Our family and cultural responsibilities limit and impact on our ability to gain and retain employment.

While the numbers may show an increase in the hiring of designated group members, particularly white women, the retention issue for Aboriginal employees illustrates the clash of cultures that occurs when Aboriginal people gain positions within institutions, such as those in academia. I have suffered throughout my law school career due to these cultural clashes and denial of my experiences. As Monture-Okanee (1992) states:

The continued denial of our experience at every corner, at every turn, from education at residential schools through to university, is violence. The denial of my experience batters me from all directions. Because others have the power to define my existence, experience and even my feelings, I am left with no place to stand and validly construct my reality. That is the violence of silence. Separateness limits remedial proceedings that could compensate for past injustice by the power of legal definition. (197-98; see also Doyle)

The law school did not recognize these issues as cultural clashes but as character flaws unique to me. The administration could also point out other "Aboriginal People" who did not have my problems.

As noted earlier, the designated group of Aboriginal lacks precise definition. As a result, some people identify as Aboriginal when in fact their cultural and community connection does not exist at all. Because employment equity depends upon self-identification, basically anyone may self-identify as Indian when in reality, their only community connections to Indians may have occurred at the first Thanksgiving. Universities love hiring these types of "Indians." Because these types of Indians have never faced poverty, racism, and oppression, they often do not carry the same baggage as First Nations people. Defined as "new Indians," Devon Mihesuah states: "many of the new Indians are not knowledge-able about their tribes" (Mihesuah and Wilson 9). Cornel Pewewardy makes a much stronger argument against institutions that rely on self identification, which allows ethnic fraud.

Ethnic fraud is the inaccurate self-identification of race by persons applying for faculty positions at mainstream colleges and universities, or for admission to special programs and for research consideration. Gonzales defines ethnic fraud as the deliberate falsification or chang-ing of ethnic identities in an attempt to achieve personal advantage or gain. (201-202)

The difficulty with the "new Indians" lies in their lack of tribal or cultural affiliation. As a result, they have no problems fitting in with the mainstream. Moreover, they tend to speak with the "authoritative voice" for all First Na-tions. As a result, they have not suffered from racism or the injuries that flow from the violence of oppression. Mainstream institutions tend to accept their experience as the norm, which further isolates those of us with community connections. Thus, these "new Indians" do not face one of the major barriers in achieving employment equity, the community and cultural connection that most Aboriginal people have maintained. Despite the lack of understanding from mainstream institutions, my cultural and community connections remains the foundation of who I am as a Mi'kmaq woman. I am connected to a large community and, I come from a very extended family. But I feel divided when my responsibilities conflict with mainstream values and mainstream institutions that refuse to acknowledge our responsibilities for our family, our community, and our cultural values.

For example, in my first year of law teaching, my mother suffered severe injuries in a car accident. My niece and nephew were also in the car with her. This occurred on a Friday afternoon. My husband, son, nephew, and I drove to Cape Breton. My mother survived the accident and had a long healing period. However, by Sunday, she had recovered sufficiently for me to return to Halifax as I had a class to teach on Monday. I did not dare miss that class. I arrived in Halifax and taught my class. None of my Mi'kmaq students attended the class. After the class, one of my Mi'kmaq students ran into me in the hall. She exclaimed, "What are you doing here, we heard that your mom was in a serious car accident." I said that that was true. My student said, "We expected you to be in Cape Breton; that is why none of us came to class. I am shocked that you are here."

And herein lies the cultural schism that I face everyday. I knew I should have stayed home in Cape Breton but I also knew that the law school would not understand if I had to miss a class for such a family emergency. My expectation came true later when I suffered three miscarriages and lost my nephew. I find it healing to tell this story because the cultural schism widened when my nephew was killed in another car accident in August 2000. I went home for the wake and funeral. I came back to Halifax because I needed to get things settled at work because I had to return to Chapel Island. After the funeral, I cried because I had so much fear of facing the law school. I knew they would not understand the loss of my nephew, the need to take care of my mom, the need to support my sister and her other children as well as my own nuclear family. But I said no; I will not prejudge. I arrived at Dalhousie and my Dean at Henson saw me, gave me a hug, and said, "Take the time you need, we understand and we are here for you."

But I still had to face the law school. Now, a few of my colleagues supported me, I believe that. But a few at the law school did not. I had to meet with senior administrators and many other people to ensure my job would be done while I was on compassionate leave. Not one person said I am sorry for the loss of your nephew. It felt like, "Oh well, another dead Indian, what can you do?" They expressed more compassion for a judge whose puppy was sick than for my family. I will never forget walking into that office and facing that hostility. I was in a very emotionally vulnerable position. While I had the permission to take the time off, I knew that I would pay a price for asserting my rights under the collective agreement for bereavement leave.

Clearly, my law school experience has further marginalized me, in terms of my self-confidence and my identity. My experience tells me that I did not fit in the law school (see *The Voices of Visible Minorities*). Those in power chose to ignore me and invalidate my experience of racism and marginalization. Historical and current oppression leaves us on the outside, looking in. Not because we don't have merit but because racial stereotypes about our lack of "appropriate qualifications" continues to rule in the mainstream (*The Voices of Visible Minorities* 4-5). The name of this article, "With the Appropriate Qualifications," reflects my experience of the subjectivity that continues to govern particular employment situations. Many employers derive their "objectivity" from racial stereotypes. Internalizing these negative stereotypes makes it difficult to speak out about racism. Maybe what they think is true? Even in my situation, filing a complaint against the law school would have further marginalized me. Pursuing human rights complaints under the provincial or federal process rips open the pain of racism and leaves the wound open for all to see, often serving to to further traumatize the victim.

The most recent case of *Moore v. Play it Again Sports*[9] is instructive in the reasons why we often fear filing a complaint and also why we cannot gain remedy in the tribunals and courts. Kateri Moore is a Mi'kmaq woman who worked at Play it Again Sports as a sales clerk. Ms. Moore's boss, she alleged, created a poisoned work environment for her by making remarks about picking Indian women up in bars as well as calling her "Kemosabi." She alleged that her boss continued to call her Kemosabi, despite her requests for him to stop. She alleged discrimination based on race/gender.

The Nova Scotia Human Rights Tribunal ruled that Ms. Moore had not been subject to discrimination by her boss when he called her Kemosabi. In reading this case, two points became clear. First, the Tribunal did not understand the experience of racism. The Tribunal called witnesses forward from the Mi'kmaq community to determine if the term Kemosabi was offensive. The Tribunal members watched hours of the Lone Ranger and Tonto television series. They also asked linguistic experts to determine the origin of the word Kemosabi. Despite intention not being a relevant consideration in the determination of discrimination, the Tribunal made reference to the respondent's state of mind in terms of his racist perspectives or lack thereof.

Second, the Tribunal appeared to blame the complainant for her circumstances. Ms. Moore did not complain right away. She accepted rides home from her boss. She appeared to be the only employee who thought her boss racist. According to the Tribunal, Ms. Moore had some sort of mental breakdown when she ended up quitting her job.

The Human Rights Commission appealed this ruling to the Nova Scotia Court of Appeal. The Nova Scotia Court of Appeal upheld the tribunal decision (*The Nova Scotia Human Rights Commission and Dorothy Kateri Moore v. Play it Again Sport Ltd., Trevor Muller and Ron Muller*). The Court stated that, "the findings of the Board clearly support the conclusion that the respondents did not, in Ms. Moore's workplace, discriminate against her by making a distinction based on her Aboriginal heritage or status" [27].

Clearly, the Tribunal and Court of Appeal ignored the social context of discrimination. By making reference to Ms. Moore's emotional state, while denying any discrimination took place, the tribunal evidently does not understand the impact of racism. The Tribunal separated her reaction from the behaviour that acted as a catalyst for creating a poisoned workplace. When I read this case, I understood my reluctance to file human rights complaints because I would become the focus. My state of mind, my reaction, my inadequacies would be on trial for all to see.

As long as we cannot find remedy in the very organization that exists to support us, we need to find other ways to ensure our workplace remains free of discrimination. Most importantly, if racism and discrimination do poison our workplace, we must come up with alternative ways to confront the problem and initiate creative solutions.

Despite the laws, constitutional protections, human rights commissions, both federal and provincial, employment equity has yet to be achieved for Aboriginal Peoples. If Mi'kmaq people cannot gain remedies at the Human Rights Tribunals, the question is: How do we rectify discrimination? How do we implement employment equity? How do we achieve fairness in the workplace? I have stayed at Dalhousie as a professor because despite my experience at the law school, Dalhousie as an institution has made strides in supporting Aboriginal and African-Canadian faculty. In the next section, I explore the changes that Dalhousie has made on the path to achieving employment equity.

MOVING TOWARDS EQUITY: THE HEALING

The struggle for employment equity goes far beyond the numbers. It depends upon not only the hiring of Aboriginal Peoples but also their retention. The difficulties arise when cultural clashes occur in employment practices such as hiring process, supervision, performance reviews, and workplace environments. Harish Jain and John Lawler argue that establishing good practices for minorities in the workplace requires more than just adherence to the law. They established an index that measures indicators such as accountability, numerical goals and guidelines, monitoring and control mechanisms, on-going publicity, employment practice review, special target or designated group recruitment and training efforts, employment equity committee or Coordinator, resources, and budget (2). By reviewing results from questionnaires, the authors concluded that racism plays a large part in the disparity in achievements between different minorities and whites in the labour market (20). Rather than debating the existence of racism, the authors advocate further studies to explore the institution from within in order to provide direct empirical evidence on the specific behaviours and attitudes that affect the employment relationship that leads to discriminatory practice (20).

L. E. Falkenburg and L. Boland also explore the development of internal mechanisms of control and enforcement instead of relying on further government intervention (97). Taking responsibility for employment equity in the workplace, from the top down, lends credence to employment equity policies. I believe this is happening at Dalhousie University.

There is no question that at Dalhousie I have experienced the schism of the vision of employment equity not meeting the reality of the situation. To Dalhousie's benefit, we met together, the administration and the Aboriginal faculty, (all three of us), and discussed freely the issues facing us at Dalhousie. We discussed the issues of mentoring, support for our community connections and work, acknowledgement of our significant workload, and the need to examine the process of tenure and promotion. With the imposition of employment equity, the merit principle took precedence. Prior to the need for "standards," the informal network of old cronies had referred each other to jobs and supported each other. Once the merit principle emerged, the need for standards created more barriers for Aboriginal academics. Not only did we need to figure out the informal network but also now we would be judged by standards not of our making; standards that ignored a social context of racism, poverty, oppression, and violence. I have faced many of these issues. Even faculty members at the law school who purport to support "equity seeking groups" have been extremely judgmental of my background, my oppression, and my community.[10]

In our candid discussions about employment equity, I felt validated for the first time with respect to my experiences at the law school. While discussing racism may encourage those in power to become defensive, the senior administrators of Dalhousie University as well as the Employment Equity officer listened attentively, without debate. Out of these meetings arose recommendations for change.

First, we identify the need of getting through the door. Even with the "appropriate qualifications," the mainstream's view of diminishing qualifications because of racial background remains constant. Employment and educational equity programs focused on Aboriginal students and others who are "racially visible" (another term I do not like because I think white people are visible, and we tend to be invisible) tend to be seen by the mainstream as people getting an education through the back door with lower qualifications and suspect degrees at the end. But as I said, getting through the door is only the first step. The university needs to reach out to the community. In some instances, qualifications for employment should be closely examined to determine if the qualifications fit the job.

Competition between equity groups often means that white women tend to win over people who are racially visible. Thus, statistics are skewed in favour of white women.[11] Deciding on priorities for employment equity means that one group is more important than the other. Again, the subjective analysis concludes that we like people who are like us. Brown faces are not white. And herein lies the problem.

However, let us assume you get through the door, through the scrutiny of your grades from graduate school, the minute examination of your thesis, and the personality tests of your professors (Indian lovers, equity seekers, liberal world changers). Once you get in the door, you must now try (or not) to fit into a culture that is different. In my experience, I learned more about my Mi'kmaq culture when I realized the deep crevice of difference between what I see as truth and what the mainstream sees as truth. I discovered that I thought differently; my values focused on family and community, and my passion for researching issues of concern to Aboriginal people to create social change all contrasted strongly with the mainstream. As noted earlier, in Mi'kmaq culture, family is all-important. Community connections remain paramount. This is in stark contrast to the culture that says individual achievements are the norm and community connection the aberration. Our community connection often translates into a significant workload for Aboriginal faculty. Managing this workload, trying to gain tenure, and being the "Aboriginal expert" takes its toll on all of us.

Despite the fear, we told our stories. Out of my story, and the stories of so many other faculty of colour, we devised the following recommendations. Given that all of us had attended Dalhousie University as students, many of the recommendations focused on students as well as faculty.

Initiatives to Recruit and Retain African-Canadian and Aboriginal Students:

- •Create an Employment Equity/Diversity Education Web site. This is ongoing.
- •Mentoring programs for African-Canadian and Aboriginal students. We recently met to develop guidelines for mentoring.
- •Scholarship support for academic excellence.
- •Accreditation of TYP courses (TYP currently offers courses not for credit to prepare students from both groups for university).
- •Exploration of other access programs similar to TYP and IB&M such as science and medicine.
- •Voluntary self-identification will be added to application forms in order to identify students for scholarships and for mentoring purposes.

Initiatives to Recruit and Retain Aboriginal and African-Canadian Faculty:

- •Faculty and departmental workloads should be defined to recognize and provide guidance to tenure and promotion committees on appropriate levels of community involvement in the assessment of the achievements of faculty members. This issue is being addressed through the new Promotion and Tenure guidelines.
- •Faculties will be encouraged to create an affirmative action program that would be used as part of the recruitment process in various units where promising designated group members who do not meet probationary tenure track criteria would enter the faculty on a convertible limited term basis. There is a planned senior administrator workshop on equity.
- •Develop Tenure and Promotion handbook orientating probationary

tenure-track faculty members and assist in guiding the committees in the tenure and promotion process. Faculties will also be encouraged to perform an annual review of probationary tenure track members to provide feedback to new faculty in order to meet the requirements for tenure and promotion.

•Faculties will be encouraged to develop a formal mentoring program.

•The President will sponsor bi-annual networking opportunities for designated group members and staff.

•Employment Equity workshops will be held for all staff/faculty such as "History of Barriers Facing African-Canadian and Aboriginal People."

•The Employment equity office will collect data and report to the President on the recruitment and retention efforts for Nova Scotia Black and Aboriginal employees.[12]

In my own experience, I feel positive about the contributions made by the Aboriginal Faculty at this meeting. I am also impressed that the senior administrators have listened to our views, adopted our recommendations, and begun the process of implementation. In my own tenure process, the committee included my community work while recognizing the many demands that flow from my workload. Often, in my experience at the law school, my community and committee work at the university was dismissed as work that took away from the law school. Thankfully, my tenure and promotion committee did not share this view. Despite false starts due to missed deadlines, I earned my tenure at Dalhousie. Focusing upon my writing, my community work, my position at Dalhousie, I did feel overwhelmed by the process. Designing and creating my dossier left me anxious and sleepless. I felt judged by people who could not understand the intricacies of my position, the community connection of TYP, and the ongoing requirement to act as the Aboriginal expert, to research and write, to counsel students whilst managing staff and budgets as well as travelling to the communities. The majority of professors do not have their work judged on so many levels. While the committee interviewed many people from the Dalhousie community, I always feared that my tenure and promotion process would not proceed smoothly. Over eight months of stress and fear, interviews, uncertainty, and the nagging doubt that perhaps I have not worked hard enough, limited my ability to maintain my position.

My Mi'kmaq world and values shape and inform my reality. To this end, the establishment of mentoring for new faculty provides information for navigating this world of academia. More than anything, having someone on your side, to assist and support you in your move to a tenured position decreases the isolation Aboriginal faculty often face in their attempt to gain a foothold in the university. I am also excited about the opportunity to be a mentor to new faculty.

I titled this section, "Moving Towards Healing." Sharing my experience will hopefully make the road easier for the next person. I carried my pain with me, and I assumed that my shortcomings prevented me from teaching and writing. I now recognize my own shortcomings, but at the same time I also acknowledge the role that systemic racism played in my experience. I am now teaching at the Faulty of Management, through the School of Resource and Environmental Studies. I teach "Indigenous Peoples and Natural Resources" with Professor Fay Cohen. Last year, due to Professor Cohen's sabbatical, I had to teach the course alone. All my old fears came back. But I faced the class, taught my curriculum, and I had a wonderful experience. Once I wrote this paper, I felt stronger within myself. I thought my working environment would be positive, friendly, and I would feel connected to those I teach and work with. But tenure brought with it the cancellation of my class, the lack of movement on the initiatives, and the need to further commit to the initiatives to support Aboriginal faculty in pursuing our dream.

The initiatives aimed at employment equity, while supported at the senior administrative level, rely on faculties and departments for implementation. It remains to be seen if faculties and departments will commit to these initiatives. Even today, some faculty deans question the level of responsibility their departments have towards meeting these objects. Today, lack of progress depends upon budgetary constraints that restrict the hiring of Aboriginal peoples and development of curriculum taught by Indigenous professors. Lack of money meant my course could not be offered. Yet at the same time, Dalhousie pursues ongoing financial commitments with the Mi'kmaq community. Dalhousie will do X if someone else pays. Yet my course, the only one on campus taught by an Indigenous professor, faces cancellation and I lose the opportunity to further my professional development.

CONCLUSION

When the conference organizers asked me to speak on Indigenous Peoples and racism in the workplace, I struggled with sharing my story, knowing the danger facing me. I never want to hurt anyone, but still the fear churned inside of me. I believe strongly in visions of equity and the need to move forward with the implementation of that vision. But underpinning my vision is the nagging voice that maybe "they" were right. Speaking out about my pain and my story can be dangerous but I want to show that I have moved beyond the law school. Yet, attending a law conference frightened me.

We often find help in unexpected places. During my visit to Washington D.C., my husband and I visited the American Museum of the American Indian. Upon walking into the first exhibit, I found the following:

> All My Relations: Entire nations perished in the wave of death that swept the Americas. Even their names are lost to us. We cannot tell you where they lived, what they believed, or what they dreamed. Their

experiences are buried and unknowable. Like much of Indian history, only fragments are left to us. This wall names many of the languages spoken by our relatives who are still here as well as those ancestors that vanished without a trace. The list can never be whole, it will always be incomplete. Nine in ten native people perished in the first century of contact between the hemispheres. One in ten survived. They didn't fear change, they embraced it. Their past lives on in our present. As descendents of the one in ten who survived, we in the twenty-first century share an inheritance of grief, loss, hope and immense riches. The achievements of our ancestors make us accountable for how we move in the world today. Their lessons instruct us and make us responsible for remembering everything, especially those things we never knew (Chaat Smith).

I recognized, finally, that possessing the strength flowing from my ancestors is their gift to me and this generation. I found the courage to speak and to write my story. I must respect my ancestors' power of resistance and survival. Flowing from that strength, I have shared my truth.

Wel'la'liak (thank you).

Originally published in Canadian Woman Studies/les cahiers de la femme, *"Indigenous Women in Canada: The Voices of First Nations, Inuit and Métis Women" 26 (3 & 4) (Winter/Spring 2008): 77-89. Reprinted with permission of the author.*

Patti Doyle-Bedwelll s a Mi'kmaq woman. She was a member of the National Association of Women and the Law (NAWL) for five years and has presented on topics such as Aboriginal women's issues such as custody, access, housing, politics, discrimination, employment equity, education, and health. She was president of the Advisory Council on the Status of Women where she developed community partnerships and made many public/media presentations on Aboriginal women's issues. She currently directs the Transition Year Program at Dalhousie University College of Continuing Education in Halifax, Nova Scotia. She has two law degrees.

[1] The Indigenous Black and Mi'kmaq Program, active since 1989, is an admissions program at Dalhousie Law School that increases the number of Aboriginal and African-Canadian students at the law school.

[2] The use of "Aboriginal" in this paper parallels the usage in *The Constitution Act, 1982*, Section 35. I use the word "peoples" rather than "people" unless specific documents or contexts use the latter. For general information about Aboriginal Peoples in Canada see Berger.

[3] Now Justice R. Abella, as she has just been appointed to the Supreme Court of Canada.

[4]The Supreme Court of Canada first interpreted s. 15 of the Charter, developed a definition of discrimination and expanded the categories of discrimination by development of enumerated and analogous grounds. Mr. Andrews wished to practice law in British Columbia but did not meet the citizenship requirement to do so. The Supreme Court found in his favour. It is also telling that Mr. Andrews found a remedy for discrimination based on citizenship using section 15(1) of the Charter when he is a white lawyer from South Africa.

[5]For further discussion of the social conditions faced by Aboriginal Peoples, please see, *The Report of the Royal Commission on Aboriginal Peoples*.

[6]Section 35(1) of the *Constitution Act 1982* being Schedule B to the *Canada Act 1982* (U.K.) states: "The existing Aboriginal and treaty rights of the Aboriginal and treaty rights of the Aboriginal peoples of Canada are hereby recognized and affirmed."

(2) In this Act, "Aboriginal peoples of Canada" includes the Indian, Inuit, and Métis peoples of Canada.

(3) "For greater certainty, in subsection (1) 'treaty rights' includes rights that now exist by way of land claims agreements or may be so acquired."

[7]For example, in Nova Scotia, besides the thirteen bands, there are four political organizations that purport to represent various groups of Aboriginal Peoples. The Union of Nova Scotia Indians represents the Cape Breton Bands, the Confederacy of Mainland Mi'kmaq represents the bands on the mainland of Nova Scotia, the Native Council of Nova Scotia represents those Aboriginal people who live off the reserve and who do not have status under the Indian Act. Whether the Native Council represents off reserve status Indians is hotly debated among the political organizations. Most recently, another group, the Nova Scotia Confederacy of Métis, has come forward, representing Aboriginal people not covered under the other groups.

[8]I use this term because one of my white students complained to the Dean that all I talked about in class was the "plight of the poor oppressed people."

[9]Tribunal Decision (On file with author). As well, please see: http://www.gov.ns.ca/humanrights/decisions/2004decisions.htm.

[10]One law faculty member who builds her career on equity questioned my work habits, and stated that I was acting like a white woman. She also sent an email to CAUT questioning my connection to my Mi'kmaq community. She is also someone who waves the flag of equity.

[11]The issues surrounding this program demand another paper.

[12]These recommendations are taken from the President's Initiatives designed to support "Recruitment and Retention of Aboriginal and African Nova Scotian Faculty and Students" (On file with author).

REFERENCES

Abella, Judge R. 1984. *Equality in Employment: A Royal Commission Report.* Ottawa: Minister of Supply and Services Canada.

Andrews v. The Law Society of British Columbia [1989] 1 S.C.R. 143.

Berger, T. R. *A Long and Terrible Shadow: White Values, Native Rights in the Americas.* Vancouver: Douglas and McIntyre, 1991.

Constitution Act 1982, c. 11 (UK).

Canadian Human Rights Commission (CHRC). Policy Guidelines. Online: <http://www.chrc-ccdp.ca/legislation_policies/Aboriginal_employment-en.asp>.

Chaat Smith, Paul. American Museum of the American Indian. Washington D.C. 2003.

Doyle, P. E. "Domestic Violence among Native Women." Unpublished Honours Thesis, submitted in partial completion of the requirements for a Bachelor's Degree in Sociology and Social Anthropology, Dalhousie University, 1990. On file with author.

Falkenburg, L. E. and L. Boland, "Eliminating the Barriers Employment Equity in the Workplace." *Journal of Business Ethics* 16 (9) (1997): 963-975.

Gunderson, Morley, Douglas Hyatt, and Sara Slinn. 2002. *Employment Equity in the United States and Canada: The Industrial Relations Research Association Proceedings.* Online: http://www.press.uillinoise.edu/journals/irra/proceedings2002

Hassman, R. Howard. "Sins of the Fathers: Canadian Civic Leaders Discuss Employment Equity." *Windsor Yearbook of Access to Justice* 21 (2002): 21.

http://www.ainc-inac.gc.ca/pr/sts/rip/rip03_e.pdf at xiii.

Henderson, J. "Empowering Treaty Federalism." *Saskatchewan Law Review* 58 (1994): 241-329.

Jain, H. and J. Lawler. "Good Practices for Visible Minorities in the Workplace." A Report prepared for Human Resources Development Canada, April 2003. Online: <http://hrsdc.gc.ca./asp/passerell.asp>.

King, Thomas. 2003. *The Truth About Native Stories: A Native Narrative.* Toronto: House of Anansi Press.

Mihesuah, D. and A. Wilson, eds. *Indigenizing the Academy: Transforming Scholarship and Empowering Communities.* Lincoln: University of Nebraska Press: Lincoln, 2004.

Monture-Angus, P. *Thunder in my Soul: A Mohawk Woman Speaks.* Halifax: Fernwood Press, 1995.

Monture-Angus, P. "Reclaiming Jus-tice: Aboriginal Women in the 1990's." The Royal Commission on Aboriginal People, *Aboriginal People and the Justice System: Report on the National Roundtable on Aboriginal Justice Issues.* Ottawa: Canadian Publishing Group, 1992. 237-266.

Monture-Okanee, P. "Introduction: Surviving the Contradictions." *Breaking Anonymity: The Chilly Climate for Women Faculty.* Eds. Chilly Collective. Waterloo: Wilfred Laurier University Press, 1995. 11-28.

Monture-Okanee, P. "The Violence We Women Do: A First Nations View." *Contemporary Times: Conference Proceedings of Contemporary Women's Movement in Canada and the United States.* Eds. David Flaherty and Constance

Backhouse. Montreal: Queen's-McGill Press, 1992. 191-200.

Moore v. Play it Again Sports Tribunal Decision. On file with author.

The Nova Scotia Human Rights Commission and Dorothy Kateri Moore v. Play it Again Sport Ltd., Trevor Muller and Ron Muller, 2004 Nova Scotia Court of Appeal, 132.

Pewewardy, C. "'So You Think You Hired an Indian Faculty Member': The Ethnic Fraud Paradox in Higher Education." *Indigenizing the Academy: Transforming Scholarship and Empowering Communities.* Eds. D. Mihesuah and A. Wilson. Lincoln: University of Nebraska Press, 2004.

Registered Indian Population by Sex and Residence, 2003. Ottawa: Ministry of Indian Affairs and Northern Development, 2004. Online: <http://www.ainc-inac.gc.ca/pr/sts/rip/rip03_e.pdf>.

Report of the Royal Commission on Aboriginal Peoples. Vols. 1-5. Ottawa: Communications Canada, 1995.

Smith, L. Tuhiwai. *Decolonizing Methodologies: Research and Indigenous Peoples.* London: Zed, 1999.

The Voices of Visible Minorities: Speaking Out on Breaking Down Barriers. Report of the Conference Board of Canada 2004. Online: <http://www.triec.ca/docs/ConfBrdCanVoicesVisibleMinorities.pdf 3>.

SUSAN JUDITH SHIP AND LAURA NORTON

HIV/AIDS AND ABORIGINAL WOMEN IN CANADA

D RAMATIC AND RAPID INCREASES in HIV and AIDS rates among Aboriginal peoples in Canada, particularly among Aboriginal women, have been
recorded despite under-reporting and the small number of documented AIDS
cases (Health Canada 2000a; 2000b). The patterns of HIV and AIDS among
Aboriginal women are markedly different from that observed for Canadian
women in general (Health Canada 2000a; Nguyen et al 1997) Epidemiological
data for 1998-1999 shows that Aboriginal women constituted 49.6 per cent of
newly diagnosed HIV cases among Aboriginal people, while non-Aboriginal
women comprise 20 per cent of newly diagnosed non-Aboriginal HIV cases
(Health Canada 2000a). Injection drug use is the major mode of HIV transmission among Aboriginal women, followed by heterosexual sexual contact. HIV
infection occurs at a younger age for Aboriginal women than for non-Aboriginal
women. Young women constitute the largest proportion of Aboriginal AIDS
cases. Consequently, the risk of HIV transmission from mothers to infants is
increasing (Health Canada 2000a). Despite these facts, Aboriginal women
continue to remain invisible in HIV/AIDS research and policy as well as face
numerous barriers in accessing services (Ship and Norton 2000).

CULTURAL DISRUPTION AND THE SUBORDINATION OF
ABORIGINAL WOMEN: THE LEGACY OF EUROPEAN CONTACT

A focus on Aboriginal women and HIV/AIDS necessarily raises the issue of
gender and women's subordination in addition to the unique historical and
socioeconomic factors that shape Aboriginal women's lives. Gender refers to
the social construction of men's and women's social roles that are historically
shaped, culturally contextualized, and class-specific (Ship 1994). Understanding
how HIV/AIDS affects women entails analysis of the socially constructed differences between men and women and how this shapes distinct female and male
experiences. Women's subordination or gender inequality among Aboriginal
peoples is largely a consequence of European contact and colonialism. The
imposition of European notions of women's social position resulted in the dispossession of Aboriginal women's rights and the devaluation of women's social

roles (Shawanda 1995). In addition to the legacies of multiple disadvantages and multi-generational abuse that affected Aboriginal communities, families, and individuals, cultural disruption served to deepen women's subordination to men (Ship and Norton 2000).

Employing a culturally-sensitive gender perspective in order to capture the unique aspects of Aboriginal women's experiences, our research explored two themes: how cultural disruption, residential schooling, family and cultural breakdown, and the legacy of multi-generational abuse affects HIV risk among Aboriginal women and how HIV affects their lives differently from men.

ABORIGINAL WOMEN IN HARD-TO-REACH COMMUNITIES AT RISK FOR HIV

Vulnerability to HIV risk has, often, more to do with, "social and environmental factors such as stigma, poverty, discrimination, sexism and racism than with individual behaviour" (Trussler and Marchand 1997: 63). Understanding how HIV risk and HIV/AIDS affect Aboriginal peoples necessarily raises the issues of the legacy of disadvantage that resulted from European contact and colonialism, which continues to impact negatively on the physical, mental-emotional, social, and spiritual health of Aboriginal peoples, families, and communities. Residential schooling, multi-generational abuse, and forced assimilation in tandem with widespread poverty, racism, sexism, loss of culture, values, and traditional ways of life have given rise to a range of pressing social problems that include alcoholism, substance abuse, high suicide rates, violence against women, and family violence (Ship and Norton 1998; ANAC 1996). High rates of sexually transmitted diseases, alcoholism, and substance abuse in tandem with low rates of condom use and high rates of teenage pregnancies continue to increase vulnerability to HIV, particularly among Aboriginal young people, who are also over-represented in high risk groups—runaways, sex trade workers, and intravenous drug users (Ship and Norton 1998). HIV risk is further compounded by the over-representation of Aboriginal people in prison and inner-city services (Health Canada 2000a).

The majority of the Inuit women involved in sex work in Montreal that we interviewed,[1] left their communities as a result of the sexual and physical abuse they suffered within the family or at the hands of a partner. (Although it is not well-publicized, the Inuit are also survivors of residential schooling.) The women chose Montreal because they had a family member there or because they knew that there are Inuit people in the city. While these women pointed out that the Inuit community in Montreal is growing, the people are spread out and there isn't a sense of community. They came to a major metropolitan centre where they do not speak the language and could not find work despite the fact that most were working as teachers, nursing assistants, and in communications back home. Victims of racism and gender discrimination, in addition to an inability to speak French, these Inuit women found themselves on the streets engaging in sex work to survive. In turn, this led to a spiralling cycle of abuse, violence, alcoholism, and drugs.

All of the ten Inuit women we interviewed were aware of the risks of HIV from unprotected sex and sharing needles. Moreover, they seemed to be aware of the existence of the Needle Exchange Program in Montreal as well as where to obtain free condoms. All expressed fear about contracting HIV. All of the women stated initially in no uncertain terms that they do not have unprotected sex (sex without condoms) with clients, even when clients offer to pay more. However, staff working with the Inuit women involved in sex work suggested that the actual use of condoms was far less frequent than the women themselves reported. We were told that many Inuit women still don't use condoms because they are afraid that the men are going to get violent. Only three women had undergone HIV testing and staff informed us that many women do not keep appointments to be tested for HIV. Racial discrimination from health professionals, the long waiting period for test results, and the lack of pre and post-counselling were cited as reasons, but many women are also afraid of the results, indicating that they most likely engage in more risky behaviour than they had revealed in the interviews.

While Inuit women in the sex trade reported using condoms more frequently with clients, they all said that they don't usually use condoms when they are involved with long term or regular partners. Most of these women expressed the view that their long-term partners were "clean" and "safe." This pattern has been identified as fairly typical among non-Aboriginal sex trade workers as well (Ship and Norton 1998).

Only one of the women reported using IV drugs. She mainlines cocaine and asserted that she never shares needles. Eight of the women we interviewed use alcohol and soft drugs such as marijuana—which they did not see as posing a risk for HIV—on a regular basis. However, it is a widely shared view that alcohol and soft drug use play a major role in risky behaviour as it clouds judgment; for example, not using condoms when engaging in casual sex increases the risk of contracting HIV.

To a much greater extent than was revealed in these interviews, sexual abuse and physical violence appear to be a pervasive factor in these women's private lives and on the street. One woman, in tears, told us that she had been the victim of what appeared to be a "gang bang." While attending a party, drugs were slipped into her drink and she woke up completely nude the next morning. One older Inuit woman confided to us that her daughter, who is an alcoholic, had beaten her up. More telling than what women actually revealed about themselves is the fact that four of the Inuit women broke down in tears during the interviews, conveying a more vivid sense of the pain and abuse they have endured.

The situation of Inuit women on the street in Montreal can only be described as one of extreme marginality, isolation, and invisibility—women, with few supports and resources, cut off from their communities. Most of the women we interviewed did not return home frequently because they did not wish to or because they could not as a result of expulsion. Most women only returned home to visit with children or attend a funeral. They fall through the cracks of the system because there are no organizations mandated to address their needs. There is no separate organization or cultural centre for Inuit people in Montreal and many of these women expressed some discomfort at patronizing the Native Friendship Centre. Although none of the Inuit women were HIV-positive at the time of the interviews, they are at high risk for HIV, as the stories of their First Nations sisters on the streets in Vancouver, now living with HIV/AIDS, reveal.

FIRST NATIONS WOMEN LIVING WITH HIV/AIDS: CULTURAL DISRUPTION AND RESIDENTIAL SCHOOLS

Our interviews with First Nations women living with HIV/AIDS revealed the painfully clear links between cultural disruption, residential schooling, family and cultural breakdown, multi-generational abuse, and HIV. Almost all of them told us that they came from families where one or both parents had attended residential schools and alcoholism was a problem. Eight HIV-positive women admitted that they had been victims of sexual abuse as children. As one HIVpositive woman who was involved in an abusive relationship explained:

> *My mother and father drank. They were products of residential schools. I was the youngest. I was placed in a foster home.... It's tough being an Aboriginal woman. I was part of an abusive relationship. What I saw in him is what I got from my family. I was sexually abused.*

Many First Nations women who have been sexually and/or physically abused leave their communities and end up on the street; this was the case of most of the women we interviewed. More often than not, abused women become victims of a spiralling cycle of abuse that includes alcoholism, drug addiction, prostitution, and violence; a cycle thatplaces them at greater risk for HIV. For some, this spiralling cycle of abuse culminates in HIV, as this positive woman confirmed:

> *I never told them. I was afraid I would get beat or they would send me away. One day I finally stood up. My uncle was sent away after my mom died.... My family is Christian. They are too proud ... to find out that their youngest girl has turned to the street and IV drugs. That's how I dealt with abuse.*

Nine of the eleven HIV-positive women we interviewed had used alcohol and drugs extensively; in some cases, since their early teens. Half of the women admitted that they were still using IV drugs, mostly cocaine and to a lesser extent heroin, despite the fact that they know it is harmful to their health; too, some were still engaging in risky behaviour such as sharing needles. Almost all of the women smoke pot and drink. Drinking and using drugs are coping mechanisms to deal with abuse and HIV, to dull the intense pain these women carry deep inside. One woman said:

> I used drugs to forget. It made me feel good ... sex and men ... but the poverty and my children. It's a coping mechanism.... The pain is overwhelming.

Some positive women do find the courage to begin the healing process and stop the cycle of abuse so that their lives and their children's lives will be different. As this woman explained:

> There is a need to reclaim family identity and community ... [that the] residential schools polluted. It's a disease of the spirit. Our people need to move beyond this. They need to love one another. My family is making a conscious effort to change that cycle. It is a healing process reclaiming family identity. My daughter won't have to deal with this as I did, as my mother did and as my grandmother did.

HIV AFFECTS FIRST NATIONS WOMEN
DIFFERENTLY FROM MEN

Unlike gay men, many First Nations women living with HIV and AIDS are parents, and most are single mothers, living below the poverty line. All but one of the women we interviewed were receiving social assistance and most were living in the East Hastings area of Vancouver, "*the poorest postal code in Canada.*" Many financial supports are geared to the needs of single men or single people. Most women do not have adequate housing for themselves and their families.

Women's social roles as primary caregivers and nurturers in the family means that for HIV-positive women, they are responsible for caring for themselves, their children, their families and their partners, and more often than not, with fewer resources. As this woman explained:

> I think for a lot of women it's scary when you find out (you're positive), you're responsible for the whole world. You're responsible for your children ... your man ... your home, for everything.

For First Nations women living with HIV and AIDS, their health and well-being is last on their list of priorities, as this mother told us:

> A lot of women I talk to are so busy taking are of everybody else's needs that

their own needs are at the bottom of life. Their own health, their well-be-ing—physical, mental, emotional and spiritual—doesn't count.

Life is a daily struggle as most positive women can barely provide the basic needs—food, clothing, shelter, and transportation—for themselves and for their children. Many women cannot afford expensive treatments and difficult choices are often made between purchasing medications for themselves and basics for their families. As this single HIV-positive mother told us:

> *Your first priority is your child. All the money that you get if you live on welfare or have a job goes to your child, to your child's well-being. Sometimes you get a little bit for yourself … money, time out, or chance to sit and share with other women.*

For many First Nations women living with HIV/AIDS, their children's health, well-being, security, and future assume a greater importance than their own health, well-being, and needs. A primary and universal concern of seropositive mothers is: who will take care of their children if they get sick and after they die. As one mother explained: "*The first thing that popped into my head [when] I found out [I was HIV-positive] was who is going to take care of my children.*" Most women expressed guilt and anxiety about how their children would cope with the knowledge of having a mother who was HIV-positive. Too, most women worried about the impact this knowledge would have on their children when discussing the illness. Caught between wanting to protect their children and feeling that their children should know the truth, deciding when, how, and to which children to disclose their HIV status is a difficult, stressful, and complex process for HIV-positive parents, but particularly for single mothers with little social and emotional support. But children are also a source of joy, hope, support, and a primary motivation for the women we interviewed to find the strength and courage to live with HIV. One woman declared: "*I have to live with it and I have to stay strong for my children.*" For women who feel that their own lives have been shattered, their hopes and their dreams are for their children.

GENDER DISCRIMINATION AS HIV-POSITIVE WOMEN

Many First Nations women live in secrecy because of the multiple forms of stigma associated with HIV/AIDS. Too, they suffer from gender discrimination because as women they carry the additional stigma of being branded "promiscuous," "a bad mother," and "deserving of HIV/AIDS." Some of the women we interviewed felt that secrecy is perhaps a bigger issue for positive women because of a need to protect not only themselves but also their children. As one woman explained: "*Women are afraid of the shame and the guilt placed on them. People will not be so accepting of them and their families.*" Many women

239

fear that disclosure of their seropositive status will bring discrimination and rejection not only for themselves but for their children. As one HIV-positive woman put it so poignantly:

It's hard being a woman with HIV [in] a society that rejects women who are HIV-positive and that rejects the children.... It's still hard being a woman with HIV because of discrimination. It seems more acceptable for a man who is HIV-positive to be accepted than it is for a woman. I fear for my children.

MULTIPLE BARRIERS TO SERVICES

Many First Nations women living with HIV/AIDS under-utilize First Nations and non-Aboriginal services for fear that their communities will find out they are seropositive. They also encounter multiple barriers based on gender, racism, and class in accessing a broad range of services. As is well-known, gender barriers persist in women's access to treatment and clinical drug trials, partly because "of their reproductive capacities," as one women pointed out. There is a lack of services and supports for positive women and their children because "most AIDS services are geared to gay men, not to women and their families." One HIV-positive woman explained:

I think that women as caretakers in society don't have a lot of places they can go and don't have a lot of support systems. There is only one organization in Vancouver that is specifically an AIDS organization for women. All the rest are 90 per cent for men. They don't discriminate against women, but there really is no place for them.

Some of the positive women we interviewed acknowledged encountering subtle forms of racism in their interaction with non-Aboriginal, mostly white, health professionals. The lack of culturally-appropriate services and counselling for First Nations women living with HIV/AIDS was noted. Almost all agreed that many health professionals needed to improve their understanding of First Nations cultures and traditions. Half the women we interviewed expressed the need for "*more Aboriginal counsellors, particularly those who know street life.*"

EXTREME ISOLATION

As a consequence of multiple stigmas and barriers to services, First Nations women living with HIV/AIDS and their children, have little, if any, emotional and social support. Many of these women live in extreme isolation. The positive women we interviewed live in urban and metropolitan centres, far from their home communities because the city provides anonymity and because they feel that there is greater acceptance of HIV-positive women there.

Many positive women desire and need to return home. One woman observed: "*I know a lot of people that have no sense of family or community and they die really quick.*" But many women fear isolation, rejection, and discrimination if they return home, not only for themselves but also for their children and their families. Community responses vary. Some communities are accepting of their members living with HIV/AIDS while others are far less so, as lack of knowledge and fear predominate. One woman was forced to leave her community:

> *When people found out, they reacted very badly. It wasn't safe for me.... It's a small community. I was the first person in the community to test positive.*

First Nations women with HIV/AIDS living far from home, family, culture, and community, hope that their children will one day be able to go home:

> *I have been told by my doctor that I am dying and have to go on antivirals. It's a hard choice to make but I'm doing it because I want to live. I have two daughters. I want them to grow up, to be good people and to be good women. I want them to be able to go home some day because I do have land and a house back home.*

ABORIGINAL WOMEN CARING FOR PEOPLE LIVING WITH HIV/AIDS

For every First Nations and Inuit person who is living with HIV or AIDS, there are many other people who are affected. Female caregivers constitute the largest proportion of Aboriginal women most immediately affected by HIV/AIDS. The majority of caregivers of Aboriginal people living with HIV/AIDS are women—mothers, sisters, aunts, grandmothers, partners, friends, and professional caregivers such as AIDS educators, community health representatives (CHRs), community health nurses (CHNs), and home support workers—a consequence of women's social roles as "nurturers" and "caretakers" in the family. As one AIDS educator pointed out:

> *Women's roles are as caregivers. I think that's why we also see mostly women in our workshops because they are in the positions of home care workers, CHRs, and CHNs. They are in those caregiving roles in the community.*

Moreover, as our interviews indicate, initial disclosure of seropositive status or AIDS by the person affected is usually made to a close female family member—an aunt, a mother, a spouse, or a partner—while initial disclosure by a female caregiver is usually made to another female friend or family member.

In some cases, the female caregiver—a wife, a mother, or a grandmother—is the anchor for the entire family. Women, as unpaid and paid caregivers, tend to form the nucleus of support for people living with HIV/AIDS. We were repeatedly told by caregivers and AIDS educators alike, that women were far more likely to be primary caregivers to people living with HIV/AIDS and commit themselves to the end while men were less likely to make this kind of commitment. We were moved by the strength and depth of the commitment of the caregivers we interviewed.

The needs and the concerns of female caregivers tend to go largely unnoticed and unattended to because caregiving is seen as the natural role of women, and because women are supposed to be the nurturers and the caregivers; they are not allowed to get sick. Female caregivers are concerned with the health of the person living with HIV/AIDS and with the health of the family; their own health is the least important priority. Many caregivers need to learn how to better take care of their own physical, mental-emotional, social, and spiritual needs and not feel guilty about this. As one caregiver told us:

I think there should be more things done for caregivers so that they can be rejuvenated and go back energized ... [such as attending] retreats where they learn meditation and give back massages.

ISOLATION OF CAREGIVERS

Isolation is the biggest problem caregivers face that negatively affects their own health and well-being, the person with HIV/AIDS, and where pertinent, the family living with HIV/AIDS. Isolation of caregivers is a consequence of the continuing stigma attached to HIV/AIDS in Aboriginal communities and the resulting dilemma of disclosure. Lack of services, counselling, and supports for the caregiver, the loved one living with HIV/AIDS, and in some cases the family, particularly those living in Aboriginal communities and smaller urban centres, serves to reinforce their isolation.

Given that the stigma of HIV/AIDS may also be associated with additional stigmas around injection drug use, homosexuality, and/or lesbianism, there is enormous anxiety about when to disclose the seropositive status of a loved one to family, friends, school, workplace, and the larger community. Reluctance to disclose the seropositive status of a loved one is also related to fear of rejection, fear of emotional and physical harm to children, fear of discrimination, and/or simply needing time to come to grips with the reality of living with HIV/AIDS. For many caregivers, the burden of silence reinforces their own isolation and negatively affects their health and well-being. As one woman explained:

I had to get it off my shoulders. I went down to the AIDS organization and talked to someone. Then I told Mike: "Mike, I had to tell someone. You don't want me to tell the family."

FEW SUPPORTS AND SERVICES

Counselling and support for caregivers are almost nonexistent. Many caregivers find it difficult to accept the diagnosis of HIV of a loved one. As one woman told us:

> *The day he told me he had AIDS, I just lost it. I didn't believe it. I said, "You're lying. You're just trying to hurt me." It was very difficult accepting it. I just couldn't believe it. I'm one of those Aboriginal people who thought we would never get AIDS in our communities.*

Caregivers need time and support in working through their complex and often contradictory feelings and undergo a grieving process just as the people living with HIV/AIDS they are caring for must undergo. As this woman explained:

> *I went through much of the same things my daughter went through—the grieving process, the denial, the anger. I tried to be supportive of her but it was much harder for her.*

Some caregivers talked about the difficulties they experienced in watching loved ones with AIDS die a slow death. Both caregivers and the person they care for may need counselling and support in dealing with death and dying. Also, the family as a whole needs support and counselling in working through their feelings throughout all stages of the disease and with respect to making difficult decisions.

Caregivers and their families may also need counselling and support in situations where the loved one is still engaged in risky behaviours such as alcoholism or drug abuse; behaviours that pose a greater health risk to their seropositive condition and that may be linked to underlying issues of cultural disruption, residential schooling, and the legacy of multi-generational abuse. Some of the caregivers we talked with expressed frustration and anger at feeling powerless to help. As one woman explained:

> *Not being able to help them, you see all the frustration. They're compounding their illness by doing negative things. They are drinking and making themselves sick. There is nothing you can do to stop them and you know they are getting worse by drinking more.*

One caregiver observed:

> *It's like living in crisis mode.... But it makes you stronger and more compassionate when you go through these hard times.... You get a lot of strength from crisis and that's the positive thing that comes from it.*

Services for caregivers and Aboriginal people living with HIV/AIDS (particularly for individuals with an advanced state of AIDS living in small communities and smaller urban centres) are inadequate. Getting appropriate information and accessing services as quickly as possible can be difficult. We were told that in one case, a young man who had come home to his reserve to die, was growing progressively sicker and because it was Good Friday, there were no services open either in the community itself or in the surrounding region that his caregivers could access. They had to call an AIDS organization in Ottawa for help.

Other caregivers felt that many health professionals needed enhanced HIV/AIDS education. As one AIDS educator explained:

> *Access to services is the biggest barrier. You go to a community that is isolated, and you don't have access. You don't have a doctor. You don't have the medications. You may not have the knowledge. You may not have the ability. At least in the city we can go to the clinic or the hospital but in the small communities, you don't even have that.*

But even where available, many Aboriginal people living with HIV/AIDS are reluctant to use services offered by AIDS organizations, health agencies, and other social service organizations because they may have experienced racial discrimination while some heterosexual men articulated discomfort utilizing services set up for single gay men. The lack of services intensifies the burden of caregiving for Aboriginal women and diminishes the quality of life for the loved one being cared for.

Aboriginal communities vary in their support for people living with HIV/ AIDS. As AIDS educators told us, denial of HIV/AIDS and fear in many communities means that they do not act until there is a crisis. Most Aboriginal people with AIDS want to go home to die, but most Aboriginal communities do not have the necessary services and trained personnel to make that journey as comfortable as possible, particularly where several infections are in evidence at the same time. Moreover, there are few supports for female caregivers. One woman told us that she drives three and a half hours to attend a support group for female Aboriginal caregivers located in another province. The cost of transportation for these trips is high, particularly as she is living on a fixed income. Increased financial assistance, better home care, respite care, and support from family, friends, and the community go a long way in easing the burden of caregiving.

For many caregivers, their spirituality—in whatever form it takes—is the glue that keeps them together. As one woman told us:

> *My brother is a traditionalist. He was a sweat lodge keeper. He earned his pipe. He told us the proper way. We prayed for him in a Native way; the whole celebration from sunrise to the end.*

For caregivers, finding joy in life gives them the strength to go on; a new addition to the family keeps the circle strong.

CONCLUSION

The over-representation of Aboriginal women in HIV/AIDS statistics demands that we place them on research and policy agendas in addition to developing a greater range of culturally appropriate, gender-specific services, supports, and counselling to reduce HIV/AIDS risk and to improve the quality of life for women living with HIV/AIDS in hard-to-reach communities, as well as for their children and caregivers.

This article was commissioned by the Maritime Centre for Excellence in Women's Health. It is reprinted with permission.

The authors gratefully acknowledge funding from the Commonwealth Secretariat, the Maritime Centre of Excellence for Women's Health, and Health Canada for this paper. This case study is based on research in a previously unpublished document by Susan Judith Ship and Laura Norton, "It's Hard Being A Woman with HIV: Aboriginal Women and HIV/AIDS. Final Research Report 1999," Kahnawake, National Indian and Inuit Community Health Representatives Organization. The section on First Nations Women Living with HIV/AIDS was taken from, "It's Hard To Be A Woman! First Nations Women Living with HIV/AIDS."

Originally published in Canadian Woman Studies/les cahiers de la femme, *"Women and HIV/AIDS," 21 (2) (Summer/Fall 2001): 25-31. Reprinted with permission of the authors.*

Susan Judith Ship has a Ph.D. in Political Science. Her doctoral thesis, inspired by this research, explored the impact of HIV/AIDS on women in Senegal from a Woman/Gender and Development perspective, with a focus on state policies. She has published in the area of gender and diversity as well as conducted research on various issues pertaining to Aboriginal health, immigration, multiculturalism and anti-racist education.

Laura Norton is a Mohawk woman from Kahnawake. She is a mind and body therapist currently enrolled in the Department of Sociology at Concordia University. She has conducted research on various issues including aging, diabetes, HIV/AIDS, environment, and occupational standards. She is currently operating Sweet Grass Alternative Therapy, which she established in 1996 (offering aromatherapy, essential oils, vibration, and herbal medicine).

[1]The interviews were conducted by Laura Norton with the assistance of Susan

Judith Ship, during the fall of 1998, as part of a larger project for the National Indian and Inuit Community Health Representatives Organization.

REFERENCES

Aboriginal Nurses Association of Canada (ANAC). "HIV/AIDS and its Impact on Aboriginal Women." Ottawa, 1996.

Health Canada. "EPI Update: HIV and AIDS Among Aboriginal People in Canada." Ottawa: Health Canada: Laboratory Centre for Disease Control, 2000a.

Health Canada. "EPI Update: AIDS and Ethnicity in Canada." Ottawa: Health Canada: Laboratory Centre for Disease Control, 2000b. Nguyen, Mai, et al. "HIV/AIDS Among Aboriginal Women in Canada: A Growing Problem." Ottawa: Health Canada: Laboratory Centre for Disease Control, 1997.

Shawanda, Bea. "Healing Journey of Native Women." *Healing Our Nations Resource Manual.* Halifax: Atlantic First Nations AIDS Task Force, 1995.

Ship, Susan Judith, and Laura Norton. "It's Hard To Be a Woman! First Nations Women Living with HIV/AIDS." *Native Social Work Journal* 3 (1) (2000): 71-89.

Ship, Susan Judith, and Laura Norton. "It's Hard Being a Woman with HIV! Aboriginal Women and HIV/AIDS Final Research Report." Kahnawake: National Indian and Inuit Community Health Representatives Organization, 1999.

Ship, Susan Judith, and Laura Norton. "Triple Jeopardy: The Dynamics of Gender, 'Race' and Class Discrimination: Aboriginal Women and HIV/AIDS." Kahnawake: National Indian and Inuit Community Health Representatives Organization, 1998.

Ship, Susan Judith. "And What About Gender? Feminism and International Relations Theory's Third Debate." *Beyond Positivism: Critical Reflections on International Relations.* Eds. Claire Turenne Sjolander and Wayne S. Cox. Boulder: Lynne Rienner, 1994. Trussler, Terry, and Rick Marchand. "Field Guide: Community HIV Health Promotion." Ottawa: Health Canada/AIDS Vancouver, 1997.

ABORGINAL WOMEN AND THE CONSTITUTIONAL DEBATES

Continuing Discrimination

ABORIGINAL WOMEN HAVE BEEN discriminated against on the basis of sex by governments of Canada for over 100 years. Aboriginal women's struggle to end the sexual discrimination began after the enactment of the Canadian Bill of Rights,[1] and continues despite the advent of section 15 of the Canadian Charter of Rights and Freedoms.[2] With amendments to the *Indian Act,* Aboriginal women were among the first women to benefit legislatively from the Charter. Despite this, Aboriginal women still have not achieved sexual equality. The struggle continues, and has expanded today to involve a recognition of Aboriginal women's rights to represent ourselves in the ongoing constitutional discussions.

HISTORY OF SEXUAL DISCRIMINATION[3]

From the introduction of the *Indian Act* into federal law in 1869,[4] Aboriginal women who married non-Indians were stripped of their legal rights, and their Indian status, banished from their communities, and barred from their families. While the *Indian Act* intruded on all aspects of Aboriginal life in Canada, Aboriginal women were most harshly restricted by the law. Not only did the *Indian Act* concern itself with whom an Indian woman married, it also allowed other Aboriginal community members to protest the paternity of any Aboriginal child suspected of having a white, or other non-Aboriginal father. This is still practised today in our communities. Such a child could be removed from the Indian registry and would not be allowed to be an Indian. This was in contrast to the treatment of men, as all offspring of Aboriginal men—legitimate or illegitimate—gained Indian status and a right to band membership.

The *Indian Act* also imposed a patriarchal system and patriarchal laws which favoured men, giving them the right to confer status and band membership, and at one time allowed only men the right to vote in band elections. By 1971, this patriarchal system was so ingrained within our communities, that "patriarchy" was seen as a "traditional trait." Even the memory of our matriarchal forms of government, and our matrilineal forms of descent were forgotten or unacknowledged.

The ongoing legal and political struggle by Aboriginal women is not only against an insensitive federal government, it is also against the Aboriginal male establishment created under the *Indian Act*. Some legal writers[5] argue that it was the federal government alone, and not Aboriginal governments, which discriminated against women. In fact, the Aboriginal male governments and organizations were part of the wall of resistance encountered by Aboriginal women in their struggle to end discrimination and they continue to ignore women's concerns and their rights.

Sexual discrimination against Aboriginal women did not end in 1985 with the passage of Bill C-31.[6] While this Bill repealed the discriminatory 'marry-out' provision in the *Indian Act*, residual discrimination remains for those whose grandmothers and great-grandmothers lost their status by marrying non-Indians. Since Bill C-31, more than 70,000 women, men, girls, and boys have been added to the federal Indian registry[7] and band lists.[8] But of these, only a few have been welcomed back into their communities.

Aboriginal women want to live within their communities, but the women are excluded because there is no land, and no housing. Aboriginal women have been shut out from their communities because the band governments do not wish to bear the costs of programs and services to which the women are entitled as Aboriginals.

Aboriginal women live in the slums. Aboriginal children prostitute themselves in Canadian cities. Our Aboriginal women, young people, and children are killing themselves with drug and alcohol abuse on Indian lands and in Canadian cities.

THE CONSTITUTIONAL DEBATES

This tragic situation will not change without our involvement in negotiating and defining self-government and without our participation in the Constitutional discussions. So far, Aboriginal men and male organizations have not represented our interests, and they are not taking the initiative to ensure that we are given a place at the table to do what they cannot.

Aboriginal women want to take their rightful place at the constitutional table. We are a "distinct and insular" minority belonging to another culture from which we have been separated. Our case is no different from that of Sandra Lovelace who successfully argued that she had suffered discrimination because she was separated from her Maliseet culture, Maliseet language, and from her people.[9] We want to reiterate that the majority of women we represent also suffer under this continuing discrimination. When our women are relegated to living in cities instead of among their own peoples, that, is discrimination. It is a denial of fundamental rights guaranteed to us in international instruments signed by Canada.

It is our right as women to have a voice in deciding upon the definition of Aboriginal government powers. Governments cannot simply choose to recognize the patriarchal forms of government that now exist in our communities. The band councils and the Chiefs who preside over our lives are not our traditional forms of government. National, regional, and band groups are not nations, and do not reflect a nationhood perspective.

The Chiefs have taken it upon themselves to decide that they will be the final rectifiers of the Aboriginal package of rights. Negotiating a right to self-government does not mean recognizing and blessing the patriarchy created in our communities by a foreign government. To Aboriginal women, this would mean chaos in our communities. We do not want this; we want the equality to which we are entitled as women.

Some Aboriginal women have said no to self-government. Some of our women do not want more power, money, and control in the hands of men in our communities. It is asking a great deal to expect us, as women, to have confidence in the men in power in our communities. We do not want the creation of Aboriginal governments with white powers and white philosophies in our communities. We do not want the western hierarchal power structure which has been forced upon us. We do not want the Chieftain overlords which have been created by the *Indian Act*. Aboriginal women must be part of the constitutional negotiation process at all stages so that we can participate in the definition of the structures and powers of our governments, and end the discrimination.

One of the major problems that currently exists is that the majority of First Nations citizens living off reserve are women. Many of these women have been reinstated under changes to the *Indian Act*, but have not been welcomed back into their communities. It is these women who are particularly excluded from the process as it currently exists. Indeed, it is often the Chiefs and councillors who supposedly represent them within the national Aboriginal organizations who are refusing to allow these women to return to their communities. This means that these women cannot get directly involved in any discussions on the reserves and do not even have a right to vote in elections on the reserves. They therefore have no direct or even indirect input in discussions whether on a national or local basis. Often, their only chance to be heard is through their provincial or national Aboriginal women's associations. But, the federal government has not funded or considered the women's associations as being at the same level as other Aboriginal (male) associations. As a result, the women's associations are being kept at the fringes of the process. This could lead to a situation in which reinstated women and others living off reserve are almost completely excluded from a process which will have a profound impact on their lives and their rights.

There are also many important issues affecting Native women living on re-serve. We are living in chaos in our communities. We have a disproportionately high rate of child sexual abuse and incest. We have wife battering, gang rapes, suicides, and substance abuse as elements of our daily lives. The development of programs, services, and policies for handling domestic violence has been placed in the hands of men, and this has not resulted in a reduction in this kind of violence. Another issue specific to women on reserves is the need for family law and matrimonial property laws to be strengthened to provide substantive equality rights to women living on reserves.

ABORIGINAL WOMEN AND THE CHARTER

Our Aboriginal leadership does not favour the application of the Canadian Charter of Rights and Freedoms to self-government. That position has not changed since 1982, when the Assembly of First nations stated the following to the Standing Committee on Aboriginal Affairs: *As Indian people we cannot afford to have individual rights override collective rights.... The Canadian Charter is in conflict with our philosophy and culture.*

The opinion is widely held that the Charter is in conflict with our Aboriginal notions of sovereignty, and further that the rights of Aboriginal citizens within their communities must be determined at the community level.

The Charter is an individual rights based document recognizing and guaranteeing fundamental human rights to Canadians. Fundamental rights and freedoms are also outlined in the Charter of the United Nations and the Universal Declaration on Human Rights. These international instruments of law celebrate the individual nature of fundamental rights and freedoms. These are the legal, political, and constitutional rights which attach to human beings because they are human beings. The Native Women's Association of Canada supports individual rights. Aboriginal women are human beings whose rights cannot be denied or removed at the whim of any government. These views are in conflict with many Aboriginal leaders and legal theoreticians who advocate Canada's recognition of sovereignty, self-government, and collective rights. It is the unwavering view of the male Aboriginal leadership that the 'collective' comes first, and that it will decide the rights of individuals.

As Aboriginal women, we can look at nations around the world which have placed collective and cultural rights ahead of women's sexual equality rights. Some nations have found sexual equality interferes with tradition, custom and history. Sexual equality rights have been guaranteed to women around the world. But, like Canada's Charter, the United Nations has allowed nations to "opt out" of these international instruments.

This is why the application of the Charter should not be left to Governments. The federal government has mistreated us as women for over 100 years. If there is a legacy we will leave for women in the future, it is to ensure women's enjoyment of all the rights granted to us by the United Nations. We want our First Nations to act within the spirit and intent of the United Nations, and not do as so many nations have done before them—opt out of sexual equality rights.

If the Charter does apply to Aboriginal governments, there is great concern that they will be given section 33 rights which grant a government the power to intentionally violate the rights protected by sections 2, 7 and 15 of the Charter. The override powers in section 33 should not be allowed to federal and provincial governments, let alone to Aboriginal governments.

As elsewhere in Canada the law of privacy generally protects homelife from close scrutiny by the State. Often that means women and children are subject to physical, psychological, and sexual abuse within the home, including wife battering, incest, and other crimes which usually go undetected and unpunished by the State. by their nature, these crimes are violations of a victim's section 7 rights to life, liberty, and security of person. We do not want to sanction the loss of these rights by allowing governments to pass laws which do not respect these rights.

While there are many groups who would like to se their Charter rights strengthened in this current round of Constitutional debates, as Aboriginal women, we are the only ones who actually risk the total loss of our Charter rights. This is not acceptable.

CONCLUSION

After 400 years of colonization, Aboriginal communities, Aboriginal families, and Aboriginal structures are devastated, and change of the systems must occur. But, there will not be self-government in our communities without the support of Aboriginal women. Our male Aboriginal leaders must realize that they cannot negotiate self-government without us, any more than they can leave out the elders, the young people, and the people living in urban centres.

As women, we are the keepers of the culture. We want to raise healthy children. We want community decision-making. We want consent powers. We want all people in the communities to decide upon their form of government. We want those Aboriginal women who are still banished from their communities to have a vote, some land, and a house in their homeland, in the community in which they were born. There are those among the Chiefs who would deny us a voice, who would deny us a place and those who wish we would simply go away until they have settled this political business. We are not going to go away. Our male leaders must make a place for us at the bargaining table.

The fact that the existing power structure and process does not seem concerned with ensuring our full and constant participation leads many of us, living both on and off reserve, to believe that we will not be heard and our rights will not be protected in the negotiations for self-government. As Native women, we must be fully involved in negotiations on self-government. Our voices must be heard.

The views expressed in this article are not necessarily reflective of the views of the Native Women's Association of Canada. While authored by the Native Women's Association of Canada in 1992, the majority of the paper was taken from an article written by Teressa Nahanee, entitled, "Indian Women, Sexual Equality and the Charter" and is thus reflective of the debate at that time.

Originally published in Canadian Woman Studies/les cahiers de la femme, *"Gender Equity and Institutional Change," 12 (3) (Spring 1992): 14-17. Reprinted with permission of the authors.*

The Native Women's Association of Canada was created in 1974 to enhance, promote, and foster the social, economic, cultural and political well-being of Aboriginal women. NWAC is the national representative of thirteen provincial and territorial organizations. It has always been NWAC's objective to provide a national voice for Aboriginal women, and to address issues of importance to Aboriginal women.

[1] S.C. 1960, c.44, reprinted in R.S.C. 970, App. II.

[2] Part I of *Constitution Act 1982*, as enacted by *Canada Act* (UK) 1982, c. 11, Schedule B.

[3] Much of this portion of the paper is taken from an article by Teressa Nahanee, entitled "Indian Women, Sexual Equality and the Charter" to be published by McGillQueen's University Press in a record of the "Canadian Women and the State Conference" held at the University of Ottawa Law School, November 1990. Paper with the Author.

[4] *An Act for the Gradual Enfranchisement of Indians, the Better Management of Indian Affairs and to Extend the Provisions of Act Thirty-First Victoria Chapter* 42, S.C. 1869, c.6.

[5] Menno Boldt and J. Anthony Long, "Tribal Philosophies and the Canadian Charter of Rights and Freedoms" in Boldt and Long, eds., *The Quest for Justice: Aboriginal Peoples and Aboriginal Rights.* Toronto: University of Toronto Press, 1985, 170. The authors note: "...the Canadian government was found guilty of denying 'Indian rights' to Indian women who married non-Indians." They also note "the Charter was exploited to create a public perception that Indian leaders are insensitive to human rights." Ibid.

[6] R.S., c. 1-6 as am. c. 10 (2nd Supp.); 1974-75-76, c. 48; 1978-79, c.11; 1980-81-82, cc.47, 110; 1985, c.27.6.2.

[7] This is a record or registry held by the Department of Indian Affairs and Northern Development which contains the names of all "registered Indians" in Canada. The provisions for entitlement are contained in the *Indian Act.*

[8] Each Indian "Band" (defined in the *Indian Act)* maintains a registry of its members, and this list is also kept, by Band, by the federal Department of Indian Affairs and Northern Development. The list is important for determining who may benefit from Indian rights, programs and services.

[9] (1982) 1 C.N.L.R. 1 (United Nations Committee on Human Rights).

LINA SUNSERI

MOVING BEYOND THE
FEMINISM VERSUS NATIONALISM DICHOTOMY

An Anti-Colonial Feminist Perspective on
Aboriginal Liberation Struggles

IN WRITING THIS PAPER, I feel that I must clearly identify my position in our "Canadian" society: I am of mixed Aboriginal-Southern White European ancestry. This mixed cultural, ethno-racial identity provides me with distinct experiences that have brought me to a point in my life where I support the anti-colonial self-determination struggles of Aboriginal peoples on this Turtle Island known as Canada. Many times I am asked by friends, intellectuals, feminists, and non-feminists, how I could support any nationalist struggle, especially in light of what has taken place in many parts of the world in the name of ethnonationalism. Indeed, I often wonder if an Aboriginal "nationalist" struggle can avoid the destructive results that have occurred elsewhere. I also wonder where I would be placed, or place myself, in this struggle given my mixed ancestry. My "hybrid" identity leaves me in what Homi Bhabha would call an "in-between" place, not quite the colonizer or the colonized. Located as I am in this ambivalent place, having the "privilege" of a mixture of cultures, it is not surprising then that I might feel both pulled and pushed towards an Aboriginal anti-colonial movement. This tension is further complicated by my feminist ideology and culture, an ideology that has expressed justifiable skepticism about "nationalisms," especially in light of the latter's relationship with women's rights.

This paper, written in the midst of all these emotions and recent events of "nationalist" movements (such as the Serbian, Croatian, Kurdish and Tamil cases), is an attempt to come to terms with my support for an Aboriginal anti-colonial nationalist movement. Mine is obviously then a situated knowledge, informed by both feminist knowledge and Aboriginal experiences, either of my own or of other Aboriginal peoples. A situated knowledge stresses and validates the importance of lived experiences and it incorporates these experiences within theory (Collins). While recognizing the limitations of past nationalist movements to liberate women, I believe that it is possible to envision a progressive nationalist liberation movement, one that could eliminate oppressive and unequal power relations. Given that Aboriginal women have lived for many centuries in an oppressive racist and sexist colonial society, which has brought them infinite political, economic, social, and cultural destruction, it is not surprising that these women would ally themselves with a movement that wants to restore and reaffirm their inherent right to govern themselves.

I will begin with an introduction to feminism, nationalism, and nation, and then briefly review the debates taking place between feminists and nationalists. I examine the contributions offered by feminist critiques of nationalism, highlighting the argument that there have been limitations to the liberatory aspects of nationalist movements. In most cases, once the postcolonial nation is formed, the position of women has not improved much and, in some cases, it has even regressed. I will argue that nationalism, in itself, is not necessarily evil, just as feminism is not, but both have the potential to be exclusionary, and therefore, on their own, cannot resolve all of Aboriginal (and non-Aboriginal) women's problems. I will then offer an overview of Aboriginal self-determination struggles. In this section, I will examine some key characteristics and assumptions of these struggles, and then address the specific dilemmas that Aboriginal women face within these struggles both with the Canadian state and with some Aboriginal organizations (e.g. the Assembly of First Nations). In my conclusion, I will attempt to move beyond the feminism versus nationalism dichotomy by arguing that Aboriginal women's participation in the self-determination of First Nations can be seen as both an anti-colonial movement and a feminist one.

DEFINING FEMINISM, NATIONALISM AND THE NATION

A core part of this paper consists of the debate between feminism and nationalism, and how the two seem incompatible. Some earlier second-wave feminists believe that women's oppression is unique and tied to a universal patriarchy (Firestone; Friedan; Millett). They sought to unite women through a sense of a shared oppression, and tended to believe that women's interests can be best achieved through a women's movement that places women's rights as the first priority in its agenda.

Many Aboriginal women, along with other women of colour and "third world" women, have felt alienated by what they view as a "western" feminist movement that has either marginalized them or not accurately represented their experiences and interests. As Nickie Charles and Helen Hintjens point out:

> In the context of the Third World, this rejection of feminism often arises from its association with western, middle-class women and with the negative consequences of modernisation.... However, feminism has also developed a critique of modernism.... Thus, western feminism recognizes that women neither automatically share a gender identity nor do they necessarily have political interests in common. Their material circumstances and experiences differ significantly and a unity of interests between women from different cultures (and within the same society) cannot be deduced from their shared gender. (20)

The marginalization of non-White European women within mainstream western feminism is a reality, and women of colour have challenged the members of the movement to analyze its own racism and its essentialist portrayal of the "universal" woman. As Charles and Hintjens indicate above, western feminism has more recently provided its own critique of modernity and taken into account the diversity of women's experience. Although western feminism has responded to the challenges presented by women of colour and third world women, and reevaluated its earlier assumptions, I still believe that more work needs to be done, especially vis-à-vis the further incorporation of issues of colonialism and racism into the theory and praxis of the movement. Until the women's movement completely faces the reality that many of its members are part of the colonial power, and therefore share some of the advantages that their male counterparts enjoy, most Aboriginal and other colonized groups will continue to view it with some skepticism. If we could all come to understand feminism as a theory and movement that wants to fight all forms of oppression, including racism and colonialism, then we could see it as a struggle for unity among all oppressed women and men. It is this meaning of feminism that I accept; that allows me to call myself "feminist" without reservation.

For the purpose of this paper, nationalism and nation are associated with movements for independence, liberation, and revolution. A classic definition of "nation" is that of Benedict Anderson, who constructs it as "an imagined community," a collectivity of individuals who feel that they belong to a shared linguistic community. Anthony Smith presents a primordial definition of nation. For him, nation refers to an ethnic collectivity with a shared past. In my analysis, nation means not only a community that may share a common culture and historical experiences, but it is also a collectivity that is "oriented towards the future" (Yuval-Davis 19). Nationalism is that ideology or discourse that promotes and shapes the formation of such communities. There are different kinds of nationalism; some rely on an exclusionary and homogeneous vision, but others can be empowering and culturally diverse. Partha Chatterjee argues, in the context of an anti-colonial project: "...the national question here is, of course, historically fused with a colonial question. The assertion of national identity was, therefore, a form of the struggle against colonial exploitation" (18).

It is precisely this anti-colonial, liberation struggle to which I refer when I speak of nationalism in this paper. Within this framework, and within an Aboriginal context, nationalism means a process to revitalize the different institutions and practices of our various Nations (Alfred). An Aboriginal perspective on nation and nationalism differs from a Western one because its basis for nationhood is not rooted in notions of territoriality, boundaries, and nation-state (Alfred). Moreover, other concepts (such as "pure" Indian, status-Indian, national and regional boundaries) are all constructs of a colonial state and are foreign, if not antithetical, to most Aboriginal cultures and ways of governance (Monture-Angus 1995).

FEMINIST CRITIQUE OF NATIONALISM

Feminist studies on nationalist and other liberation movements have revealed that, after national liberation, women generally have been pushed to domestic roles (Abdo). During nationalist struggles, women are often seen as the producers and reproducers of the national culture, and can acquire prestige and status as the bearers of "pure" culture. However, they can also become increasingly controlled, as their reproductive roles and their portrayal as bearers of culture can also be used to control their sexuality and confine them to domestic roles (Enloe).

Embedded implicitly and explicitly in this discourse of women as the bearers of culture and tradition is another discourse not exclusively tied to women: that of ethno-racial identity as immutable and connected to blood. Yet, when identity is viewed as uni-dimensional and biological, it marginalizes those who do not fit the strict categories of belonging to one specific ethnic or racial group, and in the process excludes all those individuals who have "mixed" descent, because their blood cannot be easily and exclusively connected with one group. When ethno-racial nationalist movements connect their concept of belonging to the nation to this notion of purity, we can also see that they need to regulate the sexual relationships of the members of their community. In practice, this regulation is more strictly applied, and with more negative sanctions, against women, because their reproductive roles become extremely important in the discourses of common origin and purity of blood (Yuval-Davis).

While recognizing some of the negative results of some nationalist discourses for women, we cannot ignore that some anti-colonial movements have provided the opportunity to mobilize women in their common struggle against the oppressive colonial or quasi-colonial power[1] as in the case of Algeria, South Africa, Palestine, and some Latin American countries. The women involved have increased their political consciousness and, in some cases, made the male nationalists more aware of exploitative and oppressive gender relations. Often enough though, the male nationalists argue that colonialism and/or capitalism has been the cause of women's problems and they have completely ignored or dismissed the patriarchal nature of women's oppression. Moreover, neither a nationalist nor a socialist revolution has yet integrated a feminist discourse (McClintock). Constructing a radical, alternative discourse that can smash both the sexist emperor and the sexist "colonized" is not an easy task. This project becomes even more difficult when other forces, both internal and external, such as global capitalism, religious fundamentalism, and reactionary "traditionalism" are at work, limiting the possibility of a full transformation of social relations in the postcolonial world.

ABORIGINAL SELF-DETERMINATION STRUGGLES

Aboriginal peoples of North America have in recent decades successfully articulated a discourse of "self-determination," advocating a commitment on the part of non-Aboriginals to recognize Aboriginal peoples inherent right to govern themselves. This discourse of self-determination is similar to that of self-government; however, I see it as having a much broader meaning and intent. Some may use the two terms interchangeably and argue that self-government means an inherent right of Aboriginal peoples to "be governed by rules of social, moral, political and cultural behaviour upon which they agree" (McIvor 167). However, I tend to agree more with Patricia Monture-Angus (1999) and with other Aboriginals who claim that self-government implies a perpetuation of a colonial superior government that still makes the ultimate decisions about the meaning of Aboriginal rights and how these are to be implemented. Self-government, then, is viewed by us as a "limited form of governance" (Monture-Angus 1999: 29) that maintains unacceptable and unjust colonial relations. Self-determination, on the other hand, holds a better promise for Aboriginal peoples, because it is premised on the notion that our rights to be independent and to determine our own futures were never extinguished (Monture-Angus 1999). What we demand is not merely equal opportunity within the mainstream Canadian system, but rather an inherent right of First Nations people to live by our own unique set of values (Schouls). Some of these different sets of values comprise a distinct definition of government, of land, and of land rights. For Native peoples, "government" constitutes a decision-making system based on consensus and on individuals maintaining significant responsibilities for their behaviour and decisions (Barnaby). Similarly, Aboriginals have a unique relationship to the land; in fact, this distinctive relationship to creation is reflected in our languages, hence our insistence that our rights to lands be recognized. Ours is a worldview that moves far beyond the material utility of natural resources because we view our relationship with animals, plants, water, and all other living things as a spiritual one. Land rights are, then, very different than proprietary rights. While the latter translates into individual ownership of land and is usually based on a market economy, the former "needs to be understood in a context of culture and territoriality.… Similarly, tribal sovereignty must be understood in its cultural context, one that reflects self-determination and self-sufficiency traditionally predicated on reciprocity" (Jaimes-Guerrero 102).

Many Canadians feel threatened by the demands of Aboriginal peoples; some fear they might have to relinquish any privilege they have enjoyed at the expense of Aboriginals' oppression, others feel that Aboriginal self-government may weaken an already shaky Canadian national identity. It is important to note that recognition of Aboriginal sovereignty does not automatically become national independence. As Glenn Morris argues:

> Given the difficult practical political and economic difficulties facing smaller states in the world today, most Indigenous peoples may very well not opt for complete independent state status. Many would

probably choose some type of autonomy or federation with existing states, preserving rights to internal self-governance and control as members of larger states. (78-79)

What is crucial here is that it be the choice of Aboriginal peoples to determine which course to take rather than having one imposed on them, as has been the case with the Canadian state.

As in some other anti-colonial liberation struggles, Aboriginal women have had an important role in the "national" struggle and their roles have not been free of contradictions and obstacles. Colonization of the Americas ultimately transformed all structures, including Aboriginal gender relations. Prior to this, women in most Aboriginal societies enjoyed a large amount of status and power. The Haudenosaunee (Iroquois, or a more appropriate translation, People of the Longhouse) women, for example, occupied prominent positions in all aspects of Indigenous life. Within the laws of the Haudenosaunee people (called the *Kaianerekowa* and known as the Great Law of Peace), it is clearly stated that women choose the *Oyanch* (Clan Mothers), who had a large amount of power in each clan, including the power to remove chiefs, to decide on matters of intertribal disputes, and determine the distribution of resources (Goodleaf).

The contact with European societies and the eventual colonization of Aboriginal peoples altered the conditions of Aboriginal women of Canada. As Cora Voyageur argues:

> [O]ne of the primary reasons for the situation of Indian women today is that Indians, in general, were subjugated by the immigrant European society.... The *British North American Act* of 1867 gave the power of legislative control over Indians and their lands to the federal government. The *Indian Act* of 1876 consolidated legislation already in place. The measure depriving an Indian woman of her status when she married a non-Indian was first legislated in the 1869 *Indian Act*. This Act was also the first legislation that officially discriminated against Indian women by assigning them fewer fundamental rights than Indian men. (100)

Most Aboriginal women point out that, for them, the Canadian law is at the centre of our problems and the patriarchal nature of the Canadian state has different meanings and consequences for Aboriginal women (Monture-Angus 1995). In order to fully understand how patriarchy works in Canada, we must look at the oppressive role that the Canadian state has had, and continues to have, in the everyday lives of Aboriginal women. Decolonization, therefore, is a necessary step for the full liberation of Aboriginal women, and it is the one point where Aboriginal men and women can come together as united. By "decolonization" I mean the process by which the longstanding colonial relations between Aboriginals and non-Aboriginals are abolished and new relations formed. These relations will be based on principles of mutual respect, sharing, and recognition of the inherent rights of Aboriginal peoples to follow their traditional ways of governance.

Resorting exclusively to an agenda of decolonization while simultaneously not integrating women's issues into it, as I have warned earlier, can be "dangerous" for women. We cannot be certain that the national liberation will automatically translate into a women's liberation. More often than not, failing to combine a gender analysis with an anti-colonial one can only increase the chances that colonized women's lives will not be improved, as the new male leaders will be reluctant to give up any power they have recently gained. As Aboriginal women, we have an awareness of the inequalities and injustices we suffer as women as well as Aboriginal peoples. These inequalities may have been created as a result of the colonization of our peoples, but some may have existed in some communities externally to it, and we need to look closer at this possibility. As Emma Laroque states, it is important to remember that:

> Culture is not immutable, and tradition cannot be expected to be always of value or relevant in our times. As Native women, we are faced with very difficult and painful choices, but nonetheless, we are challenged to change, create, and embrace "traditions" consistent with contemporary and international human rights standards. (14)

Canadian Indigenous women have, at times, found themselves in opposition to the male-dominated and federally funded Aboriginal associations. The two important historical moments where we witnessed this dissension between male leaders and female leaders occurred during the amendment of the *Indian Act*, which reinstated Indian status to Aboriginal women who had married non-Indian men, and then later during the Charlottetown Accord talks, when the Native Women's Association of Canada (NWAC) argued that the collective rights of Aboriginal women related to gender equality were not protected and integrated in the Accord. Throughout these moments, the Assembly of First Nations, the main Aboriginal organization recognized and funded by the Canadian state, did not fully support the positions of Aboriginal women as advanced by the NWAC, often arguing that the women's arguments were based upon an individual rights discourse that undermined the struggle of First Nations for self-determination.

This particular way of looking at the dissension between the male-dominated political associations and NWAC ignores a critical issue: "the discursive formation of ethno political identity that emerges as male and female political leaders contest each other's expressed collective aspirations and envisioned future nationhood" (Fiske 71). Many Aboriginal women's groups (which do receive support from many traditional men) use a political discourse that looks at the intersection of ethnicity, class, and gender and they want to bring back symbols and images that have been a part of most Aboriginal traditional cultures. Some of the symbols include that of "Woman as the heart of the Nation," "the centre of everything" (Fiske). What Aboriginal women envision, then, is a feminized nation, where both men and women equally give birth to it, and following a traditional Aboriginal cultural worldview, kin ties are "evoked as symbols of a community and nation: blood and culture, not law, define ethnic identity and citizenship within a nation that nurture[s] and sustains her people" (Fiske 76-77). As I expect the word "blood" to raise many eyebrows, I feel it is important to remark that as my elders and other Aboriginal peoples have told me, many Aboriginal traditional societies were very open to "adopting" members of other "tribes" who acquired their culture. At least, that was the case for the Haudenosaunee people. Therefore, it can be clarified that the notion of blood is not as rigid and exclusionary as the one more commonly used by other ethno-nationalist movements. It stands to represent one's affiliation to a clan, and one's membership to it can be obtained either by birth or adoption by the female members of the clan.

For the most part, Aboriginal male-led organizations use a different discourse, one that is masculinist and derived from the same European hegemonic power that they oppose. In this discourse, men are the natural citizens and women instead have to be accepted by the men and the Canadian state (Fiske). This masculinist discourse came into evidence during the proposed amendments to the *Indian Act* to reinstate women who had lost Indian status into their communities. In a subsequent period, in the name of protecting the constitutional "collective" rights of self-government, Aboriginal male leaders were ignoring the gender relations of power that presently exist in Aboriginal communities. Throughout both these debates, Aboriginal women asked for either reinstatement or insurance that gender equality for Aboriginal women be protected in the Constitution. Aboriginal women have always argued that, if we truly want to reaffirm our traditional way of life, women's rights are to be considered collective by nature and to be at the core of Aboriginal notions of "nation." Moreover, to argue that women's rights (as Aboriginal women) are only individual rights is a colonized way of thinking, because for Aboriginal peoples individuals are always part of the collective, not outside of or contrary to it. We must also remember that many of the dividing lines (either of status, reserve residency, blood, or membership to bands) now existing in our communities were not originally drawn by Aboriginals themselves, but by the Canadian state (Monture-Angus 1999: 144-45). During our decolonization process, we Aboriginal women must ask the men and the leaders of Aboriginal communities to respect the powerful roles Aboriginal women held and that" instead of a part of many traditional laws (e.g., the *Kaianerekowa*). In doing so, we can then equally walk together towards the same path and have a similar vision, one in which we are, in the words of Sharon McIvor, "united with our own people, on our own lands, determining our forms of government, deciding rules for membership in our Nations, and deciding who will live on our lands" (180).

CONCLUSION

In this paper, I have attempted to illustrate the complexities of the ongoing debate between feminists and nationalists. Throughout, I argue that there is not a single version of either feminism or nationalism and demonstrate that they can be either progressive or reactionary. For the most part, "western" feminism has been guilty of excluding, or at least marginalizing, women of colour and third world women and has only recently begun to integrate issues of race and colonialism in its theories. In the context of Aboriginal women's issues, feminist theories need to look more closely at the issues of land rights, sovereignty, and colonization and the impact this has had on the lives of Aboriginal women. In their critique of nationalism, feminists need to look much deeper at issues of land rights, at the colonial state's erasure of the cultural practices of Indigenous peoples, and should not be quick to define Aboriginal women's participation in nationalist struggles as non-feminist and inherently dangerous for women (Jaimes-Guerrero). However, we Aboriginal women should also be careful not to prematurely dismiss all feminist theories. Undoubtedly they have enriched our analyses of power relations, especially of those most directly related to gender. It is also true that many "mainstream" feminists have attempted to reevaluate their earlier assumptions and are beginning to question their own colonization of "others." More importantly, most of the feminist skepticism about nationalisms should be taken seriously. Historically, women's participation in anti-colonial liberation movements has been vital, but has not translated into enduring gains for women in the new nation. There are many nationalisms; but the only one that I would join is the one that offers women an emancipatory place in all phases of the liberation movement. Most importantly, identities that are defined by an ideology of purity of "race" have the potential to be oppressive and dangerous, especially for women, since they are seen as bearers of the imagined pure nation. We must also acknowledge that "tradition" is not static, but is always transformed by people; therefore, postcolonial Aboriginal nations must accommodate differences of experience and let traditional practices meet the continuously changing needs of their members.

Originally published in Canadian Woman Studies/les cahiers de la femme, *"National Identity and Gender Politics," 20 (2) (Summer 2000): 143-148. Reprinted with permission of the authors.*

Lina Sunseri is of the Oneida Nation of the Thames, Turtle Clan. Her Longhouse name is Yeliwi:saks, which means Gathering Stories, Knowledge. She also has Italian ancestry from her father's side. She is Assistant Professor, Dept. of Sociology, Brescia University College, at the University of Western Ontario.

[1]I would refer readers to the works of Jayawardena, Charles and Hintjens,

Moghadam, and Alexander and Mohanty for an overview of the mobilization of women in anti-colonial movements.

REFERENCES

Abdo, Nahla. "Nationalism and Feminism: Palestinian Women and the Intifada—No Going Back?" *Gender and National Identity*. Ed. Valerie Moghadam. London: Zed Books, 1994.

Alexander, M. Jacqui, and Chandra Talpade Mohanty, eds. *Feminist Genealogies, Colonial Legacies, Democratic Futures*. London: Routledge, 1997.

Alfred, Gerald R. *Heeding the Voices of our Ancestors: Kahnawake Mohawk Politics and the Rise of Native Nationalism*. Toronto: Oxford University Press, 1995.

Anderson, Benedict. *Imagined Communities: Reflections on the Origin and Spread of Nationalism*. London: Verso, 1983.

Barnaby, Joanne. "Culture and Sovereignty." *Nation to Nation: Aboriginal Sovereignty and the Future of Canada*. Eds. Diane Engelstad and John Bird. Concord: Anansi, 1992.

Bhabha, Homi K. *The Location of Culture*. London: Routledge, 1994.

Charles, Nickie, and Helen Hintjens, eds. *Gender, Ethnicity and Political Ideologies*. London: Routledge, 1998.

Chatterjee, Partha. *Nationalist Thought and the Colonial World: A Derivative Discourse*. London: Zed Books, 1986.

Collins, Patricia Hill. *Black Feminist Thought: Knowledge, Consciousness, and the Politics of Empowerment*. (Second Edition.) London: Routledge, 2000.

Enloe, Cynthia. *The Morning After: Sexual Politics at the End of the Cold War*. Berkeley: University of California Press, 1993.

Firestone, Shulamith. *The Dialectic of Sex*. London: The Women's Press, 1979.

Fiske, Jo-Anne. 1996. "The Womb is to the Nation as the Heart is to the Body: Ethnopolitical Discourses of the Canadian Indigenous Women's Movement." *Studies in Political Economy* 51 (1996): 65-89.

Friedan, Betty. *The Feminine Mystique*. Harmondsworth: Penguin, 1965.

Goodleaf, Donna. *Entering the War Zone: A Mohawk Perspective on Resisting Invasions*. Penticton: Theytus Books, 1995.

Jaimes-Guerrero, Marie Anna. "Civil Rights versus Sovereignty: Native American Women in Life and Land Struggles." *Feminist Genealogies, Colonial Legacies, Democratic Futures*. Eds. M. Jacqui Alexander and Chandra Talpade Mohanty. London: Routledge, 1997.

Jayawardena, Kumari. *Feminism and Nationalism in the Third World*. London: Zed Books, 1986.

LaRocque, Emma. "The Colonization of a Native Woman Scholar." *Women of the First Nations: Power, Wisdom and Strength*. Eds. Christine Miller and Patricia Chuchryk. Winnipeg: The University of Manitoba Press, 1996.

McClintock, Anne. *Imperial Leather: Race, Gender and Sexuality in the Colonial Contest*. London: Routledge, 1995.

McIvor, Sharon D. "Self-Government and Aboriginal Women." *Scratching the Surface: Canadian Anti-Racist Feminist Thought*. Eds. Enakshi Dua and Angela Robertson. Toronto: Women's Press, 1999.

Millett, Kate. *Sexual Politics*. London: Virago, 1977.

Moghadam, Valerie, ed. *Gender and National Identity*. London and New Jersey: Zed Books, 1994.

Monture-Angus, Patricia. *Thunder in My Soul: A Mohawk Woman Speaks*. Halifax: Fernwood Publishing, 1995.

Monture-Angus, Patricia. *Journeying Forward: Dreaming First Nations' Independence*. Halifax: Fernwood Publishing, 1999.

Morris, Glenn. "International Law and Politics." *The State of Native America*. Ed. M. Annette Jaimes. Boston: South End Press, 1992.

Schouls, Tim, John Olthuis, and Diane Engelstad. "The Basic Dilemma: Sovereignty or Assimilation." *Nation to Nation: Aboriginal Sovereignty and the Future of Canada*. Eds. Diane Engelstad and John Bird. Concord: Anansi Press, 1992.

Smith, Anthony. *The Ethnic Origins of Nations*. Oxford: Basil Blackwell, 1986.

Voyageur, Cora J. "Contemporary Indian Women." *Visions of the Heart: Canadian Aboriginal Issues*. Eds. David Alan Long and Olive Patricia Dickason. Toronto: Harcourt Brace and Company, 1996.

Yuval-Davis, Nira. *Gender and Nation*. London: Sage Publications, 1997.

CAROLE LECLAIR

WRITING ON THE WALL

Métis Reflections on Gerald Vizenor's Strategies for Survival

YESTERDAY I WALKED ACROSS a small inner-city park. It was just a barren-looking patch of burnt grass, a space adjacent to a concrete subsidized high-rise building. A smaller concrete structure covered in graffiti stood in the center of the park. Some of the markings were tags and throw ups, contemporary versions of "I was here," but the one that caught my attention read, "This is Canada." Who had written this concise message? I read this phrase as a fleeting irony, a political voice. Schmoo, an American graffiti writer, says "Graffiti writers are out challenging the issues of property ownership, race boundaries, and culture. They are out there making people think about what our society is, and what some of our laws really mean" (qtd. in "The Merits of Art"). The graffiti that appeared a few weeks ago on the walls of the Zibi Anishnaabeg Community Centre[1] was of a more sinister intent, with its swastikas and "white power" slogans. In his analysis of forms of graffiti, Jeff Ferrel describes this specific style of graffiti as "the ugly edge of a culture organized around economic and ethnic inequality"(5). Graffiti is also about interrupting invisibility. I was tempted for a moment to pull a marker out of my bag and write "This is Métis!" I refused the impulse, acknowledging my privilege to write and speak in the broader arena of print and classroom.

This essay seeks to illustrate ways in which oral tradition in contemporary forms underpins my scholar/activist work. Text, speaking on the page, is included in the process of gathering Aboriginal knowledges. Writers, Elders, knowledge-keepers, our elder brothers and sisters, and all living beings contribute resources that direct our actions in community collaborative work. Gerald Vizenor is among the many contemporary Indigenous writers who influence my thinking, and with his permission I have adopted his richly poetic term, "new urban earthdiver" (1981a: 6), to describe my activism. Vizenor is a mixed-blood Anishinaabe scholar who works out of the University of California, Berkeley. His amazingly prolific lifelong effort has been to write in the trickster mode of Native American traditions, using humour and ironic images to challenge received ideas, subvert the status quo, and to teach strategies of survival in what he terms "the new Indian wars," those media-driven, intellectual, and verbal skirmishes he names the "cultural word wars" (1978: viii).

THE SPEAKING SUBJECT

In "Memory Alive: Race, Religion, and Métis Identities," I briefly describe my Métis history, the land which gave me my identity, and the people I was born for. This is a necessary and time-honoured Indigenous way of establishing my right to speak as an Aboriginal person. Since writing "Memory Alive," I have joined the faculty of Wilfrid Laurier University, contributed to the development of our Indigenous Studies Program, and most recently was granted tenure. One sentence does not convey the tensions and challenges this academic process has presented for me, yet I have not lost my sense of humour and my gratitude for the gifts given on this journey.

My roots stretch deep into Red River territory. My grandmother's people walked from Minnesota into Manitoba to create the tiny Métis village of Vassar, Manitoba, in the early 1800s. My grandparent's people were from Brokenhead and St. Peters Reserves, Québec and Montana. They carried French names, and spoke Michif. They were living there on that land for many generations, building their villages along the lay of the land, using the ancient wintering camps of their tribal relatives and finding ways to live between the seams of tribal and encroaching Euro-Canadian cultures.

My grandparents were part of a generation of Métis whose lives and communities were deeply affected by the aftermath of failed uprisings, of failed resistances, in the face of sweeping loss of land, space, and the right to exist as communities. One of the many consequences of defeat at the Battle of Batoche was that the name Métis, already categorized in Euro-Canadian society by concepts of race and miscegenation, was made synonymous with crisis, rebellion, and disloyalty. My Métis parents were raised to suppress their Indigenous identities; their generation was "born into a historically scorned and jeopardized status" (Jordan 300). I think of Oka, Gustafsen Lake, Ipperwash, and the latest land reclamation efforts at Caledonia as contemporary events with similar consequences for Native peoples. For me, Métis is a verb, a being and becoming, not tied to only one historicized territory, but evident throughout what we now call Canada.

Like Vizenor, I come from a storytelling people. The stories I heard as a child were "liberative stories and strategies of survivance" (Vizenor 1993: 18). My uncle Joe worked on the railroad in Sioux Lookout and he would ride the trains to visit us. He loved to sit at the kitchen table and tell long, complicated, and richly detailed stories. His stories were about contemporary people and events in new urban settlements, told through a Métis consciousness of the past. Even in the inner cities, owls and wolves and bears inhabit our stories. The rhythms and themes of Uncle Joe's stories echoed ancient Saulteaux stories about evil gamblers and tricksters outwitting great obstacles or succumbing to defeat. It was from Joe that I learned about those other kinds of wolves, those *loups-garoux*, those shape-shifters, and those poker-playing *manitous* who rode the boxcars of Joe's train, slipping silently off into the bush and doing things unimagined in my grade school library books. I loved the imaginative freedom these stories gave me. They laid the foundation for my understanding that our stories "begin with an argument based on the idea of chance and imagination as a source of meaning, rather than going for causation, closure and authority" (Pulitano 150). Any dry discussion of race as population genetics or contentious cultural category says nothing to me about the parts that spirit and tribal memories play in constructing our physical and social selves. My grandfather often sat with his crystal set, listening to the commentator's voice drifting over the border into Vassar as the New York Yankees played baseball. My Métis Grandmother sat by kerosene lamp, sewing all the uniforms for Grandfather's team, the best and only baseball team in Vassar. I draw on Vizenor's appreciation of the vitality of Indigenous oral narrative traditions here. My grandparents joined in the dialogue, participated in the "tricky" act of the exchange between their communities and the settler worlds, what Vizenor calls:

> discussions in the best sense of the word. It's engagement.... It's imagination.... It's a discourse.... It's liberation.... It's life, it's juice, it's energy.... But it's not a theory, it's not a monologue. (qtd. in Pulitano 148)

To me, this means that we Indigenous peoples have always loved a good story, a good game, a chance to participate, and have adapted to what we find in the places where we live.

MY TASK IN ACTIVISM

Simply stated, my work within the academy and in urban settings is to bring to light Indigenous ways of understanding and acting in the world. It is a tricky task to preserve our memories and work cross-culturally. In graduate school I was offered post-colonialism, post-modernism, materialism, feminism, historicism, and contemporary theories of language as ways to theorize Native writing. I was intrigued by these approaches for what they reveal about the organizing principles of Eurocentric thinking, as they are used to probe for truths about real world experiences. Ultimately I refused them as unsuitable tools for the task of articulating Indigenous thought from within. I turned to Native writers and thinkers for some clues for how I should begin this work. Indigenous writers offer their thoughts as participants in discussion, engagement, shared discourse, not as theorists engaged in monologues. I believe that any search to clarify and share our insights must come first from ourselves: "We must determine our own identity within the parameters established by us" (Nyoongah qtd. in D'Cruz par. 5). In claiming the necessity for scholarship that is rooted in Indigenous communities we resist the genocidal gestures of appropriation. Having said this, if we are to work within the academy and within urban spaces, we are of necessity engaged in a cross-cultural dialogic. Academics interested in cross-cultural work need not approach this arena in fear and trembling. Mistakes are inevitable. When I enter the sacred space of ceremony, I leave academic logic outside. I sit in humility, grateful to be immersed in the language, the exuberance, the reverence, and the casual good humour that is so much in evidence as our communities heal and renew their ancient connections to the earth. I learn how little I know. I work hard, watching for guidance from those more competent than I am. Picture me in Sheguiandah this spring, sitting on a piece of cardboard, trying to cut up moose ribs with a pen knife. I struggled gamely with that mountainous pile, all the while feeling panicky and embarrassed by my messy incompetence. Other busy women would glance my way in disbelief and (I hoped) sympathy. Some offered their knives. Finally a much older woman wielding an efficient axe rescued me. I guess you need the right tools for the job.

For critical theorists, Gerald Vizenor's work provides the tools for creating a competent dialogic as he combines his knowledge of traditional oral traditions, contemporary Native writers and scholars, as well as academic critical theorists in order to "relocate it [the written word] for potential readers from the passive to the active realm of experience…" (Blaeser, 16). As an urban earthdiver,[2] I dig into Vizenor's vast body of writing to find many useful ideas. Choctaw scholar Louis Owens suggests that one of Vizenor's central aims is to free Indigenous identities from the "epic, absolute past that insists on stasis and tragedy for Native Americans"(Owens 231). Examples of the kind of writing, which insists on stasis and tragedy for the Métis, are Joseph Howard's "*Strange Empire*," Marcel Giraud's *Le Métis Canadien* a racist tract in two volumes, and Gerhard Ens's *Homeland to Hinterland*, which seeks to demonstrate that the Métis ceased to exist when faced with the juggernaut of western capitalism. For some tribal-affiliated writers, the cross-blood (mixed blood or Métis) characters are treated as though their condition is temporary, moving toward resolution of an ambiguous state. They remain in a confused state of identity, depicted as tragic and lost, until they return to a tribal center of culture. Some of these characters are depicted in such works as N. Scott Momaday's *House Made of Dawn*, James Welch's *Winter in the Blood*, Leslie Silko's *Ceremony*, and Louise Erdrich's *Love Medicine*.[4]

As I develop research projects and participate in community activities, I am mindful to resist mainstream and some tribal assumptions that Indigenous communities are fated to refer only to the past. Vizenor works to deconstruct what he sees as stereotypical and invented with the purpose of constructing a new authentic identity, existing at the intersections of cultures, surviving through constant struggle between subversion and balance (Blaeser 158). About the English language he says: "The English language has been the linear tongue of the colonial discoveries, racial cruelties, invented names, the simulation of tribal cultures, manifest manners, and the unheard literature of dominance in tribal communities" (1996: 105-106).

The "unheard literature of dominance" in our village and in modern urban spaces is the English language, "unheard" because it has become the ubiquitous and necessary tongue. The more my community spoke the language imposed in school, the less Michif was heard. My cousin Norman Fleury is one of the few remaining scholars of a language that linguist Peter Bakker claims is unique in all the world's languages. And yet, the outpouring of creative literature by Indigenous writers in English encourages me. Our stories of endurance, our drive to retain Indigenous oral traditions in our projects, are vehicles of cultural survival as Indigenous scholars and grassroots activists. I search out native writers in English. I teach a course on writers like Patricia Grace, (Maori) from New Zealand, Louise Erdrich, (Ojibwe) from White Earth Reservation, Minnesota, Lee Maracle, (Sto:loh First Nation), from Vancouver, Ruby Slipperjack, (Ojibwe), from Whitewater Lake Ontario, and Winona LaDuke, (Anishaabe) from White Earth Reservation, Minnesota.

In his novel *Hotline Healers: An Almost Browne Novel,* Vizenor's character Almost Browne, is born "in the back seat of an unheated station wagon ... almost on the White Earth Reservation." Subversively, Vizenor has the agency nurse write on Almost's birth certificate, "gegaa, almost on the reservation" (1997: 9-10), while the family, the nuns, and the federal agent insists on changing the actual location of his birth. Is Almost Browne earnest and believable in his constant storytelling, or is he elusive, wily and dangerous? Throughout this novel, Vizenor makes the point that the truth of native reason is flux, chance, freedom, and humour. I think about Almost Browne when I am challenged by tribal peoples and non-Natives to identify solely with their social, cultural, and political agendas. I am of this land and I care little for invented names.

Vizenor uses his writing to teach a new way of thinking, a way that deliberately violates conventional codes and obvious categories, as a tool of liberation. Listen to what he says about the academy:

> The University of California at Berkeley is a material reservation, a magic snapshot separation from the sacred, and, at the same time, this fantastic campus is a sweet place in the imagination, like an elevator filled with androgynous talebearers moving to the thirteenth floor in search of new spiritual teachers. (Vizenor 1981b: 389)

I think on these words. This vision leads me away from a defensive, exclusionary, and judgmental position as a native scholar in the academy, towards an opening up to an inherent multiplicity of experience. These words re-center my thinking within a perspective that knows that Indigenous knowledge is flux, change, chance, tease, humour, and healing.

FROM THEORY TO ACTION

How do chance, imagination, and survivance work in the academy and in community action? More than a dozen years ago, we formed the Métis Women's Circle (MWC) in response to the urgings of our elders. By chance, we were invited to submit a proposal to the Federal Government for funding. Our program manager told us what we should write. I felt constrained and defined by government language, cultural expectations, and agenda. I faltered, and looked out the window as our program manager set out the parameters of the project. Withdrawal was my only strategy. Later on, several program managers expressed the opinion that our organization was getting "too top-heavy" with academics, who were difficult to work with. Since that early beginning, the MWC has written and successfully implemented many projects with government and non-government sources of support. We have learned to turn away from strategic victimry, toward strategies of survivance, although mainstream supporters still insist on the problems and issues model, or on economic solutions to our community needs, often downplaying or refusing outright "the merely cultural" content of our work. We have learned to pose as program delivery agents, and to undermine that pose with humour, tricky strategies, and a willingness to see ourselves as tricksters, balancing between Indigenous words and Canadian institutions. The laughter and teasing during meetings is not merely a survival strategy, it bubbles up to the surface from deep wells of confidence and trust that our Aboriginal ways, gifts from our Creator, still connect us to empowerment. During our meetings and throughout our conferences and workshops, we call on our elder relatives, bear, wolf, buffalo, sweetgrass, and tobacco, to direct us. We do lean heavily on "the merely cultural" to transform and align our projects to capture desired Indigenous outcomes. Such "measurable outcomes" are sometimes hard to evaluate on final report forms.

Even though I did not write on the wall that hot summer day in the park, I do write on the wall in many ways. When I bring what I know of our Aboriginal worldviews to the academy, I write on the wall. I do not concern myself with the "manifest manners" (Vizenor's term [1996: 105]) of terminal definitions that describe Indigenous Studies Programs either as tiny niche program that will always lose money, or as political gesture. I concentrate on the students who come to my classes, and attempt to model for them a dialogic that is not a separatist one, an "us and them" approach, but rather an attempt to work together on to understand how Native writers produce their unique critical approaches to our lived experiences and what our value and meaning is within a global perspective.

The Métis Women's Circle holds cultural gatherings that bring Aboriginal people from across Canada together. At one of our gatherings we listened to Ojibwe painter Randy Charbonneau weave the traditional figures within his paintings into stories of recovery from a very long prison sentence. We sang together in an Iroquoian longhouse, to honour those who had lived in that place five hundred years or more ago, and we sat on the earth and listened to Norah Calliou from Paddle Prairie Métis Settlement in Alberta, who gave her medicine teachings cautiously, carefully, in the certain knowledge that translation from Cree into English can mean a betrayal of those teachings. Vizenor says that it is not possible to translate Native traditions and literatures into English without privileging one language and culture over another, without becoming an object of comparison, with the dominant culture as master template. And yet, English is the language he works in, the language I work in. For Vizenor, Native authors who write in English can carry forward "the shadows of tribal creative literature" (1997:13). These shadows, or remembered oral tradition, can bring life to our contemporary survival in urban places. When I see crows perched on a shopping mall roof I think of crow stories, their dances and their doings, as they have always figured in the stories of our peoples (Vizenor 1992).[5]

We participate in gatherings, at private celebrations, at powwows and Aboriginal Days and many multicultural and inter-faith events. We offer our ways of reverence and respect. We wear the Métis sash and choose to decorate our space with historic signs of identity: moccasins, beaded clothing, and Métis flags. To be visible is not necessarily to be understood as we would like, but it is a beginning, a way of re-writing ourselves into an urban landscape that has all but erased us. The powerless, the resentful, the ignorant, and the mischievous scratch or spray their messages on urban walls. We privileged few Native peoples who are academics and professionals write indigeneity into our research efforts, and in gathering elders' stories to pondering their contemporary meanings. We talk to newspaper journalists at public events and usually end up on the social events pages in (often) unflattering photos, as examples of unity in diversity. We rehearse our roots, our histories, by telling stories at live interpretation centers.

In June of 2005, the first graduate from our Indigenous Studies program attended convocation. We made him a silk ceremonial scarf, beaded with wampum beads depicting the bowl and one spoon treaty. We have honoured this treaty of friendship and sharing between the Haudenasaunee and Anishinaabe for a very long time. We did not ask permission to do this. This brought a predictable response from the academy. We could not allow this student to display his sash on the outside of his graduation gown. This would be a break with university tradition. It was a disappointing decision. However, the following year a Tuscarora beader from Six Nations was set to work, Senate permission obtained, and this past year at Wilfrid Laurier University's Convocation, our Indigenous Studies graduates, both Native and non-Native, wore their purple beaded sashes over their black robes; a sweet little triumph. Collectively, Indigenous scholars seek to challenge institutional, structural, and inter-personal tensions by carving a responsive discursive space wherein we write our indigeneity. Some of us write in elegant and precise ways, and some of us mangle moose ribs. No matter. In our collaborative efforts or in the sacred lodges, it is the spirit of openness, humility, and teachability that counts.

Originally published in Canadian Woman Studies/les cahiers de la femme, *"Indigenous Women in Canada: The Voices of First Nations, Inuit and Métis Women," 26 (3 & 4) (Winter/Spring 2008): 63-68. Reprinted with permission of the author.*

Carole Leclair is a Red River Métis, graduate of York University's Faculty of Environmental Studies, and Associate Professor of Contemporary Studies/Indigenous Studies at Wilfrid Laurier University, Brantford. Leclair is one of the increasing numbers of Indigenous women who come late to a university career. She combines many years of grassroots activism within the Métis Women's Circle with a love of the exchange of ideas in academia. She celebrates the opportunities to carry Indigenous cultural knowledge to its hallowed halls. Leclair is the current coordinator of the Indigenous Studies Program at Wilfrid Laurier University, Brantford.

[1]Zibi Anishaabeg First Nations near Maniwaki, western Québec awoke to discover their Community Centre defaced on every wall with racist slogans. A recent land claim settlement in the town of Maniwaki may have sparked the incident.

[2]Vizenor (1981a) invents this phrase, a derivative from Anishinaabe creation stories which tell of a time when the earth was covered with water and the lowly muskrat succeeded in diving to the bottom of the ocean, retrieving a small amount of earth, enough to begin to restore the earth. Urban "earthdivers" plunge into the vast multicultural ocean in order to re-create Indigenous worlds (6).

[3]For a rich assessment of the mixed-blood identity questions in Erdrich, see Peterson.

[4]See Vizenor (1992) for brilliant and subversive stories of animals in the cities.

REFERENCES

Bakker, Peter. *A Language of Our Own: The Genesis of Michif, the Mixed Cree-French Language of the Canadian Metis*. Oxford University Press, New York, 1997.

Blaeser, K. *Gerald Vizenor: Writing in the Oral Tradition*. Norman: University of Oklahoma Press, 1996.

D'Cruz, Caroline. "What Matter Who's Speaking: Authenticity and Identity in Discourses of Aboriginality in Australia." 2002. Online: <http://social.chass.ncsu.edu/jouvert/cdcr.htm>.

Ens, Gerhard. *Homeland to Hinterland: The Changing Worlds of the Red River Metis in the Nineteenth Century*. Toronto: University of Toronto Press, 1996.

Erdrich, Louise. *Love Medicine*. New York: HarperFlamingo, 1998.

Ferrel, Jeff. *Crimes of Style: Urban Graffiti and the Politics of Criminality*. Boston: Northeastern University Press, 1996.

Giraud, M. *The Métis in the Canadian West*. Trans. George Woodcock. Edmonton: University of Alberta Press, 1986.

Howard, Joseph K. *"Strange Empire: A Narrative of the Northwest."* New York: William Morrow and Co., 1943.

Jordan, June. "Waiting for a Taxi." *Names We Call Home: Autobiography on Racial Identity.* Eds. Becky Thompson and Sangeeta Tyagi. New York: Routledge, 1996.

Leclair, Carole. "Memory Alive: Race, Religion and Métis Identities." *Essays on Canadian Writing* 75 (Winter 2002): 126-144.

Momaday, N. Scott. *House Made of Dawn.* New York: Harper Perennial Modern Classics; 1st Perennial Classics Ed edition, 1999.

Owens, Louis. *Other Destinies: Understanding the American Indian Novel.* Norman: University of Oklahoma Press, 1992.

Peterson, Nancy J. "Haunted America: Louise Erdrich and Native American History." *Against Amnesia: Contemporary Women Writers and the Crises of Historical Memory.* Philadelphia: University of Pennsylvania Press, 2001. 18-50.

Pulitano, Elvira. *Toward a Native American Critical Theory.* Lincoln: University of Nebraska Press, 2003.

Silko, Leslie. *Ceremony.* New York: Penguin Press, 1986.

"The Merits of Art." No date. Hip Hop Network. <http://www.hiphop-network.com/articles/graffitiarticles/themeritsofart.asp>.

Vizenor, G. *Dead Voices: Natural Agonies in the New World.* Norman: University of Oklahoma Press, 1992.

Vizenor, G. *Earthdivers: Tribal Narratives on Mixed Descent.* Minneapolis: University of Minnesota Press, 1981a.

Vizenor, G. *Hotline Healers: An Almost Browne Novel.* Hanover: Wesleyan University Press, 1997.

Vizenor, G. *Manifest Manners: Postindian Warriors of Survivance.* Hanover: Wesleyan University Press, 1996.

Vizenor, G. *Narrative Chance: Postmodern Discourse on Native American Indian Literatures.* Norman: University of Oklahoma Press, 1993 [1989].

Vizenor, G. *Wordarrows: Indians and Whites in the New Fur Trade.* Minneapolis: University of Minnesota Press, 1978.

Vizenor, G. 1981b. "Word Cinemas." *Book Forum: American Indians Today: Thought, Literature, Art* 5 (3) (1981b): 389-95.

Welch, James. *Winter in the Blood.* New York: Harper and Row, Inc., 1974.

PATRICIA A. MONTURE

CONFRONTING POWER

Aboriginal Women and Justice Reform

I‌N WRITING ABOUT STORIES LeAnne Howe (Choctaw) notes: "Native stories are power. They create people. They author tribes. America is a tribal creation story, a tribalography" (29). These stories are always interpretative (Howe 29). Each of us has our own story about who we are and how we fit in to creation. Indigenous[1] knowledge systems acknowledge this interpretative aspect rather than organizing knowledge in a binary theoretical system of verifiable or not.[2] Luana Ross (Salish) writes: "One way in which imprisoned women can resist oppression and facilitate social change is by telling their own stories" (17). Through this telling, all oppressed groups assert themselves as subjects (hooks cited in Ross 17). Aboriginal women who are imprisoned in Canada are oppressed because of their race as well as their gender and most likely their poverty. Their imprisonment, the loss of freedom, is thus a fourth condition of their oppression. Their stories are most often stories of struggle and resistance. Sometimes, the struggles of imprisoned women receive the support of advocates who live outside the walls.

This is my story about women and justice, about activism and reform. It is a story about speaking to power. Power not only of race but the power of the prison to resist reform and continually reinvent itself as a place of coercion, power and punishment (Rothman 1971). I share with imprisoned Aboriginal women many of the experiences of oppression caused by our race and gender. I hold privilege as a Haudenosaunee woman who is both free (not sentenced) and no longer living in poverty. I am not an expert on prison never having being sentenced or incarcerated. Such an assertion of expertise on my part would violate the tenets of the Haudenosaunee knowledge system, which requires lived experience and reflection to be the basis of knowing. I do have an idea or two about activism learned from my experiences working toward reform of the Canadian criminal justice system and the sometimes harsh impacts it has had on the lives of Aboriginal women who are imprisoned federally.[3]

Any story I tell must reflect on gender and be grounded by women as knowledge among my people, the Haudenosaunee, is gendered. Teachings, shared through story, create a complex structure of knowledge. There are men's teachings and women's teaching as well as teachings for all people. And I can only know being woman as it is what I experience. As an experience based knowledge system, most often Aboriginal systems rely on reflection with self-interpretation at the core of the reflection as the grounding methodological practices. And as such, an experienced based knowledge system[4] is also necessarily about a gendered system of knowing because I can only live the experience of woman.

In the mid-1980s, while I was still a student, I started going to the prisons in the Kingston area as a volunteer. This was not a benevolent act to "help" those less fortunate than I. Rather, it was an act that was intended to create space for my own well being. I had not met First Nations people either at Queen's University where I had moved to study or seen them around town. There was no friendship centre in town and I missed the community of urban Aboriginal people I had grown up with in London, Ontario. Yet, I knew there was a Mohawk "reserve" only a half-hour drive away but as a poor student I did not have transportation. The absence of First Nation's people from town seemed very odd to me. And I knew that my survival depended on my connection to community, no matter how small or marginalized. Within a broader quest for justice, my commitment to prison began as simply a need to make community for myself.

My involvement in the prison system in Canada began in 1983, a period of time when advocates were successful in forcing penal administrators to consider the distinct experiences of women who were incarcerated. In understanding my story, reform and advocacy are concepts, which have driven both what I have dreamed and learned. But reform and advocacy are not new ideas. People have been advocating for justice reform I suspect since before the advent of the prison in North American in 1819.[5] Prison itself was a reform, a move away from harsh physical punishments often publicly displayed. Prison reform movements also resulted in the establishment of the probation system in the early 1900s. And in understanding this history of prisons, the sociological concept "net-widening" is an important consideration. As Curt Griffiths and Simon Verdun-Jones demonstrate in their discussion of youth justice reforms, reforms aimed at decarceration most often fail to diminish the numbers of people in custody but rather more often establish new populations subject to criminal sanction (559-615).

This pattern of net-widening is also seen in the years since the reporting of the Task Force on Federally Sentenced Women in 1990.[6] That Task Force was an effort aimed at addressing the impacts of discrimination carried by female federal prisoners.[7] And most obvious among this discrimination was the fact there was only one federal prison for women in such a vast country. Unlike men, women could not serve their sentence in the province where they lived unless they were from Ontario. This was a blatant denial of gender equality and a clear violation of section 15 of Canada's newly entrenched Charter of Rights and Freedoms. Since 1990, the year the Task Force reported, the situation of women who are prisoners has changed dramatically. Women are now housed in federal regional facilities in Nova Scotia, Quebec, Ontario, Saskatchewan, Alberta, and most recently British Columbia.

Despite the perception that there is increased equality in the circumstances of men and women serving sentences, maximum-security women are housed in more secure facilities than are most men or was possible at the Prison for Women. For Aboriginal women the picture is more disturbing as they are more likely to be classified as maximum-security. As a result, women are now isolated to a degree not possible under the old regime unless they were segregated. It is also important to note that Aboriginal women may be just as isolated in the new regional facilities because of the poverty they still endure and a half-day drive is just as cost prohibitive for a poor family as a cross country journey to Kingston. Women in prison have also lost the programs that compensated them for this distance from their homes (such as assistance with visiting and telephone calls as well as the family video program). When I reflect on the results of our advocacy, activism and reform efforts under the Task Force on Federally Sentenced Women, I have never been able to convince myself that our efforts to even ameliorate the geographic inequality were successful. For Aboriginal women particularly, the rates of over-representation continue to climb, more than doubling in number between 1981 and 2002 (Sinclair and Boe 17).[8]

Criminalization of Indigenous populations, which results in the present rates of over-representation is in fact a strategy of colonialism and it is therefore seen globally. And as rates of Aboriginal over-representation continue to increase it perhaps reflects that the colonial trajectory continues to increase in impact as well. In participating in the Task Force on Federally Sentenced Women, the Aboriginal women not only confronted the power of prisons both over prisoners and to re-invent themselves as places of punishment, the power of the bureaucracy to entrench itself, as well as the ability of civil servants to locate themselves in that power[9] of bureaucracy. It was also understood that each of these powers is overlain with colonial impacts including the oppression of women. A number of scholars have noted this association between colonialism and gender, but no rigorous analysis of that connection to colonialism presently exists in the Canadian literature (Acoose; Jaimes; McCaskill; Monture-Angus 1999; Smith; TFFSW).

Confronting the power of colonialism is one of the central challenges the Aboriginal women brought to the Task Force discussions as lived experiences of the Aboriginal women who are federal prisoners. And the report that was produced did force correctional officials to confront those understandings of that lived experience. As it brought, colonial history to the centre of the analysis of gender (Hayman), the report may in fact be the only government report to begin to speak inclusively to Aboriginal women's experiences in the way Aboriginal women see the issues.[10] Although the report is only 16 years old, the analysis of women, prison and colonialism was at it's best rudimentary. In those intervening years, the scholarship that considers Aboriginal women's experience of law, power, gender and legal force has been enriched significantly. Sherene Razack writes:

> Colonizers at first claim the land of the colonized as their own through a process of violent eviction, justified by notions that the land was empty or populated by peoples who had to be saved and civilized. In the colonial era, such overt racist ideologies and their accompanying spatial practices (confinement to reserves, for example) facilitate the nearly absolute geographical separation of the colonizer and the colonized. At the end of the colonial era, and particularly with urbanization in the 1950s and 1960s, the segregation of urban space replaces these earlier spatial practices: slum administration replaces colonial administration. (129)

Razack raised these concerns in her study of the trial transcripts of the two men who murdered Pamela George, a Saulteaux woman from the Sakimay First Nation. To this progression of control through spatial separations, the space of the prison must be added. The prison is a total institution that relies on various forms of isolation as the essential form of control over the prisoner in the same way that reserves isolated Aboriginal peoples.

To understand the transformative potential of the energy that Aboriginal reformers put into the Task Force, the degree to which colonial impacts were negated for female prisoners requires consideration. To date, feminist scholars have not examined the work of the Task Force or the building of the new women's facilities from this position. In fact, much of the work is silent on race (see, for example, Hannah-Moffat) or fails to consider that the six Aboriginal women who worked on the two committees did not share a singular vision of the politics of the Task Force or the prison as a coercive institution (see, for example, Hayman). In particular, not all of the Aboriginal women who participated were abolitionists. This vanishes the very real differences of Aboriginal women and places an additional pressure on Aboriginal women to be seen to agree with one another. It, as well, fosters stereotypes of Aboriginal women and pan-Indian understandings (which are often inaccurate).

What is unique about the work of the Task Force on Federally Sentenced Women, is the way in which the voices of Aboriginal women, both prisoners and advocates, were included in the report. Those voices spoke clearly to the power of colonialism that continues to this day to impact on the lives of Aboriginal women. The Task Force was not the first time that the state elected to study the situation of federally sentenced female prisoners. In fact, the Prison for Women was the subject of inquiries and commissions almost since the time the first prisoners were admitted (TFFSW 35-41). What is remarkable is that it is the first time that Aboriginal women were an integral part of the body doing the studying and this outcome is the result of efforts of both the Canadian Association of Elizabeth Fry Societies and the Native Women's Association of Canada. There were two First Nations women on the working group of the Task Force.[11] On the steering committee, there were four Aboriginal women, two of whom were federally sentenced prisoners on community release.

Fran Sugar (Cree) and Lana Fox (Saulteaux) were both members of the steering committee retained by the Task Force to study the situation of federally sentenced Aboriginal women.[12] As both these women were formerly federally sentenced women, the Task Force believed that they would have greater access to the stories that other Aboriginal women held about their incarceration. A research report entitled *Breaking Chains,* was the result of their work. It is a work that "unmaps" (Razack) and demonstrates the degree to which colonialism is a factor in the lives of Aboriginal women who are prisoners:

> No amount of tinkering with prisons can heal the before prison lives of the Aboriginal women who live or have lived within their walls. Prison cannot remedy the problem of the poverty of reserves. It cannot deal with immediate or historical memories of the genocide that Europeans worked upon our people. It cannot remedy violence, alcohol abuse, sexual assault during childhood, rape, and other violence Aboriginal women experience at the hands of men. Prison cannot heal the past abuse of foster homes, or the indifference and racism of Canada's justice system in its dealings with Aboriginal people. *However, the treatment of Aboriginal women within prisons can begin to recognize that these things* are *the realities of the lives that Aboriginal women prisoners have led.* By understanding this point, we can begin to make changes that will promote healing instead of rage. (Sugar and Fox 489, emphasis added)

The point Sugar and Fox make based both on their own experiences and their research is quite simple: acknowledge the effects of colonial imposition. This conclusion is the same one found by the Aboriginal Justice Inquiry of Manitoba, just less directly expressed by the Manitoba Commissioners who acknowledged, "the causes of Aboriginal criminal behaviour are rooted in a long history of discrimination and social inequality...." This same history has "...consigned them to the margins of Manitoba society" (Hamilton and Sinclair 85). Criminal offending, by Aboriginal people, cannot be understood as simply as an individual's malfeasance. This recognition is not intended to make victims of Aboriginal people or of all prisoners but rather its purpose is to provide a necessary and historic, contextual and structural analysis of the problem at the centre of the question being examined.

The innovative research completed by the Task Force at the insistence of Aboriginal women is one of the positive outcomes of the work reformers invested. It accomplished more than providing skills and income to two formerly federally sentenced women. It set a new standard, in my view, for other researchers conducting studies in this area that sees colonialism as a central factor in the analysis of present day social problems. The members of the Task Force believed that this piece of work was necessary in our efforts to find answers to the complex policy questions before us. It is one of the lasting contributions and because truth and knowledge operate to thwart the continuation of colonialism it is an important contribution.

Until very recently in Canadian history, Aboriginal people but particularly Aboriginal women have not had the opportunity to read our truth in government reports and thereby have it affirmed. The total impact of this outcome of the Task Force has never been the focus of study. And it is an outcome that may have impacted on the lives of the Aboriginal women who were (and in too many cases, remain) the prisoners. It is ironic that the analysis of the Task Force and the new women's facilities is critical of the outcomes often concluding that it is the women prisoners who paid the price without returning to speak to those women and without placing colonialism at the centre of the analysis. This is an ultimate irony in the analysis of the "success" or "failure" as one of the goals of the Task Force, reflected in the structure of the report, which begins with the voices of the women who are prisoners, is discussed without the very voices that the Task Force tried to centre.

Prison is also a particular kind of place, which also serves a specific albeit not always acknowledged, social function. It is equally an identity-making space, for the prisoners but not just for the prisoners. First, the fact that the prisoners also produce the prison should not be forgotten (Gaucher 43). Second, "we," those of us who are not labeled as in violation of the criminal law and are, therefore, not criminals have our identities as respectable citizens affirmed. Criminals are wrong-doers (that is not respectable and civilized) and it is therefore right and just to punish them. Thus, the prison is about a particular social function in which respectability and the accompanying social power is distributed in Canadian society.

Recognizing the parallel between the social function of the prison and its impact on Aboriginal peoples and colonialism, these are lessons I would not have learned if I had not been directly involved with prisons and prisoners. Visiting prison, seeing the control and relations of power was an early step for me in understanding the complexity of colonialism. Power, control and isolation are all visible in the prison. Uniforms distinguish prisoners from guards. The quality of the tailoring of the guards uniforms distinguish them from the prisoners as well as the keys on their belts clanking with their footsteps. Bars, control posts and looked doors make the message about who has power and who does not very clear. Power, control and isolation are key components in not only maintaining the "good order" of the institutions but were key components of colonialism. But in this country, in this century, many of these colonial vestiges are no longer visible such as the oppression of residential schools once was to Aboriginal eyes. They are now embedded.

The Task Force attempted to re-create the kind of physical space that women would serve their sentences in and as such it is an interesting study because it connects space to power, isolation and control.[13] Because many of us felt we could not "get to" the power of the prison and it's officials, we took a step back and tried to minimize the ability for exercises of power and control that result in coercion, resistance, violence and isolation. For the Aboriginal women involved, most of us had never had such an opportunity before and were willing to take risks with the hope that we could make positive changes in the experience of incarceration. The title of the report, "Creating Choices," reflects the philosophical attempt to shift the gaze from a system that corrects to one that collectively empowers women. This was an attempt to move women's corrections to a place that constructed women's criminal offending as a mere reflection of gender oppression in Canadian society (TFFSW 16, 25). It was an attempt to relocate the power to make choices in their lives out of the hands of prison officials and back to the women themselves. As noted in the preface, the consensus process engaged by the Task Force was often a painful process but through this commitment we learned that "only if people are treated with respect, only when they are empowered, can they take responsibility for their actions and make meaningful choices" (2). The report did not contain a finished plan but rather the authors urged that it be seen "as only a beginning to a much longer process of change in our justice system, and in society as a whole" (2). To obtain these goals, the Task Force attempted to reconfigure a space known as the women's prison. Whether the reconfigured spaces change women's experiences of prison generally, or specifically if the healing lodge does, remains an unexamined question. And perhaps given the degree that the implementation of the report reconfigured the vision, it may be a question that is unnecessary to examine.

It is precisely this re-focusing on empowerment as an individual responsibility that has interfered with the transformative[14] potential of the vision of "Creating Choices" and resulted in consequences often unforeseen by those of us involved with the preparation of that report. Kelly Hannah-Moffat notes that Corrections Canada has taken the feminist notion of empowerment and attached a notion of self-responsibility to it that transforms the idea of "empowering women" into something less than satisfactory (170). CSC's actions ignore the way empowerment was located at the very beginning of the report. Empowerment follows respect and only when both conditions are present can women make choices that they should be held accountable to. Hannah-Moffat concludes:

> This strong emphasis on responsibility decontextualizes feminist/ [A]boriginal constructions of women's oppression, it also disregards feminist/[A]boriginal analyses of the social economic; and political barriers experienced by women, in particular marginalized women. (176)

It is the individualization of the concept empowerment that is the problem.

Individualization when it is detached from both the other five principles the Task Force articulated, as well as from the historical analysis that acknowledges systemic patterns of colonization, gender discrimination and unequal wealth distribution, continues to complicate the problem of colonial oppression. By ignoring systemic patterns the transformative potential of *Creating Choices* is impaired. As a tool to thwart colonialism, the Task Force's work at least partially and perhaps significantly was stripped of its power to offer opportunities to decolonize.

The five "principles for change" are empowerment; meaningful and responsible choices; respect and dignity; supportive environment; and shared responsibility (TFFSW 128-135). The principles were not drafted as a checklist but are complimentary and must operate in an interlocking pattern of commitment to the women who are prisoners. One of the difficulties I often experience in justice reform efforts is that I forget to be mindful enough of the different cultural contexts—forgetting that non-Aboriginal peoples do not share the same view of the world or the same understanding of knowledge. It means never forgetting that you are different and think differently (and this is almost an impossible requirement to fulfill as it requires you to analyze each and every thought that passes through your mind or every word that crosses your lips). And who is doing the double thinking is a fact that should not escape our attention. Explaining Aboriginal traditions, worldviews and knowledge systems is insufficient to guarantee respect, understanding or reaching a shared meaning. This has been one of my hardest lessons and it indeed remains a conundrum. It is conundrum faced every time I work in a non-Aboriginal institution from the prison to the university.

More disturbingly, the result of what reformers intended to be a transformation of women's prison has instead been shifted to a recharacterization of women prisoners as dangerous. The shift can be seen in the enhanced security measures such as the "eye in the sky" surveillance camera, fences and razor wire. This recharacterization is substantiated in some instances with stereotypes of Aboriginal peoples. It is important to acknowledge that in 1990, one of the cornerstones of the TFFSW (and one of its strategies) was the acknowledgement that women prisoners were not as "dangerous" as men in prison. Coupled with this was an agreement among the majority of the Task Force that the security rating scales were not valid and some of us thought we had secured a promise that these scales were not to be used any longer at least until they had been demonstrated to be valid. Women were to be treated as women and not as a particular kind of security risk. Nowhere in the 17 pages of discussion under the heading of "The Recommended Plan" is it obvious that risk assessment would limit women's access to the new facilities including the healing lodge (TFFSW 138-154). This is because the Task Force rejected the idea of "risk management" and "risk assessment" for women prisoners (109-112). In the words of the Task Force, in response to the question, "is classification appropriate":

Initially, Task Force members supported the concept of woman-based criteria for classification as suggested by previous studies but ultimately came to the conclusion that assessment to gain better understanding of a woman's needs and experiences *is more appropriate than classification.* This conclusion is based on the Task Force perception that classification maintains the focus on security and on assigning a security rating for the women. (112)

This, in my view, is why the Task Force did not focus on women who were "hard to manage"[15] because the idea of security rating scales was fully rejected.[16] The result that women who are prisoners are now seen as dangerous both by the Service and the general public is a deeply disturbing result of our reform efforts and more damaging to women than the more common response to attempted prison reform of net-widening.

This consequence born so heavily by women prisoners may be explained as a response to a report which demanded that female prisoners be treated with respect in the post-Charter era and indeed would result in the de-prisoning of female corrections. As a government report on prisoners has not attempted this challenge to the construction of the assumed dangerousness of prisoners, a challenge that goes to the heart of the legitimacy of the prison to punish, coerce and restrain human beings could be the fatal flaw that scholars keep looking for. What is learned then, is do not challenge the legitimacy of the prison (no matter how much sense it makes) without the resources necessary to ensure that there is an opportunity for reforms to respond to the backlash as there indeed will be backlash from the prison bureaucracy.

It is important as an activist to consider why these things have happened. Kelly Hannah Moffat describes some of the consequences of the reform efforts and the countervailing need of prison administrators and staff to have control:

Enhanced security cells were expanded in each of the new regional prisons. This was in response to correctional and staff concerns about security and discipline in the new regional prisons, which up until this time had relied more heavily on dynamic (as opposed to static) security measures. "Enhanced security" cells in the new prisons have doubled in number from the original designs; they have also been modified to allow for double bunking.... *It provides housing for inmates who: exhibit violent behaviour and/or have special needs; and/or serve disciplinary sentences.* (182)

This criminalization of women and the increasing way that they are characterized as dangerous (a post-Task Force reality) was essential to re-entrenching the legitimacy of prisons to punish and coerce. In my view, this has again become, and with a vengeance, the guiding philosophy of women's incarceration in Canada.

Never before had the Correctional Service of Canada relinquished so much power to community to be involved in correctional decision-making and no mechanisms were in place to ensure that community members or organizations continued to hold some power. And this is the fatal flaw in our abilities to secure meaningful and long-term reform. Insufficient power over the long term sat and sits in the hands of the reformers. As Kim Pate notes:

> From that point forward, it has been an incredible struggle to have the voices of the women heard, much less incorporated, in the planning process. In addition, we have witnessed the appropriation of feminist language, ideas and principles. This has also happened in conjunction with the continuing decontextualizing of women's experiences and life situations. Furthermore, the CSC has developed a distressing trend toward the conversion of women's needs into criminogenic risk factors. For instance, they have commissioned researchers to study the women in prison for linkages between self-injury and violent offending. (Faith and Pate 140)

It was the advocates of women prisoners who so strongly asserted that the voices of the women had to come first. Failing to continue to include the community has jeopardized the continuity of that acknowledgement and the commitment to listen to the women who are imprisoned has continued to be lost over the years.

Reflecting on this silencing of the women prisoners' voices (and those in the community who advocate for them) is an important aspect of understanding what went wrong. It is important to recognize that during the life of the Task Force, the working environment was a women's, maybe even a feminist, environment. This made it easy to retain the feminist principles we agreed were foundational to our work. Once the Task Force's work was completed, many of the civil servants returned to the male-dominated bureaucracy of corrections where feminist values, principles and beliefs are not respected or well-regarded. This was another structural pressure well beyond the control of any individual Task Force member that diminished the reformist vision.

Despite the involvement of the Native Women's Association of Canada in the establishment of Aboriginal specific initiatives, the transformative potential here has also been contained. The report of the Task Force on Federally Sentenced Women contains a specific focus on Aboriginal women that is maintained throughout the report. The recommendations are both inclusive and separate as appropriate. The most transformative of the ideas resulted in the building of the Healing Lodge at the Nekaneet First Nation (ironically on land surrendered for the purpose of building the Lodge). This was an attempt to create Aboriginal space for women to serve their sentences in.[17]

On a visit to the Ochimaw Ochi Healing Lodge several years ago, I had occasion to sit with the Elders in the Spiritual Lodge. One of the Elders expressed to me that "there was not enough Aboriginal programming at the Lodge." This statement encapsulates the degree to which those involved with the Task Force and those charged with implementing it have been successful (or not) in creating Aboriginal space. The prison was to be in its entirety an Aboriginal "program" (or Aboriginal space). It was not to rely on discrete Aboriginal programs to supplement the core programs of CSC. Those few words from the Elder "unmapped" for me the success (or the lack thereof) of this endeavour. A word of caution is essential around this point. There is no doubt that the Healing Lodge is not all that I have imagined it to be. I, however, base my analysis on an "outsider" position, granted one who is vested in the building of the lodge. It is clear to me that individual women (both Aboriginal and non) who have served their sentences at the Lodge have benefited by being there as some of us originally envisioned.[18]

There are a number of questions I continue to ponder. The Task Force, it's implementation and the new women's facility will never be experienced as something that is either a success or failure, however you define those terms. For me, I think it will always be both. And as a woman who is not serving time, I recognize the privilege in that statement. In prisons, physical space is an important organizational quality. Compare the visual image of a maximum-security facility (and often what we conjure up reflects the reality at male prisons)—rolls and rolls of razor wire, fences or limestone walls and highly controlled offender movement. A minimum-security facility may look more like a resort than a penal institution. Although institutional-looking, the new regional facilities for women did not look like prisons prior to the enhancement of security measures in the first year of their operations. This exposes an interesting research question: how does the look of the new facilities change the experience of doing time? Or does it? What is the transformative value in changing the physical space of prisons if indeed there is one?

The physical space of the Prison for Women left little doubt about the nature of the coercion of the institution to one's imagination. Sugar and Fox explain how Aboriginal women's experience of the space of Prison for Women (P4W) was identity making:

> To be a woman and to be *seen* as violent is to be especially marked in the eyes of the administrations of the prisons where women do time, and in the eyes of the staff who guard them. In a prison with a male population, our crimes would stand out much less. Among women we do not fit stereotypes, and we are automatically feared, and labeled as in need of special handling. The label "violent" begets a self-perpetuating and destructive cycle for Aboriginal women within prisons. In P4W, everything follows this label. But the prison regime that follows serves to re-enforce the violence that it is supposedly designed to manage. It creates of P4W a place in which it is impossible for us to heal. (470)

The relationship between the colonial legacy, the portrayal of women as violent and increasingly as dangerous, and the racialization of Aboriginal women are interwoven strategies used by correctional systems. This emphasizes how important the broader context of power, while recognizing the many forms power takes, is to understanding the experiences of women who are prisoners.

When we reflect on our experiences and not just react to them, we create our stories. And those stories "are power, create people and author tribes" (Howe 29). And the land we now call Canada supports layers and layers of these Indigenous stories. Our actions, our trickster lessons and our stories have the power to turn colonialism over and our people will reclaim our power and our freedom. It is in this way that I offer my thoughts on reforming prisons and the lessons I have learned thus far. This is my small offering to that process of reclaiming just relations as prison is just one small part of a much larger problem for Aboriginal people around the world.

Originally published in Canadian Woman Studies/les cahiers de la femme, *"Canadian Feminism in Action," 25 (3 & 4) (Summer/Fall 2006): 25-33. Reprinted with permission of the author.*

Patricia A. Monture is a citizen of the Mohawk Nation, Grand River Territory. She is currently teaching in the Sociology Department at the University of Saskatchewan where she coordinates the Aboriginal Justice and Criminology Program. She is a committed activist/scholar who continues to seek justice for Aboriginal peoples and especially Aboriginal women and girls.

[1]None of the names that are commonly applied to Onkwehon:we peoples are the names we use ourselves. Indigenous is the name most often used when the global situation is the reference. In Canada, the constitution labels us as Aboriginal Peoples and more specifically the "Indian, Inuit, and Métis." "Indian" people often prefer to be called First Nations.

[2]For Indigenous peoples, often our stories, which are the foundation of our knowledge systems have been relegated to mere myth. This is a form of intellectual colonialism.

[3]In Canada, the constitution establishes that there are both federally and provincially sentenced prisoners. Federal prisoners are distinguished from provincial because their sentences are longer than two years.

[4]I am not trying to diminish the learning that comes from books although I do want to note that my time spent learning in university based systems of knowledge are also lived experience. As such, then, it is for me always about balancing learning in two very differently structured systems of knowledge (for a fuller discussion of my experience in the university please see Patricia Monture in "On Being Homeless: One Aboriginal Woman's 'Conquest of Canadian Universities, 1989-1998").

[5]New York State established a state prison at Auburn based on the congregate system. The date in itself should be an indication that the establishment of the prison and colonialism are in fact inter-connected phenomenon. For a detailed discussion of the establishment of the first prisons in North America see Rothman at 79.

[6]This is not the first time I have offered my ponderings on the Task Force. Please also see Patricia Monture–Angus, "Aboriginal Women and Correctional Practice: Reflections on the Task Force on Federally Sentenced Women."

[7]In choosing the appropriate word to describe those labeled "inmates" or "offenders," I am informed by Gayle Horii's (a lifer who served time at the Prison for Women) comments: "Prisoner is the only correct term to describe a person locked into a cage or cell within a facility not of one's choice and whose quality of existence therein depends upon the keepers" (108). In our activism we must take care to respect the expertise of those who have lived experiences.

[8]There are far fewer women incarcerated in Canada than men. In 1981, 35 federally sentenced women were Aboriginal and by 2002 they numbered 94. Sinclair and Boe report this is a relatively stable increase from 18 per cent to 20 per cent over the two decades (17). This contradicts the figure of 29 per cent reported by the Canadian Human Rights Commission in 2003 (15).

[9]This power takes several forms. At the time of the Task Force, many of the community members of the Task Force did not have access to email. Our long distance calls, facsimiles and other expenses came directly out of our pockets and were eventually reimbursed. The civil servants had unlimited resources at their immediate disposal. They had the ability to caucus on the government's dime and many worked in the same geographic area. Community members did not have this ability to caucus other than at meetings. This imbalance in resources and power impacts on the ability of the community sector to participate and results in a documentary record, such as the recording of minutes, that was really more firmly in the hands of the bureaucrats. These are significant issues that impact on the ability of reformers to see their views equally recorded.

[10]Compare this to the report of the Royal Commission on Aboriginal People where the discussion of gender is little more than the discussion of loss of status under former section 12(1)(b) of the *Indian Act* despite the fact the RCAP reported six years after the Task Force on Federally Sentenced Women.

[11]The author of this paper was one of those two women.

[12]These two women were also part of the Steering Committee of the Task Force on Federally Sentenced women.

[13]Many of these negotiations were not easy ones but ones made under the pressure of the consequences for prisoners if we did not agree as the civil servants often reminded us. I remember long, hard discussions about segregation units. I remember opining that locking me in a penthouse suite of the luxurious Royal York Hotel was still dehumanizing and a fancy place was still segregation (even if you called it something else). These are the kinds of heated discussions that were never reflected in the minutes.

[14]Laureen Snider writes: "Indeed, criminal justice systems are probably the least effective institutions to look for transformative change. Even the staunchest advocates of incarceration do not argue that prisons are successful institutions, only that they punish well" (11).

[15]Stephanie Hayman in her analysis of the work of the Task Force does not acknowledge this concession to not apply security-rating scales (see pages 231-238). This limits the results of her analysis.

[16]Both the most recent report of the Correctional Investigator (2005-2006) and the special report of the Canadian Human Rights Commission (2003) are critical that no work has been done to develop an assessment model for women.

[17]This was the first of the healing lodges built by government in Canada. There are now eight lodges that are federally funded including those that are still in the development phase with the Okimaw Ochi Healing lodge being the only female facility. These are Waseskun House in Quebec; Ochichakasipi (Crane River) in Manitoba; Willow Cree Healing Lodge in Saskatchewan, Wapatin in Saskatchewan; Stan Daniels Healing Centre in Alberta; Pe Sakawtew in Hobbema, Alberta and Kwe Kwe Kwelp in British Columbia.

[18]The birth of the healing lodge was not a well-though out plan but more of a coincidence. It was a reaction to yet another suicide at the Prison for Women. It was a spur of the moment comment about not needing another prison to warehouse Aboriginal women as my sisters kept coming home to us in boxes. It was this abolition point I was making. But I followed it with a comment about Aboriginal women needing a place to heal, a lodge. The civil servants at the table immediately embraced this idea of a healing lodge. They started to question me what such a lodge would look like. It left us stunned and I felt like I had made a mistake sharing our dream about a healing place.

REFERENCES

Acoose, Janice. *Iskewewak kah'Ki Yaw Ni Wahkoma Kaak: Neither Indian Princesses nor Easy Squaws.* Toronto: Women's Press, 1995.

Canadian Human Rights Commission. *Protecting Their Rights: A Systemic Review of Human Rights in Correctional Services for Federally Sentenced Women.* Ottawa: Canadian Human Rights Commission, 2003.

Correctional Investigator. *Annual Report of the Office of the Correctional Investigator 2005-2006.* Ottawa: Minister of Public Works and Government Services Canada, 2006.

Faith, Karlene and Kim Pate. "Personal and Political Musing on Activism: A Two Way Interview." *Ideal Prisons? Critical Essays on Women's Imprisonment in Canada.* Eds. Kelly Hannah Moffat and Margaret Shaw. Halifax: Fernwood Publishing, 2000. 136-147.

Gaucher, Bob, ed. *Writing as Resistance: The Journal of Prisoners on Prisons Anthology (1988-2002).* Toronto: Canadian Scholars Press, 2002.

Griffith, Curt T. and Simon N. Verdun Jones. *Canadian Criminal Justice.* 2nd Ed. Toronto: Harcourt Brace, 1994.

Hamilton, A. C and C. M. Sinclair. *The Report of the Aboriginal Justice Inquiry of Manitoba: The Justice System and Aboriginal People.* Winnipeg: Queen's Printer, 1991.

Hannah-Moffat, Kelly. *Punishment in Disguise: Penal Governance and Federal Imprisonment of Women in Canada.* Toronto: University of Toronto Press, 2001.

Hannah-Moffat, Kelly and Margaret Shaw, eds. *An Ideal Prison? Critical Essays on Women's Imprisonment in Canada.* Halifax: Fernwood Publishing, 2000.

Hayman, Stephanie. *Imprisoning Our Sisters: The New Federal Women's Prisons in Canada.* Montreal: McGill-Queen's University Press, 2006.

Horii, Gayle K. "Processing Humans." *Ideal Prisons? Critical Essays on Women's Imprisonment in Canada.* Eds. Kelly Hannah Moffat and Margaret Shaw. Halifax: Fernwood Publishing, 2000. 104-116.

Howe, LeAnne. "The Story of America: A Tribalography." *Clearing a Path: Theorizing the Past in Native American Studies.* Ed. Nancy Shoemaker. New York: Routledge, 2002. 29-48.

Jaimes, M. Annette, ed. *The State of Native America: Genocide, Colonization and Resistance.* Boston: South End Press, 1992.

McCaskill, Don. "Native People and the Justice System." *As Long as the Sun Shines and the Water Flows: A Reader in Canadian Native Studies.* Eds. Ian Ghetty and Antoine Lussier. Vancouver: University of British Columbia Press, 1983. 288-298.

McCaslin, Wanda, ed. *Justice as Healing: Indigenous Ways.* St. Paul, Minnesota: Living Justice Press, 2005.

Monture, Patricia. "On Being Homeless: One Aboriginal Woman's 'Conquest of Canadian Universities, 1989-1998." *Crossroads, Directions and a New Critical Race Theory.* Eds. Franscisco Valdes, Jerome McCristal Culp and Angela P. Harris. Philadelphia: Temple University Press, 2002. 274-287.

Monture, Patricia. "Aboriginal Women and Correctional Practice: Reflections on the Task Force on Federally Sentenced Women." *Ideal Prisons? Critical Essays on Women's Imprisonment in Canada.* Eds. Kelly Hannah Moffat and Margaret Shaw. Halifax: Fernwood Publishing, 2000. 52-60.

Monture-Angus, Patricia. "Considering Colonialism and Oppression: Aboriginal Women and the 'Theory" of Decolonization."010 *Native Studies Review* 12 (2) (1999): 63-94.

Razack, Sherene. "Gendered Racial Violence and Spatialized Justice: The Murder of Pamela George." *Race, Space and the Law: Unmapping a White Settler Society.* Ed. Sherene Razack. Toronto: Between the Lines, 2002. 121-156.

Ross, Luana. "Race, Gender, and Social Control: Voices of Imprisoned Native American and White Women." *Wicazo Sa Review* 10 (2) (1994): 17-37.

Rothman, David J. *The Discovery of the Asylum: Social Order and Disorder in the New Republic.* Boston: Little Brown and Company, 1971.

Sinclair, Roberta Lynn and Roger Boe. *Canadian Federal Women Offender Profiles: Trends from 1981 to 2002 (Revised).* Ottawa: Research Branch, Correctional Service of Canada, 2002.

Smith, Andrea. *Conquest: Sexual Violence and American Indian Genocide.* Cambridge: Southend Press, 2005.

Snider, Laureen. "Towards Safer Societies: Punishment, Masculinities and Violence Against Women." *British Journal of Criminology* 38 (1) (1998): 1-39.

Sugar, Fran and Lana Fox. "Nistum Peyako Séht'wawin Iskewewak: Breaking Chains." *Canadian Journal of Women and the Law* 3 (2) (1989-90): 465-482.

Task Force on Federally Sentenced Women. *Creating Choices: The Report of the Task Force on Federally Sentenced Women* (TFFSW). Ottawa: Correctional Service of Canada, 1990.

CONFRONTING COLONIALISM

PATRICIA A. MONTURE

WHITE MAN TELL ME

white man
  tell me
"I had no idea"
  white man, he,
  tell me

white man hear me
  I been
telling you 'bout
  poverty
  abuse
  jail
  foster care
  residential schools
  suicide
  bottle abuse
  rape
  crime
  battering

been telling you 'bout
  privilege I carry
  as employed,
    teacher,
      speaker,

all that, it,
don't change much
about
  the pain
i carry
it surrounds me
downs me

with knowing death and suicide
    violence and rape
    murder

spirit gone
woman gone
circle of sisters
growing smaller
not vanished

white man
what was that y'all was saying?

white man
ain't never
tole me
'bout nothing
i don't already know.

white man
don't tell me
hear me
voice crying in the wind.

white man listen:
wind is whistling
that wind
with promise of comfort
when white men
don't try tell me nothing.

as my grannies taught
the wind he promises
all them answers
in the land
this land
red land

white man listen
that wind,
he mocks you.

whistling

Originally published in CWS/cf, *"Indigenous Women in Canada: The Voices of First Nations, Inuit and Métis Women," 26 (3 & 4) (Winter/Spring 2008): 104. Reprinted with permission of the author.*

CARRIE BOURASSA, KIM MCKAY-MCNABB AND MARY HAMPTON

RACISM, SEXISM AND COLONIALISM

The Impact on the Health of Aboriginal Women in Canada

A BORIGINAL WOMEN IN CANADA carry a disproportionate burden of poor health. Aboriginal women have lower life expectancy, elevated morbidity rates, and elevated suicide rates in comparison to non-Aboriginal women (Prairie Women's Health Centre of Excellence, 2004). Aboriginal women living on reserves have significantly higher rates of coronary heart disease, cancer, cerebrovascular disease and other chronic illnesses than non-Aboriginal Canadian women (Waldram, Herring, and Young, 2000). A significantly greater percentage of Aboriginal women living off-reserve, in all age groups, report fair or poor health compared to non-Aboriginal women; 41 per cent of Aboriginal women aged 55–64 reported fair or poor health, compared to 19 per cent of women in the same age group among the total Canadian population (Statistics Canada). In addition, chronic disease disparities are more pronounced for Aboriginal women than Aboriginal men. For example, diseases such as diabetes are more prevalent among Aboriginal women than either the general population or Aboriginal men (Statistics Canada).

Epidemiologists suggest that many of these chronic health conditions are a result of the forced acculturation imposed on Aboriginal peoples (Young 1994). Yet, for Aboriginal women, low income, low social status, and exposure to violence also ontribute to poor health. Aboriginal women face the highest poverty and violence rates in Canada. Joyce Green (2000) notes that in 1991 eight out of ten Aboriginal women reported victimization by physical, sexual, psychological, or ritual abuse; this rate is twice as high as that reported by non-Aboriginal women. These issues are evident in Saskatchewan where the Saskatchewan Women's Secretariat (1999) determined that at least 57 per cent of the women who used shelters in 1995 were of Aboriginal ancestry, yet they comprised only 11 per cent of the total female population. These numbers reflect the magnitude of the problem. Redressing these injustices requires awareness of the processes that create negative health consequences and mobilization of action to correct these processes. The Saskatchewan Women's Secretariat notes: "Studies have shown that health differences are reduced when economic and status differences between people, based on things such as culture, race, age, gender and disability are reduced" (44).

Gender and ethnicity have been shown to be influential determinants of health across populations. Conceptual distinctions between definitions of "gender" and "sex" have led to our understanding that the processes of sexism (such as increased exposure to violence) are more likely to contribute to women's poor health than biological or genetic differences between women and men. Similarly, conceptual distinctions between definitions of "ethnicity" and "race" in population health research suggests that "race" is used to describe natural units or populations that share distinct biological characteristics; whereas ethnic groups are seen as being culturally distinct (Polednak). In population health research, these two terms are used interchangeably, often leaving out a discussion of the processes by which racism creates conditions of poor health for certain ethnic groups (Young 1994). Racism is a biopsychosocial stressor that has severe negative health effects on racialized individuals (Clark, Anderson, Clark and Williams). Sexism is blatantly dangerous to women's health in many ways (Lips). Racism and sexism have this in common; they operate via external power structures to contribute to poor health in certain disadvantaged groups. Research suggests that culture and cultural differences also have an impact on health (Amaratunga; Wienert). However, little is written about how what we describe as culture can be the outcome of colonial processes. Cultural groups that have lived under colonization experience a legacy of oppression that adds another level of threat to their health. Indigenous Peoples as distinct cultural groups have been exposed to genocide to further the interests of colonization (Chrisjohn and Young; Tuhiwhai Smith). We will illustrate that this colonization and its contemporary manifestations in the policies and practices that affect Aboriginal women create unique threats to their health status. Our analysis will demonstrate that the process by which the definition of "Indian" is imposed by colonial legislation in Canada constitutes a form of multiple oppressions that differentially disempower Aboriginal wo-men, conferring particular risks to their health.

LINKS BETWEEN SEXISM, RACISM, COLONIALISM
AND ABORIGINAL WOMEN'S WEALTH

Sexism, racism, and colonialism are dynamic processes rather than static, measurable determinants of health; they began historically and continue to cumulatively and negatively impact health status of Aboriginal women. Colonialism depends on the oppression of one group by another, beginning with a process described as "othering" (Gerrard and Javed). The process of "othering" occurs when society sorts people into two categories: the reference group and the "other." Women who bear their "otherness" in more than one way suffer from multiple oppressions, leaving them more vulnerable to assaults on their well-being than if they suffered from one form of oppression. The cumulative effects have painful material, social, and health consequences. We offer an example of the process of "othering" imposed on Aboriginal women through colonial legislation defining Indian identity between the years 1869–1985; these policies continue to influence women's health and well-being today. Using this example, we will deconstruct the process of colonialism and reveal its consequences for Aboriginal women and their health.

We describe ways in which the *Indian Act* differentially affects Aboriginal women and men in Canada; it is a case example of multiple oppressions. Colonial discourse has historically represented non-white populations as racially inferior. These assumptions have been used to justify social treatment of these populations that fosters inequality and social exclusion in all areas, ultimately contributing to poor health conditions in the oppressed group. Linda Tuhiwai Smith notes that racism, sexism, and colonialism (through the process of "othering") serve to describe, objectify, and represent Indigenous women in ways that have left a legacy of marginalization within Indigenous societies as much as within the colonizing society. She points out that racist and sexist notions about the role of women were imposed upon Indigenous communities by white, European settlers with patriarchal consciousness. "Colonization," she notes, "is recognized as having had a destructive effect on Indigenous gender relations which reached out across all spheres of Indigenous society." Sexism, racism, and colonialism have had a negative impact on Aboriginal women's identities, our sense of who we are, and where we belong. We argue that gender differences in the process of "othering" have forced Aboriginal women to challenge the racist, sexist, and colonial policies within and beyond our communities. We further suggest that accumulated disadvantage from past colonization and contemporary processes of ongoing colonization have a direct affect on Aboriginal women's access to social determinants of health and impedes their ability to develop a healthy sense of identity that can contribute to personal well-being.

IMPACT OF ABORIGINAL IDENTITY ON HEALTH AND WELL-BEING

An insidious result of colonialism has been the externally imposed definition of Indian identity through processes that create cultural ambiguity for Aboriginal women (Mihesuah). Bonita Lawrence (1999) argues that although Euro-Canadian legislation has affected what she terms "native identity" across gender lines, it has had greater impact on Aboriginal women. Consequently, significant gaps exist between material, social, and health outcomes for Aboriginal men and Aboriginal women. However, racist underpinnings of colonialism have also produced gaps *amongst and between* Aboriginal women themselves (Saskatchewan Women's Secretariat). For example, Métis women in Saskatchewan are more likely to be employed than status Indian women but less likely to be employed than non-Aboriginal women. Hence, sexism, racism and colonialism have converged to create a matrix of oppression that differentially affect specific Aboriginal groups and men and women within those groups.

Cultural identity evidently has implications for the status that women have in the external world and this has an impact on health. However, identity also has implications for feelings of self-worth and belonging, and this has an impact on health as well. A recent study conducted with Aboriginal women in Manitoba by the Prairie Women's Health Centre of Excellence found that Aboriginal women endorsed important links between health and wellness and their cultural identities. Cultural identities were inseparable from their family, history, community, place, and spirituality and all of these elements were integrated into a broad and holistic understanding of health and well-being. The women acknowledged that many factors shaped their health and well-being including poverty, housing, violence, and addictive behaviours, however, cultural identity served as a potential anchor to help them deal with these issues and promote health. Accordingly, they made recommendations for health practices that integrated holistic solutions that included "traditional cultural practices and understandings with respect to health and wellness" (24). This suggests that women who are Aboriginal can look to cultural identity as a foundation on which they can build healthy lives, however, for women who cannot draw on a firm sense of cultural identity, maintaining and promoting health could be more difficult. Unfortunately, there are large numbers of women who are in the latter position. It is through this removal of cultural identity and status within Aboriginal groups that Canadian legislation has produced a significant threat to the health and well-being of many Aboriginal women.

COLONIZATION AS AN INSTRUMENT OF MULTIPLE OPPRESSIONS FOR ABORIGINAL WOMEN IN CANADA

The *Indian Act*, passed in Canada in 1876, defined Indian identity and prescribed what "Indianness" meant. Because of the sexist specification inherent in this legislation, ramifications of the *Indian Act* were more severe for Aboriginal women than men, ramifications that continue to have severe impacts on our life chances today. Lawrence (2000) notes that the *Act* ordered how Aboriginal people were to think of all things "Indian" and created classifications that have become normalized as "cultural differences". She argues that the differences between Métis (or mixed ancestry people), non-status Indians, Inuit, and status Indians were created by the *Act* and those differences became accepted in Canada as being cultural in nature when, in fact, they were social constructions imposed by legislation. It should be acknowledged that cultural distinctions did and do exist within and amongst Aboriginal people; however, those cultural distinctions were never categorized nor embedded in legislation prior to 1876 and did not have the same impact until commencement of the *Act*. Indigenous scholars agree that the *Indian Act* has controlled Aboriginal identity by creating legal and non-legal categories that have consequences for rights and privileges both within and beyond Aboriginal communities (Lawrence 2000; Mihesuah).

One important consequence of the *Indian Act* is that status Indian women (hereafter referred to as Indian women) who married non-Indian men lost their Indian status and their band membership under this *Act*. Prior to 1869, the definition of Indian was fairly broad and generally referred to "all persons of Indian blood, their spouses and their descendents" (Voyageur 88). After 1869, Indian women who married non-Indians were banished from their communities since non-Indians were not allowed on reserves; this was true even if a divorce occurred (McIvor). From the government's perspective, these women had assimilated and had no use for their Indian status. The goal of assimilation was a central element of the *Indian Act 1876* because it would advance the government's policy of genocide through the process of enfranchisement: the removal of Indian status from an individual. Section 12(1)(b) of the *Act* specified that Indian women would lose their status if they married a non-Indian man. Further, Indian women could not own property, and once a woman left the reserve to marry she could not return to her reserve so she lost all property rights. This legacy of disenfranchisement was passed on to her children (Wotherspoon and Satzewich). In contrast, an Indian man who married a non-Indian woman not only retained his Indian status, but the non-Indian woman would gain status under the *Act*, as would their children. Even upon divorce or the death of her husband, a non-Indian woman who gained status under the *Act* through marriage retained her status and band membership as did her children (Voyageur). Only the identity of Indian women was defined by their husband and could be taken away. The imposition of this Euro-centric, sexist ideology on Aboriginal families was a direct disruption of traditional Aboriginal definitions of family. Under *Indian Act* legislation, enfranchised Indians were to become Canadian citizens and, as a result, they relinquished their collective ties to their Indian communities (Lawrence 1999). However, Indian women were not granted the benefit of full Canadian citizenship. Lawrence notes that until 1884, Indian women who had lost their status could not inherit any portion of their husband's land or assets after his death. After 1884, widows were allowed to inherit one-third of their husband's land(s) and assets if "a widow was living with her husband at his time of death and was determined by the Indian Agent to be 'of good moral character'" (Lawrence 1999: 56). Furthermore, if a woman married an Indian from another reserve, the *Act* stated that she must follow her husband and relinquish her band membership in order to become a member of his band. If her husband died or if she divorced him, she could not return to her reserve, as she was no longer a member. These policies governing marriage and divorce were just one of several ways that Aboriginal women were stripped of their rights and privileges. For example, from 1876 to 1951 women who married Indian men and remained on the reserve were denied the right to vote in band elections, to hold elected office, or to participate in public meetings. However, Indian men were eligible to take place in all of these activities (Voyageur). Therefore, colonization was an instrument by which sexism and racism were created and reinforced on and off reserve lands, converging in diminishing power and resources available to Aboriginal women in Canada.

Passage of the *Charter of Rights and Freedoms* made gender discrimination illegal and opened the door for Aboriginal women to challenge the Indian Act. In 1967, Aboriginal women lobbied both the federal government and Indian bands for amendment to the *Act*. Sharon McIvor notes that in *Lavell v. Her Majesty (1974)* Abori-ginal women challenged the government based on the argument that the government had been discriminating against Indian women for over 100 years via the *Indian Act*. The Supreme Court of Canada, however, ruled that since Canada had jurisdiction over Indians it could decide who was an Indian and that the *Act* was not discriminatory. Continual lobbying by Aboriginal women finally resulted in action and the *Act* was amended in 1985 through passage of *Bill C-31*.

However, despite the amendment, long-standing implications of the *Indian Act* for Aboriginal women in Canada are still evident. As Lawrence notes, the government's "social engineering process" (1999: 58) via the *Act* ensured that between 1876 and 1985 over 25,000 women lost their status and were forced to leave their communities. All of their descendants lost status and were "permanently alienated from Native culture, the scale of cultural genocide caused by gender discrimination becomes massive" (Lawrence 1999: 59). She notes that when *Bill C-31* was passed in 1985, there were only 350,000 female and male status Indians left in Canada. *Bill C-31* allowed individuals who had lost status and their children to apply for reinstatement. Approximately 100,000 individuals had regained status by 1995, but many individuals were unable to regain status. Under *Bill C-31*, grandchildren and great-grandchildren were not recognized as having Indian status and, in many cases, no longer identified as Indian (Lawrence 1999; Voyageur). In addition, legislative decision still blocked Aboriginal women from full participation in their communities. For example, the *Corbiere Decision in 1999 (John Corbiere et al. v. the Batchewana Indian Band and Her Majesty the Queen)* specified that Indian women living off-reserve could not vote in band elections because the *Indian Act* stated that Indian members must "ordinarily live on reserve" in order to vote. Thus, re-instated Indian women and their children were still at a disadvantage despite having legal recognition under the *Act*.[1]

In the end, the amendments did not repair the damage of previous legislation. Kinship ties, cultural ties, and par-ticipation in governance were significantly disrupted. Long term consequences for these women and their children would include the erosion of connections and rights that may have enabled them to work collectively to address social disparities.

It is ironic that the only recourse Aboriginal women have is to appeal to the federal government and judicial system—the same government and system that instituted and upheld the sexist, discriminatory and oppressive legislation for over 100 years. This government holds different principles of justice than traditional Aboriginal government, leaving women once again vulnerable to multiple oppressions. As Jan Langford writes, "If First Nations governments are built on the traditional Aboriginal way of governing where equity is built into the system, there wouldn't be a need for the 'white' ways of protecting rights" (35). However, band governing bodies are not working according to the traditional Aboriginal way, instead using legislation to exclude women and protect male privilege.

After fighting for the recognition of Aboriginal rights, Aboriginal women have found themselves at odds with some of their own community leaders. Indian women and their children have not been welcomed back to their communities. Since the 1980s, when the federal government began the process of devolution of control to Indian bands, band governments have been able to refuse band membership. It should be noted that there has been an influx of status Indians going to their bands to seek membership. However, the government has consistently refused to increase funding to those bands. Cora Voyageur notes that some bands have not given band membership to people given status by the federal government because they do not have the resources or the land base to do so. Most reserves are already overcrowded, and many feel that conditions will worsen if a rush of reinstated Indians want to return to the reserve. Some reinstated Indians are referred to as "C-31s," "paper Indians" or "new Indians" (Voyageur). In addition, many of these individuals may have previously been identifying with Métis or non-status Indian communities and were rejected not only by their Indian communities but also by the communities with which they had identified. As Lawrence (1999) reports that resistance to acknowledging the renewed status of those reinstated under Bill C-31 has been expressed throughout the Native press.

Furthermore, women have been formally excluded from constitutional negotiations as a result of patriarchal legislation that was applied in the federal government's decision to exclude them. The Native Women's Association of Canada (NWAC) has argued that the interests of individual Aboriginal women should not be overshadowed by collective social values and operational mandates that may be enshrined in customary law (Jackson 2000). However, Aboriginal women find themselves caught between bands who appeal to traditional practices to avoid action and a federal government that avoids involvement in deference to self-government (Green 2001).[2] In this way, government intrusion has succeeded in ensuring that divisions among Aboriginal people are maintained, if not more firmly entrenched.

Finally, as Lawrence (1999) argues, "Who am I?" and "Where do I belong?" are common questions among what she calls "people of mixed-race Native heritage." She examines the impact of the *Indian Act* and *Bill C-31* on Métis people in addition to Indian people and argues that the *Act* has externalised mixed-race Native people from Indianness and that this has implications for Native empowerment. What this discussion reveals is that other Aboriginal peoples have also been affected by these policies and this has likely had consequences for identity, empowerment, and quality of life of all Canada's Indigenous peoples.

IMPLICATIONS FOR THE HEALTH
OF ABORIGINAL WOMEN IN CANADA

A review of the post-contact history of Indigenous peoples in Canada clearly demonstrates that direct practices of genocide have transformed into legislated control of Aboriginal identity and colonization-based economic, social and political disadvantage that disproportionately affects Aboriginal women. The government's definition of who can be called Indian, who cannot and who must exist in liminal spaces where they are outsiders both on and off reserve lands clearly has implications for citizenship, but it also has implications for access to health services and ability to maintain health and well-being. With this knowledge, we must re-examine data that suggests Aboriginal women are excessively vulnerable to cerebrovascular disease, coronary heart disease, diabetes, suicide cancer, depression, substance use, HIV/AIDS, and violence/abuse in light of how colonization and post-colonial processes have conferred risks to the health of Aboriginal women, and barriers to accessing quality health care. It is these risks and barriers that contribute to rates of morbidity and mortality that are well above those of the average Canadian woman.

At a fundamental level, we understand that the colonization processes that began many years ago and continue today have material and social consequences that diminish access to social determinants of health for both Aboriginal men and Aboriginal women. Yet, as we have discussed, women have been especially marginalized through these processes and their lower social status is reflected in diminished resources and poor health. Health consequences for women have been identified, but largely within a western model of equating health with the absence of disease or illness (Newbold). The wounds that result from the cultural ambiguity imposed on Aboriginal women are harder to catalogue. They are perhaps demonstrated to us in the plight of the Aboriginal women of Vancouver's Downtown Eastside. This neighbourhood is home to thousands of Aboriginal women who have been displaced from their reserve communities and extended families (Benoit, Carroll and Chaudhry). They are socially and culturally isolated, living in poverty, and often driven to substance use, violent relationships, and the street sex trade to survive and provide for their children (Benoit *et al.*). Their material circumstances force acts of desperation, but the damage that has been done to their cultural identities can leave them without the foundation to cultivate health and well-being in their lives. Recent initiatives that have arisen out of results from the First Nations and Inuit Regional Health Survey (National Steering Committee) may offer some hope for these women, but they are still disadvantaged in benefiting from them. First, the development of culturally-appropriate services will not be useful for women who have been excluded from the definition of that culture and excluded from the decision-making structures that will determine how Aboriginal health resources are to be designed and distributed (Benoit *et al.*; Grace). Second, the research that serves as the foundation of these initiatives has not included many Aboriginal women, both because women and children have been overlooked in the work (Young 2003), and because women who do not fit into research-defined categories of "Indian" (derived from Federal categories) have not been included in the data collections.

CONCLUSIONS

In conclusion, we reiterate the fact that in Canada, Aboriginal women have faced destruction in our communities, in our families as a result of multiple oppressions. Articulating the process by which the Indian Act differentially marginalizes Indian women is important for our empowerment. Devon Mihesuah notes that there has never been a "monolithic essential Indian woman ... nor has there ever been a unitary world view among tribes" (37). She argues that this never created problems for people until after colonization and resulting genocide of Indian peoples (Chrisjohn and Young). Prior to the sexist specification of the *Indian Act* Aboriginal women were matriarchal in their families. Families thrived with their Aboriginal women's strength and support. Today, Aboriginal women suffer from poorer health than non-Aboriginal women in Canada; they suffer from more chronic diseases than Aboriginal men.

Our goal in writing this paper was to clarify our understanding of the externally-imposed oppressions facing Aboriginal women: to know where to focus our fight and our healing and to show the impact on the health of Aboriginal women. This paper has not examined the impact on Métis women specifically, but they too face similar challenges as a result of colonial policies. Today we find ourselves at peace with our identities, but vigilant against the ever-present social constructions of our identities. We can see the implications this has on our well-being and the well-being of our children. As long as we buy into the arbitrary, patriarchal, sexist, racist, socially constructed labels, we will continue to struggle not only as individuals but also as families and communities.

Originally published in Canadian Woman Studies/les cahiers de la femme, *"Women's Health and Well-Being" 24 (1) (Fall 2004): 23-29. Reprinted with permission of the authors.*

Carrie Bourassa is Métis and belongs to the Riel Métis Council of Regina. She is an Associate Professor of Indigenous Health Studies in the Department of Science at the First Nations University of Canada. Dr. Bourassa's research interests include the effects of colonization on the health of Aboriginal people, the health of Aboriginal women, culturally competent health care and Aboriginal community-based heatlh research methodology.

Kim Mckay-McNabb is an Assistant Professor of Psychology at the First Nations University of Canada in the Deaprtment of Science. She is currenlty completing her Ph.D. in Clinical Psychology at the Unviersity of Regina. Her research interests include include assisting in creating culturally competent care in health, specifically in mental health; Aboriginal community-based health reasearch methodology; Aboriginal peoples and HIV/AIDS; Aboriginal sexual health and Aboriginal people's health. Kim is a First Nations woman who is a member of the George Gordon First Nation. She resides in Regina with her husband, Patrick, and her four children, Raymond, Rowan, Shay and Isaiah.

Mary Hampton is a Professor of Psychology at Luther College, University of Regina. She is also a faculty member of SPHERU (Saskatchewan Health and Evaluation Research Unit) and Saskatchewan Academic Coordinator of RESOLVE (Research and Education for Solutions to Violence and Abuse). Her research interests include: end of life care with Aboriginal families, anti-violence feminist research, and sexual health.

[1]The *Indian Act* has had and continues to have implications for Aboriginal women in terms of identity. With the passage of *Bill C-31*, new divisions among Indian people were created. The bill limits the ability of women and their children to pass on their status beyond one generation. That is, grandchildren and great-grandchildren are generally not eligible to apply for status. In addition, while status can no longer be lost or gained through marriage, there are new restrictions on the ability to pass status on to children (Lawrence 1999). For example, the bill divides Indian people into categories by using sub-sections of the *Act*. A 6(1) Indian is defined as an Indian who had status in 1985. A 6(2) Indian is defined as a re-instated Indian under the *Act*. If a 6(1) Indian marries a non-status Indian (including a Métis) then any resulting child from that union will be considered a 6(2) Indian. If that 6(2) Indian child grows up and has a relationship with a non-status Indian the resulting child is a non-status Indian. Thus, once again, status can be eliminated in two generations and grandchildren and great-grandchildren are excluded. It should be pointed out that if a 6(1) has a relationship with a 6(2), the resulting child is a 6(1) Indian. Furthermore, if a 6(2) has a relationship with a 6(2) the resulting child is a 6(1). The message is, if you don't marry back into your race, you risk losing status for your children or grandchildren. Although assimilation policy was supposedly abandoned in 1973 (announced by the Minister of Indian Affairs, Jean Chretien), long-term effects of the *Indian Act* and *Bill C-31* still promotes assimilation. The federal government effectively controls the definition of "Indianness," but communities, families, and individuals live with the consequences and the confusion that arise from that control (Lawrence 1999).

[2]McIvor points out that these violations of civic and political rights of Aboriginal women are violations of their "existing Aboriginal and treaty rights" (35). She argues that the *Sparrow* decision *(Sparrow v. The Queen 1990)* was a landmark Supreme Court ruling that upheld the notion of existing Aboriginal and treaty rights and that this forms part of the inherent right to self-government protected under s. 35 of the *Constitution Act, 1982*. She maintains that self-government is central to Aboriginal nationhood, culture, and existence and, if it is central

to the existence of Aboriginal nations, then the ability to determine civil and political rights of members must also be central. This right to self-government thus includes the right of women to define their roles in Aboriginal communities. She states: "The right of women to establish and maintain their civic and political role has existed since time immemorial. These rights are part of customary laws of Aboriginal people and part of the right of self-government … they [rights] are those which women have exercised since the formation of their Indigenous societies. In some cases, these rights were suppressed or regulated by non-Aboriginal law, such as the *Indian Act*" (35).

REFERENCES

Amaratunga, C. *Race, Ethnicity, and Women's Health*. Nova Scotia: Atlantic Centre of Excellence for Women's Health, 2002.

Benoit, C., D. Carroll and M. Chaudhry "In Search of a Healing Place: Aboriginal Women in Vancouver's Downtown Eastside." *Social Science and Medicine* 56 (2003): 821-833.

Chrisjohn, R. D. and S. L. Young. *The Circle Game: Shadows and Substance in the Indian Residential School Experience in Canada*. Penticton, BC: Theytus-Books Ltd., 1997.

Clark, R., N. B. Anderson, V. Clark and D. R. Williams. "Racism as a Stressor for African Americans: A Biopsychosocial Model." *American Psychologist* 54 (10) (1999): 805-816.

Gerrard, N. and N. Javed. "The Psychology of Women." *Feminist Issues: Race, Class, and Sexuality*. 2nd ed. Ed. N. Mandell. Scarborough, ON: Prentice Hall Allyn and Bacon Canada, 1998. 103-131.

Grace, Sherryl L. "A Review of Aboriginal Women's Physical and Mental Health Status in Ontario." *Canadian Journal of Public Health* 94 (3) (2003): 173-175.

Green J. A. "Canaries in the Mines of Citizenship: Indian Women in Canada." *Canadian Journal of Political Science/Revue Canadienne de Science Politique* 34 (4) (2001): 715-738.

Green, J. A. "Constitutionalizing the Patriarchy." *Expressions in Canadian Native Studies*. Eds. R. F. Laliberte, P. Settee, J. B. Waldram, R. Innes, B. Macdougall, L. McBain and F. L. Barron. Saskatoon: University of Saskatchewan Extension Press, 2000. 328-354.

Jackson, Margaret. "Aboriginal Women and Self-Government." *Expressions in Canadian Native Studies*. Eds. R. F. Laliberte, P. Settee, J. B. Waldram, R. Innes, B. Macdougall, L. McBain and F. L. Barron. Saskatoon: University of Saskatchewan Extension Press, 2000. 355-373.

Lawrence, B. *"Real" Indians and Others*. Unpublished Ph.D. Dissertation. Toronto: UMI Dissertation Services, 1999.

Lawrence, B. "Mixed-Race Urban Native People: Surviving a Legacy of Policies of Genocide." *Expressions in Canadian Native Studies*. Eds. R. F. Laliberte, P.

Settee, J. B. Waldram, R. Innes, B. Macdougall, L. McBain and F. L. Barron. Saskatoon: University of Saskatchewan Extension Press, 2000. 69-94.

Langford, Jan. "First Nations Women: Leaders in Community Development." *Canadian Woman Studies/les cahiers de la femme* 14 (4) (1995): 34-36.

Lips, H. M. *A New Psychology of Women: Gender, Culture and Ethnicity,* 2nd ed. Toronto: McGraw Hill, 2003.

McIvor, S. D. "Aboriginal Women's Rights as Existing Rights." *Canadian Woman Studie/les cahiers de al femme* 14 (4) (1995): 34-38.

Mihesuah, D. A., ed. *Natives and Academics: Researching and Writing About American Indians.* Lincoln: University of Nebraska Press, 1998.

National Steering Committee. *First Nations and Inuit Regional Health Survey: Final Report.* Akwesasne Mohawk Territory, 1999.

Newbold, K. B. "Problems in Search of Solutions: Health and Canadian Aboriginals." *Journal of Community Health* 23 (1) (1998): 59-73.

Prairie Women's Health Centre of Excellence. *Living Well: Aboriginal Women, Cultural Identity and Wellness—A Manitoba Community Project.* Winnipeg: Prairie Women's Health Centre of Excellence, 2004.

Polednak, A. P. *Racial and Ethnic Differences in Disease.* New York: Oxford University Press, 1989.

Razack, S. *Race, Space and the Law: Unmapping a White Settler Society.* Toronto: Between the Lines, 2002.

Saskatchewan Women's Secretariat. *Profile of Aboriginal Women in Saskatchewan.* Regina: Saskatchewan Women's Secretariat, 1999.

Statistics Canada. *Aboriginal Peoples Survey 2001: Well-Being of the Non-Reserve Aboriginal Population.* Ottawa: Cat. no. 89-589-XIE, 2001.

Tuhiwai Smith, Linda. *Decolonizing Methodologies: Research and Indigenous Peoples.* New York: Zed Books Ltd., 2002.

Voyageur, C. "Contemporary Aboriginal Women in Canada." *Visions of the Heart: Canadian Aboriginal Issues.* Eds. David Long and Olive P. Dickason. Toronto: Harcourt Canada, 2000. 93-115.

Wienert, D. *Preventing and Controlling Cancer in North America: A Cross-Cultural Perspective.* Westport, CT: Praeger, 1999.

Waldram, J. B., D. A. Herring, and T. K. Young. *Aboriginal Health in Canada: Historical, Cultural, and Epidemiological Perspectives.* Toronto: University of Toronto Press, 2000.

Wotherspoon, T. and Satzewich, V. *First Nations: Race, Class and Gender Relations.* Regina: Canadian Plains Research Centre, 2000.

Young, I. M. *Inclusion and Democracy.* Oxford: Oxford University Press, 2000.

Young, T. K. "Review of Research on Aboriginal Populations in Canada: Relevance to their Health Needs." *British Medical Journal* 327 (2003): 419-422.

Young, T. K. *The Health of Native Americans: Toward a Biocultural Epidemiology.* New York: Oxford University Press, 1994.

CHILD SEXUAL ABUSE

Words From Concerned Women

THE SEXUAL ABUSE OF ANY CHILD is hard to understand. For thousands of children, however, sexual abuse is a reality and a hell that must no longer be ignored. As Native women, mothers and friends of victims, many of whom are very young children, we are concerned about the abuse that is happening within our own families, in our communities, and on our reserves. Some of us were ourselves victims and have had first hand experience with what sexual abuse does.

We have felt the pain and anger not only at the offenders, but at the system which tends to punish people more for damaging property than it does for damaging a child's life forever. We have realized just how difficult it is for victims who have absolutely no support services available and, sometimes, do not have family support from the non-offending parent. We have learned to quietly listen as a sixty-five-year-old grandmother, with tears in her eyes, shares the pain of her abuse at an early age. We know of other victims who have been unable to tell anyone about their abuse until years later. We have heard the stories of victims who hated their offenders (sometimes fathers and grandfathers) and how this has affected their lives. Some victims are able to talk about the abuse, years after, while others still cannot as it is too painful a memory. We know of generation after generation of our families being damaged by the abuse. We also know that sexual abuse repeats itself, often harming several generations.

Very often, violence against women is also involved; not only does the child victim live in fear, but the victim's mother is also living in hell. All too often, more than one child becomes a victim. It is a cycle that is hard to break, but it must be broken for the sake of our future and for the well being of our children and future generations.

Many people, including our own, choose to ignore the sexual abuse of children by saying such things as "no, that does't happen to my people" or "no, I've lived in this community all my life and I haven't seen any." Others claim that "only White people do that," while some White people claim "only Native people do that." Sexual abuse does not know any boundaries; it can and does happen to all people regardless of their colour, ethnic background, religion or socioeconomic class.

Specific cases need to be provided; these are documented by authorities or at least the cases in which charges have been laid, or an investigation was completed, are documented. While the reporting of abuse has increased, there are many victims who are not able to tell, while others have told and were not believed nor supported. Very often the community will be silent about the abuse and people refuse to become involved in reporting it or in supporting the victim. While this is a difficult issue to address, it will continue to damage generation after generation if we remain silent and ignore it.

Even more dangerous is the attitude of "what are you complaining about? That happens to everyone around here." The sexual abuse of children is not acceptable in any community or culture and traditionally Native people were very specific about this. The abuse of children, sexually or physically, was not tolerated and there were community standards that were followed. Incest and child molestation were not acceptable, and people were punished or banned if they broke these social standards.

When one looks at the other social conditions facing many of our people, it is not surprising this social ill also affects us. It is perhaps the worst of the social conditions. While some people feel alcohol is responsible for many problems, including sexual abuse; we feel this is a very dangerous assumption. This implies that the offender is not responsible for his actions when, in fact, he is. The sexual abuse of children is a crime; very often the offenders are not drunk at the time of their offence.

Offenders are aware of what they are doing and they know it is wrong. Some may have been victims themselves and are repeating a generational pattern. Few child molesters seek help on their own. They tend to deny their crime if they are caught; there are, however, those who plead guilty and admit the crime. In far too many cases, charges are not laid and the crime is further ignored. This enables the offender to further abuse the victim and even seek out more victims.

When sexual abuse is ignored or when the offender goes free, the victims are left without any support and may never tell again. Victims who are not helped very often go through life being further victimized. Sadly, many of our young women turn to the streets, while many victims turn to self-mutilation and/or suicide attempts. What is particularly sad is that victims are often quite young and, despite community knowledge of the crime, the offender will have a free hand at molesting yet another generation of children.

The following is a case that recently took place: A child molester in his fifties molested a six-year-old (and probably her younger siblings) and was charged but not convicted (possibly due to the young age of the victim). After this, he returned to his community and despite the efforts of some women to tell community members of his crime, he recently married a woman with several young children.

It is predictable that this offender will molest his step-children and continue to damage more generations. This should not be the case: all children have the right to healthy lives. Child molestation is perhaps the worst of all crimes.

Often, victims and their families are left without support or counselling. They are often blamed for the abuse and there is little understanding or support from family or community members. Sometimes they are told they must "forget and forgive" and to "stop bringing up the past." Worse yet, some victims are blamed for the offender's actions! The child victim is blamed for "leading on" the offender and for "letting it happen." The mother of the victim is blamed "for not treating the offender right in bed" (when she is the spouse of the offender), or otherwise. Sometimes there is the community's denial that sexual abuse exists because it is a subject that very often is too personal and too true for people to face. It *is* painful and personal, but it must be recognized as a community issue and it must be overcome. Rather than denying it is happening, we must work for solutions; the longer we deny it the worse the abuse becomes until it is generational.

When one considers the level of violence (including physical, sexual and mental abuse) towards women (and again this is ignored and considered a family problem), and how this is a power situation, similar treatment towards children is related. The abuse of children, women and Elders was not acceptable in the past and it should not be acceptable today.

We are a group of Native women who have experienced the sexual abuse of either our children, our families or ourselves. Some of us are vocal and are able to address the issue openly, while some of us are not yet able to speak. Some of our children are also able to speak about the abuse openly; others are not.

We are learning more about this crime and are beginning to realize that it has affected more Native women and children than we initially thought. It seems now that we are talking openly about this, others (usually female victims or their mothers) are able to tell us about their abuse. These are sad stories and many are similar. Sometimes when we speak to other women, we know they have been abused by the tears and pain in their eyes.

Those of us who are mothers of victims have had other victims tell us that they wish their mothers would have believed and supported them. For some, it has been the first time they have been able to speak about childhood horrors. Others have said that this is a problem that affects a lot of our people.

Many people fear the process of facing up to the abuse, but it is necessary. It is not easy; for the sake and well-being of our children, it must be done. Widespread changes must occur in our families and in our communities to put a stop to this crime, which affects generation after generation. There is a need for support services for victims and their families and, unfortunately, many communities lack these and other essential services.

Something must be done about the offenders. Some people believe treatment is effective and others feel child abuse should be treated as a family court matter. Others feel long-term jail sentences are the answer. Some victims and their mothers also feel castration is the only cure.

While no one has all the answers, communities must begin to talk about this issue and deal with it.

Awareness programming directed towards our child victims, their families and offenders, must be put in place, as must be support services. Perhaps some problems arise from the reporting procedures: people are reluctant to report abuse and "become involved." It is the law to report child abuse and it is the only way to make the offender accountable for his actions. It is difficult to report, but it must be done. Often the victim is isolated and is not willing to talk to the authorities. We must look to our own communities for groups and individuals who are prepared to support and assist victims.

Because many Native women have been, and still are oppressed, whether through violence, lack of political power, or fear, this is a difficult challenge. But who else will do this? It will not be the men in positions of power, because some of them may feel the issue is too personal or, worse yet, some may be offenders. Child molestation, incest, and sexual abuse are not popular topics that one discusses over a cup of tea, but they must be brought out and communities must develop solutions. We understand just how difficult this will be, given the present social and economic conditions of our people. But it is essential. The future of our people rests with this. Far too many of our children are suffering from abuse and, unless something is done, it will continue to repeat itself from generation to generation.

One life damaged by abuse is one too many. There are thousands of victims who are damaged and the cycle must be broken.

This article is reprinted from the newsletter of Aboriginal Women's Council of Saskatchewan , May 1988: 12-14.

Originally published in Canadian Woman Studies/les cahiers de la femme, "Native Women," 10 (2 & 3) (Summer/Fall 1989): 90-91.

ROSEMARIE KUPTANA

KEEPING THE CIRCLE STRONG IN THE NORTH

Solvent Abuse, Alcohol and Drug Strategies for the North

MOST OF US HERE KNOW the prominent role that drug and alcohol abuse play in our communities. Many, including myself, have experienced firsthand the darkness addiction inflicts upon our lives. We have seen our own families suffer. We have watched with horror the impact of alcohol on infants and children; we have seen many of our own leaders sink into alcohol and drug abuse; we have seen or even been a part of the vicious cycle of addiction, abuse, violence, poverty, despair, and finally, suicide.

We are here to help break that cycle of despair and to help strengthen the circle of healing. We have the opportunity to look closely at some of the achievements that have been made at the community level in combatting alcohol, drug, and substance abuse. We can work together to create specific goals and a sense of purpose that are essential if we are to break the spell of addiction that hangs over so many northern families and communities.

In most communities in the north, we have identified and begun to face our problems. We have done our homework, in the true sense of that word, and are listening to the testimony of mothers, children, Elders, health care workers, and one another.

We are able to say, yes—alcohol, substance, and drug abuse are issues that affect us all. Alcohol and drug addiction does not discriminate. Alcoholism and other forms of substance abuse affect everyone, everywhere—housewives, teens, children, and Elders—all races, cultures, and religions. We know that in many communities, addiction and suicide levels have reached crisis proportions and must be confronted with utmost urgency, or the community may be destroyed.

The first step is to confront directly and immediately this serious situation. We cannot approach this in a bureaucratic, political, or institutional way. We must reach our hands out to those who are in danger of losing and help them repair their broken dreams while re-establishing their hopes and the hope of their families, our families.

We must recognize that if we are to realize our large-scale dreams as peoples, we must first deal with our most specific threats to self-esteem, to our fundamental identity as Inuit, First Peoples, and northerners.

We can enrich our understanding of our own problems, and derive solutions to these problemsby sharing the experience of others.

I want to talk a little bit about community-based action and the importance of the involvement of people in the communities in dealing with solvent abuse, fetal alcohol syndrome, and suicide. I also want to address the problem of funding, and the strategies that we must develop to ensure that ideas do not simply become reports, recommendations, and goals that cannot be met because there is no money.

Substance abuse, fetal alcohol syndrome, family violence, sexual abuse, and suicide: these are expressions of the most fundamental grief and despair of our people. They are not secrets; they are not the problems of individuals only. We know too well that alcoholism, for example, is just one link in a chain that can first choke an individual, then a family, a community, and a people. Alcoholism is linked to unemployment; to inadequate housing, education, and health care; to poor nutrition; and, to the shame and confusion that attends the loss of self-respect.

One of the things we are learning as Inuit is that we must help ourselves. We have learned that we cannot and must not rely upon the government or others to do what we must do ourselves. We can have the most modern institutions, the best programs, and adequate financial resources, but if we are not ready to admit to our addictions as individuals, as families, and as a society, the cycle of abuse will continue.

Over and over again, we see proof of the fact that we must take control—of our economy, our resources, our government, our culture. Over and over again, we must break the cycle, the chain of dependency.

We can only do this ourselves.

We can draw encouragement and hope from our achievements, which, at first glance, may seem unrelated to each other. When we recognize the connection between our struggle for self-determination and our encounter with substance abuse then we will better appreciate and make use of our strengths as Inuit.

All the work and research we have undertaken in our communities emphasizes again and again the importance of integrated approaches to solving these problems. It does not work to close our eyes to the whole picture and only look at one small piece of the puzzle.

The histories of Aboriginal peoples reinforce the necessity of holistic approaches to life. We know, in our homes, that our survival depends on community, on sharing, and on cooperative solutions. These are the values that must motivate current strategies for breaking the cycle of substance abuse.

We talk of creating "models" for prevention and treatment. Let us not lose sight of the most appropriate shape for these models. It is the circle.

We must not create hierarchies or bureaucracies; we must work within the circle of the community. We must draw upon our traditional values, and use our reservoir of rituals, our sense of kinship, our way of grieving and healing. We must create our solutions on our terms, and in our own terms.

Every strategy that we propose should be measured against the circle model. Otherwise, we may not be coming around again and again to those in need. If we do not listen to the voices of those both with the greatest need and the greatest experience, we will not be able to break the cycle.

Vigilance is required by all of us; we must seek to balance vigilance and compassion. It will take vigilance and compassion on each of our parts as people in families and communities to address these issues and to help and support one another.

It will take vigilance and determination on the part of our political leaders, our youth, and our Elders to address the problem of funding for research, the training of our own health care personnel, the setting up of adequate community hospitals or nursing stations. We must integrate medical experts and techniques with our traditional ways of working together and helping one another.

It will take vigilance and determination to make sure that we control those resources, that it is our own people who look after our own people.

We must forge the circle together. Let's get started.

A version of this speech was presented in Yellowknife, North West Territories, on November 22, 1993.

Originally published in Canadian Woman Studies/les cahiers de la femme, *"Women of the North," 14 (4) (Fall 1994): 106-107. Reprinted with permission of the author.*

Rosemarie Kuptana is Past President of the Inuit Tapirisat of Canada.

CAROLINE L. TAIT

SIMPERING OUTRAGE DURING AN "EPIDEMIC" OF FETAL ALCOHOL SYNDROME

IN THIS PAPER I CRITIQUE understanding held by dominant Canadian society about the reproductive lives of Indigenous women. Specifically I explore how local reproductive relations are constituted by intersecting discourses emerging out of arenas of science, medicine, public health, and front-line service provision that empower certain categories of people to nurture and reproduce, while the reproductive futures of others are discouraged and if at all possible, avoided (Ginsburg and Rapp 3). I examine how portrayals of an "epidemic" of fetal alcohol syndrome (FAS) unfolding in Indigenous communities has been invoked to support increased surveillance and control of Indigenous women's fertility, without meaningful supports and services being put in place for them. Supporting the image of a " FAS epidemic," is the practice of non-medical labelling of Indigenous women as having fetal alcohol-related brain damage. The paper examines how, with the creation of this new population of " FAS persons," FAS prevention strategies targeting Indigenous women have expanded beyond simply preventing pregnant women from drinking alcohol, but now include as an equal focus, pregnancy prevention with approaches ranging from increased use of chemical contraception[1] to permanent sterilization. As a micro example of this larger phenomenon, the events of the workshop described in this paper help to illustrate that apart from serving as a medical diagnosis, the category FAS simultaneously exists in Canada as a means by which negative stereotypes about Indigenous women and the place of their reproductive futures in the nation's body are reinforced. This is an image that allows for certain actions to be mobilized while others are not.

GARDEN THERAPY

Looking out of the plane window, I felt relieved to be coming home. Even though I had only been away a week it felt much longer and I looked forward to seeing my son, Skender. I also hoped that returning home would lessen the unease that I felt as a result of the meeting I had just attended in Vancouver, which aimed to provide direction in areas of fetal alcohol syndrome prevention research to the newly formed Canadian Institute for Gender and Health Research. This latest trip also marked the end of my doctoral field research and I felt a sense of urgency in light of the past few days to reexamine some of my writing, and to produce a critique of what I now saw to be a blanket acceptance across Canada that Fetal Alcohol Syndrome is a health and social problem of epidemic proportions in many Indigenous communities. It was with this in mind that I arrived at Dorval airport, hopped in a taxi, and headed home.

The next morning, still feeling the effects of the Vancouver meeting, I decided to retreat to the garden to see if this would help me to reconcile my thoughts on what had transpired during the workshop. However, unlike other days where digging and pulling weeds had a therapeutic effect, today I felt increasingly worried, concerned, and even alone. Why was I the only one at the workshop who felt outraged by the federal government's lack of critical reflection in portraying the "FAS problem?" as an "Indigenous problem," when very few individuals, Indigenous or not, have actually been assessed or diagnosed with the illness and so much uncertainty remains over the actual rates of effected individuals? Why was it that my apparent outrage was met, at best, with limited concern, and at worst, dismissed out of hand by other participants? How was I to interpret the silence of other participants whom I knew shared my concerns about the gaps and numerous methodological problems with the research literature on FAS? Why did they not at least support my call for critical evaluation of government policy and programming, and for an examination of non-medical labelling by service providers of Indigenous mothers and their offspring as being alcohol-affected?[3]

As these questions occupied my thoughts, I could not help but think how fortunate it was that Lucille Bruce had attended the meeting. Lucille, a fellow Métis, and the only other Indigenous person present at the workshop, is someone I had met during my field research in Manitoba, and she had been sent to the workshop to represent the Canadian Women's Health Network.[4] My assumption was that Madeline Boscoe, the network's Executive Director, had specifically chosen Lucille because of her community activism and work with impoverished Indigenous women.

Reflecting back on the workshop, I admitted that Lucille's presence had made the experience more bearable as we worked together to push the group toward developing a critical perspective that challenged, rather than reinforced, entrenched stereotypes of Indigenous women and their children. Lucille drew upon her experiences working at a transition house for Indigenous women in Winnipeg, illustrating the barriers and gaps in programming that hinder these women to seek and comply with service demands. In turn, I put forward critiques of the current direction of FAS research, prevention, and intervention services, pointing toward racial and gender biases characteristic of these interrelated arenas of knowledge and practice. Thinking of Lucille's support, I reconsidered that maybe it had not been as bad as I first remembered. Maybe I was just feeling tired from the week of travelling and meetings. However, as I surveyed the garden for weeds, the feeling of outrage left from the meeting continued to simmer in my thoughts.

THE WORKSHOP

The workshop, "FAS and Women's Health: Setting a Women-Centered Research Agenda," was organized by the British Columbia Centre of Excellence for Women's Health. My role was as a "discussion starter" for a session focusing on FAS prevention among Indigenous women. As I sat in the garden, reflecting on the session, I was certain that the workshop organizers were less than satisfied with my decision to critique the negative stereotypes of Indigenous women that characterized FAS research literature, including the ways these images have come to shape social service and public health responses. While I felt they recognized the logic of my presentation, I was also aware that a few of the participants identified me more as an "angry Indian" than a productive "discussion starter." This, however, was not the reason I was feeling such unease; I have known many "angry Indians" who, because of their anger and determination to hold their ground on important issues, have individually and collectively transformed Indigenous and non-Indigenous relations in Canada in productive and positive ways. Rather, the unshakeable unease that followed me to my garden was the overwhelming presence of the "white man's burden," which had hung like a thick cloud over the workshop.

In Canada, the companion of "the white man's burden" is the "Indian problem"—terminology that best describes the ways in which federal and provincial governments have approached, in the past and the present, the socioeconomic, historical, and cultural/traditional realities of First Nations, Inuit, and Métis peoples. If looked at from a historical perspective, one could readily argue that Canadian governments, with support from the broader society, have ideologically framed Indigenous and non-Indigenous relations using the dichotomy that Indigenous peoples have problems, and the dominant society carries the burden of identifying, describing, and intervening in their lives in order to "fix" those problems.

A case in point is the residential school system, which theoretically was created to address the "burden" held by the colonialist government to "civilize," "Christianize," and "assimilate" Indigenous children. The government argued that the removal of Indigenous children from the care of their parents—or the supposed "immorality" of Indigenous traditions and cultures—was a proper method by which to indoctrinate them with European values and culture in order that they become productive members of society. Although stated much more subtly, the sentiments at the Vancouver workshop clearly indicated that "the white man's burden" and the "Indian problem" were central players in the twenty-first century's understanding of Indigenous persons. However, the "problem" here was not one of assimilation but of biological deficit whereby large numbers of Indigenous women believed to suffer from fetal alcohol-related brain damage give birth to "epidemic" numbers of similarly affected children. It was the "white man's burden" to come up with solutions in the form of research, interventions, and services to address this "preventable tragedy," and essentially save Indigenous peoples from themselves.

Approximately 25 people who work in FAS prevention attended the workshop. The day started with a presentation by one of the organizers who outlined the ways in which FAS prevention research, interventions, and services overwhelmingly focus on the fetus. The goal of the workshop, she stated, was to shift away from what could be described as the "uterine tradition" by advancing a "women-centered approach," that addressed the mother and fetus as a single unit. By mid-morning, it seemed evident that the workshop would prove to be productive and informative, and that the final outcome would be a positive contribution toward ensuring gender-sensitive research on pregnancy and substance abuse.

My optimism, however, was short-lived as increasingly participants struggled with the shift in focus outlined by the organizers, and much of the discussion remained focused on risk to the developing fetus posed by substance abuse. When the discussion did turn to women at risk for having children with FAS, it was mainly a discussion about Indigenous women, and there appeared to be an uncritical perception by most that Indigenous women were not only at higher risk, but that they nearly constituted the entire risk group itself.[5]

A local Vancouver pediatrician known to be an expert in FAS diagnosis was the first to make a direct link between risk, maternal FAS, and Indigenous women. During an open discussion she described her own pregnancy several years ago and how, even though she was a medical graduate, she had unwittingly placed her unborn child at risk because she was unaware of the dangers of prenatal alcohol exposure. While in previous meetings, I had heard her make reference to her own pregnancy as a way to illustrate that *all* women are at risk if they are ignorant of the public health message, on this particular occasion she used the example to illustrate that the women who give birth to children with FAS are not similar, but different from her in important ways.

Based upon my knowledge of the research literature, I expected the difference she referred to would be to socioeconomic status, because risk factors associated with poverty—particularly food insecurities, vulnerability to violence, tobacco addiction, and lack of prenatal care—in conjunction with chronic alcohol abuse are known to impact negatively upon the physiological processes of pregnancy and fetal development (Abel). Much to my surprise, however, she stated that pregnant women who give birth to children with FAS are most often women who themselves suffer from fetal alcohol brain damage and most in Canada are First Nations. While she did acknowledge poverty as a contributing factor, she emphasized that risk significantly increased because of the inability of this group of women to make "good lifestyle choices," evident, she stated, by the "common occurrence" among impoverished First Nations women of alcohol and drug abuse, and unprotected sex that fails to prevent either sexually transmitted diseases or pregnancy. I knew, however, from my research that few if any of the women the pediatrician referred to would be medically assessed for FAS because of the associated costs of obtaining a diagnosis and the inherent ambiguity within the diagnostic criteria to determine if prenatal alcohol effects are present and if so, whether they are either a primary or secondary cause of "behavioural problems."

As the physician passionately lamented that years of work on FAS had not made a significant difference to women and children, I became increasingly agitated by the unstated implications of her account. By suggesting that women who give birth to children with FAS are themselves alcohol affected and that most are First Nations, she characterized the "problem" within a larger discourse of "intergenerational trauma," that has been adopted by Indigenous peoples to explain the negative health and social impacts of colonization. However, in doing so, she recast "intergenerational trauma" not as collective suffering that at an individual level manifests itself as psychological and emotional distress, but one grounded in biology, and specifically a cognitive deficit that exists beyond the bounds of Indigenous healing.

Important to note in this context is that generally researcher-identified "risk factors" for FAS specific to Indigenous women and their children emphasize, rightly or wrongly, Indigenous ancestry, cultural practices, and collective history (Aase; Asante; Asante and Nelms-Matzke; Asante and Robinson; May). However, the pediatrician's claims effectively usurped these arguments by making the primary and overarching risk factor, widespread maternal FAS. This shift in discourse further implied that, despite First Nations women being a very high-risk group, their Indigenous identity is relatively unimportant apart from helping to identifying them. This is an argument that reminded me of one made a few years earlier by a leading FAS researcher, Anne Streissguth, who suggested that if the frequency of FAS is high enough, it becomes a "community catastrophe that threatens to wipe out any culture in just a few generations" (9). Consequently, the focus is no longer on "risk factors" present in Indigenous communities and neighbourhoods, but rather the argument contends that in certain local contexts, such as reserves or urban Indigenous ghettos, a culture of pathology has arisen, whereupon perceived widespread maternal FAS places the next generation at risk of being similarly affected.

Following her remarks, the pediatrician announced that she would not be staying at the workshop because she had to teach a class on the effects of prenatal substance use to a group of medical students, among whom I knew there would be few, if any, Indigenous students. After she left I felt a growing unease, thinking about how she had interrupted and redefined our task and legitimized references to the "Indian problem" and the "white man's burden," which would spill into the second half of our meeting.

THE "MAKING" OF AN EPIDEMIC OF FAS

Agitation is often difficult to deal with in a setting where a certain amount of decorum is required if one is to be heard. However, as I listened to a presentation later that day by a front-line worker employed by a government-funded FAS prevention program in the Burns Lake region of northern British Columbia, I found myself thinking that too much decorum was stifling in such an ill-conceived meeting. The presentation was described as "bringing a women-centered approach to broad publicly focused FAS prevention strategies." In her introduction, she stated that Burns Lake[6] is located near several First Nation reserve communities and that even though the program targets all women, the large majority of women that her program serves are Indigenous.

The Burns Lake program provides public health education on FAS and from the presenter's account, it appears to bring a level of support and out-reach services to women, their children, and the community that is generally welcomed by the people of Burns Lake, and, to a lesser degree by the surrounding reserves. The presenter began her talk by stating, "most of the moms [that the program provides services to] have had prenatal exposure to alcohol." She also referred at different times in her presentation to FAS being a serious health problem in the area, suggesting to the workshop participants that government funding and focus on FAS prevention and intervention services had hit its mark in the case of the Burns Lake area.

The Burns Lake *Healthier Babies, Brighter Futures* program was featured in a February 2001 report entitled *Fetal Alcohol Syndrome: A Call for Action in B.C.*, which was published by the Children's Commission of the B.C. Ministry for Children and Families. Under the subtitle "Innovation," the program in Burns Lake is described as a "successful prevention project" that "clearly shows that spending money on prevention and early intervention more than pays off" (24). Our presenter had written the feature piece on Burns Lake in the document, describing the program as follows:

> The program has managed to connect with very hard-to-reach families. Client profiles at intake show that 83 percent of women display FAS characteristics and behaviours. When the program began, 100 percent of the clients who came to the program were not on birth control, as it is difficult for people with FAS to remember to take a daily pill. (The Children's Commission 25)[7]

The report discusses the program's success in relation to increased birth control and pregnancy prevention, "healthier" pregnancies (abstinence or decrease in maternal substance use), birth outcomes such as "healthy birth weights," and women maintaining custody of their children. Notably, the success of the program is not measured in terms of improved health and wellness of women (clients), and instead the emphasis on birth control and pregnancy prevention suggests that success is measured, at least partially, on making the alcohol abuse of "at-risk" women less visible. More simply stated, when the women are not pregnant, their substance use/abuse and all of the problems associated with it lie outside of the range of "prevention" provided by this and other similar programs. Furthermore, increased use of contraception means that fewer babies will be born, which is perceived as a desirable "preventive" measure.

When I queried the presenter about how she knew that so many Indigenous women in the Burns Lake region had FAS, and subsequently commented that I was unclear about the intentions of her claim that "most of the moms have had prenatal exposure to alcohol," she looked surprised. However, the surprise quickly shifted back to me when she announced that to the best of her knowledge, she knew of no medical diagnoses of FAS or FAE of the mothers and their offspring in the Burns Lake region. I was further surprised that the presenter was untroubled by this fact in relation to her earlier statements.

In my determination to fully understand her claims, I pressed her for information on how she and her colleagues determined that certain individuals had FAS by asking, "was it their facial features, height or weight, or did they exhibit cognitive problems? If their lay diagnosis was not based upon assessment of physical and behavioural characteristics, how then did they know that prenatal alcohol exposure had a role to play in a woman's particular situation?" With this questioning, the presenter became defensive, arguing that high rates of FAS were present because there was so much alcohol abuse within Indigenous communities in the Burns Lake area. She added that neither her nor her colleagues labelled people based upon physical or behavioural characteristics because the problem of FAS in the area was self-evident. As indicated in the written profile of the program, which provides percentages of FAS characteristics and behaviours among the women (The Children's Commission 25), some form of in-take screening does occur. However, given the presenter's response to my questioning, it is unclear how formalized and organized this process is.

The presenter's over-emphasis on maternal FAS being a causal factor of her clients' behaviour is even more troublesome when considered in relation to her claim that it is "difficult for people with FAS to remember to take a daily pill" (The Children's Commission 25). During my field research, I found that physicians and community clinics that have high concentrations of First Nations or Métis clients commonly prescribe contraception such as Depo-Provera®,[8] sometimes to girls as young as 13 years of age, under the auspices that this contributes to the prevention of pregnancy *and* FAS. According to some outreach and social workers, DepoProvera® eliminates the need for women and girls to remember to take a pill every day or to negotiate condom use with male partners (Tait 14-15). However, public health nurses that I interviewed pointed out that DepoProvera® is not designed for adolescent girls whose bodies are still developing, nor does it address the negative health and wellness consequences of alcohol addiction/abuse or the problem of sexually-transmitted diseases. Women and girls who are given Depo-Provera® also end up falling outside of the scope of many FAS prevention programs and support services because they are not "at risk" of becoming pregnant.

My fieldwork experience suggests First Nations persons are most commonly labelled as having FAS in the absence of a medical assessment. Generally, non-medical labelling involves an "assessment" based on the opinion of one or more persons, and involves consideration of the person's body, specifically their facial characteristics, possibly consideration of their height and weight, and an "assessment" of their intelligence, cognitive abilities, and behaviour. For example, perceived memory problems of clients are interpreted as symptomatic of FAS. However, as revealed by the Burns Lake presenter's statement about birth control pills and FAS, certain actions, or in this case non-actions (not taking birth control pills), may be interpreted as pathology (poor memory) resulting from prenatal alcohol exposure, regardless of whether or not the person reports having experienced such a memory problem. The question remains as to whether or not the client population of the Burns Lake program may refrain from using birth control pills for a whole range of reasons other than poor memory, such as an exercise of personal choice, a desire to become pregnant, cultural beliefs about contraception, or concerns about health risks and side effects of different forms of contraception.

In training sessions for community workers in prevention and intervention programs, the information given to trainees is often over-simplified, offering only a basic understanding of FAS and the "typical" person with FAS. Those who have attended training sessions about FAS for community and front-line workers, report coming away with the impression that prevalence rates of FAS/FAE are very high, especially among Indigenous peoples. They also report that persons with FAS/FAE are easy to identify, and some felt that after their training they were able to identify at least some persons with FAS/FAE. Trainees also perceived themselves as having a core understanding of the "typical" person with FAS, including a perception about the " FAS behavioural profile." In this stereotypical profile, persons with FAS generally are described as being unable to distinguish between right and wrong, as having no clear understanding of the consequences that can result from their actions, trouble following instructions and rules, and poor short and long-term memory. They are also believed to be hyperactive, gullible, and easily victimized.

In Canada, medical assessment for FAS involves long waiting lists, and expensive and lengthy travel arrangements for people living in rural settings. It is also difficult to diagnose adolescents and adults, and diagnosis, if it occurs at all, commonly occurs in childhood years; therefore, front-line workers commonly employ non-medical labelling or "screening9" to identify adults they believe have FAS. Furthermore, despite scientific evidence to the contrary, the public health message claims that all levels of alcohol exposure are dangerous to the developing fetus, which suggests high prevalence rates of

FAS/FAE exist despite a lack of medical confirmation. In the example of the Burns Lake program, assumed elevated prevalence rates of FAS are determined by some form of client in-take "screening," and the program's activities are then provided based upon this process.

Returning to the presenter's response to my questioning the identification of persons with FAS, she suggested that "seeing" FAS is simply a matter of "seeing," or at least perceiving, widespread alcohol use.[10] Her response also suggested that she is "seeing" particular cohorts of First Nations and Métis people with FAS, as indicated in her statement that "most of the moms have had prenatal exposure to alcohol." This claim reinforces an image of an "epidemic" as it implies that Indigenous women with FAS intergenerationally compound the "FAS problem" by giving birth to similarly affected children.

The presenter's response further indicates that community workers are conditioned by their training to consider most women who attend their programs to have FAS/FAE, particularly if they are Indigenous. Because of this, one can speculate that these women are generally treated as having a chronic brain dysfunction, which could be used to justify actions such as increased social service surveillance, apprehension of their children, and pressure not to have children. In concert, the women themselves may adopt some form of identity associated with FAS that will influence their self-perception both positively and negatively, including the ways in which they engage in, and are perceived by the communities in which they live. This can lead to women, particularly those struggling with substance abuse, to more readily comply with contraceptive options, including sterilization, because they and others perceive of them as being ill-equipped to parent a child.

Important to the representation developed by the presenter is the identification of the Indigenous population of Burns Lake region as a "population in crisis," an image that was further reinforced during the workshop by the Chief of Pediatrics from the Prince George Regional Hospital. She stated that many contemporary Indigenous communities in northern British Columbia experience a 100 percent rate of childhood sexual abuse, which clearly indicates the level of dysfunction present in these communities. While she gave no evidence to support her claim, the assertion reinforced an image of Indigenous communities existing in a perpetual state of chaos with adults being drunkards and sexual predators, parents—in this case mothers—affected by alcohol-related pathology rendering them incapable of caring for their children or for themselves, and thus, epidemic numbers of children with FAS being victimized and neglected. Once again, Streissguth's image of the culture-less society of pathology emerged in our discussions, as the physician explained to the workshop participants how hard it was for her as a medical doctor to watch Indigenous children growing up in such circumstances. She stated that it was difficult for her to focus on the needs of the mothers when the damage they were causing to the children was so obvious and preventable.

By the end of the day I was significantly concerned with the pervasive association of Indigenous peoples, particularly First Nations women and their children, with a perceived widespread epidemic of FAS and addiction. I was equally concerned that hardly any of the workshop participants were trained as researchers and that few appeared to have a solid knowledge base of the research literature on FAS, despite the meeting's intention to influence the direction of gender-based research in this area.

Over dinner that evening Lucille Bruce and I discussed some of the implications of the day's discussion. We were both disturbed by the negative representation of Indigenous mothers and their children, especially in the Burns Lake region. Of equal concern was the workshop participants' inability to stay focused on women, such that time and time again the discussion shifted toward "protection" of the fetus. A further concern was the lack of attention paid to the inadequacies that exist in substance abuse treatment services for women, which in most regions of the country have only been modified slightly despite thirty years of knowledge about the dangers of prenatal alcohol exposure and the negative impact substance abuse has on women's health in general.

RETROSPECTIVE GARDEN THOUGHTS

In my spring garden, I concluded that the Vancouver workshop reflected much of what my field research had already illustrated about the knowledge production and practices associated with the diagnostic category FAS.[11] However, an important question to ask is whether representation of Indigenous front-line workers and leaders at the workshop would have resulted in increased support for my concerns. My research indicates that while Indigenous groups are generally concerned about the difficulties involved in obtaining diagnostic assessments, they have only limited interest in whether the scope of the "FAS problem" in their communities is being overstated by the federal and provincial governments. This I interpret as reflecting less the acceptance of an "epidemic" of FAS in their communities and more a pragmatic response to the pressures brought on by chronic under-resourcing of local and regional health care services. If a label such as FAS results in extra funding being provided to overburdened health and social services than it is unlikely that community leaders will argue against the label attached to those added resources.

Elevated fertility rates among Indigenous populations imply to many Canadians that the "Indian problem" will increase exponentially if solutions are not found. The added dimension of a serious illness such as FAS further fuels this sense of urgency, particularly when maternal FAS is perceived to be a widespread problem. As illustrated by the workshop discussions, the response to alcohol and pregnancy in Canada has resulted in increased surveillance by medical, public health, and social service agencies of the bodies and behaviours of Indigenous women, particularly during childbearing years. This has, as argued in this paper, reinvigorated enduring government strategies that historically have sought to stigmatize and control the future of Indigenous reproduction, parenting, and family life, while offering limited meaningful supports for impoverished Indigenous women and their children.

Originally published in Canadian Woman Studies/les cahiers de la femme, *"Indigenous Women in Canada: The Voices of First Nations, Inuit and Métis Women," 26 (3 & 4) (Winter/Spring 2008): 69-76. Reprinted with permission of the author.*

Caroline L. Tait is Métis from MacDowall, Saskatchewan, Canada. She received her Ph.D. from the Departments of Anthropology and Social Studies of Medicine at McGill University, Montreal, in 2003. During the 1995-1996 academic year, Caroline was a Fulbright Scholar and Visiting Fellow at Harvard University, Cambridge, Massachusetts, in the Departments of Anthropology and Social Medicine. Caroline is the past coordinator of the National Network for Aboriginal Mental Health Research funded by the Canadian Institute for Aboriginal Peoples Health Research and completed a postdoctoral fellowship in the Division of Social and Transcultural Psychiatry, Department of Psychiatry, McGill University, in May 2004. She is past Vice-chair of the Aboriginal Women's Health and Healing Research Group, a national group of Aboriginal women who are funded by the Women's Health Bureau, Health Canada. In May 2004 she joined the Indigenous Peoples' Health Research Centre and the Department of Women's and Gender Studies, University of Saskatchewan, as an Assistant Professor.

[1]Chemical contraception includes, for example, Depo Provera® and Norplant.

[2]The workshop organizers announced that for the purposes of the workshop the use of the term FAS would refer to both FAS, fetal alcohol effects (FAE) and other alcohol related birth defects.

[3]This chapter was written immediately after returning from the workshop. In later conversations with other workshop participants they expressed similar concerns, but said they were afraid or reluctant for various reasons to express them at the workshop.

[4]In an e-mail to the organizing committee later that week, I expressed my concern about the lack of Indigenous representation at the meeting. I was told that two participants who were First Nations had been invited but declined to attend the meeting. The organizers were unsure as to why these individuals had decided to decline the invitation.

[5]Some of the participants in the workshop did not contribute to the discussion during the two-day workshop except to submit written suggestions at the end of the workshop to the organizers. It is unclear why they did not verbalize their opinions, as there was sufficient opportunity for them to do so. Therefore, it is unclear if their silence meant that they concurred with the identification of

Aboriginal women as basically defining the risk group.

[6]Approximately 40 per cent of the total population of 6,000 living in Burns Lake are Indigenous. Several First Nation reserve communities are located nearby.

[7]The exact number of women in the program is not given in the publication.

[8]A prescription of DepoProvera® lasts for three months and is given to women through injection.

[9]Presently FAS screening tools for adults are limited and are likely to produce high rates of false positives. This is specifically the case for Indigenous groups where the facial features may show up naturally in the population apart from maternal alcohol exposure (Abel) and behavioral characteristics may result from socio-environmental factors that impact negatively on the person. In other cases, screening occurs as a result of local in-take tools being developed by front-line workers.

[10]Known or perceived in-utero alcohol exposure is sometimes enough for a person to be labeled as having FAS/FAE, and alcohol abuse by the mother is not seen to be necessary. In some cases, just the fact that the child is Indigenous is enough for non-medical persons to perceive prenatal alcohol exposure had occurred, especially if the child has been in foster or adoptive care, or is from certain urban or reserve communities where alcohol abuse is perceived to be high.

[11]In the weeks following the workshop, a report was produced and delivered to the IGH and to the workshop participants (Greaves, Poole and Cormier). While I gave a small amount of feedback to the organizers, at the time I could not imagine how any kind of meaningful research recommendations could come out of what felt like a very disjointed debate and discussion. However, much to my surprise and appreciation, I received a report in which the authors carefully describe and analyze the information given, producing a set of research recommendations that challenge the assumptions and questionable practices attached to the category FAS and the treatment of pregnant women. After having reviewed the report I not only feel that it signifies a successful representation of the ideas expressed and debated at the workshop, but it also attempts to redefine, at least to some degree, the ways in which research questions attached to alcohol use by pregnant women should be framed and researched in the Canadian context.

REFERENCES

Aase, J. M. "The Fetal Alcohol Syndrome in American Indians: A High Risk Group." *Neurobehavioral Toxicology and Teratology* 3 (1981): 153-156.

Abel, E. L. *Fetal Alcohol Abuse Syndrome*. New York: Plenum, 1998.

Asante, K. O. "FAS in Northwest BC and the Yukon." *BC Medical Journal* 23 (7) (1981): 331-335.

Asante, K. O. and J. Nelms-Matzke. *Survey of Children with Chronic Handicaps and Fetal Alcohol Syndrome in Yukon and Northwest British Columbia*. Ottawa:

National Native Advisory Council on Alcohol and Drug Abuse, Health and Welfare Canada, 1985.

Asante, K. O. and G. Robinson. "Pregnancy Outreach Program in British Columbia: The Prevention of Alcohol-Related Birth Defects." *Canadian Journal of Public Health* 81 (1990): 76-77.

Children's Commission of the B.C. Ministry for Children and Families. *Fetal Alcohol Syndrome: A Call for Action in B.C.* Victoria: Children's Commission of the B.C. Ministry for Children and Families, 2001.

Ginsburg, F. D. and R. Rapp. "Introduction." *Conceiving the New World Order: The Global Politics of Reproduction.* Eds. F. D. Ginsburg and R. Rapp. Berkeley: University of California Press, 1995. 1-17

Greaves, L., N. Poole and R. Cormier. *Fetal Alcohol Syndrome and Women's Health: Setting a Women-Centred Research Agenda.* Vancouver: The British Columbia Centre of Excellence in Women's Health, 2002.

May, P. A. "Fetal Alcohol Effects Among North American Indians: Evidence and Implications for Society." *Alcohol Health and Research World* 15 (3) (1991): 239-248.

Streissguth, A. P. *Fetal Alcohol Syndrome: A Guide for Families and Communities.* Toronto: Paul H. Brooks Publishing Co., 1997.

Tait, C. L. *A Study of the Service Needs of Pregnant Addicted Women in Manitoba.* Winnipeg: Prairie Women's Health Centre of Excellence, 2000.

ROBINA THOMAS

FOR KAYLA JOHN

I WAS RAISED IN THE SMALL community of Zeballos located on the West Coast of Vancouver Island. When people ask me where I am from, my response is most often met with blank stares. "Where is Zeballos?" And, I explain. I say that I am Lyackson through marriage and my grandparents were Snux'ney'mexw, Sto:olo, and Icelandic. And then I proudly proclaim that I was "raised" in Zeballos. I was in grade one when when our family moved to Zeballos in the fall of 1963.

Tragically, in the summer of 2004 this small village became front-page news when a local Indigenous girl was reported missing. Days later, thirteen-year-old Kayla John was found—essentially in her back yard—murdered. Prior to the arrest of twenty-one-year-old George Roswell Osmond for Kayla's murder, the media had portrayed Zeballos as a community where the youth were running awry and wrecking havoc on the local townspeople and businesses. I sat by the television sadly watching what was reported. I wondered how this could happen in the village that I loved as a child. I simply could not comprehend the tragedy, nor could I believe that a young person would be murdered there. In many ways, Kayla's murder rocked my foundation. This story is for Kayla.

Zeballos is located on the northern tip of Zeballos Inlet, an arm of Nootka Sound. It is the traditional territory of the Ehattesaht people. In the mid-1960s, Zeballos was a community of approximately 125 people, many from the surrounding Indigenous villages and communities, and many from our family. There were no telephones, televisions, or any other modern amenities. The village had a grocery store, a restaurant, a community hall, an elementary school, a post-office, a bakery, a liquor store, and a pub.

Zeballos was an isolated and remote community, only accessible by seaplane or boat. The main means of transportation to our community was the U'Chuck. This boat transported all our supplies: food, mail, stock, and everything else. Once a week, the boat left Gold River and worked its way eight hours up the breathtakingly beautiful West Coast of Vancouver Island to its final destination—Zeballos. When we could, we sat on the dock and greeted the crew and passengers, waiting eagerly to see if anything being unloaded was for us. I also remember the anticipation of the U'Chuck arriving when we would be boarding to leave on our annual vacation. Every summer we made our annual trip to Vancouver. Vancouver was overwhelming with its televisions, radios, traffic, and crowds; so much so it was almost more than a village girl could handle, but it was so exciting too

In Zeballos, all our social activities took place in the community hall. About once a month we had a movie night. There were always activities planned to commemorate the official holidays: Easter, Halloween, and Christmas. I remember our Christmas pageants. Everything in our small community was organized by volunteers—everyone did what they could, but more importantly, everyone in the community attended all of the events. One year our Aunty Mel (by no means a professional dancer) taught us to tap dance. Or, we at least danced wearing tap shoes. We practiced for months. It was so exciting that Saturday evening we couldn't wait to step onto our rickety stage with our headbands and short maroon silk Charleston-style dresses adorned with a sparkly silver note sign and black fringe. We danced our hearts out performing for the whole village. These events always made us feel so proud and gave us such a sense of belonging.

To the north of Zeballos was the Privateer, an abandoned gold mine. They used to say that at the height of the gold rush, the streets of the Privateer were paved of gold. In about 1942, the mine closed and for the most part, many families simply packed their personal belongings and moved, basically leaving homes almost fully furnished. We would hike the five miles up to that old mine and play for hours in those buildings. We especially loved looking at the old magazines and examining the core samples hoping that we would strike it rich by finding gold the miners failed to discover.

We spent hours on the water, usually fishing off the dock or in the Zeballos River. I remember the days when the fish ran so thick in the river they claimed you could walk across the river on their fins. I will never forget when Dad was teaching us to fly fish. I was at the edge of the river casting my line into the river, ready to catch the big one. No sooner than I cast my line, I yelled to Dad that I had caught something. I was reeling in my line as fast as I could. Meanwhile my brother was screaming behind me, but I could not understand a word he was saying. Nor was I at all interested in him as the excitement of catching a fish had my total focus. Finally my Dad yelled at me to stop reeling in. I turned around to see why. There was my young brother with my fly right through his top lip! These incidents were always scary because other than the first aid attendant, the closest facility for medical attention was the hospital at Esperanza, which was about one hour by boat down the Inlet.

Sometimes we would cross the river and visit Dolly. She was an old workhorse that was abandoned when her owners left the community. We used to think that some day we would tame her enough to ride her around the community. But Dolly had other plans. Actually, we never even got close to her. She was a wise old babe. She knew we always brought her food so she was always visible, from a distance. Only when we left would she come and eat our offerings.

Once when we were visiting her, we lost track of time and nearly got stranded on Dolly's side of the river as the tide was coming in and the river was rising fast. As it was, we had to fight the current and wade up to our hips to cross the river and get home safely.

We had so many close calls. This happened to us once when we were playing at the gold mine as well. We left the mine so late that it started getting dark. The mine was up an old logging road that had not been used for years. Of course, there were no streetlights. By the time we got home we were exhausted because we ran the whole way. With every sound we heard we ran faster, convinced we were being chased by bears or some other wild animal. By the time I got to Grama's I was crying. Her home was a haven.

Grama was the backbone of our family. Everyone was at Grama's all the time. I lived with my Grama and my cousins off and on during our time in Zeballos. We lived between Zeballos and Fleetwood because we had to take a boat to school everyday and at times, especially in the winter months, it was safer to stay at Grama's than risk the rough waters. I have such fond memories of her. Grama never drank alcohol, but loved to collect these little alcohol bottles. When anyone travelled anywhere they always brought her back those little bottles. Anywhere you looked in her house you would either see her little bottles or pictures of her grandchildren proudly displayed. She kept every card or gift we ever gave her. But mostly what I remember about Grama's place was love, and, of course, her food.

Every day we went to Grama's for lunch. The arrangement was that whoever got to the bakery first to pick up the bread got the crusts, and we all wanted the crusts. Everyday we raced to be the first to get the bread. I can still smell the freshly baked yeasty aroma of the warm bread. Once we got the bread, you had to fight the urge to bite into it so that you could arrive at Grama's with the bread intact. We fought over the bread. Sometimes by the time we got the bread home, it was all squished and doughy from us pulling and tugging at it. Grama would make one of us return to the bakery and get another loaf; this was always accompanied with a stern word about waste, and a caution not to ruin the next loaf.

Grama was a generous woman. She always remembered our birthdays and always bought us nighties or pyjamas for Christmas. These were always purchased from the local store, Wittons, or ordered from the Sears Catalogue. Sears was the Armani of the West Coast.

Grama was a strong role model. She taught us about respect through her actions. She never yelled but, when she scolded you, you felt so bad. You knew when you "got the look" or when you were "sat down" that she was disappointed in you. She always reminded us to treat people the way we wanted to be treated. She had to work extra hard to teach us this lesson when it came to school. For us, school was more a social event than a learning experience. Our favourite classroom was the outdoors!

It seemed like the teachers who couldn't get a job anywhere else came to our two-room schoolhouse. I can only remember one teacher that I actually liked. He was a visiting teacher from Fiji. Mr. Williams and his family were in Zeballos for one year on a teacher-exchange program. I often wonder what he thought of being in this community that had an average of one hundred inches of rain a year compared to the warmth of his homeland. They used to say that Zeballos had only two seasons a year—spring and fall. As children we didn't mind; we didn't know any different.

What I remember most are the bad teachers. There was a miserable old spinster who enjoyed taunting us. She always wore a knee-length black fitted dress, synched at the waist with a black belt, and buttoned up to the collar. Her outfit was accompanied with pointy black leather lace-up shoes. Her grey hair was always pulled back into a bun; not one hair out of place. She looked mean; she was mean. She sat at the back of the class and walked around with a wooden pointer that she used liberally to "keep us in our place." Being the social butterfly that I am, coupled with the fact that I was related to more than half of the students, meant that I was a regular target of her behaviour-modification tactics. Daily, I got whacked across the back of my head with that pointer. I can still remember the racist adage she taught us to memorize how to spell arithmetic: "a red Indian thought he might eat tobacco in church." Clearly, she was not concerned that the majority of the students were Indigenous. We had no respect for her.

There was one person that nearly everyone in the community did have respect for, and that was Dr. MacLean. He was the resident doctor at Esperanza, a missionary hospital down the Inlet. Not only was he the doctor, he was the priest, the dentist, the lawyer, or anything else he was required to be. Mostly he was a missionary and worked relentlessly to convert us all to Christianity. Most of us were not interested, but he never gave up hope. Dr. MacLean always tended to our emergencies.

Once I was chasing my brother through the bush because he had taken one of the grasshoppers I had been collecting for hours. He had put my grasshopper in his huge glass jar. I was angry and desperately wanted my grasshopper back (I am not sure how I knew which one was mine!). I never did catch him, but he tripped and landed right on top of the jar, which broke and cut his chest wide open. The gash was about four inches long and bled profusely. We ran frantically out of the woods, yelling for help. We finally found someone and told them what had happened. The blood was pouring down Stuart's chest and he looked pale and faint. I was convinced he was dying. I remember the boat ride to the hospital asking Dad all the way, "is he going to live?" Dad was so mad at us. Dr. MacLean stitched him up. Other than a battle wound, my bother was fine.

Every summer Dr. MacLean organized a bible camp at Camp Ferrier. I always wanted to attend, but for one reason or another it never happened. One year I just about got there. My parents had made arrangements for me to catch a ride on a small fishing boat with an old Nuu-Chah-Nulth couple from

Queen's Cove. Queen's Cove was just around the corner from the camp and the old people offered to bring me there on their way home. I was so excited. Of course, Mom had bought me new underwear, new pyjamas, shorts and t-shirts, a new sleeping bag, and all the other necessities. I headed down to the boat with my little suitcase full of treasures. I was thrilled! Off we went. We must have been travelling for about an hour when we hit something in the bay near Canada Packing Company. At the time, we didn't pay much attention because the old boat was slow and it didn't seem like we hit the deadhead very hard. But soon, water started filling the bottom of the boat. Quickly we placed an SOS call, put on our life jackets, and evacuated the boat. There I was bobbing around in the ocean and the only thing I could think of was my little suitcase with all my prized possessions. I wasn't afraid of the water, nor was I worried we wouldn't be rescued. I wanted my new undies and pj's! I was sent home that night. Dad felt so bad that he later arranged for another boat to bring me to camp, only this time with my old underwear and pajamas in tow. I made it to Camp Ferrier but only for the last few days.

I guess because we lived on the ocean, I was fearless of water. Every spring there was a pod of whales that would hang around in Nootka Sound for a few weeks feeding on the abundance of fish. For about a week, one of the young whales (maybe Luna), wanting to play and have fun, would escort our boat to and from school. We used to hang off the side of the boat clutching the ropes that were attached to the floats and trying to touch the whale. The whale was not bothered by us and we thought, like Dolly the horse, someday we would tame the whale enough to ride it too.

We knew that not all the animals in the community were friendly and welcomed our presence; in fact, the bears are as territorial as we are. There was a mother bear that lived in the mountains not far from our trailer. When her cubs were born she was so protective and fierce. We had a shed off the end of our trailer where Mom and Dad stored our canned goods and the freezer. This bear learned how to break open the cans. But more surprising, that old Mama bear learned how to get into the freezer too! She cleaned us out. Eventually Dad had to put a door on the shed and chase the bears away.

We loved our community. As a mother of three sons, I always wished that my children had the opportunity to experience the splendour of Zeballos. They have never experienced digging for clams and having a clam bake on the beach. Or hiking over the mountain from Fleetwood to Zeballos. Nor have they ever gotten lost at the gold mine and had to find their way home. They will never experience the feeling of having a whole community pull together after a fire to help a family rebuild their home. Or, organize collections to clothe and feed the family in need. I was lucky to grow up the way I did, in a community where the most frightening things were the situations that we got ourselves into as children.

Of course there were moments. We had the only liquor store and pub for miles. Especially during fishing seasons when all the fishers were on the water, a quick detour into Zeballos to unwind was common. Drinking seems to bring with it a universal set of bad and unacceptable behaviours and our community was no exception. There was violence. But even through these times, as children we did not feel threatened. There was a man that used to come down from the iron ore mine to indulge. I think he was mentally unstable. When he drank, he was completely unpredictable. We all knew this and when he was around, our parents would warn us to stay clear of the pub and liquor store areas—practically the entire downtown core of our small community.

Neither was our family immune to drinking. Most all of our family was addicted to drugs or alcohol. But we always had our grandmother. She was our sanctuary. We could stay with Grama whenever we wanted and she would always take care of us. No one would dare come around Grama's place drunk or drinking.

Much has changed since I moved from this small community. Zeballos now has road access. The population is much more transient. In fact, besides the Ehattesaht people, many folks only live there while they are employed—mostly loggers. People come and go all the time, most not invested in the ongoing well-being of Zeballos. Health services offered now are parachuted in. For example, in the local Zeballos *Privateer* newspaper, they post a medical clinic schedule. At the bottom of the posting is the following disclaimer:

> Doctors from Port McNeill Clinic travel by helicopter, arriving in Zeballos after clinics in either Holberg or Kyuquot. As such, their arrival time is dependent not only on weather, but also on how busy those clinics are and when they can leave there. Patients in Zeballos who have appointments will be notified by phone when the arrival time is known.

The same is true for social services. For the Ehattesaht people, their social service organization is located in another community. Social workers too fly into the community on an as-needed basis. Where were all the services Kayla needed to be safe in her community? It was a known fact that drugs and alcohol had reached endemic levels in the community. How is a community expected to survive when they are in crisis and there are no social services available? And then we wonder, what happened to Kayla John?

Why was Zeballos not the same haven for Kayla that is was for me? Kayla John was from the local Ehatis First Nation. In 1990, the Ehattesaht people were relocated from their traditional territory in Queen's Cove with the promise of a new and better life. I ask, new and better than what? Will anything ever replace the traditional territory of their ancestors? What teachings were left behind? Queen's Cove was struggling to supply safe drinking water and did not have telephones, hydro, or any other modern-day amenities. The solution the Department of Indian Affairs developed and offered the people was to relocate them to Zeballos. The Ehattesaht people moved. However, all the people of Ehatis ended up with were a dozen houses on a rock bed. How does this constitute a community? The children did not even have a proper playground or community hall. We have seen other communities, like Davis Inlet, where relocation has not offered improvement; in fact, relocation nearly devastated that community. What was the cost of relocation in the case of the Ehattesaht people?

So what does my story have to do with Kayla John? Why would I dare juxtapose my safe haven to the nightmare that was her life? For many reasons. First, Zeballos was not always a community with youth running awry. In fact it was a community where as a child I felt safe; I could roam and explore freely.

Second, I wanted to show that when a community is together because they want to be together, there is a sense of belonging and responsibility. As children, we never questioned our belonging to Zeballos; we knew this was our community, and we felt a sense of responsibility to the community. When I read about Kayla's death, I still felt that sense of responsibility. I had a strong urge to defend Zeballos and let people know that it is not a bad place and that Kayla's death was an isolated, tragic, and horrible incident. Who is to blame? This is a complex question to answer, but the blame surely can not rest solely on the shoulders of the youth. Where was the Department of Indian Affairs? Where were the RCMP, social workers, and other helping professionals who might have prevented what happened?

Third, and most importantly, Kayla John had a dream. Kayla was an intelligent, young, innocent girl who worked hard not only in school but also within her family. She had faith in the ability of her family and the community of Zeballos to come together and get along. She dreamed of *hish'ist'stwalk*—we are all one. She dreamed of living in a community that was violence-free. She dreamed of a community where she was allowed to be the 13-year-old girl that she was. She longed for the right to simply dream—to dream of *hish'ist'stwalk*. Kayla longed for the Zeballos that I was raised in and I feel such a sense of loss for this girl and her unmet dreams. May her dreams live on and may the people of Ehatis and the local people of Zeballos do what they can to help her dreams come true. So I write this story for Kayla John.

Since I originally wrote this story for Kayla, much has happened in Zeballos. Kayla's dream of *hish'ist'stwalk* has taken a life of its own. There are now full-time police services in the community. The village of Zeballos built a basketball court in her memory. Tolerance of drug and alcohol abuse has declined partly as a result of the Ehatis Chief and Council passing a Band Council Resolution prohibiting the use of drugs and alcohol within their traditional territories. Chief and Council has asked a number of families who choose to continue abusing drugs and alcohol to move—and they have. Volunteers from Ehattesaht have built a community hall and playground in Kayla's name. A number of young people from the community have attended rehabilitation programs and want to live a good life. The Victoria Foundation funded the development and delivery of a parenting program that has been extremely successful. On National Aboriginal Day the community will host their first cultural night. And, Kayla's parents are clean and sober, and work everyday to live as a family—to live the teachings of *hish'ist'stwalk*. Kayla John you are amazing. Many thanks to you Kayla for making me remember some of the most special times of my life.

Originally published in Canadian Woman Studies/les cahiers de la femme, *"Indigenous Women in Canada: The Voices of First Nations, Inuit and Métis Women," 26 (3 & 4) (Winter/Spring 2008): 208-212. Reprinted with permission of the author.*

Qwul'sih'yah'maht—Robina Thomas—(Lyackson of the Hul'qumi'num speaking people on Vancouver Island) is an Associate Professor in the School of Social Work at the University of Victoria.

ANITA OLSEN HARPER

IS CANADA PEACEFUL AND SAFE
FOR ABORIGINAL WOMEN?

ABORIGINAL WOMEN IN CANADA are the victims of very serious human rights violations. One blatant example is the legislative gap in both federal and provincial law in protecting a spouse's right to equal division of matrimonial real property on-reserve. All other Canadians are protected by provincial laws regarding this matter, but the same laws are not applicable on-reserve because only the federal government has jurisdiction over "lands reserved for Indians" and this includes real property on-reserve. There has never been a law enacted by the Canadian Parliament to address how real property, including matrimonial homes, will be divided when a marriage or common-law relationship breaks down. Aboriginal women and their children who reside on-reserve directly bear the brunt of this serious legislative gap. Further, because almost all reserves in Canada suffer from a severe lack of adequate housing, women who cannot remain in the family home are forced to go elsewhere with their children. This is only one example of the rights of on-reserve women remaining unprotected; a parallel situation concerning non-Aboriginal women does not exist in Canada.

These facts remain in spite of the fact that for most of the decade up to the year 2001, Canada was ranked number one among 175 countries in the world as being the best country in which to live. The United Nations' Human Development Index (HDI) makes this determination through its Quality of Life survey which examines the health, education and wealth of a country's citizens by measuring life expectancy, educational achievement, secondary and tertiary enrolment and standard of living. As well, in 2009, U.S. President Obama stated that "Canada is one of the most impressive countries in the world, the way it has managed a diverse population, a vibrant economy…" (CBC).

These findings would make one think that almost all Canadian citizens do quite well, and perhaps this is the case. For the Aboriginal people who have been living *ab initio* on these lands, however, this is simply not true. The disparity in health, educational attainment, accumulation of wealth, life expectancy and standard of living is a noticeably wide gap in comparison with the life experiences of most Canadians. Aboriginal women, in particular, suffer from inequality of status compared to both Aboriginal men and, especially, their non-Aboriginal counterparts. In this and other respects, and mostly because

Canada as a nation does not make it a priority to address issues such as these, it cannot "look in the mirror" and see a truly civilized and liberated nation.

Other countries in the world might have a difficult time comprehending that Canada hosts serious human rights problems. These beliefs and perspectives, though, do not take away from, or diminish the reality faced by many Aboriginal women in this country because of these violations. For example, Aboriginal women in Canada are subject to high rates of violence in all forms. In particular, racialized violence targeting Aboriginal women is especially disturbing because these experiences are passed on intergenerationally to children and youth in other violence-related forms such as through involvement in street gangs and other "street" misbehaviours. In far too many instances, extreme racialized violence against Aboriginal women leads to their disappearances and even murder. The life destroyed in these circumstances is not only the victim's, but those whom she has left behind: grandparents, parents, sisters, brothers, aunts, uncles, children, other relatives and friends. Could the long-standing general lack of awareness within Canada about the extreme violence against Aboriginal women mean that the public simply does not want to know? Does the public think that these "uncomfortable" issues will perhaps just somehow conveniently "go away"?

REPRESENTATION OF ABORIGINAL PEOPLE IN CANADIAN HISTORY

The way Aboriginal people have been represented in Canadian history plays an important role in how Aboriginal people, including Aboriginal women, are perceived in today's Canadian society. In these times of rapid technological and other change, any statements about the importance of history seem almost naïve; modern western societies appear to self-define according to their future plans, not from their past or history. Nonetheless, such perceptions do not take away from the validity of understanding the past in order to understand the present. Only by thoroughly comprehending the paths that have been leading to the present can appropriate and timely steps be taken to solve long-term problems, such as those faced by Aboriginal women in Canada. Incidentally, Aboriginal tradition places a high importance on expending time and effort in teaching youngsters their family and tribal history because they believe that youth with a solid understanding of the past is a youth that values its own individual and collective identity.

There are many examples that demonstrate the reality that historical representation and its subsequent presentation is not necessarily trustworthy. In Canada, most recordings of the European-Aboriginal relationships have been preserved, presented and accepted according to the values, perceptions and general life philosophies of the prevailing Euro-Canadian society. Even within the relatively short span of that society, historiography points out an interesting phenomenon: narrations over time are recorded, shaped, and fixed according to prevailing Eurocentric societal attitudes (Blaut 10). Paralleling any change in the view of the present is a change in the view of the past.

Historical presentations then, have many serious limitations. One of their functions is as a tool for propaganda to encourage thought and motivation into predetermined outcomes. The "battleground for the public mind" has always had many different fronts to serve certain specific purposes. For example, within their own societies at the time of contact, the roles of Aboriginal women were vastly different from those of European women. The latter held a status that was shared with minors and wards of the Crown; they were perceived as property—in their early lives, their father's property, and later when they married, the property of their husbands. Aboriginal women, on the other hand, headed family line,[1] exerted a great deal of power such as the authority to choose and oust their nation's chiefs, and were a vital part of consensus decision-making. Nevertheless, Canadian history presents these Aboriginal traditions in a negative light; the *Indian Act* of 1876 created the elected chief and council system thereby removing Aboriginal women's political powers by stipulating that only men could be elected as chiefs and councilors.

Canadian history shows that stereotypical images were serving a purpose for those who endorsed them. The primary overall opinion of the first Europeans was cautiously optimistic for they relied on the First Peoples for all their basic livelihood needs. They condescendingly acknowledged that these "primitive" peoples needed civilizing, but were fully confident that this could be accomplished through educational processes that they themselves would predicate. Times began to change. The true imperialist ambitions of the colonialist powers began to emerge, and the fairly balanced early relationship began to crumble to give way to the birth of the interpretation of Aboriginal people as wretched and barbaric, even demonic. Many history and children's books of the nineteenth century were based on this imagery (Francis 159-164).

Settlement in Canada's "wild west" increased, but not from invitation by the First Nations themselves, who due to decimation from foreign diseases, and other influences of oppression, increasingly found themselves on the fringes of their own territories. These times saw rampant theories of Native racial inferiority for these provided a rationale to the Europeans for indiscriminately taking lands that were not rightfully theirs (Hawkins 62). Newcomers willingly listened to academics who predicted the disappearance of the entire Indigenous peoples as God's way of using nature to weed out an inferior group in favour of a superior one (Le Conte 359-361). In the meantime, the First Peoples were being further marginalized into the undesired hinterlands and their suffering, if it was known at all, was treated with indifference by both the Canadian government and general public who were too busy and apathetic to involve themselves in any meaningful way.

INEQUALITIES LEAD TO THE "SISTERS IN SPIRIT" INITIATIVE

People treated with inequality by government are fair game for societal discrimination, and racism if they belong to a different ethnic group. Aboriginal people, meeting these conditions, are both discriminated against and suffer the consequences of racism. Further, because of the patriarchy of Canadian society, Aboriginal women are subject to even more inequality than Aboriginal men. There are many different arenas in "everyday Canadian life" in which Aboriginal women do not fare well at all.

Looking at Canada's Aboriginal women from an economic perspective, we see that, in one province (Manitoba), 42.7 per cent off-reserve live in poverty (Donner, Busch and Fontaine). The corresponding figure for non-Aboriginal women is half that number. Aboriginal women's average annual income was $13,300; Aboriginal men's was $18,200 whereas that of non-Aboriginal women was $19,350 (NAPO 2). This synopsis is a prime example of Aboriginal women's inequality in relation to both Aboriginal men and non-Aboriginal women in the area of earning power for meeting basic livelihood needs.

Canada's child welfare system continues to be disastrous for Aboriginal families. Provincial government policies target Aboriginal children for transition into various agencies and adoption into non-Native families. While these practices are now being lobbied against by Native women's and other concerned groups, policy changes are painstakingly slow. A significant but undesirable result is that, very often, the traditions and practices of most of these children, as grown adults, are not recognizable as Aboriginal and their connections to birth families tends to be weak at best. In 2004, a large proportion—30,000 out of a total of 76,000 children in care—is Aboriginal; this is an astonishing 39.5 per cent (Blackstock and Trocme 1). More disturbingly, this large number of children has all but lost its true identity; searching out family roots and ties is problematic and traumatic for most.

In the area of education, there is a particularly large gap between the rates of non and Aboriginal women with university degrees: in 2001, seven per cent of Aboriginal women over 25 years of age had a university degree, compared with 17 per cent for non-Aboriginal women within the same age group (Statistics Canada). While two-thirds of Aboriginal graduates are women, equal access to employment opportunities is still lagging; this is because gendered racism obstructs Aboriginal women's access to a fair share of the labour market (Jacobs). In the same year, 40 per cent of Aboriginal women over the age of 25 had not graduated from high school compared with 29 per cent among non-Aboriginal women. (*Women in Canada 2005* 196).

Federal, provincial and territorial justice systems are other areas that discriminate against Aboriginal women on the basis of their race, gender and class. The systemic racism of all police forces albeit some "better" than others, and not applicable to every single member, is one way of explaining this. For example, police officers need a fair and open attitude towards those working in the sex trade and must learn to treat "street people" as human beings—with dignity and respect, and this is generally not their attitude. Another area that needs serious revision is the Court system. Court personnel often fail to either recognize or acknowledge the unique forms of injury that Aboriginal women suffer when they report being sexually assaulted or raped or any number of other violations. Many Aboriginal women and girls are ostracized by their families or reserves when they go through with criminal charges; often, they themselves are blamed for their situations. This is especially harmful when so many live in the northern, more isolated areas of the country; a general lack of counseling and support services in many reserve communities does little to help and encourage these women.

The "Stolen Sisters" report by Amnesty International (Canada) made the following statements about the way in which police treat or relate to Aboriginal people:

> •Most disturbingly, the inquiry concluded that police had long been aware of white men sexually preying on Indigenous women and girls in The Pas but "did not feel that the practice necessitated any particular vigilance." (1)
>
> •The inquiry explained that many police have come to view Indigenous people not as a community deserving protection, but a community from which the rest of society must be protected. (30)
>
> •Many Indigenous families told Amnesty International that police did little when they reported a sister or daughter missing and seemed to be waiting for the woman to be found. (32)
>
> •… few police forces have specific protocols on actions to be taken when Indigenous women and girls are reported missing. (33)

Amnesty International's report concluded that Canadian authorities and most police forces do not protect Aboriginal women from violent attacks (including murder) but, instead, tend to disregard these violations when they occur and are reported.

These long-standing realities, faced by all Aboriginal women in Canada, remain mostly unaddressed and given a low priority for change by governments. The *status quo* continues to place Aboriginal women at a much greater risk of social and economic marginalization, laying fertile ground for higher risks of victimization from all types of crimes—but most likely physical and sexual crime at the forefront. So far, all levels of government have not implemented the necessary legislative action and policy direction to decrease the risks that would help protect Aboriginal women from being targets of violence and other related criminal activity.

THE SISTERS IN SPIRIT INITIATIVE

In the meantime, not awaiting government policy and legislative change to address what became known as "racialized, sexualized" violence[2] against Aboriginal women, many began working with unrelenting perseverance in lobbying and advocacy efforts. This was taking place at both the grassroots and organizational levels in the Native community; one of those was the Native Women's Association of Canada (NWAC) and its Board of Directors who were Provincial/ Territorial Member Associations (PTMAs). Many others were Aboriginal families and women themselves; they were helped by non-Aboriginal women's individuals and groups. Some of these were Amnesty International (Canada), KAIROS Canadian Ecumenical Justice Initiatives; the Canadian Association of Elizabeth Frye Societies, and the United, Anglican and other churches.

The year 2002 saw national momentum building up. Those involved pooled their efforts to raise awareness of the racially-motivated attacks on Aboriginal women. This group was known as the "National Coalition for our Stolen Sisters" and adopted a red heart-shaped logo with an inscription commemorating February 14 for "a day of love and hope and memory for our Stolen Sisters." This was the beginning of Aboriginal women's voices being heard at the national level in an area that so long was a source of frustration and distress for so long.

The Coalition, spearheaded by NWAC, was simultaneously working to cultivate federal government allies; these were Indian and Northern Affairs Canada, the Department of Justice, Canadian International Development Agency, Public Safety and Emergency Preparedness Canada (part of which is the Royal Canadian Mounted Police), Foreign Affairs Canada and Status of Women Canada (SWC). Only one department made a formal agreement with NWAC. In November 2005, SWC committed five-year[3] funding for Sisters in Spirit and this moved the campaign into a full research, education, national-awareness and policy initiative. Qualitative research in the form of life histories is being undertaken with the victims' family members and friends to gain a better understanding of the circumstances, root causes and trends that surround these cases. The terms of the funding agreement provide NWAC with the fiscal and human resources to work in collaboration with other non and Aboriginal women's organizations and with various federal government departments to improve the human rights of Aboriginal women in Canada, and to target the racialized and/or sexualized violence directed at this particular group.

Sisters in Spirit's update includes an exegesis of the recent history of violence against Aboriginal women. From the 1980s through to the 2000s, concern for the safety of Aboriginal women was steadily increasing and posters of missing women were becoming a common sight anywhere Aboriginal people congregated—in community halls, stores and band offices, for example. Websites began to appear, listing the names of missing women, many being Aboriginal. Families of those missing and/or found murdered were starting to voice the pain, isolation, and trauma they were experiencing, and talked about the lack of support from police and other authorities when they tried to report on status of their loved ones.

In the early 1990s, sex trade workers in Vancouver's downtown east-side were noticing that, for at least the past decade, many of their peers were simply vanishing, never being heard from again. For those friends and family members trying to get help from police, interactions were generally not fruitful. For example, in April 1999, there was a move to get police to offer a reward for information leading to information on the missing women, but instead the City of Vancouver[4] suggested offering $5,000 to any of the missing women to come forward. This offer reveals that authorities did not believe that the women were indeed missing, but had perhaps simply had gone off somewhere. Then, the media became knowledgeable, and curious and involved. Journalists began to ask the same questions that family members had been asking for years. The eventual result was the formation of a joint Vancouver City Police/ RCMP Taskforce; more than 70 women were listed as missing. An arrest was made in early 2002 and Robert Pickton was charged with 27 murders. It is believed that at least one-third of his victims were Aboriginal.

Statistically, Vancouver's Aboriginal population is about seven per cent (Vancouver/Richmond Health Board 7). There is a high prevalence of prostitution in the city's downtown east-side where many Aboriginal women go missing. Aboriginal women are significantly overrepre-sented in Vancouver's sex trade and this "reflects not only their poverty but also their marginalized and devalued status as Canadians" (Farley, Lynne and Cotton 256). The city of Victoria reports a similar overrepresentation: 15 per cent of women in escort prostitution are Aboriginal, although the Aboriginal population is only around two per cent (Benoit and Millar 18).

Vancouver is not the only "hot spot" in the province, however. Another area is now known as the "Highway of Tears" because of the large number of missing and/or murdered Aboriginal women along this nearly 500-mile stretch between Prince Rupert and Prince George. These murders starting coming to light around 1994/ 1995 when three 15-year-old Aboriginal girls were found, in three separate instances, murdered in Prince George and Smithers. In March 2006, concerned community and family members held the "Highway of Tears Symposium" to address the urgent issue of the missing and murdered women along this highway. Eighteen families are now officially listed as having members of their family go missing—including an entire family. Only one young woman was non-Aboriginal.

The Symposium made four broad recommendations:

> •Emergency readiness must include an enhanced "amber alert" program which fast-tracks a public alert when someone goes missing, and preparation of an inventory of violent offenders for release into communities.
> •Prevention programs must involve both families and communities as advocates for policy change in the area of regulations regarding missing persons; installing well-lit emergency telephones along this stretch of highway; creation of a hitch-hiker tracking system that would work somewhat like a block watch program; and, development of youth awareness programs such as "street smarts" and "stranger danger."
> •Community development to address racism and oppression; identify

339

"safe homes" along Highway 16; and, placing coordinators in Prince George and Terrace to move identified action plans.
•Counseling and support services that offer an Aboriginal focus on spirituality; advocates working with the RCMP in victim services.

Over the years since the time that these recommendations were made, however, none have been implemented. When asked about what she saw as the reason for this, Carrier Sekani Family Services coordinator Mavis Erickson stated, "Aboriginal women's lives are not a priority in Canada for the government or its institutions."

Sisters in Spirit works to support initiatives like the Highway of Tears Symposium. NWAC President, Beverley Jacobs, speaking at various functions, articulates the integral connection of colonization to the displacement of Aboriginal women in this country, and that an undeniably strong example is the missing/murdered in this region. She also mentions the need for collaboration among all those working to draw national, regional ,and local attention to the missing women and how awareness itself can help guard against further disappearances and murders. Ms. Jacobs always speaks of hope and words of encouragement to all those families who suffer from losses of loved ones.

The Sisters in Spirit initiative has other related objectives that are directed at cultivating strength and support for Aboriginal families and entire communities. These include helping to mobilize the caring power of the family and community; providing tools accessible by Internet to help the families of victims familiarize themselves with the justice and other related systems; and providing links to community organizations for front-line delivery service (such as grief counseling, therapy, Legal Aid and discussion circles).

The strategic outcome for Sisters in Spirit is gender equality for all Aboriginal women in Canada, and their full participation in the economic, social, cultural and political arenas that are available to all other citizens in this country.

CONCLUSION

The Sisters in Spirit initiative works to reduce the risks and increase the safety and security of all Aboriginal women in Canada, regardless of where they work or where they live. The initiative also works to draw attention, recognition, and dignity to those Aboriginal women and girls who are still missing and those already found murdered. While this number is still unknown, most Aboriginal people, both men and women, would say that they know at least one person who simply disappeared; many would know at least one who was murdered.

It is not hard to make the connection between being socially, economically and politically marginalized to being targets of hatred, violence and murder. This is exactly the plight of Aboriginal people in Canada, particularly Aboriginal women. The effects of Canada's historical grounding are proving to be, without a doubt, disastrous for Aboriginal women. The way and means of Canadian history being interpreted and presented in educational and other fundamental institutions portrays a "logical rationale," convoluted and pejorative as it is, that allows and perpetuates Aboriginal women continuing as targets of violence and death just because of their gender and racial identity.

Clearly, Aboriginal women's self-interpreted and self-defined concerns must be allowed in all modalities of expression within Canadian society. We need our distinct voices heard in re-defining a better society in which we are included in positive and meaningful ways, ones that elevate our historic positions as significant decision-makers, choosers of chiefs, and land-owners. Indigenous truths, as a whole, need to be communicated everywhere in this country; our worldviews and cosmologies must be known in educational institutions and political establishments, for example; no longer should room be made for the kind of cultural bigotry that see our thoughts and concerns as unsophisticated, undeveloped, or simply inapplicable in a contemporary highly-technological global society. Historically, the "Fathers of Confederation" deliberately excluded us as Aboriginal people, both men and women, from vital nation-building processes, and now there is a crucial need to restore our contributions to an honourable and rightful place, and to recognize the enormous challenges we still face because of Canada's continuing discriminatory laws and practices.

Sisters in Spirit, striving to eliminate the objectification and dehumanizing activities that Aboriginal women have been subjected to since European contact, has a definite and significant role in helping to change the attitudes, practices, policies and awareness levels of everyday Canadians. Undoubtedly, Canada still manages to maintain a relatively high global image—but for this country's Aboriginal women, continuing to suffer from large scale inequalities, this has little meaning and no relevance.

Originally published in Canadian Woman Studies/les cahiers de la femme, *"Ending Woman Abuse," 25 (1 & 2) (Winter/Spring 2006): 33-38. Reprinted with permission of the author.*

Anita Olsen Harper is a Ph.D. student at the Faculty of Education, University of Ottawa. Her dissertation (in progress) is on the interpretation of resilience in the context of domestic violence in Aboriginal communities. She is Ojibwaa from the Lac Seul First Nation, Ontario and lives in Ottawa with her husband, former MP Elijah Harper.

[1]They were matrilineal and matriarchal, generally speaking.
[2]This is violence directed at a person because of their gender and race.
[3]The initiative ends in 2010.
[4]Vancouver, meanwhile, was being placed high on the annual Quality of Life survey. Other major Canadian cities were honoured for high levels of "personal safety and security" ("Vancouver 3rd in world in quality of life survey").

REFERENCES

Amnesty International. *Stolen Sisters: A Human Rights Response to Discrimination and Violence Against Aboriginal Women in Canada.* Ottawa: Author, 2004.

Benoit, C. and A. Millar. "Dispelling Myths and Understanding Realities: Working Conditions, Health Status and Exiting Experiences of Sex Workers." 2001. Online: http://web.uvic.ca/~cbenoit/papers/DispMyths.pdf. Accessed May 13, 2006.

Blackstock, Cindy and Nico Trocme. *Community Based Child Welfare for Aboriginal Children: Supporting Resilience Through Structural change.* First Nations Child and Family Caring Society and Centre of Excellence for Child Welfare, University of Toronto, Ocober 9, 2004.

Blaut, I. M. *The Colonizer's Model of the World: Geographical Diffusionism and Eurocentric History.* New York: Guilford Press, 1993.

CBC Television. "Mansbridge One on One." Ottawa, February 19, 2009.

Donner, Lissa, Angela Busch and Nahanni Fontaine. "Women, Income and Health in Manitoba: An Overview and Ideas for Action." Women's Health Clinic website, 2002. <http://www.womens healthcli-nic.org/resources/wih/wih.html. Accessed June 2, 2006.

Erickson, M. Personal communications. 10 September 2009.

Farley, Melissa, Jacqueline Lynne and Ann J. Cotton. "Prostitution in Vancouver: Violence and the Colonization of First Nations Women." *Transcultural Psychiatry* 42 (2) (June 2005): 242 271.

Francis, Daniel. *The Imaginary Indian: The Image of the Indian in Canadian Culture.* Vancouver: Arsenal Pulp Press, 1995.

Hawkins, M. *Social Darwinism in European and American Thought.* Cambridge: Cambridge University Press, 1997.

"Highway of Tears" Symposium Broad Recom-mendations. Online: http://www.highwayoftears.ca/recommendations.htm

Jacobs, Beverley. "Review of Beijing from an Indigenous Perspective; Secretariat Permanent Forum on Indigenous Issues." Paper presented at the Secretariat Permanent Forum on Indigenous Issues. New York, March 3, 2005.

Le Conte, J. "The Race Problem in the South." *Evolution Series No. 29: Man and the State.* New York: Appleton and Co, 1982.

National Anti-Poverty Organization (NAPO). *The Face of Poverty in Canada: An Overview* (updated January 2006). Online: www.napo-onap.ca/en/issues/2006POVERTYinCANADA.pdf

Statistics Canada. "Aboriginal Women in Canada." *Women in Canada 2005.* Catalogue No. 89-503-XIE. Ottawa: Statistics Canada, 2005.

"Vancouver 3rd in world in quality of life survey." CBC News, Sun. 13 March 2005, 17:56:35 EST.

Vancouver/Richmond Health Board. *Healing Ways: Aboriginal Health and Service Review.* October 1999.

APRYL GLADUE

A CULTURE OF LOSS

The Mourning Period of Paper Indians

I WAS THIRTY-FIVE WHEN my mother died. She was fifty-eight. I cried for a few days then took up my life again, as it was not so different a life than when she was alive. Mine is a life of loss. It is only in the early mornings or when I found myself in a still house without my children that my mind would turn to her loss.

Loss was the basis of the relationship between my mother and me. I have known this feeling of loss all of my life. It is such a central part of me that I can not distinguish it from other parts of my identity—being short, having brown hair, being raised on a farm, not able to bend the first joint on my left thumb from having cut the tendon there as a child. When I was three, my brother and I went to live with our father's parents, our grandparents, our non-native family. Our mother had left and it was only when we were older that we began to piece together some of the reasons. Many we would never know or understand. Yet, we carried with us, inside us, all the reasons and circumstances of that time. Unanswered questions were a way of life.

We were fed and clothed and given an identity deriving from European pioneering roots. My grandfather was a soldier and a farmer homesteading in northern Alberta. In 1945 he brought his Dutch war-bride home and in succession they raised a son and daughter, took care of his ailing mother, and then their two half-blood grandchildren. It was not that we were taught to see the world in a different way; it's just that we were only taught one side. We were never encouraged or given the opportunity to know our mother's family, even though our *kohkum* (grandmother) lived in the neighbouring community. We were white, or at least we looked white, but we had a dark secret that was only publicly acknowledged when our school fees for grade nine and ten were paid for through Treaty benefits. As members of the Lubicon Lake First Nation and then of the newly formed Woodland Cree First Nation in 1989, my brother and I were eligible for education benefits. Treaty 8 was signed in 1899 when the Queen's representatives came to Lesser Slave Lake looking to expand the railway and open the West for settlement. Eighty-five years later when my grandparents needed help to pay our school fees, the promises of Treaty 8 were fulfilled in a legally sanctioned act and I, and my brother, became

Native. It was only in later years that I enrolled in Native Studies and then law school, in an attempt to further understand my own circumstance and that of my family and my country.

In my adult life I found comfort in identifying with my Nativeness through the lens of school, history, and educational opportunities. I sought out Native classmates, Native courses, Native scholars, Native writings. But my interest in all things Native was confined to the campus. I never brought Native friends home to meet my husband and daughter. I was still uncomfortable with this side of myself. It took many more years and a divorce before I was able to bring more balance to my life and identity, though I still feel like a "paper" Indian.

Native, Indian, Treaty, First Nations, Métis, Aboriginal, Indigenous. Even within this segment of Canadian society there are so many labels and divisions. There are so many existing laws, regulations, and policies, and new legislation and solutions being proposed daily. There is so much paper. Since the Royal Proclamation of 1763 Canadian Indians have been suffocated with rules and categories and paper. The many variations of the *Indian Act*, the 1969 White Paper, the 1996 Report of the Royal Commission, and on and on. Numerous inquiries, commissions, reports, legislation, and policies record the progress of the Indian "problem" in this country. National policies have gone from assimilation to integration to reconciliation. Reconciliation sounds like a good idea but how will it be possible if we don't yet understand each other? How can I teach you who I am if I still have open wounds? Where can we even start? Is there any point in questioning how things could have been or should have been different?

I wonder sometimes how different I would have been if I had been raised by my mother. I would have been exposed to my Cree heritage and relatives. I would have been taught my mother's tongue. I would have been lulled to sleep in a moss bag, comforted by the smell of burning sweetgrass. It is only on paper, only sometimes in my writing, that I can touch a reality that never was, that should have been. I am left to ponder why a child should grow up wondering who she really is and where she belongs; why she wasn't given the things she needed to comfort her. My mother would have given me these things if she had been given the chance to learn them herself.

My mother was a survivor of the residential school system. As with many survivors, the treatment they received in the schools affected their relationships, their behaviours, and their circumstances. My mother's relationship with her family suffered at times, and she found herself living a life of poverty, violence, abuse, and addiction. She had lost one child and given up three others before given the chance to raise another. She regularly faced prejudice and racism in small towns, cities, and a variety of institutions. Finally, at the end of her life, she had to face a debilitating liver disease resulting from her addictive past. As is common in our communities, the toxicity of daily life shows up in the health of our people in everything from alcoholism to diabetes. My mother had many problems with her health from childhood tuberculosis to two heart attacks to numerous major surgeries for which she was hospital-ized, once for over six months. In April of 2004 she became very ill and was diagnosed with liver cancer and cirrhosis that June; she survived the surgery to remove the tumour in the summer and had a three-week stay in intensive care. In the fall, she was rejected for a liver transplant because the cancer was too far advanced and the next February, one week to the third anniversary of her own mother's death, she left us. My mother could not give me what I needed as she was on her own arduous journey.

In many ways I was a tourist in my own life. I never felt like I "fit in." I accepted funding dollars set aside for Band members and became wary of backlash from the reserve community I was never a part of. I swore an oath to Her Majesty the Queen as I was admitted to the legal Bar. I pursued a career as a civil servant with the Canadian state. I act as legal counsel for the Department of Indian and Northern Development Canada (DIAND) in its capacity as a modern-day Indian agent. I cautiously and tentatively express a political awareness and an Indigenousness through safe venues of committee work and workplace duties. I confine my contributions to the theoretical areas of law and policy.

In my work and on paper I can create an identity that is mine alone and has nothing to do with quantum of blood or community acceptance or traditional teachings. I write, therefore I am. I make my way as a woman in a profession seen by many in Indian country as one of the new warriors, fighting for justice with words and legal principles, turning the tables on the British common law, finding spaces for Aboriginal legal perspectives and agendas, being a role model, and trying always to find and follow the heartbeat of my own distant drum.

It's always been difficult choosing to step into this world without any sense of culture or ingrained identity. In law school I felt they took something away from me that I didn't have to lose in the first place. I was taught how to think like a lawyer; I was given an inside view and a familiarity with the legal prin-ciples that form the basis of our society and institutions and government. That same government employs me now. It is difficult to be an Aboriginal person in this government department where the Crown litigates/defends against Aboriginals; where we as solicitors are the go-betweens among the DIAND and the First Nations, advising on what can and cannot be done with reserve lands and Indian monies. It is difficult because there are many fantastic people here who do an excellent job in spite of the regulatory and historical mess, yet there is much room for change and improvement. There are ideas that need to be talked about, solutions that need to be discovered, policies and assump-tions that need to be questioned in order to get the work done and reach the goal of true reconciliation.

I am not a radical person, I was not raised that way, and the words feel funny in my mouth. I only understand a fraction of all the possible arguments and counter-arguments and I'm only a small voice and a tiny cog in this machine. Yet, I do believe that the best way to change the system is from within. This is where the policies are made, the laws drafted, the files managed; it's where the human beings are on the front lines of the Crown-Aboriginal relationship making small daily decisions. I would like to believe that it only takes a few open-minded, sympathetic, properly placed people to change things, to change minds, to change perspectives. I try myself to understand others' perspectives so that I can understand the systemic impulses. Possibly, if we share our common frustrations, we can learn patience and tolerance together. I don't want to be a spokesperson yet I don't want to be invisible; I don't want to be isolated or silenced, yet I don't want to be a government puppet; it's a tough road, requiring skills that I know I haven't fully developed.

In my personal life I want to be able to give my children something more than a culture of loss and legacy of colonialism, of residential school trauma, of a *kohkum* they barely knew, of traditions that their mother lacks the ability and genuineness to guide them in. For what do I know of Native culture and traditions?

What I know of being Native I learned from growing up and going to school in a mixed Native and non-Native rural setting. We lived in a small farming community and commuted to school in the neighbouring mostly First Nations village and then later to high school in the mostly non-Native populated town. Though I knew my mother was Native, the kids at school categorized me as *mooniyaw* or "white-man" because my closest friends were non-Native. I felt more comfortable with the non-Native kids but I knew in the back of my mind that I had closer ties with the Native families of the community; many of their mothers and aunties knew my mother's family and even babysat my brother and me when we were smaller. Unsure of how to make my way in the world, I soon formed my own identity in academics. Rather than being known as the white kid or the Métis girl. I was known as the smarty-pants.

What I know then of being Aboriginal I learned from books and media and my post-secondary education. I acquired an intellectual understanding of issues and theories in a pan-Aboriginal context. As I did not have a guide into the world of my ancestors, I immersed myself in studying largely non-Aboriginal views of Aboriginal Canadian history, politics, and law.

What I know then about being Indian I learned through school and through my job as a federal government lawyer interpreting and applying the *Indian Act* and other legislation applicable to Aboriginal people and their lands. I know about laws and history and politics and I have a unique perspective on legal theory, case law, and government policies as they relate to Indians. All this knowledge has been mostly book knowledge, mostly paper knowledge. Words on a page provide refuge but also unintended distance from people and community.

The only things I know about being First Nations I learned from being a member of my mother's Band and having off-reserve voting rights. My mother's people in northern Alberta went from identifying themselves as the Lubicon Lake Band to the Lubicon Lake First Nation. Now, as part of the neighbouring Woodland Cree First Nation who received a settlement from the federal government in 1989, I receive referendum packages in the mail whenever there is an important community issue. On my admittance to the Alberta Bar and Law Society, the Band Council sent a representative who presented me with handcrafted gifts, which I display in my office as a reminder of how close and how distant I am from my mother's people.

Similarly what I know about having Treaty status I learned from receiving certain benefits such as education funding and healthcare. Though these provisions are in the Treaties, the kind of membership and benefits they bring are government-driven and are not meaningful to my identity search. I still have no real connections to the people and the community of my First Nation. Over the years in my search I have found connections with other similarly situated people, students, researchers. I have formed bonds with a like-minded and accessible group, the Métis.

What I know about being Métis, I learned from my new husband, his family, and our friends who belong to this wonderful strong and proud community who have merged two cultures. I feel accepted here and at home. I will continue to try to learn what I can about my Cree culture and background. I have the opportunity to do so through my mother's extended family, uncles, and aunts and cousins. Depending on where my journey takes me I may always feel like a paper Indian, and I may never be able to fully reconcile all the parts of my Aboriginal and non-Aboriginal identity, but with time and through building connections I hope I can become more comfortable with those parts of my identity that were lost.

When my brother and I were separated from our mother, it was not only the loss of a parent that we had to live with, it was the loss of a cohesive identity. It was a part of ourselves that was not understood and not encouraged by our non-Native grandparents. And what about my mother's identity? What about her story? Who is qualified to tell it? From the day she left us, everything that went wrong in my brother's life and my life, our mother would feel guilty about. My divorce, my brother's health problems, his dissatisfaction with his job, my bouts of unhappiness. Besides this self-imposed guilt, there were many other obstacles and challenges my mother faced in her life, some of her own making, others arising from the unlucky fact that she was a Native person in a certain period of history in her country.

In the end, I only had the opportunity of knowing my mother for a short period in both our lives. I will have to learn how to negotiate this grief. This mourning, though not completely unfamiliar, will not necessarily have a recognizable end. We've lost a shared future—a future of family and life events, weddings, births, celebrations, accomplishments. She did not raise me, I was denied this. She cannot now be my adult parent and my direct link to a lost culture; this is denied as well. Perhaps paper Indians are only accorded this legacy of denial and culture of loss.

I and other women with similar experiences must parent ourselves; we must deal with our own loss and the dysfunctions in our families and communities. I wanted a *kohkum* for my children. I wanted so many things that were taken from me before I even knew I wanted them. Perhaps that is why paper Indians, like me, choose to live in a paper world. We find it difficult sometimes to live in a world where nothing is made up, where everything is real, where people suffer and children hurt and mothers die.

I search for meaning in my mother's life story, in her Nativeness, in mine. I must learn what is needed of me. My voice wavers with the weight of it. My tears blur my vision. My anger betrays me. My eyes strain to see who is friend. My ears listen between the lines. My hands work for answers to questions posed at the dawn of my country. My skills and my intelligence guide me through the landscape of misconceptions, mistakes, mismanagement. My quest is for a kind of justice previously unknown in this country, a justice that honours our parents' journeys and gives our children hope.

I was three when my mother left the first time. I was thirty-five when she left for good. She was too young. Too damaged. Too innocent. And sadly, in this post-colonial world, her experience is all too common.

Originally published in Canadian Woman Studies/les cahiers de la femme, *"Indigenous Women in Canada: The Voices of First Nations, Inuit and Métis Women," 26 (3 & 4) (Winter/Spring 2008): 204-207. Reprinted with permission of the author.*

Apryl Gladue is of Cree and English/Dutch descent and makes her life in Edmonton, Alberta, with her husband, Lorne, and their children and step-children. She is a member of the Woodland Cree First Nation. She obtained her law degree from the University of Alberta in 1998 and works for Justice Canada as a Solicitor in the Aboriginal Law Section. She is part of various government committees focused on reconciliation and Aboriginal employment issues. She is also a published short-story writer.

CONFRONTING THE
CANADIAN LEGAL SYSTEM

KATE MONTURE

FREEDOM

Smashed bottles, cover the floor.
Like a liquid mirror.
All I can see is the old us.
Back to the old us, who were strong,
but now we are breakable, like bottles.
I try picking up those pieces,
knowing that I may never find all of them.
I want us to be the liquid in the bottle.
It is so lucky, always flowing as one;
it can easily fit back together if separated.
It will always belong to that liquid chaos.
I wish we had that,
that invisible wall, that strong sturdy wall.
It seems so great at times,
always protects them.

But we are like broken bottles,
strong and sturdy, when together.
But when broken, when separated,
we are weak.
We should be the liquid in the bottle,
working as one, flowing as one,
so when the walls crumble,
we can flow over those pieces,
and be free.

Published in Canadian Woman Studies/les cahiers de la femme, *"Women and Canadian Multiculturalism," 27 (2 & 3) (Summer/Fall 2009). Reprinted with permission of the author.*

Kate Monture is Mohawk from Grand River Territory and also has ties through her father to the Thunderchild First Nation (Cree) in Saskatchewan.

"THE LEAST MEMBERS OF OUR SOCIETY"

*T*HIS ELOQUENT PLEA WAS *presented to the Canadian government in 1978. It chronicles the desperate situation of Indian women who have lost their Indian status through their marriage to Indians without status or to non-Indians. A speech given by Native activist Mary Two-Axe Early at the Canadian Research Institute on the Advancement of Women conference in Edmonton in October 1979 is also included.*

"We, the Mohawk Indian women of Caughnawaga who have lost our status through marriage to Indians without status or non-Indians, present our plea for justice and for the recognition of our legitimate rights to the Canadian people.

Some of us live on the Caughnawaga Indian Reserve, our Iroquois tribal lands that date back to 1674. We live under the constant threat of eviction by the Band Council. Others have already been forced off the Reserve and live in homes in and around Montreal.

Our tribal Chiefs were abolished in the 1890s. The government then instituted the elective system which had its origins in Europe. This was supposed to be a temporary measure but it has continued to the present day. According to anthropologists and leading North American historians, the Iroquois Indians had a strong sociopolitical structure. The great Iroquois Confederacy was held together by a sociopolitical system of clans, headed by women, in a true matrilineal political and familial system, the like of which was never witnessed in other tribes of North or South American Native Peoples. The clan system of family, government, and social organization was the foundation upon which a political structure was built. This uniquely democratic structure of government has been acclaimed by historians to be the model for modern democratic representative government.

It seems strange that a people nurtured by such a heritage would adopt a foreign patriarchal system and then that they would use this system as a legal basis for stripping us women, who have married non-Indians or Indians without status, of our cultural identity and our legal status as Indians. It seems inconceivable that our biological constitution should be reason enough for our birthright and heritage to be arbitrarily divested at the moment that we enter into a sacred union with another child of God. Although the same blood flows in our veins and the same views and beliefs are forever a part of our self-conscious being; the same memories of our traditions, folklore and customs are imprinted in our subconscious; the same Indian words pass over our tongues; we are said to have lost these our Indian cultural assets, as though they were tangibles that can be freely given or taken.

Let us chronicle our pain, point by point:

1. When the Great Spirit calls us we cannot be buried alongside our ancestors in the traditional burial grounds where their bodies have gone to rest. This is the most cruel condition of our imposed exile. Yet people from the neighbouring city of Montreal can bury their dogs on selected plots of Reserve land.

2. We cannot inherit property given to us by our ancestors or bestow property to our children. It is as though we were non-entities, not to be accorded the normal recognition afforded to all free people.

3. We are prohibited from exercising the right to political participation, including the right to vote and to advocate the candidacy of those worthwhile persons who could be an asset to our people.

4. We cannot be Indian in word or action. We are the victims of cultural genocide.

In 1968, thirty of us Mohawk Indian women, who had lost our status by marriage to non-Indians, came together under the leadership of Mary Two-Axe Early, a grandmother of wholly Indian blood and of proud spirit. It was the beginning of our struggle to create a public awareness of our plight.

We prepared a brief, chartered a bus and travelled to Ottawa to present the brief to the Royal Commission on the Status of Women. In Ottawa, we were met by the Honourable Grace McGinnis, MP, and by Senator Thérèse Casgrain, the foremost fighter for women's rights in Quebec. She was to become one of our staunchest allies.

The main arguments of our presentation can be briefly summarized:

1. A non-Indian woman who marries a male member of the Band assumes all the rights and privileges that their Indian husbands possess, as specified in the *Indian Act*. They can vote on major issues affecting the life of the community. They are also allowed to participate in the direct election of Band councilors. There are over two hundred male members of the Band who are married to non-Indian women of Danish, Irish, French, German, Italian, Polish or English ancestry. We feel that their voting block represents a continuous threat to the preservation of Indian cultural life. It is Indian women who can enlighten the non-Indian wives on Indian thought and culture so that it can be perpetuated. We believe that we should retain the right to vote along with our non-Indian sisters.

2. The children of marriages between Indian males and non-Indian females are accorded the full rights and privileges of the father. Children raised by white mothers tend to identify with white culture because mothers are the culture

bearers of the society. Our children are raised in the customs and traditions of the Indian people, yet they are not recognized as Indians by the *Indian Act*.

3. The Indians of Canada are entitled to educational benefits at a primary, secondary and post-secondary level. With marriage to a non-Indian, the Indian woman loses these benefits, and although our educational needs may be much greater than those of our white sisters, it is the non-Indian wife who gains these benefits. On our Reserve, the children of Indian women who have lost their status are bused many miles to white schools, where they often encounter racist attitudes against them. In the United States, the Department of the Interior extends educational benefits to all persons of one-quarter Indian blood regardless of lineage. We should follow the example set by the United States.

4. According to the *Indian Act*, an Indian woman who marries outside of the Band must sell or dispose of her property within ninety days. This infringes upon a woman's natural right to use her property. We believe that it should be our right to inherit and bequeath property as we choose, as long as this property remains among the people of one-quarter or more Indian ancestry.

Our brief was well received and positive recommendations to end the discrimination of the *Indian Act* appeared in the final report of the Royal Commission on the Status of Women.

In 1973, we affiliated our group with *Indian Rights for Indian Women*, a national organization based in Edmonton. The history of these first Indian women's rights groups will become a part of the history of Canada, because our struggle has become a unifying force as the women of Canada rally behind our cause.

In 1975, the United Nations International Year of Women, the base of support spread to women's groups across Canada, backed by the support of the National Action Committee on the Status of Women. When we discovered that Indian women were not to be represented by the official Canadian delegation to the International Women's Conference in Mexico, an appeal was launched for funds to send our president, Mary Two-Axe Early. Money was donated by the National Action Committee and by a sympathetic Quebec government.

While she was in Mexico attending the conference, Mary Two-Axe received the news that she had been evicted from her family home on the Reserve. Mary spoke from the podium at the Tribunal with passionate anger and sorrow and three thousand women delegates from all over the world listened and, for the first time, learned of the shameful treatment accorded to the Indian women of Canada. The delegates unanimously voted their support and cablegrams were sent to Prime Minister Trudeau; the Minister responsible for the Status of Women, Marc Lalonde; and the Minister of Indian Affairs, Judd Buchanan. With the resulting world publicity, the cause of the nonstatus Indian women became an international issue.

The government of Canada not only failed to respond to this international pressure but also, in June, 1977, passed to the Senate Committee for approval Bill C-25, the new Human Rights legislation, which made no provisions for the protection of the rights of Indian women. It might have passed without comment but for the intervention and courageous protest of Senator Joan Neiman. We are grateful for the friendship of Canadian women who have taken personal and political risks to raise their voices in our defence.

It is important for the Canadian people to know how the provisions of the *Indian Act*, which discriminate against Indian women, put Canada in violation of its obligations to the United Nations.

The Charter of the United Nations recognizes the equal rights of men and women in the Preamble and Purposes. Article 2 expressly imposes upon members the duty of fulfilling 'in good faith, the obligations assumed by them in accordance with the present charter.' Provisions of the *Indian Act* which violate the equality of men and women under the Charter therefore violate Canada's obligations to the United Nations.

The Universal Declaration of Human Rights Article 16 (1) provides that men and women 'are entitled to equal rights as to marriage, during marriage and at its dissolution.' Article 16 (3) states that 'the family is entitled to protection by society and the state.' When the Indian Act protects only the rights of male Indians, it is in violation of this Declaration.

The Convention on the Nationality of Married Women provides that marriage shall not affect the nationality of women. Canada has ratified this Convention. It is a clear violation of the spirit of this Convention, if not the actual wording, for Canada to use the *Indian Act* to take away an Indian woman's Indian 'nationality.'

If Canada whishes to continue to enjoy world esteem as a free and democratic country, it must give equality to Indian women. We have no wish to shame our country in the eyes of the world but the United Nations may become our last court of appeal.

There is still time to resolve this injustice within Canada and with honour.

The *Indian Act* was proclaimed into law in 1951, without prior consultation with the Indian people. The National Indian Brotherhood is presently working with a joint government committee to draft legislation for a new act to be ready by 1980. Indian women are not represented on that committee and their opinions have not been solicited.

Our brothers have betrayed us. We have suffered with them the indignities of the white man's *Indian Act*. Now we walk the trail alone through the 'Peaks of Hope' and the 'Valleys of Despair': the 'Peaks of Hope' in knowing that millions of fair-minded and justice-seeking citizens of Canada and other democratic countries support our position and empathize with our efforts, and the Valleys of Despair in the realization that chauvinistic men, steeped in patriarchal heritage, would see injustice in the name of 'Well that's the law, Babe.' A 'Valley of Despair' as each sun sets with the knowledge that another day has passed wherein thousands of Indian women have had to live as second class citizens, facing the world and their people as non-entities. Days filled with tension and the stress of dealing with families who are divided by these issues.

"…We Indian women stand before you as 'the least members of your society.' You may ask yourself why. First, we are excluded from the protections of the *Canadian Bill of Rights* or the intercession of human rights commission because the *Indian Act* supercedes the laws governing the majority. Second we are subject to a law wherein the only equality is the unequality of treatment of both status and non-status women. Third, we are subject to the punitive actions of dictatorial chiefs half-crazed with newly acquired powers bestowed by a government concerned with their self-determination. Fourth, we are stripped naked of any legal protection and raped by those who would take advantage of the inequities afforded by the *Indian Act*.

Raped because we cannot be buried beside the mothers who bore us and the fathers who begot us:

•Because we are subject to eviction from the domiciles of our families and expulsion from the tribal roles.

•Because we must forfeit any inheritance or ownership of property.

•Because we are divested of the right to vote.

•Because we are ruled by chiefs steeped in chauvinistic patriarchy who are supported by the *Indian Act*, drafted by the rulers of this country over one hundred years ago.

•Because we are unable to pass our Indianness and the Indian culture that is engendered by a mother to her children.

•Because we live in a country acclaimed to be one the greatest cradles for democracy on earth offering asylum to Vietnamese refugees and other suppressed peoples while within its borders its Native sisters are experiencing the same suppression that has caused thes peoples to seek refuge by the great mother known as 'Canada.'

Three score and ten years ago I started my life's journey. I have seen man land on the moon, the development of air travel, a nation linked by modern highways, the advent of radio and television, the age of cybernetics, the development of a body of scientists so vast that here are more scientists alive today than in the whole of our past development. There was never a better or more exciting time to live on this earth or in this country. I am excited for having lived during a period that has witnessed the greatest social, political, technical and scientific advances. I am excited that this is a time of great social change for women and with your help it could be a time of great social change for Indian women, 'the least members of your society.' Perhaps tomorrow the rest of the free world will look upon the great mother 'Canada' with respect and admiration for she will have responded to our cries, amended the *Indian Act*, created a Human Rights Commission that would affect Indian women.

I have the utmost confidence that the great mother 'Canada' will engender the leadership and afford the courage to effect these changes."

—Mary Two-Axe Early

Where the weak would give up the fight, we continue to find the strength deep within ourselves to continue our search for justice.

At a press conference on June 9, 1978, Indian Affairs Minister Hugh Faulkner said that he would ask the next Parliament to eliminate discrimination against Indian women in the *Indian Act*, even if he does not have the consent of most of the Indian people. However this would not be retroactive and thus it would not help the women in the Indian women's rights groups who have been campaigning for change.

Can the Minister believe that we, who have fought so long and so hard will give up our claim to justice? Are we to abandon the sick and aged widows who seek only to end their days in the Indian community of their birthplace and to be laid to rest in their traditional burial grounds? Are we to deny the deserted wives and children the security of family life on their reserve land?

We demand in the name of humanity that the government act now to give us back our status and to alleviate the distress of these widows and mothers of children who live in fear from day to day, under the threat of eviction.

Prime Minister Pierre Elliot Trudeau, speaking in Vancouver, said: 'What can we do to redeem the past, to compensate for the injustices? We will be just today. This is all we can do. We must be just today.'

This is what we ask justice today and for all the tomorrows.

We are dedicated to Indian unity within a Canadian unity. Allied with the women of Canada, we will continue the fight against racism and poverty, neglect and despair. With our non-Indian sisters, we will become an invincible force in the cause of peace and unity."

Originally published in Canadian Woman Studies/les cahiers de la femme, *"The Decade/La décennie 1970-1980," 2 (2) (1980): 64-66.*

AKI-KWE/MARY ELLEN TURPEL

ABORIGINAL PEOPLES AND THE
CANADIAN CHARTER OF RIGHTS AND FREEDOMS

Contradictions and Challenges

Whereas Canada is founded upon principles that recognize the supremacy of God and the rule of law....
—Preamble to Part I, *Canadian Charter of Rights and Freedoms*

****

Your religion was written upon tables of stone by the iron finger of your God so that you could not forget. The Red Aboriginal people could never comprehend nor remember it. Our religion is the traditions of our ancestors—the dreams of our old men, given them in solemn hours of night by the Great Spirit; and the visions of our sachems: and it is written in the hearts of our people.
—Chief Seattle to the Governor of Washington Territory, 1854

When anthropologists, government officials, and churchmen have argued that our ways have been lost to us, they are fulfilling one of their own tribal rituals—wish fulfillment.
—Chief George Manuel, *The Fourth World*

THE CONTEMPORARY WORLD of Aboriginal politics is inhabited by discussions about rights—the right to self-government, the right to title to land, the right to equality, the right to social services, and the right to practice spiritual beliefs. None of this is very new, nor is it surprising, given that non-Aboriginal people have been writing on behalf of the "rights" of Aboriginal People since the sixteenth century.

The earliest of these works were concerned primarily with how the colonial powers (Spain) should treat the "uncivilized" and savage peoples discovered in America.[1] Many would argue that there have been no real advances in "rights" for Aboriginal people in America since the sixteenth century, but to seek advances in "rights" presupposes the acceptance of terminology. It strikes me that when Aboriginal people discuss rights and borrow the rhetoric of human rights

358

in contemporary struggle, we are using the paradigm of human rights, both nationally and internationally, as an instrument for the recognition of historic claims—and in many cases as the "only" resort. Is that really buying into the distinctly western and liberal vision of human rights concepts?

Underlying the use of human rights terminology is a plea for recognition of a different way of life, a different idea of community, of politics, of spirituality—ideas that have existed since time immemorial, but have been cast as differences to be repressed and discouraged since colonization. In asking for recognition by another culture of the existence of your own, and for toleration of, and respect for, the practical difference that it brings with it, there seems to be something at stake which is larger than human rights, and certainly larger than the texts of particular documents which guarantee human rights, such as the *Canadian Charter of Rights and Freedoms:* a more basic request—the request to be recognized as peoples. I believe that from early colonization up to the present, no government or monarch has ever genuinely recognized Aboriginal Peoples as distinct Peoples with cultures different from their own. In other words, as Peoples whose ways of life should be tolerated and respected, even though certain customs may challenge the cultural assumptions of the newcomers.

I also believe that one reason for this, aside from the obvious one of the assertion of government power and the quest for economic dominance, is that Aboriginal ways have been and still are presumed to be primitive, in the sense of "lesser" states of development. This presumption denies genuine differences by presuming that another culture is the same, just not quite as "civilized" yet. Hence, it is important for the colonial governments to take jurisdiction over Aboriginal Peoples in order to guide them to a more reasoned state of being where they can become just like them (it is not surprising here that the church was usually the state's best ally).

No government has ever dealt with Aboriginal Peoples on an equal basis—without seeing us as means to an economic goal (settlement and development), as noble savages, the pagans without civilization, or as specimens for anthropological investigation and scientific collection.[2] Genuinely recognizing another People as another culture is more than recognizing rights of certain persons. It's not simply recognizing Peoples of another colour, translated in European terms as "race," nor is it recognizing the presence of a minority because the minority is always defined by and in subordination to the majority. Placing the emphasis on race or minority (and consequently on rights) has the effect of covering over the differences at work to the majority's advantage. Aboriginal cultures are not simply difference "races"—a difference explained in terms of biology (or colour): Aboriginal cultures are the manifestations of a different human (collective) imagination.

To borrow the words of a non-Aboriginal writer, Aboriginal cultures "are oriented as wholes in different directions. They are travelling along different roads in pursuit of different ends, and these ends and these means in one society cannot be judged in terms of those of another society because essentially they are incommensurable...."[3] While it seems that, in the Canadian context, Aboriginal Peoples and non-Aboriginal persons have some understanding and recognition of each other, it seems that Aboriginal Peoples have been the ones who have had to suffer for tolerance (even by force and imprisonment).[4] It is true that there have been treaties between Aboriginal Peoples and the British Crown. However, these do not amount, in my view, to a genuine recognition of diverse Indigenous cultures; they were really western-style (written in a highly legalistic form in most cases) methods to make way for progress, with "progress" defined according to the standards of the newcomers. After all, it was the British practice in almost all of the colonies, irrespective of cultural differences among those they "discovered" or "conquered." It is no wonder then, that in studying the law of treaties, we quickly learn that, according to Anglo-Canadian legal standards, treaties (even before Confederation) are not seen as agreements between sovereign Peoples or nations. When we inquire as to why treaties are not viewed as agreements between two (or more) sovereign Peoples, we are generally led to the theory that Aboriginal People (either at the time of treaty-making or now) were not sufficiently "civilized" and organized to qualify as "sovereign" Peoples, or that they had already "lost" their sovereignty through some predestined and mysterious process (for example, by virtue of being "discovered").

Of course, there is no compelling reason, according to the doctrines and principles of international law, to view treaties between Aboriginal Peoples and the Crown as anything other than treaties between sovereigns, or *international* treaties. Nor does there seem to be any com pelling reason for continuing to pretend that Aboriginal Peoples do not have distinct cultures, cultures which are deserving of recognition by the dominant (European) one which has been imposed in Canada. Why is it then that Aboriginal Peoples, and Aboriginal claims, must be "fit in" to the categories and concepts of a dominant culture, in some form of equivalence, in order to be acknowledged? There appears to be a contradiction at work in areas like human rights—that is, a contradiction between pretending, on the one hand, to accept Aboriginal Peoples as distinct Peoples, and, on the other, of accepting something called Aboriginal Peoples' rights. This contradiction, which I explore briefly in the following pages, has lead to a great deal of misunderstanding, and has given the dominant culture (as represented by the government of Canada) plenty of scope in which to manoeuvre, while avoiding a difference-based approach to Aboriginal Peoples as equals or as sovereigns.

"Aboriginal rights" are a category, primarily a category of law, in which most discussions about our historic claims and cultural differences are carried out in Canadian society. It is a category with severe limitations politically and legally; limitations which have been set, whether or not intentionally, by those who thought up the category—mostly non-Aboriginal people. It is a realm in which discussions focusing on strange expressions like "title," "usufructory rights," "mere premises," "status," "referential incorporation," "extinguishment," and "existing" take on enormous significance, even though they do not seem to have anything to do with the everyday lives of Aboriginal people. A frightening and frustrating thing about the centrality of these expressions is that they were thought up by the same non-Aboriginal people that brought us the "rights" category: they seem incompatible with Aboriginal ideas about land, family, social life, and spirituality. Yet somehow they are supposed to be helping us out, assisting us in our struggle to continue to practice our cultures. Could it be that they just serve to limit the possibilities for genuine acknowledgement of the existence of Aboriginal Peoples as distinct cultures and political communities possessing the ability to live without external regulation and control?

I chose the first two quotations prefacing this article to illustrate the contradiction here—a Charter based on the supremacy of a foreign God and the (Anglo-American) rule of law just doesn't seem to be the kind of constitution that Aboriginal Peoples can get too excited about. Rather, it is the kind of constitution that we can get angry about because it has the effect of excluding Aboriginal vision(s) and (diverse) views about the land and the society now called Canada. Clearly, as a historical document, it represents only one story of Canada—that is, the story of the colonialists. As a document held out to be the "supreme law of Canada" (according to Section 52 of the *Constitution Act*, 1982), it represents an act of ethno-centrism and domination, acknowledging at no point The Great Law of customary laws of the First Peoples of this territory (except unless through wish-fulfillment; section 35 is read this way).[5]

Could Aboriginal spirituality ever be represented by the likes of the preamble to the *Canadian Charter of Rights and Freedoms*? Do Chief Seattle's words render this impossible? Are we travelling along a different road, one that doesn't need formal written declarations to convince ourselves of what kinds of societies we are? Should we even try to do things this way? Who are we trying to please in doing so? Is it inevitable that Aboriginal traditions and customs have to take the form of "rights" which are brought to courts, proven to exist then enforced? Isn't the fundamental problem here the fact that everything has to be adjusted to fit the terms of the dominant system?

I view the problems in the Aboriginal Peoples-human rights area as further evidence of the fact that the dominant culture has never recognized Aboriginal Peoples as distinct Peoples and cultures. I suppose that the exclusion or repression of the "Aboriginal fact" of Canada in the present *Constitution Act*, in a strange way, bolsters the idea that Aboriginal Peoples are sovereign and distinct (yet entrapped) nations. Unless there was a conscious strategy of "ignore them and they'll go away," one would presume more ink would have been spilt on setting out the nature of the relationship between the Crown and the First Peoples of Canada; or at least mentioning it more directly than in two perfunctory sections in the *Constitution Act*.

Larger questions loom over all of these problems. What does it mean for Aboriginal Peoples to advance claims enveloped in the rhetoric of human rights? While there is no question that there are serious human problems in Aboriginal communities that seem to warrant redress as "human rights" violations, are such claims too piecemeal? Is there a difference between having discrete "rights" incrementally recognized, and being recognized as a People? What alternative to rights-based claims are available? In the very pragmatic-oriented work of human rights lawyers and activists in Canada—in discourses about litigation strategies and legal doctrines—there hardly seems to be an opportunity to stop and consider these kinds of questions about Aboriginal rights and the *Canadian Charter of Rights and Freedoms*. I wonder to what extent those who support struggles for the recognition of Aboriginal rights have considered these issues?

Generally, we have never had to address these problems during the first five years of the *Charter* because we were preoccupied with negotiations to recognize (both within the *Charter* and within another specific section of the *Constitution Act*) the "right to self-government."[6] When these negotiations failed miserably at the final meeting of First Ministers in 1986, a failure which was something of a foregone conclusion given that Aboriginal Peoples were never seen as equal parties in the negotiation process from the beginning (instead we were given special "observer" status), people returned to the *Charter* and the vague provision on Aboriginal Rights in section 35 of the *Constitution Act* to consider legal challenges and claims based upon these provisions. It is my belief that questions regarding which forums and laws are especially urgent now and can hardly be avoided any longer, especially in light of the fact that Aboriginal Peoples are turning more so to the *Charter* for recognition of their rights *vis-a-vis* the Canadian Crown, and perhaps more disturbingly, turning to the *Charter* to fight out internal battles in communities.

I would like to explore some of the layers of contradiction or conflict that are raised in the context of Aboriginal Peoples' claims and the *Charter,* and describe briefly an effort to meet one aspect of these contradictions which has been made by Aboriginal women through the Native Women's Association of Canada. The views put forward here are my own, many of which have been developed in the course of advising the Native Women's Association of Canada on human rights matters in recent years. I have been greatly influenced in these questions by situations facing the Association and its constituents, and by both my mixed education and ancestry![7] I don't propose to consider in any detail traditional and customary practices of specific Aboriginal Peoples, both for reasons of the limits of space here and because I have reservations about the extent to which knowledge about these matters can be transmitted in such a medium. There is valuable information on Iroquois customs and the idea of rights in the article in this collection entitled, "Our World," by Osennontion and Skonaganleh:rá.

THE ORIGINS OF HUMAN RIGHTS

While it might seem obvious that human rights and the *Canadian Charter of Rights and Freedoms* are incompatible with Aboriginal culture and traditions, it is helpful to trace the origin of the idea of human rights in the modern era in order to locate the differences here. The Anglo-American concept of rights was set out, for the most part, by two seventeenth century English political theorists, Thomas Hobbes and John Locke. Locke is the more famous of the two on these matters. He developed a theory of "natural rights"—later "human" came to be substituted for "natural," after the recognition (post-Holocaust) that Peoples are capable of barbaric actions in the name of what is "natural." Locke's theory of natural rights was based around his idea that every *man* (and emphasis should be on *man* because Locke is also famous for his theory that society was naturally patriarchal) possesses a right to private property, or the right to own property. This right, he suggested, flowed from the fact the human beings are God's property ("God" as in the preamble to the *Canadian Charter*). He argued that people enter into "civil society" for the central, and negatively conceived, purpose of protecting their right to private property against random attack (see Locke).

The idea of the absolute right to property, as an exclusive zone of ownership, capable of being transmitted through the family (through males according to a doctrine called "primogenitor"), is the cornerstone of the idea of rights—the idea that there is a zone of absolute individual right where the individual can do what he chooses: "The right is a loaded gun that the right holder may shoot at will in his corner of town" (Unger). It doesn't take much of a stretch of the imagination to see where slavery and the subordination of women found legitimacy in the Anglo-American tradition—with absolute ownership of property, and autonomous domains, "naturally"rights will extend "even to another person's body" (Hobbes).

Although there is no pan-Aboriginal culture of an ironclad system of beliefs, this notion of rights based on individual ownership is antithetical to the widely shared understanding of creation and stewardship responsibilities of First Nations Peoples for the land or for Mother Earth. Moreover, to my knowledge, there are nonotions among Aboriginal Nations of living together for the purposes of protecting an individual interest in property. Aboriginal life has been set out in stories handed down through generations and in customary laws sometimes represented by wampum belts, sacred pipes, medicine bundles and rock paintings. For example, the teachings of the Four Directions is that life is based on four principles—trust, kindness, sharing and strength. While these are responsibilities that each person owes to others, they represent the larger function of social life—that is, to honour and respect Mother Earth. There is no equivalent of "rights" here because there is no equivalent to the ownership of private property. The collective or communal bases of Aboriginal life does not have a parallel to individual rights; they are incommensurable. To try to explain to an Elder that, under Canadian law, there are carefully worked over doctrines pertaining to who owns every square inch of the country, the sky, the ocean, and even the moon, would provoke disbelief and profound sadness.

THE STRUCTURE OF THE CANADIAN CHARTER

Nevertheless, the Canadian human rights system, having been distanced in time and space somewhat from its origin and conceptual basis in the theories about the right to individual ownership to property seems a little less foreign, especially since so much is said of Aboriginal matters in the context of human rights. Some writers even argue that in Canada, thee *Charter* recognized certain collective rights, such as Aboriginal rights, and not merely individual rights. However, my reading of the law leads me to believe that the individual property basis of human rights is still entirely with us and is revealed clearly in the text of the *Canadian Charter*, as well as in recent cases that have been decided under the *Charter*. The language of the *Charter* refers to the human rights enjoyed by "every citizen of Canada," "every one," "every individual," "any person," etc. The section of the *Charter* on enforcement applies to "[a]ny *one* whose rights or freedoms ... have been infringed," permitting them to apply to a court for the order the court considers appropriate in the circumstances—almost always the singular subject.

The extent to which a human rights law set out in such individualist terms could ever either (i) be interpreted as including a collective understanding of rights, or (ii) lead to judges acknowledging that other Peoples might not base their social relations on these individual "rights" notions, is highly questionable. There is nothing strong enough in the *Charter* to allow for either a collectivist idea of rights (or responsibilities), if such a theory is conceivable, or toleration of a community organized around collective values. When cases involving Aboriginal Peoples come before the courts, it is doubtful that different standards of legal analysis will be applied. Already the case law has taken a disturbing course from the viewpoint of Aboriginal Peoples.

With shades of private property notions in mind, the Supreme Court of Canada in the recent Morgentaler case on abortion, suggested that "the rights guaranteed in the *Charter* erect around each individual, metaphorically speaking, an invisible fence over which the state will not be allowed to trespass. The role of the courts is to map out, piece by piece, the parameters of the fence" (*Morgentaler et al v. The Queen and Att. Gen. of Canada* 1988). In an earlier decision, involving Aboriginal persons (*Bovery, Canada*), the Federal Court (1986) of Canada took the view that, "in the absence of legal provisions to the contrary, the interests of individual persons will be deemed to have precedence over collective rights. In the absence of law to the contrary, this must be as true of Indian Canadians as of others."

Even in the area of language rights—an area said to be a cornerstone of collective rights in the *Charter*—the Supreme Court of Canada in the recent case involving Quebec's former *Bill 101* has indicated that the basic understanding of this right is somehow both an individual and a collective one: "Language itself indicates, a means by which a people may express its cultural identity. It is also the means by which the individual expresses his or her personal identity and sense of individuality" (*The Attorney General of Quebec & Brown & Ford & McKenna et al. v. La Chaussure Brown's Inc.*)"? Or place case title and date in in-text citation? How to go about reconciling these two aspects when they con flict is no easy task, and the Court gives little guidance here on its view of collective rights— except to say that the individual's rights to speak their language must be protected at law against the community's prohibition of it.

Even in the area of equality rights, as recognized in section 15 of the *Charter*, the text applies to "every individual." This provision has been interpreted by the courts not as a general recognition of the idea of equality (which if read as "sameness" would be deeply disturbing to Aboriginal people), but simply as a principle relating to the application of given laws. In a recent equality case, the Supreme Court of Canada stated that section 15, "is not a general guarantee of equality, it does not provide for equality between individuals or groups within society in a general or abstract sense, nor does it impose on individuals or groups an obligation to accord equality treatment to others. *It is concerned with the application of the law*" (*Law Society of British Columbia et al v. Andrews et al.*, emphasis added). The scope for Aboriginal rights claims under section 15 is limited, even if such a course was seen as desirable by Aboriginal leaders.

Moreover, we can begin to see the broader implications of these cases for Aboriginal Peoples or Aboriginal claims. It is difficult to move in a certain direction as a People if individuals can challenge collective decisions based on infringements of their individual rights and if collective goals will not be understood or prioritized. Some people may view this as the triumph of democracy, but it makes the preservation of a different culture and the pursuit of collective political goals almost impossible.

In Aboriginal communities where customary political and spiritual institutions are the guiding force (even alongside the imposed *Indian Act* system of Band Councils), such as the Haudenosaunee of the Iroquois Confederates, recourse to an individual-rights based law like the *Charter* could result in further weakening the cultural identity of the community. This could take one of two forms: either a member of the community would challenge Aboriginal laws based on individual rights protections in the *Charter* arguing that they have not been respected by their government (an internal challenge); or a non-Aboriginal person could challenge the laws of an Aboriginal government on the basis that they do not conform with *Charter* standards (an external challenge).

In the case of an external challenge, for example, on the basis of voting or candidacy rights where a non-Aboriginal complainant argued that they could not vote or stand for elections in an Aboriginal community because of cultural restrictions, the court would be given the authority to decide an important part of the future of an Aboriginal community. It would have to consider the protections of Aboriginal rights in the *Charter* and weigh these against the individual right to vote recognized in section 3. Should Canadian courts (and non-Aboriginal judges) have authority in these cases? Given the highly individualistic basis of the *Charter*, and of the history of human rights, would the collective Aboriginal right stand a chance? I doubt it. As the Assembly of First Nations argued, before the Parliamentary Committee on Aboriginal Affairs in 1982: "As Indian people we cannot afford to have individual rights override collective rights. Our societies have never been structured that way, unlike yours, and that is where die clash comes.... If you isolate the individual rights from the collective rights, then you are heading down another path that is even more discriminatory.... The *Canadian Charter of Rights* is in conflict with our philosophy and culture...." (Canada).

The other possible challenge, the internal challenge, where a member of an Aboriginal community felt dissatisfied with a particular course of action the Aboriginal government was taking, and turned to the *Charter* for the recognition of a right, is equally if not more worrisome. This kind of challenge would be a dangerous opportunity for a Canadian court to rule on individual versus collective rights *vis-a-vis* Aboriginal Peoples; it would also break down community methods of dispute-resolution and restoration. Here, the example of the *Indian Civil Rights Act l6* in the United States is instructive. This Act, based on the idea that protections for the *American Bill of Rights* should be extended to Aboriginal communities, along with the establishment of tribal courts that would have the same function as American courts generally, has been greatly criticized by Aboriginal people as imposing alien ways of life.

As noted scholars, Vine Deloria, Jr. and Clifford M. Lytle suggest:

> In philosophical terms, it is much easier to describe the impact of the ... Act. Traditional Indian society understood itself as a complex of responsibilities and duties. The [Act] merely transposed this belief into a society based on rights against government and eliminated any sense of responsibility that the people might have felt for one another. Granted that many of the customs that made duties and responsibilities a serious matter of individual action had eroded badly in the decades since the tribes had agreed to move to reservations, the impact of the [Act] was to make these responsibilities impossible to perform because the Act inserted the trial court as an institution between the people and their responsibilities. People did not have to confront one another before their community and resolve their problems; they had only to file suit in tribal court.

The lessons of the *American Indian Civil Rights Act*, and of the establishment of tribal courts, are important ones in light of the *Charter*. If internal disputes are brought before Canadian courts, it will seriously undermine the Aboriginal system of government based on responsibility (like the Four Directions) and interpose a system of individual-based rights. It also has the effect of encouraging people to go outside the community, and outside of custom, to settle disputes in formal courts—instead of having to deal with a problem within the community.

This might sound like a hard line to take, especially when one considers the extent to which customs and traditional methods of governance and dispute-resolution have been dislodged in Aboriginal communities after more than a century of life under the *Indian Act*. The experience of gender-based discrimination was employed as a technique of assimilation up until the 1985 amendments to the *Indian Act* (many see the gender-based discriminatory provisions as having continuing effect despite the amendments), and scarred many Aboriginal communities as male-dominated Band councils frequently sided against women and with the Canadian government in the belief that to do otherwise would undermine the Crown's trust responsibility for Aboriginal Peoples.

As a consequence, women were forced to go outside the community to resolve the injustices of gender discrimination, so cases were brought under the *Canadian Bill of Rights* and eventually under the *United Nations Covenant on Civil and Political Rights*. Changes were made to the *Indian Act*, but many of the after effects of gender discrimination still plague Aboriginal communities, including problems associated with women returning to communities, and being able to take up residence, educate their children, share in social services, and receive per capital payments from resource exploitation on Aboriginal lands.

Communities have been slow to address questions related to the aftermath of gender discrimination in the *Indian Act*, and the mechanisms available to resolve disputes according to customary practices are not necessarily available. This places a great deal of pressure on Aboriginal communities, which could lead to cases being taken to Canadian courts pursuant to the *Charter* for recognition of rights against Aboriginal governments. As a result of concern over what this could lead to, in light of the individual-based notions of rights under Canadian law, and in light of lessons derived from the United States experience with the *Indian Civil Rights Act*, Aboriginal women have been working on projects to encourage the development of First Nations laws in areas like "citizenship" and human rights and responsibilities—laws based, as far as possible, on inherent First Nation jurisdiction and customary practices.

AN ALTERNATIVE APPROACH:
FIRST NATIONS HUMAN RIGHTS AND RESPONSIBILITIES LAWS

The Native Women's Association of Canada has addressed questions relating to gender discrimination in the *Indian Act*, and related problems in Aboriginal communities since the late 1970s. In 1985, when amendments to the *Indian*

Act aimed at eliminating gender discrimination were finally passed, the Native Women's Association took the position that, while Aboriginal women could support the end of unfair bias against women, they could not simply support the Federal government's efforts to "improve" the *Indian Act* and the extension of legislative control over the lives of Aboriginal Peoples through its paternalistic provisions. Consequently, the Association turned its attention to the development of a "First Nation Citizenship Code," or a model law that would address the issues of membership or citizenship in a First Nation, but would base its principles and jurisdiction not on Canadian law, but on the inherent jurisdiction of First Nations to regulate citizenship as practices since time immemorial.

The model codes were distributed to every Aboriginal community in Canada with a letter encouraging communities to take a First Nations approach to citizenship, and not an *Indian Act* approach, and to set up local mechanisms based, as much as possible, on customary principles for settling disputes, so that problems regarding citizenship could be addressed in the community itself and not in Canadian courts. As it became clear that citizenship was not the only area of concern in communities (although the issue of Indian status was by far the most divisive), it was evident that some other efforts would need to be expended to discourage internal challenges of Aboriginal government actions getting into Canadian courts under the *Charter*. In 1986 the Native Women's Association of Canada began to consider the development of another model law, parallel to the Citizenship Codes, which would be a First Nations human rights and responsibilities law.

It appears that this Code, which at the time of writing is still in the draft stages, will be based on the inherent jurisdiction of First Nations to make laws for their Peoples. It will include a very loosely and generously worded part on human rights and responsibilities, corresponding to four groups of rights and responsibilities that come from the teachings of the Four Directions. Hence, there are the following responsibilities and rights:

- *kindness*—social rights
- *honesty*—political and civil rights
- *sharing*—economic rights
- *strength*—cultural rights.

For example, the responsibility and rights category of strength/cultural rights would include provisions on the right to pursue traditional occupations; the right to education in Aboriginal languages; the right to customary marriage and adoptions; the right to participate in ceremonies according to the laws and traditions of the Nation; and, most importantly, the recognition of the fundamental importance of Elders and spiritual leaders in the preservation of ancestral and customary law and in the health and well-being of the community as a whole.

The provisions on the model law developed by the Native Women's Association on dispute-resolution provide options for a particular community to consider in creating a law which that fits in its customs and aspirations. These include mediation, the establishment of a Human Rights Committee, and a Council of Elders. Also included are options for setting up methods to deal with conflicts on a regional basis (e.g., an Iroquois or Ojibway council of Elders). It is hoped that the work of the Association will contribute to the development of community laws and less formal community solutions to reduce the possibilities that individual members of First Nations communities will have to go outside their communities (to foreign courts) for redress of grievances. It seems that the development of community codes is the best available solution to the problems in communities and to the threat of the (further) imposition of a western individualistic human rights system on Aboriginal Communities.

FUTURE CHALLENGES

The work of the Native Women's Association of Canada only addresses the problem of internal challenges based on the *Charter* by members of First Nations communities. It does not attempt to deal with other areas of concern, such as external challenges, or claims brought by non-Aboriginal Peoples pursuant to the *Charter*, calling into question the collective basis of Aboriginal communities.[8] Even claims brought by Aboriginal communities against the Federal Government based on provisions of the *Charter* seem to present a dangerous opportunity for the court to take a restrictive view of collective-based community goals. Any case which presents a Canadian court with the opportunity to balance or weigh an individual right against a collective right, or Aboriginal collective understanding of community, will be an opportunity to delimit the recognition of Aboriginal Peoples as distinct cultures.

This is something different than dealing on an equal footing with Aboriginal Peoples about historic claims and cultural differences which have to be addressed and settled. These cases permit the court to say, "Yes, we do have jurisdiction over you, and we will decide what is best for you under Canadian law." It is not that different from the imposed system of *rule* under the *Indian Act*; except in *Charter* cases, the court can cloak its decision in the rhetoric of democratic freedom, emancipation, multiculturalism, and human rights for "all Canadians." The only way to really consider the political and cultural differences between Aboriginal Peoples and the Canadian state is through discussions that are quasi-international so that the respective "sovereignty" of the parties will be respected.

Aboriginal Peoples have been trying to pursue this (international) course during the past decade. The United Nations has established a special Working Group on Indigenous Populations to consider the human rights violations (really historic claims under international law) of Indigenous Peoples from around the globe. During the past seven years, there have been six meetings of the Working group, and recently efforts have been directed at the development of a United Nations Declaration on Indigenous Rights. Although Aboriginal Peoples have been participating quite actively in this process of development of a United Nations Declaration, once again, we are really on the outside of the United Nations system. Nevertheless, certain States that are part of the United Nations structure have been willing to advocate for the recognition of Indigenous Rights in a Declaration.[9]

The matters dealt with in the proceedings of the Working Group and in the Draft Declaration can hardly be ignored, when one considers the extent to which they are present in all areas of the globe. As one noted international scholar, Richard Falk, has suggested, "The peoples of entrapped nations are a sleeping giant in the workings of power politics" (Falk 1987). A cornerstone of an eventual declaration would have to be, from the Aboriginal perspective, a recognition and explicit extension of self-determination to Indigenous Peoples under international law. There are persuasive arguments that, even without a specific declaration, international law already recognizes the right of all Peoples (including Aboriginal Peoples) to self-determination. Self-determination is something different from self-government, although it could include the latter. Self-government (which has been the pinnacle of all human rights discussions in the Canadian context) implies that Aboriginal Peoples, who were not previously able to govern themselves because they were not at an advanced enough stage of civilization, can however now take on some responsibility for their own affairs.[10] Very few people make a distinction between self-government and self-determination. In a recent report by the Canadian Bar Association special committee on Native justice, the idea of self-government is used throughout without any distinction as to its historical context or political implications.[11] On this point, Aboriginal women in Canada, through the voice of the Native Women's Association, have again made their position in support of self-determination over self-government quite clear.[12]

In the international context, the draft declaration on Indigenous rights is silent on the issue of self-determination. It contains many disturbing provisions on lesser notions like "autonomy ... in local affairs" and the "right to exist." While these might seem progressive in some situations where the very life of Aboriginal People is systematically threatened on a daily basis, the provisions do not go far enough in recognizing Aboriginal Peoples as distinct cultures and political entities, equally as capable of governing and making decisions as European sovereigns, except with different political and cultural goals.

A great deal more work will have to be done in the next few years to ensure that the text of the Draft Declaration is one that will recognize Indigenous Peoples as legitimate, though different, governments and cultures. The only way to do this, in international law and in national law, is through a recognition of self-determination. To do this will require broad-based support from international society, manifested in the work of non-government organizations, women's movements, and sympa thetic States. The Canadian government and Canadian people could do much to assist the international process if the Government would simply recognize Aboriginal Peoples as distinct Peoples with different but equally legitimate cul tures and ways of life. This can't be done through Canadian courts and in the rhetoric of Canadian human rights—it has to be done through a joint Aboriginal-Canadian discussion process where, unlike the series of discussions held on Canadian constitutional amendments, Aboriginal Peoples are equal participants in the process, along with the Prime Minister and perhaps Provincial Premiers.

In the meantime, Aboriginal women will continue to do what can be done to ensure that Aboriginal communities are governed by customary laws and practices, through the development of First Nations laws, and through the political and spiritual voice of the Native Women's Association of Canada as guided by its Elders and affiliated women's organizations.

Originally published in Canadian Woman Studies/les cahiers de la femme, *"Native Women," 10 (2 & 3) (Summer/Fall 1989): 149-157. Reprinted with permission of the author.*

Mary Ellen Turpel-Lafond is Cree and Scottish. She was appointed British Columbia's first Representative for Children and Youth—an independent officer of the Legislature who works to support vulnerable children, particularly Aboriginal children and youth—in November 2006, for a five-year term. Ms Turpel-Lafond, who took a five-year leave from the Saskatchewan Provincial Court, was appointed to the bench in 1998. She was the Administrative Judge for Saskatoon, involved in the administration of the Provincial Court of Saskatchewan in relation to access to justice, Aboriginal justice and healing, and public outreach. She has also worked as a criminal law judge in youth and adult courts, which led her to work at developing partnerships to better serve the needs of young people in the justice system. Prior to her judicial appointment, Ms Turpel-Lafond was a lawyer in Nova Scotia and Saskatchewan and a tenured professor of law at Dalhousie University Faculty of Law. As a practicing lawyer, she has appeared before all levels of Courts in Canada, including the Supreme Court of Canada, on behalf of Aboriginal individuals, bands, and organizations. She has received numerous awards, scholarships, grants and honours, including three honourary doctorates from the University of Regina (2003), Mount Saint Vincent University (2005), and Thompson Rivers University (2009). Ms Turpel-Lafond is a member of the Muskeg Lake Cree Nation in Saskatchewan and the mother of four children, which she considers her greatest opportunity for learning and growth as a person. The article appearing in this collection was written when Ms Turpel-Lafond was a professor of law at Dalhousie Law School many years ago.

[1]See, for instance, Bartolomé de Las Casa, *The Tears of the Indians* (tr. John Phillips, 1656), and Francisco deVitoria, *De Indis Et De Ivre Belli Relectiones* (tr. Ernest Nys, 1917).

[2]Here I am mindful of the rise of the museums of so-called "natural history", which were dedicated to the study of primitive peoples and the collection of cultural objects for display as curiosities. It was not only cultural or spiritual objects that were collected during the rise of the museum and curatorial science, but also human specimens. For example, see Kenn Harper, *Give Me My Father's Body*, or a recent article in *Harper's Magazine* (March 1989) suggesting that the New York Museum of Natural History has the skeletal remains of 15,000 Aboriginal persons in its collection, each carefully boxed and numbered.

[3]See Ruth Benedict, *Patterns of Culture.*

[4]To cite just a few examples, the prohibition of the potlatch under the *Indian Act*, the burning of the longhouses of the Iroquois Confederacy at the turn of the century, and the convictions of the Innu in Labrador for protesting low-level military flights over their territory.

[5]Aboriginal rights are mentioned only twice within the text of the *Constitution Act*, 1982. The first is in the *Charter*, in section 25 interpretative provision which provides (in part) that "[t]he guarantee in this *Charter* of certain rights and freedoms shall not be construed to abrogate or derogate from any Aboriginal, treaty or other rights or freedoms that pertain to the Aboriginal peoples of Canada..."; the second is in Part II of the *Constitution Act* in section 35 which recognizes and affirms "existing Aboriginal and treaty rights."

[6]Of course, not all Aboriginal Peoples participated in this process of negotiation. Many perceived it as a process designed to compromise historic claims and treaties in a document (the *Canadian Constitution*), which would suit the needs of the Federal and Provincial governments first, and Aboriginal Peoples second.

[7]Mixed education meaning both formal legal training, and the significant teachings of my Grandmothers, Sisters, and the Lodge; and mixed ancestry—Cree and Anglo-Canadian, which seems to focus the mind on contradictions like those discussed in this article.

[8]Section 25 of the *Charter* mentioned in footnote 5 above is supposed to guard against such challenges, but it is difficult to predict whether the court will take a generous view in favour of collective rights, especially when everything else in the *Charter*, and in the history of human rights, seems to be directed to the protection of the individual from the community or government.

[9]The Scandinavian states have been particularly supportive here.

[10]The idea that Aboriginal communities are not sufficiently advanced enough to control their own affairs is recognized in the *Indian Act*, where, under the provisions for Band Council control over financial decisions, a band can make laws for financial issues only when the Minister determines whether or not they reached a sufficient stage of "development."

[11]See, *Aboriginal Rights in Canada: An Agenda for Action.*

[12]They have done so through a special declaration adopted (unanimously) at an Annual Meeting (Whitehorse, 1986).

REFERENCES

Aboriginal Rights in Canada: An Agenda for Action. Ottawa: Canadian Bar Association, 1988.

Andrews et al v. Law Society of British Columbia et al. [1989] 1 S.C.R. 143, 36 C.R.R. 193 (Mr. Justice McIntyre).

Benedict, Ruth. *Patterns of Culture.* New York: New American Library, c1934.

Bovery, Canada. [1986] 35 N.R. 305. (Mr. Justice MacGuigan).

Canada. Parliament. House of Commons. Standing Committee on Aboriginal Affairs. (Minutes and Proceedings ... Evidence no. 58, September 29, 1982).

Casa, Bartolomé de Las. *The Tears of the Indians.* Tr. John Phillips. London: Printed by J. C. for Nath. Brook, 1656.

Deloria, Jr., Vine, and Clifford M. Lytle. *The Nations Within: The Past and Future of American Indian Sovereignty.* New York: Pantheon Books, 1984.

Falk, Richard. "Promise of Natural Communities." *The Rights of Indigenous Peoples in International Law.* Ed. Ruth Thompson. Saskatoon: University of Saskatchewan, Native Law Centre: 1987.

Harper, Kenn. *Give Me My Father's Body: The Life of Minik, the New York Eskimo.* Frobisher Bay, N.W.T.: Blacklead Books, cke, J1986.

Hobbes, Thomas. *Leviathan.* New York: Dutton, 1973 [1651].

Indian Civil Rights Act 16. U.S. Statutes at Large, 82: 77.

Locke, John. *Two Treatises of Government.* New York: Hafner, 1947 [1689].

Morgentaler, Smoling and Scott v. Her Majesty the Queen and the Attorney General of Canada. [1988] 1 S.C.R. 164. (Madame Justice Wilson).

The Attorney General of Quebec v. La Chaussure Brown's Inc. and Ford and McKenna Inc. et al, [1988] 2 S.C.R. 712.

Unger, Roberto Mangabeira. *The Critical Legal Studies Movement.* Cambridge: Harvard University Press, 1986.

Vitoria, Francisco de. *De Indis et De Ivre Belli Relectiones.* Tr. Ernest Nys. Washington: The Carnegie Institute of Washington, 1917.

SHARON D. MCIVOR

ABORIGINAL WOMEN'S RIGHTS AS "EXISTING RIGHTS"

ABORIGINAL WOMEN OF CANADA have struggled since 1967 to have their right to identity and their civil and political rights recognized. Part of this battle included changing century-old provisions in the *Indian Act* which banished women from their families and communities by forcing them to give up their Indian status, Band membership, and, essentially, their identity as Aboriginal women if they married outside their race (Leslie and Macguire 25).[1] The Tory government amended the *Indian Act* in June 1985 through Bill C-31. Aboriginal women's struggle continues, however, as some Indian Chiefs are trying to overturn the amendments in court, claiming they interfere with their jurisdiction to determine membership in their own communities. It is my position that the civil and political rights of Indian women are fundamental human rights, and that they are Aboriginal rights which are now recognized under section 35(1) of the *Constitution Act, 1982*.[2] These rights have never be extinguished and they continue to exist.

Under the *Indian Act*, when Indian women married non-Indians they were banished from their communities and their legal right to be "Indian" was stripped from them. Indian women who married members of the "settler" community were excommunicated from Indian reserves and never allowed to return, even upon divorce. This denied their right and their ability to participate in elections of *Indian Act* Chiefs and Councillors, as well as removing their ability to choose to live on the reserve and to remain part of their Aboriginal community. The *Indian Act* provisions directly affected 12,000 Indian women, and constituted a severe restriction on their exercise of their civil and political rights. In 1985, these women and approximately 40,000 descendants were restored to their previous Indian status and Band membership.

One form of regulation with respect to political rights was removed when the intermarriage provisions were amended. Sex discrimination still exists in the *Indian Act* in the area of civil and property rights, however, and needs to be challenged under the *Canadian Charter of Rights and Freedoms* (hereafter *Charter)*. Because marital property rights for Canadians is governed by provincial law and not federal law, in cases of Indian divorces involving land on Indian reserves, the wife is legally disadvantaged compared to other Canadian women.

374

There is no federal law granting rights to women in cases of marital dispute or separation, and the Supreme Court of Canada has held in *Derrickson U. Derrickson* and *Paul v. Paul* that where there is a conflict between federal and provincial law, federal law prevails in the case of Indians. Also, wives of Indians living on reserve cannot enjoy any benefits related to possession of land in the event of divorce from an Indian male unless they own the land in their own name, with the blessing of the Band Council and the Minister of Indian and Northern Affairs. There is also continuing sex discrimination against Indian women which impacts upon their voting or political rights because 98 per cent of reinstated women and their children cannot vote for Chiefs and Council because they do not live on the reserve This is an estimated 12,000 Indian women who regained status and their estimated 40,000 descendants in the first generation. Their second-generation descendants are discriminated against compared to their cousins from male Indians. Sex discrimination continues in the *Indian Act.*

The recent *Sparrow* decision will be extremely significant for Aboriginal women in arguing that their political and civil rights are existing Aboriginal rights which have not been extinguished, in spite of the intermarriage provisions in the *Indian Act.* It will also be vital in arguing that any other existing and hture discriminatory measures imposed by government or by Aboriginal communities are contrary to section 35(1) of the *Constitution.*

Before *Sparrow* and before section 35(1) of the *Constitution Act,* 1982, the Government of Canada could and did discriminate against Indian women on the basis of sex. For over 100 years Indian women who married non-Indians lost their Band Membership and Indian status and their right to live in and return to their home communities. Not only did they deny them the right to live with their own families and people, but it denied them access to their Aboriginal languages, cultures, and traditions as was found in the *Lovelace v. Canada* case decided by the United Nations Committee on Human Rights. The Supreme Court of Canada in *Lavell v. Her Majesty* in 1974 upheld the right of Canada to discriminate declaring that parliamentary supremacy meant if Canada had jurisdiction over Indians it could decide "who was an Indian." Parliament for 100 years decided Indian women were no longer Indians when they married non-Indians, and it decided non-Indian women were "Indians" when they married male Indians. These practices ended in 1985 with Bill C-31, *An Act to Amend the Indian Act.*

Prior to 1982, federal Indian matters were governed solely by section 91(24) of the *Constitution Act, 1867* (formerly called the *British North America Act*), under which authority Parliament passed successive versions of the *Indian Act.* Parliamentary supremacy ensured that Indians had no rights except those granted in legislation. This changed in 1982 with constitutional amendments recognizing the "existing" Aboriginal and treaty rights of Aboriginal peoples of Canada. Parliamentary supremacy is no longer enough. If Aboriginal and treaty rights are to be extinguished, they must be done so explicitly in law, and likely with the consent of Aboriginal peoples. What the *Sparrow* decision added was a reinterpretation of the regulation of rights versus the extinguishment of rights. The Supreme Court held that just because Aboriginal (fishing) rights were regulated for 100 years did not mean they were extinguished. Similarly for Aboriginal women's civil and political rights. Even if they were heavily regulated under the *Indian Act* for 100 years, it did not mean these rights were extinguished.

In the *Sparrow* case, which is a landmark case indicating the legal interpretation that will be given to section 35(1) of the *Constitution Act, 1982,* the Government attempted to prove that the right of Musqueam Indians to fish in the Fraser River had been extinguished by regulation prior to 1982, and therefore could not be recognized as an existing right under section 35(1). The Supreme Court disagreed with this position, and held that the fact "[t]hat the right is controlled in great detail by the regulations does not mean that the right is thereby extinguished" (*Sparrow* 400). If a right is not extinguished, it exists. Furthermore, the court ruled that:

> an existing Aboriginal right cannot be read so as to incorporate the specific manner in which it was regulated before 1982. The notion of freezing existing rights would incorporate into the Constitution a crazy patchwork of regulations. (*Sparrow* 396)

The Supreme Court agreed with Brian Slattery that "existing" means "unextinguished" instead of "exercisable at a certain time in history" (*Sparrow* 396),[3] and held that the term "existing" must be interpreted flexibly to permit its evolution over time (*Sparrow* 397).

Sparrow is significant in holding that certain Aboriginal and treaty rights may be regulated without being extinguished as a result. Aboriginal women's civil and political rights were regulated from 1867 to 1985 by the intermarriage provisions in the Indian Act, but I argue, that the fundamental human rights of Aboriginal women—including civil and political rights—form part of the inherent right to Aboriginal self-government which is now recognized and protected under section 35(1) of the *Constitution Act, 1982*. The decision in Sparrow provides a framework within which to make this argument.

The civil and political rights of Aboriginal women differ according to culture and tribal traditions. Most Aboriginal societies were traditionally matriarchal and matrilineal, including hunting and gathering societies. Aboriginal women's civil and political rights are foundational and do not derive their existence from documents or treaties (*Sparrow* 390). The right of women to establish and maintain their civic and political role has existed since time immemorial. These rights are part of customary laws of Aboriginal people and part of the right of Aboriginal self-government. "Such practices or forms of social organization do not require the imprimatur of state action to qualify as rights" (Sparrow 506).

Self-government is central to Aboriginal nationhood, culture, and existence, and the civil and political rights of women are central to traditional, matriarchal, and egalitarian forms of government. If Aboriginal self-government is central to the existence of Aboriginal nations, so must also the ability to determine civil and political rights of members be central to the exercise of the right of Aboriginal self-government (Asch and Macklem 505). This includes the right of women to define their roles in Aboriginal communities.

The rights of women were not explicitly recognized in the treaties between the Aboriginal peoples and the settlers, but they are rights which women have exercised since the formation of their Indigenous societies. In some cases, these rights were suppressed or regulated by non-Aboriginal law, such as the *Indian Act*.

The *Sparrow* decision makes it dear, however, that Aboriginal women's civil and political rights were not frozen in their regulated form when section 35(1) recognized and affirmed "existing" Aboriginal rights. Using the Court's interpretation, the civil and political rights of Aboriginal women were affirmed in 1982 in their contemporary form "rather than in their primeval simplicity and vigour" (*Sparrow* 397), or in the form they had been restricted to under the *Indian Act*. Moreover, even if women's rights were so restricted that women were banished from Aboriginal communities, this in itself does not lead to extinguishment of their rights. There *can* be no "extinguishment by regulation" of Aboriginal rights (*Sparrow 391*). Moreover, fundamental human rights, like civil and political rights of Aboriginal women, *can* never be extinguished. Therefore, these rights existed in some form in 1982, and are now recognized and affirmed in their full, unregulated form under section 35(1).

Sparrow held that there must be a "dear and plain" intention on the part of the Government where it intends to extinguish Aboriginal and treaty rights. This holding relied on a statement by Justice Hall in *Calder* that: "the onus of proving that the Sovereign intended to extinguish the Indian title lies on the respondent and that intention must be 'dear and plain'" (216). The Court also noted that in "the context of Aboriginal rights, it could be argued that before 1982, an Aboriginal right was automatically extinguished to the extent that it was inconsistent with a statute" (*Sparrow* 401). On this point, Aboriginal women would have had to overcome the argument that their political and civil rights were necessarily inconsistent with the Indian Act, had Bill C-31 not reinstated them and attempted to end *sex* discrimination against Indian women.

Prior to the 1985 amendments to the Indian Act, Parliament made it clear in law that Indian women who married with non-Indian men lost their civil and political rights within their communities. The *Luvell* decision of the Supreme Court of Canada agreed that parliamentary supremacy and the federal power to pass laws in relation to Indians and lands reserved for Indians under section 91(24) of the *Constitution Act, 1867* gave parliamentarians the right to determine who had Indian status.

After the 1985 amendments to the *Indian Act*, Parliament's clear and plain intention was restorative of rights that had been regulated (*Sparrow* 401). It reinstated Indian women and their children to their communities and ended legislated sex discrimination. Even if an Indian woman had lost status forty years earlier than 1985, she could have that status restored. If she had since died, she could still have her status restored. In either case, her descendants could apply to have Indian status and Band membership. The legislation also restored control of band membership and regulation of Indian lands to Indian Act governments. The legislation effectively restored the civil and political rights of Indian women who regained their Band membership and right to vote in Band elections.

The scope of modern-day Aboriginal women's civil and political rights will be determined in the context of the inherent right of self-government. Over the past few years, organized Aboriginal women's groups like the Native Women's Association of Canada have fought for participatory rights. In other words, they demand, as women, to be part of the policy and legislative processes that are being set up to define, develop and interpret their forms of Aboriginal government. This process includes defining who is a member of the "group" or of the "collective." What Bill C-31 did was to restore women and their descendants to the "base group," Band or Tribe that will exercise the right of self-government.

Some Aboriginal leaders and some governments will look to the nature of Aboriginal women's civil and political rights and believe that the manner in which the rights were regulated under the *Indian Act* will determine the scope of the rights. The Court in *Sparrow* rejected that approach. Aboriginal women, themselves, must be part of the process of delineating their civil and political rights. The Court also held that any future restriction on Aboriginal rights "must be in keeping with section 35(1) (*Sparrow* 401). As a result, Aboriginal women can use section 35(1) as a point of negotiation for definition of their modern civil and political rights.

The Court in *Sparrow* also stated that section 35(1) was to be interpreted in a purposive way: "[W] hen the purposes of the affirmation of Aboriginal rights are considered, it is clear that a generous, liberal interpretation of the words in the constitutional provision is demanded" (407). This provides further support for the argument that section 35(1) recognized and affirmed the civil and political rights of Aboriginal women as part of the inherent right of Aboriginal self-government.

The Supreme Court of Canada has also held that Aboriginal and treaty rights should be interpreted by taking into account Aboriginal history and tradition (*Sparrow* 408).[4] In interpreting Aboriginal women's civil and political rights as Aboriginal and treaty rights under section 35(1), the Court must take into account the historic roles of women within their traditional as well as contemporary Aboriginal societies. In this context, it is argued that the federal government has an active responsibility to respect and protect the rights of Aboriginal women as part of its fiduciary duty toward Aboriginal people.

> The relationship between the government and Aboriginals is trust-like, rather than adversarial, and contemporary recognition and affirmation of Aboriginal rights must be defined in light of this historic relationship. (*Guerin*)

This trust responsibility may also require the Government of Canada to protect the civil and political roles of Aboriginal women within their societies.

One of the purposes of Bill C-31 was to remove sex discrimination from the *Indian Act* and bring the legislation in line with the *Canadian Charter of Rights and Freedom*. Discrimination on the basis of *sex* is no longer allowed under section 15 of the *Charter of Rights and Freedom*. Furthermore, in 1983, Aboriginal women were successful in lobbying federal and provincial governments, and Aboriginal leaders, to have section 35(4) added to the *Constitution Act, 1982* which affirms that Aboriginal and treaty rights are guaranteed equally to men and women. This, to women, is a double confirmation of their rights. The section did not create new rights, but confirmed that women's rights are contained in section 35(1) *(Nowegijick* 198). Both of these instruments prevent Parliament from establishing new ales in the *Indian Act* in the future that discriminate on the basis of sex.

International law also dictates the recognition of fundamental civil and political rights of Aboriginal women under the *International Covenant on Civil and Political Rights;* the *Convention on the Elimination of All Forms of Discrimination Against Women*, and the *Universal Declaration of Human Rights*. Other sections of the *Charter of Rights and Freedom* also require governments to respect the civil and political rights of all women, including Aboriginal women. Human rights codes of the provinces and territories call for the adherence to fundamental human rights without discrimination based on race or sex. All of these instruments should prevent both Parliament and Aboriginal communities from discriminating against Aboriginal women on the basis of sex or race in future. At least some of them will be valuable in challenging existing discrimination that is still going on.

Three events have occurred in constitutional history that lead to the conclusion that Aboriginal women's civil and political rights are "existing" Aboriginal and treaty rights. In 1982, the *Constitution Act* recognized gender equality in sections 15 and 28 at the same time that it also recognized existing Aboriginal and treaty rights. In 1983, all First Ministers and Aboriginal representatives endorsed the inclusion of section 35(4) in the *Constitution Act, 1982* to recognize that men and women equally enjoy Aboriginal and treaty rights. In 1985, Parliament passed amendments to the *Indian* Act purportedly to eradicate *sex* discrimination against Indian women. What the *Sparrow* decision adds is an end to the federal theory that Aboriginal rights have been extinguished by regulations. Just as the Aboriginal right to fish was not extinguished by specific fisheries legislation, so, too, the *Indian Act* has not extinguished female civil and political rights. There can be no extinguishment by regulation of Aboriginal women's civil, political and property rights.[5]

Originally published in Canadian Woman Studies/les cahiers de la femme, *"Women's Rights are Human Rights," 15 (2 & 3) (Spring/Summer 1995): 34-38. Reprinted with permission of the author.*

Sharon D. McIvor is a member of the Lower Nicola Indian Band. She graduated from the University of Victoria Law School in 1986 and is a currently an LL.M candidate at Queen's University Faculty of Law in Kingston, Ontario. She is a practicing and active member of the Bar of British Columbia; Counsel to the "Coalition" Intervenants, O'Connor v. Her Majesty, at the Supreme Court of Canada; Justice Coordinator for the Native Women's Association of Canada; and a member of the National Aboriginal Advisory Committee to the Commissioner of the Correctional Service of Canada.

[1]Leslie and Macguire note that *An Act of 1851*, 14-15 Victoria, c. 59, was the first to exclude white men married to Indian women from being "legal Indians," but white women married to Indian men and their children would henceforth be "Indians." At page 55, the authors report that the *Act* of 1869 "was the first Canadian statute governing status of native women after marriage to non-Indians, or to Indians of other bands." The 1876 *Act* disenfranchised illegitimate children, Indians who lived continuously outside Canada for five years and to half-breeds.

[2]Section 35(1) states: "The existing Aboriginal and treaty rights of the Aboriginal peoples of Canada are hereby recognized and affirmed."

[3]See Slattery (781-82); McNeil (258); Pentney.

[4]In this context, the Court is citing *Agawa*: "The second principle ... emphasized the importance of Indian history and traditions as well as the perceived effect of a treaty at the time of its execution. He also cautioned against determining Indian rights in avacuum. The honour of the Crown is involved in the interpretation of Indian treaties, as a consequence, Fairness to the Indians is a governing consideration.... This view is reflected in recent judicial decisions which have emphasized the responsibility of government to protect the rights of Indians arising from the special trust relationship created by history, treaties and legislation: see *Guerin v. The Queen* (1984), 13 D.L.R. (4th) 321" (215-16).

[5]"In fact, extinguishment by regulation has for many years been a premise of the federal Indian claims policy. If the doctrine has 'no merit', which is certainly the view for the time being of the Supreme Court of Canada, then a substantial chunk of the governmental defences against Aboriginal rights claims across Canada ... may collapse" (Binnie 226).

REFERENCES

Asch, Michael and Patrick Macklem. "Aboriginal Rights and Canadian Sovereignty: An Essay on R. v. Sparrow." *Alberta Law Reports* 29 (2) (1991): 498.

Bill C-31, An Act to Amend the Indian Act, R.S.C. 1985, *c.*32 (1st Supp. 1985).

Binnie, W.I.C. "The Sparrow Doctrine: Beginning of the End or End of the Beginning?" *Queen's Law Journal* 15 (1992): 217.

Calder v. *Attorney-General (British Columbia)*. (1973), 34 D.L.R. (3d) 145.

Canadian Charter of Rights and Freedoms, Part I of the *Constitution Act, 1982*, being Schedule B to the *Canada Act 1982 (U.K.)*, 1982, c. 11.

Indian Act, R.S.C. 1970, C.1-6, S.12(L)(B).

Leslie, John and Ron MacGuire. *The Historical Development of the Indian Act*. Ottawa: Department of Indian and Northern Affairs Canada, 1979.

McNeil, Kent. "The Constitutional Rights of Aboriginal Peoples of Canada." *Supreme Court Law Review* 4 (1982): 255.

Nowegijick v. The Queen (1983), 144 D.L.R. (3d) 193 at 198.

Pentney, William. "The Rights of the Aboriginal Peoples of Canada in the *Constitution Act, 1982*, Part 11, Section 35: The Substantive Guarantee." *University of British Columbia Law Review* 22 (1987): 207.

R. v. Sparrow (1990), 70 D.L.R. (4th) 385 (S.C.C.).

R. v. Agawa (1988), 43 C.C.C. (3d) 266,28 O.A.C. 201.

Slattery, Brian. "Understanding Aboriginal Rights." *Canadian Bar Review* 66 (1987): 27.

WOMEN AND THE CANADIAN LEGAL SYSTEM

Examining Situations of Hyper-Responsibility

IN THE ADVOCACY WORK of the Canadian Association of Elizabeth Fry Societies (CAEFS) and the Native Women's Association of Canada (NWAC), we have noticed the emergence of a number of patterns that demonstrate the degree to which women face systemic discrimination in the Canadian legal system. These patterns are especially problematic when women are marginalized in intersectional ways across race, class, poverty, language, ability and sexual orientation. Taking the opportunity to share and compare stories and experiences of advocacy activities allows us to learn more about the systemic nature of the ways women are experiencing Canadian legal processes and the degree to which rights paradigms (such as the Charter) are not yet able to provide full remedies for women.

Canadian law is often built around expectations that individuals take responsibility for their actions and nowhere is this truer than in matters of criminal law. What we have noticed over the years is a number of situations where women (particularly when they are racialized, have a disability or a mental illness, are poor or a sexual minority) are expected by the legal system to take more responsibility than others. This is the situation we are referring to as hyper-responsibility.

Situations of hyper-responsibility of women through Canadian law often occur when women resist violence. Violence in our view, is a broad term which extends to all situations where harm is done to a person. Violence is, then, not just about physical harming but in our definition also includes psychological, emotional, sexual, economic and spiritual woundings. Both individuals and the state perpetuate violence against women. Secondary violence is experienced by the women who are in support or advocacy roles and is often evidenced in our growing frustration with the denial of justice to women in this country.

With monies secured from the Court Challenges Program (CCP), CAEFS and NWAC were able to convene a two and a half day meeting in Winnipeg at the end of February 2008. It was a first opportunity to have a focused discussion beyond the small discussions one has with activist friends on the situations of hyper responsibility of women demanded by the legal system. One of the principles that the meeting proceeded on was the need to move from talk to action. The goal of this discussion paper is to extend the conversation and examination of hyper-responsibilization of women in the Canadian legal system beyond the circle of twenty who were able to meet in Winnipeg. It is clear to us that there is much work that remains to be done to protect women's human rights and their right to live in a just, safe and peaceful society.

It has now been 26 years since the *Charter of Rights and Freedoms* became the supreme law of the land. Although sometimes, through small incremental steps, the *Charter* has improved the circumstances for women in Canada through the anti-discrimination provisions found in section 15(1) and (2), our continued work with women who stand up for their rights, despite the consequences, is now pointing to some of the limitations that section 15 presents. It is clear that we need to move beyond incidental advocacy and challenge the systemic and structural barriers that still exist in Canadian law for women.

PATTERNS OF HYPER-RESPONSIBILITY

Women's advocates began to see the issues that surround the hyper-respon-sibilization of women in Canadian law through their individual attempts at supporting women charged with offences, often when they had protected themselves from batterers. Since the Ratushny review was completed:

> ... researchers have noted that women are increasingly vulnerable to criminalization when they use violence in self-defence and, under rigorous zero tolerance policies, women continue to be countercharged for domestic assault—even when they call the police for help. (Balfour 2000a: 294)

Throughout our discussions one predominant theme emerged. Women who are experiencing and responding to the violence around them are not receiving adequate protection from the Canadian legal system. We were able to correlate our concerns about patterns of hyper-responsibility under several headings.

WOMEN IN PRISON

Prisoners are among the most disadvantaged members of society in countries around the world (Stern 2006) and this is as true for women. When we cast our gaze on the experiences of the most disadvantaged, the range and scope of the inequalities women in Canada face becomes illuminated. If we cannot improve the situation of women serving sentences, either provincially or federally, then there is very little chance that we have ameliorated the disadvantages women face in Canadian society. When the scope of our inquiry is the violence that is perpetrated against women, then examining the individual circumstances where women have resisted enhances our understanding of inequalities that remain embedded in Canadian law. As many of these women are criminalized for their resistance, we access their stories through our anti-prison activism.

Especially since the 1990s, the situation of women in prisons and jails in this country has received more scholarly and research attention than it did in the past (Balfour 2006b; Balfour and Comack 2004, 2006; Hannah-Moffat 2000, 2001; Hannah-Moffat and Shaw; Monture 2000, 2006; Neve and Pate; Pate 1999a, 1999b, 2005). A number of reports have raised concerns about inequalities women in custody face and these include the lack of access to gender-relevant programming; the lack of community-based release options; the lack of opportunity to serve their sentences in minimum security facility and the likelihood of being over-classified resulting in a maximum security conditions (CHRC; Auditor General of Canada). Women have been forced to engage in litigation to close the women's maximum-security units in prisons for men as well as to ensure that the only minimum security for women in Canada remains open. It is our view that this kind of litigation is a drain of women's energy as well as the financial resources of the state. Our view of equality demands that the state take positive and progressive action when state officials are aware that their conduct discriminates against women.

Despite the report of the Task Force on Federally Sentenced Women, which was implemented in part in the 1990s, women are still being treated more harshly than men in the prison. The five principles the Task Force articulated (empowerment; meaningful and responsible choices; respect and dignity; supportive environment; and shared responsibility) have been divested of their feminist and collective meanings and used by the system to demand from women a level of accountability for their crimes not expected of men (Hannah-Moffat 2001; Hayman). These philosophical shifts have become even more problematic in these neo-liberal times, which produce the law and order environment currently prevalent in Canada.

One of our most pressing concerns is the super-maximum-security management protocol to which three Aboriginal women are currently subjected. The conditions of confinement under the protocol are more stringent than those of men in "Special Handling Units" and too many of the behavioural standards set in these protocols are impossible to meet. For instance, the Correctional Service of Canada (CSC) has demanded that women "not swear" or "demonstrate anger or disrespectful behaviour" (emotions we believe help the women cope in a super-maximum-security environment) and has then attached a six month time frame for the assessment of "appropriate and expected behaviour." These are conditions that we believe would be seen as ridiculous if suggested in a male correctional environment but because women continue to be cast stereotypically by the penal regime it is not challenged. This introduces another theme. Women in prison have received equality with a vengeance.

Over the years we have seen an increase in the attempts to label women as dangerous offenders. The best-known case is Lisa Neve (Neve and Pate). An examination of her criminal record reveals the negligible risk she posed to society.

This exposes a glaring gender difference when that record is compared against the records men who have been signified as dangerous offenders. Currently, a woman who started a three-year sentence is now serving more than 20 years in prison and is facing this court process as a result of charges incurred *inside* the institution. Information such as this makes the category "dangerous" a suspicious one and also points to the fact that the women's prison environment begets violence rather than "correction."

With the patterns of state oppression and violence directed at women we see within the prison regime in Canada, there is another pattern of criminalization of Aboriginal women (and other women of colour). All of the women on the optional protocols, for example, are Aboriginal women. Many have noted with alarm the over-representation of Aboriginal women in federal custody (in 2004, 29 percent of the federally sentenced woman population were Aboriginal and a full 46 percent of the maximum security population (CHRC) and once in prison, an Aboriginal woman is more likely to serve her sentence in a maximum-security environment (Monture 2000). These facts demonstrate the point that started this discussion on women in prison. It is the most disadvantaged who find their way to prison or jail.

CRIMINAL JUSTICE RESOURCES

Resources in the community, particularly local resources (such as court workers and Elders), at times, are not meeting women's needs. We acknowledge that this is a very difficult topic to discuss and we are not laying blame. The problem is particularly acute for women who are charged with serious offences. We are concerned that the implications that flow from individualized systems of legal responsibility (such as those that provide the foundation for Canada's criminal law) may not be well understood by individuals who come from more community-focused and collective cultures. When such persons offer advice to an accused person that might be appropriate in a collective culture (e.g. accept responsibility or heal the family), the woman accepting such advice might become more vulnerable in the courts. We acknowledge that this is a very difficult topic to discuss because of the ease to which any comment is seen as criticism of Aboriginal ways and that is clearly not our intent. What we see is the pattern of continued conflict between Canadian legal practices and Aboriginal ways which continues to have a negative impact on Aboriginal women's lives.

Resources in the community, particularly local resources, are not meeting women's needs in other ways as well. For example, chronic lack of affordable housing and temporary shelter beds limit women's ability to be released on bail.

One particular case in the prairie region of the country was discussed at length. During a house party on a reserve about an hour from a major urban centre, a young man was killed. This story is not unlike many other stories we heard during the course of our meetings or that we are familiar with because of our advocacy work.

During the work on this case of several of the advocates who attended the Winnipeg meeting, it became clear to them that the woman who had been charged had not murdered the young man. This was disturbing because the court process had already been underway for about a year. The police stopped investigating immediately because they had a "confession." After it was determined that she may not have been the appropriate person charged, it was too late. Valuable evidence at the scene had already been lost. Despite the best efforts of advocates and lawyers, the woman eventually pled guilty to manslaughter.

On the videotape recorded immediately after her arrest, the women did say she was responsible for the young man's death. The woman took responsibility because the young man was her nephew, she had helped raise him and on the evening in question she knew he was about to receive some troubling news. In Aboriginal ways, Auntie's are responsible for their nephews. She had given him a drink even though she knew he had drinking problems. Her admission of responsibility was *not* an admission that properly supported the conclusion that she was criminally responsible.

This is not the end of the troubling facets of this case. When the nephew received the bad news, he started fighting. The police were called and they did *not* respond. The police were called a second time after the young man was stabbed. The police did not respond until there was a dead body. This communicates a loud message to Aboriginal people: our lives are not valuable in the eyes of the police. The work of organizations such as NWAC and Amnesty International on the number of murdered and missing Aboriginal women in this country also emphasizes the many missed opportunities for the police to respond appropriately to Aboriginal concerns for their family members or for their own individual safety. This concern on its own should be cause for action. However, the impact on Aboriginal people is even greater. We see that the state has effectively trained many Aboriginal women to believe they are on their own in circumstances where they face violence. Women are then faced with the prospect of no hope and likely death or the need to fight. When women are forced to meet violence with violence, the travesty is they are then susceptible to facing criminal charges. The lack of response by the police thus becomes a self-fulfilling prophecy and the stereotype that Aboriginal people are criminal is reinforced.[1]

In our advocacy efforts we have also noted that women are susceptible to entering guilty pleas at a very high rate. Concerns were also raised that women face additional pressures in plea-bargaining. Often women, especially when the context is a battering relationship, plead guilty to protect their children and sometimes to protect the batterer. Overcharging also results in women pleading guilty to more serious charges (such as second degree murder instead of manslaughter). Unfortunately, as statistics are not readily available on these concerns, systemic arguments cannot be made in courts that would assist women who have faced or are facing these circumstances. We believe that a government funded review, developed in true partnership with NWAC and CAEFS, should occur for women who have pled guilty to serious offences. We see it as essential that the state begin to take responsibility for the circumstances where women are facing inequalities in the legal system.

Additional concerns were raised about the sentencing process. Section 718.2(e) of the *Canadian Criminal Code* first acknowledges that Canada over-relies on sentences of incarceration and that this has had a particular impact on Aboriginal peoples. The section then directs sentencing judges to consider alternatives to incarcerations, particularly for Aboriginal peoples. The *Gladue* decision provides further guidance on this matter (see Turpel Lafond 1999). What is not known is the degree to which the *Criminal Code* and the *Gladue* decision are of assistance to women. This is an area where further research is recommended to determine if women receive access to the *Gladue* provisions and the degree to which the court's analysis of race that *Gladue* demands is coupled with a gendered analysis.

MOTHERS AND CHILDREN

The consequences for women facing criminal charges include the loss of their children to child welfare authorities. When charges are dropped, women are found not guilty or wrongful convictions are reversed, it is often too late as the children are already lost to the system. Racialized women are more likely to lose their children, especially Aboriginal women.

We are particularly concerned with the ways in which the state interferes with Aboriginal women's parenting. Even when the woman is not involved in the legal process, she may lose her children because she is seen as not having fulfilled her responsibilities to them because they are living in poverty or there is violence in the home. However, what is actually happening is that the state is looking to the mother to correct the systemic conditions of poverty and violence affecting Aboriginal families and punishing her with the loss of her children if she fails (Kline). These conditions are systemic and they require systemic solutions, not an allocation of individual blame. It has been noted that the lion's share of federal funding to First Nations child welfare authorities is heavily weighted toward removal of the children (Fontaine), and does not fund assistance to the family to improve parental strategies or life circumstances.

While incarcerated, women are separated from their children except in rare circumstances. The mother and child program at the Okimaw Ohci Healing Lodge has been closed for several years now. Recently, in British Columbia a woman convicted of manslaughter and now serving a four-year sentence was allowed to have her child with her at the new federal facility in that province (Culbert and Bellett). However, this permission was only secured with the activism of several lawyers and community groups. Programs and options for women and their children should not rely on individual cases of advocacy but should exist as a matter of policy.

Again, concern was raised that they are very few, if any, resources for women who are facing state-sanctioned removal of their children. While the Supreme Court of Canada has recognized that a woman may be entitled to legal assistance from the state in these cases (*New Brunswick (Minister of Health and Community Services) v. G.(J.)* 1999), there are no systems in place to provide such assistance. A complex individual application to the very court hearing the proceedings is the only way to seek such assistance, and it will not be granted in every case. This remains an ongoing problem that needs further state redress. Perhaps, the court-worker system developed in the criminal law could also be provided for child welfare matters.

RESISTING STATE VIOLENCE

In ways similar to the treatment of women who resist personal violence, Aboriginal people who acknowledge their traditional responsibilities as caretakers of the land are increasingly being criminalized by the Canadian state. Canada, in fact, has a long history of criminalizing the traditional practices and ceremonies of Aboriginal peoples. The outlawing of the potlatch and the sun dance, through criminal provisions in the *Indian Act*[2] failed to obliterate these practices, thanks to the peoples who continued them at great personal risk during the period of interdict (Backhouse). Although the criminal sanctions against potlatch and sun dance were removed decades ago,[3] Canada continues to criminalize the assertion of traditional rights and the exercise of traditional duties to protect Mother Earth. The state awards to corporations permits for the exploration or development of "Crown" land without regard for the rights and claims of First Peoples to that land, and then will use the Criminal Code, with its provisions against trespass, intimidation and public mischief, to punish the Aboriginal protesters who challenge defilement of the land and overriding of Aboriginal rights and title. Moreover, corporations holding such permits successfully apply to court for injunctions to stop protests against development, and courts are now readily convicting and imposing heavy sentences on Aboriginal leaders and activists for "contempt of court" when they resist the courts' commands to respect the corporations' rights over Aboriginal land. State practices, actualized by bureaucrats, police, and courts, thus amount to a form of legalized violence against Aboriginal peoples who assert stewardship over their traditional lands.

Examples of this deployment of state power to privilege corporate development of traditional lands, and punish efforts to protect it, are numerous. Women have been in the forefront of opposition to development, and have figured prominently among those incarcerated for alleged violations of the Criminal Code or "contempt of court" for defying injunctions secured to protect corporate interests. Women are also in the forefront of the legal movement to resist criminalization for fulfilling their traditional duties toward the land.

Recent Ontario cases where protesters were jailed for contempt of court for ignoring injunctions protecting permits granted for mineral exploration and development highlight the adverse consequences to Aboriginal people of accepting responsibility for one's actions, within the context of the legal system. Demonstrators from the Ardoch Algonquin First Nation and the Kitchenuhmaykoosib Inninuwug First Nation accepted responsibility for barring resource companies' access to their traditional lands, pursuant to their traditional duty to protect the land (see *Frontenac Ventures Corporation* v. *Ardoch Algonquin First Nations* 2008 and *Platinex* v. *Kitchenuhmaykoosib Inninuwug First Nation* 2008). However, in both cases, the courts saw this open acceptance of responsibility for the Earth, and for their actions, as demonstrators' aggravated defiance of court orders allowing the companies access to the land. Heavy jail sentences were imposed for contempt of court.

Similar cases have proceeded in British Columbia as well. Nicole and Beverly Manuel are members of the Secwepemc (Shuswap) First Nation and the Neskonlith Indian Band. They participated in a roadblock on Sun Peaks Road near Kamloops, B.C. in August 2001. They were convicted in Provincial Court on September 16, 2002 of unlawfully obstructing a highway and mischief, contrary to sections 423(1) and 430(1)(c) of the Criminal Code. Nicole, the mother of young children, was sentenced to 45 days in jail, and put on probation for 12 months, and her mother Beverly received a suspended sentence and one year's probation. The imposition of probation is itself a way of inhibiting protest, as breach of the conditions of probation by further protesting will attract a jail term. These convictions were upheld on appeal to the Supreme Court of British Columbia on November 12, 2004. (*R.* v *Manuel* 2007 para. 2; Canadian Press).

Nicole and Beverly Manuel appealed their convictions to the British Columbia Court of Appeal. Here, they asserted once again the arguments which had been rejected by the first two courts: namely, that they had a legal right to block Sun Peaks Road under the natural laws of their people and the laws of the Creator, which imposed a duty on the Manuels and other members of their Nation to take care of and preserve the land. In the technical language of the law of trespass, this defence was that they had a "colour of right" to be on the road they had been accused of blocking and a right to keep others off it. In the court below, and in other courts dealing with charges against other demonstrators, the belief asserted by the Manuels had been characterized as a "moral" belief that was insufficient to justify a breach of the law (*R.* v *Manuel* 2007, paragraphs 4-6).

At the next level of Manuels' appeal, the BC Court of Appeal recognized that their beliefs in their people's title to the land and the obligations imposed by the law of Creator were beliefs in legal rights, because Aboriginal law is not a separate legal system, or moral code. It is part of Canadian law. The Court of

Appeal thus ruled that it was incorrect to characterize the Manuels' beliefs as beliefs only in moral rights (*Manuel* 2008).

Although this ruling is important in the overall development of the law, the Court of Appeal's final decision was very disturbing. A person must have an honest belief about her legal rights in order to claim a "colour of right" defence, and the Court ruled that to be characterized as honest, a belief must be reasonable. Then it went on to hold that the Manuels' belief that their Aboriginal legal rights gave them the right to block the road was not reasonable (and thus not honest) because they knew that the federal government had refused to recognize their land claim for reserve lands lost, and the status of their Aboriginal title to the land was unclear because their had been no litigation to settle it (*Manuel*).

The decision leaves First Nations totally at the mercy of the government. Government can deny in negotiation, or delay in litigation, the resolution of Aboriginal claims, and at the same time issue to corporations permits to develop Crown land affected by those claims. Even if the First Nations are successful in the long run, the land will have been devastated by the development permitted in the short run. There is an urgent need to challenge the ultimate ruling on reasonableness/honesty arrived at by the BC Court of Appeal. Until that is done, First Nations and individual protesters may be able to benefit from the Court's acceptance of Aboriginal law as part of Canadian law, not just a system of "moral beliefs," and each protest will have to be back-grounded with a clear legal opinion setting out Aboriginal title and the right to the land.

The risks for Aboriginal women who demonstrate to protect their peoples' traditional lands are very high. Mothers are separated from their children by jail sentences, and thus run the risk of child welfare authorities' involvement. On January 25, 2007, Harriet Nahanee, a Squamish Elder aged 71, was sentenced to 14 days in the Surrey Pretrial Centre, a men's prison with two segregated maximum units for women, for her role in the Eagleridge protest. Fellow demonstrator Betty Krawczyk advised Justice Brenda Brown of Ms. Nahanee's frail health to no result. Shortly after her release from prison, Ms. Nahanee was hospitalized with pneumonia, and she died February 24, 2007. It is clear that Aboriginal people are experiencing serious consequences when the state fails to take a balanced approach (including their legal duty to consult First Nations) to economic development on reserve lands.

MEDIA

The media do not cover well issues of concern to women. For example, most of the wrongful conviction cases highlighted in the media involve men. Even after the Rathushny review the wrongful conviction cases involving women receive scant attention. The media pay little attention, if any, when Aboriginal people go missing.

When the media response is not silence then the image of women the media portrays are problematic in various ways (Faith 256). Concerns were also raised at the Winnipeg meetings about the stereotyping of Aboriginal peoples involvement in criminal activity. The best example is the discussion of gang members in the prairies as though there were only Aboriginal gangs. It was also noted anecdotally that in prairie papers, only the race of Aboriginal persons are noted in stories about arrests, convictions or offences.

Sociologists have long noted that the media play a significant role in creating public perceptions about crime (Schneider). In 1978, Mark Fishman noted the mass media have often produced "crime waves" despite the fact that statistics reveal that crime was actually decreasing (cited in Schneider). Schneider notes that crime news is good news because people are interested and it is a "cheap, easy to get hold of" news which sells papers. Since the Task Force on Federally Sentenced Women which was brokered on the fact that women were not as dangerous men, we have seen the media in Canada capitalize through reporting of stories that cast women as dangerous. Furthermore, Laureen Snider points out: "in a neo-liberal, punishment-obsessed culture, any evidence of "leniency" will instantly be seized by sensationalistic media eager both to foment and capitalize on anti-feminist backlash" (Balfour and Comack 324). Unfortunately, little scholarly attention has been paid to the way the media portray women, particularly women involved in crime.

OTHER CONCERNS

There are also other situations that need to be examined and these include: prostitution and sexual exploitation of girls and young women, who are too often blamed and disrespected; the number of murdered and missing Aboriginal women (as a particular way that Aboriginal women experience violence and victimization); lack of or delayed police responses to situations of violence against women; forced addiction treatment for pregnant women; and, the way the *Indian Act* encouraged and still encourages violence against women. There are a number of ways these issues in Canada have international overlaps. More work needs to be done to fully examine all of the situations of hyper-responsibility and prepare responses to the situations of discrimination they produce.

ACADEMIC LITERATURE

Since the mid-1990s, academics have been developing theories around the concepts of responsibilization and governmentality. These are tools that help us understand the structure and functioning of the neo-liberal state. In 1996, British scholar David Garland published a paper, "The Limits of the Sovereign State: Strategies of Crime Control in Contemporary Society." Garland's argument begins by noting that most contemporary western societies have, since the 1960s and extending at least into the late 1990s, experienced increasing crime rates. In some countries (including Canada), this trend has now reversed. Equally the fear of crime has become widespread as a result of media representations and the politicization of crime control. Garland also notes that crime "has an uneven social distribution." The dispossessed are more likely to be victimized. Yet, "… for most people, crime is no longer an aberration or an unexpected, abnormal event" (446).

The shift in how crime is experienced as an everyday phenomenon has cyclical impacts on the actions of the state and the ways crime control is justified. Within this new mode of governing, Garland argues, the central government is "seeking to act upon crime not in a direct fashion through state agencies (police, courts, prisons, social work, etc.) but instead by acting indirectly, seeking to activate action on the part of non-state agencies and organizations" (1996: 452). Thus, as a result of the state's responsibilization strategy, what was previously a sovereign power of the state is now a responsibility of the citizen. This downloading strategy is couched in terms of the freedom of the citizens to choose to act in an appropriate way. This shift in accountability from state to citizen (and community group or organization) must make suspect recent strategies and funding for prevention.

Looking specifically at the way Great Britain's laws on youth crime control have recently changed, John Muncie notes that:

> What is clear is that traditional justice versus welfare or welfare versus punishment debates are particularly inadequate in unraveling how youth justice acts on an amalgam of rationales, oscillating around, but also beyond, the caring ethos of social services, the neo-liberal legalistic ethos of responsibility and the neoconservative ethos of coercion and punishment (771).

Debates about when punishment is justified in criminal justice systems are now more complex and it is more difficult to determine the underlying rationales under a neo-liberal system of governance. Canada too has experienced recent periods of rapid change in its youth justice laws since 1983, first enacting a new law called the *Young Offenders Act* (proclaimed into force in 1984) and then the *Youth Criminal Justice Act* (2002 and revised in 2004). The experiences of girls and young women are far too often absent from these academic debates and articles; thus, their experiences of hyper-responsibility or their treatment under responsibilization strategies are not as clearly visible.

The Canadian literature on responsibilization in crime control sectors of society focuses on studies of examples of the state's ability to make citizens responsible for their own "correction." Kelly Hannah Moffat (2000) argues that the implementation strategies of the federal crown regarding the work of the Task Force on Federally Sentenced Women have turned the feminist concept of empowerment inside out. It becomes a way of holding women prisoners accountable for their criminogenic factors and offending, a standard much higher than male prisoners are held accountable to. Steven Bittle considers anti-prostitution in Alberta while Patrick Paranby analyzes risk as the new justification for intervention. What is key in the responsibilization discourse is the illumination of a new "freedom" individuals have to make responsible choices away from poverty, addiction and criminal behaviour rather than having a government provide a social safety net.[4] Canadian scholars have not been discussing in the academic literature either the theoretical framework of responsibilization and governmentality in a national context nor have they been asking questions about the impacts that this shift in policy has had on those who are criminalized and imprisoned, including young men and women. Women and gender are again not central in the discussion.

Absent from Garland's work is the presence of women as well as young persons. "The treatment of women with in the criminal justice system has been closely tied to their social characteristics... " (Gelsthorpe 77) or in other words the way women are socially constructed. In terms of Garland's own work this is unfortunate as "the recent huge increases in the number of women sentenced to imprisonment are simply inexplicable and point to a paradox that well exemplifies the situation Garland is trying to explain (Gelsthorpe 77). It is more than disappointing to note that the consideration of feminist theories of criminalization are absent from the literature written about responsibilization within the criminal justice system.

Feminist criminologists in Canada have indeed noted their frustration with their ability to positively influence the inequalities women continue to face in the Canadian legal system (see for example Balfour 2006a; Comack; Monture 2000, 2006; Snider). These criticisms grow not just from theoretical positions but also from the activism that good feminist praxis demands be joined to theorizing. It is worth quoting Laureen Snider at length on the realizations that have been gained:

> The criminal justice system in the modern democratic state is structur-
> ally ill equipped to deliver empowerment or amelioration.... Criminal
> justice does not have a Janus-like quality, a legitimating, positive or
> life-affirming mission to balance its repressive side. The official role
> of institutions of criminal justice is to discipline those designated as
> lawbreakers, to control them legally and equally, regardless of race,
> class or gender. This means that institutions of criminal justice are
> not like other institutions—schools, for example are charged with
> educating, hospitals with healing—because they are charged only
> with delivering "equal-opportunity social control." The favoured con-
> sciousness raising strategy of progressive groups—calling institutions
> to account for not delivering on their official promises—has limited
> potential here. Police, prisons, and courts cannot be named, blamed
> or shamed for failing to empower women or failing to provide them

with life-affirming choices. They can only be castigated for failing to punish women equally with men (324).

Laws, which have as their goal social control, are equally implicit in this conclusion. Following Snider's argument, further reforming the prison in the best interest of women will not take us to a true form of equality.

Understanding the rate at which feminist criminology has progressed in the last four decades, is informative to the considerations of women's legal inequality which brought us together in Winnipeg. The first wave of feminist criminology began to emerge in the 1970s and had as its focus a critique of the exclusion of women from "malestream" criminology (Comack 28). But critiques neither solve the problems women encounter in the legal system nor do they provide a sound theoretical basis for feminist (or any other) theory. The 1980s were "heady times ... as they watched decades of activism finally begin to pay off" (Balfour 2006a: 737). Reforms were underway in the federal correctional system, domestic violence seemed to be taken more seriously and important changes were made to the rape laws, which became known as sexual assault to reinforce that the crime was indeed one of violence. The most recent wave of feminist criminology began as a response to the recognition that many of the gains perceived by feminists in the 1980s were double-edged as seen in the charges and countercharges brought against women who were merely defending themselves against violence, often the violence of their partners. In fact, some have concluded that reliance on the law including the criminal law is misguided (cited in Snider 323). Laureen Snider, however, concludes that the "first and most obvious lesson of the reform efforts of the past is that making change is a complex and complicated activity" (325). This acknowledgement brings us to the place where the literature on responsibilization can compliment our thinking as feminists.

The literature on responsibilization and governmentality illuminates certain realities on the prairies. First, applying Garland's recognition that "crime has an unequal social distribution," we can acknowledge that not only those committing crimes are more likely to be poor, socially excluded and racialized but that the victims are more likely to come from this same social grouping. In the west, Aboriginal persons are even more disproportionately both the victims and the perpetrators (Aboriginal Justice Inquiry of Manitoba; Monture 2006). A second realization should be emphasized. Despite decreasing crime rates in the province, we do not yet seem to be experiencing a reduced fear of crime, a decrease on the "tough on crime" policy and political frameworks or a reduction in police demands for more officers and resources to fulfill the "tough on crime" mandate. As a result, policy and government funding allocations to crime are no longer driven by statistical evidence. Third, looking to the academic literature, the position of women and girls is not an emphasis. The same exclusion exists in what grants are funded and not. There is a need to ensure that more scholarly and other research endeavors incorporate gender into their analysis. Often one of the problems we face as advocates is a lack of research, which supports gendered understandings of the struggles women continue to face.

The literature on responsibilization within criminal justice systems does parallel our concerns about the hyper-responsibility being demanded of women. However, the conversation about hyper-responsibility may not necessarily fit squarely within the academic discussion on responsibilization. Our challenge, and our priority, is to bring the lived experience of women to the debate and find ways to advance our understandings while providing real opportunities to end the hyper-responsibilization of women in Canadian law.

CONCLUSION

What is required is action! For the part of CAEFS and NWAC, the organizations have committed to signing an agreement regarding their future work together on these issues. The group who met in Winnipeg agreed on the following objectives[5] that will guide the work to eliminate state and personal violence against women and their children:

> 1. Denounce, resist and eliminate criminalization of women who resist state and personal violence towards them and their children.
> 2. Denounce, resist and eliminate hyper-responsibilization of women who resist state and personal violence against them and their children.
> 3. Develop ways of acknowledging responsibility that do not criminalize women.

There is much work that needs to be done and funding will be a key issue. Projects discussed include:

> •preparing a resource kit(s) for courtworkers, advocates and lawyers that discusses the situations women and their children face when resisting personal or state violence;
> •accessing funds to ensure that adequate research is completed on the systemic inequalities women face in the Canadian legal system. Both quantitative and qualitative studies are needed to document the experiences of women, their children and their families;
> •legal action, documentation and research is also needed. Concerns were raised about two specific instances: women's ability to access to the sentencing provisions of section 718.2(e) of the Criminal Code as interpreted in the Gladue ruling as well as the lack of privilege (legal confidentiality) accorded to Elders;
> •develop public education strategies that show the multiple ways in which women are being treated unequally in Canada's legal system.

It was clear to the women gathered in Winnipeg, that there is a profound need to change the system's perception of women's resistance to personal and state violence. The goal is to prevent the criminalization of women who resist and prevent their continued hyper-responsibilization. There is a need to de-criminalize and deinstitutionalize the response to women who resist violence. This requires a change in institutional practices such as police and prosecutorial guidelines. These aims will prevent more women from being criminalized in the Canadian legal system. However, we must not forget the cases presently before the courts or the women who are presently serving sentences. There is a need to find ways to interfere in these ongoing cases and to remedy the historic cases.

The Canadian Association of Elizabeth Fry Societies and the Native Women's Association of Canada would like to thank Elizabeth Bastien, Yvonne Boyer, Mary Eberts and Patricia Monture for their efforts in preparing this paper. Reprinted with permission.

Originally published in Canadian Woman Studies/les cahiers de la femme, *"Indigenous Women in Canada: The Voices of First Nations, Inuit and Métis Women,"* 26 (3 & 4) (Winter/Spring 2008): 94-104. Reprinted with permission.

[1]For a fuller discussion of how these factors operate in the justice system please see David M. Tanovich. Unfortunately, this work does not contain a gender analysis.

[2]The ban was originally enacted by *An Act further to amend the Indian Act 1880*, S.C. 1884, c. 27, s.3, which became R.S.C. 1886, c.43, s.114. The ban was enlarged by R.S.C. 1886, c.43, s.6, and this was included as s.149 of R.S.C. 1906, c.81. The ban was further enlarged by S.C. 1914, c. 35, s.8, and appeared in R.S.C. 1927, c. 98, as s.140.

[3]The ban contained in R.S.C. 1927, c. 98, s.140 was amended once, by S.C. 1932-33, c.42, s.10, and continued until 1951. The *Indian Act* was substantially overhauled in 1951, and no ban appeared in the 1951 Act: S.C. 1951, c. 29.

[4]This key element has been embraced by the Chief Justice of Canada, and the majority of the Court, in the decision in *Gosselin* v *Quebec (Attorney General)*, [2002] 4 S.C.R. 429. The Supreme Court upheld the constitutional validity of a Quebec workfare scheme for young adults, ruling that id did not violate their dignity because it gave them the opportunity to learn a skill and enter the workface. The decision was reached despite evidence that there were insufficient training opportunities attached to the program, and even those who wanted to "work" could not get it, and would thus continue to draw the below-subsistence allowances provided to those not participating in workfare.

[5]These objectives and commitments have not yet received the endorsement of the Boards of Directors of either organization.

REFERENCES

Aboriginal Justice Inquiry of Manitoba. (Commissioners A. C. Hamilton and C. M. Sinclair). *The Report of the Aboriginal Justice Inquiry of Manitoba: The Justice System and Aboriginal People.* Winnipeg: Queen's Printer, 1991.

Auditor General of Canada. *Report of the Auditor General of Canada to the House of Commons.* Ottawa: Minister of Public Works and Government Services, 2003.

Backhouse, Constance. "'Bedecked in Gaudy Feathers': The Legal Prohibition of Aboriginal Dance: Wanduta's Trial, Manitoba, 1903." *Colour-Coded: A Legal History of Racism in Canada, 1900-1950.* Constance Backhouse. Toronto: University of Toronto Press, 1999. 56-102.

Balfour, Gillian. "Introduction." *Criminalizing Women: Gender and (In)justice in Neo-liberal Times.* Eds. Gillian Balfour and Elizabeth Comack. Black Point, NS: Fernwood Books, 2006a. 1-21.

Balfour, Gillian. "Re-imagining a Feminist Criminology." *Canadian Journal of Criminology and Criminal Justice* 48 (5) (2006b): 735-752.

Balfour, Gillian. 2004. *The Power to Criminalize: Inequality and the Law.* Halifax: Fernwood Books.

Balfour, Gillian and Elizabeth Comack. *Criminalizing Women: Gender and (In)justice in Neo-liberal Times.* Black Point, NS: Fernwood Books, 2006.

Balfour, Gillian and Elizabeth Comack. *The Power to Criminalize: Violence, Inequality and the Law.* Halifax, NS: Fernwood Books, 2004.

Bittle, Steven. "When Protection is Punishment: Neo-Liberalism and Secure Care Approaches to Youth Prostitution." *Canadian Journal of Criminology* 44 (3) (2002): 317-350.

Canadian Human Rights Commission (CHRC). *Protecting Their Rights: A Systemic Review of Human Rights in Correctional Services for Federally Sentenced Women.* Ottawa: CHRC, 2003.

Canadian Press. "Woman sentenced to 45 days in jail over native protest at Sun Peaks." October 22, 2002. Online: <http://www.geocities.com/ericsquire/articles/delta/cp021022.htm>. Retrieved 3/29/08.

Comack, Elizabeth. "The Feminist Engagement with Criminology." *Criminalizing Women: Gender and (In)justice in Neo-liberal Times.* Eds. Gillian Balfour and Elizabeth Comack. Black Point, NS: Fernwood Books, 2006. 22-55.

Culbert, Lori and Gerry Bellett. "Prison Mom Focused on Raising Child." *Vancouver Sun* February 7, 2008. Retrieved from <www.canada.com/topics/news/national/story.html?k=17812&id=f7bcadfe-2647-4c87-92cc-400f2f11864b>.

Faith, Karlene. *Unruly Women: The Politics of Confinement and Resistance.* Vancouver: Press Gang, 1993.

Fontaine, Phil. "Funding Plan Hurts Aboriginal Children." Toronto Star, January 20, 2005: A21.

Garland, David. "The Limits of the Sovereign State: Strategies of Crime

Control in Contemporary Society." *British Journal of Criminology* 36 (1996): 445-471.

Gelsthorpe, Loraine. "Back to Basics in Crime Control: Weaving Women In." *Critical Review of International Social and Political Philosophy* 7 (2) (2004): 76-103.

Hannah-Moffat, Kelly. "Prisons that Empower: Neo-Liberal Governance in Canadian Women's Prisons." *British Journal of Criminology* 40 (2000): 510-531.

Hannah-Moffat, Kelly. *Punishment in Disguise: Penal Governance and Federal Imprisonment of Women in Canada.* Toronto: University of Toronto Press, 2001

Hannah-Moffat, Kelly and Margaret Shaw, eds. *An Ideal Prison? Critical Essays on Women's Imprisonment in Canada.* Halifax: Fernwood Books, 2000.

Hayman, Stephanie. *Imprisoning Our Sisters: The New Federal Women's Prisons in Canada.* Montreal & Kingson: McGill-Queen's University Press, 2006.

Jacobs, Beverley and Andrea J. Williams. *Legacy of Residential Schools: Missing and Murdered Aboriginal Women.* Ottawa: Aboriginal Healing Foundation, 2008.

Kline, Marlee. "The Colour of Law: Ideological Representations of First Nations in Legal Discourse." *Social and Legal Studies* 3 (1994): 451-476.

Monture, Patricia. "Confronting Power: Aboriginal Women and Justice Reform." *Canadian Woman Studies/les cahiers de la femme* 25 (3,4) (2006): 25-33.

Monture, Patricia. "Aboriginal Women and Correctional Practice: Reflections on the Task Force on Federally Sentenced Women." *An Ideal Prison? Critical Essays on Women's Imprisonment in Canada.* Eds. Kelly Hannah-Moffat, and Margaret Shaw. Halifax: Fernwood Books, 2000. 52-59.

Muncie, John. "Governing Young People: Coherence and Contradiction in Contemporary Youth Justice." *Critical Social Policy* 26 (2006): 770-793.

Neve, Lisa and Kim Pate. "Challenging the Criminalization of Women Who Resist." *Global Lockdown: Race, Gender, and the Prison Industrial Complex.* Ed. Julia Sudbury. New York: Routledge, 2005. 19-33.

Parnaby, Patrick. "Crime Prevention through Environmental Design: Discourses of Risk, Social Control, and a Neo-Liberal Context." *Canadian Journal of Criminology and Criminal Justice* (2006): 1-29.

Pate, Kim. "CSC and the 2 Per Cent Solution." *Canadian Woman Studies/les cahiers de la femme* 19 (1,2) (Spring/Summer 1999a): 145-153.

Pate, Kim. "Prisons: Canada's Default Response to Homelessness, Poverty, and Mental Illness—Especially for Women." Paper presented at the United Nations Congress on Criminal Justice and Crime Prevention, Bangkok, 2005. Available at www.elizabethfry.ca/pubs/bangkok/1.htm.

Pate, Kim. "Young Women and Violent Offences: Myth and Realities." *Canadian Woman Studies/les cahiers de la femme* 19 (1,2) (Spring/Summer 1999b): 39-43.

Ratushny, Lynn. *Self Defence Review: Final Report.* Ottawa: Minister of Justice and Solicitor General of Canada, 1997.

Schneider, Hans Joachim. "The Media World of Crime: A Study of Social Learning Theory and Symbolic Interactionism." *Advances in Criminological Theory, Volume 2*. Eds. William S. Laufer and Fred Alder. London: Transaction Publishers, 1990. 115-143.

Snider, Laureen. "Making Changes in Neoliberal Times." *Criminalizing Women: Gender and (In)justice in Neoliberal Times*. Eds. Gillian Balfour and Elizabeth Comack. Black Point, NS: Fernwood Books, 2006. 2006. 323-342.

Stern, Vivien. *Creating Criminals: Prisons and People in a Market Society*. Halifax: Fernwood, 2006.

Tanovich, David M. *The Colour of Justice: Policing Race in Canada*. Toronto: Irwin Law, 2006.

Task Force on Federally Sentenced Women. *Creating Choices: The Report of the Task Force on Federally Sentenced Women*. Ottawa: Correctional Service of Canada, 1990.

Turpel-Lafond, Mary Ellen. "Sentencing within a Restorative Justice Paradigm: Procedural Implications of *R. v Gladue*. *Criminal Law Quarterly* 43 (1) (1999): 34-50.

Cases Cited:

Frontenac Ventures Corporation v. *Ardoch Algonquin First Nations*, [2008] Can LII 8427 (On.S.C.).

Gosselin v *Quebec (Attorney General)*, [2002] 4 *S.C.R.* 429 (S.C.C.)

New Brunswick (Minister of Health and Community Services) v. *G.(J.)* [1999] 3 *S.C.R.* 46.

Platinex v. *Kitchenuhmaykoosib Inninuwug First Nation*, [2008] CanLII 11049 (On.S.C.).

R. v *Gladue*, [1999], 133 *C.C.C.* (3d) 385 (S.C.C.).

R. v *Manuel*, [2007] BCCA 581.

R. v *Manuel*, [2008] BCCA 143.

FRAN SUGAR

ENTRENCHED SOCIAL CATASTROPHE

Native Women in Prison

NATIVE PEOPLE LEAD the *KKKountry* in statistical categories such as unemployment, alcoholism, early death rates from infant mortality, violence, and criminally-related activities. According to a recent study by Trent University, the *Dangerous Offenders Act*, Bills C-67 and C-68, Native people in the criminal justice system are more likely to be gated under this bill, and are, therefore, deemed the most dangerous and most violent offenders in Canada.

Native women face double, triple, and quadruple standards when entering the prison system. Number one is because we are women; number two, we are Native; number three, we are poor; and, number four, we do not usually possess the education necessarily equivalent to the status quo.

PROFILE

Ms. Cree is eighteen years old, a single parent with two children. She lives in the city of _____ where the offence took place. She was convicted of manslaughter and sentenced to four years. Her parents are deceased. She has two sisters and two brothers. Ms. Cree was a housewife whose sole income was social assistance.

Ms. Cree entered the institution with a grade-four level of education. She quit school due to problems in her foster home. Ms. Cree has not been involved in an education upgrading program. She has been offered a job cleaning yet has refused this placement beasue she feels the school supervisor does not treat her or other Native sutdents properly. As a result, she will not work anywhere in the institution.

Ms. Cree was first arrested at age sixteen for uttering and forging documents. She was put on one year's probation, which she completed successfully. The subject displays no responsibility for her criminal involvement. The subject clearly has a drug and alcohol problem. Her institutional participation is limited to Native Sisterhood. The writer strongly suggests that Ms. Cree remain a maximum security inmate. The writer is not in support of community release at this time. Day parole denied. Full parole

---

denied. Escorted temporary absence denied for one year. Ms. Cree was involved in a would-be serious incident with a number of her friends on May 1, 19—, when security staff were proceeding to dispel an incident in another part of the building. As a result of Ms. Cree not being able to remain charge-free for any length of time, her cavalier attidude, her activities and friendships with many know drug dealers in the institution, it is the writer's opinion that Ms. Cree meets number two and number three criteria under Bill C67-68.

Ms. Cree is a danger to society, to herself, and to the staff members of the institution. Ms. Cree is being referred under Bill C67-68. Ms. Cree's sentence expires January 199–. Next case management review scheduled for December, 198–."

This is a fictional profile, but it closely resembles a perceived reality on the part of the bureaucracy who assess the Native woman as she enters prison. Those who assess us come from an opposite life experience. The average case management person is Caucasian, married, has one to two children, a university degree, is from an upper-middle-class background with no comparable experiences to a Native woman.

Obviously there are going to be some very profound difficulties that the Native woman will have in making adjustments within the institution and in serving out her sentence. Almost every Sister I have talked to has told me they were raised in foster homes, sent to juvenile detention centres, were victims of sexual abuse, were victims of rape. And finally entering Prison for Women, we have all become victims of bureaucracy because we do not have the right colour of skin, the right kind of education, the right kind of social skills, and the right kind of principles to get out of here.

Most often, criminal defense lawyers in conjunction with crown prosecutors and judges, agree that a guilty plea with a lengthy sentence will correct past lifestyles, our way of thinking, and make us into law abiding "cityzens." It is an absurd, *phucking* joke to think that the criminal *just-us cystem* with their residential care, treatment, programming, counselling, and mental health programs are specifically designed programs to meet the needs of Native women when we have never had an equal footing in the case management strategic planning sessions that take place. The bureaucracy and paper pushing outweighs the importance of listening to what the Native woman says she needs.

Usually the woman in the cage is too busy *surviving* the new rules, new regulations of daily life in la-la land to even consider what the future holds after she is finished her sentence.

When we come to prison, we need to adjust to greater and greater violence in our lives. We adjust to increasingly deadly conditions, and come to accept them as "natural." We adjust to having freedoms stolen from us, to having fewer and fewer choices, and, less and less voice in the decisions that affect our lives. We come to believe that making $4.20 a day and things we can buy with it are the most important life goals. We have adjusted to deafening silence, because it is now mandatory to wear headphones. We have adjusted to the deafening noises and screams coming from segregation when our Sister has just been stripped of her clothes and maced in the face. We have adjusted to the deadening entertainment of bingo games that give out prized bags of taco chips and we hear glees of happiness at this score, because some pathetic individual hasn't tasted taco chips since 1979. We have adjusted to the lack of conversation, because some days there is absolutely nothing of significance or meaning to a few cheap words. We have adjusted to dreaming of our futures. We have adjusted to divorcing ourselves from relationships with our husbands. We keep adapting to new and ever more dangerous conditions and ideas in the name of survival.

We forget how life once was, how blue the sky is, how good food tasted. We forget because the changes are gradual and unannounced. No one can forewarn us of what lies ahead. If we could imagine ourselves taking pleasure in a slave job like cleaning floors over and over again, day after day, year after year, and see ourselves as fanatical psychos when our freshly waxed floor gets a scratch on it and ruins our entire day, we would recoil with horror and shame because our minds and values become as twisted and irrational as the ones that impose these conditions upon our lives.

We *become so phucking* numb from the incredible *b/sh* we are exposed to: trying to see a case management officer to get a call to our children is a major, major event. It is no wonder that so many of us cut our throats, lacerate our bodies, hang ourselves. It is no wonder that we need to identify our pain onto our physical bodies, because our whole lives have been filled with incredible pain and traumatizing experiences—psychic pain, physical pain, spiritual pain.

When you ask a Native woman why she was placed in a foster home, she'll likely tell you it was because Children's "Aid" arrested her because her parents didn't send her to school regularly. When you ask a Native woman where she was sexually abused, she'll likely respond it took place in the foster homes. When you ask a Native woman why she killed somebody, she'll tell you she was a battered wife and she lost control of her senses when she was taking another beating. She didn't mean to kill her husband, her lover, her friend, she was just so spun out after each licking she lived through—she just was so spun out.

I am your typical Native woman and one who has survived the Criminal *"Just-us"* system. When I think about my time in prisons, I often wonder how I maintained my sanity. I never conformed in my heart or in my mind, but my body danced. I learned how to cope with lies. I believe justice does not exist for Native people. The battle of will is to see through the wall, to see through the screws and their power plays—their bureaucratic games of power and pleasure.

I learned there is a certain degree of hypocrisy in the groups that represent women in prison. The money and efforts that go into "services" is a mere band-aid effort in conspiracy with the criminal *just-us cystem*. The money and effort would be better directed at commuting the families of the incarcerated women to the prisons. The time that is spent on conducting study upon study is wasted time because statistics stay the same, and the pain stays the same, only the faces of the women change—but the stories are identical.

I entered Prison for Women as a young. poorly-educated, Native woman and I will soon be released with similar characteristics. But, you can add another deficiency—after seven years—I am now an *angry*, young, poor, uneducated, Native woman!

Signed In the Blood of My Sisters,
Ms. Cree XO

This article first appeared in Tightwire *20 (4)*: 26-28.

Also published in Canadian Woman Studies/les cahiers de la femme, *"Native Women," 10 (2 & 3) (Summer/Fall 1989): 87-89. Reprinted with permission of the author.*

A SUITABLE PLACE

Positive Change for Federally-Sentenced Aboriginal Women in Canada

FOR SIXTY YEARS THERE HAVE been calls to close Canada's Prison for Women in Kingston, Ontario. There have also been dozens of commissions and inquiries into the conditions of federally sentenced women in Canada. However, until recently the specific needs of Aboriginal women were not addressed in terms of cultural and historical understandings of their positions in prison and in society.[1] In 1989, the Canadian government convened the Task Force on Federally Sentenced Women. The Task Force, made up of Aboriginal and non-Aboriginal women, addressed the issues of women's incarceration and for the first time, listened to the voices of federally sentenced women. The Task Force resolved to build already being implemented, such as the Okimaw Ohci Healing Lodge, which would allow Aboriginal women the choice of a better life physically, spiritually, emotionally, and culturally.

Unfortunately, literature available on federally-sentenced women and the struggles they face is scarce. When the focus is Aboriginal federally-sentenced women, documents often become overlapping and repetitive. If not for *Creating Choices: The Report on The Task Force on Federally Sentenced Women*, the voices of Aboriginal women who are incarcerated in Canada would be silenced. *Creating Choices* offers us a firsthand look at the lives of federally sentenced women prior to and during their contact with the justice system.

In 1996, the *Report* of *the Inquiry Into Certain Events at the Prison far Women* was published. This report addressed a myriad of issues surrounding the internal problems facing prisoners and staff at Kingston's Prison for Women. The Honourable Madam Justice Louise Arbour headed this commission and in her own words, summed up the situation that Aboriginal women faced with regards to the Canadian criminal justice system: "If the history of women's imprisonment is one of neglect and indifference, it will come as no surprise that the history of Aboriginal women's imprisonment is an exaggeration of the same" (218). The report made recommendations for changing the situation and supports some of the changes that were the creation of the Healing Lodge.

It is important to understand how the lives of federally-sentenced women were affected by the previous facilities and programming—that in some aspects, outside of the Healing Lodge, still exist—which were neither culturally or gender appropriate. I will use the words of Fran Sugar,[2] sister, friend, as well as speaker for many federally sentenced women:

> When we come to prison, we need to adjust to greater and greater violence in our lives. We adjust to increasingly deadly conditions, and come to accept them as "natural." We adjust to having freedoms stolen away from us, to having fewer and fewer choices, less and less voice in the decisions that affect our lives. We come to believe that making $4.20 a day and things we can buy with it are the most important life goals. We have adjusted to deafening silence, because it is now mandatory to wear headphones. We have adjusted to the deafening noises and screams coming from segregation when our Sister has just been stripped of her clothes and maced in the face. We have adjusted to the deadening entertainment of bingo games that give out prized bags of taco chips and we hear glees of happiness at this score, because some pathetic individual hasn't tasted taco chips since 1979.... We have adjusted to dreaming of our futures.
>
> We become so *phucking* numb from the incredible *b/sh* we are exposed to: trying to see a case management officer to get a call to our children is a major, major event. It is no wonder that so many of us cut our throats, lacerate our bodies, hang ourselves. It is no wonder that we need to identify our pain onto our physical bodies, because our whole lives have been filled with incredible pain and traumatizing experiences—psychic pain, physical pain, spiritual pain. I entered Prison for Women as a young, poorly-educated, Native women and I will soon be released with similar characteristics. But, you can add another deficiency—after seven years—I am now an *angry,* young, poor, uneducated, Native woman! (Sugar 89)[3]

This quote speaks to the lives of federally sentenced women and how often life's little moments are taken for granted by those of us on this side of the wall. What is not clear from this reference, (and has been brought to my attention by Patricia Monture-Angus) is that inmates at the Prison for Women were being "maced in the face" long before Louise Arbour's Commission inquired into events at the prison, which took place in April 1994. To be more concise, Sugar wrote about the macing and stripping of prisoners in 1989, while Arbour's Inquiry revolved around events five years later. It is obvious that these inhumane practices were not isolated incidents. When we look at what went "before" in terms of positive change in the lives of federally sentenced Aboriginal women, we find:

> Almost all of the healing experiences that Aboriginal women who have been in prison report lie outside of the conventional prison order. They come through bonds formed with other women in prison,

405

through the support of people on the outside, and from the activities of Native Sisterhood. (Sugar and Fox 478)

This suggests that the need for meaningful change must involve the realization that Aboriginal women have their own methods of healing. Given the time and space, Aboriginal women are capable of implementing support networks which address their specific needs.

The Task Force on Federally-Sentenced Women was thus set up to research and make suggestions toward changing the circumstances of federally sentenced women. Although it might appear to the casual observer that the time constraints (March to October 1989) faced by the Task Force would be too narrow to allow for proper research and development of meaningful recommendations, the Task Force did look to the women in prison for their input, enabling them to come up with their recommendations in less time to come up with their suggestions than those who looked for solutions in books, government institutions, and previous task forces. One has only to observe that there were 26 separate commissions/reports (Shaw 86-7), to realize that a third-party view of federally sentenced women was not sufficient to bring about meaningful change to their condition in prison; the women needed to be heard.

The Task Force then put forth the idea that, "[just] as we cannot tack women on to a men-oriented system of corrections, so we cannot tack Aboriginal women onto any system be it for men or women" (99). They therefore examined not only what it is that makes female offender different from men, but more specifically how Aboriginal women differ from non-Aboriginal men and women in their offending patterns and needs.

For someone looking at the Canadian criminal justice system for the first time, it is hard to imagine why one group of women would need to be seen as separate, or different, from another. To better understand this, we need to look at some of the marked differences between federally sentenced Aboriginal and non-Aboriginal women. I cannot put into words the differences that exist for Aboriginal and non-Aboriginal federally sentenced women and I would not take that liberty because it is not mine to speak of. I can only echo the words of Fran Sugar and Lana Fox, who themselves have firsthand experience of prison and the absence of justice within it's walls and who aided the Task Force by listening and writing the words of 39 federally sentenced Aboriginal women:

...[Prison] and release from prison are not the starting point. Aboriginal women who end up in prison grow up in prison, although the prisons in which they grow up are not the ones to which they are sentenced under law.

No amount of tinkering with prisons can heal the before prison lives of the Aboriginal women who live or have lived within their walls. Prison cannot remedy the problem of poverty on reserves. It cannot deal with immediate or historical genocide that Europeans worked upon our people. It cannot remedy violence, alcohol abuse, sexual assault during childhood, rape, and other violence Aboriginal women experience at the hands of men. Prison cannot heal the past abuse of foster homes, or the indifference and racism of Canada's justice system in its dealings with Aboriginal people. However, the treatment of Aboriginal women within prisons can begin to recognize that these things *are* the realities of the lives that Aboriginal women prisoners have led. (469)

Patricia Monture-Angus advocates the separate system approach by outlining some of the seldom-acknowledged differences between Aboriginal and non-Aboriginal women in her book, *Thunder in My Soul: A Mohawk Woman Speaks:*

> [It] cannot be (and should not be) concluded or assumed that Aboriginal women will construct a response to rape, battering and other instances of abuse, incest, child welfare laws and abortion in the same way that the mainstream feminist movement has. Nor can it be assumed that the dispute resolution mechanisms that Aboriginal women will advance will look the same as those advanced by the mainstream women's movement. (234)

The Task Force on Federally Sentenced Women listened to the voices of federal female offenders and what they needed. They also heard from the families of these women as well as Aboriginal women and men who are concerned about members of their communities (104). Together, with the stories of federally-sentenced women, and the understanding of women's different needs, the Task Force came up with five principles for meaningful change for federally sentenced women.

The first principle for meaningful change was *empowerment.* Empowerment means improving the self-esteem of women whose lives have led them to prison (Task Force 105-6). Empowerment also means giving women the strength, mentally, spiritually, emotionally, and physically to make the choices the task force recommends.

When I look at this recommendation, I see Aboriginal women being returned to the positions they once occupied, and in some communities still occupy, in terms of having a voice and the respect of fellow Aboriginal people. Basically, this is an across-the-board understanding of the knowledge and contribution of Aboriginal women to the community. As an Aboriginal woman, I see my own disempowerment leading to anger, frustration, violence, and self-destruction.

The second guiding principle of change for the Task Force was *meaningful and responsible choices.* In order for federally-sentenced women to empower themselves, in any way, they must be given the option to choose. The availability of choice in the lives of federally sentenced women prepares them for release in the sense that it builds self-sufficiency and the ability to take responsibility for themselves as well as their families (Task Force 107-8).

The third and perhaps most fundamental principle of the Task Force when looking toward making meaningful change in the lives of federally-sentenced women are the principles of *respect and dignity*. Many of us who live our lives on this side of prison walls[4] assume that respect and dignity are givens in daily life. They are not. Respect for the all things is fundamental to Aboriginal spirituality and culture and must be looked at as the first stepping stone to helping federally sentenced Aboriginal women retrieve some of what they have lost, or possibly, never had (Task Force 109).

The fourth principle for change involves a *supportive environment*. There can be no healing without the support of those around you. Healing is not an individual thing, just as getting to a place of violence and selfd-estructiveness is not an individual phenomenon (Task Force 110).

The fifth principle for change is *shared responsibility*. This principle reinforces the notion that the community, as well as the government, and corrections officials must actively participate in and support programs and initiatives that present meaningful choices to federally-sentenced women (Task Force 111).

The Task Force recommended the establishment of five regional facilities, an Aboriginal healing lodge, and additional community release programs. The healing lodge would look to the knowledge of Aboriginal women for structure and programming (Task Force 114-5). The Task Force clearly had a vision for federal female corrections that had never been seen before in the world, both in terms of size and availability of choice.

There is a place in southeastern Saskatchewan the Cree call *Okimaw Ohci* (in translation, "thunder hills"). It is here that the Neekaneet First Nation has leant sacred land to Correctional Services Canada for the site of the Healing Lodge so that federally-sentenced Aboriginal women can begin to heal themselves. The Healing Lodge is also open to non-Aboriginal women whose own life plans show that they will benefit from the kinds of spirituality and healing offered at Okimaw Ohci. These women must apply to be sent to the Lodge (Correctional Service Canada 1997a). The site of the Lodge was chosen on the part of Correctional Service Canada, because the Neekaneet First Nation:

> [Demonstrated] a long tradition of Aboriginal and non-Aboriginal cooperation, an offering of sacred rural land, a sincere interest in making the Healing Lodge part of their communities, and a strong sense of responsibility towards Aboriginal women under sentence. (Correctional Service Canada 1997b)

From the Task Force on Federally-Sentenced Women's recommendations arose a planning committee to "carry out assessments, facility design and overall plan" (Correctional Service Canada 1997b) for the Healing Lodge. The Planning Circle consisted of government and non-government people, Aboriginal groups as well as delegates from the town of Maple Creek. It was the job of this committee to oversee the implementation of the Task Force's recommendations through structure and policy for the Healing Lodge. An Elder's Circle worked closely with the committee as spiritual guides (Correctional Service Canada 1997a).

When planning was completed and the Healing Lodge opened November of 1995, the Planning Committee was replaced by Kekunwemkonawuk, or "Keepers of the Vision" (Correction Service of Canada 1997a). It is their job to ensure that the initiatives recommended by The Task Force are maintained (correction Service of Canada 1997a).

Although the booklet on Okimaw Ohci Healing Lodge—published by Correctional Service Canada [n.d.]—is quite useful in terms of making available information that does not exist elsewhere.[5] I am under the impression[6] that some of this information is bordering on Sacred and some of the stories/wording(s) have possibly been appropriated without proper accreditation or respect. Another problem I have with the booklet is that it comes across as incredibly patronizing and insensitive to the realities of federally-sentenced women. For instance, in one section there is a statement that says, the "[health care] model will mirror *real life* as much as possible" (emphasis added) (Correctional Service Canada [n.d.]: 15). For many Aboriginal women, prison is the only reality that exists—it is *real life*.

Okimaw Ohci Healing Lodge is so removed from the traditional prison system that for those who visit, it is easy to forget that it is still a prison. There are no concrete walls, no razor-wire, and no metal bars. The geography of the land is such that you can see for miles along the treeline, hear the creek splashing below the Spirit Lodge, and see where the beavers make their home. On any summer day you can see children playing in the playground, and even hear the drums and voices of the pow-wow if the season is right. The main building is circular and from the air, one can see that the entire structure, including the residential units and the Spirit Lodge,[7] are built in the shape of an eagle (Wiebe and Johnson 7). To the Cree,[8] the eagle carries great spiritual meaning, thereby reinforcing the tie between spirituality and the Lodge.

The external physical structure gives way to the internal guiding structures of the Lodge. The warden is not called a warden, instead she is called, *Kikawinaw*—Cree for "Our Mother" (Correctional Service Canada 1997b). The other staff members also have (Cree) family designations (Wiebe and Johnson 7). These people oversee the daily operations of the Lodge. In casual conversation there is no delineating of "us" and "them," however, the presence of cameras and paperwork act as reminders that this place is still a prison.

There are several programs in place at Okimaw Ohci that allow federally-sentenced women to expand their knowledge and skills. These programs may be mandatory such as literacy, or elective such as crafts workshops. The programs include (but are not limited to): drug and alcohol treatment, education, and work programs. The residents can also participate in anger management groups, participate in Sentenced Women's survivors' groups, first-aid certificates and food handling (Correctional Service Canada [n.d.]: 4). The programs promote healthy lifestyles with a blend of Aboriginally-focused programs as well as skills that ensure successful reintegration into the community upon release.

Perhaps the most significant change to the lives of federally sentenced Aboriginal women, outside of having meaningful choices, is the option of having their children with them during the child's pre-school years. According to the Task Force on Federally Sentenced Women, "Two out of three federally-sentenced women are mothers, who said they had primary responsibility for their children" (Task Force 101). The Task Force also found that, "Federally-sentenced women who chose to remain in their home provinces, under Exchange of Services Agreements ... did so to maintain regular contact with their children"[9] (Task Force 101). It has also become increasingly apparent that:

> experience with the criminal justice system is intergenerational and that the children of incarcerated parents may be at greater risk than their peers for future involvement with the criminal justice system. Thus the impact of incarceration becomes multigenerational. (Bloom 28)

So we can see that it is not only the mother and child who suffer when women are incarcerated, it is future generations of children as well.

The sacred understanding of the land and how its boundaries are outlined helps one to better appreciate the freedom and respect that Aboriginal women have been allowed at the Healing Lodge:

> [The] Elders tied four ceremonial flags to the trees on the limits of the land at the four directions, to let the Creator and Spirit World acknowledge the place. So thespiritual boundor fencing are needed here because if you cross the boundaries of the four colours you defy the Creator and the Spirits, the ultimate disrespect.... (Wiebe Johnson 7)

It is this spirituality and cultural sensitivity that will ensure the continued healing journeys of federally sentenced Aboriginal women now and in the future.

The Okimaw Ohci Healing Lodge at Neekaneet is the most peaceful place I have ever had the opportunity to visit. From the moment I drove onto the land, I felt an inner peace that I was not even aware of at first. As I drove along the road I tried to imagine why I felt so at peace, and then I realized that it was because I was among people who understand. They understand what it is to live on the margins of society, to be shunned in public, and to struggle with addictions and abuse in its many forms. They understand that acceptance is the most fundamental aspect of life, an aspect we all seek, and hope to find in the hearts and eyes of others. As I drove along, I realized that the reason for the Healing Lodge being in this place was for all of these reasons; because these are some of the very same experiences that have led Aboriginal women to prison.[10]

It has been evident for a number of years that the Canadian criminal justice system has failed Aboriginal people and, more specifically, Aboriginal women. It has only been within the last decade that there been movement toward changing the face of corrections for federally sentenced women in Canada. The change began with the formation of the Task Force on Federally Sentenced Women, which recognized that in order to make meaningful change, women in prison must have a voice. From that arose, *Creating Choices: The Report on The Task Force on Federally Sentenced Women.* This 134-page report detailed the thoughts and feelings of federally-sentenced women and came up with a list of meaningful recommendations for changing women's corrections in Canada. For Aboriginal women, this meant the creation of a HealingLodge on Sacred land on the Neekaneet First Nation. The Okimaw Ohci Healing Lodge was built to accommodate 40 women and up to four children. It observes the cultural understanding of the four directions and a policy of respecting the traditions of all Aboriginal nations considering it houses Aboriginal and non-Aboriginal women from across Canada (Correctional Service Canada [n.d.]: 4-6).

The Okimaw Ohci Healing Lodge also respects the cultural understanding of Aboriginal women and how the absence of positive life choices have led most of the residents into conflict with the Canadian criminal justice system. It speaks to the belief that healing is not a solitary process, and that according to tradition it involves the community, the family, and the children. Thus, the women at Okimaw Ohci are given the opportunity to choose their life paths and journey on the trails that best suit their needs; rather than those impressed upon them by the Canadian criminal justice system which operates on a different value system than thar of the Aboriginal community (Ross; Correctional Service Canada 1997b).

The Healing Lodge has moved justice forward (Monture-Angus 249), for federally-sentenced Aboriginal women, their children, families, and communities. By doing so, Okimaw Ohci will serve to better the tomorrows of all Aboriginal people. The experiences of federally-sentenced Aboriginal women in Canada, have, and will, act as a guide for tolerance and understanding in relationships between Aboriginal and non-Aboriginal people the world over.

Originally published in Canadian Woman Studies/les cahiers de la femme, *"Women and Justice," 19 (1 & 2) (Spring/Summer 1999): 87-89. Reprinted with permission of the author.*

Lori Sparling holds a Bachelor of Arts in English and has an advanced honours certificate in Native Studies. She is the Health Director for Clearwater River Dene Nation where she lives with her six-year-old son.

[1]For the purposes of this paper, I will use the term Aboriginal or Aboriginal people, which according to its constitutional definition includes Indian, Inuit, and Métis.

[2]1 will not disrespect the experiences and realities of the women whom I am speaking of by pretending to understand or even be able to properly paraphrase the experiences of federally sentenced women.

[3]Fran Sugar's article is reprinted in this volume, pgs. 387-390.

[3]I do not assert that those of us who are not incarcerated in a federal institution are entirely better off in circumstance than federally sentenced women. For many who live out their days without food, shelter, or close bonds with families and friends, life on this side of the wall is not always so appealing. I was told once that many of the women in prison have, in prison, what they do not have on the outside-namely relationships, security, and knowledge of knowing what will happen next as well as respect of friends and fellow human beings. I do not think for one minute that I am above any of these women or that life on this side of the wall is the most desired goal for everyonebecause I know that it is not.

[4]Due to the fact that this book is published by Correctional Services Canada, it does not offer what I consider to be a neutral view of the Lodge. However, it does provide information on a subject for which information is, at best, rare.

[5]I use the word "impression" due to a lack of specific knowledge of Sacred Teachings on my part. This *impression* is my own and any error in understanding is my own.

[6]The Spirit Lodge is built in the shape of a tee-pee (Wiebe and Johnson 8).

[7]1 am Cree and my husband is Saulteaux/Cree; he has shared his understanding of the eagle with me.

[8]According to Patricia Monture-Angus, task force member and research advisor, a mother-child program was the number one item that federally sentenced women asked for.

[9]These, of course, are my own perceptions and reasonings, not those of the Task Force, planning committee or *Kekunwemkonawuk.*

REFERENCES

Arbour, Louise. *Report of the Inquiry into Certain Events at the Prison for Women in Kingston.* Ottawa: Canada Communication Group, 1996.

Bloom, Barbara. "Imprisoned Mothers." *Children of Incarcerated Parents.* Eds. Katherine Gabel et al. Toronto: Lexington Books, 1995.

Correctional Service Canada (CSC). "Okimaw Ohci Healing Lodge." Pamphlet. Ottawa: CSC [n.d.].

Correctional Service Canada (CSC). *Federally Sentenced Women Initiative: The Healing Lodge.* Ottawa: CSC, 1997a.

Correctional Service Canada (CSC). *Okimaw Ohci Healing Lodge for Federally Sentenced Women.* Ottawa: CSC, 1997b.

Monture-Angus, Patricia. *Thunder In My Soul: A Mohawk Woman Speaks.* Halifax: Fernwood Publishing, 1995.

Ross, Rupert. *Returning to the Teachings: Exploring Aboriginal Justice.* Toronto: Penguin Books, 1996.

Shaw, Margaret. *The Federal Female Offender.* Ottawa: Minister of Supply and Services Canada, 1989.

Sugar, Fran. "Entrenched Social Catastrophe: Native Women in Prison." *Canadian Woman Studies/les cahiers de la femme* 10 (2-3) (1989): 87-89.

Sugar, Fran, and Lana Fox. *"Nistum Peyako Seht wawin Iskwewak:* Breaking Chains." *Canadian Journal of Women and the Law* 3 (1989-1990): 465-82.

Task Force on Federally Sentenced Women. *Creating Choices: The Report of the Task Force on Federally Sentenced Women.* Ottawa: Minister of Supply and Services Canada, 1990.

Wiebe, Rudy, and Yvonne Johnson. *Stolen Life: Journey of a Cree Woman.* Toronto: AlfredA. Knopf Canada, 1998.

PATRICIA A. MONTURE

WOMEN AND RISK

Aboriginal Women, Colonialism and Correctional Practice

I OFTEN FEEL THAT THE STORIES I have to tell begin outside of the words and ideas that have been placed on pages. There is nowhere that this is more true than when the issue is the contact and experience that Aboriginal people, and especially Aboriginal women, have with the Canadian criminal justice system. Given the thousands of pages of government reports which examine the issue of Aboriginal overrepresentation in the Canadian criminal justice system, this may come as a great surprise to many people. However, the truth remains that much of what I have read about Aboriginal people and Canadian criminal justice is not what I have experienced and been taught were the central issues.

The most recent report on Aboriginal people and the Canadian justice system, is the *Report of the Royal Commission on Aboriginal Peoples.* The justice materials were compiled in a separate report, titled *Bridging the Cultural Divide,*[1] released in 1996 just prior to the Commissioner's six-volume final report. This most recent report is an excellent example of the gap that still exists between Aboriginal understandings of our justice struggles and the words that have been written on the page. It is also essential to note that this report will not be helpful in examining the questions which come to the fore regarding Aboriginal women and the administration of their prison sentences including the issues of risk assessment, risk management, and security classification.[2] The *Report,* in fact, is silent on how to remedy the negative experiences of Aboriginal women from in prison (see Monture-Angus 1999). This is troubling.

It is important to note the nature and scope of the discussion in the Royal Comission on Aboriginal Peoples (RCAP) report. Their first recommendation states:

> Federal, provincial and territorial governments recognize the right of Aboriginal nations to establish and administer their own systems of justice pursuant to their inherent right of self-government, including the power to make laws, within the Aboriginal nation's territory. (RCAP 1996a: 312)

Although I do not disagree in principle with this statement, it is not very realistic in practical terms. As a result of the colonial legacy of Canada, Aboriginal nations are not represented as nations in the way our political organizations have been structured. Rather, these Aboriginal nations are organized around the classifications which arise out of the *Indian Act* regime either because of registration as an "Indian" or the lack of such a legal recognition. This must be seen as a demonstration of the degree to which colonial policy and practice has fragmented and re-structured Aboriginal governing structures. For example, the Assembly of First Nations is an organization which represents *Indian Act* Chiefs while the Congress of Aboriginal People represents those who are not entitled to be registered or maintain off-reserve residency which disentitles them to many of the benefits of the *Indian Act*. If the power to have justice relationships is not maintained at the community level but at the nation level, as the Royal Commission on Aboriginal Peoples endorses, then the power for Aboriginal persons to exercise their jurisdiction in justice matters is seriously compromised if not fully limited. Although this first recommendation is an eloquent statement of principle, it means very little in practical terms as our nations no longer remain significantly organized in this political way. Therefore, celebrating the wisdom of the Royal Commission that saw fit to acknowledge the self-governing power of Aboriginal nations must be cautiously undertaken. The impact of colonialism was discounted by the Commission, if not fully ignored, and as a result no real opportunity exists to transform the recommendations from mere words into reality.

It is equally important to note that the justice recommendations of the Royal Commission did not significantly focus on the circumstances and experiences of Aboriginal people in prison. The rate at which Aboriginal women are overrepresented in Canadian institutions of incarceration is higher than the rate of overrepresentation for Aboriginal men if national figures are used as the base.[3] So if the silence of the Royal Commission on prison circumstances is noted, the double silence regarding the situation of Aboriginal women in prison is of greater consequence as their experiences are often based on the denial of their race/culture and concurrently their gender.[4] Granted, I do believe that it is essential that we look to the future when reclaiming Aboriginal justice practices. I do not agree that this task can be allowed to force us to sacrifice the current generation housed in federal, provincial, and youth institutions of confinement for the mere hope that future generations will not have to face the imposition of Canadian criminal justice law and practices. Hope after all guarantees nothing.

Turning to the six-volume final *Report of the Royal Commission on Aboriginal Peoples* to understand more about the manner in which the Commissioners included Aboriginal women in their work, identifies further problem areas. The Commission believes that we, as women, hold "perspectives"[5] and neatly identifies two issues which are of (by implication) special concern *only* to Aboriginal women.[6] This is an insufficient way to characterize the position of Aboriginal women in our nations. These two issues are violence and loss of status under former section 12(l)(b).[7] Although I do believe that these are important issues, they do not reflect the full diversity of concerns that Aboriginal women possess. They do not reflect my "perspective" on being an Aboriginal (more accurately, Mohawk) woman. Some deconstruction of these ideas and the way they limit my race/culture-based knowledge of gender is necessary.

First, section 12(1)(b) is just one small example of the way Aboriginal governments have been interfered with by the imposition of Canadian ways of and ideas about governing. This includes the way that women's roles were diminished in the government forms that were brought to the Aboriginal territories now known as Canada. This is not a correct construction of the gender-balanced roles in Aboriginal societies. Second, to suggest that the place of Aboriginal women is a "perspective" is to do serious harm to the governing structure of Aboriginal nations that would be described as matrilineal. Gender in these governments is a fundamental part of the way that government responsibilities are distributed.[8]

Both the fact that Aboriginal governments have been interfered with and the specific manner that this interference was gender-based is important to understanding the justice obstacles Aboriginal people now face. Logically then, it can be easily surmised that as women were and *are* central to the structure of Aboriginal governments, women also played a significant role and possessed authority in matters of (criminal) justice. I have heard from Aboriginal people all over the continent: "Grandmother made the rules and Grandfather enforced them." If this is the case, then Aboriginal women had (and still have) a fundamental responsibility with and to justice relations in our communities. The imposition of foreign forms and relations of governance must be seen to have significantly interfered with Aboriginal justice traditions. This does not mean that traditions have been destroyed or that they no longer exist. It simply means that colonialism has had, and continues to have, a negative impact on the ability of Aboriginal people to maintain peaceful and orderly communities.

Since the Task Force on Federally Sentenced Women in 1990, the direction that First Nation[9] communities have taken with justice matters is also of importance to this discussion. The Task Force recommended the building of a Healing Lodge for Aboriginal women. This recommendation was realized with the opening of Okimaw Ochi Healing Lodge at the Nekaneet First Nation in 1995. Since then at least two more lodges[10] have been opened in the prairie provinces with negotiations occurring in other areas of the country as well.[11] Little research[12] has been completed on the introduction of these new institutions no matter how much Aboriginal culture and tradition inspires their contour, shape, and form. This direction demonstrates the degree to which Aboriginal communities have been willing to embrace conventional correctional practice.

The government of the Nekaneet First Nation understood that the Healing Lodge was a part of the legal and bureaucratic structure of the Canadian prison system. In their negotiations, the community addressed this concern by recognizing that the building of the Lodge was only a first step and not a final step. Their vision was that as time passed the Lodge would move more and more toward community control and administration. This was also the vision of the Aboriginal women who participated in the Task Force. Anecdotal evidence clearly suggests that this is not what has happened. Rather, as time passes, the philosophical foundation of the Lodge has shifted toward the Canadian correctional mentality. Chief Larry Oakes of the Nekaneet First Nation had at least one meeting with the Commissioner of Corrections in the fall of 1998 to disuss the community vision and further community involvement. There are no negotiations underway based on this community vision (Oakes) and, in my view, this is unacceptable.

As a result of the willingness of some prairie First Nations to embrace conventional correctional practices such as risk prediction, even as a starting point for taking control of justice matters in their communities, demonstrates the need to examine risk from an Aboriginal standpoint. A "standpoint" is different from a "perspective." The women's facility is designated as a medium-security facility. The federal male institution at Hobemma is a minimum-security facility. This is despite the fact that it has been known for some time that Aboriginal men and women are overrepresented within the maximum-security classification. This is very frustrating.

As a member of the Task Force on Federally Sentenced Women, I believe that my contributions and values have been profoundly disrespected by the Correctional Service of Canada.[13] These "Aboriginal" institutions are based on the borrowed notion of security classification. Therefore, work undertaken after the women's Task Force reported on developing better risk scales by Corrections Canada has a direct, but generally invisible, impact on the institutions that were envisioned by First Nations. Unfortunately, this impact has not been expressed in any of the literature that I have seen on the development of risk predictors or on the new Aboriginal institutions. The isolation in which Aboriginal initiatives are developed in this federal bureaucracy has a profoundly negative impact on the amount of Aboriginal visioning that is possible. As many First Nations communities do not have access to the professionalization of justice relationships, I worry that these consequences are not necessarily always visible. Our dreams are limited by correctional expectations that we will accept certain ideas such as risk management and risk prediction scales. This must be seen for what it is. It is a clear form of systemic and structural disadvantage.

An idea such as risk management is one that is contrary to the community vision of Aboriginal justice and further to how I was raised as an Aboriginal person to think about involvement. As I have noted in other writings, relationships are the central construct in "Indian" law as I understand it (see "Roles and Responsibilities" in Monture-Angus 1996a). People (or any "thing" with spirit) were not intended to be managed but rather respected. The conclusion is that one of the foundational ideas of current correctional philosophy is, in my opinion, incompatible with Aboriginal cultures, law, and tradition. This incompatibility is a greater obstacle than simple theories of cultural conflict. This opinion is a substantive criticism that is much larger than questioning the cultural relevance of programming within correctional institutions which has been a significant preoccupation in the many justice reports that address Aboriginal experiences and concerns.

This discussion has now brought me to the place where I can make some comments about the idea popular among prison administrators regarding their ability to determine risk. These risk scales are all individualized instruments. Applying these instruments to Aboriginal people (male or female) is a significant and central problem. The individualizing of risk absolutely fails to take into account the impact of colonial oppression on the lives of Aboriginal men and women. Equally, colonial oppression has not only had a devastating impact on individuals but concurrently on our communities and nations (see Monture-Angus 1996b). This impact cannot be artificially pulled apart as the impact on the individual and the impact on the community are interconnected.

For example, in the *Report of the Aboriginal Justice Inquiry of Manitoba,* it is noted that Aboriginal "women move to urban centres to escape family or community problems. Men on the other hand, cite employment as the reason for moving" (485). Once in the city, many Aboriginal women face issues that they had not expected from systemic and overt to subtle forms of racism as well as lack of opportunities. The Manitoba Justice Inquiry notes that "what they were forced to run to is often as bad as what they had to run from" (485). And often, what they experience in the city (from shoplifting to prostitution, drug abuse to violence) as a result of poverty and racism, leads them into contact with the criminal justice system. Yet, a criminal court is not interested in hearing about this long trail of individualized and systemic colonialism which leads to conflict with the law. Courts are only interested in whether you committed a wrong act with a guilty mind. This is a clear example of how the individualized nature of law obscures systemic and structural factors. This is a problem that exists within the court process but also in other justice decision-making practices and bodies such as security classification, risk assessment, penitentiary placement, parole, and so on.

Examination of the risk prediction scales identifies many common considerations taken into account to predict security classifications which influence the conditions of confinement. For example,

> [t]he Case Needs Identification and Analysis protocol identifies seven need dimensions, including *employment, marital/family, associates, substance abuse, community functioning, personal/emotional and attitudes.* (Motiuk 19; emphasis added)

Several of these dimensions are particularly problematic for Aboriginal "offenders." Aboriginal people do not always belong to communities that are functional and healthy (and colonialism is significantly responsible for this fact). Therefore, constructing a "community functioning" category ensures that Aboriginal people will not have access to scoring well in this category. This is not a factor for which individuals can be held solely accountable. Rather than measuring risk this dimension merely affirms that Aboriginal persons have been negatively impacted by colonialism. The same kind of assessment can be put forward for the dimensions of "marital/family" and "associates" as the incidence of individuals with criminal records is greater in Aboriginal communities. It has been frequently noted that the issue of substance abuse in Aboriginal communities is a symptom[14] of a much larger problem. Therefore, this simple analysis demonstrates that scoring higher on these categories is predetermined for Aboriginal prisoners because of the very structure of the instruments. What is being measured is not "risk" but one's experiences as part of an oppressed group.

The work that assesses the validity of these risk prediction scales is also a problem because it does not do race (Aboriginal) and gender (female) as categories that are inclusive (see Motiuk; Blanchette; Bonta; Collin). The studies tend to examine the validity of these scales for Aboriginal people but not for Aboriginal women. Despite this fact, prison administrators and senior bureaucrats remain committed to applying these "tests" and concepts to the structure of individual Aboriginal women's prison sentences as well as to the manner in which the prisons in which Aboriginal women serve their sentence are structured.

In my opinion, this is a violation of the *Canadian Charter of Rights and Freedoms'* section 15 equality provisions. It also strains the common sense interpretation of section 28 of the *Corrections and Conditional Release Act,* which provides that persons confined in a penitentiary shall be confined in the least restrictive environment. If risk prediction scales are not valid for Aboriginal women (and I have not seen convincing documentation that they are), then security decisions based on these scales cannot be reasonably applied to Aboriginal women.

Enough has been said and written about the devastating effects of the Canadian criminal justice system on both Aboriginal citizens and our nations. Despite this fact, little has been accomplished to do more than accommodate Aboriginal persons within the mainstream system. There has been no systemic change of Canadian justice institutions. As we approach the tenth anniversary of the report of the Task Force on Federally Sentenced Women, perhaps it is time to revisit the work of the last decade and see how true it has remained to the original vision of the women who were asked to participate in this project. This project should take place within some formal structure. I am quite confident that I am not the only former Task Force participant who is bitterly disappointed.

The author would like to acknowledge the guidance of the late Elder, Dr. Art Solomon and the many Aboriginal women who have served federal sentences who have demonstrated their patience and understanding when teaching her. Any errors are the author's and not the teachers'.

This paper was originally presented at the Interdisciplinary Workshop on Risk Assessment, Risk Management, and Classification organized by Professors Kelly Hannah Moffat (Brock University) and Margaret Shaw (Concordia University) held in Toronto on May 21-23, 1999. The support of Status of Women Canada is gratefully acknowledged.

Originally published in Canadian Woman Studies/les cahiers de la femme, *"Women and Justice," 19 (1 & 2) (Spring/Summer 1999): 24-29. Reprinted with permission of the author.*

Patricia A. Monture is a citizen of the Mohawk Nation, Grand River Territory. She is currently teaching in the Sociology Department at the University of Saskatchewan where she coordinates the Aboriginal Justice and Criminology Program. She is a committed activist/scholar who continues to seek justice for Aboriginal peoples and especially Aboriginal women and girls.

[1]It is my understanding that the justice materials were released early as a way of noting the seriousness with which the Commissioners saw this topic.

[2]Pages 139-147 of *Bridging the Cultural Divide* discusses the experiences of Aboriginal women in prison. This discussion does not move beyond the descriptive and no recommendations are made. The Commissioners did attend a special hearing at the Kingston Prison for Women, and the women shared their stories (often very painful stories) with them. The end result is that the Commission "borrowed" the pain of Aboriginal women prisoners and gave nothing beyond a few pages of descriptive discussion back to the women. This fails to meet the standards of responsibility that I was raised with as a Mohawk woman. If you take from a person, you are obligated to give back at least what you took. The irony that this is what occurred in a Commission that was meant to be Aboriginal-specific and Aboriginal-focused has not escaped me.

[3]The national figures do disguise some of the circumstances that Aboriginal men who are incarcerated experience. Although the national rate of overrepresentation is a figure lower than twenty per cent (depending who counts and how the counting is being done) for Aboriginal men, this figure hides the fact that Aboriginal men make up approximately eighty per cent of the population at Saskatchewan Penitentiary.

[4]My point is not numerical and I realize that there are far fewer women incarcerated in Canadian prisons than men.

[5]The section on Aboriginal women is titled, "Women's Perspectives" and appears as Chapter 2 of the volume titled, "Perspectives and Realities." The chapter

devoted to women begins on page 7 and the discussion ends on page 96 (totaling 90 pages). Not including introductions and conclusion, the discussion appears under the headings: "Historical Position and Role of Aboriginal Women: A Brief Overview" (3.5 pages); "Reversing a Pattern of Exclusion-Women's Priorities for Change" (less than a page); "Aboriginal Women and Indian Policy: Evolution and Impact" (31 pages); "Health and Social Services: A Priority on Healing" (9.5 pages); "The Need for Places of Refuge" (6.5 pages); "The Rise of Aboriginal Women's Organizations" (3 pages); "the Need for Fairness and Accountability (12 pages); and, "The Family" (12 pages). The longest discussion deals with issues of status and membership under the *Indian Act*. The relationship between violence in communities and the overrepresentation of Aboriginal women in corrections institutions is not made.

[6]The way the Commission has constructed gender is highly problematic. Violence against women is not a women's problem. It is a community problem. Further, the section on "family" appears in the women's section. Are men no longer part of our families with particular gender-based responsibilities?

[7]This section of the *Indian Act* stripped Indian women of their status if they "married out." The same prohibition was not extended to women who "married in." I am not familiar with any research which examines if there is a relationship between being stripped of your status and contact with the criminal justice system. The idea that such research might yield interesting results occurs because many Indian women who go to the city do not have and have not had access to educational opportunities or employment. This is another example of the gaps that exist in the written record.

[8]See, for example, Aboriginal Justice Inquiry of Manitoba, 475-477.

[9]The change of language from Aboriginal to First Nations is intentional. It indicates that my comments focus on the experiences of "Indians" to the exclusion of Metis and Inuit peoples.

[10]The Prince Albert Grand Council operates a facility on the Wahpeton (Dakota) First Nation near the city of Prince Albert, Saskatchewan. This facility holds only male offenders primarily serving provincial sentences with five federal beds. The Pe'Sakastew Centre is located on the Hobemma (Cree) First Nation in Alberta. It is a federal minimum security facility.

[11]This is one of the ways that First Nations have chosen to participate in reclaiming traditional justice practices.

[12]The most significant research was completed by Connie Braun (Cree) in her M.A. thesis (1998). In this work she documents the experiences of Aboriginal men at the Hobemma facility against their experiences of conventional prisons.

[13]Please see Chapter 2 of the Task Force Report, *Creating Choices*, for a discussion of the hesitations the Aboriginal women had with regard to participating in the Task Force. I do understand that the degree to which I feel violated in this process arises out of my Aboriginal values and teachings about respect.

[14]Further research, research that is conducted with the primary involvement

(meaning control) of Aboriginal persons (including women) is needed in this area.

REFERENCES

Aboriginal Justice Inquiry of Manitoba. *Report of the Aboriginal Justice Inquiry of Manitoba.* Winnipeg: Queen's Printer, 1991.

Blanchette Kelly. "Classifying Female Offenders for Correctional Interventions." *Forum (on Corrections Research)* 9 (1) (January 1997): 36-41.

Bonta, James. "Do We Need Theory for Offender Risk Assessment?" *Forum (on Corrections Research)* 9 (1) (January 1997): 42-45.

Braun, Connie. "Colonization, Destruction, and Renewal: Stories from Aboriginal Men at the Pe'Sakastew Centre." M.A. Thesis. University of Saskatchewan, 1998.

Collin, Jeannette. "Legal Aspects of Inmates's Security Classification." *Forum (on Corrections Research)* 9 (1) (January 1997): 55-57.

Monture-Angus, Patricia. "The Justice *Report of the Royal Commission on Aboriginal Peoples:* Breaking with the Past?" Paper presented at "Building the Momentum: A Conference on Implementing the Recommendations of the Royal Commission on Aboriginal Peoples." Osgoode Hall, Toronto, Ontario. 22-24 April 1999. Online: <www.Indigenousbar.ca>.

Monture-Angus, Patricia. *Thunder in My Soul: A Mohawk Woman Speaks.* Halifax: Fernwood Books, 1996a.

Monture-Angus, Patricia. "Lessons in Decolonization: Aboriginal Over-Representation in Canadian Criminal Justice." *Visions of the Heart.* Eds. David Long and Ovide Dickason. Toronto: Harcourt Brace, 199610.

Motiuk, Larry. "Classification for Correctional Programminmg: The Offender Intake Assessment (OIA) Process." *Forum (on Corrections Research)* 9 (1) (January 1997): 18-22.

Oakes, Chief Larry. Personal interview. 27 April 1999.

Royal Commission on Aboriginal Peoples (RCAP). *Bridging the Cultural Divide.* Ottawa: Supply and Services, 1996a.

Royal Commission on Aboriginal Peoples (RCAP). *Report of the Royal Commission on Aboriginal Peoples.* Ottawa: Supply and Services, 1996b.

Task Force on Federally Sentenced Women. *Creating Choices: The Report of the Task Force on Federally Sentenced Women.* Ottawa: Minister of Supply and Services Canada, 1990.

M. CÉLESTE MCKAY

INTERNATIONAL HUMAN RIGHTS STANDARDS AND INSTRUMENTS RELEVANT TO INDIGENOUS WOMEN

THERE ARE SEVERAL INTERNATIONAL human rights standards and laws that are relevant to advancing the human rights of Indigenous women—as members of Indigenous nations and as individual women. The lived experiences of Indigenous women call for protection to be sought from a variety of sources—those that protect individual rights, such as the right to live free from violence, which has been developed under the framework of "women's rights" as well as those rights that protect Indigenous Peoples as peoples, most notably, the United Nations *Declaration on the Rights of Indigenous Peoples.* For example, Indigenous women suffer from many human rights violations, as noted below:

> Indigenous women in many areas of the world are suffering from the alarming deterioration of health conditions within their communities. Inadequate and limited access to health services, lack of culturally appropriate approaches to health care, lack of outreach clinics in remote areas, deteriorating quality of air, water and land due to unchecked industrial development are just a few of the factors contributing to this downward trend. Other socio-economic factors, such as the alarming number of indigenous women, (especially in Asia) being trafficked and sold into prostitution, have led to the rapid spread of the HIV/AIDS epidemic and other sexually transmitted diseases into indigenous communities, destroying their social fabric. Changes in the traditional social, cultural and political institutions have led to an erosion or loss of practices and culturally appropriate health rules and codes of behaviour which have been instrumental in ensuring gender-sensitive approaches to health.[1]

These inequalities and challenges facing Indigenous women can only be overcome by advocacy at all levels—local, national and international. Below, key international instruments that can be used by Indigenous women in Canada and globally are outlined. Many times, international advocacy efforts can work in tandem with local and national efforts aimed at improving the human rights of Indigenous women. International avenues of recourse often place political pressure on Canada to live up to their international obligations, shaming them into action.

The rights outlined below are set out according to the categories of rights, rather than by instrument. These include the rights to equality and non-discrimination, the right to self-determination, the right to live free from violence, the right to an adequate standard of living, the right to culture, the right to free, prior and informed consent, the right to participate in decision-making and the right to property.

THE RIGHTS TO EQUALITY AND NON-DISCRIMINATION

The rights to equality and non-discrimination are well established under international law. These rights are important both in relation to equality and non-discrimination between non-Indigenous individuals and Indigenous individuals (such as matrimonial property rights, for example) as well as between Indigenous women and Indigenous men (in relation to the right to live free from violence, for example).

Indigenous women often experience inequalities, both in comparison to non-Indigenous women and in comparison to their male counterparts. For example, Indigenous women may suffer from discrimination in housing and employment in urban settings from non-Indigenous peoples. At the same time, Indigenous women often face greater risk of domestic violence within their own communities. Thus, rights to equality and non-discrimination are necessary in order to reduce inequality within Indigenous societies and between Indigenous and non-Indigenous women.

This must be done in a way that promotes self-determination without subverting gender equality.[2] For example, it could be asserted that a patriarchal Indigenous society does not need to institute protections for the female members of their society (such as matrimonial property laws that promote equal distribution of lands between a wife and a husband) and that their right to self-determination grants them the authority to disregard the equality rights of the women in their communities. This type of argument can be refuted by the assertion that the members of these communities have equality rights, or rights to non-discrimination, that are recognized not only in national but international instruments. International instruments apply universally, a fact that has been recognized by Indigenous Peoples who have worked within the United Nations system for its recognition of their right to self-determination for over 20 years (through the development of the UN Declaration on the Rights of Indigenous Peoples) and throughout the history of the UN.[3]

This legal principle of equality is often bolstered by traditional norms and customs of Indigenous Peoples, even in patriarchal societies, where egalitarian principles were traditionally upheld. In some countries, such as Canada, colonization has had an impact on the egalitarian treatment of women in these societies. This is where the application of the principles of equality and non-discrimination can be very helpful.

These rights are contained within the following instruments:

Right to Equality:
•Articles 1 and 7 of the UN *Universal Declaration of Human Rights* (UDHR);
•Articles 3 of the UN *International Covenant on Economic, Social and Cultural Rights* (the ICESCR) and the *International Covenant on Civil and Political Rights* (the ICCPR), (specifically in relation to equality between men and women);
•Articles 2 and 44 of the UN *Declaration on the Rights of Indigenous Peoples* (DRIP).

The Convention on the Elimination of All Forms of Discrimination against Women (the CEDAW) provides for equality between men and women. In particular, article 16(1)(c) of the CEDAW provides for appropriate measures to be taken by States to ensure "the same rights and responsibilities during marriage and at its dissolution" between men and women.

Right to Non-Discrimination:
•Article 2 of the UDHR;
•Article 2 (2) of the ICESCR;
•Article 2(1) of the ICCPR;
•Article 2 of the DRIP.

The International Convention on the Elimination of All Forms of Racial Discrimination (CERD) provides for the elimination of racial discrimination.

THE RIGHT TO SELF-DETERMINATION

Gaining recognition of the right to self-determination is critical to indigenous women in addressing the historic wrongs experienced by their nations. This has been expressed by the International Indigenous Women's Forum (FIMI) in its Beijing +10 Declaration, where it states:

We maintain that the advancement of Indigenous Women's human rights is inextricably linked to the struggle to protect, respect and fulfill both the rights of our Peoples as a whole and our rights as women within our communities and at the national and international level.[4]

The right of self-determination, along with two important sub-sets of this right, the right to free, prior and informed consent and the right to participate in decision-making are discussed.

The right of self-determination is protected by article 1 of both the ICCPR and the ICESCR (although the application of article 1 to Indigenous Peoples is contentious).[5] Article 1(1) of both the ICCPR and the ICESCR states that, "All peoples have the right of self-determination. By virtue of that right they freely determine their political status and freely pursue their economic, social and cultural development." This wording is replicated in the DRIP, except the word "All" is replaced with "Indigenous."[6]

This right should be used as a foundational principle in recognizing the legal systems of the particular Indigenous People concerned. As discussed above, fears about the protection of individual rights can be allayed by the understanding that all self-determining nations are accountable to act in a manner that is respectful of all international peremptory norms, including equality and non-discrimination.

This right is contained within the following additional provisions:

Article 3 of the DRIP explicitly recognizes the right to self-determination of Indigenous peoples. Other articles, such as article 4, 5 and 7 elaborate upon the right of self-determination contained under article 3. The United Nations General Assembly adopted the Declaration on September 13, 2007.

The International Labor Organization's Indigenous and Tribal Peoples Convention, 1989 (No. 169) (the ILO Convention 169) provides for a right to self-determination but this is generally recognized to be of a lower standard to that of the UN DRIP.[7]

FREE, PRIOR AND INFORMED CONSENT

The principle that a state is required to obtain the free, prior and informed consent of Indigenous Peoples prior to development or removal of their lands, territories and resources is gaining recognition under international law.[8] This is a right that should inform any legislative framework. Without adequate protection of the right of Indigenous Peoples to make their own decisions over lands, resources and territories, the right to self-determination will remain unfulfilled in a meaningful way. Meaningful application of the principle of free, prior and informed consent must be built on the full and effective participation of members of the particular community.

In the case of matrimonial property concerns, it is clear that the dispossession of First Nations from their lands and the imposition of the *Indian Act* is what lead to the current situation of inequalities. A specific approach to matrimonial property regime is required immediately to remedy the violations of the rights of individual members, but this must be done in tandem with efforts to resolve outstanding land claims and larger reforms aimed at ending the post-colonial relationship between Indigenous peoples and the Canadian government. In practical terms, this could be done by weighing whether particular reform options will lead to upholding or negating this principle of free, prior and informed consent. This should not be viewed as conflicting with individual human rights, since a meaningful application of the principle of free, prior and informed consent would be built on the full and effective participation of members of the community in question, as discussed below.

This right is contained in the following instruments:

•Articles 10, 19 and 32 of the DRIP
•Article 16 of the ILO Convention 169
•Article 8 (j) of the Convention on Biological Diversity

THE RIGHT TO PARTICIPATE IN DECISION-MAKING

Indigenous Peoples' right to participate in decision-making on matters affecting their rights is related to the above principle of FPIC. It is particularly pertinent to assertions that Indigenous women must have an equal voice at the legislative and policy levels. Under international law, the principle of the right to participate in decision-making is recognized in implementing economic, social and cultural rights.[9] This is also a principle contained within national legislation, including section 15 of the Charter and section 35(4) of the Canadian Constitution. In Canada, Indigenous women have not achieved this equal voice due to colonial influences such as the *Indian Act* which historically forbade women from holding office as Chiefs or Band Councillors. One study found that out of 633 chiefs, only 87 were women.[10]

The right of Indigenous women to participate in decision-making processes is critical to the development, implementation and evaluation of any and all policy and legislative initiatives affecting them. This is because systemic discrimination in many circumstances has prevented Indigenous women from exercising their right to participate in decision-making.

This right is contained within the following instruments:

•Articles 18 and 22 of the DRIP;
•Article 7 of the CEDAW.

THE RIGHT TO LIVE FREE FROM VIOLENCE

The right to live free from violence is strongly inter-related to the promotion of the overall socio-economic status of Indigenous women. This right under international law has developed over time.[11] This right is highly inter-related numerous other rights, such as equality, non-discrimination, sexual and reproductive rights and matrimonial property rights. It is well-recognized that where Indigenous women face violence they are left vulnerable to other human rights violations, such as lack of housing, lack of sexual and reproductive rights, etc. Statistics and the daily experiences of Indigenous women make it clear that this is a problem that disproportionately affects Indigenous women, as compared to both non-Indigenous women and Indigenous men.[12]

This right can be found in the following instruments:

•Article 22 of the DRIP;
•Article 5 (b) of the CERD;
•The UN Declaration on the Elimination of Violence against Women.

THE RIGHT TO AN ADEQUATE STANDARD OF LIVING

The right to an adequate standard of living is particularly important to improving the socio-economic status of Indigenous women and is essential to ensuring that their basic human needs are not jeopardized. Currently, Indigenous women suffer from, for example, inadequate housing, food insecurity, ill health and disabilities at disproportionate rates. The lack of the right to an adequate standard of living realized by Aboriginal women in Canada has been the subject of grave criticism by the international and national human rights community.[13]

Similar to the right to live free from violence, the right to an adequate standard of living calls for legislative and policy reforms aimed at ensuring that the underlying socio-economic conditions are addressed through effective measures.

This right is contained within the following instruments:

•Article 25 of the UDHR;
•Article 11 of the ICESCR.

THE RIGHT TO CULTURE

The right to culture is important in asserting the rights of Indigenous women from a holistic perspective:

Aboriginal women must take their rightful place in Aboriginal governments, and in shaping the future of Aboriginal nations. Capacity development and Aboriginal women's leadership, as well as the restoration of the traditional roles of Aboriginal women are essential to the restoration of Aboriginal governance.[14]

In Canada, the right to culture was successfully used by Sandra Lovelace to claim her right to live in her community when she was excluded under section 12(1)(b) of the *Indian Act*, which was inherently sexist and granted different rights to status to women than men. The United Nations Human Rights Commission ruled in favour of Ms Lovelace, determining that the provisions of the *Indian Act* were unilaterally enacted by the government of the day in violation of her right to culture.

The promotion of the right to culture must be understood in a way that recognizes the right of all members of the society on an equal, non-discriminatory basis. Framing the right in such a manner requires a nuanced approach to understanding the universality of human rights and culture as a fluid concept, as discussed above.[15] In this manner, forms of self-determination that do not respect peremptory norms such as equality and non-discrimination are challenged, as are forms of continued colonialism where oppression from states on Indigenous Peoples' rights to self-determination lead to continued suppression of Indigenous cultures.

This right is contained within the following instruments:

•Article 27 of the iccpr provides that persons belonging to "…minorities shall not be denied the right, in community with the other members of their group, to enjoy their culture…" (*Lovelace v. Canada* (24/1977)(R.6/24), iccpr, A/ 36/40 (30 July 1981) 166);
•Article 15. 1 (a) of the icescr provides for the right of everyone to "take part in cultural life";
•Article 5 of the drip provides for a right of Indigenous peoples to their distinct cultural institutions (as well as political, economic, legal and social ones);
•Article 8 of the drip provides for protection against "forced assimilation or destruction of their culture";
•Article 9 of the drip provides for the right to belong to an Indigenous nation in accordance with community customs and traditions. Regarding the protection of customs, languages and traditions, see also Articles 11 to 16, 27, 33, 34, 35 and 36 of the drip;
•Article 5 (e) (vi) of the cerd;
•Article 30 of the Convention on the Rights of the Child.

THE RIGHT TO PROPERTY

The right to property is a basic human right that requires all individuals and collectivities, or in this case, all Indigenous persons and all Indigenous Peoples, respectively, to own property without arbitrary distinctions being made. For example, in this context, a claim that a traditional society could discriminate against women, on the basis of their right to self-determination, is inconsistent with this international right. Other instruments outlined below make it clear as well that non-discrimination on the basis of gender, race, etc. must be upheld in relation to property division.

Indigenous women have faced many violations to their right to property, particularly in the context of matrimonial property rights on reserve. While individuals living off reserve have matrimonial real property protections (such as equal division of the matrimonial home) found in provincial and territorial laws, these protections do not extend to individuals living on reserve where the *Indian Act* governs land management, rendering provincial and territorial laws inapplicable.[16] This causes grave injustices to Indigenous women who may be left without access to the matrimonial home on reserve upon marital breakdown. Indigenous women facing violence are even more vulnerable due to these lack of property rights.

The right to property without discrimination and on an equal basis to others, is contained within the following instruments:

•Article 17 of the UDHR provides that everyone has a right to own property individually and collectively and that no one should "be arbitrarily deprived" of one's property;
•Article 21 of the DRIP provides for the right, without discrimination, to socio-economic improvements, including housing;
•Article 5 (d) (v) of the CERD;
•Article 16 (1)(h) of the CEDAW.

CONCLUSION

The reality is that in Canada and across the world, many Indigenous women suffer from grave human rights violations, at all levels—from the right to live free from violence, to the right to self-determination to the right to own property, to name only a few examples. It is hoped that this summary of some of the key human rights instruments and standards available to advance the human rights of Indigenous women will be of assistance in remedying the human rights violations facing Indigenous women, their families and their nations.

This article is adapted from previous article written by M. Céleste McKay for the Native Women's Association of Canada entitled, "International Human Rights Standards and Instruments Relevant to Indigenous Women: An Information Paper Prepared for the National Aboriginal Women's Summit, June 20-22, 2007 in Corner Brook, Newfoundland.

Originally published in Canadian Woman Studies/les cahiers de la femme, *"Indigenous Women in Canada: The Voices of First Nations, Inuit and Métis Women," 26 (3 & 4) (Winter/Spring 2008): 147-152. Reprinted with permission of the author.*

M. Céleste McKay is a Métis woman from Manitoba. She has a Bachelor of Social Work degree from the University of Manitoba, a LL.B. degree from the University of Victoria and a LL.M. from the University of Ottawa that focused on the international right to health of Indigenous women in Canada. Céleste has worked in the areas of human rights, policy, research and advocacy work, primarily on behalf of Indigenous women's organizations. She is the Director of Human Rights and International

Affairs for the Native Women's Association of Canada. Her greatest source of joy is her son, Evan Raoul Chartrand.

[1]Permanent Forum on Indigenous Issues, Report of the Third Session (10-21 May 2004), UN Doc. No. E/C.19/2004/23, p. 23.

[2]See article 46(2) of the United Nations *Declaration on the Rights of Indigenous Peoples* which calls for a balancing of human rights and fundamental freedoms of all and article 46(3) which sets out the principles of "justice, democracy, respect for human rights, equality, non-discrimination, good governance and good faith" in the interpretation of the rights contained in the Declaration.

[3]See MADRE/FIMI, Marin Iwanka Raya: *Indigenous Women Stand Against Violence: A Companion Report to the United Nations Secretary-General's Study on Violence Against Women* (New York: MADRE/FIMI, 2007) at 29 where the "rights versus culture" discourse is identified as a false dichotomy: "By the 1990s, the notion of culture as the exclusive purview of Indigenous, eastern, or other 'primitive' people had lost much of its legitimacy. But a new doctrine of 'cultural relativity' emerged, arguing an inherent tension between universal human rights standards and local cultural practices. The dichotomy maintains the assumption that cultures are monolithic and homogeneous, rather than dynamic, fluid processes." The authors call for an integrated understanding of human rights, noting that "the work of Indigenous anti-violence activists is not predicated on a rejection of their culture as merely a site of oppression, but is grounded in the understanding that culture can be deployed in multiple, even conflicting, ways, including in defense of women's human rights. Along with the notion of culture as static and sacred, there is another conception of culture that threatens Indigenous women, rooted in western colonial conquest. This view suggests that 'culture' is found only in 'primitive' or backward places, not in 'western civilization.' (Thus, date rape and child beauty pageants in the U.S. are not considered harmful cultural practice" [at 29].)

[4]FIMI, Declaration of the International Indigenous Women's Forum, Indigenous women beyond the ten-year review of the Beijing Declaration and Program of Action, 2005.

[5]Indigenous peoples have asserted this right to self-determination on an equal basis to all other peoples throughout history. The UN General Assembly strongly recognized and reaffirmed this right when it adopted the UN Declaration in September 2007. For a discussion on the development of this right under international law see S. James Anaya, *Indigenous Peoples in International Law: Second Edition* (Oxford: Oxford University Press, 2004) at 8 and at 49 where he states, "Shaped by Western perspectives and political power, international law developed a complicity with the often brutal forces that wrested lands from indigenous peoples, suppressed their cultures and institutions, and left them among the poorest of the poor." See also Rodríguez-Piñero *supra* note 4 at 261-262, "The political discourse of the international indigenous movement was founded on a critical reformulation of the bases of international law that

did not recognize the legal personality of indigenous peoples and relegated them to a predicament of internal colonialism within their own territories. Indigenous peoples reminded the world that the consequences of colonialism persisted after formal decolonization, and pleaded for recognition of their right to a full measure of self-determination as the cornerstone of their aspirations to cultural preservation and development, the exercise of full-government and jurisdiction, and control over their traditional lands and natural resources. The indigenous movement was successful in articulating those aspirations in human rights terms, contributing to the generation of new normative understandings concerning the specific catalogue of rights pertaining to these peoples *qua* peoples. [References omitted].

[6]Article 3 of the UN *Declaration on the Rights of Indigenous Peoples.*

[7]For a full discussion of the ILO Convention No. 169 see Luis Rodríguez-Piñero, *Indigenous Peoples, Postcolonialism, and International Law: The ILO Regime (1919-1989)* (Oxford: Oxford University Press Inc., 2005). There are many regional examples of instruments that recognize the right to self-determination, but it is beyond the scope of this paper to discuss these instruments.

[8]See *Report of the International Workshop on Methodologies regarding Free, Prior and Informed Consent and Indigenous Peoples*, UN Permanent Forum on Indigenous Issues, 4th Sess., UN Doc. E/C.19/2005/3, (2005) (PFII FPIC) which outlines the origins of this right. In its Conclusions at 10, the report states that, "Various international instruments, such as the ILO Convention (no. 169) concerning Indigenous and Tribal Peoples in Independent Countries, and the Convention on Biological Diversity, as well as pronouncements of international human rights treaty bodies, provide a normative basis for free, prior and informed consent." For a complete listing of these instruments, see *ibid* at 24. See also *General Comment 23 supra* note 133. See also I/A Comm. H. R. *Mayagna (Sumo) Awas Tingni Community v. Nicaragua*, Judgment of August 31, 2001, Ser. C. No. 79 (2001) (*Awas Tingni*).

[9]See for example, *Women and Health (Article 12) (General Recommendation No. 24)*, UN Committee on the Elimination of Discrimination against Women, 20th Sess., UN Doc. A/54/38 (1999) 5 at para. 31 (a).

[10]Judith F. Sayers and Kelly A. MacDonald, "A Strong and Meaningful Role for First Nations Women in Governance" in Judith F. Sayers et al. *First Nations Women, Governance and the Indian Act: A Collection of Policy Research Reports* (Ottawa: Status of Women Canada, 2001) at 11.

[11]See *CEDAW, supra* note 10, arts 1, 2, 5, 6. While CEDAW does not specifically include the right to live free from violence, several of its provisions are related to eliminating discrimination against women, for example, Articles 1, 2 and 5, as well as Article 6, which requires States to take appropriate measures to "suppress all forms of traffic in women and exploitation of prostitution of women". However, the Committee on the Elimination of Discrimination against Women clarified that the right to live free from violence is a right contained in CEDAW in its General Recommendation No. 19: *Violence against*

women (General Recommendation No. 19), UN Committee on the Elimination of Discrimination against Women, 11th Sess., UN Doc. CEDAW /C/1992/L.1/ Add.15 (1992).

[12]See: *Consideration of Reports Submitted by States Parties Under Article 40 of the Covenant, Advanced Unedited Version: Canada*, UN Human Rights Committee, 85th Sess., UN Doc. CCPR/C/CAN/CO/5/ at para. 23, where it states that, "The State party should gather accurate statistical data throughout the country on violence against Aboriginal women, fully address the root causes of this phenomenon, including the economic and social marginalization of Aboriginal women, and ensure their effective access to the justice system. The State party should also ensure that prompt and adequate response is provided by the police in such cases, through training and regulations."

[13]Standing Senate Committee on Human Rights, "Seventeenth Report To Examine and Report Upon Key Legal Issues Relating to the Division of On-Reserve Matrimonial Real Property," (Ottawa: Standing Senate Committee on Human Rights, 2005); Standing Senate Committee on Human Rights, A Hard Bed to Lie In: Matrimonial Real Property on Reserve: Interim Report of the Standing Senate Committee on Human Rights (Ottawa: Standing Senate Committee on Human Rights, 2003); Report of the Special Rapporteur on the situation of human rights and fundamental freedoms of indigenous people, Rodolfo Stavenhagen, Addendum, Mission to Canada, UN Commission on Human Rights, 61st Sess., UN Doc. E/CN.4/2005/88/Add.3 (2004) at para. 90 [Stavenhagen Report]; Consideration of Reports Submitted by States Parties under Articles 16 and 17 of the Covenant: Concluding Observations of the Committee on Economic, Social and Cultural Rights: Canada, UN Committee on Economic, Social and Cultural Rights, 36th Sess., UN Doc. E/C.12/CAN/CO/4 E/C.12/CAN/CO/5 (2006) at para. 45; Consideration of Reports Submitted by States Parties Under Article 40 of the Covenant, Advanced Unedited Version: Canada, UN Human Rights Committee, 85th Sess., UN Doc. CCPR/C/CAN/CO/5/ at para. 22 [HRC Concluding Observations 2005]; UN Human Settlements Programme (UN-HABITAT) and Office of the High Commissioner for Human Rights (OHCHR), Indigenous peoples' right to adequate housing: A global overview (Nairobi: UN-HABITAT and OHCHR, 2005) [UN-HABITAT] at 89.

[14]Native Women's Association of Canada, "Restoring Balance, Addressing Poverty and Building Healthy Communities: A Policy Paper Prepared for the Second National Aboriginal Women's Summit II" (Ottawa: NWAC, 2008) at 7.

[15]*Supra*, footnote 3.

[16]1986, *Derrickson v. Derrickson.*

INDIGENOUS KNOWLEDGES

WHEN I WAS A CHILD

When I was a child
I used to go fishing
along with my bap pa

He used to say to me
Listen! Ndan—senh!
Listen to the sounds of the boat.

Do you hear water splashing
against our boat?
and I'd say,
ah yes, Bap pa!

He said, *the wood of the boat*
is talking to the water spirit.
Ssh! Listen!
They are singing together!

And when I listened
My ears became sharp
to the sounds of the outside world

The sound of the boat groaned and cried
for she, the Noodin (The Wind),
was getting old.

Noodin creaked, squeal, and squeak,
sometimes rusty, her voice sometimes clear.
Her songs combined with sounds
of water
splashing against her

made beautiful songs.

They sang and sang
about a child
called Shir-o-lee.

Shir -o-lee!
I am Noodin, the wind
I will carry you
and your bap-pa, Shan-zii-moo!

My bap pa used to say
Always listen!
Always be aware!
for your ears are not
for decorations!

Take a look —
See the beauty of the world
Use your eyes to see the beauty
for when you see something
only you can see it.

Only you can interpret
what you see.
Look how clear the water is.
When I looked
I saw — Beauty! Water
shining and dancing
before my eyes.

To see, to look,
to appreciate beauty of things
is a prayer, he said
Then, I felt good.

I felt gladness.
I felt joy.
I felt whole.
Beauty!
Life so precious
it's a gift of Master.

My bap-pa used to say

Use everything you have
and always give thanks
for what you see
for some day you may not see.

In the morning always face the sun
for Giizis gives heat and light.
Be sure to day
Miigwech!

When night comes
wait for the moon.
She provides night light
to us to see
so we won't get lost.

Shir-o-lee, my daughter
let us stop to fish
for we are near the rocks.

Look into the "nbiing" water
until you see three large rocks
for that's our fishing mark.

Shh — hear the rocks speak
for they have spirit, too.
Whenever you are in trouble
speak to a rock
for you have a special "asin," too.

The "asin" we have is the
foundation of us
for we need
a stone to stand on
for when we're weak.

Life is like sharp rocks
full of mountains to climb.
climb hard, my daughter,
and you will be strong

Always, my child,
look and listen.
Use your eyes to see

the world.
Breathe Noodin, the wind
for you will feel whole, he said.

Then, I felt
a bite on my line.
It's a fish!, I yelled.

Bap-pa smiled
then laughed so hard
that I lost my line!

Let's go home, he said.
Miigwech! Noodin!
Then I heard Noodin sing.

We will go home, Shir-o-lee.
I will carry you home!

—1986 (updated 2009)

Ojibway words:
Asin — stone
Bap-Pa — my father
Giizis — Sun
Miigwech — thank you
Nbiing — in the watewater
Ndan-senh — my daughter
Noodin — wind
Shan-zii-moo —John Simon
Shir-o-lee — Shirley

Originally published in Canadian Woman Studies/les cahiers de la femme, *"Native Women," 10 (2 & 3) (Summer/Fall 1989): 44. Reprinted with permission of the author.*

Shirley Ida Williams-Pheasant is a member of the Bird Clan of the Ojibwa and Odawa First Nations of Canada. Her Indigenous name is "Migizi-ow-Kwe," meaning Eagle Woman. She was born and raised at Wikwemikong, Manitoulin Island and attended St. Joseph's Residential School in Spanish, Ontario. She received her BA in Indigenous Studies at Trent University and her Native Language Instructors Program diploma from Lakehead University in Thunder Bay. Shirley received her Masters degree from York University in Environmental Studies in June of 1996. She worked at Trent University for many years and is currently retired.

ALICE OLSEN WILLIAMS

THE SPIRIT OF MY QUILTS

THE WORK IN MY QUILTS and quilted wall-hangings depicts my double heritage. My mother, who is Anishinaabe, gave me the core of my Being, my Anishinaabe (Ojibwe) culture, while my father, who was born in Norway, gave me the traditions of the White culture which would make it possible for me to live more easily in the milieu of the dominant society.

Traditionally, women rearing their daughters and sons cultivate a more intimate relationship with their children than do men. Thus, it is mainly women who pass on the cultural norms and values. Because it was my Anishinaabe mother who raised me during the formative years of my life, the essence of my Being is experienced in terms of the Anishinaabe, the Ojibwe people. I represent this part of my heritage in my work by portraying in the centre of my quilts, birds or animals that figure heavily in the Anishinaabe way of Life. Since it was not given me to draw, Curve Lake artist Norman Knott makes me sketches using the pictographic style of the Anishinaabe art form. These I transfer onto fabric.

Because I would one day have to go to school and live outside of the Anishinaabe culture, which was in those days essentially communal and non-competitive, my parents realized they had to prepare me to live in the culture of a competitive capitalist society. My White father taught me the norms and values I should adopt and adapt to so that it would be easier for White people to accept me. These non-Indian cultural traits I perceive as clothing to cover up my Ojibwe self so I can "succeed" or "make it." The heritage my father gave me is represented in the quilting blocks I use which either surround the central theme, or decorate the Anishinaabe-inspired picture. The quilting blocks are traditional and contemporary White North American designs.

The circular symbol in the sky of the quilts is my personal symbol and I now display it in all the quilts I make. This symbol helps me to recognize and be thankful for the gifts of Life that have been given to me. It represents the teachings of respect embedded in our Anishinaabe culture. Sometimes these sets of teachings are called 'The Medicine Wheel" or "The Wheel of Life." I prefer to call it "The Search for Pimaatisiwin." Pimaatisiwin is the aim and

hope of living a Good Life on this Earth. The four directions, East, South, West and North, are represented respectively by the colours red, yellow, black, and white. Within these colours are the Lands that were given to the Human Race to love and cherish and look after so that we may have a Good Life on our Mother Earth; the four colours of Human Beings: the Red People, the Yellow People, The Black People, and the White People; the four Life-givers: food, sun, water, air; the four seasons: spring, summer, fall, winter; the four little Rascals: inferiority, jealousy, resentment, not caring; the four moral principles: sharing, humbleness, kindness, and caring. The East gives us the animals, who teach us about sharing. From the South we get the trees, which teach us about honesty; and from the West we are given the grasses, which talk to us about kindness. The North gives us the rocks, which speak to us of strength. All things in this Life were, and are, given to us by the Mother of us all, Our Mother, the Earth. She is represented by the green (sometimes brown) circle, which encompasses the four colours and all that we experience.

Lines that radiate from the "Pimaatisiwin Wheel" tell us that each Being in Creation affects all that comes into contact with her/him. The centre, where all the colours touch, is the soul. Our belief is that all Beings, all animate objects, have a Soul or Spirit. The Mother Earth circle represents the physical existence of all things. The lines radiating from the physical circle show that we have a physical effect on our surroundings, while lines from the centre, the

Soul, show that our Souls also have just as great an effect on all things that touch our lives.

Creation has given all people knowledge and wisdom, each in her/his own way; no one is for gotten. To our Indian peoples, and to others who live close to our Mother Earth, we are given knowledge and wisdom through dreams, visions, fasting and prayer: we are blessed with the gift of seeing the many les sons that have been put in Nature and in the world around us.

The loons (or geese) in this quilt represent patience and devotion to working together for Pimaatisiwin, that is, trying to live a Good Life. The loons show us that they can float and swim and dive superbly. They speak to us of caring and sharing and faith. They say to us:

> *My feet and my wings are perfectly balanced. I am like the Peoples of the Earth. Time and Nature is all around me and I listen and wait patiently to know when and where my next move shall be.*

> *My wings work in harmony and balance. One wing is Woman, and the other is Man. When both Woman and Man have equal power and they are balanced, then the people of the world will live to their highest limits.*

The next time we see loons they will tell us even more.

The water in this quilt represents humility, strength and perseverance. Look at the wisdom that the Creator has put into the Water. Feel the Water. See how gently and lovingly it touches your hands. Water gives Life to all living

THE PIMAATISIWIN CIRCLE

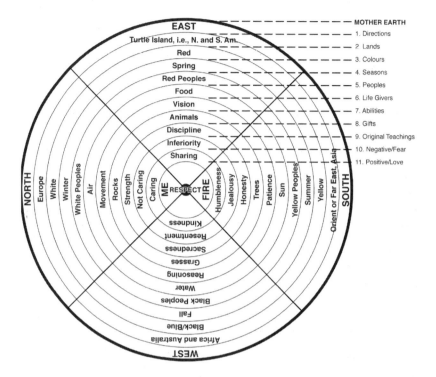

things and yet always seeks the lowest spot to show how humble She is. And no matter what we do to Her, She always remains herself and never turns her back on anyone. Although She is humble, She has great strength, patience, and faith.

> *For even if a mountain or an island were to stand in a little stream's path, the Water would keep moving until finally, she would find a path to continue on her journey. She would never give up...*

The trees represent helpfulness and thankfulness. If we are to have peace in the world, we must be as the trees. The lilac doesn't order the oak tree to move over; the maple doesn't tell the birch to move over. All of the different trees stand together with their arms upraised in prayer and thanksgiving; they support and protect one another against adversity.

We, the sacred Creation, must remember to gather beneath the Sacred Tree of Life—the Sacred Tree of Hope, with its ever-lasting branches spreading across and sheltering all the people.

In the quilt, the sky and clouds represent giving. The Sky holds for us the

Air we breathe, the Sun that warms us, the Moon that guides us, the stars that give us pleasure and direct our movements, and the Clouds that wet the Earth and all its Creation.

When we offer up the sacred smoke from the pipe we turn—

First, we smoke to the East where the red sun rises, and from whence comes New Life, and we call upon the Gifts of the new mornings.

Then to the South, where the Sun shines the strongest and gives the most of its Gifts.

Then we turn to the West where thunder and lightning flash across the skywe ask those Powers for help.

Then to the North where the snow and cold winds live, and ask for their help and blessings.

Then we offer the tobacco to our Life Giver, the Sky, in honour of the Great Spirit and all those who have gone on to the Spirit World.

Finally, we offer the gift of sweet-smelling, purifying smoke to our Mother, the Mother of us all, Mother Earth, who brings forth and sustains all Life.

We are thankful for Pimaatisiwin, the purpose in Life, and we remember that the Good Creation speaks to each one of us in our own time and place. Meanwhile, we share the best we have to help one another find Pimaatisiwin, a balance in giving and receiving a Life of kindness, loving, and compassion.

I wish to acknowledge the inspiration I received from Walking with Grandfather and Great Wolf and Little Mouse, *a curriculum guide by Dick Hastings and Dan Vaillain-court (Kipohtakaw EducationCentre, P.O. Box 510, Morinville, Alta. T0G 1P0 (403) 939-3551); with the editorial assistance of the staff of the Four Worlds Development Project, Faculty of Education, University of Lethbridge, Alta.*

Originally published in Canadian Woman Studies/les cahiers de la femme, *"Native Women," 10 (2 & 3) (Summer/Fall 1989): 49-51. Reprinted with permission of the author.*

Alice Olsen Williams is a Curve Lake First Nation member known for her beautiful quilt-work. Alice blends expressions of Anishinaabe beliefs, traditions, and ideology, while combining reflections on social issues such as racism and violence against women. In the centre of her quilts are animals and birds which figure intimately in the lives of the Anishinaabeg. Often, she also uses the floral designs which Anishinaabe-Kwewag continue to use in their beadwork, quiltwork, embroidery, and other creative media. Her quilts and wall-hangings have been exhibited at the Smithsonian Institution's National Museum of the American Indian, Michigan State University Museum, Wanuskewin Heritage Park, the Thunder Bay Art Gallery, Peterborough Art Gallery, and many other museums and art galleries. One of Alice's goals is to show how quilting can bring healing, companionship, and comfort to women, by sharing experiences and expressing their feelings through the arts.

OUR WORLD

W E FOUND OURSELVES ON April 4, 1989, still without the article we had promised to submit for this special edition of *Canadian Woman Studies*. Being Kanien'kehá:ka (Mohawk) women, and therefore notorious for "talking," we decided to record a conversation between ourselves. We spoke of everything from our initial apprehension to contribute to a so-called "feminist" journal and our views on "feminism," to our very deep beliefs of who we are and where we want to go. What follows is our significantly condensed and revised (to say the least!) version of our spoken words. It is our sincere hope that these words will provide our readers an opportunity to begin to recognize, to understand, and to respect the Aboriginal woman for who she is.

Skonaganleh:rá: Frankly, I'm very *tired* of having other women interpret for us, other women empathize for us, other women sympathize with us. I'm interested in articulating our own directions, our own aspirations, our own past, *in our own words*. I saw the opportunity, through this journal, to do this—to communicate to the women who teach women's studies and their students. At the same time, I want to tell our own young women that we don't need to grow up wanting to be like "Dick and Jane." I want them to know that it's not only all right, it's *necessary* for us to grow up in a way that we have articulated ourselves: we don't need governments, laws, or legislative frameworks to articulate the whole concept of self-government and self-direction. When I pulled all these things together, I decided, given some discomfort with the concepts around a feminist journal, that I was prepared to become involved.

Osennontion: Not considering myself to be "feminist" necessarily, nor a "writer," I had some difficulty deciding whether this was a good thing to do. I was also not sure about what I would submit, and then you suggested a co-authorship. I am most concerned with how we can best affect the readership—how we can get the message across to them that *we are absolutely different*! If the educators are going to teach anybody, and if their students are going to learn anything, then we have to try as much as possible to get them to at least *realize* that they are going to have to twist their minds a little bit (or a lot) to try to get into the same frame of mind as us, or to try to get on the same wavelength. They must realize that their own thinking cannot be applied to what we are going to say, so that what we say "fits"—there seems to be a tendency for that to happen. We must somehow get them to empty their heads of what they may think they know about us, so that they are prepared to begin to learn the truth.

Skonaganleh:rá: It's important for me to say a few things about why I suggested a co-authorship. I want to show that it's possible to work together and to co-operate. While you and I share common views on self-government, and the direction in which Aboriginal people are going (and Aboriginal women are being dragged), these are not always shared one hundred per cent. However, it is possible to disagree, *and* to still work together. This is, unfortunately, something that we don't see in our community often enough. We see cliques and little power circles form, but we rarely see genuine co-operation. It seemed to me that we could be an example to the women who read the journal, and to our own women.

WHO WE ARE/WHO WE ARE NOT

Skonaganleh:rá: We must begin by explaining who we are. We are both Kanien'kehá:ka, and we both believe in the Haudenosaunee (the Five Nation Iroquois Confederacy) having been created and operating long before anyone came here. In that context of who we are, we believe that woman came first—that the first one, the first being to come amongst our relatives, came from a sky world, a world that we cannot define in nice anthropological terms, as some would have us do, but nevertheless, for us, there is no doubt in our minds. This first woman who came carried a child, and this firstborn was a woman. We must remind ourselves and the Grandfathers, Fathers, Uncles, Brothers, Husbands, and Sons amongst us, that they borrowed and adopted "other" ways and that those other ways of looking at us are just not acceptable.

Osennontion: I want to emphasize that we *believe* our Creation Story—that we don't need any other explanations nor does there need to be any great analysis or any great scientific substantiation for it, because we believe it! You are right when you say that we know it to be the truth, and so if someone believes otherwise, then let that one prove to us that it is *not* the truth.

Skonaganleh:rá: The Elders and Traditional People, with whom I have spoken, talk about when peoples of all colours came here and how we came to be and how everybody had her/his own medicine wheel. In that medicine wheel, ir-respective of colour, was everything that s/he needed. Inside those medicine wheels were the values and beliefs, and social mores, about how we were to get along. It was only as time went on that certain of these colours of peoples forgot what was in their medicine wheels and by forgetting what was in them and forgetting to honour them, they created a whole false society. This society rooted itself in what we consider to be this falseness. The people who came here to co-exist on Turtle Island have not done so very successfully—co-existed that is.

Osennontion: We are taught that we have a relationship to the natural world and so we are natural human beings. We have names, very descriptive names of who we are (Kanien'kehá:ka are people of the flint) and how we differ. Our own languages enable us to do that, generally, in a respectful way. You speak often of the young ones whom you are responsible for; how they have their own "Indian" names by which they are known, and how important these names are. One of the very small girls understands at three years old, the teaching of the sweetgrass braid—how weak one strand is, how easy it is to break it up, and it's gone. She knows, however, that many strands, braided together, cannot be torn apart. She carries that name and is being taught the responsibilities that go along with her name.

Skonaganleh:rá: She is being taught, as are the small boys, to understand respect, to respect all of her relations, and to understand and respect the role she has to play with regards to those relations. We want to ensure that she can honour her name—that she is prepared to accept the responsibility to see that we are braided together, that we do not stand alone as a single blade of grass.

I think a few words should also be said about *who we are not*. One of the big social phenomena of the time that we live in centres around definitions like "Indian" and Métis. Perhaps too many of our people very passionately want to be the label that has been ascribed to them. We must remember that those labels are not ours. Those who believe the story that "Indians" are called "Indian" because the lost ones thought they had reached India when they arrived here, are surely grateful that some other place, which might have suggested a less flattering name, was not the target. I'm not sure about Métis. I appreciate that it reflects the concept of mixed blood, but a self-defined Métis person who considers that s/he is Aboriginal, is only that because s/he has an origin that comes from the Onkwehonwe, Anishinabe, or one of the other natural beings. If we put our minds, particularly the women, more to acting like good natural human beings and less to pursuing these political labels that come from foreign governments, we might find it easier to get along with some of the other groups. When we use *their* words and *their* weapons, *their* issues around law and behaviour and expectations, we can't ever expect to measure up.

SELF-DETERMINATION

Osennontion: The term "self-government" has become a universal buzz word, widely used throughout the world, when the issues of Aboriginal/Indigenous peoples are discussed. I have difficulty with the word, myself, and with what it represents. Just as other Nations of peoples, like those who call themselves Canadians, have their own system of government, so do we. Presumably, Canadians consider that their government is such that it allows them to govern their affairs—to govern themselves. Of course, *we* know that they go far beyond that and impose their system on others like us, but to make the point—their government is a self-governing one, only they do not describe it as such. I guess the concept that *we* might have our own government, which also allows us to govern ourselves, is just too much to take, so the "others" refer to us as wanting "self-government." It should be said that when we were given our own ways to live, we were never given a government for any others *but* ourselves, and to this day, *we* maintain our end of the original agreement to co-exist, not to impose our ways on others.

Naturally, our own people, as continues to happen time and time again, have wholeheartedly embraced the buzzword. Of course, the word itself is not the culprit; what it means to people, how it is interpreted, or misinterpreted, and how it comes about are causes for debate and dissension. When the Feds talk of recognizing "self-government," they mean delegated authority to "Indians," for example, to govern their affairs on the reserves wherein they were displaced, and this is accomplished through *their* legislation. When an Aboriginal person, who knows what s/he is talking about, speaks of "self-government," s/he means the particular system of government that was given to the people when they were placed in their territory on Turtle Island. This government needs no sanction through legislation or otherwise; rather, the "others" need only honour the original agreements to co-exist, and through their actions, show respect for our ways. However, because so many of our people don't know our ways, they have become involved in processes whereby they have attempted to gain recognition of our "right to self-government," instead of working on finding ways to effectively assert and exercise our own governments. Before I knew better, I myself supported and took part in some of those processes—this was before I knew what things like "Nationhood" and "Sovereignty" *really* meant. I came to realize *my* mistakes; I am praying for others to do the same before any more damage is done on behalf of "the people."

If we are going to use the English language, I prefer the term "self-determination," as it better describes, for me, the action that needs to be taken. The establishment, exercise and enforcement of government is only one aspect of "self-determination." In our own language, we have a word that, of course, even better describes what we have been instructed to do. *Tewatatha:wi* best translates into "we carry ourselves"—a rather simple concept, some might say, but *I* think it says it all.

Skonaganleh:rá: In our community, we want to define ourselves and not in somebody else's context (which is what we see the "feminist" definition to be, for example). We want to define ourselves in our own context, and I'm not

449

convinced that in that self-definition, which is where self-government comes from—exploring one's self—we are going to find terms that can be shared with and understood by the "others." Ours are going to be very different. The object of the self-government exercise seems to be to permit all of the voices to articulate themselves in very different ways, with very different aspirations, and yet to be able to co-exist in the houses that we built—be those political, economic, social or cultural houses. We are not going to find that outside, because we see "them" as tending to define themselves collectively—be they women or men, adult or child. We have a problem with that, with the way that they seem to want to "box" us. A lot of times when we try to interact with other women's groups, particularly groups that call themselves "feminist" groups, they come to the table with equally as passionate, as strong, opinions about that "box" that we don't want to be in. They try to make it more palatable because, after all, we have this universal sisterhood; *we* know that this does not exist. We protest the notion that the "box" is good, and we deny the attempts to have us attracted to it.

Somehow there seems to be this attitude that there is one answer for all Aboriginal people in Canada, or all Aboriginal peoples on Turtle Island. There isn't. Just as our creation stories all differ, our clans or totems all differ. So does the answer to how we will re-assume responsibility for our own affairs; the care and protection of our own people are going to be different. Yet we have followed a path that says somehow there is going to be one great lodge and in that lodge we are all going to come to an understanding that things are going to be done a certain way. Certainly when we go to meetings we see that. We see people trying to do things that probably would have been traditional, like trying to come to one good mind—one good mind! However, "one good mind" had always meant in the context of *our own relationships*.

It hadn't meant that we were going to go from our territorial homeland out to what's now called British Columbia, and say "there is the way that you have to do things," although this might work there, since our peoples are close in that they have longhouses where women play very primary roles. However, to take the same issue to the Plains Cree, Southern United States, or where Inuit or Inuvialuit people live would likely not work. Yet this whole nature of Confederation—of somehow people banding together and affiliating, giving them some sense of protection, direction, ownership and community—that we've adopted is not necessarily the best answer or resolution for our communities. At least *I'm* not convinced it is.

Osennontion: There were a number of processes that still exist in the longhouses today where you try to get people to come to a good mind. Where you can't have everybody agree to see a good mind, then you wait, and you set the decision aside, and you talk about it—the women talk about it, and the men talk about it, and the clans talk about it and then you all talk about it again. If there still is no good mind, well, you set it aside again. However, outside of the longhouse, somehow there is a sense of chasing ourselves, that we're in a big hurry to do something, that it has to be resolved right now.

Skonaganleh:rá: We have a law that came from the creator and in that law was *absolutely* everything that we needed! Kanien'kehá:ka call it the *kaianere'ko:wa*. Some people call it the Great Law, or the Great Law of Peace, and it is. This law, our law, does not define "rights;" nor does it defend "rights." In our ways, there are no "rights," only responsibilities: to observe the clans, to bring honour, trust, friendship and respect; to be kind; honest; share and have strength; to maintain a relationship with all of the natural world.

With those things that we were given, came strength. In very modern times, strength is perceived as force, as something external. In our ways, strength is perceived as internal. It was always represented by the rock, who doesn't change whether you speak softly or lovingly to it, or if you are standing there yelling at it. The rock is the rock—it is the Grandmother/Grandfather. That's the way it is; it doesn't change.

Our relationship with the natural world has all but been forgotten. We pursue strength as force, either as a political movement as we see some of the big powers in the world doing, or force in the way of personal relationships between men and women. We see a very downside of a syndrome, when the nature of strength is really a very internal issue. I have been taught that I am strong enough and have the wherewithal to be the very best human being I can be—not the strongest, not the most aggressive, not the biggest, not the one whose dogma and dicta says, "because they're the best, they must be followed by all the people." In the context of the whole world around me, I understand those things given by the Great Mystery. I understand the code, the law, that I am to follow. I understand that I have the strength of my relationships to honour the smallest plant and the smallest child and the most sacred of ceremonies. In the context of all that, I don't have to change myself. I don't need a big stick, a loud voice, a women's group to represent me. I must not let my ego get in the way.

Osennontion: Talking about what woman was and certainly what we want her to be again, is not negating anybody else's role in creation. It is honouring, respecting, saying that there is a relationship—that we all need to get along. We all need to get along now, whether we are whatever. We need to get along because the Mother is getting sicker. The world is getting smaller; there are more and more people who are less and less careful. It is fine for the so-called leaders of the Soviet Union and the United States to say this is the way things are going to be in the world. However, frankly, if we don't honour our relationships with the natural world, *they* are going to tell us how it is going to be—nobody else is going to! Not one of us, female or male, complete or not, young or old, is going to be able to do anything about that and that is something that, I think, our young people have to soon start putting their minds to.

451

RELATIONSHIPS

Osennontion: Our relationship to the natural world and our observance of our laws began to change with the coming of the "others"—the "visitors," the "boat people." Different relationships and happenings in other peoples' times and countries and environments discredited a number of things. Women were looked upon as possessions by the "others," and children were to be seen and not heard; in our own ways, women were looked upon as sacred and, in our councils, even the smallest child had a voice. The whole "discovery" theory had an impact on our people. The "boat people" neglected to recognize that *they* were sick and lost offshore and that if *we* had not "discovered" *them* perhaps we would have been able to delay what happened here by a few decades if not centuries. Historical impacts bastardized relationships in the family and in the community with the lack of recognition of clans. In a political context, we were forced into a relationship with the Crown, through the *Indian Act*, and we found out that not everyone was an "Indian." With the introduction of alcohol (and then later, drugs and other addictive substances), our people established a relationship with the bottle, a relationship that has escalated over the ages.

In the last one or two decades, we have begun to rethink those relationships. We want to be healthy again, to re-assert, to re-discover, to re-whatever—to do again the kinds of things that we were instructed to do. We have begun to talk about government as *we* understood it—in the form of *responsibility*: that we have responsibilities for the earth, for the water, for all of our relatives, on and in it, and equally, they have responsibilities, and if they don't observe one of their responsibilities, then we die!

If we continue to forget our responsibilities and find ourselves in situations where there is still a wholesale destruction of Aboriginal people, all around the globe—be it the cutting down of the rainforests; be it marching in what is now known as Central or Southern America under some popular movement as a political initiative and Indian people are being killed; be it the outright starvation and destruction of Aboriginal peoples' self-image; or, be it the wholesale attempt at massive assimilation, as is occurring in what is known as the United States and here—then, how can we endure as the peoples that we are? For these and a multitude of other reasons, we have had to come to new decisions. With the disruption of our ways, came racism. I remember listening to an Elder talk about racism: "If you truly want to conquer a people, you withdraw, but you leave your education system behind, and you won't have to do anything to them. By using the tool, the very important and powerful tool they left behind, you'll do it to yourselves! While we may want 'Indian Control over Indian Education'—educating our own to guarantee our own future—we're not even doing that yet with our own resources." People don't know the original law, and have been raised in such a way that denies the existence of our ways, particularly the men who are the elected "Chiefs" and other so-called "leaders." So they define our future in a context that results exactly in what those people—"the boat people," the "visitors"—wanted us to do. They do it in the context of foreign law. They look to the *Indian Act* for "self-government" enactment—there *is* no sense of self. We are then left to ask ourselves, particularly the women, what we have to do to look at raising our heads and dealing with our children and making sure there *is* a future!

WOMAN'S ROLE AND RESPONSIBILITIES

Skonaganleh:rá: In our community, the woman was defined as nourisher, and the man, protector, and as protector, he had the role of helper. He only reacted; she acted. She was responsible for the establishment of all of the norms—whether they were political, economic, social or spiritual. She lived in a very co-opera-tive environment, where power needed not be lorded over.

Osennontion: She did not have to compete with her partner in the running of the home and the caring of the family. She had her specific responsibili-ties to creation, which were different, but certainly no less important, than his. In fact, if anything, with the gifts given her, woman was perhaps *more* important.

Skonaganleh:rá: There was an understanding that the woman in many respects, certainly spiritually, was more powerful and complete and this was because she had a direct relationship to Mother Earth, Grandmother Moon, and to the female elements of the waters, all of which we cannot live without. The men understood that gifts were given them by the Great Mystery—ceremonies and teachings—and that there were things they had to do to be able to walk the same road beside her, because she had been given the responsibility for completing creation, something that she still carries, even now. She shared a true partnership with her man. Two halves, with very different elements and very different responsibilities, make up the medicine wheel, and both halves have to be there to make it complete.

Woman has had a traditional role as Centre, maintaining the fire—the fire that is at the centre of our beliefs. She is the Keeper of the Culture. She has been able to play that role, even in a home divided. She has maintained that role even though church dogma has suggested that our families need be structured in a different way; that we teach "Dick and Jane;" that there are certain aspirations that young boys should have, and differing and somehow lesser ones that young girls should have. She has maintained her role despite intermarriage, which caused her to be cut off from her roots, both legislatively and sometimes physically. Her home has been divided as a result of education. A wholesale taking away of our children to schools diminished her role and her 100 per cent right to teach her children, by imposing laws which require her to hand over that child, who comes home and checks everything her mother says in the context of what the teacher said, and this, when teachers are poorly equipped to deal with, from our perspective—an Aboriginal perspective—what the children *should* be taught.

Her home is divided as well, as a result of economics. If he works, he may or may not be able to work in their home community; in the communities where we come from, many, many of the men are gone from late Sunday night to late Friday night and there is a substantial number of women left to be the heads of the household during the week, while the men work away in high steel, auto plants, or wherever they can get a job. In more traditional environments, because of the requirements for schooling, women end up staying at home, while the men are out hunting and trapping; under other circumstances that would have been a family initiative and children would have been taught in that manner. So her home is very much divided as a result of that.

Her home has been divided because of the whole nature of family. She traditionally was able to rely on her mother, her grandmother, her older aunties to help her—to help her in the norms around raising a young family and around how a home got run. She participated in getting information, of being schooled through women getting together to quilt, to do crafts, or to do a variety of other things that just are not around anymore. So her home has been divided and sub-divided again, and they have attacked her sacred space from a number of perspectives. Families don't do things together now—little boys go to hockey; little girls go over there and do this thing; young people go and hang out at the drop-in centre; *he* has *his* activities and *she* has *hers*, so there's no longer that traditional nature of interaction there. There are obviously education issues that are very different, right to the point where informal education systems, people are divided physically—one doesn't even interact with other age groups and sometimes males go off to auto shop and girls are sent to home economics.

It's still a divisive issue. We're finding more and more as we go places, and people attempt to return to tradition, that there are things that we are not sharing with each other because, oh, those are women's responsibilities, and those are men's responsibilities; women's ceremonies and men's ceremonies; women's teachings and men's teachings, women's circles and … so you can't share that. Men are beginning to follow that and while we had the split in ceremonial life between genders, it was merely to learn and understand our own role so that when we went out and interacted, we would do so in an appropriate manner.

Certainly there are issues around economics. Despite all of the wonderful heartfelt feelings of sisterhood in the world, our women are still the poorest, still have the poorest health, and still have the shortest life expectancy. In those contexts, I don't know how many more ways you can divide her house and she'll continue to maintain that fire—*but she will!*

Osennontion: In addition to all of the responsibilities already talked about, perhaps the most daunting for woman is her responsibility for the men—how they conduct themselves, how they behave, how they treat her. She has to remind them of their responsibilities and she has to know when and how to correct them when they stray from those.

At the beginning, when the "others" first came here, we held our rightful positions in our societies, and held the respect due us by the men, because that's the way things were then, when we were following our ways. At that time, the European woman was considered an appendage to her husband, his possession. Contact with that European male and the imposition of his ways on our people resulted in our being assimilated into those ways. We forgot our women's responsibilities and the men forgot theirs.

Because the woman is still the one who bears the children, she has not moved all that far from her original instructions, despite great adversity. The man, on the other hand, is oftentimes virtually helpless in even attempting to carry out his role as protector/helper, because *his* connection to the natural world has all but been severed. The environment is no longer the same, the lands and its resources are not necessarily there for him anymore. So our men are hurting, they are suffering because they're physically removed, they are locked out; their self-image issues around fulfilling their role cannot be met. The environment in which they have come to exist has caused them to turn to ways that are not particularly appropriate in terms of "helping" forces, alcohol and drugs being the worst of them—the biggest and worst cause of wholesale destruction of our culture that could happen. The woman is responsible for picking that man up and bringing him back to health.

In our Nation, while there is no question that the woman is the central figure in the scheme of things, our official government leaders are still men. That is how our government was given to us, and that is what is in our *kaianere'ko: wa* (great law). They are called *rotiane*, the best translation being "good men." So our leaders, who are more often referred to as "Chiefs," are to be good, upright men. At this time, only a few of our Nation's nine *rotianer* positions are filled. This is a sign that all is not well in *Kanien'kehá:ka* territory, and this too becomes the responsibility of the women, for we have to select and groom the men for these positions. Once they are there, we are also responsible for making sure that they *are* "good men," that they remember that they are to serve the people, and not exercise their responsibilities in the same manner as those leaders of the "others." A *rotanier* is considered to have been given great and serious responsibilities when he assumes the position; he is not considered to be at the top of an hierarchy with authority that is subject to abuse, as on the outside. Again, the women must ensure that her *rotianer* are carrying out their responsibilities or they will see to them being reprimanded and ultimately removed, when necessary.

These positions cannot be confused with the elected "Chiefs" positions as prescribed by the *Indian Act*. Too often we hear men protesting women's attempts to gain these positions by reminding us that, in our ways, the "Chiefs" are men. I, for one, have promoted women becoming involved in the Band Council system, not because I think it is a good one that should be perpetuated, and not because I think there should be "equal" representation of women to men. Rather I believe that women have a responsibility to make sure that we don't lose any more, that we don't do any more damage, while we work on getting our original government system back in good working order.

So, our women have massive responsibilities and therefore a great deal of work to do. Along with that comes the necessity for women to "learn." We must be properly educated in *our ways*, so that we know what we must do, and so we will have the strength to do it.

FEMINISM AND THE FEMINIST MOVEMENT

Osennontion: Earlier I stated that I did not necessarily consider myself to be a feminist. I feel this way mainly because I have had many occasions to observe the "feminists" at work, and decided that I did not really identify with the behaviours demonstrated, did not like what I saw, and so did not want to be one.

While, in what I now refer to as my past life, I was very actively involved in our movement—the Aboriginal women's movement—and so was a fervent advocate for our women, I could never separate my gender from my origin. That is, I never and still do not see myself as strictly woman. That is because I am a *Kanien'kehá:ka* woman. In my experiences, many of our women have been expected to make the separation. We are expected to believe that because we are women, we can automatically share in the sisterhood with other women, regardless of the fact that we may have almost nothing else in common. We are not the only ones who suffer with this expectation. At almost any gathering of women from many origins, one can first notice that there tends to be very, very, few women who are not white. The next thing that one can notice is that these few women tend to gravitate toward each other and tend to make similar statements on the issues at hand.

We attempt to get the "others" to understand that we encounter problems and obstacles that oftentimes go far beyond those that are referred to as "women's issues." We often talk about the rampant racism that continues to flourish in this country and become extremely aware that "racism" is a very dirty word, especially in Canada, which basks in its international lily-white reputation as the most human and activist of human rights activists. We have found ourselves considered difficult because too many times for the "others'" liking, we just could not "go along;" we just could not believe in and uphold the slogan that "Sisterhood is Global." We have even, in some fora, because we actually have stated *our own* positions on *Indian Act* amendments, for instance, been publicly confronted by mainstream women's organizations who do not share our views. This *has* happened despite the fact that these "others" claimed to want to support us "in the struggle." It has been particularly distasteful to endure such treatment from other women, because they *are* women! We didn't *expect* better from men, so it is not too surprising that *they* perpetuate a paternalistic attitude and approach. On the other hand, we oftentimes cannot distinguish the "female" view from the "male," and so we find ourselves having to deal with maternalism as well as paternalism. In Nairobi, at the Women's Forum, I was especially appalled with the behaviour of women toward other women, and this at a world event commemorating the United Nations Decade of Women. I left there wondering how far anyone had progressed in ensuring better conditions for women and our families!

Skonaganleh:rá: I agree we had a hard time with this thing called "feminism" and writing for a "feminist" journal. *The Concise Oxford Dictionary* tells me that, "feminism" is "advocacy, extended recognition, of the claims of women." *The New Lexicon Webster's Dictionary of the English Language* tells me that it is "the policy, practice or advocacy of political, economic, and social equality for women," and that a "feminist" is "an advocate of feminism." While I can read these definitions and comprehend them, I don't really understand. I understand the nature of being defined as a "feminist," and wanting some sense of equality, but frankly, I don't want equality. I want to go back to where women, in Aboriginal communities, were complete, where they were beautiful, where they were treated as more than equal—where man was helper and woman was the centre of that environment, that community. So, while I suppose equality is a nice thing and while I suppose we can never go back all the way, I want to make an effort at going back to at least respecting the role that women played in communities.

Osennontion: I would at least like to see us have our rightful place back. To me, when these women, who call themselves "feminist," or get called "feminist," talk about equality, they mean sameness. They appear to want to be the *same* as a man. They want to be treated the same as a man, make the same money as a man...and, they consider all women, regardless of origin, to be the same, to share the same concerns. I, for one, maintain that Aboriginal women are *different*, as are the women who are burdened with such labels as "immigrant women" or "visible minority women." I certainly do not want to be a "man!"

Skonaganleh:rá: The "others" have to start to think differently and they have to look in their own mirror, at their own selves, and their own baggage that they're carrying and where that came from. They should not look at a universal sisterhood, so much as we should be looking at creating a situation where all people of many colours can peacefully exist. I agree that we all have certain goals that we want out of life, one of which is peace in all of our relationships. However, we cannot have peace in our relationships if we don't have peace inside ourselves. We can't have peace inside ourselves if there is no credence or credibility given to the way that we define ourselves.

LEADERSHIP

Osennontion: In the absence of our *real* leaders, or in too many cases due to ignorance about, or worse, lack of recognition of, our *real* leaders, too many of our people have again gone the way of the "white man" and opt for and participate in systems that allow for elected leadership. These "leaders" are the ones who get recognized as the official spokespersons for our people and these are the ones who represent us in so-called "negotiations" with the Federal and Provincial Territorial Governments, for example.

Skonaganleh:rá: There *are* a lot of people who go out into that system, particularly the elected system, and females and males alike, because of the pressures that are there, because of the shiny objects that government is waving all the time, because of the blown-up image the "Indian" organizations have created for themselves, then end up perpetuating the system. They may come in with wonderful motivation to change things, and instead become part of the system. It is a phenomenon that happens anywhere. It's one that is particularly troublesome to us in the whole context of the way that we are evolving; "self-government" has become one's image of oneself being defined in somebody else's context.

Osennontion: I think the major problem with the representation that we have is that the so-called "leaders" do not have an understanding of what "self-determination," or "sovereignty," or "Nationhood" mean. Either they don't have knowledgeable people around to tell them, or they haven't looked, or they *have had* the opportunity to learn, but didn't like what they were told and so chose to ignore it. I suppose the other possibility is that teachings have been misinterpreted and therefore have not been put into practice, *or* have they just *not* understood!

I have great difficulty with all of this, because the teachers that I have had the good fortune to meet have passed on rather simple and uncomplicated messages about how things should be done and that they *have* to be done. We have basically been told to get back to our ways before any more is lost. The existing "leadership" does a lot of talking about our peoples' origins and philosophies and laws, but has yet to put these into practice. The existing organizations, from the community Band Councils to national bodies, may have names that suggest that they are "self-determining," but really they operate in mimicry of the outside organization, which in turn legitimizes them by recognizing them as the "voice of the people."

As far as I am concerned, too often an Aboriginal spokesperson or organization is extended recognition and prominence because it is ultimately convenient to the "others" to do so. This is especially true of the male-dominated organizations, which have always had more funding and they believe more power, but are apparently more easily led into the hands of the foreign governments. For instance, because they have been led to believe that they are a force to contend with, our people, in good faith most times, let down their guards, and forget that they are facing an enemy who will agree only to something that is in that enemy's best interests. I remain to be convinced that an outside government system, even with substantial Aboriginal representation, *can* and *will* ever do anything that is ultimately in the best interests of *our people*. I think we are seriously kidding ourselves if we believe that this is possible.

Instead, I would feel better if I knew for sure that they were doing these things only as part of a plan or a strategy to foil the enemy while, behind the "front," they were living and working *our ways*, which is the *only* way to go. I know this *not* to be the case. I am not discounting those who have tried, through reorganization or constitutional changes, to conduct themselves in a more appropriate manner. While it is a start and a good one, I have observed that these kinds of changes alone do not necessarily reflect the behaviours of the people involved. We have lots and lots of "members" and "leaders" who are obviously *lost* when it comes to our ways, even though they may be active participants in organizations that espouse the promotion of original values and beliefs.

I am highly critical of organizations that establish Elders Councils or invite Elders to provide guidance and direction to them in the running of their affairs, but then use them to do opening and closing prayers, and that's all. I have witnessed too many occasions where invited guests have not been taken care of. I have met an Elder in an airport who was not sure where to go and had to rely on an organizational representative, who had had too much to drink on the same flight, to take him to the hotel. I often wondered how these people who invite Elders to their meetings, treat guests to their homes. However, the absolute worst abuse that I have witnessed is the deliberate attempt by "leaders" to use Elders to get their way.

I will never forget my first national meeting, as a delegate, where avowed traditional men and women fed information to the Elders present with the intent to have us, the delegates, adopt their proposals. Because we have been taught to listen to our Elders, the plan would have succeeded, but too many of the Elders and delegates saw through the plan and so it failed, *that time*.

Skonaganleh:rá: I think some of it, though, is also an issue of timing. It's been about twenty-five years that I've been trying, *and only trying* to find the traditional road, that good red road, that sweetgrass path. It has taken active trying, and it has taken changes that must occur— first, inside the individual: changes in attitude, in the way one presents oneself, even in the way one thinks and feels. There are some things that are given sunlight, and grow, and are legitimized, and there are things that we had to do away with. There have been experiences in both of our short-lived political lives that suggest "window-dressing." People are saying "we are changing," and yet we hear the same stories, the same criticisms; we don't hear the kind words. We hear lots about honesty—everyone wants to go out and be honest, but they forget the four directions, the first teachings. Then we are to share, and through the sharing, we will have strength.

It took four hundred years for us to get to the point where we are now. Changes that *you* would like to see cannot have happened this quickly. We, I think, are both very eager to admit that we are young, very young, in our learning, but we've gone to at least look. However, there are people who sit in some circles that we had, or talked about it one time, who suddenly *know*. They added water, mixed, put it into a microwave, and now culture can be served. This is not the way it is. This everyday good living that we are looking for starts with the individual, then it goes to the family, then to the clan, and finally it goes to the Nation.

Nowadays, even when we talk, we have other ways that it must go, because we have certain concepts of communities. The political organizations have decided that our communities are "First Nations." There is only one *Kanien'kehá:ka* Nation, spread out over seven communities, yet many of those communities now call themselves "First Nations of such and such." So they, too, contribute to dividing our house even further. No longer is there a sense, even amongst our women, *Kanien'kehá:ka* women, that we could have a sisterhood in one community or another. No, we have to have it only within that "First Nation" context, essentially defined by our so-called "leadership," or the organizations, which you have suggested are at the convenience of, and are playing into the hands of, the foreign governments. If we are going to do anything about it, we have to return to the "grassroots." Best as I know, "grassroots" is very clean, very shiny, very humble; it is connected to the earth, it accepts its responsibilities—it's not airport people or airport politicians.

THE FUTURE DIRECTION

Skonaganleh:rá: We have got to begin in this process of "self-identification," and again, the only place we can look is in our past. We can't do that if the woman doesn't go back and pick up those things that were left behind, if the men don't protect us while we're doing that journey, and if everything is being given away in the context of negotiations. The way it has been is that "Indian" people, Aboriginal people, "negotiated" and governments "consulted." I think now is the time for Aboriginal peoples to "consult" with each other and for governments to begin to "negotiate." In "negotiating," a focus should be "consultation"—true "consultation"—and not a giving-away, not a "some win, some lose, some compromise situation." Recognition must be given to the prophecy, which says that the ones who would visit here would come to a time when their life was dying and their life was falling apart around them, and they would recognize the wisdom of our ways and our words.

I want to be *awake* when that time comes. I want to be able to remember what is. When they come and knock on our door and say: " We are killing the earth, help us," how can we help? There *are* some helpers, the fire continues to be passed; I see children in my travels throughout Turtle Island who are raised this way. Wouldn't it be wonderful if all the children were growing that way? For them we would be able to turn the time around rather quickly. The reality, I suppose, is that we are becoming very urban, even those who live on the reserves; those in northern and isolated communities have southern and satellite influence and have forgotten to be natural.

That is not to say that we have to turn back the clock and that we can no longer learn from our brothers and sisters across the country. If we are going to learn from them, if we are going to adopt their ways too, we still have to answer the question, individually, of *who I am*. We still have to make sure our own houses are in order, and if you want to know who is a true traditional person of all of the people who are out there, our Elders and Traditional People have told us that the proof is in the pudding. You look at their family and how they behave; you look at their grandchildren and how they behave; you don't look at what they say, you look at *how they are*. Very recently, a Seneca Grandmother told us: "You watch their body, because their body, that 'non-verbal,' doesn't lie; you do question what comes out of their mouth."

We've also been told to quit using our heads to think, to start feeling, because when we feel, when we think with our hearts, which was what we were first instructed to do, we tend to at least think about being kind first—not how much money will this cost, can we do it?—but what good will it do? If it will do good, then all of the water, all of the trees, all of the rocks, and all of the earth energy that needs to be applied for that good to come up, *will*. But if we say: "How much does it cost and who has the power, and so-and-so got more than I did," we might as well cover it all with concrete, because what will grow out of there will not be something that will help all of the people.

We have to begin, as Aboriginal women, to think about all of our relations, not just ourselves and getting ahead, but all of our relations! How do we do that in the context of there being benefit, there being good, there being this ripple effect of the water, that helps everybody? The more and more that we buy into the government programming and servicing, the more and more we contribute to dividing our house. If we keep letting them divide us so that we have to have an alcohol and drug organization, social service organization, a cultural organization, political organization, etc., etc., then we are contributing now to dividing our house.

If we continue to take that approach, that attitude, what will we leave the seventh generation? Through our thoughts, our actions, our words, *today*, we're supposed to be thinking about their well-being, I hope everyone knows, whether they are female or male, that this time that we have, these resources that we have, we are only borrowing from our children, our grandchildren, and our great-grandchildren; that they're not ours. We are not motivated the same way as perhaps others are here, to work really, really hard in order to leave a whole bunch of money and vast holdings in property to our children, because we are only borrowing this time that we live in, this place that we live in, from those seven generations who sit and who watch us and upon whom our thoughts and deeds and actions impact. If in seven generations, they are sitting in council, as children, as young people, as women and men, as Elders and Grandparents, and they're saying: "Why did they do this to us, why did they hurry, why did they rush along?" we will be held responsible for not having made the best decisions when we had the chance. Meeting processes do not permit people to stop and wonder: "What am I doing to my children, what am I leaving them?"

I've had conversations with my parents and with my aunts and uncles about why they made decisions they made around our language, around our education, the church, around Children's Aid, around letting people come into our communities to do what they did. They say, *now*, as they are aging: "We thought we were helping, we thought there wasn't anything left. There was no language, there weren't going to be any ceremonies, there weren't going to be all of the things that go into culture—everyday good living—and there were other things that we had to do." Most of them seriously regret their decisions now—now that their grandchildren are here. If they had just held on a little longer, perhaps our communities might not be as sick as they are—*and they are sick*—and it seems to me that when somebody is sick in our family, it's usually the woman, it's usually the mother who goes and does the administering to that issue. It seems to me that while we need to be very respectful of the role that everybody plays in the community and we need to be very respectful, in particular, of those responsibilities of men; at the same time, we have to get ourselves in gear and start to do some kind of healing. There's a need for Aboriginal women to understand that they have to get going—that they are the ones who always have the responsibility when people are sick in a house, and even when they're not sick. If your children are sick or if your partner is sick, you have got to keep going and it seems to me, that if there's this un-healthiness in our communities, that responsibility also rests with us.

It is necessary for all of us, from the very youngest to the very oldest, in our communities, to recognize the truth that was provided us by the Great Mystery when we were lowered here to Turtle Island. In that medicine wheel, that way of life we were given, that good life, that good mind, is everything we need. Some of it needs to be interpreted into modem concepts, but in interpretation, we must not lose the truth, we must not find ourselves glibly quoting from other dogmas because those are good words and they seem to fit into the context. We have to remember the truth. We have to go and find it. We have to go and wake up our Elders and our Traditional People, our true teachers, whether they are young or old, and not be so much on our high horse and our ego, so busy pursuing our *per diem*, running off to this meeting, and sitting on that inter-ministerial committee, and having this heavy, heavy title of Grand Chief, leader of all, "don't question me." We have to go to those people and say: "Tell us, because I've lost my age of learning, my true wisdom of the medicine wheel, and I have come to my time of adoption and borrowing—this from those people and that from that society—and I don't know what's my own anymore."

I can't go and I cannot speak with a good mind, in a heartfelt way for the people, if I don't know who I am. We have been taught by Elders and Traditional People that one cannot answer the question "who am I?" until one knows where s/he comes from, and one cannot find where s/he comes from in books, policy/position papers, *Robert's Rules of Order*. You have to go out and be with your first teacher, your mother, the earth. You have to take off those other clothes, those other glasses that you put on to present yourself to the "other" world, and see what it is that we had.

There are things that are going to change. We are not advocating that things don't change, but we are advocating that we think them through, twice; that we "double understand" as one beloved Elder tells us, before we are going to go in a certain direction. Before we go off to those meetings where our minds get changed, we need to be very firmly rooted in all of the peoples' opinions, not in a democratic process of 50 per cent + 1, but in the minds of all of our people. And if we have to talk about it for five years or ten years before we come to a common mind themselves, then so be it. The quicker we run now, the further apart the moccasin tracks (if there are any left), the further the space for the ones who will come after, and the more we give away.

There need to be councils created where the children, the young people, the men, the women, the Elders, the seniors, the Traditional People in communities, can come together. When they come together, when you've dropped that rock into that water and the message has been sent out, then we are going to have something to talk about. We will have something—very, very strong seeds that will have been planted, that will make it even harder for the next round of threat and attack in our community, on our society. It will be harder to uproot those as we make them stronger, but it's going to be very easy for that wind of change to blow through if we are planting them in the sky, if we're planting them by typing them on paper—if our relationships are not firmly rooted in where we've come from.

Osennontion: What can I add to the teaching that you've just given, but to say that we recognize what the Aboriginal woman has done in the face of adversity, and we congratulate her and we encourage her to continue—we don't do this often enough. We must remember that despite all that has happened to us and our people, you and I can still sit here in 1989 and talk about our ways, and about the problems, and about how we would like to see things and that, as far as we are concerned, the solution is to learn our ways: that's where the answers are because we were given it all. We may have screwed up along the way, but we said: "Okay, no more!" We have heard the truth and it is our responsibility to make sure that that truth is not twisted any more; that, in fact, it is shined up, and we had better start relaying that truth. We can't lie any more and we can't hide what we know for the sake of appearances, or to spare people's feelings—we have to tell the truth!

Osennontion & Skonaganleh:rá: In closing, we want to say that we realize that perhaps we have given you, the readers, too much; or is it that we haven't given you enough? Either way, we apologize. We trust that we have been able to convey to you that the Aboriginal woman has begun to add fuel to the fire that she keeps so that other people can see that fire and can come themselves to get warm and to get nourished. She sees, too, those "other" fires where she can go for help. We need to look at these things and we need to encourage our own women when they are trying to look at getting healthy in their communities, when they are trying to attack the issues of alcohol and drugs, lack of employment opportunities, lack of real and appropriate education opportunities, and lack of community support mechanisms that had existed prior to us adopting this modern approach to living that has resulted.

We wish to tell all the women to use all of the senses that you have, to keep your eyes open, your ears open, and to not be afraid to touch things in a good way and to embrace new ideas, as well as people who are in need of help. Don't be afraid to speak what you have to say, and to speak from the heart. Use this physical vessel that we were given to really do the work of the people; in doing so, maybe there will come a time when we can truly find peace in all of our relationships.

Originally published in Canadian Woman Studies/les cahiers de la femme, *"Native Women," 10 (2 & 3) (Summer/Fall 1989): 7-19. Reprinted with permission of the authors.*

Osennontion was born and raised in Kahnawake, where she is now living. She is a granddaughter and her parents' eldest and only daughter, the older sister to five brothers, and an aunt to a niece and nephews, and a relative to many, many others. In her past life, she has been a student at Bishop's University, an employee of Parks Canada and Indian and Inuit Affairs, a staff member of the Native Women's Association of Canada (NWAC), and an active "mover" in the Aboriginal women's movement, from the Ottawa Local of the Ontario Native Women's Association (ONWA) to the NWAC. She left that whole scene in the fall of 1987 and moved "home," where she has become a community activist of sorts. She is a "beginner" when it comes to learning her language and her ways, but she is a strong believer, her entering colour and sacred space being red, which is the colour of faith. She currently travels Turtle Island sharing good life teachings and learning traditional ways.

Skonaganleh:rá was born and raised (mostly) at Tyendinaga. She is a granddaughter, daughter, sister, auntie, friend and relative to many. Skonaganleh:rá is a Kanien'kehá:ka woman and was born into the Wolf Clan. Skonaganleh:rá is a student of traditional ways: Wolf Clan teachings, medicine wheels, colour teachings and life. She has been involved with the Friendship Centre movement for over thirty-five years. Skonaganleh:rá has provided advice and support over the years to a number of Native women's organizations. She is a reformed and recovering politician. She is currently employed at the Ontario Federation of Indian Friendship Centres as Executive Director. Her work ensures she works in many fields. She continues to learn her traditional ways and teachings.

LESLEY MALLOCH

INDIAN MEDICINE, INDIAN HEALTH

IT IS DIFFICULT TO WRITE about traditional Indian medicine and Indian values relating to health because the Indian tradition is an oral one and an active one. In other words, Indian medicine is spoken and practiced, but it is not written. It is also difficult to talk about Indian medicine and Indian values without relating them to a whole way of life, a traditional way of life of which they were a vital part.

Nevertheless, in this article I have tried to summarize the underlying perceptions and principles that have always guided traditional Indian health maintenance and healing practices as they were seen in 1982. I have not tried to describe the specific details of Indian medicine, such as the names of medicines and how they are used. That was not the intention of this article. Instead, I have tried to clarify Indian values related to health so that the committee can then consider how best to incorporate these values into policy statements on Indian health.

The information presented here represents the teachings that have been passed down by successive generations of Elders right up to the present day. These principles continue to guide the practice of true Indian medicine, where it is still practiced today. While these values may not be the values of all Indian people today, they remain important to those people who are trying to live a life compatible with the traditional teachings of their people.

In compiling this information, I spoke to several Anishnaabe Elders, as well as to some younger people who are rediscovering the traditional teaching of their culture. I also drew on some written material, including the workshop transcripts, and on earlier conversations with Elders and young people from other Indian nations. Before including information which I received from non-Anishnaabe sources, I checked that information out with my Anishnaabe contacts just to make sure that the perceptions, principles, and values were consistent with a traditional Anishnaabe worldview. This process of cross-checking confirmed my own hunch that the underlying values of Indian people throughout the country, with regard to health and healing, are very similar. It is only the specific practices and methods by which those values are applied that differ from culture to culture, from nation to nation.

466

TRADITIONAL INDIAN PRINCIPLES OF HEALTH[1]

Good health is a gift from the Creator and it is our responsibility to take care of it. When we show respect for ourselves and our health, we show our appreciation of the Creator's gifts. When we neglect our health or abuse ourselves, we are showing disrespect for the Creator.

Good health is a balance of physical, mental, emotional, and spiritual elements. All four interact together to form a strong, healthy person. If we neglect one of these elements, we get out of balance and our health suffers in all areas. For example, a troubled mind or spirit may cause sickness in the body; a poorly nourished body may weaken a person's mental function or contribute to mental illness.

Prevention of sickness goes hand in hand with a traditional healthy lifestyle. Good health is ours when we live in a balanced relationship with the Earth and the natural world. Everything we need has been provided by our common mother, the Earth: whole foods, pure water and air, medicines, and the laws and teachings which show us how to use these things wisely. When we combine these gifts with an active lifestyle, a positive attitude, and peaceful and harmonious relations with other people and the spiritual world, good health will be ours. When we get sick it is usually because we are out of balance in some way. Perhaps we have failed to take care of our bodies by eating the proper foods, getting the right kind of exercise, fasting, cleansing, etc. Or perhaps we are out of balance in our minds. Even our own negative thoughts can come back on us and cause us to become sick. Or perhaps our spirit is not well: we may have failed to observe certain ways of living that show respect for our spirit. Any of these imbalances can cause us to become sick. Sickness may also be the result of something that someone has done to us. If we do not protect ourselves, someone can direct negative energy towards us that will cause us to get out of balance.

Parents must be particularly careful of the way in which they live and behave because they are responsible for their children's welfare and even their grand children's, and great-grandchildren's. A parent who fails to heed the teachings of the Creator and of Mother Earth risks injury to his or her child.

Since the coming of the White man, we have put aside many of our ways, and forgotten the teachings of Mother Earth. We no longer eat the natural foods we were meant to—we eat White man's food, full of sugar and chemicals. We no longer drink pure water—we drink black tea and coffee, even alcohol. Many other things have been forgotten. This is why we have become sick and weak.

TRADITIONAL ROLES OF MEN AND WOMEN IN HEALTH AND HEALING[2]

Woman is the Earth, the centre of the circle of life. She brings forth life; she is the caretaker of life. She nourishes, nurtures, and heals in the same way that the Earth does. Her reproductive power is sacred and she has great natural healing powers that derive from her spiritual connection with the Earth.

A traditional Indian woman practices preventative medicine in the home. She has a working knowledge of the foods and plants that are essential to her family's health. She also has a knowledge of basic home remedies for treating illness.

Woman also nurtures the spiritual and mental health of her children by means of the natural way in which she bears her children and rears them. Natural child birth, bonding, breastfeeding, security, and establishing a positive self-image in the home are examples of this. This process is transmitted to the children as much by example as it is by instruction. Some women also fulfill the special role of midwife in their community.

Man fulfills his role in a different way. Because he is not born with the same relationship to the Earth and lifegiving powers as is a woman, he must strive throughout his life to develop that relationship. This he does through ceremonies, the sweat, fasting, and serving the people.

Man must seek knowledge and powers through suffering and self-sacrifice. If he is blessed with power and knowledge, it is not for his own personal gain but rather for the benefit of the people (for example, his family, his community).

Men are usually the ones chosen to be the "medicine" people in the Anishnaabe way—that is, medicine men who doctor the sick with medicines and through spiritual ceremonies. The reason for this is that women are already fulfilling their role as lifegivers and healers. It is the men who must fulfill their role and relationship to the Creation as servants of the people, as "medicine men." At the same time, some women may be recognized for their knowledge and skill (or gift) in the use of herbal medicines. Different people have different gifts and act appropriately.

TRADITIONAL INDIAN UNDERSTANDING OF MEDICINE AND HEALERS[3]

Medicines that come from the Earth, from the natural world, are a gift from the Creator and are sacred. Medicines must be gathered, handled, prepared, and administered with respect and proper care. The spirit of the medicine must be honoured. This is why we make an offering of tobacco before picking medicines or when we ask for a spiritual healing. Medicines are not for sale.

It is important that we pick medicine at its own correct time. We are instructed to take both the adult male and female plant. We are to speak to the medicine first and tell it we are asking for its power and that we are offering tobacco for its help. After acknowledging its contribution to the life cycle, we carefully put out our tobacco and pick what we need.

People picking medicines must ensure they are taking care of themselves. From the time of moon to pick, what to pick, by whom, and how to ensure attention is paid to picking in a good way, some of the medicine will help.

Indian medicine does not just treat the symptoms, but works on the cause of the illness. In some cases, Indian medicine works more slowly but is more thorough and effective than western pharmacology.

There are different types of traditional healers or medicine people. Each traditional healer has been given his (or her) own role to fulfill and no two healers are exactly alike. It should be reiterated that both men and women may fulfill this role. In the Anishnaawbe way, and for the purposes of arriving at a general understanding of Indian medicine, several observations can be made:

The term "medicine man" is generally reserved to describe a man with a great deal of knowledge and a wide range of healing abilities. This man is one who doctors people through spiritual ceremonies, as well as with herbal medicines. However, this same term is sometimes used to describe a herbalist, one who works with the healing powers of plants, but who does not conduct spiritual healing ceremonies. While the medicine man and the herbalist fulffill different roles, they are both traditional healers in their own right.

The term "Elder" is used to describe someone who has knowledge and understanding of the traditional ways of his or her people, both the physical culture of the people and their spiritual tradition. An Elder may be a traditional healer also, but is not necessarily one. While an Elder is generally an older person with a rich life experience, he or she need not be Elderly in order to gain that position of respect within the community. It is a person's knowledge and wisdom, coupled with the recognition and respect of people in the community, which are the important criteria in the definition of an Elder.

The medicine man is a physician, psychiatrist, psychologist, family counsellor, and spiritual advisor all in one. He is concerned with the body, mind, and spirit, and their balanced relationship. In treating sick peoople, he helps to restore the individual's balance. He stresses preventative medicine.

The healing powers of the medicine man (and of traditional healers) are really the healing powers of Creation which flow through him. He is the servant of the Creator, a vehicle or medium for the natural healing powers of the Creation. Thus, the medicine man is governed by the natural laws of the Earth and of the Universe, and carries out his duty in accordance with the instructions he has re ceived from his Elders and from the Creator.

The medicine man is accountable to the Creator and to the people. He is a servant to both. In this way, the medicine man does not charge money for his services. His reward is in seeing the recovery of those who come to him for help. Gifts may also be given to him by the people in recognition of the help that he gives them. This amounts to support from the people to enable him to continue fulfilling his role.

The medicine man is often born with a natural gift for healing, but he must also study under the guidance of Elders, as well as pursue his learning through expe rience and spiritual development.

Because medicine is sacred, medicine people are careful about whom they transmit knowledge to and how they do it. Information is handed down to the next generation by oral tradition, and is not generally written down. Individual in struction or apprenticeship is also generally preferred to group or classroom in struction. The student of Indian medicine must be sincere and committed, and must have the right intention, that is, to help the people.

In medicine, as in the natural world, there is both the good and the bad. The medicine man's role is to practice good medicine to help the people, but he must also understand the negative force in order that he can balance it with the positive. For example, in treating physical, mental, or spiritual sickness, the medicine man must understand where the sickness comes from in order to deal with it. Another example: the medicine man must under stand the power of those medicines which are not used because they work contrary to the Creator's wishes, for example, abortifacients.

When we look around us, we see that mistakes, flaws and accidents do occur in nature. So it is with human beings that abnormalities occur such as developmental delays, physical handicaps, and birth defects. These are part of nature and it is not the medicine man's role to tamper with or try to correct these conditions. Nor should we reject people who suffer from these disabilities. They are human beings and have a place and or worth in our society.

THE ROLE OF THE TRADITIONAL MIDWIFE[4]

Birth is a sacred event in the circle of life. It must be respected in this way. It is a powerful celebration of life that can strengthen the family and the nation. Birth is a natural process and must be protected rather than interfered with.

Women are the caretakers of the birth process. This is a responsibility and a power which women have. This is why, in the traditional Indian way, midwives attended the birth. A midwife is more than just a woman who catches a baby. She has to know about nutrition, herbology, gynecology, and obstetrics. She has to be able to counsel a woman and a couple (family counsellor). A midwife is a mother herself who knows the power of the female side of life. In helping other women through their pregnancy and at the time of their delivery, she helps them also to discover and take responsibility for their female power.

On the other side of the pain experienced in childbirth is knowledge, strength, and power; men acquire that through fasting, sweating, and sun-dancing.

Pre-natal care, natural childbirth and breastfeeding, as practiced in the traditional way, contribute to the physical and emotional health of mother and child. These are aspects of the nurturing role which a woman fulfills in the same way that the Earth nurtures the people.

A midwife, like other traditional healers in the Indian community, does not charge money for her services. Families may give her gifts or money in recognition of her help, or support her in other ways.

Midwives, in the contemporary context, have adapted and integrated some western medical procedures into their practice (taking blood pressure, blood tests, urine tests, fetoscope, resuscitation equipment, etc.). These are viewed as appropriate and helpful adaptations of the purely traditional methods. The combination of traditional practices and attitudes, and western medical technology is welcomed, in so far as it does not unduly interfere with the natural birth process or take away from the sacredness of the birth event.

A COMPARISON OF VALUES

In this section, I have set out a comparison of the underlying values or guiding principles of traditional Indian medicine and of western (Euro-American) medicine. This comparison will help to clarify the differences (and similarities) between the two systems of medicine. This, in turn, may help to determine if or how it is possible to work with both systems to achieve Indian control of Indian health.

It can be seen, from this comparison, that many of the underlying principles of Indian medicine and western medicine are in direct opposition to each other. This suggests that it will be difficult to combine them, in such a way, as to arrive at a single, unified system of " "Indian-Western"" medicine. In fact, several Elders stressed to me the importance of retaining a clear distinction between the two ways of medicine and the people who practice them. In the view of these Elders, the two different systems of medicine cannot be combined into a new brand of medicine without undermining the integrity of traditional Indian medicine.

However, this does not rule out the possibility that Indian medicine and western medicine can coexist and complement each other. In the next section, I discuss the apparent features of both kinds of medicine and look at the ways in which they can complement each other.

In order to give some perspective on the respective roles that Indian and western medicine may possibly play in Indian health care, I begin with several observations on the current state of both systems.

Indian Medicine

The degree to which traditional Indian medicine is still active in any given Anishnabe community depends on the unique history and cultural experience of that community. In broad terms, however, it would seem that on many reserves the people have become largely dependent on the western medical system to meet their health needs. Indian medicine has been suppressed and undermined by the western medical values and practices that have accompanied colonialism, and the Indian ways have been put aside or have gone underground. In some cases, Indian people themselves have rejected Indian medicine in favour of the western technological system that they have come to believe is superior to their traditional system.

TRADITIONAL INDIAN MEDICINE AND WESTERN MEDICINE:
A COMPARISON OF VALUES

Traditional Indian Medicine

•integrated, holistic approach to health: body, mind, and spirit interact together to form person;
•emphasis on prevention of sickness;
•personal responsibility for health and sickness;
•health and sickness understood in terms of the laws of nature;
•man living in balance with nature, with natural law;
•traditional medicine governed by the laws of the Creation: everything we need comes from the Earth—our food, medicines, water, education, religion, and laws;
•a medicine man is accountable to the Creator, to the people, to the Elders of his medicine society;
•medicine is not for sale, and not-for-profit—it is a gift to be shared;
•the land and the people support the medicine man and his practice;
•encourages self-sufficiency, self-care, and responsibility, and control by the people.

Western Medicine

•Analytic approach: separation of body, mind, and spirit (total split between medicine and religion);
•emphasis on disease, treatment;
•impersonal, "scientific" approach to health and sickness;
•health and sickness understood in terms. of quantifiable, scientific data;
•man controlling nature, manipulating natural variables;
•western medicine governed by laws of the state, man-made laws that grow out of a political-economic system;
•doctor is accountable to the government, and to his professional association;
•medicine is a business, the patient is the consumer, the doctor and the medical industry profit;
•the government, the taxpayer, and the consumer support the doctor, and the practice of medicine;
•encourages dependency and abdication of self-government by the people.

This state of dependence on western medicine can be seen in the fact that many Indian people are no longer familiar with the philosophy or practice of Indian medicine, and bona fide traditional medicine people are now few and far between. Indian medicine kept appearing on the agenda of the future workshops, along with comments such as the"need more information on Indian medicine," "still confused about Indian medicine," or "need more on Indian values." These comments indicate a genuine interest in learning more about the subject, but also point out the current lack of knowledge among some people at the reserve level. Both Ron Wakegijig and Bobby Woods commented on the scarcity of medicine people today because Indian medicine has gone through a period of remaining largely underground. It is only in recent years that the interest in Indian medicine has been openly revived.

It must be noted that on some reserves Indian medicine remains a way of life for some, if not all, of the residents. It would seem to be the elderly people who have retained the most knowledge of, and faith in, Indian medicine. But there is evidence of a growing interest on the part of young people to learn once more the traditional Indian principles of health and healing.Gatherings such as the annual meeting of Elders at Birch Island (sponsored by the Ojibway Cultural Foundation) provide an opportunity for Elders to meet and share their experiences, as well as for young people to listen and learn. Though still relatively few, there are a number of young people who have begun to apprentice with herbalists or medicine men. The renewed interest in Indian medicine, which both young and old have demonstrated in recent years, suggests that the role of traditional medicine, in meeting the health needs of contemporary Anishnaabe, must be given careful consideration.

Western Medicine

While the underlying principles of mainstream western medicine are quite clearly at odds with the principles of traditional Indian medicine, it is important to recognize that counter-trends do exist in the western medical profession. These trends can be seen in the way that some doctors have returned to a more holistic approach to treating the person, taking into account the importance of body, mind, and spirit. There has also been a growing emphasis within the medical profession on prevention of illness and promotion of health promotion. This has been translated into practical areas such as nutrition, lifestyle counselling, and stress management, to name a few. Naturopathy, a branch of medicine dealing with natural medicines and treatments, while still outside of the mainstream western medical profession, is receiving renewed interest also.

A "radical minority" of the consumers (patients) and professionals (doctors, nurses, etc.) have been active in the area of encouraging people to take a greater degree of responsibility for their health, and a larger measure of control over their health services. This trend can be seen in the growth of self-help programs and consumer-controlled programs.

These counter-trends seem to have been on the increase in recent years as the disillusionment with the existing medical system has grown on the part of both consumers and professionals. To the extent that these counter-trends represent values and principles that are more closely aligned with Indian medicine (holistic approach, emphasis on prevention, personal responsibility, etc.), the doctors and nurses within the western medical profession who support these trends may be valuable allies of Indian people working to build their own health care system around Indian values.

The observations outlined above lead me to identify two principles concerning the roles of Indian medicine and western medicine in the development of an Indian-controlled health care system: Indian people must continue to have access to traditional Indian medicine, or to western scientific medicine, or to both, and the choice must remain with the people.

In spite of the apparent contradictions between the traditional Indian medicine and western scientific medicine, there is room for mutually respectful co-operation and coexistence. Within the parameters of Indian control of Indian health, Indian people must determine ways to protect and enhance the on-going practice of traditional Indian medicine. And, in conjunction with the medical profession, Indian people must determine ways of making the western medical system more responsive to Indian values and more supportive of traditional Indian medicine.

I believe that these principles are consistent with the positions held by the Elders and traditional practitioners with whom I spoke. Perhaps I can summarize what they said in this way:

Western medicine does have a role to play, today, for several reasons. First of all, the people have become dependent on it and we can't hope to change attitudes and behaviours overnight.

Secondly, there are some diseases that were unknown to the Indian people before the coming of the White man. While we have Indian medicines that can treat some of these diseases, some times we have to turn to western medicine for treatment. And thirdly, there are some aspects of the scientific and technological developments of western medicine which are truly beneficial and which we can make use of.

At the same time, however, it is very important that we return to our Indian values to guide us in rebuilding our health (prevention), and return to our Indian medicines where they are known to work as well, if not better than western medicine (decreasing the dependency). This is the only way the people will become strong again.

TRANSLATING PRINCIPLES INTO POLICY DIRECTIONS

Two principles have been identified with respect to the roles of traditional Indian medicine and western scientific medicine in the development of Indian health. What follows is a number of examples of how these principles could be translated into policy directions, or applied in a practical way to activities at the reserve level:

1) One way of increasing access to western medical services for Indian people is to support the establishment of Indian-contrtolled clinics on the reserve. A clinic designed to meet the specific needs of the community it serves could go far in increasing a full spectrum of medical services to community residents.

One example of such a clinic is the one now operating at Rama. Located on the reserve and staffed, in part, by members of the community, the Rama Clinic is able to make available to the people preventative care, primary treatment, and follow-up services in a way that the doctors and hospital in town are not able to. The Rama Clinic was established as a result of the initiative and resourcefulness of community members and some outside support. The Medical Services Branch (MSB) to date has provided only minimal support in the way of funds for the rental of office spaces, renovations to the clinic, and minimal supplies.

Policy development in this area is very much needed if any meaningful support is going to come from MSB for similar initiatives from Bands elsewhere. At the present time there is no comprehensive policy with regard to the establishment and operation of clinics on reserves. As a result, the people responsible for the Rama Clinic have had to pull together bits and pieces of funding from diverse govern ment sources in order to keep their program going. Policy needs to be defined not only with respect to support for the day-to-day operation of a clinic (administration, professional staff, support staff, equipment, supplies, etc.), but also with respect to support for related programs, such as community education, follow-up services, etc.

2) One way of increasing access to traditional Indian medicine is to provide finmancial assistance to medicine people who must travel in order to provide consultation to patients, to gather medicines, and to attend meetings of medicine people or Elders. This kind of support is necessary in order to maximize the limited human resources that exist today in the field of Indian medicine. If every community had its own medicine man, the need to subsidize travel would not be so great. But at the present time, a very few traditional healers are being called upon to respond to the requests of the people who live throughout a large geographic area. Support to Elders to travel to meetings, such as the one held each year at Birch Island, is a way of contributing to the preservation and growth of knowledge about Indian medicine.

It must be noted that policy development in this area is a delicate matter because it involves the provision of funds, by the government, for an activity that remains within the domain of Indian medicine. The difficulty here is not so much in the acceptance of such funds by Indian medicine people, for the funds are merely for subsidizing travel and not renumeration for services. Rather, the problem relates to regulation and accountability procedures that accompany such funds. Medicine men are firm in their stance that they are accountable to the people and their fellow Elders, but not to the government for their activities.

Thus, while prepared to accept minimal accounting procedures, medicine people are not prepared to accept prescribed regulations laid down by the government, which might dictate details of how the money must be spent This particular example is only one which could be used to illustrate the dilemma that occurs when strings are attached to government funds earmarked for "Indian-controlled" programs or, in fact, when "Indian-controlled" programs receive government funds at all.

3) One way of encouraging cooperation and sharing between the Indian medicine system and western medical system is through a community nutrition project. Such a project could build on the Indian principles of preventative health care as they are related to food and nutrition, as well as incorporate the scientific understanding of nutrition that comes from the western system. Through the development of culturally-appropriate educational materials, nutrition classes, and projects in the schools and the community, and individual nutrition counselling, a wide range of nutrition issues could be addressed. Examples of these issues are preventative or optimum nutrition, diabetes, pre-natal nutrition, food processing and preservation, and obesity. Indian culture contains a wealth of information related to nutrition and Elders should be encouraged to participate actively in such a project.

This approach to nutrition education could also serve to strengthen a positive identification between health and Indian cultural identity. Nutritionists involved in such a project, while able to contribute their specialized knowledge of the chemical dynamics of nutrition, must be receptive to and respectful of the Indian cultural expertise in the field of nutrition. The success of such a project would depend to a great extent on the vision and creativity of the individuals involved in its planning and implementation. Bearing this in mind, it is critical that policy development reflect the principle that Indian people must have control over the selection of professionals who work in Indian communities. Even the most brilliantly conceived community nutrition project, designed to incorporate the expertise of both the Indian and western systems, would fail miserably if a professional nutritionist with the wrong kind of attitude was sent into the community to take a leading role in the project. (A further note: In order for this kind of project to receive support from MSB, policy development will have to reflect the principle that preventative health care is at least of equal importance alongside the treatment of disease or dysfunction.)

4) Another way of encouraging the harmonious coexistence of the western medical profession and the traditional Indian way is through the development of the role of the Community Health Representative (CHR). While the CHR's role is often seen as one of liaison between the community and western medical system (to increase the people's access to such services), the CHR

could play a unique role in helping to make the western medical system more responsive to Indian values and more supportive of traditional Indian medicine. In order for this aspect of the CHR's role to be developed, the training that is provided her (or him) must be made more culturally relevant. The CHR should be familiar with the underlying principles of Indian health philosophy and the Indian approach to treating sickness. This is not to say that the CHR should study the actual practice of Indian medicine. Such an activity would amount to an apprenticeship with a traditional healer and would take the individual outside the realm of the paraprofessional. But it would be possible to incorporate some study of the underlying Indian values related to health into the training of the CHR.

This would not only contribute other greater awareness and understanding of the role of traditional healers today, but would also put her in a better position to encourage the western medical profession to be more supportive of traditional Indian health maintenance and healing practices. Culturally-relevant training might also enrich the CHR's concept of her own role in the promotion of health within her community. For example, the traditional value associated with the role of the woman as caretaker of the health of her family could act as a source of support for the role of the CHR in her community.

5) Another area of health care that lends itself to the cooperation between western medical knowledge and the expertise of traditional Indian practices is the area of pre-natal care, labour coaching and delivery, and post-natal care. While different approaches can be taken with respect to the degree to which a traditional Indian perspective serves as a guiding philosophy, most projects undertaken in this area to date have reinforced the principle that maternal and infant care is most appropriately provided at home, in the community, by women who are themselves members of the community. It would also appear that lay practitioners in this area of health care are more readily able to incorporate elements of western medical technology and traditional Indian medicine into their practice, without compromising the principles of Indian medicine.

One project worthy of examination is the Women's Dance Health Program at Akwesasne. Four Indian women work together to provide complete maternal and infant care to women who choose to have their babies at home. Two of the women are registered nurses, while two are trained midwives. All the members of the team combine selected aspects of western medical science and procedure with a traditional Indian approach to childbirth and comprehensive female health care. The midwives have managed to enlist the support and back-up assistance of several local doctors.

However, they advocate the position that a normal pregnancy and labour can best be managed at home, with the support of family and competent midwives, and that the intervention of the medical profession is only warranted in the case of exceptional complications. They also maintain that community-based midwives are able to provide more personalized and individualized care to the women they serve, thus generally providing a higher quality of care than the hospitals and medical professionals are able to provide. (Note: the assumption here is that the more time spent with a woman, and, therefore, the more personal and individually-tailored care she receives are factors that contribute to a higher level of quality of care. In fact, these factors may be regarded as among the criteria which determine levels of quality.)

It must be noted that the Women's Dance Health Program is strictly a voluntary program. The midwives charge nothing for their services and are not supported by the federal Indian Health Services Program (USA). In this way, they are guided by the principles of Indian medicine. The program is supported by the midwives, the families they serve, and whatever means of financial support they are able to raise independently. It is, no doubt, this independent way in which they operate that has permitted them the freedom to develop the program in such a unique way, incorporating elements of western medicine along with the age-old wisdom of Indian cultural experience. The independence of the program itself is an issue of sovereignty as the state of New York (which surrounds the Mohawk Nation at Akwesasne) does not sanction the practice of midwifery or the delivery of babies at home.

The Women's Dance Health Program at Akwesasne is an example of an independent community-based initiative in the field of maternal and infant care which that offers an alternative for women who do not wish to rely on the western medical profession. A different model has been developed in the Sioux Lookout Zone of Northwestern Ontario in the form of a "self-help" program provided by local Indian women in collaboration with the medical profession.

In the case of the Sioux Lookout Zone Program, four Indian women provide pre-natal and post-natal counselling to mothers in their communities about diet, exercise, infant care, personal counselling, etc. In this capacity, the members of the self-help team are able to provide more frequent and personalized services than the medical professionals would be able to provide, given the shortage of medical personnel, the remoteness of some of the communities, and the language and cultural barriers which impede the delivery of western medical services. In this respect, the women who work on the program fulfill somewhat of a dual role, providing some paraprofessional primary care and, at the same time, acting as a liaison between the community and the doctor, who is called in the case of complications and at the time of delivery of the baby. Some in-service training is provided to the workers to supplement their own culturally-derived knowledge related to maternal and infant care, and full back-up services are always at their disposal in the form of the zone hospital and the doctors attached to it.

Although not a standard program within the MSB, the "self-help" program has been endorsed and supported by the management of the Sioux Lookout Zone, and funds for a pilot project have been provided by the Hospital for Sick Children Foundation. (The workers are paid positions, and travel, equipment, and supplies account for other costs.) As the end of the term of the pilot project approaches, the future of the program is a little uncertain. Efforts are being made to secure on-going funds from the federal government.

The Sioux Lookout Zone Program differs from the Women's Dance Health Program in that it has not been set up as an independent alternative to the existing federal health care system. Rather it had been designed to make the existing health care system more responsive to community needs, and at the same time, return some measure of responsibility to com munity members themselves. Related to this difference is the fact that the workers on the Sioux Lookout Zone Program do not provide comprehensive services, including labour coaching and home birth attendance, as do the midwives at Akwesasne.

This article is an abridged version of a paper prepared by Lesley Malloch for the Union of Ontario Indians' Health Steering Committee. The contents of the article were garnered from discussions with many Elders and traditional peoples. It was originally prepared in 1982 as a general discussion paper.

Originally published in Canadian Woman Studies/les cahiers de la femme, *"Native Women," 10 (2 & 3) (Summer/Fall 1989): 105-112.*

[1] In this section, source material came from the following: Transcripts by R. Wakegijig, Dan Pine, Bobby Woods, and Damien McShane. Interviews conducted with R. Wakegijig and Joe Yellowhead. Oral Tradition, transmitted to this day by many Elders.

[2] In this section, source material came from the following: Transcripts by Bobby Woods. Interviews conducted with R. Wakegijig, Vern and Pauline Harper, Edna Manitowabi, and Katsi Cook. Further written material provided by Art Solomon and Katsi Cook.

[3] In this section, source material came from the following: Oral tradition, traditional practice, and transcripts by D. Pine, B. Woods, and R. Wakegijig. Conversations with R. Wakegijig, Joe Yellowhead, Vern and Pauline Harper, and Edna Manitowabi.

[4] In this section, source material came from the following: Katsi Cook, Women's Dance Health Program, Akwesasne; , Edna Manitowabi, Gladys Taylor, and Elsie Knott at Curve Lake, HSC Workshop.

MONIQUE MOJICA

CHOCOLATE WOMAN DREAMS THE MILKY WAY

I HAVE BEEN THINKING FOR quite awhile about knowing and not knowing. What we know and *how* we know it. There's a saying in Spanish—*saber sabiendo*—literally "to know knowingly." But it also carries the connotation of knowing the unknown, the intuitively known, or what we don't know that we know.

Most of the work that I have done over the past two decades reflects tapping this kind of knowing. I haven't always done it consciously and I haven't done it alone. Since 1991, I have collaborated with Floyd Favel and Muriel Miguel, among others, in performance research and laboratories searching out how to do consciously what we do *un*consciously. This work has resulted in studio investigations and produced performances that aim to identify and hone a methodology that Floyd has called Native Performance Culture. These two visionary directors have had an enormous influence on me and I will talk more about them later.

So, I have been doing this performance thing for a long time. It has been 50 years since I first started training (!), 27 years since I first worked with an all Native theatre company: *Indian Time Theater*, directed by Bruce King, out of the now defunct Native American Center for the Living Arts in Niagara Falls, New York. It has been 24 years since I moved to Toronto to be one of the early Artistic Directors of *Native Earth Performing Arts*. Those were the times just preceding the infamous "Native theatre explosion" in Toronto when our small circle included the Highway brothers, Tomson and René, Billy Merasty, Makka Kleist, Maariu Olsen, Gary Farmer, Shirley Cheechoo, Graham Greene, and Doris Linklater. Over the years, I have accumulated quite a bit of material. Some there is no record of; some is in the form of drafts lost on floppy discs that my computer can no longer read. Some drafts hide in my not so organized filing cabinet, and still others are scraps of paper folded into notebooks: fragments of stories and notations of improvisations. As someone whose writing process includes doing laundry, making lists, and sifting though papers, I excavated some two-decade old writings, dusted them off, and had a look. What I found is that not only could I recognize recurring themes and imagery, but I could also trace a trajectory, a personal transformation as an artist and as an Aboriginal woman. This trajectory transforms amnesia through stories drawn from conscious memory, muscle memory, blood memory, then births organic texts, allowing me to emerge trusting the Indigenous knowledge encoded in my dreams, in my waking visions, and in my DNA.

***

I have organized this chronologically so I am going to begin with some fragments from a writing exercise written during the development of *Princess Pocahontas and the Blue Spots* (1988), dramaturged by Djanet Sears. When I uncrinkled this and read it, it occurred to me that it contains many of the themes that I have worked with since and that it is something of a prophecy for my life's path.

> *Once upon a time there was a little girl who lived in a stone cave, not entirely by herself—but almost. She lived that way, away from other people, because she was not entirely invisible—but almost (maybe about half). It made other people very uncomfortable that they couldn't see the other half of her even though she referred to it often and insisted that it actually was there and that it would bleed if she scraped it, and even scab over and get well.*
>
> *One day, the girl got tired of waiting in her stone cave for some one to believe her and she decided to leave. But she didn't know where she was going so she didn't know how to get there. So, she called to the spirit of heartbreak and sadness, the spirit of blood and rebellion, the spirit of back-breaking endurance, and the spirit of transformation to help her make a map.*

The part of the story that follows has been lost but this is the next recovered fragment:

> *"Easy for you to say," said the girl, "but I only have one foot!"*
> *"Ah, ahhh," said the Grandmother spirits, "but just because other people cannot see your other foot doesn't mean it doesn't make an imprint when you walk. One foot in front of the other. Follow your own path, which is ours."*
> *So she did.*

This is how elements from this exercise appeared in the final *Princess Pocahontas and the Blue Spots* script:

CONTEMPORARY WOMAN NO. 1:
No map, no trail, no footprint, no way home; only darkness, a cold wind whistling by my ears. The only light comes from the stars.
Nowhere to set my feet.

No place to stand. (rising)
No map, no trail, no footprint, no way home.

Sees basin of water; brings it to center.

He said, "It's time for the women to pick up their medicine in order
for the people to continue." *(washes hands, arms)*
She asked him, "What is the women's medicine?" The only answer
he found was, "The women are the medicine, so we must heal the
women.

Washes from basin head, arms, legs, feet. Tiple theme begins.

*Squatting over basin in a birthing position, she lifts a newborn from
between her legs, holding baby in front of her, she rises.*

When I was born, the umbilical cord was wrapped around my neck
and my face was blue.
When I was born, my mother turned me over to check for the blue
spot at the base of the spine—the sign of Indian blood.
When my child was born, after counting the fingers and the toes, I
turned it over to check for the blue spot at the base of the spine.
Even among the half-breeds, it's one of the last things to go.
(19-20)

"No map, no trail, no footprint, no way home," is a refrain echoed by the
character, Lady Rebecca, as Pocahontas was renamed when she was converted
to Christianity and then taken to England's Elizabethan court as an advertising
gimmick. The theme of being lost in my motherland, finding no trail to follow
because my grandmothers and great-grandmothers left no written records of
themselves or their experiences, weaves through my early work. Narratives of
wandering without a map, having forgotten my way, evolved to another recurring theme: memory /remembering/memorializing.

The following text fragment is from a writing exercise on "amnesia" from
Un(tit)led (1993), a piece co-written with Djanet Sears and Kate Lushington
that explored the borders and boundaries of race and women's friendship. It
was presented by Nightwood Theatre as a workshop production, facilitated by
Clarissa Chandler, animated by Bañuta Rubess and directed by Muriel Miguel,
with a set designed by Teresa Przybylski.

Amnesia fragments

Amnesia.
Long nightmare hallways,

lost, wandering.
Memory just slipped away.
All recognition of myself,
 who I was or am or might be.
Where does the spirit of an amnesiac go to find refuge?
Does it hang around waiting to be recognized, brought home,
fed and warmed as the relatives on the other side do
when we forget to acknowledge them?
Plastic Halloween costumes,
 remnants of some vague need for ritual,
 walking in the night—not to wander
 nor to play but to be fed—Day of the Dead.
Sacred time to eat,
to celebrate,
to consecrate,
to pacify,
to subdue.
Smoke filled hollows of spaces long neglected needing
 to be filled and fulfilled with the brimming nurturing
 sustenance of food
 of flavors on the tongues of we who are we who are we
who make fire,
 who plant,
who hands in the cornmeal bless the masa dough
facing East.

I forgot.
I forgot the ant spray.
I forgot where I've been.
I forgot where I walked
I forgot what it's like to walk on sand,
 to be in the ocean everyday,
to sleep in a hammock,
to wake at dawn and go with the other
women in dugout canoes to the mainland
to get water from the river in the forest.
I forgot what it's like to climb coconut trees and
 to know the jaguar watches over us.
I forgot to remember.

The following is the piece that was actually scripted from this exercise and
presented. It began as a monologue that I wrote and then we broke it up and
Djanet and Kate added some character-specific images.

Forbidden Territory

MONIQUE: In this forbidden territory, the landscape itself is treacherous.

DJANET: No Exit.

MONIQUE: No entrance.

KATE: No admittance.

ALL: (whisper) Only, only us.

MONIQUE: White lies in twisted words of "Discover America!" (singing) "See the USA in your Chevrolet!"

KATE: Poor Dinah.

MONIQUE: Twisted words of nice hiding behind a Sunday school smile.

DJANET: Sssh, it's a secret.

KATE: (singing) "Someone's in the kitchen with Dinah."

MONIQUE: I always thought that meant Dinah Shore.

KATE: Poor Dinah.

MONIQUE: In this treacherous landscape where we by our natures are forbidden.

KATE: In secret we meet.

DJANET: It's a secret manoeuvre.

KATE: Sssh.

MONIQUE: Covert operation. Undercover. Under wraps. Under the stars, under the cover of night.

DJANET: Dinah never fooled me; I always knew she was Black.

KATE: In the shadows, in the margins …

DJANET: … our spines pressed flat against the wall, bellies pushed against our spines …

KATE: We gasp for breath to fortify us in our vigilance. Vigilance, unless I keep constant vigilance, I will forget everything.

DJANET: … like a flower, a Black Cosmos, pushing up through the concrete.

KATE: I have forgotten who I am, I have forgotten who you are, I have forgotten why we are important to one another. The stars are going out inside my mind. I used to remember; how to dance, Pythagoras theorem, the capital of Australia.

ALL: We who are we who are we who are we … (continues under)

DJANET: … we who jump the borderline into this forbidden territory. Clandestine.

KATE: Clandestine.

MONIQUE: Clandestine mass graves—bones of my ancestors, bones of my ancestors, bones of my ancestors.

DJANET: (singing) "Dong dong bell, bodies in a well! Who put them in?"

DJANET: Sssh, it's a secret.

MONIQUE: The souls of amnesiac Indians on the land roam like trick-or-treaters on a Halloween night in the suburbs.

DJANET: (singing) "See the USA in your Chevrolet!"

MONIQUE: White lies fall apart, shattered into millions of metallic mirrored pieces only to reproduce as mutant thoughts in the bodies of our unborn children.

KATE: Poor Dinah.

DJANET: Incognito we advance. Masked, veiled, disguised and hidden.

KATE: Subversive.

MONIQUE: We meet with a password:

ALL: Now!

The voice in the previous piece became a character I named Rebelda. Here is Rebelda's story:

> *There once was a woman named Rebelda. She has a plan. She has a memory. Rebelda knows they will come knock on your door, take you away and kill you. Rebelda knows they will burn your homes. Rebelda has no time to cry. Rebelda plans. Rebelda makes allies. Rebelda strategizes. Rebelda will not be wiped out.*
>
> *She carries memorized in code: a recipe for cornbread, a song for birthing babies while under fire. Propaganda in her hand and propagation on her mind. A baby on each hip and a weapon in her hand. Rebelda has no time to cry. Rebelda plans. Rebelda makes allies. Rebelda strategizes. Rebelda will not be wiped out.*
>
> *Like the coyotes, they haven't built a trap that will hold her. Like the raccoons, Rebelda spreads her brood. Rebelda steals. Rebelda eats garbage. Rebelda will not be wiped out.*

***

Another one of the recurring images in my work is the bag of bones-carrying girl/woman. A character I will refer to as Bag of Bones/Rebecca first appeared in an early Native Earth production, *Double Take/A Second Look* (1983), written by Billy Merasty, Gloria Miguel, Maariu Olsen, and myself and directed by Muriel Miguel. Rebelda is another aspect of the same character. In retrospect, they are both early versions of Esperanza, my massacre-collecting atrocity tour guide from Turtle Gals" *The Scrubbing Project* (2002 and 2005). My original inspiration for this character came from Gabriel García Márquez's *One Hundred Years of Solitude*, which I read for the first time at age sixteen. This is a passage from García Márquez's magical novel:

That Sunday, in fact, Rebecca arrived. She was only eleven years old....

> Her entire baggage consisted of a small trunk, a little rocking chair with small hand-painted flowers, and a canvas sack which kept making a *cloc-cloc-cloc* sound, where she carried her parent's bones. (47)

I carried this bag of bones around for a long time—these "bones of my ancestors," and with the bones, the history of Native women on this continent. The history of being the sexual commodities for the conquest, the stories from the female side of the colonization experience, were not being told in the course of the "Native theatre explosion." I wanted to work with other Native women who felt the void and who had the courage to tell their own stories.

Jani Lauzon, Michelle St. John, and I first worked together in 1990 on the set of a CBC mini-series, *Conspiracy of Silence*. At that time, during pre-dawn conversations on the way to the set in sub-zero temperatures, we discovered a common interest in a theme that had left its mark on us all. Each of us had, or knew some one who had, tried to scrub off or bleach out her colour. These conversations and recognitions were the first seeds of *The Scrubbing Project*. It was not until nearly ten years later that we gathered to create the work.

In 1999 Turtle Gals Performance Ensemble was formed. Its founding members included Jani Lauzon, Michelle St. John, Sandra Laronde, and myself. For the first two workshop presentations in Nightwood Theatre's Groundswell and Native Earth's Weesageechak Begins to Dance, *The Scrubbing Project* was performed by a four-woman ensemble. By our second Groundswell presentation in 2000, we had become a trio.

In *The Scrubbing Project*, the Bag of Bones / Rebecca / Rebelda character was fully developed and her story expanded to include the massacre imagery that I had been working with since The Centre for Indigenous Theatre's residency at the Banff Centre in the winter of 1995. This was a program that Floyd Favel and I co-directed that included Muriel Miguel, Pura Fé, Michelle St. John, Archer Pechawis, Maariu Olsen, Jennifer Podemski, Alex Thompson, and others. There were several questions from this residency that carried over into the creation process of *The Scrubbing Project*. They were: 1) What are the consequences of creating art out of atrocity? 2) Is there such a thing as internalized genocide? (If so, what does it look like?) A question from a subsequent research project on memorials I did with Floyd Favel was: How do we create memorials to the holocaust in the Americas? To which Turtle Gals added: 1) Once Native women have put down the bundles of grief and multi-generational trauma that we collectively carry—then what? And 2) How do we get from victim to victory?

The Scrubbing Project is a study of the manifestations of internalized racism and genocide. Esperanza, my Earthplane character is a persona formed from my deepest victimization. She carries with her at all times a bag of bones she recovered from a clandestine mass grave: bones that she scrubs, feeds and cares for. She also carries a bag filled with shoes she collected from massacre sites, which she treats as prayers and offerings, which the play's three characters transform into tobacco ties, to honour them—to memorialize.

Esperanza was further informed by this quotation from a document entitled *Guatamala: Memory of Silence: Conclusions and Recommendations* from the Report of the Commission for the Clarification of History (CEH) in 1999 (see Tomuschat). This is an excerpt of testimony made by a witness to the commission who arrived carrying human remains. I put these words in Esperanza's mouth:

> It is very painful to carry them ... it's like carrying death ... I'm not going to bury them yet.... Yes, I want them to rest, I want to rest too, but I can't yet.... They are the proof of my declaration.... I'm not going to bury them yet, I want a paper that tells me "they killed them" ... and they had committed no crime, they were innocent. Then we will rest.

In contrast, my Starworld character, Winged Victory, was created from my strongest vision of victory: the huge copper and bronze winged beings, round breasted and full in the thigh, who crown the tops of the triumphant neo-Greco/Roman statuary our colonizers have erected in order to commemorate *their* victories. She is also rooted to the knowledge that the Tule Revolution of 1925, led by Nele Kantule, and the Mayan uprising of 1994, led by the Zapatistas, are evidence that sometimes we get to win.

This is an excerpt from *The Scrubbing Project* where Esperanza crosses a threshold into a "Massacre Portal" and tells the story of the recovery of the bones. By the end of the story she cradles the bones in her arms and addresses them. When Turtle Gals performs this, there are pieces of text woven into the story and the character Ophelia's "Passion Portal" unfolds out of the "Massacre Portal" like a kaleidoscope before its conclusion. Here, I've put the sections back together in order to read it as a whole.

Massacre Portal

ESPERANZA: Crack! / Thud! Crack! / Thud!
BRANDA tries to hang on to tradition. DOVE spirals down to Earthplane, back to
OPHELIA.
ESPERANZA: It's that once you see you can't ever pretend you don't see.
And I see,
I see the men lined up on one side, the women trembling on the other. I've never
witnessed a massacre/I see them all the time.

I see the soldiers raise their rifles—

I see
Skulls shatter
I see
Bodies fall:
Friends
Companions
Husband
Crack! Thud! (x 2)
I've never seen a body fall under the crack of
Bullet splintering bone / I see them all the time
And once you've seen, you can't ever pretend you don't see
And I see …
ESP & OPH: Little rivulets of blood …
ESPERANZA: … soaked up by the thirsty earth.
ESP & OPH: All the coulours of the rainbow …
ESPERANZA: … dried to a rusty brown crust.
I've never seen my relatives" bodies piled on the
blood soaked earth/I see them all the time.
Spit on blood fades the stain.

But once you've seen, you can't ever pretend you don't see
and I see.
(*as she gathers up bones*)
I will carry you, I will care for you, I will feed you, and I
will sing you songs of comfort.
I will wash away the dirt, and the ragged flecks of flesh and
skin
And you will be warm
And you will be loved
And I will build memory.

I am very grateful to the process that Turtle Gals went through diving headlong into the dark places of our victimization. The willingness to go there has allowed me to use those depths as a springboard—a trampoline that offers me the possibility of grounding myself in another place: a place where I cease to identify with my own victimization and no longer recognize my reflection as "the victim."

***

I would now like to talk about two veteran theatre directors whom I consider to be light-bearers in our movement. They have consistently held up a beacon, shed light on the path and given me a direction through their incredible vision. They are: Floyd Favel of Takwakin Performance Lab on the Poundmaker Reserve in Saskatchewan and my aunt, Muriel Miguel of

Spiderwoman Theatre in New York City.

I will start with this equation that Floyd created, and although it is somewhat "tongue in cheek" and pseudo-scientific, I think it works.

Trad (social/ritual) x M = NpC
Or, Tradition, social or ritual x Methodology = Native Performance Culture.

Instead of trying to interpret what Floyd means, I will offer a quotation from an article he wrote called "The Shadowed Path":

> One of the ideas of Native Performance Culture is to search for accessible ritual and social structures that can act as a catalyst for creative action. I believe that there needs to be a bridge from a ritual and social action to the professional stage. Tradition needs to be filtered and transformed for the objective needs of the theatre. Without this bridge, theatre risks presenting "Artificial Trees" on stage. "Artificial Trees" is the superficial or clichéd presentation of ritual and social structures on the professional stage.

In another article entitled "Waskawewin," published in 2005 for *Topoi*, an international philosophy journal published in the Netherlands, Floyd defines the concept of "Artificial Trees" this way:

> to take the traditional sacred dance as it is and transplant this to the modern stage. This process I feel turns the dance into folklore, or an "artificial tree." A tree cut off from its roots, a facsimile of culture and sacredness. (114)

He describes the methodology for Native Performance Culture he has been searching for in these words:

> One would have to isolate the technical principles of the dance and use these as starting points for contemporary performance. What is meant by technical principles is: the position of the body to the earth, the relationship of the feet to the ground, the head to the sky, the different oppositions in the body, balance. It is the enigmatic relationship between these technical principles that create the dance. These enigmatic relationships are the shadow zone where ancestors and the unknown dwell, and this is where creativity is born, where the impulse is born.
>
> In Japan, they call this the Ma, the pause between beats and notes. In my tradition, they say the ancestors dwell in the space between the dancers. (114)

One of the things that I love about Floyd is that he doesn't get stuck in his own dogma. He warns against his equation being applied as a formula, saying that each artist must work from his or her own equation. In a recent phone conversation he also said, ""Artificial trees" is its own valid form." And that is true. It is what my grandpa did performing Indian medicine shows—it is the "Lakota" commercial. Which provides the perfect segue to … Spiderwoman Theater.

I have known Muriel Miguel all my life; she is my mother's youngest sister. I grew up watching her, my mother, Gloria Miguel and their older sister, Lisa Mayo, perform long before Spiderwoman Theater was founded. They are my lineage and I am proud of the precious gifts that I have inherited from them.

As the director that I have worked with most consistently over the past two decades, Muriel has truly been the one to mold the raw material of my writing into performances. This is how she describes what she does. It is from the director's notes from *The Scrubbing Project* program.

As Indigenous people, we see all disciplines as inter-connected, with roots in traditional forms of storytelling. As the artistic director of Spiderwoman Theater, I have, over the past 30 years been using a methodology called *storyweaving* to entwine stories and fragments of stories with words, music, song, film, dance and movement, thereby creating a production that is multi-layered and complex; an emotional, cultural and political tapestry.

I have been thinking about the way Muriel works when she directs. She helps generate materials, she dramaturgs that material and weaves it together in a way that is very intuitive—not at all an intellectual process. In fact, it is a mistake to even try to justify something to her intellectually. She will wave it away with her wrist and say, "That sounds very intellectual"—as if to also say, "I can't do anything with *that*, Dearie—you're going to have to go deeper." Muriel does not allow an actor/creator to stay in her head. Muriel works from that place of what is unconsciously known, intuitively known—*saber sabiendo*: to know knowingly. Nor is she satisfied for a piece of theatre to be one or two-dimensional when it could be three, six, nine or even twelve dimensional. And dynamics!—do not play her the same note!

Then I had a brain flash. Maybe it was just menopause, but I could see, I thought, what Muriel does. She makes *molas* out of theatre. *Molas* are her palette and her dramaturgical tool. *Molas*: the art of Kuna women.

Molas are the traditional textiles of the Kuna nation from the autonomous territory of Kuna Yala, in what is known as Panama. Kuna women are renowned for their skills in creating their designs and combining colour. Originally the designs were painted and tattooed on our bodies. Kuna women wear two *mola* panels—front and back—sewn together to form blouses. Each *mola* tells a story. Each story is a layered narrative. When the women walk it is said, "We are walking stories." Kuna perception, Kuna cosmology, Kuna identity is encoded in the layers of our *molas*.

Molas are made by the combined techniques of reverse appliqué, appliqué and embroidery. They require several layers of fabric and the designs are cut out free-hand to allow the colours from the layers underneath to show through. Stitching the edges of the designs with the tiniest of stitches is the most fastidious part because it is what connects the layers. The *mola* gets thicker and thicker. Sometimes a corner will be torn apart and another colour or pattern of cloth will be inserted. Some areas will be built up with appliqué and details embroidered on. There are no even edges and although symmetry and duality are central principles, even two panels of the same blouse will not be exactly the same. Ironically, sewing machines were introduced to make Kuna women's work faster, a more economically sound enterprise. They did make the work faster but these *molas* are thin with square edges to their designs and inferior overall. It is possible to trace the design of a *mola* and reproduce its outline but it would lack the multi-dimensional layers of meaning that make it Kuna. I have never made a *mola*, neither has my mother nor my aunts, but we all grew up living with them, touching them, tracing their texture and designs, smelling them, sleeping on them and wearing them. It is this thickness, this multi-dimensional knowing applied from the principles of Kuna women's art, that I believe is my inheritance from Spiderwoman's theatrical methodology. And I want that thickness in my work.

I still have a *mola* that was my mother's since before I was born. When I was very small I used to put in on to dance around our apartment. It was too long and fell almost to my knees; it would slip off my shoulders. I always wore it accompanied by a little red ballet tutu, and I would dance and create performances all by myself. I would spend hours dancing in my *mola* and red tutu to Tschaikowsky, Mendelssohn, Rimsky-Korsokov. I have not thought about that outfit in fifty years, but I can feel myself going back to where I began, only now with more experience and more information. *Saber sabiendo.*

In November 2007 I had the unique opportunity to try these ideas in a studio/laboratory setting starting from a clear premise and intent. *Chocolate Woman Dreams the Milky Way* is a multidisciplinary collaboration among three senior artists; myself as writer/performer, Floyd Favel as director and Kuna visual artist Oswaldo (Achu) DeLeon Kantule as painter, design and cultural consultant. Our proposal was: 1) to collaboratively create a multidisciplinary live theatre piece that integrates traditional and contemporary art forms and incorporates visual imagery with text and performance, and 2) to build on a methodology of Native Performance Culture by applying principles and structures from traditional visual story narratives to script development. We also wanted to explore: a) how organically generated text and story narrative can support (not explain) the visual image and b) how a performer can embody the visual image such that it can be used as the framework for a narrative structure.

The first three days of the workshop process were spent looking at paintings from Achu's considerable body of work—stunning contemporary paintings rooted in the aesthetic of *mola* designs and pictographic writing. Then we poured through piles of *molas*, with Achu making us familiar with the principles in *mola* art from the most abstract (most traditional) to the most representational or figurative (most modern). We studied the *molas*" dissection of designs, their dualities, multiples of dualities and thematic abstractions. We then turned to the pictographic writings that notate the chants of the traditional Kuna healers and identified the literary structure of the chants: a repetition that builds through the accumulation of verbs—*dramatic action*.

From these principles, rooted in an Indigenous cosmology, identity and aesthetic, we employed abstractions (a process Achu has been using in his paintings for some time) to create the beginnings of a form and a structure for *Chocolate Woman Dreams the Milky Way*. We also used the Kuna principles of presenting image and story metaphorically as if through the smoke screen of Chocolate Woman's smudge in order to protect its true meaning by encoding it.

We knew from the first improvisation "on my feet" that we were onto a process that worked; however, we were quite astonished when I was instructed by Floyd to notate that first improvisation using the process and my text emerged as pictographs written from right to left, then left to right.[1] We have now taken a first step towards developing a dramaturgy specific to an Indigenous aesthetic and literary structure—in this case, one rooted in the principles of traditional Kuna visual art and literature. In Achu's words, "We are reclaiming cultural history." What is more, this same model could be adapted and applied by an Ojibwe artist investigating the bark scrolls, an Inuit artist examining the syllabic writing system, a Pueblo artist looking at rock paintings or a Mayan artist deciphering the glyphs.

This collaboration also gave space to a discussion about the evolution of Floyd's "formula" for Native Performance Culture. He has grown away from the term "methodology" as connoting something too fixed and product-oriented. He now prefers to call the transformative journey to the stage (and back to our origins) simply "process." So the "formula" now looks like this:

Tradition ⇔ Process ⇔ Performance.

It is a fluid, multi-directional continuum where the three elements all relate to each other in an equal manner.

Tracing the themes in my work over the past two decades has allowed me to see up close my trajectory from victim to victory. Returning to the fragment from the development of *Princess Pocahontas* noted at the beginning of this piece, I can say that today I am no longer willing to call to the "spirits of heartbreak and sadness, blood and rebellion, or back breaking endurance." I spent a long time digging around in massacre imagery and now I must call out to other spirits because transformation *is* a continuum and I must conjure myself into another place on my map. My writings and the theatre I create

Monique Mojica performs "Chocolate Woman Dreams the Milky Way,"
Macdonald Stewart Art Centre, 21 Nov. 2007. Photo: Dawn Owen

from them are my offerings, my prayers, my healing chants, my history, my identity—my *molas*. This is what the stories in *Chocolate Woman Dreams the Milky Way* are about.

Siagua, cacao beans, are what chocolate is made from. In the central part of the Americas (from Mexico south) they are very important. They are used as currency, they are burned as smudge to purify, pray and heal and they are an important part of the traditional diet. *Siagua.* Without it many Kuna have developed diabetes and high blood pressure. I have started eating these beans. In Kuna culture all the medicines are women, so *siagua* is referred to as Cacao Woman—*Puna Siagua.* Intrigued by the yummy image of a chocolate woman I began calling to Cacao Woman just as *Ixquic,* Blood Woman from the Mayan creation story, did when, bereft and alone, she cried out for help. This title piece of a new multidisciplinary collaboration evolved, in part, from a dream I had about ten years ago.

CHOCOLATE WOMAN DREAMS THE MILKY WAY

An invocation

In this time when my blood is held inside,
the cries of my dolphin children are carried farther out to sea into the arms of
Muu Bili, Grandmother Ocean.

Now that my blood is held inside,

Purified by the smoke of Red Cacao Woman's beads—*siagua*—here
on *Abya Yala* Land of Blood.

Puna Siagua, Siagua kinnit!
Be an anwe be sagua waale waaletgine
Wrap me in the arms of your purifying smoke

*

Olowaili, the morning star is the sister of the sun.
  My grandfather whose broad chest was tattooed with an eagle's
wingspan open full,
saw *Olowaili* fall to earth over New York harbour and named me
for her.
Olowaili, swirl and dance!
  Spiral and place your feet in mine!
  Fill my belly with starlight!
Olowaili guile birya birya!
Be nak odoe an nakine!
Be an saban enoge nizgana guallu gine

*

In heavy chocolate dreams I swim to shore
I am naked as the warm turquoise water breaks over my face.
  I can see the shoreline. There are houses made from cane stalks
lashed together
their palm-thatched roofs hang low.
  Swaying and rebounding in the sea breeze are the palms them-
selves.
The beach burns brilliant.
Sand blinding white. *Kuna Yala!*

I stand and walk out of the sea. Salt water slides off my naked
skin.
Against the starkness of the sand there are *molas* neatly laid out.
A blanket of red layered and encoded with meaning.

To my left, a few steps away from the *molas*, stands a beautiful young
woman.

She wears the clothes of *Kuna* women: a red *mola* blouse, sarong skirt, a red
and gold head-scarf, *winis*—beads wrapped tightly around her wrists almost
to the elbow, adorning her ankles almost to the knee, a gold nose-ring and
a gold necklace that falls over her entire chest like a breast-plate. A delicate
line of blue-black paint traces the centerline of her nose. Her round cheeks

are shiny with moisture and stained *achiote* red. Her black hair cropped short frames her face. There is something on her head like ... a golden bowl whose sides undulate in constant motion.

She is smiling. Smiling at me. Her arms outstretched, fingers spread wide. She shows me her *molas,* neatly arranged in rows on the sand. She is proud of her work. She begins to spin and spin and spin. Faster and faster.

Olowaili, guile birya birya!
Be nak odoe an nakine!
Be an saban enoge nizgana guallu gine
Puna Siagua! Siagua kinnit!
Be an anwe be sagua waale waaletgine
Let my smile mirror the spinning girl on the beach!

*

Full moon hangs low over the Ocean.
It is December. The air is humid and night cocoons the narrow thread of highway. Sugarcane fields whip past.
Shards of moonlight like fragments of broken disco ball bob in the black water—laying a path of stars to the Milky Way—*negaduu.*

If I could place my feet upon those stars like stepping stones, I would follow them to visit my ancestors. And we would drink cacao—*siagua* mixed with ground, roasted corn from gourds. We would smack our lips; wipe our mouths on the backs of our hands and talk. Wouldn't we talk! *Tegi!*

I, too, am a granddaughter fallen from the stars
I call to Sky Woman: send me your courage!
The courage of the valiant Morning Star, *Olowaili,* when she rises each morning to greet her brother, *Ibeler,* the sun, at daybreak
And there, for some moments, we hang in the liquid pigment of a watercolour sky.

This essay is a revised version of two oral presentations, the first offered at the Distinguished Lecture Series, University of Toronto, in January 2006, and the second at the Honouring Spiderwoman Conference, Native American Women Playwrights Archive, Miami University, in February 2007. It was revised and updated in January 2008. An earlier version will appear in a forthcoming volume of essays on North American Native performance, edited by Steve Wilmer, to be published by Arizona University Press.

"Chocolate Woman Dreams the Milky Way" by Monique Mojica used with permission. Originally published in Bruce Barton, ed., Collective Creation, Collabora-

tion and Devising, *Toronto: Playwrights Canada Press, 2008. Recently published in* Performing Worlds into Being: Native American Women's Theater *(pages 114-125), edited by Ann Elizabeth Armstrong, Kelli Lyon Johnson, and William A. Wortman (Oxford,* OH: *Miami University Press, 2009). See the publisher's website: http://www.orgs.muohio.edu/mupress/details/wortman_performingworlds.html.*

Also published in Canadian Woman Studies/les cahiers de la femme, *"Indigenous Women in Canada: The Voices of First Nations, Inuit and Métis Women," 26 (3 & 4) (Winter/Spring 2008): 160-176. Reprinted with permission of the author.*

Monique Mojica is an actor and published playwright from the Kuna and Rappahannock nations. Based in Toronto since 1983, she began training at the age of three and belongs to the second generation spun directly from the web of New York's Spiderwoman Theater. Her play "Princess Pocahontas and the Blue Spots" was produced by Nightwood Theatre and Theatre Passe Muraille in 1990, on radio by CBC *and published by Women's Press in 1991. She is the co-editor, with Ric Knowles, of* Staging Coyote's Dream: An Anthology of First Nations Drama in English, *Vols. I & II (Playwrights Canada Press). Monique is a long-time collaborator with Floyd Favel on various research and performance projects investigating Native Performance Culture. Theatre credits include: "The Rez Sisters" (Native Earth), "Red River" (Crow's Theatre) "The Adventures of a Black Girl in Search of God" (Nightwood Theatre/Obsidian/Mirvish) and "Home Is My Road" (Factory Theatre) as well as the one-woman show, "Governor of the Dew" by Floyd Favel (NAC/Globe Theatre). Monique received a Best Supporting Actress nomination from the First Americans in the Arts for her role as Grandma Builds-the-Fire in Sherman Alexie's film* Smoke Signals. *She was the Artist in Residence for American Indian Studies at the University of Illinois in Spring 2008. She continues to explore art as healing, as an act of reclaiming historical/cultural memory and as an act of resistance.*

[1]For much of the public reading of this work-in-progress presentation my text was read from pictographs.

REFERENCES

Favel, Floyd. "The Shadowed Path." Unpublished.

Favel, Floyd. "Waskawewin." *Topoi* 24 (1) (2005):113-115.

García Márquez, Gabriel. *One Hundred Years of Solitude.* New York: Avon, 1971.

Mojica, Monique. *Princess Poca-hontas and the Blue Spots.* Toronto: Women's Press, 1991.

Tomuschat, Christian, Otilia Lux de Cotí and Alfredo Balsells Tojo. "Guatemala: Memory of Silence. Report of the Commission for Historical Clarification. Conclusions and Recommendations." Februray 1999. Online: <http://shr.aaas.org/guatemala/ceh/report/english/toc.html> Accessed 23 January 2008.

EMERANCE BAKER

LOCATING OURSELVES IN THE PLACE OF CREATION

The Academy as *Kitsu'lt melkiko'tin*[1]

"Reconciliation"

We are waking up to our history
from a forced slumber
We are breathing into our lungs
so it will be a part of us again
It will make us angry at first
because we will see how much you stole from us
and for how long you watched us suffer
we will see how you see us
and how when we copied your ways
it killed our own.
We will cry and cry
because we can never be the same
But we will go home to cry
and we will see ourselves in this huge mess
and we will gently whisper the circle back
and it will be old and it will be new .
— R. Tababodong

IN A PREVIOUS PAPER I ESTABLISHED the necessity of recognizing that Indigenous women's writing, as it is grounded in our teachings and ways of knowing, produces something that is mostly missing from so much scholarly discourse *about* Indigenous Peoples; that is, a "loving perception" of Indianess. (Baker). For the purpose of this paper, I want to shift from how writing *by, for, and about* ourselves is grounded in "loving Indianess," to why we *need* to write about ourselves. The intent of this paper is to make clear that, as Indigenous researchers and scholars, we need to produce Indigenous research[2] *by, for, and about* ourselves—informed by our own principles of "kindness, caring, sharing, and respect"—to better claim a place for ourselves in the space in which we do this; namely the academy (Weber-Pillwax 80). Aboriginal theorist, James (Sàkéj) Youngblood Henderson, provides a way to better understand what I mean by "space" with the Mi'kmaq word *kitsu'lt melkiko'tin* which translates more fully to "place of creation" (257). The goal of this paper is to mindfully locate ourselves as Aboriginal scholars in this "place of creation." Specifically, to link the physical space of the academy with our hearts and minds in our production of Aboriginal scholarly discourse or as Gregory Cajete writes a "way to express your true self. "your heart and your face"(183).[3]

As mentioned earlier, in "Loving Indianess: Native Women's Storytelling as Survivance" (Baker), I talked about the necessity of writing from our experiences in Indigenous women's production of contemporary Indigenous critical pedagogy. This loving perception is grounded in Indigenous women writers respect for Indigenous Knowledge, teachings, empirical observations, and revelations (Castellano 2000b: 23). Writing Indigeneity from a loving perspective is also grounded in what Shawn Wilson calls "the lifelong learning and relationship that goes into it" (179).

Much of the Indigenous scholarly discourse emerging now, while still cognizant of the limits of the academic institutions in which it is created, is clearly informed by the "cultural protocols and values" of relational accountability that we get from living and being in our communities (Steinhauer). To write from within our culture isn't simply going to achieve the relational accountability that informs Aboriginal epistemology, but when we engage our teachings (and for some us who go and seek out those teachings) we better understand what is needed to guide and inform our research. As Cora Weber-Pillwax writes, the values and principles that guide Aboriginal research can be attributed to

> The interconnectedness of all living things … our motives and intentions … the foundations of research as lived Indigenous experience … our theories grounded in an Indigenous epistemology … the transformative nature of research … the sacredness and responsibility of maintaining personal and community integrity … and the recognition of languages and cultures as living processes. (31-32)

As writers producing scholarly Indigenous discourse we also need to be mindful of the ways that the institutions in which we work (our places of creation) limits the efficacy of our research process and devalues our Indigenous Knowledge bases. As Weber-Pillwax explains, "the argument for exclusive use of institutional standards and/or forms … to guide research has the weight of efficacy on its side: less time and money are spent if researchers accept their work is guided by one set of ethics and embedded in one culture" (79). What gets lost in this process for all scholars is that knowledge is fluid and always changing. As Weber-Pillwax suggests, it is the "effectiveness" of this type of "efficient" scholarship, in which the benefit to the community is either "ignored or not addressed" at all, that gets lost (79). The reason this is important for us as Aboriginal scholars is that much of our work gets carried out in communities that are close to our hearts. Following Weber Pillwax's argument, it is imperative that we recognize and change the ways the academy privileges the structures of research, often perceived as taking place in "hypothetical communities" with objective researchers, which in turn creates challenges for our own material and tangible relations to our own communities (80). As Leroy Little Bear says, "when jagged worldviews collide" as they often do for those of us working in the academy, it becomes clear that "objectivity is an illusion" (85).

A particular interest of this paper is to better understand how our location in the place of creation—kitsu'lt melkiko'tin— defines the production of cultural and personal identity within Indigenous scholarship as it relates to our personal and the collective sovereignty of our communities. This focus has most recently come home, as it were, in my most recent incarnation as an Aboriginal postsecondary supports coordinator. In this role I am reminded time and again how imperative it is to have resources and materials which speak to the differing but similar life experiences of the Indigenous students (my children's generation) now attending our universities. I would like to say, that for emergent Indigenous scholars, the playing field has changed in that they have the privilege of working in a space that recognizes and values Indigenous Knowledge. Sadly, for the most part, I would be wrong. Wilson explains that much of what is written about us as Indigenous Peoples reflects the mainstream ideology that knowledge is an "individual entity" and that the "researcher is an individual" who "gains" knowledge, so much so that it fails to ever really recognize us as Indigenous Peoples (179). Within the academy there is still a strong current of Aboriginalist theory written about us (Aboriginals) flowing in and out of our classrooms and minds. Mainstream research, as many Indigenous theorists contend, is still understood as ethical and valid in the academy even though the outcomes of such research rarely benefit our Aboriginal communities. Not only have Aboriginal people grown up surrounded by research about them, but they also bear witness to the outcomes of that research not benefiting themselves, their families or communities, whilst misrepresenting their identities or ignoring their most obvious needs. Marlene Brant Castellano (2004) relates her story of being a member of the Royal Commission on Aboriginal Peoples inquiry and meeting with Elders to talk about the need for Aboriginal communities to engage the research process. The Elders told her "We've been researched to death!" (97). "The workshop was not off to a promising start" Castellano goes on to say, "until an Elder who had opened the meeting spoke quietly from a corner of the room. 'If we have been researched to death,' he said, 'maybe it's time we started researching ourselves back to life'" (97). This Elder's call for an active shift in focus from being "researched" to "researching" actively compels and implicates Indigenous researchers and writers in the uptake of relationally accountable research. Indigenous scholarship needs to focus less on decolonizing the academy. We need to focus more on understanding how Indigenous Peoples are implicated as a part of this colonized space so that we can better develop our relational accountability no matter where we operate.

In consideration of this, my interest becomes less about what the "mainstream" is doing and more about what we as Indigenous writers are doing and where we are doing this.

A challenge inherent in this shift in focus is addressing the need for a fuller and more accurate representation of Indigenous Knowledges in the academy while prioritizing the need for Indigenous communities to recognize the importance of their involvement in research and the production of local, critical Indigenous Knowledges. In this work I'm more closely focused on the impact of Indigenous researchers, writers, and theorists developing a pedagogy within the academy for the coming generations of Indigenous scholars. To be clear, my intent is not to suggest that by filling the academy with Indigenous scholarship we will somehow have "all the answers." While sometimes when I'm tired I would like to have all the answers (mostly) readily at hand, I am reminded by Evelyn Steinhauer, that Aboriginal epistemology doesn't necessarily have the "right answers" as a desired end point:

> A topic such as the articulation of an Indigenous research methodology is new, and like myself, many Indigenous students are searching for answers. I don't know if I can provide these answers, but what I do attempt to do is compile the works of Indigenous scholars who have written and spoken to me directly about this topic." (69)

So, while the search for answers is meaningful it is not fully commensurate with the production of Indigenous Knowledges. Most often, gathering, talking about, writing, and sharing Indigenous Knowledge is the best way to "give voice to and legitimize the knowledge of our people" (Steinhauer 70). As Little Bear writes, "This is why we engage in conversation. So I can share my experiences with you and make you understand what I am feeling. And when you respond you are doing the same with me" (85). My intent here is to forward this as the foundation of an Indigenous epistemology.

A positive, while at times frustrating, part of working in and having close relations within Indigenous communities is that we are often intimately tied to the awareness of what is needed in our communities and therefore have a personal stake in addressing and meeting these needs. This intimate knowledge comes from our worldview and relations with those around us. I have come to realize that understanding this worldview is a lifelong process. As Henderson suggests, the difficulty for most Indigenous people working in the academy is that you have to learn yet another "world-view" and "this is a lifetime project that requires time and patience" (261).

Fifteen years ago, as an undergraduate student, I didn't meet many other Indigenous students in the university I attended. Talking with Indigenous graduates from other universities, I learned that I wasn't the only person who ate lunch in my car. Eight years ago, the university where I started my graduate work did not have an Indigenous scholar to supervise and guide my research. Today, while some of that is changing it is not changing fast enough to meet the increasing need. Recent trends in increased Aboriginal high school achievement and enrollment in postsecondary programs (though still below the national average for non-Aboriginal students[4]) means that more and more Indigenous youth are completing high school and entering postsecondary than in previous generations[5] (Siggner and Costa). With an increased participation in postsecondary educational programs, many institutions are now faced with an increased need for culturally relevant resources that specifically address the needs of these students.[6] However, the point of this paper is not to discuss who or what institution addresses these needs better or worse. The point here is to better understand how Indigenous students (Indigenous Knowledge makers in the making) benefit from and need resources created by Indigenous scholars, writers, researchers, teachers, elders, and even themselves so that they can better navigate the kitsu'lt melkiko'tin.

Starting from the premise that our desire to be located in the academy is to positively contribute to the overall well-being of Indigenous Peoples in Canada means that we need to find ways to better understand how to make the academy our kitsu'lt melkiko'tin; our place of creation. Weber-Pillwax says, "Many, if not most, Indigenous scholars engage in contemporary research for the explicit purpose of bringing benefits to their communities and their people" (78). She goes on to say "they are usually unprepared for these challenges" even though "an interest in research is one of the reasons the people associate themselves with a university" (80). My concern here is with these "challenges" that Weber-Pillwax mentions. As we are primarily talking about the location of Indigenous scholarship within academia, it is critical that we first address the difficulties of producing Indigenous scholarly discourse within the academy. For many of us this means starting by discussing our own entry into the Indigenous Knowledge field. Steinhauer relates what many Indigenous students experienced when she says, "It was not until I started the Masters Program in First Nations Education at the University of Alberta that I was exposed to the concept of Indigenous Knowledge" (70). Like Steinhauer, many of us starting out in Indigenous research felt and knew that our education left us unprepared, as it was at best partial and at worst damaging steeped in what Marie Battiste calls "cognitive imperialism—the persisting ideologies from our colonial past that remain a part of our education system. Australian Aboriginal scholar, Martin Nakata says these feelings of under-preparedness can be best attributed to the works we studied about us. Nakata says,

> In studying texts that have been written about them, scholars are negotiating the representations of themselves, their ancestors and their experiences. Negotiating these texts is not simply an intellectual process. It is also an emotional journey that often involves outrage, pain, humiliation, guilt and depression. (3)

Nakata's statement begins to speak to the strange duality many Aboriginal scholars in mainstream academies experience when faced with a reading about them selves that they feel is somehow wrong. This is what Leroy Little Bear calls "jagged world-views colliding." Gregory Cajete calls "ping geh heh" or "split-mind" and Patricia Monture-Angus calls, "contradictions." Each author is referring to their location, as Indigenous scholars, in the academy (the place of creation) as an often painful duality of simultaneously positive and negative experiences.

WRITING AS SOLUTION OF THE "SPLIT MIND:
PING GEH HEH"

Monture-Angus's paper, "Flint Woman: Surviving the Contradictions in Academia" was, and still is, a work that better allowed me to do more than just "survive" the academy. Monture-Angus's ability to "name and describe" the contradictions she was experiencing as an Aboriginal scholar in mainstream academia is a strategy that I still use today (53). Monture-Angus's writing provides a "roadmap" of survivance by explaining how to negotiate the emotional conflicts that arise as a product of working within what Cajete calls the "split-mind: *ping geh heh*" of the academy. Monture Angus says as, "I have felt either confused or uncomfortable…. This feeling is rooted in my difference either as a woman or as an "Indian" or some combination of the above" (54). Monture-Angus named these uncomfortable and confusing experiences "contradictions," which was for her the "state of being that I often slam into headfirst and the experience leaves me overwhelmed and motionless" (54). Having the ability to identify and name what she was experiencing in the "push and pull" of academia allowed Monture-Angus to "understand my relationship with the university as a process of negotiating those contradictions" which she says was "no good solution" but "the solution I can hope to secure" (54). The pain and frustration of living the "split-mind" for many Aboriginal writers, researchers, and scholars has developed in us an urgent need to create from that contradictory space so that those coming after us can better understand it and have solutions for themselves. Castellano, Lynne Davis, and Louise Lahache suggest that writing, creating from this painful "spilt-mind" space is exactly what we need to move out of it. They say we can "see it as introducing a new set of ideas, a way of thinking and talking that pushes against existing boundaries, enlarging the space for new possibilities" (254). Like Castellano, Davis, and Lahache, I also argue that this "space for new possibilities" as it has emerged from our "split-mind" space, allows for new thoughts and ideas that would not have been able to exist before. Castellano, Davis, and Lahache conclude, "it becomes the grounds on which further discourse is generated" (254). This is *kitsu'lt melkiko'tin*; the creative place.

For many writers like Monture-Angus, Cajete, and Leroy Little Bear, their place of creation—their kitsu'lt melkiko'tin—may physically be the academies in which they work, but more specifically their place of creation is located in their writing. Monture-Angus writes,

> Things happen and I write them all down ... writing—talking back—is the process through which I come to terms with my pain, anger and emotions. Often only through the process of writing does the feeling of contradiction become actuated. It is real because I make it appear in bold black letters against stark white paper. Writing is the place where I have found both strength and empowerment. (55)

Years have passed and I am still energized by Monture-Angus's writing. For me and many other Aboriginal theorists, writing is a place of empowerment and strength. Our ability to imagine solutions that meet the needs of our communities and write them down is in keeping with my worldview and the possibility of making them real. This is why I write; because I've had a vision that writing ourselves into the academy benefits not only us, but the academy as well. Our writing softens the blows when our "jagged worldviews collide". It creates the space of kitsu'lt melkiko'tin that more fully makes visible the still present flaws of character and hidden agendas within the academy so that we can name and describe and change them. It is imperative to note that our location in the academy is not a "reclaimed" space; it is our claimed space. Our location in academia signals to me that we are still here and we have never left.

CONCLUSION

The purpose of this paper is to better understand what we need as Indigenous scholars working in the academy. As Marie Battiste says, what we "Aboriginal people""need" is "a new story" and "ultimately this new story is about empowering Indigenous worldviews, languages, knowledges, cultures, and most important, Indigenous peoples and communities" (viii). We need to write from our hearts and minds as Indigenous writers, because our youth, our contemporaries, and our Elders need to see themselves in the loving light our words cast.[7] We need to write about what it's like to be Indigenous in the here and now so that those who follow us are able to see themselves better reflected back to them when they enter the academy. This is the real issue. Our young people are entering the academy in droves. They are seeking out for themselves what it means to be Indigenous and an academic. We need to be there because the academy is slow to change. When the academy isn't ready to be relationally accountable, then Indigenous scholars need to provide that balance. We need to make real those loving images and words about our Peoples so that new scholars too can believe that the Indigenous Knowledges they hold will carry them into the future. Our youth are the keepers of our knowledge and they will be the ones to write about us in the years to come. Lighting their way is our path to becoming sovereign peoples.

Originally published in Canadian Woman Studies/les cahiers de la femme, *"Indigenous Women in Canada: The Voices of First Nations, Inuit and Métis Women," 26 (3 & 4) (Winter/Spring 2008): 15-25. Reprinted with permission of the author.*

Emerance Baker, Cayuga/Mohawk-Hungarian, is the mother of four wonderful children. She currently works with Indigenous youth at the University of Waterloo's Aboriginal Services Office. Emerance's field of study was in Social Sciences specializing in community-based research ethics and methodology. Emerance's work in the field of women's health and community-based research with Cancer Care Ontario, the Cancer Survivors and Healing Arts Pilot Project in Newfoundland, and with the CIHR Aboriginal Women's Cancer Care Project out of Wilfrid Laurier University allowed her to work extensively with First Nations communities across Canada.

[1]Mi'kmaq word for "space" or "place of creation" (Henderson).

[2]Marlene Brant Castellano (2004) defines "Aboriginal research" as a " research that touches the life and well-being of Aboriginal Peoples. It may involve Aboriginal Peoples and their communities directly. It may assemble data that describes or claims to describe Aboriginal Peoples and their heritage. Or, it may affect the human and natural environment in which Aboriginal Peoples live" (99).

[3]See Willie Ermine's "Aboriginal Epistemology" for a clearer understanding of the ways we need to link our hearts and minds to the process of Indigenous knowledge creation.

[4]See Siggner and Costa's *Overview of Educations Conditions of Urban Aboriginal Populations in Canada.* The 2001 statistics show that urban Aboriginal youth university and college degree attainment is significantly less than urban non-Aboriginal students, yet higher than reserve youth attainment.

[5]The importance of accessibility and participation for these students will only grow in the next six years (2011), when the Aboriginal 20 to 24 age group is expected to peak.

[6]"The gap between Aboriginal and non-Aboriginal participation rates is often attributed to a variety of barriers that are unique to this population group. While the specific barriers vary greatly, it has been recognized that in order to effectively address access, each barrier must be addressed comprehensively. Specific barriers have been listed to include: the impact of the Residential School system, the assimilative nature of post-secondary education, lack of academic preparation, social discrimination, unemployment and poverty, cultural differences faced by Aboriginal students at post-secondary institutions, and family and personal barriers specific to Aboriginal students" ("Ontario Undergraduate Student Alliance and McMaster Student Union).

[7]Monture-Angus states, "Encouraging positive self-images must be a fundamental building block on which Aboriginal inspirations are built into the education system" (78).

REFERENCES

Baker, E. "Loving Indianess: Native Women's Storytelling as Survivance." *Atlantis* 29 (2) (2005): 1-15.

Battiste, M. "Foreword." *Aboriginal Education: Fulfilling the Promise.* Eds. Marlene Brant Castellano, Lynne Davis, Louise Lahache. Vancouver: University of British Columbia Press, 2000. vii-ix.

Cajete, G. "Indigenous Knowledge: the Pueblo Metaphor of Indigenous Education." *Reclaiming Indigenous Voice and Vision.* Ed. M. Battiste. Vancouver: University of British Columbia Press, 2000. 180-191.

Castellano, M. B. "Conclusion." *Aboriginal Education: Fulfilling the Promise.* Eds. Marlene Brant Castellano, Lynne Davis, and Louise Lahache. Vancouver: University of British Columbia Press, 2000a.

Castellano, M. B. "Updating Aboriginal Traditions of Knowledge." *Indigenous Knowledges in Global Contexts.* Eds. George J. Sefa Dei, Budd L. Hall, and Dorothy Goldin Rosenberg. Toronto: University of Toronto Press, 2000b. 22-36.

Castellano, M. B. "Ethics of Aboriginal Research." *Pimatisiwin: A Journal of Aboriginal and Indigenous Community Health* 2 (1) (2004): 98-114.

Ermine, W. "Aboriginal Epistemology." *First Nations Education in Canada: The Circle Unfolds.* Eds. M. Battiste and J. Barman. Vancouver: University of British Columbia Press, 1995. 101-111.

Henderson Youngblood, (Sákéj) J. "Ayukpachi: Empowering Aboriginal Thought." *Reclaiming Indigenous Voice and Vision.* Ed. M. Battiste. Vancouver: University of British Columbia Press, 2000. 248-278.

Little Bear, L. "Jagged Worldviews Colliding." *Reclaiming Indigenous Voice and Vision.* Ed. M. Battiste. Vancouver: University of British Columbia Press, 2000. 177-185.

Monture-Angus, P. "Flint Woman: Surviving the Contradictions in Academia." *Thunder in My Soul: A Mohawk Woman Speaks.* Halifax: Fernwood, 1995.

Nakata, Martin. "Anthropological Texts and Indigenous Standpoints." *Australian Aboriginal Studies* 2 (1998): 3-12.

Ontario Undergraduate Student Alliance and McMaster Student Union. "Aboriginal Students in Ontario's Post-secondary Education System." 2005. Online: <www.msu.mcmaster.ca/cbp/2006_2007/OUSA/Aboriginal_Students.pdf>.

O'Reilly-Scanlon, Kathleen. "Pathways to Understanding: 'Wahkohtowin' as a Research Method." *McGill Journal of Education* 39 (1) (Winter 2004): 29-44.

Siggner, A. and R. Costa. *Overview of Educations Conditions of Urban Aboriginal Populations in Canada.* Ottawa: Statistics Canada, 2005.

Smith, L. T. *Decolonizing Methodologies: Research and Indigenous Peoples.* London: Zed Books Ltd., 1999.

Steinhauer, E. "Thoughts in an Indigenous Research Methodology." *Canadian*

Journal of Native Education 26 (2) (2002): 69-75.

Tababodong, R. "Reconciliation." Eds. John Bird, Lorraine Land, Murray Macadam, and Diane Engelstad. *Nation to Nation: Aboriginal Sovereignty and the Future of Canada.* Toronto: Irwin Publishing, 2002. xi.

Weber-Pillwax, C. "Indigenous Researchers and Indigenous Research Methods: Cultural Influences or Cultural Determinants of Research Methods." *Pimatisiwin: A Journal of Aboriginal and Indigenous Community Health* 2 (1) (2004.): 77-89.

Wilson, S. "What is an Indigenous Research Methodology?" *Canadian Journal of Native Education* 25 (2001): 175-179.

KIM ANDERSON

NOTOKWE OPIKIHEET—"OLD LADY RAISED"

Aboriginal Women's Reflections
on Ethics and Methodologies in Health

RESEARCH INTO THE HEALTH of First Nation, Métis, and Inuit Peoples in Canada is of increasing interest and concern, and has been the locus of much activity in recent years. At the core of this emerging research agenda is dialogue around appropriate methodologies and ethical considerations, with a focus on promoting Aboriginal leadership and community-based approaches to achieving health and wellness. Within this dialogue, my interest has been in exploring culture-based approaches to health research, in particular how they relate to Aboriginal women. Drawing on interviews that I carried out in 2005 with seven First Nation, Métis, and Inuit grandmothers from across Canada, this article provides a glimpse into the leadership provided by Aboriginal women as health providers, healers, and health researchers in the recent past.[1] The analysis supports my assumption that when these women were girls, Aboriginal women played a critical role in managing health and wellness in their communities, and that health research has always been part of Aboriginal "women's work."

Although culturally diverse and from vastly different geographic locales, the seven grandmothers who participated in this research all shared their experiences of having grown up in communities where survival was dependent on a close relationship with the land. It is also important to note that all of these women are "young" as Elders, mostly in their fifties or sixties. The time period that they talked about was therefore relatively recent, referring mostly to the 1940s, 1950s, and 1960s. The women who shared their knowledge with me were as follows[2]: Be'sha Blondin, Dene (Northwest Territories); Maria Campbell, Métis (Saskatchewan); Madeleine Dion Stout, Cree (Alberta); Reepa Evic-Carleton, Inuit (Nunavut); Sally Johnson, Mi'kmaw (Nova Scotia); Dorris Peters, Sto:lo (British Columbia); and Helen Thundercloud, Algonquin (Québec).

Each participant was asked questions about the role of Aboriginal women in the health care of their girlhood communities, and about how women went about doing research and solving health-related problems. The interviews also covered questions related to research ethics and knowledge translation practices. While these were broad and complex questions asked of a small interview sample, and while there is limited space for exploration of these issues in this article, the grandmothers' stories provide valuable insights into how we might govern our work as researchers concerned with the current state of health in our communities.

WOMEN'S TRADITIONAL ROLES IN COMMUNITY-BASED HEALTH CARE SYSTEMS

The grandmothers spoke about the multiple health management roles they had witnessed among women in their lifetimes. As girls, they saw women in their communities practice as midwives, medicine women, and traditional doctors. Women were also responsible for disease prevention and health promotion. Overall, women administered to the sick and oversaw the healthy development of their communities.

Women as Midwives[3]

Several of the women spoke about midwifery, noting that they and their siblings were born with the assistance of a community-based midwife. Helen Thundercloud discussed the comprehensive nature of a traditional midwife's work, drawing on her own experience of growing up with her grandmother:

> The business of birthing, I recall, was a long one. That is to say, my grandmother did not just attend the actual "catching" of the baby. She spent time with the mother, prior to the event and probably the rest of the day and night. I know this because I lost her for that period of time. I also remember gatherings of new mothers, maybe two or three women, all nursing their babies and my grandma talking about [the] care of the baby, but also [the] care of themselves.

Reepa Evic-Carleton talked about the experience of having a midwife attend her birth, and how traditional midwifery practices were grounded in the sacred:

> I was born into the world by a midwife back when the Inuit were still living in small little camps. My mother told me that when I came out, that midwife who delivered me predicted certain things about me. Inuit did that when a baby was born. What they predicted was always positive.

Be'sha Blondin is a traditional midwife. In her interview she described some of the practices of midwives in her culture, which demonstrate how long-term relationships based in the sacred are at the heart of Dene childbirth practices:

> We have ceremonies for everything. It's the woman who prepares all the ceremonies. It's the woman who cradles the baby. As soon as the baby is

born, they whisper in the baby's ear who they are. "I'm Be'sha." I would blow into the baby's nose so the baby knows my breath. I would touch the baby so it knows my feel. So all the women, we call them aunties to that baby, they would all do the same thing so that the baby would never forget who they are.

Blondin also noted that modern midwifery practices and training are often void of the sacred aspects of traditional midwifery. She talked about the lack of community and the spiritual disconnect that contemporary people experience from land and community, emphasizing the need to return to the old ways.

Traditional Doctoring and Health Care

Traditionally, Aboriginal women were also well-established as medicine people, ceremonialists, and doctors in their communities. Sally Johnson recalled that there were several female healers in her childhood community, and "they used the traditional medicines and all the different variations of trying to help individuals that had certain ailments." Helen Thundercloud also offered memories of a medicine woman—her grandmother—as follows:

My grandmother's role was doing medicine, so my memories of her are related to her work. She was healthy, and that was probably because she worked hard, she was always engaged in some activity. If she was not actually practicing medicine, she was gathering medicine. We lived in the bush a lot of the time, and she spent her days harvesting various plants, roots, bark, and different kinds of leaves and branches.

A few of the other grandmothers mentioned that it was typically the women of their communities who tended to physical health conditions. Reepa Evic-Carleton recalled:

I believe it was more so the women's role [to do the doctoring] because they knew how to read a boil or infection, using the skin of a lemming to open that infection. I also remember the overall health issues—that they knew what to get from the land and from the animals. I don't remember the men doing that so much. It was mostly the women.

Similarly, Dorris Peters commented that she did not remember many male health practitioners in her childhood community and that "the women did the major work in that area."

As mothers, women were also required to learn the skills needed to administer the health of their own families. Be'sha Blondin commented that each individual family had to have knowledge of traditional medicines, because they lived on the land and only gathered in community settings for two months of the summer. She described the traditional system of health care, in which women of different ages and generations had specific roles: older women were typically leaders in administering healing practices, and younger women were always involved as apprentices, taking on the tasks that were more physically challenging. In her interview, Blondin stated:

> *The young women took responsibility; looking after the person for cleansing, to wash the hair, clean the body, that sort of thing. It was the young women who did this because the young women had the strength to move the sick person.*

Women were also central in the management of broader health crises and epidemics that affected their families and communities. Dorris Peters talked about the influenza pandemic of 1918-1919 during which her parents lost six children. She asserted, "It was the women in our area who dealt with it; the men were helpful but they were more scared." Be'sha Blondin stated that when new or unknown illnesses like the flu pandemic came to her community, patients would be isolated and "only certain groups of women were allowed to work with them." Some of the other grandmothers noted that men were more removed from the epidemic crises because they were often hunting and thus away from the community.

All of these stories demonstrate that women—older women in particular—had skills and knowledge that were central to the well-being of their families and communities. This knowledge had to have come from research, which leads one to ask: what methods and ethics were employed in their research and knowledge transfer practices?

EXPLORING ABORIGINAL WOMEN'S TRADITIONAL APPROACHES TO RESEARCH

Relationships to the Natural and Supernatural Worlds

All of the grandmothers talked about how research in the past was based on trial and error, grounded in spiritual practice, and informed by a well-established web of relationships. Madeleine Dion Stout remarked, "The evidence that was gathered was very much based on intuition, based on dreams, on trial and error, and on relationships with other beings, whether they were natural or supernatural." A relationship with the natural world was thus critical to Aboriginal women's approaches to research in the past, as elaborated on by Dion Stout:

> *Animals and nature were the greatest teachers and the greatest forces of information for what had to be done. Animals were used or invoked by women to come and teach us life's lessons. That educated us. Coyote and owl*

were good teachers, and often we were told that their powers would be a message. Of course, the eagles were these powerful beings as well. We knew the source of the knowledge, and the source of knowledge was definitely not books, it was animals, it was older people, it was our mothers.

Connection to the land was equally important to the research that Aboriginal women carried out in the past. Maria Campbell noted that her grandmother's style of research would have been disrupted by settler encroachment, as this interfered with relationships to the land that were necessary for her research. This notion was also touched on by Dorris Peters who recalled that in her youth, medicine people would practice in isolated areas. This was likely because certain places held a special significance and had particular medicines, but it may also have been because of a need to escape settler interference, which became an increasing threat over the years.

The Importance of Respect and Reciprocity

Respectful relationships were at the core of the research and knowledge generation that the grandmothers witnessed as girls. Some of them talked about relationships of respect in the context of traditional healing: illness or disease had to be researched and addressed through reciprocal exchange. This can be seen in the way that we continue to interact with traditional healers, in that we always offer a gift to strengthen our relationship to them, and ensure the work that needs to be done gets done. However, the grandmothers' stories provide further insight into Aboriginal principles of respect and reciprocity, as some also talked about what the *healer* needs to give to the person that they wish to treat. Be'sha Blondin explained:

> *Say that someone is very, very ill. You can't just go there to the people who are ill and say "I'm going to do this for you." You have to offer something to them. It might be a kerchief if an elderly lady got sick. You would go there and say, "I would like to come and help you and this is what I give you, from me, to help you." Because we believe when you give something for them to receive help, they know you are sincere, that you are going to give 100 per cent in looking after them. Not to be there for your ego. You have respect for that Elder and you want to help them.*

As researchers, traditional healers were mindful that they had to give something for the knowledge they received through treating their patients.

Reciprocity is something that needs to be established with *all* our relations, if we are to seek answers using traditional approaches to research. For instance, Dorris Peters told a story that demonstrates the type of reciprocal relationships that need to be established when using plant medicines. She remembered being ill, and being sent by her grandmother to pick the medicines that she needed to use to get better. Peters was so young that she couldn't count, but she remembered picking the plants according to her grandmother's directions:

> *I was just a little kid and my grandma would tell me, "Put something on the ground," and she would give me something because we didn't have tobacco in those days. She didn't really explain what that was, but she made sure to tell me, "Here are a lot of plants." She said, "You don't take any one leaf from one plant. You just take from there, there, and there." So there was a nice big plant and I would pick one leaf from there, and then I would look at her, and she would nod her head. I would go to another one quite a ways away and I would look at her, and so on.*

Peters concluded her story by saying, "That's ethics—to give, return, or give something for something that you are going to use in a good way."

USING RESEARCH "IN A GOOD WAY": THE QUESTION OF ETHICS

It is worth sharing a story told by Maria Campbell that highlights *unethical* approaches to research and knowledge translation. Her story provides an example of how outsiders have so often operated without regard for, or awareness of, Aboriginal principles of respect, communication, and reciprocity. Campbell described a visit by a nurse to her community after her aunt contracted typhoid from a water supply outside of their community:

> *[The nurse] was going around checking everybody's water.... I remember my grandmother and I were home alone. She couldn't speak English, so I was translating for her, and I wasn't very good at it. The nurse was trying to explain to me that [the] water was full of bacteria, and I couldn't find a word to translate the word "bacteria." I'd never heard it before. She tried the best she could and finally she said the water was full of bugs. She had a jar of our water and she wanted to talk to my granny about boiling water before she used it. Well, in Cree, the word for "bugs," at least the one I used, was pretty strong. It was munchoskuk. It sounds awful—especially to an old lady who was very careful and made sure that everyone was healthy, and who boiled all the drinking water. My granny was very upset and ran [the nurse] off the property.*

Campbell pointed out that the nurse should have found out about what kind of procedures the community members were taking to purify their water *before* offering them her advice, but instead "she came in and just decided that we didn't know how to keep things clean." The nurse's act was seen to be particularly insulting because the women in the community were so vigilant in their care for the water.

In contrast, Sally Johnson talked about the kind of ethics that *are* necessary to ensure positive research results:

> *Doing research in a good way would include community involvement. It involves understanding the culture and understanding the individual, knowing what their background is. It means knowing what their knowledge level is, the language used, making it simple and to the point. It means recognizing the quality of life, and making sure that their voices are heard.*

Some of the other grandmothers responded to the question about ethics by talking about the need to maintain confidentiality when working as healers or health researchers. Maria Campbell talked about the rigour and professionalism of the health practitioners in her childhood community:

> *The healers, medicine people, and herbalists were trusted. They learned about medicines, plant recipes, and often ceremony for these things, and they were only shared with their students. If anyone broke that trust, they would not only lose the people's confidence, but also the spirit helpers could leave them and the medicine and power to heal would be gone. Yes, some plant [medicines] and healing practices were taught, and still are taught to everyone, but most of it takes years to learn. It is not something one does lightly. If you made a mistake, you could hurt, or maybe even kill someone. It is no different than a doctor today. They don't learn overnight.*

Helen Thundercloud noted that ethical conduct was a way of life for health care practitioners and researchers of the past. She talked about how her own grandmother demonstrated ethical behaviour in both her life and practice. Thundercloud stated that her grandmother "never lectured or scolded" but would call upon peer influence, use stories, and invoke the supernatural to ensure that people were mindful of their behaviour:

> *Mostly, she would invoke Windigo. Windigo is the Trickster, and the admonition was phrased something like: "Windigo will seal your lips—that's what happens to people who talk like that." Then, of course, there would be laughter and the others would make mocking sounds at the "offender" and collapse with laughter. Grandmother would wait patiently, and then continue with the teaching, saying that Windigo knows that people have forgotten how to be good to one another, and they say and do wicked things. It's Windigo's job to "fix" a person up.*

Thundercloud's grandmother played interconnected roles of doctor, healer, researcher, and ethicist in her community. Each role fed into the other to define her vocation, which could not be separated from who she was and how she lived her life. As Thundercloud further noted: "She lived in a way that we only begin to touch on when we speak of being "holistic" these days. That is to say, everything in her life was integrated as part of one greater whole: her work was her spiritual practice, her community role was her work, and so on."

NOTOKWE OPIKIHEET—"OLD-LADY RAISED": KNOWLEDGE TRANSFER PRACTICES AMONG ABORIGINAL WOMEN HEALERS

In the childhood communities of the women interviewed, research was grounded in relationships with the natural and supernatural worlds, but also based on relationships with other people in their communities. This included particular systems of intergenerational collaboration and knowledge transfer among women, as well as collaborative work among healers.

The grandmothers were asked if they remembered "conferences" of healers and researchers taking place in their girlhood communities, and many spoke of regular gatherings, typically in the spring or summer when larger communities would come together. Be'sha Blondin talked about traditional ways of sharing knowledge among healers from the Great Bear Lake area in the Northwest Territories:

In July when all of the ice was melted, they would all meet from five different communities in this place. They would meet there and they would talk for two months, and share dance and stories. They did all that. That's where the medicine people would all gather together and talk about their area, the medicines they had just learned about. They shared medicines and they would talk about all the sick people that they worked with on healing. They talked about the medicines that they shared with each other, how to make it, how to work with it, what it's good for.

These gatherings were also a time for transferring knowledge to the younger generations, as Blondin further explained:

So the medicine people would gather like that and you would see a lot of young medicine people, very young—some even at the age of five years old. They would all gather together and talk. That's their time; no one interrupts them. Then they would take off in the bush and they would look at medicines, they would talk about it, what it was good for.

Blondin also noted that the healers also conducted many ceremonies at this time, which were part of the knowledge transfer and research process. She stated:

Some of them go on to their fast. They go into the mountains and walk on the sheep trails and that's the fasting. Some would go up to seven or eight days without food and water, just so they can go above one more stage and talk about all of the songs that were given to them by very spiritual people from the spiritual world.

Maria Campbell also shared some stories about "old lady" gatherings that took place in her home community in northern Saskatchewan. Her stories offer a vivid insight into the governing role that older women held, in terms of the health and well-being of their communities:

My granny used to have all of these old ladies come to visit her in the summer, and of course we would travel and visit other old ladies. These old ladies would come and stay with us for a week and my dad would put the tent up for them beside the house and that's where they would all sleep and visit. There were three or four of them and some of them were my granny's relatives who were also her friends. They ranged in age from their fifties to my grandmother's age. They would sit and visit inside the tent all day long. They would talk about all sorts of things. There would be exchanges of medicine and sharing information about who was marrying who, who was related to who, and the kinds of things that women talk about. They were the matriarchs of the families and so there would be a lot of exchanges about all kinds of information. I was often allowed to listen as I was their helper/runner, but sometimes I would be sent away.

In addition to having regular "conferences," healers and their apprentices engaged in ongoing intergenerational training and knowledge transfer activities. Be'sha Blondin's stories about her development as a healer demonstrate that training was a community responsibility, overseen by elders:

I was chosen to be a medicine person, so all the Elders looked after me. They make sure of everything they feed me. [They gave me] their teachings, taking me out on the land, teaching me about medicines, about the water medicines, about the animal medicines, how do I connect myself to mother earth. I have to be able to be a good hunter, good trapper, good everything, because for me to be able to get the animals, I have to learn to trap them—because I might need their gall bladder. So the men had to train me how to do that. The whole community is responsible to make sure that I get that training.

Maria Campbell's stories also speak to the intergenerational transfer of knowledge between women. The old ladies of the previously-mentioned summer gatherings always had young women and girls who tended to them, and in so doing learned their ways. Campbell talked about her own experiences as a helper to the grannies:

I think I was influenced by those old ladies because I was one who looked after them. I would make their tea, haul their wood, look after the fire … whatever. No one ever just sat around doing nothing, that's for sure. They would be doing their work, be it sewing, beading, grinding medicine or playing handgames—they did that often. And it was my job to be there for them.

Campbell talked about this as one system of knowledge transfer, stating, "I would listen to everything they said and observe everything. The stories, the teachings, all the values, laws—anything you need is in those stories, and one began learning by first listening, and always by being a helper."

Campbell also talked of another method of knowledge transfer. In many traditional societies, it was the grandparents who raised and educated children, and in many societies there were specific children who were very deliberately "given" to Elders for their upbringing. Campbell pointed out how this worked in her case:

I was taught things that the rest of my family didn't have to learn, and that was because I was the oldest and was given to my grannies. There is a word in Cree for someone who is raised by the grannies: it is notokwe opikiheet, which means "old-lady raised." This ensures that if children are snatched away, then someone in the family will know the language and will have some, if not all of the information.

Children who were chosen to be knowledge-keepers were thus "old-lady raised" because they maintained close relationships with the Elders who taught them traditional skills and practices.

DISCUSSION

These stories about Aboriginal women's traditional roles, practices, and knowledge systems have practical applications for our current work in health and healing research. First, the stories teach us that in the past, Aboriginal women played central and critical roles in their communities as health care researchers and practitioners, and they did so in ways that were distinct to their gender and cultures. We can reclaim many of the roles traditionally carried out by women—roles that included health research—and in so doing, we need to call on our grandmothers to assist us, as the answers are in their stories.

Researchers may want to consider the types of evidence used by our foremothers. For instance, Madeleine Dion Stout's assertion that "the evidence that was gathered was very much based on intuition, based on dreams, on trial and error and on relationships with other beings, whether they were natural or supernatural" warrants our attention. We may not be ready to footnote coyote or owl in our research papers, but we can certainly call on these relations in thoughtful meditation, ceremony, or prayer to guide us in our work. In my own experience, time spent on the land and in the company of relations—both natural and supernatural—has been critical in guiding my research and my practices around knowledge transfer. As we evolve as researchers and research organizations, we can connect with these powers by bringing ceremony into our daily business or by going on retreats where we can learn from the wisdom of the land.

In terms of how we might better govern ourselves as researchers, Be'sha Blondin's description of how she works as a healer is directly applicable. Ultimately, there needs to be respect. The fundamental principle of reciprocity must be respected, as mutual exchange must take place to ensure successful results in healing and in research. As Blondin explained, one can not simply go to the people and say "I'm going to do this for you." In order to gain knowledge through research, we must give something first. If we look at the example of storytelling, we must *earn* the right to tell a story, and each time this will involve a different process of relationship-building. If research is viewed as a process of gathering and retelling stories, these same principles can apply. In talking about not being "there for your own ego," Be'sha Blondin inspires us to remember to always consider our intent. The way in which we govern our work is directly tied to the way in which we govern ourselves. This was also demonstrated in Helen Thundercloud's description of the life and "work" of her grandmother.

Dorris Peters' story about picking medicine with her grandmother contains lessons about the importance of intergenerational knowledge transfer, reciprocity, responsibility, and the significance of relationships. In the story, the young Peters was directed by her grandmother to go out and find the plants that she needed for her own healing. As noted earlier, the grandmother sent Peters to pick the medicines by herself, in spite of her age. She had to do the work herself in order to benefit from the research and knowledge at hand. This shows us how the knowledge that we seek as researchers is often connected to the relationships that we establish in the process. If we don't have direct contact with the community of our work, we may come away with a watered down version of the knowledge we are seeking, and thus come out with weaker results.

Peters was also directed to be responsible about how much she was taking from the land. She was careful not to deplete the resources, or to come away having damaged the environment she went into. Rather, she took one step at a time, always looking back to her grandmother for guidance, who watched from a distance. Likewise, as researchers and research organizations, we need our grandmothers to watch us from a distant place; to guide us so that we can be sure that we are stepping lightly in our quest for knowledge. If we pay attention to their wisdom, we will not go charging into the woods picking everything that looks good at first glance. A more careful and guided walk will allow us to consider what kind of research we engage in, how we carry it out, as well as a consideration of what we will leave behind.

We must also be mindful of the damage caused by disrespectful and ill-informed researchers of the past. Outsiders going into communities have made—and continue to make—assumptions about Aboriginal people and communities that are unfounded. In Maria Campbell's story, the public health nurse failed to do the background research that would have better informed her about community strategies for purifying water. Instead, she made the unfounded (and no doubt racist) assumption that the Aboriginal community was responsible for the waterborne disease. The nurse also made several other mistakes: she (or the organization she represented) was not invited into the community; she lacked the means to communicate in the local language; and, she made no apparent effort to establish relationships before doing her research. She did not even consider inviting the community to define the real "research" question at hand (i.e., where the typhoid originally came from). We can draw out some important lessons from this story: researchers need to know the communities that they work with; they need to establish relationships of respect; they need to invite the community to help in defining the work, or be invited in by a community that has already defined their own research objectives; and, they need to consider how they are going to communicate in a culturally appropriate manner.

CONCLUSION

As Aboriginal women, we have been organizing, helping, healing, and researching throughout history. This has been possible because of the types of relationships, connections, and knowledge exchange systems that we have established among ourselves and with the human, natural, and supernatural worlds around us. There are some overall principles that we can take away from the stories shared by the grandmothers. These include valuing relationship-building with all our relations, the importance of reciprocity, and the need for ongoing processes of intergenerational knowledge transfer. These principles can ground us in Aboriginal research that is based on our own ways of knowing, being, and doing. As we move forward in the development of research focused on Aboriginal women's health and healing practices, we must continue to gather together, share our thoughts, and seek out opportunities to apply the principle of being *notokwe opihikeet*, "old-lady raised," within a modern context, so that our research can enhance the life, health, and well-being of our people.

This article is dedicated to my friend and teacher, Helen Thundercloud, who passed away suddenly on May 14, 2007.

Originally published in Canadian Woman Studies/les cahiers de la femme, *"Indigenous Women in Canada: The Voices of First Nations, Inuit and Métis Women," 26 (3 & 4) (Winter/Spring 2008): 6-12. Reprinted with permission of the author.*

Kim Anderson is the author of A Recognition of Being: Reconstructing Native Womanhood *(Sumach Press, 2000) and the co-editor, with Bonita Lawrence, of* Strong Women Stories: Native Vision and Community Survival *(Sumach Press, 2003).*

[1]In selecting research participants for this paper, I looked for a sample that would represent some of the cultural and regional diversity of the country. I sought out women who—as traditional healers, health workers, teachers and educators—could speak to issues of health research, ethics and knowledge transfer processes in their childhood communities. Some of these women are my friends, while others were recommended to me by colleagues.

[2]I recognize that it is a common qualitative research practice for participants to maintain anonymity, and that this is considered ethically responsible in terms of protecting the privacy of the interviewees. In this paper, however, participants have been identified with their consent, as this is more in keeping with practices of Indigenous knowledge transfer where we identify our teachers. In this way, we honour the teacher and validate the source of knowledge.

[3]I refer to midwives of the past in this section, but wish to note that these traditional roles and relationships are now being re-adopted by Aboriginal midwives in communities across Canada.

PATRICIA D. MCGUIRE AND PATRICIA A. MONTURE

CONCLUSION

T HIS BOOK IS AN OFFERING. Accompanying it, we offer our prayers and hopes for a brighter future for Aboriginal women in this country now known as Canada. Understanding Aboriginal women and our great diversities is necessary to building new relationships with our people based on respect, peace, sharing, and friendship. Seeing in writing the things that Aboriginal women have survived since colonial contact is sometimes very difficult. But when we move past our tears and sadness, we come to a different place where we are able to acknowledge the pride we feel in the strength of Aboriginal woman. We celebrate the Aboriginal women in this volume, their vision, wisdom, and courage. And then we offer our prayers for the future.

There are a number of questions we hope each reader will continue to consider. We also hope that each reader will come to his or her own questions. And of course, we hope that we all have the courage to answer the questions this material raises, even the hard ones. We offer a few of our own questions here. What does the future hold for Indigenous women in this country and around the world? And for Indigenous women who are writers and scholars? What can we conclude about the diversity of the women's writings that have been offered in this text? Many of these writings are stamped by the time that they were written. One of the strong themes in this text is the demonstration that Indigenous women are questioning the way things are in Canada. We do not accept that we are passive victims of colonialism, racism, sexism, and violence. The writings offered demonstrate the multiple ways Aboriginal women create and sustain change in our own lives and in our communities. How do Indigenous women talk about the needed changes? Each section of this book was developed using our traditional values and teachings with the intention that these groupings would help the reader build their knowledge about Aboriginal women and thus be able to deal with some of the hard questions raised. On this base of knowledge, it is our hope the each reader will be able to continue to question, learn, and challenge.

In "Profiles of Aboriginal Women," the life histories detailed give concrete examples of Aboriginal women who thirsted for social change in their communities. These Indigenous women's lives act as a foundation for us and we know these stories are familiar ones found all across Turtle Island. These Aboriginal women could be your grandmothers, mothers, aunts, sisters, cousins, friends, or teachers. Ultimately, Indigenous women's life stories are meant as teachings for us. They tell us that we are not limited by what is happening to us. We always have to the ability to transform ourselves. We also have the ability to transform our lives, our families, and the communities that comprise our nations. We draw great strength from our sisters and their journeys. We acknowledge that we come from peoples who have survived great hardship, often with strength, grace, creativity, and courage. Often our writing is an act of survival.

Much has been written on Indigenous "Identity." Many stereotypes of Aboriginal peoples come from these writings by outsiders who offer us inert portrayals of Aboriginal peoples and what they suppose our identities were (or are). The historical record is full of examples of this difficulty. Yet, in the writings by Aboriginal women included in this book; vibrant, inclusive, and contemporary ideas about identity emerge. These women say that we are not just Aboriginal in the traditional past, but we are Aboriginal now! We are not authentic "Indians" because we live on reserve or were raised on reserve. After all, the reserve is a good colonial idea, not a good Indigenous one! Our identities come from our families, clans, nations, and territories. The women also say that the unchanging features of our identities are still wrapped up in our lands and our sovereignties. These things are not lost but rather have been damaged and interfered with by colonialism.

The "Territory" that Aboriginal women story about is our source(s) of re-newal, family, and responsibility. The land is also the source of many Indigenous laws and law-making traditions. Indigenous women are apprehensive about the health of the environment because of our experience in who is setting the agenda regarding the land and her wealth as well as the policies that arise from that agenda. We know that our earth needs healing and nurturance. The earth has suffered under imperialism and colonialism as much as we have. Sustainable ideologies and practices are still very much part of the worldviews of Indigenous communities on Turtle Island. It is often Aboriginal women who are resurrecting these ideas and putting them to work in our everyday lives. Indigenous knowledges about sustainable environmental practices are even more important today than they were in the past given the harm that has been done to the land and waters. We acknowledge that today it is important, necessary even, to share these teachings with others outside of our cultures and traditions. Ultimately, it is the healing of the earth that matters.

There has been a wide range of Aboriginal women's "Activism" in Canada. Activists have seen the need to both challenge and support our communities. Indigenous women first take action by remembering who we are and what our responsibilities are. Aboriginal women's activism has involved individuals who responded to challenges even when they were not previously known for their activist stance. Shrewd grandmothers, Two-Spirited peoples, participators and creators of human rights dialogues have all contributed to the change and healing that is occurring in our communities. We acknowledge the social liberators of uniquely Aboriginal traditions and the Aboriginal women concerned about the legal system. These are women who are not scared of challenging and changing the power contained within the laws of Canada. Their critiques offer an analysis of power using their astute sharp minds to challenge the shape of systems such as education, health, law, and jurisprudence. These critiques also offer an analysis of privilege and ultimately fiercely question the status quo in Canada.

In the section titled, "Confronting Colonialism," we offer Aboriginal women reflections on the search for the causes of what has happened to us, to our communities, and to our nations. Social challenges in our communities have affected all of us. The symbiotic relationships between colonialism, racism, and sexism in Canada have been long-lasting. The marginalization of Aboriginal women can be directly related to this symbiosis. Challenges to our nations, sexual abuse, violence, substance abuse and its effects, reproductive health, violence against women, and our rights being violated by the existing power structures, require a matrix of responses. Aboriginal women are leading these needed confrontations even when there are significant consequences including the criminalization of their actions. Indigenous women confronted by the veneers of colonial ideologies have looked to our own ways as sources of renewal and resiliency. Here we have found the tools to combat oppression using our Indigenous ideas and philosophies.

Important work has also been accomplished through challenges to the "Canadian Legal System" and we offer a series of papers in this section that provide examples of the kind of work that has been started and that must continue. At the center of many of the oppressions we have faced, and continue to face, are the laws of Canada. Thus, we know that our work within Canada's legal system will continue and perhaps only end when we have recovered all of our own legal systems. Some Aboriginal women in Canada have changed the Canadian constitutional order by embracing the Canadian Charter of Rights and Freedoms as a tool for change. These leaders have been able to have significant impact both on the rights of Aboriginal women and for all women in Canada. Aboriginal women have lead adroit critiques and debates of laws and jurisprudence that question, challenge, and confront. These efforts have forced recognition that legal, social, and political change in Canada is essential. These women have made impacts on many government policies. Having generations of our people in prisons is not acceptable to us. Indigenous women remember our past responsibilities in law and governance and we are reviving these traditions today. The renewal and respect for our civil and political rights and responsibilities as Indigenous women and as Indigenous peoples are at the core of these challenges to Canadian laws and legal practices.

In the final section of the book, "Indigenous Knowledges," discussions about the future of our scholarship and creative endeavours for the next generation of Aboriginal women is established. How will we interpret how we see the world for ourselves and for others? What do we share about our Indigenous knowledge traditions? Does knowledge translation make Indigenous knowledge a commodity? How much of our theories and methodologies of transmitting knowledge do we share? Does learning how we see our worlds mean that others become us when we share our knowledges? How do we discuss who we are? How should others discuss who we are? Where do we want to go as Aboriginal nations and as Aboriginal women? Our stories about our worlds must be told for ourselves, our families, our communities, and our nations. We are the ones who must choose how we will tell them and why. These considerations can help us create, re-create, and remember the time when our nations were strong and balanced.

Many of the issues that we as Indigenous women have been facing remain the same since the time of first contact: sexualized violence, abuse, and marginalization. The impact is a loss of respect and honour for us as women within our own societies and within our communities. Colonialism also results in poverty for many Aboriginal peoples and many communities. Colonization was and is a multidimensional force with many tentacles reaching outwards toward us and within us as Indigenous peoples. The removal of these forces takes time and requires leadership from Indigenous women. As women, we recognize that even with change efforts occurring on multiple levels, we are forever changed by colonialism. Yet, our peoples of Turtle Island were and are comfortable with change and movement; even violent upheavals that change us forever. Our cultures were dynamic and vibrant at first contact because of our familiarity with change. Our cultures are remembering this familiarity now as we face this future. Time is cyclical to us. This stage of our collective history will pass and we will remain, as we always have been, changing and adapting who we are as Indigenous peoples on our own terms.

Colonialism, however, is not just about Aboriginal women. We have our grief to carry about the oppressions our ancestors and our relatives have survived. But colonialism also requires those who do the oppressing change. We acknowledge that many Canadians carry guilt over what has happened to Aboriginal peoples across the span of Canada's history. And as much as we have had to carry our own grief, Canadians too must work through the guilt. This guilt is not (and cannot be) the responsibility of Aboriginal peoples. This is, we believe, a more profound responsibility than simply dealing with what academics and anti-racist activists would call "white privilege." Although a dated document, Peggy McIntosh's work on this issue, titled "White Privilege: Unpacking the Invisible Knapsack," remains one of the best resources for beginning to understanding this social phenomenon. It is easily found in an internet search of either the author's name or the title of the article.

During the process of working on this book, there were mentors, teachers, students, laughter, and humour. We followed our traditions in times of challenge and in times of thankfulness. Tobacco was placed down when needed for guidance, to offer prayers, and for being asked to do this work. Prayers were offered for the experience of working with accomplished mentors. Women often do not realize that we are always teaching others and are unaware of how others see our work or see us. We were honoured by being given the opportunity to work with talented writers, students, and teachers, Patricia Monture, Luciana Ricciutelli, Patricia McGuire, and all of the women who were courageous enough to share their stories in this reader. Tobacco was offered in thanksgiving and gratitude for the wonder of beauty and creation that we carry within us as women of this earth.

REFERENCES

McIntosh, Peggy. "White Privilege: Unpacking the Invisible Knapsack." *Independent Schools* 29 (2) (1990): 31-36.

PHOTO CREDITS

Page vii: Kate Monture, 2003-2009. Photo courtesy Monture family collection.

Page 7: Kigishabun, Patricia McGuire's paternal great grandmother, and her daughter Ella. Photo courtesy McGuire Jackfish Island collection.

Page 63: Waiting for Sealift, Pangnirtunjg, 1984. Photo: Valerie Alia.

Page 127: Larissa Grant, stripping cedar bark from a tree, Musqueam territory. Photo: Nadia Joe. Courtesy Musqueam Indian Band collection.

Page 183: Walk4Justice, one of a series of vigils for missing and murdered Aboriginal women held in 30 communities across Canada, October 4, 2008. Photo courtesy Amnesty International.

Page 289: Cedar bark stripping, Musqueam territory. From left to right, Rosalind Campbell, Tracy Point, Vivian Campbell, Cindy Sparrow and Marie Grant. Photo: Nadia Joe. Courtesy Musqueam Indian Band collection.

Page 349: Patricia Monture at a rally in support of Six Nations land reclamation at Douglas Creek. Photo: Darlene Rose Okemaysim.

Page 435: Monique Mojica performs *Chocolate Woman Dreams the Milky Way.* Macdonald Stewart Art Centre, 21 November 2007. Photo: Dawn Owen.

INDEX

G